General Motors N-cars Automotive Repair Manual

by Richard Lindwall and John H Haynes

Member of the Guild of Motoring Writers

Models covered:

Buick Skylark - 1986 thru 1995
Buick Somerset - 1985 thru 1987
Oldsmobile Achieva - 1992 thru 1995
Oldsmobile Calais - 1985 thru 1991
Pontiac Grand Am - 1985 thru 1995

(2B9 - 38025)
(1420)

ABCD

AUTOMOTIVE PARTS & ACCESSORIES ASSOCIATION MEMBER

Haynes Publishing Group
Sparkford Nr Yeovil
Somerset BA22 7JJ England

Haynes North America, Inc
861 Lawrence Drive
Newbury Park
California 91320 USA

About this manual

Its purpose

The purpose of this manual is to help you get the best value from your vehicle. It can do so in several ways. It can help you decide what work must be done, even if you choose to have it done by a dealer service department or a repair shop; it provides information and procedures for routine maintenance and servicing; and it offers diagnostic and repair procedures to follow when trouble occurs.

We hope you use the manual to tackle the work yourself. For many simpler jobs, doing it yourself may be quicker than arranging an appointment to get the vehicle into a shop and making the trips to leave it and pick it up. More importantly, a lot of money can be saved by avoiding the expense the shop must pass on to you to cover its labor and overhead costs. An added benefit is the sense of satisfaction and accomplishment that you feel after doing the job yourself.

Using the manual

The manual is divided into Chapters. Each Chapter is divided into numbered Sections, which are headed in bold type between horizontal lines. Each Section consists of consecutively numbered paragraphs.

At the beginning of each numbered Section you will be referred to any illustrations which apply to the procedures in that Section. The reference numbers used in illustration captions pinpoint the pertinent Section and the Step within that Section. That is, illustration 3.2 means the illustration refers to Section 3 and Step (or paragraph) 2 within that Section.

Procedures, once described in the text, are not normally repeated. When it's necessary to refer to another Chapter, the reference will be given as Chapter and Section number. Cross references given without use of the word "Chapter" apply to Sections and/or paragraphs in the same Chapter. For example, "see Section 8" means in the same Chapter.

References to the left or right side of the vehicle assume you are sitting in the driver's seat, facing forward.

Even though we have prepared this manual with extreme care, neither the publisher nor the author can accept responsibility for any errors in, or omissions from, the information given.

NOTE

A **Note** provides information necessary to properly complete a procedure or information which will make the procedure easier to understand.

CAUTION

A **Caution** provides a special procedure or special steps which must be taken while completing the procedure where the Caution is found. Not heeding a Caution can result in damage to the assembly being worked on.

WARNING

A **Warning** provides a special procedure or special steps which must be taken while completing the procedure where the Warning is found. Not heeding a Warning can result in personal injury.

Acknowledgements

Wiring diagrams originated exclusively for Haynes North America, Inc. by Valley Forge Technical Communications. Technical writers who contributed to this project include Ralph Rendina and Jeff Killingsworth.

© **Haynes North America, Inc.** 1988, 1990, 1991, 1995, 1998

With permission from J.H. Haynes & Co. Ltd.

A book in the Haynes Automotive Repair Manual Series

Printed in the U.S.A.

ISBN 1 56392 123 5

Library of Congress Catalog Card Number 94-74482

Contents

Haynes mechanic, author and photographer with Pontiac Grand Am

Introduction to the General Motors N-Cars

General Motors introduced the N-car line in 1985 with the Buick Somerset, the Oldsmobile Calais and the Pontiac Grand Am. In 1986, the Buick division of General Motors added a second model to the N-car line by redesigning their popular Skylark, using the N-car chassis. Buick discontinued the Somerset after the 1987 model year. These models are available in 2-door coupe and 4-door sedan body styles featuring coil spring suspension and front wheel drive.

In 1992 the Oldsmobile Calais was replaced by the more stylish and aerodynamic Achieva. Both the Buick Skylark and

the Pontiac Grand Am received new interior design and more aerodynamic body styling in 1992.

The transversely mounted, inline four-cylinder or V6 engines used in these models are equipped with either Throttle Body Injection (TBI) or multi-port fuel injection systems. Some four-cylinder models may be turbocharged.

The engine drives the front wheels through either a manual or automatic transaxle via unequal length driveaxles. The power assisted rack-and-pinion steering gear assembly is mounted behind the engine

against the firewall.

The front suspension consists of independent coil spring/MacPherson strut units, three point lower control arms and a stabilizer bar. The rear suspension consists of a solid axle mounted to the chassis with integral trailing arms and shock absorbers. The chassis is supported over the rear axle with coil springs.

Power assisted brakes are standard. All models use disc at the front and drum-type at the rear. Some later models are equipped with an Anti-lock Brake System (ABS).

Vehicle identification numbers

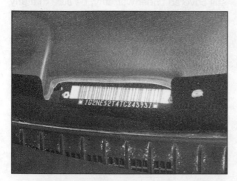

The Vehicle Identification Number (VIN) is on a plate attached to the top left of the instrument panel where it can be seen from outside the vehicle

Modifications are a continuing and unpublished process in vehicle manufacturing. Since spare part manuals are compiled on a numerical basis, the individual vehicle numbers are essential to correctly identify the component required.

Vehicle identification number (VIN)

This very important identification number is located on a plate attached to the top left corner of the dashboard of the vehicle **(see illustration)**. The VIN also appears on the Vehicle Certificate of Title and Registration. It contains valuable information such as where the vehicle was manufactured, the model year, the engine family and the body style.

Body identification plate

This metal plate is located on the top side of the radiator support. Like the VIN, it contains information concerning the production of the vehicle as well as information about how the vehicle came equipped from the factory. It's especially useful for matching the original color and type of paint.

Service parts identification label

This label is located in the trunk. It is attached to either the spare tire cover or to the inside of the trunk lid. It lists the VIN number, the wheelbase, paint number, options and other vehicle specific information. Always refer to this label when ordering parts.

Engine identification number

The engine ID number on the 2.0 liter OHC four-cylinder engine is located on the left front side of the block casting adjacent to the transaxle bellhousing **(see illustration)**.

The 2.3 liter OHC (Quad-4) engine ID number is located on the left rear of the engine block next to the starter motor **(see illustration)**. The Quad-4 engine also has a code label attached to the rear edge of the timing belt housing.

On the 2.5 liter four-cylinder, the ID number is located on the left front of the engine block below the cylinder head or on the rear of the cylinder head **(see illustrations)**.

On the 3.1 liter V6 engine, the ID number is located on the center of the engine block

between the timing cover and intake manifold or on the left front vertical web of the engine block near the starter motor **(see illustration)**.

On 3.0 and 3.3 liter V6 engines, the number is located adjacent to the timing chain cover, just below and forward of the water pump.

All late model V6 engines have an engine code label attached to the front valve cover.

Manual transaxle number

The identification number on the Isuzu five-speed transaxle is stamped into the front or upper edge of the case, where it joins the bellhousing. The Muncie transaxle has an adhesive-backed label attached to the rear of the case and an ID number stamped into the front of the case. If the transaxle number is unreadable, use the Service parts identification label to determine which transaxle was installed at the factory.

Automatic transaxle number

The identification number is located on a flange pad at the top of the transaxle case and the model code is located on the lower front edge near the dipstick.

Vehicle Emissions Control information label

The Vehicle Emissions Control label is attached to the front shock tower or to the engine air intake in the engine compartment (see Chapter 6 for an illustration of the label).

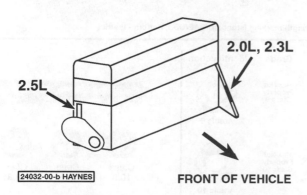

2.0L, 2.3L
2.5L
24032-00-b HAYNES   **FRONT OF VEHICLE**

Engine number locations - four-cylinder engines

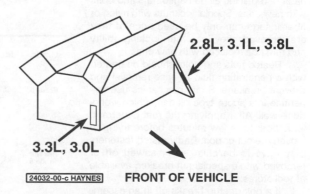

2.8L, 3.1L, 3.8L
3.3L, 3.0L
24032-00-c HAYNES   **FRONT OF VEHICLE**

Engine number locations - V6 engines

Buying parts

Replacement parts are available from many sources, which generally fall into one of two categories - authorized dealer parts departments and independent retail auto parts stores. Our advice concerning these parts is as follows:

Retail auto parts stores: Good auto parts stores will stock frequently needed components which wear out relatively fast, such as clutch components, exhaust systems, brake parts, tune-up parts, etc. These stores often supply new or reconditioned parts on an exchange basis, which can save a considerable amount of money. Discount auto parts stores are often very good places to buy materials and parts needed for general vehicle maintenance such as oil, grease, filters, spark plugs, belts, touch-up paint, bulbs, etc. They also usually sell tools and general accessories, have convenient hours, charge lower prices and can often be found not far from home.

Authorized dealer parts department: This is the best source for parts which are unique to the vehicle and not generally available elsewhere (such as major engine parts, transmission parts, trim pieces, etc.).

Warranty information: If the vehicle is still covered under warranty, be sure that any replacement parts purchased - regardless of the source - do not invalidate the warranty!

To be sure of obtaining the correct parts, have engine and chassis numbers available and, if possible, take the old parts along for positive identification.

Maintenance techniques, tools and working facilities

Maintenance techniques

There are a number of techniques involved in maintenance and repair that will be referred to throughout this manual. Application of these techniques will enable the home mechanic to be more efficient, better organized and capable of performing the various tasks properly, which will ensure that the repair job is thorough and complete.

Fasteners

Fasteners are nuts, bolts, studs and screws used to hold two or more parts together. There are a few things to keep in mind when working with fasteners. Almost all of them use a locking device of some type, either a lockwasher, locknut, locking tab or thread adhesive. All threaded fasteners should be clean and straight, with undamaged threads and undamaged corners on the hex head where the wrench fits. Develop the habit of replacing all damaged nuts and bolts with new ones. Special locknuts with nylon or fiber inserts can only be used once. If they are removed, they lose their locking ability and must be replaced with new ones.

Rusted nuts and bolts should be treated with a penetrating fluid to ease removal and prevent breakage. Some mechanics use turpentine in a spout-type oil can, which works quite well. After applying the rust penetrant, let it work for a few minutes before trying to loosen the nut or bolt. Badly rusted fasteners may have to be chiseled or sawed off or removed with a special nut breaker, available at tool stores.

If a bolt or stud breaks off in an assembly, it can be drilled and removed with a special tool commonly available for this purpose.

Most automotive machine shops can perform this task, as well as other repair procedures, such as the repair of threaded holes that have been stripped out.

Flat washers and lockwashers, when removed from an assembly, should always be replaced exactly as removed. Replace any damaged washers with new ones. Never use a lockwasher on any soft metal surface (such as aluminum), thin sheet metal or plastic.

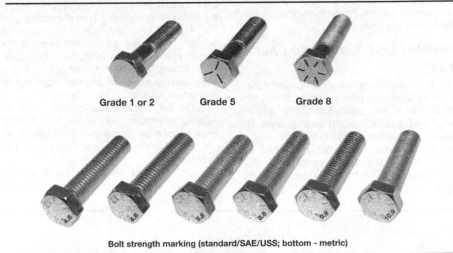

Grade 1 or 2   Grade 5   Grade 8

Bolt strength marking (standard/SAE/USS; bottom - metric)

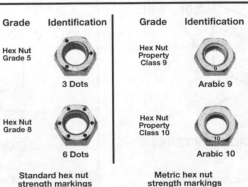

Grade	Identification	Grade	Identification
Hex Nut Grade 5	3 Dots	Hex Nut Property Class 9	Arabic 9
Hex Nut Grade 8	6 Dots	Hex Nut Property Class 10	Arabic 10

Standard hex nut strength markings

Metric hex nut strength markings

Class 10.9   Class 9.8   Class 8.8

Metric stud strength markings

00-1 HAYNES

Fastener sizes

For a number of reasons, automobile manufacturers are making wider and wider use of metric fasteners. Therefore, it is important to be able to tell the difference between standard (sometimes called U.S. or SAE) and metric hardware, since they cannot be interchanged.

All bolts, whether standard or metric, are sized according to diameter, thread pitch and length. For example, a standard 1/2 - 13 x 1 bolt is 1/2 inch in diameter, has 13 threads per inch and is 1 inch long. An M12 - 1.75 x 25 metric bolt is 12 mm in diameter, has a thread pitch of 1.75 mm (the distance between threads) and is 25 mm long. The two bolts are nearly identical, and easily confused, but they are not interchangeable.

In addition to the differences in diameter, thread pitch and length, metric and standard bolts can also be distinguished by examining the bolt heads. To begin with, the distance across the flats on a standard bolt head is measured in inches, while the same dimension on a metric bolt is sized in millimeters (the same is true for nuts). As a result, a standard wrench should not be used on a metric bolt and a metric wrench should not be used on a standard bolt. Also, most standard bolts have slashes radiating out from the center of the head to denote the grade or strength of the bolt, which is an indication of the amount of torque that can be applied to it. The greater the number of slashes, the greater the strength of the bolt. Grades 0 through 5 are commonly used on automobiles. Metric bolts have a property class (grade) number, rather than a slash, molded into their heads to indicate bolt strength. In this case, the higher the number, the stronger the bolt. Property class numbers 8.8, 9.8 and 10.9 are commonly used on automobiles.

Strength markings can also be used to distinguish standard hex nuts from metric hex nuts. Many standard nuts have dots stamped into one side, while metric nuts are marked with a number. The greater the number of dots, or the higher the number, the greater the strength of the nut.

Metric studs are also marked on their ends according to property class (grade). Larger studs are numbered (the same as metric bolts), while smaller studs carry a geometric code to denote grade.

It should be noted that many fasteners, especially Grades 0 through 2, have no distinguishing marks on them. When such is the case, the only way to determine whether it is standard or metric is to measure the thread pitch or compare it to a known fastener of the same size.

Standard fasteners are often referred to as SAE, as opposed to metric. However, it should be noted that SAE technically refers to a non-metric fine thread fastener only. Coarse thread non-metric fasteners are referred to as USS sizes.

Since fasteners of the same size (both standard and metric) may have different

Metric thread sizes	Ft-lbs	Nm
M-6	6 to 9	9 to 12
M-8	14 to 21	19 to 28
M-10	28 to 40	38 to 54
M-12	50 to 71	68 to 96
M-14	80 to 140	109 to 154

Pipe thread sizes	Ft-lbs	Nm
1/8	5 to 8	7 to 10
1/4	12 to 18	17 to 24
3/8	22 to 33	30 to 44
1/2	25 to 35	34 to 47

U.S. thread sizes	Ft-lbs	Nm
1/4 - 20	6 to 9	9 to 12
5/16 - 18	12 to 18	17 to 24
5/16 - 24	14 to 20	19 to 27
3/8 - 16	22 to 32	30 to 43
3/8 - 24	27 to 38	37 to 51
7/16 - 14	40 to 55	55 to 74
7/16 - 20	40 to 60	55 to 81
1/2 - 13	55 to 80	75 to 108

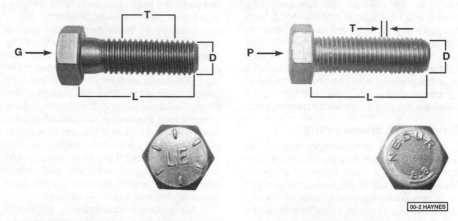

Standard (SAE and USS) bolt dimensions/grade marks

G   Grade marks (bolt strength)
L   Length (in inches)
T   Thread pitch (number of threads per inch)
D   Nominal diameter (in inches)

Metric bolt dimensions/grade marks

P   Property class (bolt strength)
L   Length (in millimeters)
T   Thread pitch (distance between threads in millimeters)
D   Diameter

strength ratings, be sure to reinstall any bolts, studs or nuts removed from your vehicle in their original locations. Also, when replacing a fastener with a new one, make sure that the new one has a strength rating equal to or greater than the original.

Tightening sequences and procedures

Most threaded fasteners should be tightened to a specific torque value (torque is the twisting force applied to a threaded component such as a nut or bolt). Overtightening the fastener can weaken it and cause it to break, while undertightening can cause it to eventually come loose. Bolts, screws and studs, depending on the material they are

made of and their thread diameters, have specific torque values, many of which are noted in the Specifications at the beginning of each Chapter. Be sure to follow the torque recommendations closely. For fasteners not assigned a specific torque, a general torque value chart is presented here as a guide. These torque values are for dry (unlubricated) fasteners threaded into steel or cast iron (not aluminum). As was previously mentioned, the size and grade of a fastener determine the amount of torque that can safely be applied to it. The figures listed here are approximate for Grade 2 and Grade 3 fasteners. Higher grades can tolerate higher torque values.

Fasteners laid out in a pattern, such as cylinder head bolts, oil pan bolts, differential cover bolts, etc., must be loosened or tight-

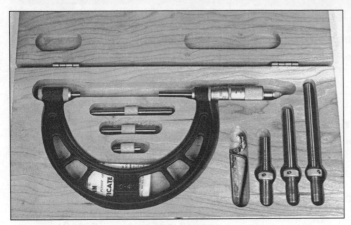

Micrometer set

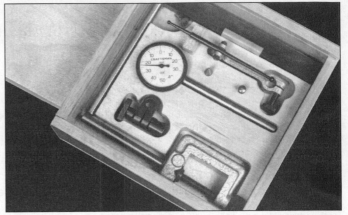

Dial indicator set

ened in sequence to avoid warping the component. This sequence will normally be shown in the appropriate Chapter. If a specific pattern is not given, the following procedures can be used to prevent warping.

Initially, the bolts or nuts should be assembled finger-tight only. Next, they should be tightened one full turn each, in a criss-cross or diagonal pattern. After each one has been tightened one full turn, return to the first one and tighten them all one-half turn, following the same pattern. Finally, tighten each of them one-quarter turn at a time until each fastener has been tightened to the proper torque. To loosen and remove the fasteners, the procedure would be reversed.

Component disassembly

Component disassembly should be done with care and purpose to help ensure that the parts go back together properly. Always keep track of the sequence in which parts are removed. Make note of special characteristics or marks on parts that can be installed more than one way, such as a grooved thrust washer on a shaft. It is a good idea to lay the disassembled parts out on a clean surface in the order that they were removed. It may also be helpful to make sketches or take instant photos of components before removal.

When removing fasteners from a component, keep track of their locations. Sometimes threading a bolt back in a part, or putting the washers and nut back on a stud, can prevent mix-ups later. If nuts and bolts cannot be returned to their original locations, they should be kept in a compartmented box or a series of small boxes. A cupcake or muffin tin is ideal for this purpose, since each cavity can hold the bolts and nuts from a particular area (i.e. oil pan bolts, valve cover bolts, engine mount bolts, etc.). A pan of this type is especially helpful when working on assemblies with very small parts, such as the carburetor, alternator, valve train or interior dash and trim pieces. The cavities can be marked with paint or tape to identify the contents.

Whenever wiring looms, harnesses or connectors are separated, it is a good idea to identify the two halves with numbered pieces of masking tape so they can be easily reconnected.

Gasket sealing surfaces

Throughout any vehicle, gaskets are used to seal the mating surfaces between two parts and keep lubricants, fluids, vacuum or pressure contained in an assembly.

Many times these gaskets are coated with a liquid or paste-type gasket sealing compound before assembly. Age, heat and pressure can sometimes cause the two parts to stick together so tightly that they are very difficult to separate. Often, the assembly can be loosened by striking it with a soft-face hammer near the mating surfaces. A regular hammer can be used if a block of wood is placed between the hammer and the part. Do not hammer on cast parts or parts that could be easily damaged. With any particularly stubborn part, always recheck to make sure that every fastener has been removed.

Avoid using a screwdriver or bar to pry apart an assembly, as they can easily mar the gasket sealing surfaces of the parts, which must remain smooth. If prying is absolutely necessary, use an old broom handle, but keep in mind that extra clean up will be necessary if the wood splinters.

After the parts are separated, the old gasket must be carefully scraped off and the gasket surfaces cleaned. Stubborn gasket material can be soaked with rust penetrant or treated with a special chemical to soften it so it can be easily scraped off. A scraper can be fashioned from a piece of copper tubing by flattening and sharpening one end. Copper is recommended because it is usually softer than the surfaces to be scraped, which reduces the chance of gouging the part. Some gaskets can be removed with a wire brush, but regardless of the method used, the mating surfaces must be left clean and smooth. If for some reason the gasket surface is gouged, then a gasket sealer thick enough to fill scratches will have to be used during reassembly of the components. For most applications, a non-drying (or semi-drying) gasket sealer should be used.

Hose removal tips

Warning: *If the vehicle is equipped with air conditioning, do not disconnect any of the A/C hoses without first having the system depressurized by a dealer service department or a service station.*

Hose removal precautions closely parallel gasket removal precautions. Avoid scratching or gouging the surface that the hose mates against or the connection may leak. This is especially true for radiator hoses. Because of various chemical reactions, the rubber in hoses can bond itself to the metal spigot that the hose fits over. To remove a hose, first loosen the hose clamps that secure it to the spigot. Then, with slip-joint pliers, grab the hose at the clamp and rotate it around the spigot. Work it back and forth until it is completely free, then pull it off. Silicone or other lubricants will ease removal if they can be applied between the hose and the outside of the spigot. Apply the same lubricant to the inside of the hose and the outside of the spigot to simplify installation.

As a last resort (and if the hose is to be replaced with a new one anyway), the rubber can be slit with a knife and the hose peeled from the spigot. If this must be done, be careful that the metal connection is not damaged.

If a hose clamp is broken or damaged, do not reuse it. Wire-type clamps usually weaken with age, so it is a good idea to replace them with screw-type clamps whenever a hose is removed.

Tools

A selection of good tools is a basic requirement for anyone who plans to maintain and repair his or her own vehicle. For the owner who has few tools, the initial investment might seem high, but when compared to the spiraling costs of professional auto maintenance and repair, it is a wise one.

To help the owner decide which tools are needed to perform the tasks detailed in this manual, the following tool lists are offered: *Maintenance and minor repair, Repair/overhaul* and *Special*.

The newcomer to practical mechanics

Dial caliper

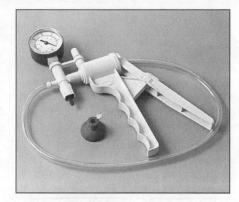

Hand-operated vacuum pump

Timing light

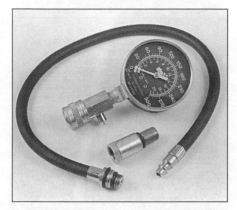

Compression gauge with spark plug
hole adapter

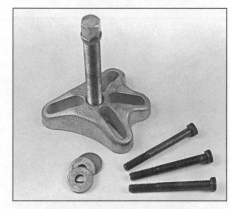

Damper/steering wheel puller

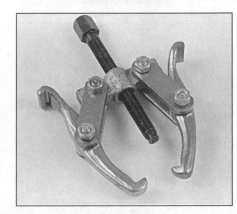

General purpose puller

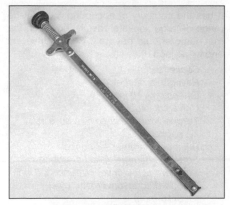

Hydraulic lifter removal tool

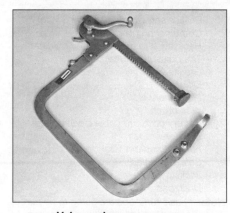

Valve spring compressor

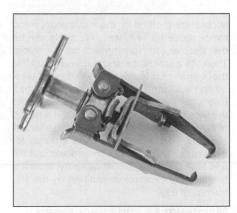

Valve spring compressor

Ridge reamer

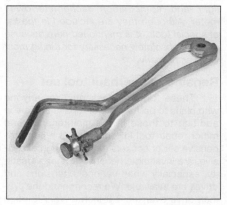

Piston ring groove cleaning tool

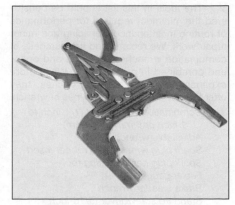

Ring removal/installation tool

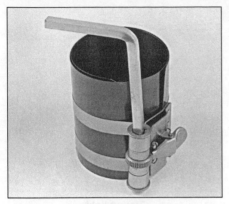

Ring compressor

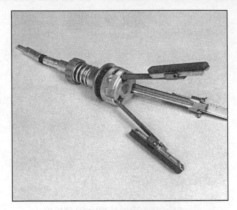

Cylinder hone

Brake hold-down spring tool

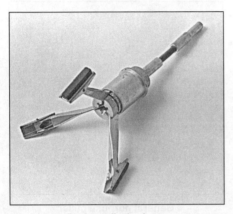

Brake cylinder hone

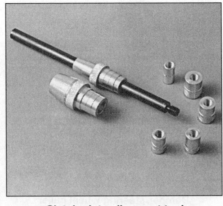

Clutch plate alignment tool

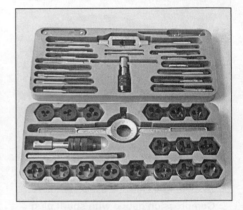

Tap and die set

should start off with the *maintenance and minor repair* tool kit, which is adequate for the simpler jobs performed on a vehicle. Then, as confidence and experience grow, the owner can tackle more difficult tasks, buying additional tools as they are needed. Eventually the basic kit will be expanded into the *repair and overhaul* tool set. Over a period of time, the experienced do-it-yourselfer will assemble a tool set complete enough for most repair and overhaul procedures and will add tools from the special category when it is felt that the expense is justified by the frequency of use.

Maintenance and minor repair tool kit

The tools in this list should be considered the minimum required for performance of routine maintenance, servicing and minor repair work. We recommend the purchase of combination wrenches (box-end and open-end combined in one wrench). While more expensive than open end wrenches, they offer the advantages of both types of wrench.

Combination wrench set (1/4-inch to 1 inch or 6 mm to 19 mm)
Adjustable wrench, 8 inch
Spark plug wrench with rubber insert
Spark plug gap adjusting tool
Feeler gauge set
Brake bleeder wrench
Standard screwdriver (5/16-inch x 6 inch)

Phillips screwdriver (No. 2 x 6 inch)
Combination pliers - 6 inch
Hacksaw and assortment of blades
Tire pressure gauge
Grease gun
Oil can
Fine emery cloth
Wire brush
Battery post and cable cleaning tool
Oil filter wrench
Funnel (medium size)
Safety goggles
Jackstands (2)
Drain pan

Note: *If basic tune-ups are going to be part of routine maintenance, it will be necessary to purchase a good quality stroboscopic timing light and combination tachometer/dwell meter. Although they are included in the list of special tools, it is mentioned here because they are absolutely necessary for tuning most vehicles properly.*

Repair and overhaul tool set

These tools are essential for anyone who plans to perform major repairs and are in addition to those in the maintenance and minor repair tool kit. Included is a comprehensive set of sockets which, though expensive, are invaluable because of their versatility, especially when various extensions and drives are available. We recommend the 1/2-inch drive over the 3/8-inch drive. Although the larger drive is bulky and more expensive,

it has the capacity of accepting a very wide range of large sockets. Ideally, however, the mechanic should have a 3/8-inch drive set and a 1/2-inch drive set.

Socket set(s)
Reversible ratchet
Extension - 10 inch
Universal joint
Torque wrench (same size drive as sockets)
Ball peen hammer - 8 ounce
Soft-face hammer (plastic/rubber)
Standard screwdriver (1/4-inch x 6 inch)
Standard screwdriver (stubby - 5/16-inch)
Phillips screwdriver (No. 3 x 8 inch)
Phillips screwdriver (stubby - No. 2)
Pliers - vise grip
Pliers - lineman's
Pliers - needle nose
Pliers - snap-ring (internal and external)
Cold chisel - 1/2-inch
Scribe
Scraper (made from flattened copper tubing)
Centerpunch
Pin punches (1/16, 1/8, 3/16-inch)
Steel rule/straightedge - 12 inch
Allen wrench set (1/8 to 3/8-inch or 4 mm to 10 mm)
A selection of files
Wire brush (large)
Jackstands (second set)
Jack (scissor or hydraulic type)

Note: *Another tool which is often useful is an electric drill with a chuck capacity of 3/8-inch and a set of good quality drill bits.*

Special tools

The tools in this list include those which are not used regularly, are expensive to buy, or which need to be used in accordance with their manufacturer's instructions. Unless these tools will be used frequently, it is not very economical to purchase many of them. A consideration would be to split the cost and use between yourself and a friend or friends. In addition, most of these tools can be obtained from a tool rental shop on a temporary basis.

This list primarily contains only those tools and instruments widely available to the public, and not those special tools produced by the vehicle manufacturer for distribution to dealer service departments. Occasionally, references to the manufacturer's special tools are included in the text of this manual. Generally, an alternative method of doing the job without the special tool is offered. However, sometimes there is no alternative to their use. Where this is the case, and the tool cannot be purchased or borrowed, the work should be turned over to the dealer service department or an automotive repair shop.

Valve spring compressor
Piston ring groove cleaning tool
Piston ring compressor
Piston ring installation tool
Cylinder compression gauge
Cylinder ridge reamer
Cylinder surfacing hone
Cylinder bore gauge
Micrometers and/or dial calipers
Hydraulic lifter removal tool
Balljoint separator
Universal-type puller
Impact screwdriver
Dial indicator set
Stroboscopic timing light (inductive pick-up)
Hand operated vacuum/pressure pump
Tachometer/dwell meter
Universal electrical multimeter
Cable hoist
Brake spring removal and installation tools
Floor jack

Buying tools

For the do-it-yourselfer who is just starting to get involved in vehicle maintenance and repair, there are a number of options available when purchasing tools. If maintenance and minor repair is the extent of the work to be done, the purchase of individual tools is satisfactory. If, on the other hand, extensive work is planned, it would be a good idea to purchase a modest tool set from one of the large retail chain stores. A set can usually be bought at a substantial savings over the individual tool prices, and they often come with a tool box. As additional tools are needed, add-on sets, individual tools and a larger tool box can be purchased to expand the tool selection. Building a tool set gradually allows the cost of the tools to be spread over a longer period of time and gives the mechanic the freedom to choose only those tools that will actually be used.

Tool stores will often be the only source of some of the special tools that are needed, but regardless of where tools are bought, try to avoid cheap ones, especially when buying screwdrivers and sockets, because they won't last very long. The expense involved in replacing cheap tools will eventually be greater than the initial cost of quality tools.

Care and maintenance of tools

Good tools are expensive, so it makes sense to treat them with respect. Keep them clean and in usable condition and store them properly when not in use. Always wipe off any dirt, grease or metal chips before putting them away. Never leave tools lying around in the work area. Upon completion of a job, always check closely under the hood for tools that may have been left there so they won't get lost during a test drive.

Some tools, such as screwdrivers, pliers, wrenches and sockets, can be hung on a panel mounted on the garage or workshop wall, while others should be kept in a tool box or tray. Measuring instruments, gauges, meters, etc. must be carefully stored where they cannot be damaged by weather or impact from other tools.

When tools are used with care and stored properly, they will last a very long time. Even with the best of care, though, tools will wear out if used frequently. When a tool is damaged or worn out, replace it. Subsequent jobs will be safer and more enjoyable if you do.

How to repair damaged threads

Sometimes, the internal threads of a nut or bolt hole can become stripped, usually from overtightening. Stripping threads is an all-too-common occurrence, especially when working with aluminum parts, because aluminum is so soft that it easily strips out.

Usually, external or internal threads are only partially stripped. After they've been cleaned up with a tap or die, they'll still work. Sometimes, however, threads are badly damaged. When this happens, you've got three choices:

1) *Drill and tap the hole to the next suitable oversize and install a larger diameter bolt, screw or stud.*
2) *Drill and tap the hole to accept a threaded plug, then drill and tap the plug to the original screw size. You can also buy a plug already threaded to the original size. Then you simply drill a hole to the specified size, then run the threaded plug into the hole with a bolt and jam*
nut. *Once the plug is fully seated, remove the jam nut and bolt.*
3) *The third method uses a patented thread repair kit like Heli-Coil or Slimsert. These easy-to-use kits are designed to repair damaged threads in straight-through holes and blind holes. Both are available as kits which can handle a variety of sizes and thread patterns. Drill the hole, then tap it with the special included tap. Install the Heli-Coil and the hole is back to its original diameter and thread pitch.*

Regardless of which method you use, be sure to proceed calmly and carefully. A little impatience or carelessness during one of these relatively simple procedures can ruin your whole day's work and cost you a bundle if you wreck an expensive part.

Working facilities

Not to be overlooked when discussing tools is the workshop. If anything more than routine maintenance is to be carried out, some sort of suitable work area is essential.

It is understood, and appreciated, that many home mechanics do not have a good workshop or garage available, and end up removing an engine or doing major repairs outside. It is recommended, however, that the overhaul or repair be completed under the cover of a roof.

A clean, flat workbench or table of comfortable working height is an absolute necessity. The workbench should be equipped with a vise that has a jaw opening of at least four inches.

As mentioned previously, some clean, dry storage space is also required for tools, as well as the lubricants, fluids, cleaning solvents, etc. which soon become necessary.

Sometimes waste oil and fluids, drained from the engine or cooling system during normal maintenance or repairs, present a disposal problem. To avoid pouring them on the ground or into a sewage system, pour the used fluids into large containers, seal them with caps and take them to an authorized disposal site or recycling center. Plastic jugs, such as old antifreeze containers, are ideal for this purpose.

Always keep a supply of old newspapers and clean rags available. Old towels are excellent for mopping up spills. Many mechanics use rolls of paper towels for most work because they are readily available and disposable. To help keep the area under the vehicle clean, a large cardboard box can be cut open and flattened to protect the garage or shop floor.

Whenever working over a painted surface, such as when leaning over a fender to service something under the hood, always cover it with an old blanket or bedspread to protect the finish. Vinyl covered pads, made especially for this purpose, are available at auto parts stores.

Jacking and towing

Jacking

The jack supplied with the vehicle should only be used for raising the vehicle when changing a tire or placing jackstands under the frame. **Warning:** *Never work under the vehicle or start the engine while this jack is being used as the only means of support.*

The vehicle should be on level ground with the wheels blocked and the transmission in Park (automatic) or Reverse (manual). Pry off the hub cap (if equipped) using the tapered end of the lug wrench. Loosen the wheel nuts one-half turn and leave them in place until the wheel is raised off the ground.

Place the jack under the side of the vehicle in the indicated position and place the jack lever in the "up" position. Raise the jack until the jack head groove fits into the rocker panel flange notch **(see illustration)**. Operate the jack with a slow, smooth motion, using your hand or foot to pump the handle until the wheel is raised off the ground. Remove the wheel nuts, pull off the wheel and replace it with the spare. (If you have a stowaway spare, refer to the instructions accompanying the supplied inflator.)

With the beveled side in, replace the wheel nuts and tighten them until snug. Place the jack lever in the "down" position and lower the vehicle. Remove the jack and tighten the nuts in a criss-cross sequence by turning the wrench clockwise. Replace the hub cap (if equipped) by placing it into position and using the heel of your hand or a rubber mallet to seat it.

Towing

The vehicle can be towed with all four wheels on the ground, provided that speeds do not exceed 35 mph and the distance is not over 50 miles, otherwise transmission damage can result.

Towing equipment specifically designed for this purpose should be used and should be attached to the main structural members of the vehicle and not the bumper or brackets.

Safety is a major consideration when towing and all applicable state and local laws must be obeyed. A safety chain system must be used for all towing.

While towing, the parking brake should be released and the transmission should be in Neutral. The steering must be unlocked (ignition switch in the Off position). Remember that power steering and power brakes will not work with the engine off.

Location of the rocker panel flange notches used for jack placement

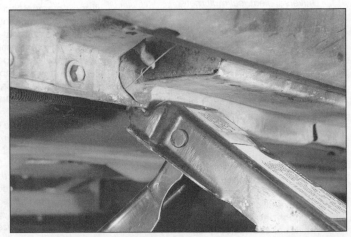

Placement and operation of the jack for tire changing

Delco Loc II anti-theft audio system

General information

1   Some 1992 and later models are equipped with the Delco Loc II audio system, which includes an anti-theft feature that will render the stereo inoperative if stolen. If the power source to the stereo is cut with the anti-theft feature activated, the stereo will be inoperative. Even if the power source is immediately re-connected, the stereo will not function. If your vehicle is equipped with this anti-theft system, do not disconnect the battery, remove the stereo or disconnect related components unless you have either turned off the feature or have the individual ID (code) number for the stereo.

2   Refer to your vehicle owner's manual for more complete information on this audio system and its anti-theft feature.

Disabling the anti-theft feature

3   Press the stereo's l and 4 buttons at the same time for five seconds with the ignition on and the radio power off. The display will show SEC, indicating the unit is in the secure mode (anti-theft feature enabled).

4   Press the SET button. The display will show "000."

5   Press the SEEK button to make the first number appear.

6   Rotate the TUNE knob right or left to make the last two numbers agree with your code. The numbers will be displayed as entered.

7   Press the lower BAND knob. "000" will be displayed.

8   Enter the second three digits of the code.

9   Press the lower BAND knob. If the display shows "_ _," you have successfully disabled the anti-theft feature. If SEC is displayed, the code you entered was incorrect and the anti-theft feature is still enabled.

Unlocking the stereo after a power loss

10   When power is restored to the stereo, the stereo won't turn on and LOC will appear on the display. Enter your ID code as follows; pause no more than 15 seconds between Steps.

11   Turn the ignition switch to ON, but leave the stereo off.

12   Press the SET button. "000" should display.

13   Press the SEEK button to make the first number appear.

14   Rotate the TUNE knob right or left to make the last two numbers agree with your code.

15   Repeat Steps 2 through 4 for the last three digits of your code.

16   Press the lower BAND knob. The time should appear, indicating the stereo is unlocked. If SEC appears, the numbers you entered were not correct and the stereo is still inoperative.

Booster battery (jump) starting

Observe these precautions when using a booster battery to start a vehicle:

a) Before connecting the booster battery, make sure the ignition switch is in the Off position.
b) Turn off the lights, heater and other electrical loads.
c) Your eyes should be shielded. Safety goggles are a good idea.
d) Make sure the booster battery is the same voltage as the dead one in the vehicle.
e) The two vehicles MUST NOT TOUCH each other!
f) Make sure the transaxle is in Neutral (manual) or Park (automatic).
g) If the booster battery is not a maintenance-free type, remove the vent caps and lay a cloth over the vent holes.

Connect the red jumper cable to the positive (+) terminals of each battery (see illustration).

Connect one end of the black jumper cable to the negative (-) terminal of the booster battery. The other end of this cable should be connected to a good ground on the vehicle to be started, such as a bolt or bracket on the body.

Start the engine using the booster battery, then, with the engine running at idle speed, disconnect the jumper cables in the reverse order of connection.

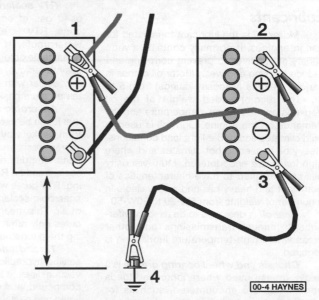

00-4 HAYNES

Make the booster battery cable connections in the numerical order shown (note that the negative cable of the booster battery is NOT attached to the negative terminal of the dead battery)

Automotive chemicals and lubricants

A number of automotive chemicals and lubricants are available for use during vehicle maintenance and repair. They include a wide variety of products ranging from cleaning solvents and degreasers to lubricants and protective sprays for rubber, plastic and vinyl.

Cleaners

Carburetor cleaner and choke cleaner is a strong solvent for gum, varnish and carbon. Most carburetor cleaners leave a dry-type lubricant film which will not harden or gum up. Because of this film it is not recommended for use on electrical components.

Brake system cleaner is used to remove grease and brake fluid from the brake system, where clean surfaces are absolutely necessary. It leaves no residue and often eliminates brake squeal caused by contaminants.

Electrical cleaner removes oxidation, corrosion and carbon deposits from electrical contacts, restoring full current flow. It can also be used to clean spark plugs, carburetor jets, voltage regulators and other parts where an oil-free surface is desired.

Demoisturants remove water and moisture from electrical components such as alternators, voltage regulators, electrical connectors and fuse blocks. They are non-conductive, non-corrosive and non-flammable.

Degreasers are heavy-duty solvents used to remove grease from the outside of the engine and from chassis components. They can be sprayed or brushed on and, depending on the type, are rinsed off either with water or solvent.

Lubricants

Motor oil is the lubricant formulated for use in engines. It normally contains a wide variety of additives to prevent corrosion and reduce foaming and wear. Motor oil comes in various weights (viscosity ratings) from 5 to 80. The recommended weight of the oil depends on the season, temperature and the demands on the engine. Light oil is used in cold climates and under light load conditions. Heavy oil is used in hot climates and where high loads are encountered. Multi-viscosity oils are designed to have characteristics of both light and heavy oils and are available in a number of weights from 5W-20 to 20W-50.

Gear oil is designed to be used in differentials, manual transmissions and other areas where high-temperature lubrication is required.

Chassis and wheel bearing grease is a heavy grease used where increased loads and friction are encountered, such as for wheel bearings, balljoints, tie-rod ends and universal joints.

High-temperature wheel bearing grease is designed to withstand the extreme temperatures encountered by wheel bearings in disc brake equipped vehicles. It usually contains molybdenum disulfide (moly), which is a dry-type lubricant.

White grease is a heavy grease for metal-to-metal applications where water is a problem. White grease stays soft under both low and high temperatures (usually from -100 to +190-degrees F), and will not wash off or dilute in the presence of water.

Assembly lube is a special extreme pressure lubricant, usually containing moly, used to lubricate high-load parts (such as main and rod bearings and cam lobes) for initial start-up of a new engine. The assembly lube lubricates the parts without being squeezed out or washed away until the engine oiling system begins to function.

Silicone lubricants are used to protect rubber, plastic, vinyl and nylon parts.

Graphite lubricants are used where oils cannot be used due to contamination problems, such as in locks. The dry graphite will lubricate metal parts while remaining uncontaminated by dirt, water, oil or acids. It is electrically conductive and will not foul electrical contacts in locks such as the ignition switch.

Moly penetrants loosen and lubricate frozen, rusted and corroded fasteners and prevent future rusting or freezing.

Heat-sink grease is a special electrically non-conductive grease that is used for mounting electronic ignition modules where it is essential that heat is transferred away from the module.

Sealants

RTV sealant is one of the most widely used gasket compounds. Made from silicone, RTV is air curing, it seals, bonds, waterproofs, fills surface irregularities, remains flexible, doesn't shrink, is relatively easy to remove, and is used as a supplementary sealer with almost all low and medium temperature gaskets.

Anaerobic sealant is much like RTV in that it can be used either to seal gaskets or to form gaskets by itself. It remains flexible, is solvent resistant and fills surface imperfections. The difference between an anaerobic sealant and an RTV-type sealant is in the curing. RTV cures when exposed to air, while an anaerobic sealant cures only in the absence of air. This means that an anaerobic sealant cures only after the assembly of parts, sealing them together.

Thread and pipe sealant is used for sealing hydraulic and pneumatic fittings and vacuum lines. It is usually made from a Teflon compound, and comes in a spray, a paint-on liquid and as a wrap-around tape.

Chemicals

Anti-seize compound prevents seizing, galling, cold welding, rust and corrosion in fasteners. High-temperature ant-seize, usually made with copper and graphite lubricants, is used for exhaust system and exhaust manifold bolts.

Anaerobic locking compounds are used to keep fasteners from vibrating or working loose and cure only after installation, in the absence of air. Medium strength locking compound is used for small nuts, bolts and screws that may be removed later. High-strength locking compound is for large nuts, bolts and studs which aren't removed on a regular basis.

Oil additives range from viscosity index improvers to chemical treatments that claim to reduce internal engine friction. It should be noted that most oil manufacturers caution against using additives with their oils.

Gas additives perform several functions, depending on their chemical makeup. They usually contain solvents that help dissolve gum and varnish that build up on carburetor, fuel injection and intake parts. They also serve to break down carbon deposits that form on the inside surfaces of the combustion chambers. Some additives contain upper cylinder lubricants for valves and piston rings, and others contain chemicals to remove condensation from the gas tank.

Miscellaneous

Brake fluid is specially formulated hydraulic fluid that can withstand the heat and pressure encountered in brake systems. Care must be taken so this fluid does not come in contact with painted surfaces or plastics. An opened container should always be resealed to prevent contamination by water or dirt.

Weatherstrip adhesive is used to bond weatherstripping around doors, windows and trunk lids. It is sometimes used to attach trim pieces.

Undercoating is a petroleum-based, tar-like substance that is designed to protect metal surfaces on the underside of the vehicle from corrosion. It also acts as a sound-deadening agent by insulating the bottom of the vehicle.

Waxes and polishes are used to help protect painted and plated surfaces from the weather. Different types of paint may require the use of different types of wax and polish. Some polishes utilize a chemical or abrasive cleaner to help remove the top layer of oxidized (dull) paint on older vehicles. In recent years many non-wax polishes that contain a wide variety of chemicals such as polymers and silicones have been introduced. These non-wax polishes are usually easier to apply and last longer than conventional waxes and polishes.

Conversion factors

Length (distance)

Inches (in)	X 25.4	= Millimetres (mm)	X 0.0394	= Inches (in)
Feet (ft)	X 0.305	= Metres (m)	X 3.281	= Feet (ft)
Miles	X 1.609	= Kilometres (km)	X 0.621	= Miles

Volume (capacity)

Cubic inches (cu in; in³)	X 16.387	= Cubic centimetres (cc; cm³)	X 0.061	= Cubic inches (cu in; in³)
Imperial pints (Imp pt)	X 0.568	= Litres (l)	X 1.76	= Imperial pints (Imp pt)
Imperial quarts (Imp qt)	X 1.137	= Litres (l)	X 0.88	= Imperial quarts (Imp qt)
Imperial quarts (Imp qt)	X 1.201	= US quarts (US qt)	X 0.833	= Imperial quarts (Imp qt)
US quarts (US qt)	X 0.946	= Litres (l)	X 1.057	= US quarts (US qt)
Imperial gallons (Imp gal)	X 4.546	= Litres (l)	X 0.22	= Imperial gallons (Imp gal)
Imperial gallons (Imp gal)	X 1.201	= US gallons (US gal)	X 0.833	= Imperial gallons (Imp gal)
US gallons (US gal)	X 3.785	= Litres (l)	X 0.264	= US gallons (US gal)

Mass (weight)

Ounces (oz)	X 28.35	= Grams (g)	X 0.035	= Ounces (oz)
Pounds (lb)	X 0.454	= Kilograms (kg)	X 2.205	= Pounds (lb)

Force

Ounces-force (ozf; oz)	X 0.278	= Newtons (N)	X 3.6	= Ounces-force (ozf; oz)
Pounds-force (lbf; lb)	X 4.448	= Newtons (N)	X 0.225	= Pounds-force (lbf; lb)
Newtons (N)	X 0.1	= Kilograms-force (kgf; kg)	X 9.81	= Newtons (N)

Pressure

Pounds-force per square inch (psi; lbf/in²; lb/in²)	X 0.070	= Kilograms-force per square centimetre (kgf/cm²; kg/cm²)	X 14.223	= Pounds-force per square inch (psi; lbf/in²; lb/in²)
Pounds-force per square inch (psi; lbf/in²; lb/in²)	X 0.068	= Atmospheres (atm)	X 14.696	= Pounds-force per square inch (psi; lbf/in²; lb/in²)
Pounds-force per square inch (psi; lbf/in²; lb/in²)	X 0.069	= Bars	X 14.5	= Pounds-force per square inch (psi; lbf/in²; lb/in²)
Pounds-force per square inch (psi; lbf/in²; lb/in²)	X 6.895	= Kilopascals (kPa)	X 0.145	= Pounds-force per square inch (psi; lbf/in²; lb/in²)
Kilopascals (kPa)	X 0.01	= Kilograms-force per square centimetre (kgf/cm²; kg/cm²)	X 98.1	= Kilopascals (kPa)

Torque (moment of force)

Pounds-force inches (lbf in; lb in)	X 1.152	= Kilograms-force centimetre (kgf cm; kg cm)	X 0.868	= Pounds-force inches (lbf in; lb in)
Pounds-force inches (lbf in; lb in)	X 0.113	= Newton metres (Nm)	X 8.85	= Pounds-force inches (lbf in; lb in)
Pounds-force inches (lbf in; lb in)	X 0.083	= Pounds-force feet (lbf ft; lb ft)	X 12	= Pounds-force inches (lbf in; lb in)
Pounds-force feet (lbf ft; lb ft)	X 0.138	= Kilograms-force metres (kgf m; kg m)	X 7.233	= Pounds-force feet (lbf ft; lb ft)
Pounds-force feet (lbf ft; lb ft)	X 1.356	= Newton metres (Nm)	X 0.738	= Pounds-force feet (lbf ft; lb ft)
Newton metres (Nm)	X 0.102	= Kilograms-force metres (kgf m; kg m)	X 9.804	= Newton metres (Nm)

Vacuum

Inches mercury (in. Hg)	X 3.377	= Kilopascals (kPa)	X 0.2961	= Inches mercury
Inches mercury (in. Hg)	X 25.4	= Millimeters mercury (mm Hg)	X 0.0394	= Inches mercury

Power

Horsepower (hp)	X 745.7	= Watts (W)	X 0.0013	= Horsepower (hp)

Velocity (speed)

Miles per hour (miles/hr; mph)	X 1.609	= Kilometres per hour (km/hr; kph)	X 0.621	= Miles per hour (miles/hr; mph)

Fuel consumption*

Miles per gallon, Imperial (mpg)	X 0.354	= Kilometres per litre (km/l)	X 2.825	= Miles per gallon, Imperial (mpg)
Miles per gallon, US (mpg)	X 0.425	= Kilometres per litre (km/l)	X 2.352	= Miles per gallon, US (mpg)

Temperature

Degrees Fahrenheit = (°C x 1.8) + 32

Degrees Celsius (Degrees Centigrade; °C) = (°F - 32) x 0.56

*It is common practice to convert from miles per gallon (mpg) to litres/100 kilometres (l/100km),
where mpg (Imperial) x l/100 km = 282 and mpg (US) x l/100 km = 235

Safety first!

Regardless of how enthusiastic you may be about getting on with the job at hand, take the time to ensure that your safety is not jeopardized. A moment's lack of attention can result in an accident, as can failure to observe certain simple safety precautions. The possibility of an accident will always exist, and the following points should not be considered a comprehensive list of all dangers. Rather, they are intended to make you aware of the risks and to encourage a safety conscious approach to all work you carry out on your vehicle.

Essential DOs and DON'Ts

DON'T rely on a jack when working under the vehicle. Always use approved jackstands to support the weight of the vehicle and place them under the recommended lift or support points.

DON'T attempt to loosen extremely tight fasteners (i.e. wheel lug nuts) while the vehicle is on a jack - it may fall.

DON'T start the engine without first making sure that the transmission is in Neutral (or Park where applicable) and the parking brake is set.

DON'T remove the radiator cap from a hot cooling system - let it cool or cover it with a cloth and release the pressure gradually.

DON'T attempt to drain the engine oil until you are sure it has cooled to the point that it will not burn you.

DON'T touch any part of the engine or exhaust system until it has cooled sufficiently to avoid burns.

DON'T siphon toxic liquids such as gasoline, antifreeze and brake fluid by mouth, or allow them to remain on your skin.

DON'T inhale brake lining dust - it is potentially hazardous (see *Asbestos* below).

DON'T allow spilled oil or grease to remain on the floor - wipe it up before someone slips on it.

DON'T use loose fitting wrenches or other tools which may slip and cause injury.

DON'T push on wrenches when loosening or tightening nuts or bolts. Always try to pull the wrench toward you. If the situation calls for pushing the wrench away, push with an open hand to avoid scraped knuckles if the wrench should slip.

DON'T attempt to lift a heavy component alone - get someone to help you.

DON'T rush or take unsafe shortcuts to finish a job.

DON'T allow children or animals in or around the vehicle while you are working on it.

DO wear eye protection when using power tools such as a drill, sander, bench grinder, etc. and when working under a vehicle.

DO keep loose clothing and long hair well out of the way of moving parts.

DO make sure that any hoist used has a safe working load rating adequate for the job.

DO get someone to check on you periodically when working alone on a vehicle.

DO carry out work in a logical sequence and make sure that everything is correctly assembled and tightened.

DO keep chemicals and fluids tightly capped and out of the reach of children and pets.

DO remember that your vehicle's safety affects that of yourself and others. If in doubt on any point, get professional advice.

Asbestos

Certain friction, insulating, sealing, and other products - such as brake linings, brake bands, clutch linings, torque converters, gaskets, etc. - may contain asbestos. Extreme care must be taken to avoid inhalation of dust from such products, since it is hazardous to health. If in doubt, assume that they do contain asbestos.

Fire

Remember at all times that gasoline is highly flammable. Never smoke or have any kind of open flame around when working on a vehicle. But the risk does not end there. A spark caused by an electrical short circuit, by two metal surfaces contacting each other, or even by static electricity built up in your body under certain conditions, can ignite gasoline vapors, which in a confined space are highly explosive. Do not, under any circumstances, use gasoline for cleaning parts. Use an approved safety solvent.

Always disconnect the battery ground (-) cable at the battery before working on any part of the fuel system or electrical system. Never risk spilling fuel on a hot engine or exhaust component. It is strongly recommended that a fire extinguisher suitable for use on fuel and electrical fires be kept handy in the garage or workshop at all times. Never try to extinguish a fuel or electrical fire with water.

Fumes

Certain fumes are highly toxic and can quickly cause unconsciousness and even death if inhaled to any extent. Gasoline vapor falls into this category, as do the vapors from some cleaning solvents. Any draining or pouring of such volatile fluids should be done in a well ventilated area.

When using cleaning fluids and solvents, read the instructions on the container carefully. Never use materials from unmarked containers.

Never run the engine in an enclosed space, such as a garage. Exhaust fumes contain carbon monoxide, which is extremely poisonous. If you need to run the engine, always do so in the open air, or at least have the rear of the vehicle outside the work area.

If you are fortunate enough to have the use of an inspection pit, never drain or pour gasoline and never run the engine while the vehicle is over the pit. The fumes, being heavier than air, will concentrate in the pit with possibly lethal results.

The battery

Never create a spark or allow a bare light bulb near a battery. They normally give off a certain amount of hydrogen gas, which is highly explosive.

Always disconnect the battery ground (-) cable at the battery before working on the fuel or electrical systems.

If possible, loosen the filler caps or cover when charging the battery from an external source (this does not apply to sealed or maintenance-free batteries). Do not charge at an excessive rate or the battery may burst.

Take care when adding water to a non maintenance-free battery and when carrying a battery. The electrolyte, even when diluted, is very corrosive and should not be allowed to contact clothing or skin.

Always wear eye protection when cleaning the battery to prevent the caustic deposits from entering your eyes.

Household current

When using an electric power tool, inspection light, etc., which operates on household current, always make sure that the tool is correctly connected to its plug and that, where necessary, it is properly grounded. Do not use such items in damp conditions and, again, do not create a spark or apply excessive heat in the vicinity of fuel or fuel vapor.

Secondary ignition system voltage

A severe electric shock can result from touching certain parts of the ignition system (such as the spark plug wires) when the engine is running or being cranked, particularly if components are damp or the insulation is defective. In the case of an electronic ignition system, the secondary system voltage is much higher and could prove fatal.

Troubleshooting

Contents

This section provides an easy reference guide to the more common problems which may occur during the operation of your vehicle. These problems and their possible causes are grouped under headings denoting various components or systems, such as Engine, Cooling system, etc. They also refer you to the Chapter and/or Section which deals with the problem.

Remember that successful troubleshooting is not a mysterious art practiced only by professional mechanics. It is simply the result of the right knowledge combined with an intelligent, systematic approach to the problem. Always work by a process of elimination, starting with the simplest solution and working through to the most complex - and never overlook the obvious. Anyone can run the gas tank dry or leave the lights on overnight, so don't assume that you are exempt from such oversights.

Finally, always establish a clear idea of why a problem has occurred and take steps to ensure that it doesn't happen again. If the electrical system fails because of a poor connection, check all other connections in the system to make sure that they don't fail as well. If a particular fuse continues to blow, find out why - don't just replace one fuse after another. Remember, failure of a small component can often be indicative of potential failure or incorrect functioning of a more important component or system.

Engine

1   Engine will not rotate when attempting to start

1   Battery terminal connections loose or corroded (Chapter 1).
2   Battery discharged or faulty (Chapter 1).
3   Automatic transaxle not completely engaged in Park (Chapter 7) or clutch not completely depressed (Chapter 8).
4   Broken, loose or disconnected wiring in the starting circuit (Chapters 5 and 12).
5   Starter motor pinion jammed in flywheel ring gear (Chapter 5).
6   Starter solenoid faulty (Chapter 5).
7   Starter motor faulty (Chapter 5).
8   Ignition switch faulty (Chapter 12).
9   Starter pinion or flywheel teeth worn or broken (Chapter 5).

2   Engine rotates but will not start

1   Fuel tank empty.
2   Battery discharged (engine rotates slowly) (Chapter 5).
3   Battery terminal connections loose or corroded (Chapter 1).
4   Leaking fuel injector(s), fuel pump, pressure regulator, etc. (Chapter 4).
5   Fuel not reaching fuel injection system (Chapter 4).
6   Ignition components damp or damaged (Chapter 5).
7   Worn, faulty or incorrectly gapped spark plugs (Chapter 1).
8   Broken, loose or disconnected wiring in the starting circuit (Chapter 5).
9   Loose distributor is changing ignition timing (Chapter 5).
10   Broken, loose or disconnected wires at the ignition coil or faulty coil (Chapter 5).
11   Timing belt stripped or broken (2.0L OHC only).

3   Engine hard to start when cold

1   Battery discharged or low (Chapter 1).
2   Fuel system malfunctioning (Chapter 4).
3   Injector(s) leaking (Chapter 4).
4   Distributor rotor carbon tracked (Chapter 1).

4   Engine hard to start when hot

1   Air filter clogged (Chapter 1).
2   Fuel not reaching the fuel injection system (Chapter 4).
3   Corroded battery connections, especially ground (Chapter 1).

5   Starter motor noisy or excessively rough in engagement

1   Pinion or flywheel gear teeth worn or broken (Chapter 5).
2   Starter motor mounting bolts loose or missing (Chapter 5).

6   Engine starts but stops immediately

1   Loose or faulty electrical connections at distributor, coil or alternator (Chapter 5).
2   Insufficient fuel reaching the fuel injectors (Chapter 4).
3   Vacuum leak at the gasket between the intake manifold/plenum and throttle body (Chapters 1 and 4).

7   Oil puddle under engine

1   Oil pan gasket and/or oil pan drain bolt seal leaking (Chapter 2).
2   Oil pressure sending unit leaking (Chapter 2).
3   Rocker cover gaskets leaking (Chapter 2).
4   Engine oil seals leaking (Chapter 2).
5   Timing cover sealant or sealing flange leaking (Chapter 2).

8   Engine lopes while idling or idles erratically

1   Vacuum leakage (Chapter 4).
2   Leaking EGR valve or plugged PCV valve (Chapters 1 and 6).
3   Air filter clogged (Chapter 1).
4   Fuel pump not delivering sufficient fuel to the fuel injection system (Chapter 4).
5   Leaking head gasket (Chapter 2).
6   Timing chain and/or gears worn (Chapter 2).
7   Camshaft lobes worn (Chapter 2).

9   Engine misses at idle speed

1   Spark plugs worn or not gapped properly (Chapter 1).
2   Faulty spark plug wires (Chapter 1).
3   Vacuum leaks (Chapters 1 and 4).
4   Incorrect ignition timing (Chapter 5).
5   Uneven or low compression (Chapter 2).

10   Engine misses throughout driving speed range

1   Fuel filter clogged and/or impurities in the fuel system (Chapters 1 and 4).
2   Low fuel output at the injector (Chapter 4).
3   Faulty or incorrectly gapped spark plugs (Chapter 1).
4   Incorrect ignition timing (Chapter 5).
5   Cracked distributor cap, disconnected distributor wires or damaged distributor components (Chapter 1).
6   Leaking spark plug wires (Chapter 1).
7   Faulty emission system components (Chapter 6).
8   Low or uneven cylinder compression pressures (Chapter 2).
9   Weak or faulty ignition system (Chapter 5).
10   Vacuum leak in fuel injection system, intake manifold or vacuum hoses (Chapter 4).

11   Engine stumbles on acceleration

1   Spark plugs fouled (Chapter 1).
2   Fuel injection system malfunction (Chapter 4).
3   Fuel filter clogged (Chapter 1).
4   Incorrect ignition timing (Chapter 5).
5   Intake manifold air leak (Chapter 4).

12   Engine surges while holding accelerator steady

1   Intake air leak (Chapter 4).
2   Fuel pump faulty (Chapter 4).
3   Loose fuel injector harness connections (Chapter 4).
4   Defective ECM (Chapter 6).

13   Engine hard to start and surges when cold

1   Faulty idle control system or ECM (Chapter 6).
2   Incorrect PROM installed in ECM. See your dealer for a list of available service PROMs.

14   Engine stalls

1   Idle speed incorrect (Chapters 1 and 4).
2   Fuel filter clogged and/or water and impurities in the fuel system (Chapters 1 and 4).
3   Distributor components damp or damaged (Chapter 5).
4   Faulty emissions system components or sensor (Chapter 6).
5   Faulty or incorrectly gapped spark plugs (Chapter 1).
6   Faulty spark plug wires (Chapter 1).
7   Vacuum leak in the fuel injection system, intake manifold or vacuum hoses (Chapter 4).

15 Engine lacks power

1 Incorrect ignition timing (Chapter 5).
2 Excessive play in distributor shaft (Chapter 5).
3 Worn rotor, distributor cap or wires (Chapter 1).
4 Faulty or incorrectly gapped spark plugs (Chapter 1).
5 Fuel injection system malfunctioning (Chapter 4).
6 Faulty coil (Chapter 5).
7 Brakes binding (Chapter 1).
8 Automatic transaxle fluid level incorrect (Chapter 1).
9 Clutch slipping (Chapter 8).
10 Fuel filter clogged and/or impurities in the fuel system (Chapter 1).
11 Emission control system malfunctioning (Chapter 6).
12 Low or uneven cylinder compression pressures (Chapter 2).

16 Engine backfires

1 Emissions system malfunctioning (Chapter 6).
2 Ignition timing incorrect (Chapter 5).
3 Faulty secondary ignition system (cracked spark plug insulator, faulty plug wires, distributor cap and/or rotor) (Chapter 1).
4 Fuel injection system malfunctioning (Chapter 4).
5 Vacuum leak at fuel injectors, intake manifold or vacuum hoses (Chapter 4).
6 Valves sticking (Chapter 2).

17 Pinging or knocking engine sounds during acceleration or uphill

1 Incorrect grade of fuel.
2 Ignition timing incorrect (Chapter 5).
3 Fuel injection system malfunctioning (Chapter 4).
4 Improper or damaged spark plugs or wires (Chapter 1).
5 Worn or damaged distributor components (Chapter 5).
6 Faulty emissions system components or sensor (Chapter 6).
7 Vacuum leak (Chapter 4).

18 Engine runs with oil pressure light on

1 Low oil level (Chapter 1).
2 Idle rpm below specification (Chapter 1).
3 Short in wiring circuit (Chapter 12).
4 Faulty oil pressure sender (Chapter 2).
5 Worn engine bearings and/or oil pump (Chapter 2).

19 Engine diesels (continues to run) after switching off

1 Idle speed too high (Chapters 1 and 4).
2 Thermo-controlled air cleaner heat valve not operating properly (TBI equipped engines only) (Chapter 6).
3 Excessive engine operating temperature (Chapter 3).

Engine electrical system

20 Battery will not hold a charge

1 Alternator drivebelt defective or not adjusted properly (Chapter 1).
2 Battery terminals loose or corroded (Chapter 1).
3 Alternator not charging properly (Chapter 5).
4 Loose, broken or faulty wiring in the charging circuit (Chapter 5).
5 Short in vehicle wiring (Chapters 5 and 12).
6 Internally defective battery (Chapters 1 and 5).

21 Voltage warning light fails to go out

1 Faulty alternator or charging circuit (Chapter 5).
2 Alternator drivebelt defective or out of adjustment (Chapter 1).
3 Alternator voltage regulator inoperative (Chapter 5).

22 Voltage warning light fails to come on when key is turned on

1 Warning light bulb defective (Chapter 12).
2 Fault in the printed circuit, dash wiring or bulb holder (Chapter 12).

Fuel system

23 Excessive fuel consumption

1 Dirty or clogged air filter element (Chapter 1).
2 Incorrectly set ignition timing (Chapter 5).
3 Emissions system malfunctioning (Chapter 6).
4 Fuel injection system malfunctioning (Chapter 4).
5 Low tire pressure or incorrect tire size (Chapter 1).

24 Fuel leakage and/or fuel odor

1 Leak in a fuel feed or vent line (Chapter 4).
2 Tank overfilled.
3 Evaporative canister filter clogged (Chapters 1 and 6).
4 Fuel injection system malfunctioning (Chapter 4).

Cooling system

25 Overheating

1 Insufficient coolant in system (Chapter 1).
2 Water pump drivebelt defective or out of adjustment (Chapter 1).
3 Radiator core blocked or grille restricted (Chapter 3).
4 Thermostat faulty (Chapter 3).
5 Electric cooling fan faulty, or blades broken or cracked (Chapter 3).
6 Radiator cap not maintaining proper pressure (Chapter 3).
7 Ignition timing incorrect (Chapter 5).

26 Overcooling

Faulty thermostat (Chapter 3).

27 External coolant leakage

1 Deteriorated/damaged hoses or loose clamps (Chapters 1 and 3).
2 Water pump seal defective (Chapters 1 and 3).
3 Leakage from radiator core or header tank (Chapter 3).
4 Engine drain or water jacket core plugs leaking (Chapter 2).

28 Internal coolant leakage

1 Leaking cylinder head gasket (Chapter 2).
2 Cracked cylinder bore or cylinder head (Chapter 2).
3 Leaking intake manifold gasket (Chapter 2).

29 Coolant loss

1 Too much coolant in system (Chapter 1).
2 Coolant boiling away because of overheating (Chapter 3).
3 Internal or external leakage (Chapter 3).
4 Faulty radiator cap (Chapter 3).

30 Poor coolant circulation

1 Inoperative water pump (Chapter 3).
2 Restriction in cooling system (Chapters 1 and 3).
3 Water pump drivebelt defective or out of adjustment (Chapter 1).
4 Thermostat sticking (Chapter 3).

31 Drivebelt squeals or chirps

1 Defective drivebelt (Chapter 1).
2 Defective drivebelt tensioner (Chapter 3).
3 Drivebelt pulleys not in alignment.

Clutch

32 Pedal travels to floor - no pressure or very little resistance

1 Master or slave cylinder faulty (Chapter 8).
2 Hose/pipe burst or leaking (Chapter 8).
3 Connections leaking (Chapter 8).
4 No fluid in reservoir (Chapter 8).
5 If fluid is present in master cylinder dust cover, rear master cylinder seal has failed (Chapter 8).
6 If fluid level in reservoir rises as pedal is depressed, master cylinder center valve seal is faulty (Chapter 8).
7 Broken release bearing or fork (Chapter 8).

33 Fluid in area of master cylinder dust cover and on pedal

Rear seal failure in master cylinder (Chapter 8).

34 Fluid on slave cylinder

Slave cylinder seal faulty (Chapter 8).

35 Pedal feels spongy when depressed

Air in system (Chapter 8).

36 Unable to select gears

1 Faulty transaxle (Chapter 7).
2 Faulty clutch disc (Chapter 8).
3 Fork and bearing not assembled properly (Chapter 8).
4 Faulty pressure plate (Chapter 8).
5 Pressure plate-to-flywheel bolts loose (Chapter 8).

37 Clutch slips (engine speed increases with no increase in vehicle speed)

1 Clutch plate worn (Chapter 8).
2 Clutch plate is oil soaked by leaking rear main seal (Chapter 8).
3 Clutch plate not seated. It may take 30 or 40 normal starts for a new one to seat.
4 Warped pressure plate or flywheel (Chapter 8).
5 Weak diaphragm spring (Chapter 8).
6 Clutch plate overheated. Allow to cool.

38 Grabbing (chattering) as clutch is engaged

1 Oil soaked, burned or glazed lining (Chapter 8).
2 Worn or loose engine or transaxle mounts (Chapters 2 and 7).
3 Worn splines on clutch plate hub (Chapter 8).
4 Warped pressure plate or flywheel (Chapter 8).

39 Noise in clutch area

1 Fork shaft improperly installed (Chapter 8).
2 Faulty release bearing (Chapter 8).

40 Clutch pedal stays on floor

1 Fork shaft binding in housing (Chapter 8).
2 Broken release bearing or fork (Chapter 8).

41 High pedal effort

1 Fork shaft binding in housing (Chapter 8).
2 Pressure plate faulty (Chapter 8).

Manual transaxle

42 Vibration

1 Rough wheel bearing (Chapter 10).
2 Damaged driveaxle (Chapter 8).
3 Out-of-round tires (Chapter 1).
4 Tire out-of-balance (Chapter 10).
5 Worn or damaged CV joint (Chapter 8).

43 Noisy in Neutral with engine running

Damaged clutch release bearing (Chapter 8).

44 Noisy in one particular gear

1 Damaged or worn constant mesh gears (Chapter 7).
2 Damaged or worn synchronizers (Chapter 7).

45 Noisy in all gears

1 Insufficient lubricant (Chapter 1).
2 Damaged or worn bearings (Chapter 7).
3 Worn or damaged input gear shaft and/or output gear shaft (Chapter 7).

46 Slips out of gear

1 Worn or improperly adjusted linkage (Chapter 7).
2 Transaxle loose on engine (Chapter 7).
3 Shift linkage does not work freely, binds (Chapter 7).
4 Input shaft bearing retainer broken or loose (Chapter 7).
5 Dirt between clutch cover and engine housing (Chapter 7).
6 Worn shift fork (Chapter 7).

47 Leaks lubricant

1 Excessive amount of lubricant in transaxle (Chapter 1).
2 Loose or broken input shaft bearing retainer (Chapter 7).
3 Input shaft bearing retainer O-ring and/or lip seal damaged (Chapter 7).
4 Driveaxle oil seal(s) leaking (Chapter 7).

Automatic transaxle

Note: *Due to the complexity of the automatic transaxle, it is difficult for the home mechanic to properly diagnose and service this component. For problems other than the following, the vehicle should be taken to a dealer or transmission shop.*

48 Fluid leakage

1 Automatic transmission fluid is a deep red color. Fluid leaks should not be confused with engine oil, which can easily be blown by air flow to the transaxle.
2 To pinpoint a leak, first remove all built-up dirt and grime from the transaxle housing with degreasing agents and/or steam cleaning. Drive the vehicle at low speeds so air flow will not blow the leak far from its source. Raise the vehicle and determine where the leak is coming from. Common areas of leakage are:

a) *Pan (Chapters 1 and 7)*
b) *Filler pipe (Chapter 7)*
c) *Transaxle oil lines (Chapter 7)*
d) *Speedometer gear or sensor (Chapter 7)*
e) *Driveaxle oil seals (Chapter 7)*

49 Transaxle fluid brown or has a burned smell

Transaxle overheated. Change fluid (Chapter 1).

50 General shift mechanism problems

1   Chapter 7 Part B deals with checking and adjusting the shift linkage on automatic transaxles. Common problems which may be attributed to poorly adjusted linkage are:
   a) *Engine starting in gears other than Park or Neutral.*
   b) *Indicator on shifter pointing to a gear other than the one actually being used.*
   c) *Vehicle moves when in Park.*
2   Refer to Chapter 7 Part B for the shift linkage adjustment procedure.

51 Transaxle will not downshift with accelerator pedal pressed to the floor

Throttle valve (TV) cable out of adjustment (Chapter 7).

52 Engine will start in gears other than Park or Neutral

Starter safety switch malfunctioning (Chapter 7).

53 Transaxle slips, shifts roughly, is noisy or has no drive in forward or reverse gears

There are many probable causes for the above problems, but the home mechanic should be concerned with only one possibility - fluid level. Before taking the vehicle to a repair shop, check the level and condition of the fluid as described in Chapter 1.
   Correct the fluid level as necessary or change the fluid and filter if needed. If the problem persists, have a professional diagnose the probable cause.

Driveaxles

54 Clicking noise in turns

Worn or damaged outer CV joint. Check for cut or damaged boots (Chapter 1). Repair as necessary (Chapter 8).

55 Knock or clunk when accelerating after coasting

Worn or damaged outer CV joint. Check for cut or damaged boots (Chapter 1). Repair as necessary (Chapter 8).

56 Shudder or vibration during acceleration

1   Excessive inner CV joint angle. Check and correct as necessary (Chapter 8).
2   Worn or damaged CV joints. Repair or replace as necessary (Chapter 8).
3   Sticking inboard joint assembly. Correct or replace as necessary (Chapter 8).

Brakes

Note: *Before assuming that a brake problem exists, make sure that:*
   a) *The tires are in good condition and properly inflated (Chapter 1).*
   b) *The front end alignment is correct (Chapter 10).*
   c) *The vehicle is not loaded with weight in an unequal manner.*

57 Vehicle pulls to one side during braking

1   Incorrect tire pressures (Chapter 1).
2   Front end out of line (have the front end aligned).
3   Unmatched tires on same axle.
4   Restricted brake lines or hoses (Chapter 9).
5   Malfunctioning brake assembly (Chapter 9).
6   Loose suspension parts (Chapter 10).
7   Loose brake calipers (Chapter 9).

58 Noise (high-pitched squeal when the brakes are applied)

Front disc brake pads worn out. The noise comes from the wear sensor rubbing against the disc. Replace pads with new ones immediately (Chapter 9).

59 Brake roughness or chatter (pedal pulsates)

1   Excessive front brake disc lateral runout (Chapter 9).
2   Parallelism not within specifications (Chapter 9).
3   Uneven pad wear caused by caliper not sliding due to improper clearance or dirt (Chapter 9).
4   Defective brake disc (Chapter 9).
5   Rear brake drum out-of-round.

60 Excessive pedal effort required to stop vehicle

1   Malfunctioning power brake booster (Chapter 9).

2   Partial system failure (Chapter 9).
3   Excessively worn pads or shoes (Chapter 9).
4   One or more caliper pistons or wheel cylinders seized or sticking (Chapter 9).
5   Brake pads or shoes contaminated with oil or grease (Chapter 9).
6   New pads or shoes installed and not yet seated. It will take a while for the new material to seat.

61 Excessive brake pedal travel

1   Partial brake system failure (Chapter 9).
2   Insufficient fluid in master cylinder (Chapters 1 and 9).
3   Air trapped in system (Chapters 1 and 9).

62 Dragging brakes

1   Master cylinder pistons not returning correctly (Chapter 9).
2   Restricted brakes lines or hoses (Chapters 1 and 9).
3   Incorrect parking brake adjustment (Chapter 9).

63 Grabbing or uneven braking action

1   Malfunction of proportioner valves (Chapter 9).
2   Malfunction of power brake booster unit (Chapter 9).
3   Binding brake pedal mechanism (Chapter 9).

64 Brake pedal feels spongy when depressed

1   Air in hydraulic lines (Chapter 9).
2   Master cylinder mounting bolts loose (Chapter 9).
3   Master cylinder defective (Chapter 9).

65 Brake pedal travels to the floor with little resistance

Little or no fluid in the master cylinder reservoir caused by leaking caliper or wheel cylinder pistons, loose, damaged or disconnected brake lines (Chapter 9).

66 Parking brake does not hold

Parking brake linkage improperly adjusted (Chapter 9).

Suspension and steering systems

Note: *Before attempting to diagnose the suspension and steering systems, perform the following preliminary checks:*

  a) Tires for wrong pressure and uneven wear.
  b) Steering universal joints or coupling from the column to the steering gear for loose fasteners or wear.
  c) Front and rear suspension and the steering gear assembly for loose or damaged parts.
  d) Out-of-round or out-of-balance tires, bent rims and loose and/or rough wheel bearings.

67 Vehicle pulls to one side

1   Mismatched or uneven tires (Chapter 10).
2   Broken or sagging springs (Chapter 10).
3   Front wheel alignment incorrect (Chapter 10).
4   Front brakes dragging (Chapter 9).

68 Abnormal or excessive tire wear

1   Front wheel alignment incorrect (Chapter 10).
2   Sagging or broken springs (Chapter 10).
3   Tire out-of-balance (Chapter 10).
4   Worn shock absorber (Chapter 10).
5   Overloaded vehicle.
6   Tires not rotated regularly.

69 Wheel makes a "thumping" noise

1   Blister or bump on tire (Chapter 1).
2   Improper shock absorber action (Chapter 10).

70 Shimmy, shake or vibration

1   Tire or wheel out-of-balance or out-of-round (Chapter 10).
2   Loose or worn wheel bearings (Chapter 10).
3   Worn tie-rod ends (Chapter 10).
4   Worn balljoints (Chapter 10).
5   Excessive wheel runout (Chapter 10).
6   Blister or bump on tire (Chapter 1).

71 Hard steering

1   Lack of lubrication at balljoints, tie-rod ends and steering gear assembly (Chapter 10).
2   Front wheel alignment incorrect (Chapter 10).
3   Low tire pressure (Chapter 1).

72 Steering wheel does not return to center position correctly

1   Lack of lubrication at balljoints and tie-rod ends (Chapter 10).
2   Binding in steering column (Chapter 10).
3   Lack of lubricant in steering gear assembly (Chapter 10).
4   Front wheel alignment (Chapter 10).

73 Squeaking or squawking noise from the front suspension

Check the stabilizer bar bushings for wear and replace if necessary (Chapter 10).

74 Abnormal noise at the front end

1   Lack of lubrication at balljoints and tie-rod ends (Chapter 1).
2   Loose upper strut mounting (Chapter 10).
3   Worn tie-rod ends (Chapter 10).
4   Loose stabilizer bar (Chapter 10).
5   Loose wheel lug nuts (Chapters 1 and 10).
6   Loose suspension bolts (Chapter 10).

75 Wander or poor steering stability

1   Mismatched or uneven tires (Chapter 10).
2   Lack of lubrication at balljoints or tie-rod ends (Chapters 1 and 10).
3   Worn shock absorbers (Chapter 10).
4   Loose stabilizer bar (Chapter 10).
5   Broken or sagging springs (Chapter 10).
6   Front wheel alignment incorrect (Chapter 10).
7   Worn steering gear clamp bushings (Chapter 10).

76 Erratic steering when braking

1   Wheel bearings worn (Chapters 8 and 10).
2   Broken or sagging springs (Chapter 10).
3   Leaking wheel cylinder or caliper (Chapter 10).
4   Warped rotors or brake drums (Chapter 10).
5   Worn steering gear clamp bushings (Chapter 10).

77 Excessive pitching and/or rolling around corners or during braking

1   Loose stabilizer bar (Chapter 10).
2   Worn shock absorbers or mounts (Chapter 10).
3   Broken or sagging springs (Chapter 10).
4   Overloaded vehicle.

78 Suspension bottoms

1   Overloaded vehicle.
2   Worn shock absorbers (Chapter 10).
3   Incorrect, broken or sagging springs (Chapter 10).

79 Cupped tires

1   Front wheel alignment incorrect (Chapter 10).
2   Worn shock absorbers (Chapter 10).
3   Wheel bearings worn (Chapters 8 and 10).
4   Excessive tire or wheel runout (Chapter 10).
5   Worn balljoints (Chapter 10).

80 Excessive tire wear on outside edge

1   Inflation pressures incorrect (Chapter 1).
2   Excessive speed in turns.
3   Front end alignment incorrect (excessive toe-in or positive camber). Have professionally aligned.
4   Suspension arm bent or twisted (Chapter 10).

81 Excessive tire wear on inside edge

1   Inflation pressures incorrect (Chapter 1).
2   Front end alignment incorrect (toe-out or excessive negative camber). Have professionally aligned.
3   Loose or damaged steering components (Chapter 10).

82 Tire tread worn in one place

1   Tires out-of-balance.
2   Damaged or buckled wheel. Inspect and replace if necessary.
3   Defective tire (Chapter 1).

83 Excessive play or looseness in steering system

1   Wheel bearings worn (Chapter 10).
2   Tie-rod end loose or worn (Chapter 10).
3   Steering gear loose (Chapter 10).

84 Rattling or clicking noise in rack and pinion

Steering gear clamps loose (Chapter 10).

Chapter 1
Tune up and routine maintenance

Contents

Specifications

Recommended lubricants and fluids

Note: *Listed here are manufacturer recommendations at the time this manual was printed. Manufacturers occasionally upgrade their fluid and lubricant specifications, so check with your local auto parts store for the most current recommendations.*

Engine oil type .... API grade SG, SH, SG/CD or SH/CD multigrade and fuel efficient oil
Engine oil viscosity .... See accompanying charts

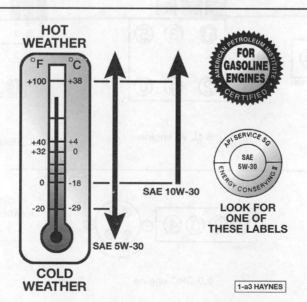

Engine oil viscosity recommendations

1-a3 HAYNES

Recommended lubricants and fluids

Automatic transaxle fluid .... Dexron type automatic transmission fluid
Manual transaxle lubricant... GM Synchromesh Transmission Fluid (part no. 12345349) or equivalent
Engine coolant. .... Mixture of water and ethylene glycol-base antifreeze
Brake fluid.. DOT 3 brake fluid
Clutch fluid... DOT 3 brake fluid
Power steering fluid .... GM power steering fluid or equivalent
Chassis lubrication .... NLGI #2 multi-purpose lithium-base chassis grease

Capacities*

Engine oil
(**Note**: *When changing the oil filter, one additional quart of oil may be needed*)
    2.5L four-cylinder engine
        With manual transaxle .... 4.0 qts
        With automatic transaxle .... 3.0 qts
    All others .... 4.0 qts
Automatic transaxle fluid (filter change and refill)........................... 4.0 qts
Manual transaxle lubricant.. 3.0 qts
Cooling system .... 7.5 to 12.9 quarts (depending on engine and cooling system option)

* All capacities approximate. Add as necessary to bring to the appropriate level.

General engine

Radiator cap opening pressure .... 15 psi
Thermostat
    Starts to open... 188 to 193-degrees F
    Fully open.. 212-degrees F
Engine idle speed*
    Automatic transaxle .... 700 rpm
    Manual transaxle .... 750 rpm
Drivebelt deflection (V-belt) .... 1/4 to 1/2 inch
Serpentine drivebelt tension
    2.3L power steering pump .... 100 lbs
    All other models .... Automatically adjusted

* Refer to the Vehicle Emission Control Information label in the engine compartment and follow the information on the label if it differs from the information shown here.

2.5L engines

3.1L V6 engine

3.0L V6 engine

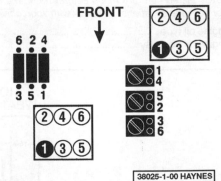

FRONT

3.3L V6 engine

38025-1-00 HAYNES

2.3L engine (Quad-4)

2.0 OHC engine

Cylinder location and distributor rotation/coil terminal location diagrams

The blackened terminal shown on the distributor cap indicates the Number One spark plug wire position

Ignition system

Firing order

Four-cylinder engines... 1-3-4-2
3.1L V6 engines... 1-2-3-4-5-6
3.0L and 3.3L V6 engines.. 1-6-5-4-3-2

Spark plug type and gap*

	Type	Gap
Four-cylinder engines		
2.0L OHC		
1985 and 1986 models	AC R44CTS or equivalent	0.035 inch
1987 models	AC R44XLS6 or equivalent	0.060 inch
2.3L		
1990 and earlier	AC FR3LS or equivalent	0.035 inch
1991 and later		
Exc. H.O. or manual transaxle	AC 41-603** or equivalent	0.035 inch
H.O. or with manual transaxle	AC 41-602** or equivalent	0.035 inch
2.5L	AC R43TS6 or equivalent	0.060 inch
V6 engines		
3.0L	AC R44LTS or equivalent	0.045 inch
3.1L	AC 41-600 or equivalent	0.060 inch
3.3L		
1992 and earlier	AC R45LTS6 or equivalent	0.060 inch
1993 on	AC 41-600 or equivalent	0.060 inch

Ignition timing (models with distributors only)*

1986 and earlier models

   2.0L OHC four-cylinder engine .... 6-degrees BTDC @ idle
   2.5L four-cylinder engine .... 8-degrees BTDC @ idle

1987 on .... 8-degrees BTDC @ idle

Refer to the Vehicle Emission Control Information label in the engine compartment and follow the information on the label if it differs from that shown here.

**Can substitute as follows: AC 41-602 can use AC FR2LSK or FR2LS (Gap = 0.035 inch); AC 41-603 can use AC FR3LSK or FR3LS (Gap = 0.035 inch)*

Brakes

Disc brake pads - minimum thickness. .... 1/8 inch
Drum brake shoes - minimum thickness. .... 1/16 inch

Torque specifications   **Ft-lbs** (unless otherwise indicated)

Spark plugs

   1991 and earlier... 84 to 180 in-lbs
   1992 and later .... 132 in-lbs
Automatic transaxle fluid pan bolts .... 120 in-lbs
TBI mounting nuts/bolts .... 156 in-lbs
Wheel lug nuts

   Steel wheels 80
   Aluminum wheels 100

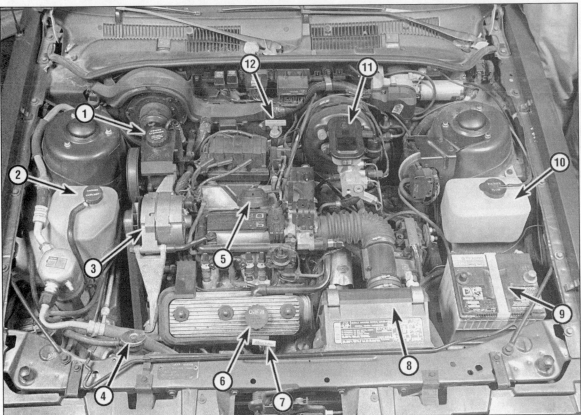

Typical 3.0L V6 engine compartment component layout

1   Power steering fluid dipstick
2   Coolant reservoir
3   Alternator
4   Radiator cap
5   EGR valve
6   Engine oil filler cap
7   Engine oil dipstick
8   Air cleaner assembly
9   Battery
10 Windshield washer fluid reservoir
11 Brake fluid reservoir
12 Automatic transaxle dipstick

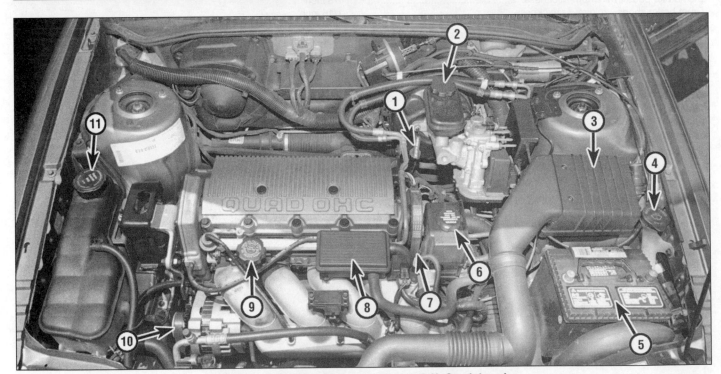

Engine compartment component layout - 2.3L Quad-4 engine

1	Automatic transmission fluid dipstick	5	Battery	9	Engine oil filler cap/dipstick
2	Brake fluid reservoir	6	Power steering fluid reservoir	10	Drivebelt
3	Air cleaner housing	7	Drivebelt	11	Coolant reservoir/expansion tank
4	Windsield washer fluid reservoir	8	Crankcase ventilation air/oil separator		

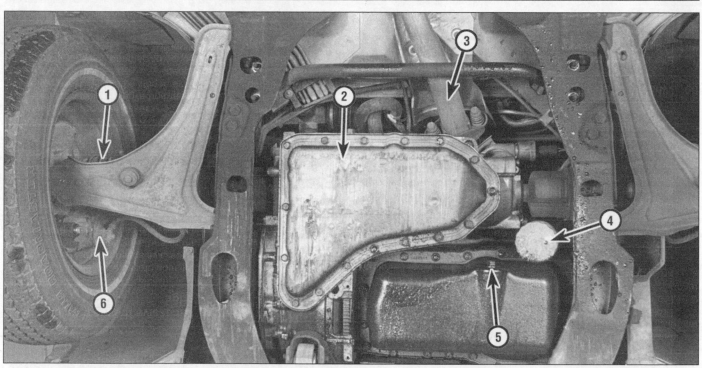

Underside view of engine/transaxle (V6 model shown)

1 CV joint boot	3 Exhaust pipe	5 Engine oil drain plug
2 Automatic transaxle	4 Engine oil filter	6 Disc brake caliper

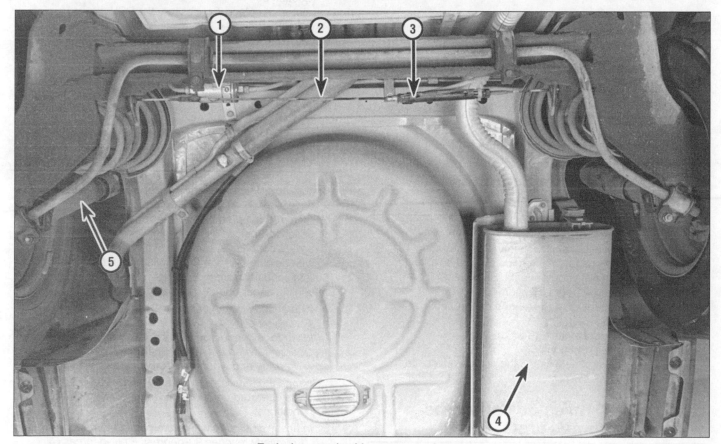

Typical rear underside component layout

1 Fuel filter	3 Parking brake cable	5 Shock absorber
2 Fuel tank filler hose and pipe	4 Muffler	

1

1 GM N-car maintenance schedule

The following maintenance recommendations assume that the vehicle owner will be doing the maintenance and service work. Although the time and mileage intervals are based on factory recommendations, most have been shortened to ensure that lubricants and fluids are checked or changed at intervals that promote maximum engine and driveline service life. If the owner interested in keeping their vehicle in peak condition, many of the maintenance procedures can be performed more often than recommended in the following schedule. We encourage such owner initiative.

Every 250 miles or weekly, whichever comes first

Check the engine oil level (Section 4)
Check the engine coolant level (Section 4)
Check the windshield washer fluid level (Section 4)
Check the brake and clutch fluid levels (Section 4)
Check the tires and tire pressures (Section 5)

Every 3000 miles or 3 months, whichever comes first

All items listed above plus:
Check the automatic transaxle fluid level (Section 4)*
Check the power steering fluid level (Section 4)*
Check and service the battery (Section 6)
Check the cooling system (Section 7)
Inspect and replace if necessary all underhood hoses (Section 8)
Inspect and replace if necessary the windshield wiper blades (Section 9)
Change the engine oil and filter (Section 10)

Every 6000 miles or 6 months, whichever comes first

All items listed above plus:
Check the manual transaxle lubricant level (Section 4)*
Adjust the clutch pedal (1985 models) (Section 11)
Lubricate the chassis components (Section 12)
Check the driveaxle boots (Section 13)
Inspect the suspension and steering components (Section 14)*
Inspect the exhaust system (Section 15)*
Check the brakes (Section 16)*
Check and adjust, if necessary, the engine drivebelts (Section 17)

Every 12,000 miles or 12 months, whichever comes first

Rotate the tires (Section 18)
Inspect the fuel system (Section 19)
Replace the fuel filter (Section 20)

Check the throttle body mounting nut torque (Section 21)
Check the accelerator cable and linkage (Section 22)
Check the thermostatically-controlled air cleaner (2.5L engine) (Section 23)
Check the air filter and PCV filter (Section 24)

Every 24,000 miles or 24 months, whichever comes first

Check the wheel bearings (Section 25)
Check the EGR system (Section 26)
Check the ignition timing (Section 27)

Every 30,000 miles or 30 months, whichever comes first

All items listed above plus:
Change the automatic transaxle fluid and filter (Section 28)**
Change the manual transaxle lubricant (Section 29)
Service the cooling system (drain, flush and refill) (Section 30)
Inspect and replace if necessary the PCV valve (Section 31)
Inspect the Evaporative Emissions Control System (Section 32)
Replace the spark plugs (Section 33)
Inspect the spark plug wires, distributor cap and rotor (Section 34)

Every 48,000 miles or 48 months, whichever comes first

Check the oxygen sensor (Chapter 6) and replace it, if necessary
*This item is affected by "severe" operating condition as described below. If your vehicle is operated under severe conditions, perform all maintenance indicated with an asterisk (*) at 3000 mile/3 month intervals.
Severe conditions are indicated if you mainly operate your vehicle under one or more of the following:

Operating in dusty areas
Towing a trailer
Idling for extended periods and/or low speed operation
Operating when outside temperatures remain below freezing and when most trips are less than 4 miles

**Change the automatic transaxle fluid every 15,000 miles if it is operated under one or more of the following conditions:

In heavy city traffic where the outside temperature regularly reaches 90-degrees F (32-degrees C) or higher
In hilly or mountainous terrain
Frequent trailer pulling

2 Introduction

This Chapter is designed to help the home mechanic maintain the GM N-car with the goals of maximum performance, economy, safety and reliability in mind. Included on page 1-6 is a master maintenance schedule, followed by procedures dealing specifically with each item on the schedule. Visual checks, adjustments, component replacement and other helpful items are included. Refer to the accompanying illustrations of the engine compartment and the underside of the vehicle for the locations of various components.

Servicing your vehicle according to the maintenance schedule and the step-by-step procedures will result in a planned maintenance program that should produce a long and reliable service life. Keep in mind that it is a comprehensive plan, so maintaining some items but not others at the specified intervals will not produce the same results.

As you service your vehicle, you will discover that many of the procedures can - and should - be grouped together because of the nature of the procedure you're performing or because of the close proximity of the otherwise unrelated components.

For example, if the vehicle is raised for chassis lubrication, you should inspect the exhaust, suspension, steering and fuel systems while you're under the vehicle. When you're rotating the tires, it makes good sense to check the brakes since the wheels are already removed. Finally, let's suppose you have to borrow or rent a torque wrench. Even if you only need it to tighten the spark plugs, you might as well check the torque of as many critical fasteners as time allows.

The first step in this maintenance program is to prepare yourself before the actual work begins. Read through all the procedures you're planning to do, then gather up all the parts and tools needed. If it looks as if you might run into problems during a particular job, seek advice from a mechanic or an experienced do-it-yourselfer. **Caution:** *If the vehicle is equipped with a Delco Loc II audio system, make sure you have the correct activation code before disconnecting the battery. See the information at the front of this manual for the radio re-activation procedure.*

3 Tune-up general information

The term tune-up in this manual represents a combination of individual operations rather than one specific procedure.

If the routine maintenance schedule is followed closely and frequent checks are made of fluid levels and high wear items, the vehicle will be kept in relatively good condition and the need for additional work will be minimized.

More likely than not, however, there will be times when the engine is running poorly due to lack of regular maintenance. This is even more likely if a used vehicle, that has not received regular and frequent maintenance checks, is bought. In such cases, perform an engine tune-up outside the regular routine maintenance interval.

The first step in any tune-up or diagnostic procedure to help correct a poor running engine is a cylinder compression check. A compression check (see Chapter 2 Part D) will help determine the condition of internal engine components and as a guide for tune-up and repair procedures. If, for instance, a compression check indicates serious internal engine wear, a conventional tune-up will not improve the performance of the engine and would be a waste of time and money.

The following procedures are those most often needed to bring a generally poor running engine back into a proper state of tune.

Minor tune-up

Check all engine related fluids (Section 4)
Clean, inspect and test the battery (Section 6)
Check the cooling system (Section 7)
Check all underhood hoses (Section 8)
Check and adjust the drivebelts (Section 17)
Check the air and PCV filters (Section 24)
Check and adjust the ignition timing (models with distributors only) (Section 27)
Check the PCV valve (Section 30)
Replace the spark plugs (Section 33)
Inspect the distributor cap and rotor (Section 34)
Inspect the spark plug and coil wires (Section 34)

Major tune-up

All items listed under Minor tune-up plus . . .

Check the fuel system (Section 19)
Replace the air and PCV filters (Section 24)
Check the EGR valve (Section 26)
Replace the distributor cap and rotor (Section 34)
Replace the spark plug wires (Section 34)
Check the ignition system (Chapter 5)
Check the charging system (Chapter 5)
Check the EGR system (Chapter 6)

4 Fluid level checks (every 250 miles or weekly)

Note: *These fluid level checks are to be done on a 250 mile or weekly basis. Additional fluid level checks can be found in specific maintenance procedures that follow. Regardless of intervals, be alert to fluid leaks under the vehicle that would indicate a problem to be corrected immediately.*

1   Fluids are an essential part of the lubrication, cooling, brake and windshield washer systems. Because the fluids gradually become depleted and/or contaminated during normal operation of the vehicle, they must be periodically replenished. See *Recommended lubricants and fluids* at the beginning of this Chapter before adding fluid to any of the following components. **Note:** *The vehicle must be on level ground when checking fluid levels.*

Engine oil

Refer to illustration 4.4
2   The engine oil level is checked with a dipstick located at the side of the engine block. The dipstick extends through a metal tube down into the oil pan.
3   The oil level should be checked before being started or about 15 minutes after the engine has been shut off. If the oil is checked immediately after running, some of the oil will remain in the upper part of the engine, resulting in an inaccurate reading on the dipstick.
4   Pull the dipstick from the tube and wipe all the oil from the end with a clean rag or paper towel. Insert the clean dipstick all the way back into the tube and pull it out again. Note the oil at the end of the dipstick. Add oil as necessary to keep the level above the ADD mark on the dipstick **(see illustration).**
5   Do not overfill the engine by adding too much oil since this may result in oil fouled spark plugs, oil leaks or oil seal failures.
6   Add oil to the engine after removing a twist off cap located on the valve cover. A funnel may help to reduce spills.
7   Checking the oil level is an important preventive maintenance step. A consistently low oil level indicates oil leakage through damaged seals, defective gaskets or past

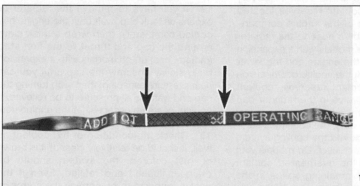

4.4 The oil level should be in the cross-hatched area - if it's below the ADD line, add enough oil to bring the level near the upper line (it takes one quart to raise the level from the lower to the top mark)

4.9 The coolant level must be maintained between the FULL HOT and FULL COLD marks on the reservoir or expansion tank

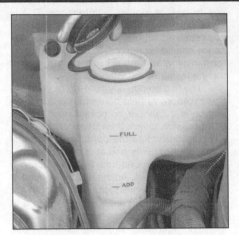

4.14 The windshield washer fluid level should be kept between the FULL and ADD marks

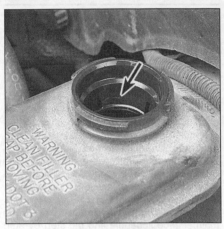

4.18a On black plastic reservoirs, unscrew the cap and make sure the brake fluid level is up to the bottom of the slot in the neck

worn rings or valve guides. If the oil looks milky in color or has water droplets in it, the head gasket may be blown or the head or block may be cracked. The engine should be checked immediately. The condition of the oil should also be checked. Whenever you check the oil level, slide your thumb and index finger up the dipstick before wiping off the oil. If you see dirt or metal particles clinging to the dipstick, the oil should be changed (see Section 10).

Engine coolant

Refer to illustration 4.9
Warning: *Do not allow antifreeze to contact your skin or painted surfaces of the vehicle. Rinse off spills immediately with plenty of water. Antifreeze is highly toxic if ingested. Never leave antifreeze lying around in an open container or in puddles on the floor; children and pets are attracted by its sweet smell and may drink it. Check with local authorities about disposing of used antifreeze. Many communities have collection centers that will dispose of antifreeze safely.*
Note: *When draining antifreeze, it's recommended to use a plastic or other non-galvanized drain pan and container. The galvanized coating can contaminate the antifreeze.*
8   All vehicles covered by this manual are equipped with a pressurized coolant recovery system. A plastic coolant reservoir located along the right side of the engine compartment is connected by a hose to the radiator filler neck or, on later models with a expansion tank, connected to the engine and the lower part of the radiator. If the engine overheats on a model with a coolant reservoir, coolant escapes through a valve in the radiator cap and travels through the hose into the reservoir. As the engine cools, the coolant is automatically drawn back into the cooling system to maintain the correct level. On models with a expansion tank, the overheated coolant expands to fill the remaining space in the tank, but will flow past the valve in the cap and out of an overflow hose if it fills up completely and exceeds a certain temperature.

Warning: *Do not remove the radiator cap (or expansion tank cap on later models) to check the coolant level when the engine is warm.*
9   The coolant level in the reservoir/expansion tank should be checked regularly. The level varies with the temperature of the engine. When the engine is cold, the coolant level should be at or slightly above the FULL COLD mark. Once the engine has warmed up, the level should be at or near the FULL HOT mark **(see illustration)**. If it isn't, allow the engine to cool, then remove the cap and add a 50/50 mixture of ethylene glycol based antifreeze and water.
10   Drive the vehicle and recheck the coolant level. If only a small amount of coolant is required to bring the system up to the proper level, water can be used. However, repeated additions of water will dilute the antifreeze and water solution. In order to maintain the proper ratio of antifreeze and water, always top up the coolant level with the correct mixture. An empty plastic milk jug or bleach bottle makes an excellent container for mixing coolant. Do not use rust inhibitors or additives.
11   If the coolant level drops consistently, there may be a leak in the system. Inspect the radiator, hoses, filler cap, drain plugs and water pump (see Section 7). If no leaks are noted, have the radiator cap pressure tested by a service station.
12   If you have to remove the radiator or expansion tank cap, wait until the engine has cooled completely, then wrap a thick cloth around the cap and turn it to the first stop (radiator cap) or, on models with a expansion tank, slowly unscrew the cap until you can hear pressure escaping, then stop turning the cap and wait for all pressure to be relieved. If coolant or steam escapes, let the engine cool down longer, then remove the cap.
13   Check the condition of the coolant as well. It should be relatively clear. If it is brown or rust colored, the system should be drained, flushed and refilled. Even if the coolant appears to be normal, the corrosion inhibitors wear out, so it must be replaced at the specified intervals.

Windshield washer fluid

Refer to illustration 4.14
14   Fluid for the windshield washer is located in a plastic reservoir in the engine compartment **(see illustration)**. In milder climates, plain water can be used in the reservoir, but it should be kept no more than 2/3 full to allow for expansion if the water freezes. In colder climates, use windshield washer system antifreeze to lower the freezing point of the fluid. Mix the antifreeze with water according to the manufacturer's directions on the container. **Caution:** *Do not use cooling system antifreeze - it will damage the vehicle's paint.*
15   To help prevent icing in cold weather, warm the windshield with the defroster before using the washer.

Battery electrolyte

16   All vehicles that this manual is concerned are equipped with a battery that is permanently sealed (except for vent holes) and has no filler caps. Water does not have to be added to these batteries at any time. If, however, an aftermarket battery has been installed and it is a type that requires regular maintenance, refer to Section 6 for the electrolyte level checking procedure.

Brake and clutch fluid

Refer to illustrations 4.18a and 4.18b
17   The brake master cylinder is mounted on the front of the power booster in the engine compartment. The clutch cylinder used on manual transaxles is mounted next to it on the firewall.
18   On black plastic reservoirs, unscrew the cap and make sure the fluid level is even with the bottom of the filler cap **(see illustration)**. On translucent white plastic reservoirs, the fluid inside is readily visible. The level should be above the MIN marks on the reservoir. If a low level is indicated, be sure to wipe the top of the reservoir cover with a clean rag to pre-

4.18b The fluid level inside the translucent brake reservoir is easily checked through the inspection windows (when adding fluid, grasp the tabs and rotate the cover up as shown)

4.25 The manual transaxle dipstick (arrow) is located adjacent to the master cylinder

4.26 Follow the manual transaxle oil level checking procedure printed on the dipstick

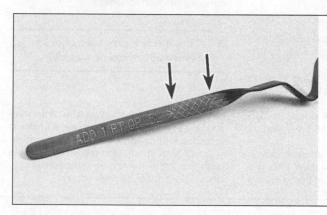

4.34 The automatic transaxle fluid level must be maintained within the cross-hatched area on the dipstick

vent contamination of the brake and/or clutch system before removing the cover (see illustration).

19   When adding fluid, avoid spilling it onto surrounding painted surfaces. Be sure the specified fluid is used, since mixing different types of brake fluid can cause damage to the system. See *Recommended lubricants and fluids* at the front of this Chapter or your owner's manual. **Warning:** *Brake fluid can harm your eyes and damage painted surfaces, so use extreme caution when handling or pouring it. Do not use brake fluid that has been standing open or is more than one year old. Brake fluid absorbs moisture from the air. Excess moisture can cause a dangerous loss of braking effectiveness.*

20   At this time the fluid and cylinder can be inspected for contamination. The system should be drained and refilled if deposits, dirt particles or water droplets are seen in the fluid.

21   After filling the reservoir to the proper level, make sure the lid is on tight to prevent fluid leakage.

22   The fluid level in the master cylinder will drop slightly as the pads and the brake shoes at each wheel wear down during normal operation. If the master cylinder requires repeated replenishing to keep it at the proper level, this indicates leakage in the brake system, which should be corrected immediately. Check all brake lines and connections (see Section 16 for more information).

23   If upon checking the fluid level, you find one or both reservoirs empty or nearly empty, bleed the brake system (see Chapter 9).

Manual transaxle lubricant

Refer to illustrations 4.25 and 4.26

24   A dipstick is used for checking the lubricant level in the manual transaxles used on these models.

25   The transaxle should be cool to the touch and the vehicle parked on a level surface. Remove the dipstick from the filler tube

located at the left rear of the engine compartment, near the brake master cylinder (see illustration).

26   The level must be even with our slightly above the FULL COLD mark on the dipstick (see illustration). Make sure the level is at the FULL COLD mark because lubricant may appear on the end of the dipstick even when the transaxle is several pints low.

27   If the level is low, add the specified lubricant through the filler tube, using a funnel.

28   Replace the dipstick into the filler tube and seat it securely.

Automatic transaxle fluid

Refer to illustration 4.34

29   The automatic transaxle fluid level should be carefully maintained. Low fluid level can lead to slipping or loss of drive, while overfilling can cause foaming and loss of fluid.

30   With the parking brake set, start the engine, then move the shift lever through all the gear ranges, ending in Park. The fluid level must be checked with the vehicle level and the engine running at idle. **Note:** *Incorrect fluid level readings will result if the vehicle has just been driven at high speeds for an extended period, in hot weather in city traffic, or if it has been pulling a trailer. If any of these conditions apply, wait until the fluid has*

cooled (about 30 minutes).

31   With the transaxle at normal operating temperature, remove the dipstick from the filler tube. The dipstick is located at the rear of the engine compartment and is clearly marked "TRANS FLUID".

32   Carefully touch the fluid at the end of the dipstick to determine if the fluid is cool, warm or hot. Wipe the fluid from the dipstick with a clean rag and push it back into the filler tube until the cap seats.

33   Pull the dipstick out again and note the fluid level.

34   If the fluid felt cool, the level should be about 1/8-to-3/8 inch below the ADD mark (see illustration). If it felt warm, the level should be close to the ADD mark. If the fluid was hot, the level should be at the FULL mark. If additional fluid is required, pour it directly into the tube using a funnel. It takes about one pint to raise the level from the ADD mark to the FULL mark with a hot transaxle, so add the fluid a little at a time and keep checking the level until it's correct.

35   The condition of the fluid should also be checked along with the level. If the fluid at the end of the dipstick is a dark reddish-brown color, or if the fluid has a burned smell, the fluid should be changed. If you are in doubt about the condition of the fluid, purchase some new fluid and compare the two for color and smell.

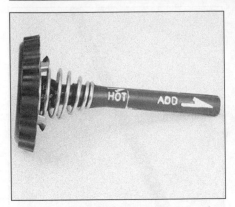

4.41 The markings on the power steering fluid dipstick indicate the safe range

Power steering fluid level check

Refer to illustration 4.41

36   Unlike manual steering, the power steering system relies on fluid that may, over a time, require replenishing.

37   The fluid reservoir for the power steering pump is located with the power steering pump on the engine.

38   For the check, the front wheels should be pointed straight ahead and the engine should be off.

39   Use a clean rag to wipe off the reservoir cap and the area around the cap. This will help prevent any foreign matter from entering

the reservoir during the check.

40   Twist off the cap and check the temperature of the fluid.

41   Wipe off the fluid with a clean rag, reinsert it, then withdraw it and read the fluid level. The level should be at the HOT mark if the fluid was hot to the touch **(see illustration)**. It should be at the COLD mark if the fluid was cool to the touch. Note that on some models the marks (Full Hot and Cold) are on opposite sides of the dipstick. The fluid level should never drop below the ADD mark.

42   If additional fluid is required, pour the specified type directly into the reservoir, using a funnel to prevent spills.

43   If the reservoir requires frequent fluid additions, all power steering hoses, hose connections, the power steering pump and the rack-and-pinion assembly should be carefully checked for leaks.

5   Tire and tire pressure checks (every 250 miles or weekly)

Refer to illustrations 5.2, 5.3, 5.4a, 5.4b and 5.8

1   Periodic inspection of the tires may spare you from the inconvenience of being stranded with a flat tire. It can also provide you with vital information regarding possible problems in the steering and suspension systems before major damage occurs.

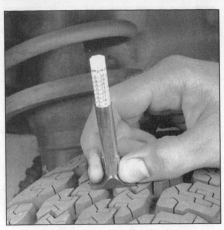

5.2 A tire tread depth indicator should be used to monitor tire wear - they are available at auto parts stores and service stations and cost very little

2   Normal tread wear can be monitored with a simple, inexpensive device known as a tread depth indicator **(see illustration)**. When the tread depth reaches the specified minimum, replace the tire(s).

3   Note any abnormal tread wear **(see illustration)**. Tread pattern irregularities such as cupping, flat spots and more wear on one side than the other are indications of front end alignment and/or balance problems. If any of these conditions are noted, take the vehicle to a tire shop or service station to cor-

UNDERINFLATION

CUPPING

Cupping may be caused by:

● Underinflation and/or mechanical irregularities such as out-of-balance condition of wheel and/or tire, and bent or damaged wheel.
● Loose or worn steering tie-rod or steering idler arm.
● Loose, damaged or worn front suspension parts.

OVERINFLATION

INCORRECT TOE-IN OR EXTREME CAMBER

FEATHERING DUE TO MISALIGNMENT

5.3 This chart will help you determine the condition of your tires, the probable cause(s) of abnormal wear and the corrective action necessary

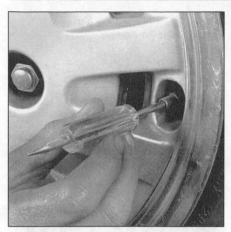

5.4a If a tire loses air on a steady basis, check the valve core first to make sure it's snug (special inexpensive wrenches are commonly available at auto parts stores)

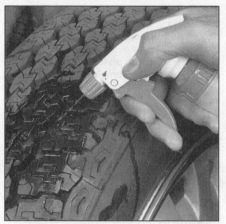

5.4b If the valve core is tight, raise the corner of the vehicle with the low tire and spray a soapy water solution onto the tread as the tire is turned slowly - slow leaks will cause small bubbles to appear

5.8 To extend the life of your tires, check the air pressure at least once a week with an accurate gauge (don't forget the spare!)

1

rect the problem.

4   Look closely for cuts, punctures and embedded nails or tacks. Sometimes a tire will hold its air pressure for a short time or leak down very slowly even after a nail has embedded itself into the tread. If a slow leak persists, check the valve stem core to make sure it is tight **(see illustration)**. Examine the tread for an object that may have embedded itself into the tire or for a "plug" that may have begun to leak (radial tire punctures are repaired with a plug that is installed in a puncture). If a puncture is suspected, it can be easily verified by spraying a solution of soapy water onto the puncture area **(see illustration)**. The soapy solution will bubble if there is a leak. Unless the puncture is inordinately large, a tire shop or gas station can usually repair the punctured tire.

5   Carefully inspect the inner sidewall of each tire for evidence of brake fluid leakage. If you see any, inspect the brakes immediately.

6   Correct tire air pressure adds miles to the lifespan of the tires, improves mileage and enhances overall ride quality. Tire pressure cannot be accurately estimated by looking at a tire, particularly if it is a radial. A tire pressure gauge is therefore essential. Keep an accurate gauge in the glovebox. The pressure gauges fitted to the nozzles of air hoses at gas stations are often inaccurate.

7   Always check tire pressure when the tires are cold. "Cold," in this case, means the vehicle has not been driven over a mile in the three hours preceding a tire pressure check. A pressure rise of four to eight pounds is not uncommon once the tires are warm.

8   Unscrew the valve cap protruding from the wheel or hubcap and push the gauge firmly onto the valve **(see illustration)**. Note the reading on the gauge and compare this figure to the recommended tire pressure shown on the tire placard on the left door. Be sure to reinstall the valve cap to keep dirt and moisture out of the valve stem mechanism. Check all four tires and, if necessary, add

enough air to bring them up to the recommended pressure levels.

9   Don't forget to keep the spare tire inflated to the specified pressure (consult your owner's manual). Note that the air pressure specified for the compact spare is significantly higher than the pressure of the regular tires.

6   Battery check, maintenance and charging (every 3000 miles or 3 months)

Check and maintenance

Refer to illustrations 6.1 and 6.7
Warning: *Certain precautions must be followed when checking and servicing the battery. Hydrogen gas, which is highly flammable, is always present in the battery cells, so keep lighted tobacco and all other flames and sparks away from it. The electrolyte inside the battery is a dilute sulfuric acid, which will cause injury if splashed on your skin or in your eyes. It will also ruin clothes and painted surfaces. When removing the battery cables, always detach the negative cable first and hook it up last!*
Caution: *If the vehicle is equipped with a Delco Loc II audio system, make sure you have the correct activation code before disconnecting the battery. See the information at the front of this manual for the radio re-activation procedure.*

1   Battery maintenance is an important procedure that will help ensure that you are not stranded because of a dead battery. Several tools are required for this procedure **(see illustration)**.

2   Before servicing the battery, always turn the engine and all accessories off and disconnect the cable from the negative terminal of the battery.

3   A sealed (sometimes called mainte-

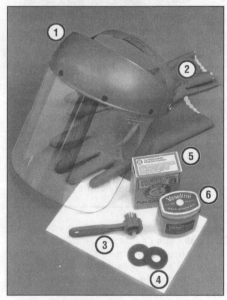

6.1 Tools and materials required for battery maintenance

1   *Face shield/safety goggles - When removing corrosion with a brush, the acidic particles can easily fly up into your eyes*
2   *Rubber gloves - Another safety item to consider when servicing the battery - remember that's acid inside the battery!*
3   *Battery terminal/cable cleaner - This wire brush cleaning tool will remove all traces of corrosion from the battery and cable*
4   *Treated felt washers - Placing one of these on each terminal, directly under the cable end, will help prevent corrosion (be sure to get the correct type for side-terminal batteries)*
5   *Baking soda - A solution of baking soda and water can be used to neutralize corrosion*
6   *Petroleum jelly - A layer of this on the battery terminal bolts will help prevent corrosion*

Terminal end corrosion or damage.

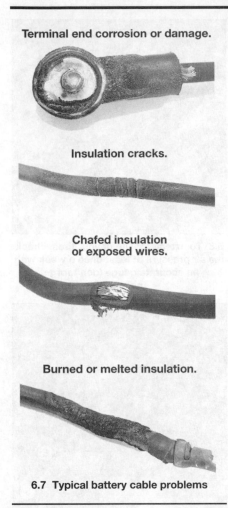

Insulation cracks.

Chafed insulation or exposed wires.

Burned or melted insulation.

6.7 Typical battery cable problems

nance free) battery is standard equipment. The cell caps cannot be removed, no electrolyte checks are required and water cannot be added to the cells. However, if an aftermarket battery has been installed and it is a type that requires regular maintenance, the following procedures can be used.

4   Remove the cell caps and check the electrolyte level in each of the battery cells. It must be above the plates. There's usually a split-ring indicator in each cell to indicate the correct level. If the level is low, add distilled water only, then install the cell caps. **Caution:** *Overfilling the cells may cause electrolyte to spill over during periods of heavy charging, causing corrosion and damage to nearby components.*

5   If the positive terminal and cable clamp on your vehicle's battery is equipped with a rubber or plastic protector, make sure that it's not torn or damaged. It should completely cover the terminal.

6   The external condition of the battery should be checked periodically. Look for damage such as a cracked case.

7   Check the tightness of the battery cable terminals to ensure good electrical connections and inspect the entire length of each cable, looking for cracked or abraded insulation and frayed conductors **(see illustration)**.

8   If corrosion (visible as white, fluffy

deposits) is evident, remove the cables from the terminals, clean them with a battery brush and reinstall them. Corrosion can be kept to a minimum by installing specially treated washers available at auto parts stores or by applying a layer of petroleum jelly or grease to the terminals and cable clamps after they are assembled.

9   Make sure the battery carrier is in good condition and that the hold-down clamp bolt is tight. If the battery is removed (see Chapter 5 for the removal and installation procedure), make sure that no parts remain in the bottom of the carrier when it's reinstalled. When reinstalling the hold-down clamp, don't over tighten the bolt.

Cleaning

10   Corrosion on the carrier, battery case and surrounding areas can be removed with a solution of water and baking soda. Apply the mixture with a small brush, let it work, then rinse it off with plenty of clean water.

11   Any metal parts of the vehicle damaged by corrosion should be coated with a zinc-based primer, then painted.

12   Additional information on the battery and jump starting can be found in Chapter 5 and at the front of this manual.

Charging

13   Remove all of the cell caps (if equipped) and cover the holes with a clean cloth to prevent spattering electrolyte. Disconnect the negative battery cable and hook the battery charger leads to the battery posts (positive to positive, negative to negative), then plug in the charger. Make sure it is set at 12-volts if it has a selector switch.

14   If you're using a charger with a rate higher than two amps, check the battery regularly during charging to make sure it doesn't overheat. If you're using a trickle charger, you can safely let the battery charge overnight after you've checked it regularly for the first couple of hours.

15   If the battery has removable cell caps, measure the specific gravity with a hydrometer every hour during the last few hours of the charging cycle. Hydrometers are available inexpensively from auto parts stores - follow the instructions that come with the hydrometer. Consider the battery charged when there's no change in the specific gravity reading for two hours and the electrolyte in the cells is gassing (bubbling) freely. The specific gravity reading from each cell should be very close to the others. If not, the battery probably has a bad cell(s).

16   Some batteries with sealed tops have built-in hydrometers on the top that indicate the state of charge by the color displayed in the hydrometer window. Normally, a bright-colored hydrometer indicates a full charge and a dark hydrometer indicates the battery still needs charging. Check the battery manufacturer's instructions to be sure you know what the colors mean.

17   If the battery has a sealed top and no built-in hydrometer, you can hook up a volt-

Check for a chafed area that could fail prematurely.

Check for a soft area indicating the hose has deteriorated inside.

Overtightening the clamp on a hardened hose will damage the hose and cause a leak.

Check each hose for swelling and oil-soaked ends. Cracks and breaks can be located by squeezing the hose.

7.4 Hoses, like drivebelts, have a habit of failing at the worst possible time - to prevent the inconvenience of a blown radiator or heater hose, inspect them carefully as shown here

meter across the battery terminals to check the charge. A fully charged battery should read 12.6-volts or higher.

18   Further information on the battery and jump starting can be found in Chapter 5 and at the front of this manual.

7   Cooling system check (every 3000 miles or 3 months)

Refer to illustration 7.4

1   Many major engine failures can be attributed to a faulty cooling system. If the vehicle is equipped with an automatic transaxle, the cooling system also cools the transaxle fluid and thus plays an important role in prolonging transaxle life.

2   The cooling system should be checked with the engine cold. Do this before the vehi-

cle is driven for the day or after it has been shut off for at least three hours.

3   On models with a radiator cap, remove the cap by turning it to the left until it reaches a stop. If you hear any hissing sound (indicating there is still pressure in the system), wait until it stops. Now press down on the cap with the palm of your hand and continue turning to the left until the cap can be removed. On models with a expansion tank cap, slowly unscrew the cap until you hear pressure escaping. Wait until all pressure is relieved, then continue to unscrew the cap. Thoroughly clean the cap, inside and out, with clean water. Also clean the filler neck on the radiator or the expansion tank opening. All traces of corrosion should be removed. The coolant inside the radiator or expansion tank should be relatively transparent. If it is rust colored, the system should be drained and refilled (see Section 30). If the coolant level is not up to the top, add additional anti-freeze/coolant mixture (see Section 4).

4   Carefully check the large upper and lower radiator hoses along with any smaller diameter heater hoses which run from the engine to the firewall. Inspect each hose along its entire length, replacing any hose that is cracked, swollen or shows signs of deterioration. Cracks may become more apparent if the hose is squeezed **(see illustration)**.

5   Make sure that all hose connections are tight. A leak in the cooling system will usually show up as white or rust colored deposits on the areas adjoining the leak. If wire-type clamps are used at the ends of the hoses, it may be wise to replace them with more secure screw type clamps.

6   Use compressed air or a soft brush to remove bugs, leaves, etc. from the front of the radiator or air conditioning condenser. Be careful not to damage the delicate cooling fins or cut yourself on them.

7   Every other inspection, or at the first indication of cooling system problems, have the cap and system pressure tested. If you do not have a pressure tester, most gas stations and repair shops will do this for a minimal charge.

8   Underhood hose check and replacement (every 3000 miles or 3 months)

Refer to illustration 8.1

General

1   **Caution:** *Replacement of air conditioning hoses must be left to a dealer service department or air conditioning shop that has the equipment to depressurize the system safely. Never remove an air conditioning component or hose* **(see illustration)** *until the system has been depressurized.*

2   High temperatures under the hood can cause the deterioration of the rubber and plastic hoses used for engine, accessory and emission systems operation. Periodic inspection should be made for cracks, loose clamps, material hardening and leaks. Information specific to the cooling system hoses can be found in Section 7.

3   Some, but not all, hoses are secured to the fittings with clamps. Where clamps are used, check to be sure they haven't lost their tension, allowing the hose to leak. If clamps aren't used, make sure the hose has not expanded and/or hardened where it slips over the fitting, allowing it to leak.

Vacuum hoses

4   It is quite common for vacuum hoses to be color coded or identified by colored stripes molded into each hose. Various systems require hoses with different wall thickness, collapse resistance and temperature resistance. When replacing hoses, be sure the new ones are made of the same material.

5   Often the only effective way to check a hose is to remove it completely from the vehicle. If more than one hose is removed, be sure to label the hoses and fittings to ensure correct installation.

6   When checking vacuum hoses, be sure to include any plastic T-fittings in the check. Inspect the fittings for cracks and the hose where it fits over the fitting for distortion, which could cause leakage.

7   A small piece of vacuum hose (1/4-inch inside diameter) can be used as a stethoscope to detect vacuum leaks. Hold one end of the hose to your ear and probe around vacuum hoses and fittings, listening for the hissing sound characteristic of a vacuum leak. **Warning:** *When probing with the vacuum hose stethoscope, be careful not to allow your body or the hose to come into contact with moving engine components such as the drivebelt, cooling fan, etc.*

Fuel hose

Warning: *There are certain precautions that must be taken when inspecting or servicing*

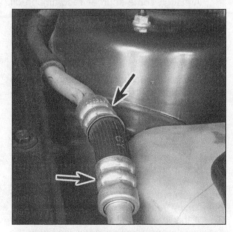

8.1 Air conditioning hoses are best identified by the metal tubes used at all bends (arrows) - DO NOT disconnect or accidentally damage the air conditioning hoses as the system is under high pressure

fuel system components. Work in a well-ventilated area and do not allow open flames (cigarettes, appliance pilot lights, etc.) or bare light bulbs near the work area. Mop up any spills immediately and do not store fuel soaked rags where they could ignite. The fuel system is under pressure, so if any fuel lines are to be disconnected, the pressure in the system must be relieved first (see Chapter 4 for more information).

8   Check all flexible fuel lines for deterioration and chafing. Check especially for cracks in areas where the hose bends and just before fittings, such as where a hose attaches to the fuel filter and fuel injection unit.

9   High quality fuel line, intended specifically for usage with fuel injection systems, should be used for fuel line replacement. Never, under any circumstances, use standard fuel hose, unreinforced vacuum line, clear plastic tubing or water hose for fuel lines.

10   Spring-type clamps are commonly used on fuel lines. These clamps often lose their tension over a time, and can be "sprung" during the removal process. It's recommended that all spring-type clamps be replaced with screw clamps whenever a hose is replaced.

Metal lines

11   Sections of metal line are often used for fuel line between the fuel pump and fuel injection unit. Check carefully to be sure the line is not bent or crimped and that no cracks have started in the line.

12   If a section of metal fuel line must be replaced, only seamless steel tubing should be used, since copper and aluminum tubing do not have the strength necessary to withstand normal engine vibration.

13   Check the metal brake lines where they enter the master cylinder and brake proportioning unit (if used) for cracks in the lines and loose fittings. Any sign of brake fluid leakage calls for an immediate thorough inspection of the brake system.

9   Wiper blade inspection and replacement (every 3000 miles or 3 months)

Refer to illustrations 9.5a, 9.5b and 9.7

1   The windshield wiper and blade assembly should be inspected periodically for damage, loose components and cracked or worn blade elements.

2   Road film can build up on the wiper blades and affect their efficiency, so they should be washed regularly with a mild detergent solution.

3   The action of the wiping mechanism can loosen the bolts, nuts and fasteners, so they should be checked and tightened, as necessary, at the same time the wiper blades are checked.

4   If the wiper blade elements (sometimes called inserts) are cracked, worn or warped,

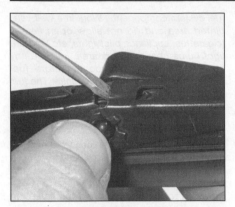

9.5a Using a small screwdriver, gently pry on the spring at the center of the windshield wiper arm . . .

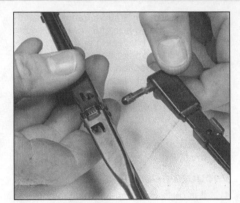

9.5b . . . while pulling the blade assembly away from the arm

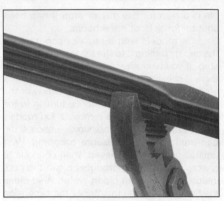

9.7 The rubber element is retained in the blade by small clips - the metal backing of the rubber element can be compressed with pliers, allowing the element to slide out of the clips

they should be replaced with new ones.

5   Remove the wiper blade assembly from the wiper arm by inserting a small screwdriver into the opening and gently prying on

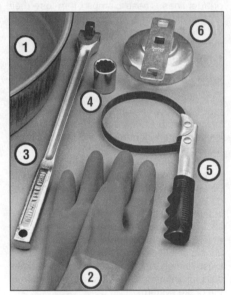

10.3 These tools are required when changing the engine oil and filter

1   Drain pan - It should be fairly shallow in depth, but wide in order to prevent spills

2   Rubber gloves - When ,removing the drain plug and filter it is inevitable that you will get oil on your hands (the gloves will prevent burns)

3   Breaker bar - Sometimes the oil drain plug is pretty tight and along breaker bar is needed to loosen it

4   Socket - To be used with the breaker bar or a ratchet (must be the correct size to fit the drain plug)

5   Filter wrench - This is a metal band-type wrench, which requires clearance around the filter to be effective

6   Filter wrench - This type fits on the bottom of the filter and can be turned with a ratchet or breaker bar (different size wrenches are available for different types of filters)

the spring while pulling on the blade to release it **(see illustrations)**.

6   With the blade removed from the vehicle, you can remove the rubber element from the blade.

7   Using pliers, pinch the metal backing of the element **(see illustration)** and then slide the element out of the blade assembly.

8   Compare the new element with the old for length, design, etc.

9   Slide the new element into place. It will automatically lock at the correct location.

10   Reinstall the blade assembly on the arm, wet the windshield glass and test for proper operation.

10   Engine oil and filter change (every 3000 miles or 3 months)

Refer to illustrations 10.3, 10.10 and 10.15

1   Frequent oil changes are the most important preventive maintenance procedures that can be done by the home mechanic. As engine oil ages, it becomes diluted and contaminated, which leads to premature engine wear.

2   Although some sources recommend oil filter changes every other oil change, we feel that the minimal cost of an oil filter and the relative ease that it is installed dictate that a new filter be used every time the oil is changed.

3   Gather all necessary tools and materials before beginning the procedure **(see illustration)**.

4   In addition, you should have plenty of clean rags and newspapers handy to mop up any spills. Access to the underside of the vehicle is greatly improved if the vehicle can be lifted on a hoist, driven onto ramps or supported by jackstands. **Warning:** *Do not work under a vehicle that is supported only by a bumper, hydraulic or scissors-type jack.*

5   If this is your first oil change, get under the vehicle and familiarize yourself with the locations of the oil drain plug and the oil filter. The engine and exhaust components will be warm during the actual work, so note how they are situated to avoid touching them when working under the vehicle.

6   Warm the engine to normal operating temperature. If the new oil or any tools are needed, use this warm-up time to gather everything necessary for the job. The correct type of oil for your application can be found in *Recommended lubricants and fluids* at the beginning of this Chapter.

7   With the engine oil warm (warm engine oil will drain better and more built-up sludge will be removed with the oil), raise and support the vehicle. Make sure it's safely supported.

8   Move all necessary tools, rags and newspapers under the vehicle. Position the drain pan under the drain plug. Keep in mind that the oil will initially flow from the pan with some force, so place the pan accordingly.

9   Two different oil change procedures are used on these models, depending on whether the oil filter is mounted on the engine block or in the oil pan. All V6 engines and most four-cylinder models are equipped with a block-mounted filter, while some later four-cylinder models have an oil pan-mounted filter.

10   Be careful not to touch any of the hot exhaust components. Depending upon which style of filter the vehicle is equipped with, remove either the drain plug at the bottom of the oil pan or the filter access cover **(see**

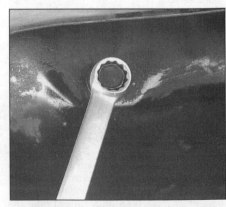

10.10 The oil drain plug is located at the bottom or rear of the oil pan (V6 shown) - it's usually very tight, so use a box-end wrench to avoid rounding off the hex

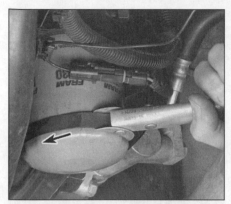

10.15 The oil filter is usually on very tight and will require a special wrench for removal - DO NOT use the wrench to tighten the new filter!

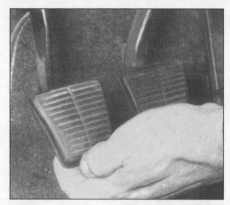

11.2 Pull the clutch pedal back to the stop, then depress it slowly to adjust the freeplay

illustration). If the oil is hot, you may want to wear gloves while unscrewing the plug the final few turns.

11   Allow the old oil to drain into the pan. It may be necessary to move the pan farther under the engine as the oil flow slows to a trickle.

12   After all the oil has drained, wipe off the drain plug with a clean rag. Small metal particles may cling to the plug which would immediately contaminate the new oil.

13   Clean the area around the drain plug opening and reinstall the plug. Tighten the plug securely with the wrench. If a torque wrench is available, use it to tighten the plug.

14   Move the drain pan into position under the oil filter.

Engine block-mounted oil filter

15   Use the filter wrench to loosen the oil filter **(see illustration)**. Chain or metal band filter wrenches may distort the filter canister, but this is of no concern as the filter will be discarded anyway.

16   Completely unscrew the old filter. Be careful, as it is full of oil. Pour the oil inside the filter into the drain pan.

17   Compare the old filter with the new one to make sure they are the same type.

18   Use a clean rag to remove all oil, dirt and sludge from the area where the oil filter seats on the engine. Check to make sure the rubber gasket is not stuck to the engine mounting surface. If the gasket is stuck to the engine (use a flashlight if necessary), remove it.

19   Apply a light coat of oil around the full circumference of the rubber gasket of the new oil filter. Open a can of oil and partially fill the oil filter with fresh oil. Oil pressure will not build in the engine until the oil pump has filled the filter with oil, so partially filling the filter at this time will reduce the amount of time the engine runs with no oil pressure.

20   Attach the new filter to the engine, following the tightening directions printed on the filter canister or packing box. Most filter manufacturers recommend against using a

filter wrench due to the possibility of over-tightening and damage to the seal.

Oil pan-mounted oil filter

21   Reach up inside the filter access hole with a pair of pliers, grasp the filter securely, pull it down using a twisting motion and remove it from the oil pan.

22   Check the filter to make sure the rubber O-ring has come out with it. If it hasn't, reach up inside the pan opening and remove it.

23   Coat the new O-ring (included with the new filter) with clean engine oil and then slide it into position, all the way up in the filter opening.

24   Coat the inside of the grommet on the top of the new filter with clean engine oil.

25   Slide the new oil filter up into the oil pan opening as far as possible without forcing it.

26   Wipe off the filter plug with a clean cloth. Inspect the gasket, replacing it with a new one if necessary, and coat it with clean engine oil.

27   Clean the area around the filter plug opening. Reinstall the plug, tighten it by hand until the gasket contacts the oil pan, then tighten it an additional 1/4-turn with a wrench.

All models

28   Remove all tools, rags, etc. from under the vehicle, being careful not to spill the oil in the drain pan, then lower the vehicle.

29   Move to the engine compartment and locate the oil filler cap.

30   Pour three quarts of fresh oil into the engine. Wait a few minutes to allow the oil to drain into the pan, then check the level on the dipstick (see Section 4 if necessary). If the oil level is above the ADD mark, start the engine and allow the new oil to circulate.

31   Run the engine for only about a minute and then shut it off. Immediately look under the vehicle and check for leaks at the oil pan drain plug and around the oil filter. If either is leaking, tighten with a bit more force.

32   With the new oil circulated and the filter now completely full, recheck the level on the dipstick and add more oil as necessary.

33   During the first few trips after an oil

change, make it a point to check frequently for leaks and proper oil level.

34   The old oil drained from the engine cannot be reused in its present state and should be disposed of. Oil reclamation centers, auto repair shops and gas stations will normally accept the oil, which can be refined and used again. After the oil has cooled it can be drained into a suitable container (capped plastic jugs, topped bottles, milk cartons, etc.) for transport to one of these disposal sites.

11   Clutch pedal adjustment (1985 models only) (every 6000 miles or 6 months)

Refer to illustration 11.2

1   At the specified interval the clutch pedal must be adjusted to maintain a constant tension on the clutch self-adjusting mechanism cable.

2   Grasp the pedal and pull it up to the rubber stop, then depress the pedal slowly **(see illustration)**.

12   Chassis lubrication (every 6000 miles or 6 months)

Refer to illustrations 12.1 and 12.6

1   Refer to Recommended lubricants and fluids at the front of this Chapter to obtain the

12.1 Tools and materials necessary for chassis lubrication

1   Engine oil - Light engine oil in a can like this can be used for door and hood hinges

2   Graphite spray - Used to lubricate lock cylinders

3   Grease - Grease, in a variety of types and weights, is available for use in a grease gun. Check the Specifications for vehicle requirements

4   Grease gun - A common grease gun, shown here with a detachable hose and nozzle, is for chassis lubrication.

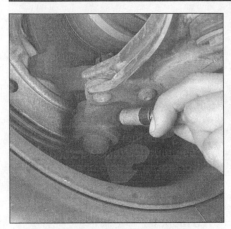

12.6 After wiping the grease fitting clean, push the nozzle firmly into place and pump the grease into the component (usually about two pumps of the gun will be sufficient)

13.2 Push on the driveaxle boots to check for cracks

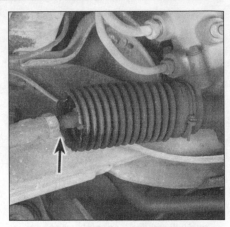

14.5 Check the steering gear for ripped or torn boots which could cause the steering gear to fail prematurely

necessary grease, etc. You will also need a grease gun **(see illustration)**. Occasionally plugs will be installed rather than grease fittings. If so, grease fittings will have to be purchased and installed.

2   Look under the vehicle and see if grease fittings or plugs are installed in the balljoints and tie-rod ends. If there are plugs, remove them and buy grease fittings that will thread into the component. An auto parts store will be able to supply the correct fittings. Straight, as well as angled, fittings are available.

3   For easier access under the vehicle, raise it with a jack and place jackstands under the frame. Make sure it is securely supported by the stands. If the wheels are to be removed at this interval for rotation or brake inspection, loosen the lug nuts slightly while the vehicle is still on the ground.

4   Before beginning, force a little grease out of the nozzle to remove any dirt from the end of the gun. Wipe the nozzle clean with a rag.

5   With the grease gun and plenty of clean rags, crawl under the vehicle and begin lubricating the components.

6   Wipe the grease fitting clean and push the nozzle firmly over it **(see illustration)**. Squeeze the trigger on the grease gun to force grease into the component. The balljoints and tie-rod ends should be lubricated until each rubber seal is firm to the touch. Do not pump too much grease into the fitting or it could rupture the seal. If the grease escapes around the grease gun nozzle, the fitting is clogged or the nozzle is not completely seated on the fitting. Reattach the gun nozzle to the fitting and try again. If necessary, replace the fitting with a new one.

7   Wipe the excess grease from the components and the grease fitting. Repeat the procedure for the remaining fittings.

8   If equipped with a manual transaxle, lubricate the shift linkage with a little multipurpose grease. While you are under the vehicle, clean and lubricate the parking brake cable along with the cable guides and levers.

This can be done by smearing some of the chassis grease onto the cable and its related parts with your fingers.

9   Open the hood and smear a little chassis grease on the hood latch mechanism. Have an assistant pull the hood release lever from inside the vehicle as you lubricate the cable at the latch.

10   Lubricate all the hinges (door, hood, etc.) with engine oil to keep them in proper working order.

11   The key lock cylinders can be lubricated with spray-on graphite or silicone lubricant, which is available at auto parts stores. **Caution:** *The manufacturer does not recommend using oil in black plastic lock cylinders as it could damage them by washing out the factory applied lubricant.*

12   Lubricate the door weather-stripping with silicone spray. This will reduce chafing and retard wear.

13   Driveaxle boot check (every 6000 miles or 6 months)

Refer to illustration 13.2

1   The driveaxle boots are very important because they prevent dirt, water and foreign material from entering and damaging the constant velocity (CV) joints. Oil and grease can cause the boot material to deteriorate prematurely so it's a good idea to wash the boots with soap and water.

2   Inspect the boots for tears and cracks as well as loose clamps **(see illustration)**. If there is any evidence of cracks or leaking lubricant, they must be replaced as described in Chapter 8.

14   Suspension and steering check (every 6000 miles or 6 months)

Refer to illustration 14.5

1   Raise the front of the vehicle periodically and visually check the suspension and steer-

ing components for wear.

2   Indications of a fault in these systems are excessive play in the steering wheel before the front wheels react, excessive sway around corners, body movement over rough roads or binding at some point as the steering wheel is turned.

3   Raise the front end of the vehicle and support it securely on jackstands placed under the frame rails. Because of the work to be done, make sure the vehicle cannot fall from the stands.

4   Check the front wheel hub nuts for looseness and make sure they are securely locked in place.

5   From under the vehicle check for loose bolts, broken or disconnected parts and deteriorated rubber bushings on all suspension and steering components. Look for grease or fluid leaking from the steering gear **(see illustration)**. Check the power steering hoses and connections for leaks.

6   Have an assistant turn the steering wheel from side-to-side and check the steering components for free movement, chafing and binding. If the steering does not react with the movement of the steering wheel, try to determine where the slack is located.

15   Exhaust system check (every 6000 miles or 6 months)

Refer to illustration 15.2

1   With the engine cold (at least three hours after the vehicle has been driven), check the complete exhaust system from the engine to the end of the tailpipe. Ideally, the inspection should be done with the vehicle on a hoist to permit unrestricted access. If a hoist is not available, raise the vehicle and support it securely on jackstands.

2   Check the exhaust pipes and connections for evidence of leaks, severe corrosion and damage **(see illustration)**. Make sure that all brackets and hangers are in good condition and tight.

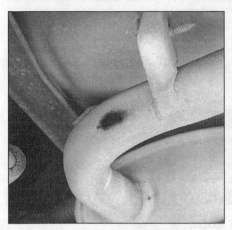

15.2 Check the pipes and connections for signs of leakage - this stain around a small hole is indicative of a tailpipe needing replacement

16.6a The amount of disc pad material remaining can be checked by looking through the opening in the caliper

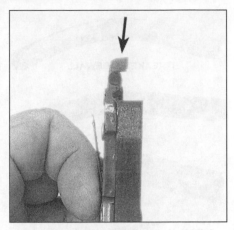

16.6b The disc brake pads have built in wear indicators that contact the rotor and emit a squealing sound when the pads have worn to their limit

3   At the same time, inspect the underside of the body for holes, corrosion, open seams, etc., which may allow exhaust gases to enter the passenger compartment. Seal all body openings with silicone or body putty.

4   Rattles and other noises can often be traced to the exhaust system, especially the mounts and hangers. Try to move the pipes, muffler and catalytic converter. If the components can come in contact with the body or suspension parts, secure the exhaust system with new mounts.

5   Check the running condition of the engine by inspecting inside the end of the tailpipe. The exhaust deposits here are an indication of engine state-of-tune. If the pipe is black and sooty or coated with white deposits, the engine is in need of a tune-up and/or a thorough fuel system inspection.

16   Brake check (every 6000 miles or 6 months)

Refer to illustrations 16.6a, 16.6b and 16.13
Warning: *The dust created by the brake system may contain asbestos, which is harmful to your health. Never blow it out with compressed air or inhale any of it. An approved filtering mask should be worn when working on the brakes. Do not, under any circumstances, use petroleum-based solvents to clean brake parts. Use brake system cleaner only!*
Note: *For detailed photographs of the brake system, see Chapter 9.*
1   The brakes should be inspected every time the wheels are removed or whenever a defect is suspected. Indications of a potential brake system defect are:
  a) *The vehicle pulls to one side when the brake pedal is depressed.*
  b) *Noises coming from the brakes when they are applied.*
  c) *Excessive brake pedal travel.*
  d) *Pulsating pedal.*
  e) *Leakage of fluid, usually seen on the inside of the tire or wheel.*

Disc brakes

2   Both front and rear disc brakes (if the rear is so equipped) can be visually checked without removing any parts except the wheels.
3   Raise the vehicle and place it securely on jackstands. Remove the wheels (see *Jacking and towing* at the front of the manual).
4   The disc brake calipers, which contain the pads, are now visible. There is an outer pad and an inner pad in each caliper. All pads should be inspected.
5   The outer pads on the front wheels are equipped with a wear sensor. This is a small, bent piece of metal that is visible from the inboard side of the brake caliper. When the pads wear to the danger limit the metal sensor rubs against the disc and makes a screeching sound.
6   Check the pad thickness by looking at each end of the caliper and through the inspection hole in the caliper body **(see illustrations)**. If the wear sensor clip is very close to the disc, or if the lining material is 1/8-inch or less in thickness, the pads should be replaced. Keep in mind that the lining material is riveted or bonded to a metal backing shoe and the metal portion is not included in this measurement.
7   Remove the pads for further inspection or replacement if you are in doubt as to the condition of the pad (see Chapter 9).
8   Before installing the wheels, check for leakage around the brake hose connections leading to the caliper and damage (cracking, splitting, etc.) to the brake hose. Replace the hose or fittings as necessary, referring to Chapter 9.
9   Check the condition of the disc. Look for scoring, gouging and burned spots. If these conditions exist the disc should be removed for servicing (see Chapter 9).

Drum brakes

10   Using a scribe or chalk, mark the drum and hub so the drum can be reinstalled in the same position on the hub.

11   Remove and discard the retaining clip and pull the brake drum off the axle and brake assembly. If this proves difficult, make sure the parking brake is released, then squirt some penetrating oil around the center hub area. Allow the oil to soak in and try to pull the drum off again. If the drum still can't be pulled off, the brake shoes will have to be retracted. This is done by first removing the lanced knock-out in the backing plate with a hammer and chisel. With the lanced area punched in, use a small hooked tool to pull the self-adjusting lever off the star wheel and use a small screwdriver to turn the wheel, which will move the shoes away from the drum.
12   With the drum removed, clean the assembly with brake system cleaner.
13   Note the thickness of the lining material on the brake shoes **(see illustration)**. If the material is worn to within 1/16-inch of the recessed rivets or metal backing, the shoes should be replaced. If the linings look worn,

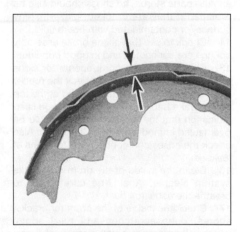

16.13 If the lining is bonded to the brake shoe, measure the lining thickness from the outer surface to the metal shoe, as shown here; if the lining is riveted to the shoe, measure from the lining outer surface to the rivet head

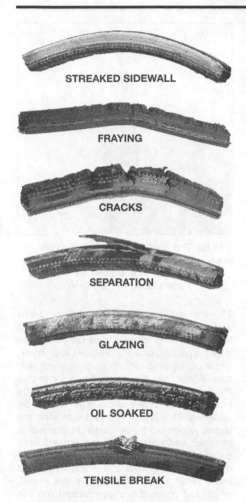

17.1 Here are some of the more common problems associated with drivebelts (check the belts carefully to prevent an untimely breakdown

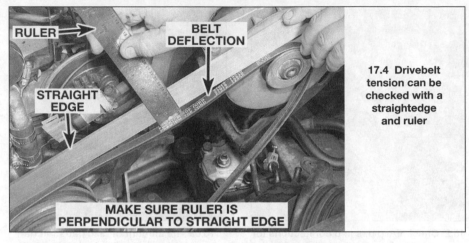

17.4 Drivebelt tension can be checked with a straightedge and ruler

but you are unable to determine their exact thickness, compare them with a new set at an auto parts store. The shoes should also be replaced if they are cracked, glazed (shiny surface) or contaminated with brake fluid.

14 Check to see that all the brake assembly springs are connected and in good condition.

15 Check the brake components for signs of fluid leakage. Carefully pry back the rubber cups on the wheel cylinder, located at the top of the brake backing plate. Any leakage is an indication that the wheel cylinders should be overhauled immediately (see Chapter 9). Also check the hoses and connections for signs of leakage.

16 Clean the inside of the drum with brake system cleaner. Again, be careful not to breathe the asbestos dust.

17 Check the inside of the drum for cracks, scores, deep scratches and hard spots, which will appear as small discolored areas. If imperfections cannot be removed with fine emery cloth the drum must be taken to a machine shop for resurfacing.

18 After the inspection process, if all parts are found to be in good condition, reinstall

the brake drum. Install the wheel and lower the vehicle to the ground.

Parking brake

19 The easiest way to check the operation of the parking brake is to park the vehicle on a steep hill with the parking brake set and the transmission in Neutral (stay in the car while performing this check). If the parking brake can't prevent the vehicle from rolling, it is in need of adjustment (see Chapter 9).

17   Drivebelt check and adjustment (every 6000 miles or 6 months)

V-belts

Refer to illustrations 17.1, 17.4 and 17.6

1 The drivebelts, or V-belts as they are often called, are located at the front of the engine and play an important role in the overall operation of the vehicle and its components. Due to their function and material make-up, the belts are prone to failure after a period of time and should be inspected and adjusted periodically to prevent major engine damage **(see illustration)**.

2 The number of belts used on a particular vehicle depends on the accessories installed. Drivebelts are used to turn the generator/alternator, power steering pump, water pump and air-conditioning compressor. Depending on the pulley arrangement, more than one of these components may be driven by a single belt.

3 With the engine off, open the hood and locate the various belts at the front of the engine. Using your fingers (and a flashlight, if necessary), move along the belts checking for cracks and separation of the belt plies. Also check for fraying and glazing, which gives the belt a shiny appearance. Both sides of the belt should be inspected, which means you will have to twist the belt to check the underside.

4 The tension of each belt is checked by pushing on the belt at a distance halfway between the pulleys. Push firmly with your thumb and see how much the belt moves

(deflects). A rule of thumb is that if the distance from pulley center to pulley center is between 7 and 11 inches, the belt should deflect 1/4-inch. If the belt travels between pulleys spaced 12 to 16 inches apart, the belt should deflect 1/2-inch **(see illustration)**.

5 If it is necessary to adjust the belt tension, either to make the belt tighter or looser, it is done by moving the belt-driven accessory on the bracket.

6 For each component there will be an adjusting bolt and a pivot bolt. Both bolts must be loosened slightly to enable you to move the component **(see illustration)**.

7 After the two bolts have been loosened, move the component away from the engine to tighten the belt or toward the engine to loosen the belt. Hold the accessory in position and check the belt tension. If it is correct, tighten the two bolts until just snug, then recheck the tension. If the tension is all right, tighten the bolts.

8 It will often be necessary to use some sort of prybar to move the accessory while the belt is adjusted. If this must be done to gain the proper leverage, be very careful not to damage the component being moved or the part being pried against.

Serpentine belts

Refer to illustrations 17.9a, 17.9b, 17.9c, 17.9d, 17.9e and 17.9f

9 Later models are equipped with a single "serpentine" drivebelt that powers all engine accessories. This style belt requires no adjustment; it is handled by a spring-loaded tensioner pulley. The belt should be inspected regularly for missing ribs and frayed plies. Cracks in the belt ribs do not necessarily indicate a faulty or damaged belt, since they will not impair belt performance **(see illustrations)**. **Caution:** *It is critical to route the belt properly to ensure the correct rotation of the water pump. The illustrations referred to in Step 9 are typical routing diagrams. Note the actual routing of the belt on the vehicle before removing it from any pulley. Most vehicles will have a diagram for the belt routing on the power steering pump reservoir, on the plastic belt guard or on a sticker in the engine compartment.*

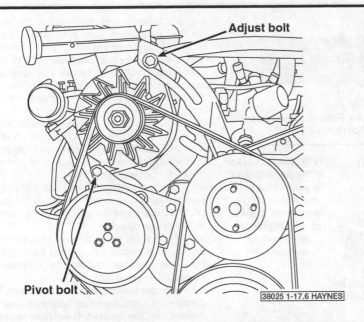

Adjust bolt

Pivot bolt

38025 1-17.6 HAYNES

17.6 Typical alternator drivebelt adjustment details

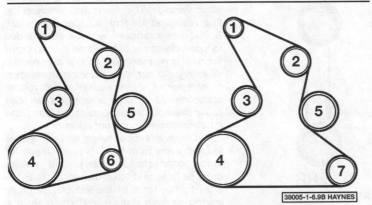

38005-1-6.9B HAYNES

Without air conditioning   **With air conditioning**

17.9c Serpentine drivebelt routing diagram - 3.1L V6 engines

1	Alternator	5	Water pump
2	Power steering pump	6	Idler pulley
3	Belt tensioner	7	Air conditioning
4	Crankshaft pulley		compressor

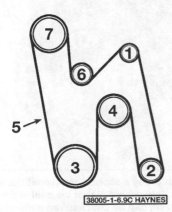

38005-1-6.9C HAYNES

17.9d Serpentine drivebelt routing diagram - 3.0 and 3.3L V6 engines

1 Alternator pulley
2 Air conditioning compressor
3 Crankshaft balancer
4 Water pump pulley
5 Serpentine belt
6 Belt tensioner

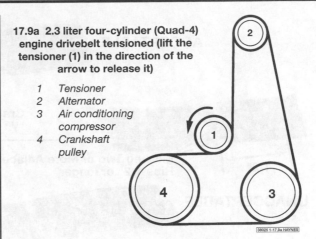

17.9a 2.3 liter four-cylinder (Quad-4) engine drivebelt tensioned (lift the tensioner (1) in the direction of the arrow to release it)

1 Tensioner
2 Alternator
3 Air conditioning compressor
4 Crankshaft pulley

38025 1-17.9a HAYNES

1

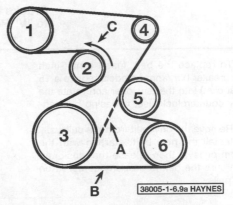

38005-1-6.9a HAYNES

17.9b Serpentine drivebelt routing diagram - 2.5L four-cylinder engines

1	Power steering pulley	A	Without air conditioning
2	Belt tensioner		
3	Crankshaft pulley	B	With air conditioning
4	Alternator	C	Tensioner - rotate in
5	Idler pulley		direction of arrow to
6	Air conditioning compressor pulley		remove or install belt

17.9e Replace the serpentine drivebelt when the pointer (2) on the moveable portion of the tensioner lines up with the minimum tension range (1)

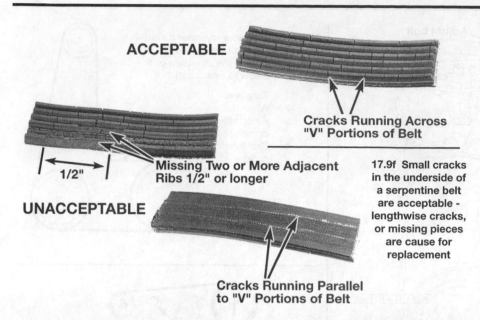

ACCEPTABLE

Cracks Running Across "V" Portions of Belt

1/2"

Missing Two or More Adjacent Ribs 1/2" or longer

UNACCEPTABLE

17.9f Small cracks in the underside of a serpentine belt are acceptable - lengthwise cracks, or missing pieces are cause for replacement

Cracks Running Parallel to "V" Portions of Belt

10   To replace the belt, insert a half-inch drive breaker bar (some models require a 15 mm socket) into the tensioner and rotate the pulley counterclockwise, releasing belt tension.
11   Remove the drivebelt from the pulleys.
12   Install the new belt, starting with the bottom pulleys, then release the tensioner. Make sure the belt is properly centered on each pulley.

18   Tire rotation (every 12,000 miles or 12 months)

Refer to illustration 18.2
1   The tires should be rotated at the specified intervals and whenever uneven wear is noticed. With the vehicle raised and the tires removed, you can also check the brakes (see Section 16) and the wheel bearings (see Section 25).
2   Refer to the accompanying illustration of the preferred tire rotation patterns **(see illustration)**.
3   Before raising the vehicle, loosen, but so not remove, the wheel lug nuts. Refer to the information in *Jacking and towing* at the front of this manual for the proper procedures to follow when raising the vehicle and changing a tire. If the brakes are to be checked, do not apply the parking brake as stated. Make sure the tires are blocked to prevent the vehicle from rolling.
4   Preferably, the entire vehicle should be raised at the same time. This can be done on a hoist or by jacking up each corner and then lowering the vehicle onto jackstands placed under the frame rails. Always use four jackstands and make sure the vehicle is securely supported.
5   After rotation, check and adjust the tire pressures as necessary and be sure to check the lug nut torque.

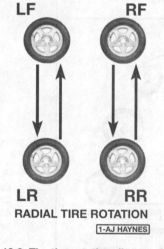

LF   RF

LR   RR

RADIAL TIRE ROTATION
1-AJ HAYNES

18.2 The tire rotation diagram for these models

19   Fuel system check (every 12,000 miles or 12 months)

Refer to illustration 19.5
Warning: *Gasoline is extremely flammable, so take extra precautions when you work on any part of the fuel system. Don't smoke or allow open flames or bare light bulbs near the work area, and don't work in a garage where a natural gas-type appliance (such as a water heater or clothes dryer) with a pilot light is present. Since gasoline is carcinogenic, wear latex gloves when there's a possibility of being exposed to fuel, and, if you spill any fuel on your skin, rinse it off immediately with soap and water. Mop up any spills immediately and do not store fuel-soaked rags where they could ignite. The fuel system is under constant pressure, so, if any fuel lines are to be disconnected, the fuel pressure in the system must be relieved first (see Chapter 4 for more infor-*

mation). When you perform any kind of work on the fuel system, wear safety glasses and have a Class B type fire extinguisher on hand.
1   Refer to the fuel pressure relief procedure (see Chapter 4) before servicing any component of the fuel system. Also, remove the fuel tank cap to relieve the pressure in the tank.
2   Before any fuel lines are disconnected for servicing, be prepared to catch the fuel as it spurts out. Plug all disconnected fuel lines immediately after disconnection to prevent the tank from emptying itself.
3   The fuel system is most easily checked with the vehicle raised on a hoist so the components underneath the vehicle are readily visible and accessible.
4   If the smell of gasoline is noticed while driving or after the vehicle has been in the sun, the system should be thoroughly inspected immediately.
5   Remove the gas filler cap and check for damage, corrosion and an unbroken sealing imprint on the gasket **(see illustration)**. Replace the cap with a new one if necessary.
6   With the vehicle raised, inspect the gas tank and filler neck for punctures, cracks or other damage. The connection between the filler neck and the tank is especially critical. Sometimes a rubber filler neck will leak due to loose clamps or deteriorated rubber, problems a home mechanic can usually rectify. **Warning:** *Do not, under any circumstances, try to repair a fuel tank yourself (except rubber components). A torch or even a spark can easily cause the fuel vapors to explode if the proper precautions are not taken.*
7   Check all rubber hoses and metal lines leading away from the fuel tank. Check for loose connections, deteriorated hoses, crimped lines and other damage. Follow the lines to the front of the vehicle, carefully inspecting them all the way. Repair or replace damaged sections as necessary.
8   If a fuel odor is still evident after the inspection, check the evaporative emissions control system (see Section 32).

19.5 With today's sophisticated emissions systems, it is essential that the seal in the gas tank cap be checked regularly

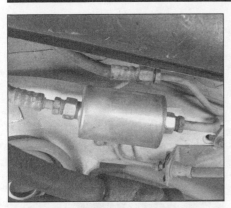

20.1 Typical frame-mounted fuel filter used with Multi-port Fuel Injection

21.4 Check the tightness of the throttle body mounting fasteners (arrows)

22.1 Remove the accelerator cable retaining clips (arrows), then check the cable for freedom of movement

20   Fuel filter replacement (every 12,000 miles or 12 months)

Refer to illustrations 20.1

Warning: *Gasoline is extremely flammable, so take extra precautions when you work on any part of the fuel system. Don't smoke or allow open flames or bare light bulbs near the work area, and don't work in a garage where a natural gas-type appliance (such as a water heater or clothes dryer) with a pilot light is present. Since gasoline is carcinogenic, wear latex gloves when there's a possibility of being exposed to fuel, and, if you spill any fuel on your skin, rinse it off immediately with soap and water. Mop up any spills immediately and do not store fuel-soaked rags where they could ignite. The fuel system is under constant pressure, so, if any fuel lines are to be disconnected, the fuel pressure in the system must be relieved first (see Chapter 4 for more information). When you perform any kind of work on the fuel system, wear safety glasses and have a Class B type fire extinguisher on hand.*

1   The models covered in this manual employ a stainless steel in-line fuel filter. On TBI engines it is located at the left rear of the engine, clamped to the cylinder head. On Multi-Port Fuel Injected models the filter is attached to the frame rail near the fuel tank **(see illustration)**.

2   Relieve the fuel system pressure (see Chapter 4).

3   With the engine cold, place a container under the fuel filter. Remove any bolts attach-ing the fuel filter bracket to the engine.

4   Loosen the clamps or fittings at each end of the filter, then detach the lines. On filters with threaded fittings, be sure to use a back-up wrench on the filter to prevent twisting the lines. On filters with quick-disconnect fittings, refer to Chapter 4 for release methods.

5   Loosen the clamp bolt and slide the filter out of the clamp.

6   Install the new filter by reversing the removal procedure. Do not over-tighten the fuel fittings.

21   Throttle Body Injection (TBI) mounting fastener torque check (2.5L engine only) (every 12,000 miles or 12 months)

Refer to illustration 21.4

1   The TBI throttle body is attached to the top of the intake manifold by two studs and nuts. These fasteners can sometimes work loose from vibration and temperature changes during normal engine operation and cause a vacuum leak.

2   If you suspect that a vacuum leak exists at the bottom of the throttle body, obtain a length of fuel hose. Start the engine and place one end of the hose next to your ear as you probe around the base of the throttle body with the other end. You will hear a hiss-ing sound if a leak exists.

3   Remove the air filter housing, tagging each hose to be disconnected to make reassembly easier.

4   Locate the mounting bolts or nuts on the throttle body **(see illustration).**

5   Tighten the bolts or nuts to the torque listed in this Chapter's Specifications. Do not over-tighten the fasteners.

6   If a vacuum leak still exists, the throttle body must be removed and a new base gas-ket installed.

7   After tightening, install the air filter hous-ing and return all hoses to their original posi-tion.

22   Accelerator cable check and maintenance (every 12,000 miles or 12 months)

Refer to illustration 22.1

1   The accelerator linkage is a cable type and although there are no adjustments to the linkage itself, periodic maintenance is neces-sary to assure its proper function **(see illus-tration)**.

2   Remove the air filter housing so the entire linkage is visible.

3   Check the entire length of the cable to make sure that it is not binding.

4   Check all the nylon bushings for wear, replacing them with new ones as necessary.

5   Lubricate the cable mechanisms with engine oil at the pivot points, but do not lubri-cate the cable itself.

23   Thermostatically controlled air cleaner (THERMAC) check (every 12,000 miles or 12 months)

Refer to illustration 23.3

Note: *This procedure applies to Throttle Body Injected (TBI) models only.*

1   Throttle Body Injected models are equipped with a thermostatically controlled air cleaner that draws air to the throttle body from different locations, depending upon engine temperature.

2   This is a visual check. If access is lim-ited, a small mirror may have to be used.

3   Open the hood and locate the damper

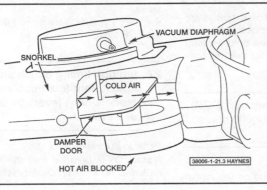

23.3 Thermac assembly shown with the snorkel passage (damper door) open

VACUUM DIAPHRAGM

SNORKEL

COLD AIR

DAMPER DOOR

HOT AIR BLOCKED

38005-1-21.3 HAYNES

24.4 On flat, pleated paper filters, note the direction the pleats face for correct reinstallation

24.8a Remove the clip and withdraw the PCV filter housing from the air cleaner (TBI equipped engines)

24.8b Pull the PCV filter element out of the holder (TBI equipped engines)

door inside the air cleaner assembly. It will be located inside the long snorkel of the metal air filter housing **(see illustration)**.

4   If there is a flexible air duct attached to the end of the snorkel, leading to an area behind the grille, disconnect it at the snorkel. This will enable you to look through the end of the snorkel and see the damper inside.

5   The check should be done when the engine is cold. Start the engine and look through the snorkel at the damper, which should move to a closed position. With the damper closed. air can't enter through the end of the snorkel, but instead enters the air cleaner through the flexible duct attached to the exhaust manifold and the heat stove passage.

6   As the engine warms up to operating temperature, the damper should open to allow air through the snorkel end. Depending on ambient temperature, this may take 10 to 15 minutes. To speed up this check you can reconnect the snorkel air duct, drive the vehicle, then check to see if the damper is completely open.

7   If the thermo-controlled air cleaner is not operating properly see Chapter 6 for more information.

24   Air filter and PCV filter replacement (every 12,000 miles or 12 months)

Refer to illustrations 24.4, 24.8a and 24.8b

1   At the specified intervals, the air filter and PCV filter should be replaced with new ones. Thorough preventative maintenance calls for the two filters to be inspected between changes.

2   On some models, the air filter is located inside the air filter housing on the top of the engine. On other models the air filter housing is located on the left side of the engine compartment. On some models the filter is replaced by removing the wing nut at the top of the air filter housing and lifting off the cover. On other models, spring clips or

screws hold the plastic cover on the housing.

3   While the air filter housing is open, be careful not to drop anything into the intake duct or down the throttle bore.

4   Lift the air filter element out of the housing. On models with a flat, pleated paper filter element, be sure to note which way the filter is installed **(see illustration)**.

5   Wipe out the inside of the air filter housing with a clean rag.

6   Place the new filter into the air filter housing. Make sure it seats properly in the bottom of the housing.

7   The PCV filter is also located inside the air filter housing. Remove the top plate and air filter as described previously, then locate the PCV filter on the side of the housing.

8   Remove the PCV filter housing clip and filter **(see illustrations)**.

9   Install a new PCV filter and the air filter.

10   Install the top plate and any hoses that were disconnected.

25   Wheel bearing check (every 24,000 miles or 24 months)

1   With the vehicle securely supported on jackstands, spin the wheels and check for noise, rolling resistance and freeplay. Grasp the top of the tire with one hand and the bottom of the tire with the other. Move the tire in and out. If it moves more than 0.005-inch, the bearings should be checked and, if necessary, replaced.

2   The wheel bearings on these models are of the sealed type that cannot be serviced and must be replaced with new ones if a fault develops. See Chapter 10 for the replacement procedure.

26   Exhaust Gas Recirculation (EGR) valve check (every 24,000 miles or 24 months)

Refer to illustration 26.2

1   The EGR valve is located on the intake

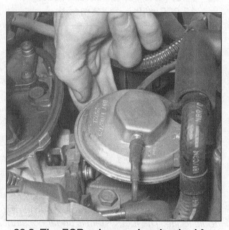

26.2 The EGR valve can be checked for free movement by pushing up on the diaphragm

manifold. Most problems in the emissions control system are due to a stuck or corroded EGR valve.

2   With the engine cold to prevent burns, reach under the EGR valve and manually push on the diaphragm. Using moderate pressure, you should be able to press the diaphragm up and down inside the housing **(see illustration)**.

3   If the diaphragm does not move or moves only with much effort, replace the EGR valve with a new one. If in doubt about the condition of the valve, compare the free movement of your EGR valve with a new valve.

4   See Chapter 6 for more information on the EGR system.

27   Ignition timing check and adjustment (distributor ignition models only) (every 24,000 miles or 24 months)

Refer to illustration 27.2

Note: *It is imperative that the procedures included on the Vehicle Emissions Control*

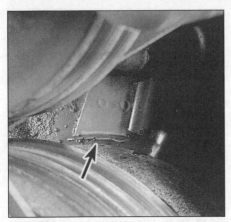

27.2 Typical timing scale (arrow)

28.7 Loosen the bolts at one end of the automatic transaxle drain pan, then pry one corner of the pan to break the seal and allow the fluid to drain - be careful, the fluid will gush out with considerable force

28.9 Separate the pan and lower it carefully - there is still some residual fluid in it

Information label be followed when adjusting the ignition timing. The label will include all information concerning preliminary steps to be performed before adjusting the timing as well as the timing specifications. Two different methods of timing are used. The conventional method and on some four-cylinder models the averaging method. The VECI label will tell you which method is used with your engine.

1   Locate the VECI label under the hood and read through and perform all preliminary instructions concerning ignition timing.

2   Locate the timing scale located beside the crankshaft pulley **(see illustration)**. The "T" mark represents Top Dead Center (TDC). The pointer plate will be marked in either one or two-degree increments and should have the proper timing mark for your particular vehicle noted. If not, count back from the "T" mark the correct number of degrees BTDC (*Before* Top Dead Center), as noted on the VECI label, and mark the scale.

3   Locate the notch on the crankshaft balancer or pulley and mark it with chalk or a dab of paint so it will be visible under the timing light.

4   Start the engine, warm it up to the normal operating temperature and shut it off. Turn off all lights and other electrical loads.

5   With the ignition off, connect the pick-up lead of the timing light to the number one spark plug wire. Connect the timing light power leads according to the manufacturer's instructions.

6   Start the engine, aim the timing light at the timing mark by the crankshaft pulley and note which timing mark the notch on the pulley is lining up with.

7   If the notch is not lining up with the correct mark. loosen the distributor hold-down bolt and rotate the distributor until the notch is lined up with the correct timing mark.

8   Retighten the hold-down bolt and recheck the timing.

9   Turn off the engine and disconnect the timing light. Reconnect the number one spark plug wire, if removed, and any other components which were disconnected.

Averaging method

10   The averaging method is used to bring the timing of each cylinder into alignment with the base timing specification. Models using the averaging method have a double-notched crankshaft pulley with the notch for the number one cylinder scribed across all three edges of the pulley. Another notch, scribed across only the center section of the pulley, is located 180-degrees away. The coil wire, instead of the number one spark plug wire, is used to trigger the timing light. Because the trigger signal is picked up at the coil wire, each spark firing causes a flash from the timing light. This makes the timing notch appear to jiggle since each firing is indicated. Adjustment is accomplished by centering the total apparent notch width over the specified timing mark.

11   On electronic spark timing equipped models disconnect the four terminal EST plug at the distributor so the engine will operate in the bypass timing mode.

12   Connect the timing light, following the manufacturer's instructions. Be very careful not to tangle the wires in moving engine parts.

13   Clamp the timing light inductive pickup around the high tension coil wire. Peel back the protective plastic sheath on the wire when installing the timing light inductive pickup.

14   Loosen the distributor clamp nut sufficiently to allow the distributor to be rotated for adjustment.

15   Start the engine, aim the timing light at the timing tab and, if necessary, rotate the distributor to center the notch width over the specified mark. Remember that a slight jiggling of the pulley notch is normal.

16   Shut the engine off and tighten the distributor clamp nut, taking care not to move the distributor.

17   Recheck the timing and repeat the adjustment if necessary.

18   Plug in the EST connector, replace the plastic cover on the coil wire and remove the

timing light. **Note:** *On some models it will be necessary to remove and replace the ECM 1 fuse to clear the trouble code memory.*

28   Automatic transaxle fluid and filter change (every 30,000 miles or 30 months)

Refer to illustrations 28.7, 28.9, 28.11 and 28.17

1   At the specified time intervals the automatic transaxle fluid should be changed and the filter replaced.

2   Since there is no drain plug, the transaxle oil pan must be removed to drain the fluid. Before beginning work, purchase the specified transmission fluid (see *Recommended lubricants and fluids* at the front of this Chapter), and a new filter.

3   Other tools necessary for this job include jackstands to support the vehicle in a raised position, a drain pan capable of holding at least eight pints, newspapers and clean rags.

4   The fluid should be drained immediately after the vehicle has been driven. This will remove any built-up sediment better than if the fluid were cold. Because of this, it is wise to wear protective gloves. Fluid temperature can exceed 350-degrees in a hot transaxle.

5   After the vehicle has been driven to warm up the fluid. raise it and place it on jackstands for access underneath.

6   Move the necessary equipment under the vehicle, being careful not to touch any of the hot exhaust components.

7   Place the drain pan under the transaxle fluid pan and loosen, but do not remove, the bolts at one end of the pan **(see illustration)**.

8   Moving around the pan, loosen all the bolts a little at a time. Be sure the drain pan is in position, as fluid will begin dripping out. Continue in this manner until all of the bolts are removed except for one at each of the corners.

9   While supporting the pan, remove the remaining bolts and lower the pan **(see illustration)**. If necessary, use a screwdriver to break the gasket seal, but be careful not to

damage the pan or transaxle gasket surfaces. Drain the remaining fluid into the drain pan. As this is done check the fluid for metal particles, which may be an indication of internal failure.

10 Now visible at the bottom of the transaxle is the filter/strainer.

11 Remove the filter and O-ring seal **(see illustration). Caution:** *If the O-ring doesn't come off with the filter, be sure to retrieve it from the hole.*

12 Thoroughly clean the transaxle fluid pan with solvent. Check for metal filings or foreign material. Dry with compressed air if available. It is important that all remaining gasket material be removed from the pan mounting flange. Use a gasket scraper or putty knife for this.

13 Clean the filter mounting surface on the valve body. Again, this surface should be smooth and free of any leftover gasket material.

14 Install the new filter with a new O-ring seal.

15 Press the new gasket into place on the pan, making sure all bolt holes line up.

16 Lift the pan up to the bottom of the transaxle and install the mounting bolts. Tighten the bolts in a diagonal pattern working around the pan. Using a torque wrench, tighten the bolts in a criss-cross pattern to the torque listed in this Chapter's Specifications.

17 When reinstalling the pan on a 3-speed transaxle, you must apply thread locking compound to the threads of bolt A **(see illustration)** to prevent fluid leaks.

18 Lower the vehicle.

19 Open the hood and remove the transaxle fluid dipstick.

20 Add the specified amount and type of fluid to the transaxle through the filler tube. Use a funnel to prevent spills. It is best to add a little fluid at a time, continually checking the level with the dipstick. Allow the fluid time to drain into the pan.

21 With the selector lever in Park, apply the parking brake and start the engine without depressing the accelerator pedal (if possible). Do not race the engine - run it at idle only.

22 With the engine idling, check the level on the dipstick. Look under the vehicle for leaks around the transaxle oil pan mating surface.

23 Check the fluid level to make sure it is just below the Add mark on the dipstick. Do not allow the fluid level to go above this point as the transaxle would then be overfilled, necessitating the removal of the pan to drain excess fluid.

24 Push the dipstick firmly back into its tube and let the engine idle, with the transaxle in Park, for three minutes. Check the fluid level again and add as necessary to bring the level to just above the add mark. Now drive the vehicle far enough to reach normal operating temperature in the transaxle. This should take just a few miles of highway driving, slightly less in the city. Park the vehicle on a level surface and check the

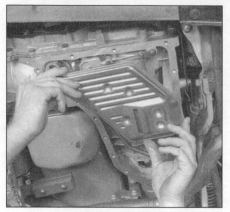

28.11 Detach the filter and lower it carefully because it also contains some fluid

fluid level on the dipstick with the engine idling and the transaxle in Park. The level should now be at the F mark on the dipstick. If not, add more fluid, a little at a time, to bring the level up to this point. Again, do not overfill.

29 Manual transaxle lubricant change (every 30,000 miles or 30 months)

1 Remove the dipstick, raise the vehicle and support it securely on jackstands.

2 Move a drain pan, rags, newspapers and wrenches under the transaxle.

3 Remove the transaxle drain plug at the bottom of the case and allow the oil to drain into the pan.

4 After the oil has drained completely, reinstall the plug and tighten it securely.

5 Lower the vehicle.

6 Remove the dipstick and using a funnel, fill the transaxle with the correct amount of the specified lubricant. Use the dipstick to check the level (see Section 4). If it is low, add more lubricant, a little at a time, to bring the level up to the specified point. Be careful not to overfill it.

30 Cooling system servicing (draining, flushing and refilling) (every 30,000 miles or 30 months)

Warning: *Do not allow antifreeze to come in contact with your skin or painted surfaces of the vehicle. Rinse off spills immediately with plenty of water. Antifreeze is highly toxic if ingested. Never leave antifreeze lying around in an open container or in puddles on the floor; children and pets are attracted by it's sweet smell and may drink it. Check with local authorities about disposing of used antifreeze. Many communities have collection centers that will see that antifreeze is disposed of safely.*

1 Periodically the cooling system should

28.17 On certain models, be sure to apply thread locking compound to the threads of bolt A

be drained, flushed and refilled to replenish the antifreeze mixture and prevent formation of rust and corrosion, which can impair the performance of the cooling system and cause engine damage.

2 At the same time the cooling system is serviced, all hoses and the radiator/surge tank cap should be inspected and, if necessary, replaced (see Section 7).

3 Since antifreeze is a poisonous solution, be careful not to spill any of the coolant mixture on the vehicle's paint or your skin. If this happens, rinse immediately with plenty of clean water. Consult your local authorities about the dumping of antifreeze before draining the cooling system. In many areas reclamation centers have been set up to collect automobile oil and drained antifreeze/water mixtures, rather than allowing them to be added to the sewage system.

4 With the engine cold, remove the radiator cap.

5 Move a large container under the radiator to catch the coolant as it is drained.

6 Drain the radiator. Most models are equipped with a drain plug at the bottom. If this drain has excessive corrosion and cannot be turned easily, or if the radiator is not equipped with a drain, disconnect the lower radiator hose to allow the coolant to drain. Be careful that none of the solution is splashed on your skin or into your eyes.

7 If accessible, remove the engine block drain plugs. There is usually a plug on the side of the engine about halfway back, on the lower edge near the oil pan rail. On V6 engines there are two plugs, one on each side of the engine block. These will allow the coolant to drain from the engine itself.

8 Disconnect the hose from the coolant reservoir and remove the reservoir. Flush it out with clean water.

9 Place a garden hose in the radiator filler neck and flush the system until the water runs clear at all drain points.

10 In severe cases of contamination or clogging of the radiator, remove it (see Chapter 3) and reverse flush it. This involves inserting the hose in the bottom radiator outlet to

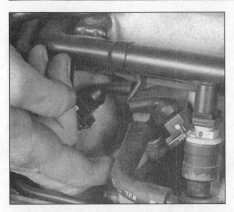

31.1 On some models the PCV valve plugs into the intake manifold

31.2 Removing the PCV valve from the valve cover

32.2 The EECS canister is located at the front corner of the engine compartment

1

allow the clear water to run against the normal flow, draining through the top. A radiator repair shop should be consulted if further cleaning or repair is necessary.

11   When the coolant is regularly drained and the system refilled with the correct antifreeze/water mixture, there should be no need to use chemical cleaners or descalers.

12   To refill the system, reconnect the radiator hoses and install the drain plugs securely in the engine. Teflon thread-sealing tape, available at auto parts stores, should be used on the drain plugs. Install the reservoir and the overflow hose where applicable.

13   On models with a coolant reservoir, fill the radiator to the base of the filler neck and then add more coolant to the reservoir until it reaches the Full Cold mark. On models with a surge tank, slowly fill the surge tank until the level is up to the Full Cold mark.

14   Run the engine until normal operating temperature is reached and, with the engine idling, add coolant to the Full Hot level. Install the pressure cap and, on models so equipped, the reservoir cap.

15   Always refill the system with a mixture of high quality antifreeze and water in the proportion called for on the antifreeze container or in your owner's manual. Chapter 3 also contains information on antifreeze mixtures.

16   Keep a close watch on the coolant level and the various cooling system hoses during the first few miles of driving. Tighten the hose clamps and add more coolant as necessary.

31   Positive Crankcase Ventilation (PCV) valve check and replacement (every 30,000 miles or 30 months)

Refer to illustrations 31.1 and 31.2

1   On some models the PCV valve is located in the valve cover. A hose runs from the valve to the throttle body base plate or intake manifold. On other models, the valve plugs into the intake manifold and is connected to the valve cover by a hose **(see illustration)**. **Note:** *The 2.3L (Quad-4) engine does not use a PCV valve - instead an oil/air separator is used. The oil/air separator does*

not require service. Replace it if it becomes plugged.

2   Pull the valve (with hose attached) from the rubber grommet in the valve cover **(see illustration)** or, on models with the valve mounted in the intake manifold, detach the PCV hose from its fitting on the valve cover.

3   Start the engine and bring it to normal operating temperature.

4   Place your finger over the end of the valve or hose. If the engine speed drops, the valve is working properly. If the speed doesn't drop the valve is faulty and should be replaced with a new one.

5   To replace the valve. pull it from the end of the hose or out of the manifold, noting its installed position and direction.

6   When purchasing a replacement PCV valve, make sure it is for your particular vehicle, model year and engine size. Compare the old valve with the new one to make sure they are the same. Push the valve into the end of the hose until it is seated.

7   Inspect the rubber grommet for damage and replace it with a new one if necessary.

8   Push the PCV valve and hose securely into position.

9   More information on the PCV system can be found in Chapter 6.

32   Evaporative Emissions Control System (EECS) check (every 30,000 miles or 30 months)

Refer to illustration 32.2

1   The function of the Evaporative Emissions Control System is to capture fuel vapors from the fuel tank and intake manifold before they can escape into the atmosphere, store them in a charcoal canister and then burn them during normal engine operation.

2   The most common symptom of a fault in the evaporative emissions system is a strong fuel odor in the engine compartment. If a fuel odor is detected, inspect the charcoal canister, located at the front corner of the engine compartment, and system hoses **(see illustration)**.

3   A simple check of system operation on early models is to place your hand under the

canister with the engine at normal operating temperature and slowly increase engine speed. If air can be felt being sucked into the bottom of the canister the system is operating properly.

4   The evaporative emissions control system is explained in more detail in Chapter 6.

33   Spark plug replacement (every 30,000 miles or 30 months)

Refer to illustrations 33.1, 33.5a, 33.5b and 33.10

1   In most cases, tools necessary for a spark plug replacement include a plug wrench or spark plug socket that fits onto a

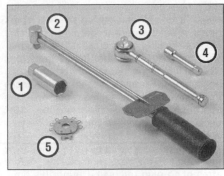

33.1 Tools necessary for changing spark plugs

1   **Spark plug socket** - *This will have special padding inside to protect the spark plug porcelain insulator*

2   **Torque wrench** - *Although not mandatory, use of this tool is the best way to ensure that the plugs are tightened properly*

3   **Ratchet** - *Standard hand tool to fit the plug socket*

4   **Extension** - *Depending on model and accessories, you may need special extensions and universal joints to reach one or more of the plugs*

5   **Spark plug gap gauge** - *This gauge for checking the gap comes in a variety of styles. Make sure the gap for your engine is included*

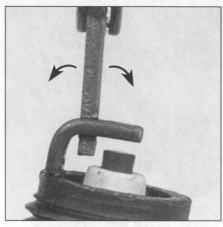

33.10 A length of rubber hose eases the job of installing a spark plug in difficult to reach areas

33.5a Spark plug manufacturers recommend using a wire-type gauge when checking the gap - if the wire does not slide between the electrodes with a slight drag, adjustment is required

33.5b To change the gap, bend the side electrode only, as indicated by the arrows, and be very careful not to crack or chip the porcelain insulator surrounding the center electrode

ratchet wrench (this special socket will be insulated inside to protect the porcelain insulator) and a wire-type feeler gauge to check and adjust the spark plug gap (see illustration).

2   The spark plugs are located on each side of V6 engines, on the front (radiator) side on 2.0 and 2.5L four-cylinder engines and in the center of the engine on 2.3L (Quad-4) engines.

3   The best procedure to follow when replacing the spark plugs is to purchase the new spark plugs beforehand, adjust them to the proper gap and then replace each plug one at a time. When buying the new spark plugs, it is important to obtain the correct plugs for your specific engine. This information can be found on the Vehicle Emissions Control Information label, located under the hood, or in the owner's manual. If differences exist between these sources, purchase the spark plug type specified on the label because the information was printed for your specific engine.

4   With the new spark plugs at hand, allow the engine to cool completely before attempting plug removal. During this time, each of the new spark plugs can be inspected for defects and the gaps can be checked.

5   The gap is checked by inserting the proper thickness gauge between the electrodes at the tip of the plug. The gap between the electrodes should be the same as that given in this Chapter's Specifications or on the Vehicle Emissions Control Information label. The wire should just touch each of the electrodes (see illustration). If the gap is incorrect, use the notched adjuster on the feeler gauge body to bend the curved side electrode slightly until the proper gap is achieved (see illustration). If the side electrode is not exactly over the center electrode, use the notched adjuster to align the two. Check for cracks in the porcelain insulator, indicating the spark plug should not be used.

6   With the engine cool, remove the spark plug wire from one spark plug. Do this by grabbing the boot at the end of the wire, not the wire itself. Sometimes it is necessary to use a twisting motion while the boot and plug wire are pulled free. Note: If you're working on a 2.3L four-cylinder engine ("Quad-4"), refer to Chapter 5, Section 10, Step 69, for the Integrated Direct Ignition (IDI) unit removal procedure (no spark plug wires are used on this engine).

7   If compressed air is available, use it to blow any dirt or foreign material away from the spark plug area. The idea here is to eliminate the possibility of material falling into the cylinder as the spark plug is removed.

8   Place the spark plug wrench or socket over the plug and remove it from the engine by turning in a counterclockwise direction.

9   Compare the spark plug with those shown on the inside back cover of this manual to get an indication of the overall running condition of the engine.

10   Due to the angle at which the spark plugs must be installed on most engines, installation will be simplified by inserting the end of the new spark plug into a snug-fitting rubber hose, a few inches long (see illustration). This procedure serves two purposes. The rubber hose gives you flexibility for establishing the proper angle of plug insertion in the head and, should the threads be improperly aligned, the rubber hose will slip on the spark plug when it meets resistance, preventing cross-threading into the head.

11   After installing the plug to the limit of the hose grip, tighten it with the socket. It is a good idea to use a torque wrench for this to insure that the plug is seated correctly. The correct torque figure is included in this Chapter's Specifications.

12   Before pushing the spark plug wire onto the end of the plug, inspect it following the procedures outlined in Section 34.

13   Attach the plug wire to the new spark plug, again using a twisting motion on the

boot until it is firmly seated on the spark plug. Make sure the wire is routed away from the exhaust manifold.

14   Allow the above procedure for the remaining spark plugs, replacing them one at a time to prevent mixing up the spark plug wires.

---

34   Spark plug wires, distributor cap and rotor check and replacement (every 30,000 miles or 30 months)

Refer to illustrations 34.3, 34.4, 34.6, 34.7, 34.17a and 34.17b

Note: Most models are equipped with Direct Ignition Systems (DIS) which does not use a distributor. Consequently, on these models only the spark plug wires and connections need to be checked.

1   Begin this procedure by making a visual check of the spark plug wires while the engine is running. In a darkened garage (do this at night with the garage door open) start the engine and observe each plug wire. Be careful not to come into contact with any moving engine parts. If there is a break in the wire, you will see arcing or a small spark at the damaged area. If arcing is noticed, make a note to obtain new wires, then allow the engine to cool and check the distributor cap and rotor.

2   Disconnect the negative cable from the battery. Caution: If the vehicle is equipped with a Delco Loc II audio system, make sure you have the correct activation code before disconnecting the battery. See the information at the front of this manual for the radio re-activation procedure. At the distributor, disconnect the ECM connector and the coil connector (coil-in-cap models) or coil wire (models with a separately mounted coil).

3   Remove the distributor cap by placing a screwdriver on the slotted head of each latch. Press down on the latch and turn it 90-degrees to release the hooked end at the bottom (see illustration). On some engines, due to restricted working room, a stubby screwdriver will work best. With all latches disengaged, separate the cap from the distributor with the spark plug wires still attached. Note: Some models may use

34.3 Releasing the distributor cap hold-down latches

34.4 Inspect the distributor cap for cracks and carbon tracks and the terminals (arrow) for corrosion and damage

34.6 Removing the rotor

screws instead of latches.

4   Inspect the cap for cracks and other damage. Closely examine the terminals on the inside of the cap for excessive corrosion **(see illustration)**. Slight pitting is normal. Deposits on the terminals may be removed with a small file.

5   If the inspection reveals damage to the cap, make a note to obtain a replacement for your particular engine, then examine the rotor.

6   The rotor is visible, with the cap removed, at the top of the distributor shaft. It is held in place by two screws. Remove the screws and the rotor **(see illustration)**.

7   Inspect the rotor for cracks and other damage. Carefully check the condition of the metal contact at the top of the rotor for excessive burning and pitting **(see illustration)**. On coil-in-cap models, also check the top of the rotor for carbon tracks. This is a sign of moisture contamination due to a leaking seal between the distributor cap and the coil. The rotor and seal should be replaced with new ones if carbon tracks are visible.

8   If it is determined that a new rotor is required, make a note to that effect. If the rotor and cap are in good condition, reinstall them at this time. Be sure to apply a small

dab of silicone lubricant to the terminals inside the cap before installing it. Note that most rotors have two raised pegs on the bottom and have a wide slot and a narrow slot. Make sure that the slots are correctly aligned and that the pegs are firmly seated with the rotor is installed.

9   If the cap must be replaced, do not reinstall it. Leave it off the distributor with the wires still connected.

10   If the spark plug wires are being replaced, now is the time to obtain a new set, along with a new cap and rotor as determined in the checks above. Purchase a wire set for your particular engine, pre-cut to the proper size, with the rubber boots already installed.

11   If the spark plug wires passed the check in Step 1, they should be checked further as follows.

12   Examine the wires one at a time to avoid mixing them up.

13   Disconnect the plug wire from the spark plug. A removal tool can be used for this, or you can grab the rubber boot, twist slightly and then pull the wire free. Do not pull on the wire itself, only on the rubber boot.

14   Inspect inside the boot for corrosion, which will look like a white crusty powder. Some models use a conductive white silicone lubricant, that should not be mistaken for corrosion.

15   Push the wire and boot back onto the end of the spark plug. It should be a tight fit on the plug end. If not, remove the wire and use pliers to carefully crimp the metal connector inside the wire boot until the fit is snug.

16   Using a clean rag, clean the entire length of the wire. Remove all built-up dirt and grease. As this is done, check for burns, cracks and any other form of damage. Bend the wires in several places to ensure that the conductive wire inside has not hardened.

17   The wires should be checked at the distributor cap (or coils, on models with a distributorless ignition system) in the same manner. On four-cylinder engines and later model V6 engines, remove the wire from the cap by pulling on the boot, again examining the wires one at a time, and reinstalling each one after examination. Apply new silicone lubricant before installation. On early models with V6 engines, the spark plug wire boots are connected to a circular retaining ring attached to the distributor cap. Release the

34.7 Close-up of the metal contact on this rotor reveals a normal wear pattern

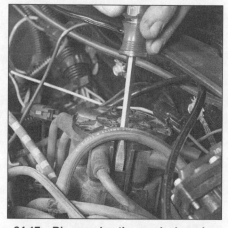

34.17a Disengaging the spark plug wire retaining ring clip from the top of the distributor cap

34.17b Removing the plug wire retainer from the cap

locking tabs, turn the ring upside down and check all wire boots at the same time **(see illustrations)**.

18   If the wires appear to be in good condition, reinstall the retaining ring (some models) and make sure that all wires are secure at both ends. If the cap and rotor are also in good condition, the check is finished. Reconnect the wires at the distributor (or coil) and the battery.

19   If it was determined that new wires are required, obtain them at this time, along with a new cap and rotor if so determined by the checks above.

20   If a new cap is being installed on a coil-in-cap type distributor, the coil and cover from the cap being replaced should be transferred to the new cap.

21   Remove the three coil attaching screws and lift off the cover.

22   Remove the coil attaching screws, disconnect the leads and separate the coil from the distributor.

23   Attach the new coil to the cap by reversing Steps 21 and 22. Use a new seal between the coil and cap and be sure to lubricate the seal with multi-purpose grease.

24   Attach the rotor to the distributor. Make

sure that the carbon brush is properly installed in the cap, as a side gap between the carbon brush and the rotor will cause rotor burn-through and/or damage to the distributor cap.

25   If new wires are being installed, replace them one at a time. **Note**: *It is important to replace wires one at a time, noting the routing as each wire is removed and installed, to maintain the correct firing order and to prevent cross-firing.*

26   Attach the cap to the distributor, reconnecting all wires disconnected earlier, then reconnect the battery cable.

Chapter 2 Part A
2.0L overhead cam (OHC) four-cylinder engine

Contents

Specifications

General
Cylinder numbers (timing belt end-to-transaxle end) 1-2-3-4
Firing order 1-3-4-2

Camshaft
Lobe lift (intake and exhaust) .... 0.2409 inch
Endplay .... 0.016 to 0.064 inch
Journal diameters
    No. 1 .... 1.6720 to 1.6714 inches
    No. 2 .... 1.6816 to 1.6812 inches
    No. 3 .... 1.6917 to 1.6911 inches
    No. 4 .... 1.7015 to 1.7009 inches
    No. 5 .... 1.7114 to 1.7108 inches
Bearing oil clearance .... 0.0008 inch

Oil Pump
Idler gear-to-body clearance .... 0.004 to 0.007 inch
Drive gear-to-body clearance .... 0.007 to 0.010 inch
Gear-to-cover clearance .... 0.001 to 0.004 inch

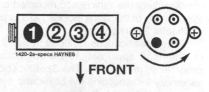

1420-2a-specs HAYNES

↓ **FRONT**

**Cylinder location and
distributor rotation**

*The blackened terminal shown on the
distributor cap indicates the Number
One spark plug wire position*

Torque specifications

Ft-lbs (unless otherwise noted)

Camshaft carrier/cylinder head bolts	
Step 1	18
Step 2	tighten an additional 60 degrees
Step 3	tighten an additional 60 degrees
Step 4	tighten an additional 60 degrees
Step 5	tighten an additional 30 to 50 degrees (with the engine hot)
Camshaft cover bolts	72 inch-lbs
Camshaft retainer plate bolts	72 inch-lbs
Camshaft sprocket retaining bolt	34
Crankshaft pulley-to-sprocket bolts	15
Crankshaft sprocket retaining bolt	115
Driveplate-to-crankshaft bolts	48
Exhaust manifold bolts	16
Flywheel-to-crankshaft bolts*	
Step 1	48
Step 2	Turn an additional 30 degrees
Intake manifold nuts	16
Oil drain hose (both ends)	35
Oil feed pipe union	144 inch-lbs
Oil feed pipe-to-block	144 inch-lbs
Oil feed pipe-to-turbocharger	144 inch-lbs
Oil pan bolts	48 inch-lbs
Oil pick-up tube-to-block bolts	60 inch-lbs
Oil pick-up tube-to-oil pump bolts	60 inch-lbs
Oil pump mounting bolts	60 inch-lbs
Oil pump plug	180 inch-lbs
Turbocharger support bracket	
Lower bolt	37
Retaining nut	18
Turbocharger-to-exhaust manifold	18
Turbocharger-to-outlet elbow	18

Discard the bolts each time they're removed and use new ones for installation - be sure to follow the detailed tightening procedure in the text

1   General information

This part of Chapter 2 is devoted to in-vehicle repair procedures for the 2.0L OHC turbocharged four-cylinder engine.

Information concerning engine removal and installation, as well as engine block and cylinder head overhaul, is in Part F of this Chapter.

The following repair procedures are based on the assumption that the engine is installed in the vehicle. If the engine has been removed from the vehicle and mounted on a stand, many of the steps included in this part of Chapter 2 will not apply.

The specifications included in this Part of Chapter 2 apply only to the engine and procedures in this Part. The Specifications necessary for rebuilding the block and cylinder head are found in Part F.

2   Repair operations possible with the engine in the vehicle

Many major repair operations can be accomplished without removing the engine from the vehicle.

Clean the engine compartment and the exterior of the engine with some type of pressure washer before any work is done. A clean engine will make the job easier and will help keep dirt out of the internal areas of the engine.

Depending on the components involved, it may be a good idea to remove the hood to improve access to the engine as repairs are performed (see Chapter 11 if necessary).

If vacuum, exhaust, oil or coolant leaks develop, indicating a need for gasket or seal replacement, the repairs can generally be made with the engine in the vehicle. The intake and exhaust manifold gaskets, oil pan gasket and cylinder head gasket are all accessible with the engine in place.

Exterior engine components such as the intake and exhaust manifolds, the oil pan, the oil pump, the water pump, the starter motor, the alternator, the distributor, the turbocharger and the fuel injection system can be removed for repair with the engine in place.

Since the cylinder head can be removed without pulling the engine, camshaft and valve component servicing can also be accomplished with the engine in the vehicle.

In extreme cases caused by a lack of necessary equipment, repair or replacement of piston rings, pistons, connecting rods and rod bearings is possible with the engine in the vehicle. However, this practice is not recommended because of the cleaning and preparation work that must be done to the components involved.

3   Camshaft cover - removal and installation

Refer to illustrations 3.3, 3.4 and 3.5

1   Detach the induction tube.

2   Remove the crankcase breather hoses.

3   Remove the bolts and separate the cover from the engine. It may be necessary to break the gasket seal by tapping the cover with a soft-face hammer. If it's really stuck, use a knife, gasket scraper or chisel to

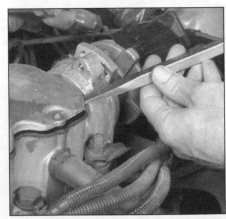

3.3 Break the camshaft cover gasket seal with a chisel and hammer - be careful not to damage the sealing surfaces!

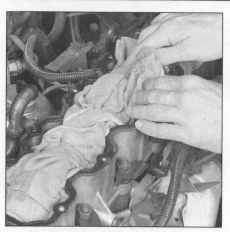

3.4 Rags placed in the camshaft gallery will keep foreign material out

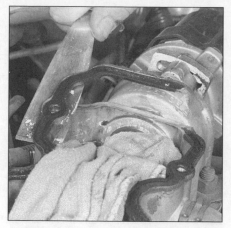

3.5 When removing the camshaft cover gasket with a scraper, be careful not to nick or gouge the carrier

4.3 Locations of the timing belt front cover bolts

2A

remove it, but be very careful not to damage the gasket sealing surface of the cover or housing (see illustration).

4   Place clean rags in the camshaft gallery to keep foreign material out of the engine (see illustration).

5   Remove all traces of gasket material from the cover and housing. Be careful not to nick or gouge the soft aluminum (see illustration). Clean the mating surfaces with lacquer thinner or acetone.

6   Reinstall the cover with a new gasket - no sealant is required. Install the bolts and tighten them to the specified torque in a criss-cross pattern.

7   Reinstall the induction tube and breather hoses.

4   Timing belt front cover - removal and installation

Refer to illustration 4.3

1   Detach the battery cable from the negative battery terminal.

2   Remove the serpentine drivebelt (see Chapter 1). Remove the tensioner bolt and swing the tensioner down, out of the way.

3   On 1988 and earlier models, unsnap the retaining clips and detach the upper and lower covers from the engine. On 1989 and later models, remove the outer cover retaining nuts/bolts and remove the cover (see illustration).

4   Installation is the reverse of removal.

5   Timing belt rear cover - removal and installation

1   Remove the timing belt front cover (see Section 4) and the timing belt (see Section 6).

2   Remove the camshaft and crankshaft sprockets (see Sections 7 and 8). On 1989 and later models, remove the timing belt tensioner assembly.

3   Remove the bolts and separate the rear

cover from the engine.

4   Installation is the reversal of removal. Pay special attention to tightening the bolts and rubber grommets on 1988 and earlier models to avoid rubbing of the belt.

6   Timing belt - removal, installation and adjustment

Refer to illustrations 6.7a, 6.7b, 6.12, 6.13 and 6.17

Caution: Incorrect installation or adjustment of the timing belt could result in engine damage. Although a skilled mechanic may be able to set timing belt tension without them, we recommend the use of a tension gauge tool, available at most auto parts stores. DO NOT turn the camshaft with a wrench on the sprocket bolt. When necessary, turn the camshaft with an open-end wrench on the machined hex above cylinder number four (inside the camshaft cover).

6.7a On 1988 and earlier models, the crankshaft pulley notch must be aligned with the 10 degree BTDC mark (arrows) before the timing belt is removed

Removal

1   Disconnect the cable from the negative battery terminal.

2   Drain the coolant (see Chapter 1).

3   Remove the timing belt front cover (see Section 4).

4   Remove the coolant reservoir.

5   Raise the vehicle and support it securely on jackstands.

6   Remove the right front wheel. Remove the bolts and detach the inner splash panel from the wheel well.

7   On 1988 and earlier, rotate the crankshaft until the timing mark on the crankshaft pulley is aligned with the ten degree BTDC mark on the indicator scale and the camshaft sprocket mark lines up with the mark on the camshaft carrier (see illustrations).

8   On 1989 and later, rotate the crankshaft and camshaft until the marks on the timing belt sprockets are aligned with the marks on the rear cover.

6.7b The valve timing marks are easy to see grooves cast into the camshaft sprocket and carrier (arrows)

6.12 Carefully pry out on the water pump to break the gasket seal, . . .

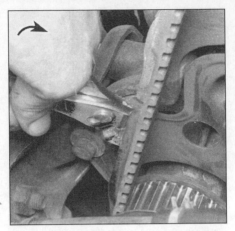

6.13 . . . then rotate the water pump in the direction shown (arrow) to release the timing belt tension

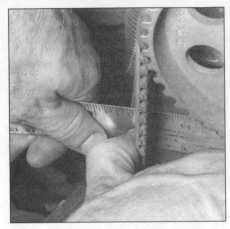

6.17 Use a ruler to check the timing belt tension

9   Remove the bolts and detach the pulley from the crankshaft sprocket.

10   On 1988 and earlier models, remove the timing probe for bolt access.

11   On all years, loosen the water pump bolts.

12   Use a large screwdriver to break the water pump gasket seal **(see illustration)**.

13   Grasp the water pump with a pair of pliers and release the tension from the timing belt by rotating the pump toward the engine **(see illustration)**.

14   Slip the belt off the sprockets. **Caution:** *Don't rotate the crankshaft or camshaft while the belt is off.*

Installation and adjustment - 1988 and earlier (without a factory tool)

15   Slip the new belt onto the sprockets, install the crankshaft pulley and make sure the crankshaft and camshaft marks are aligned.

16   Rotate the water pump to apply tension to the timing belt and tighten the water pump bolts.

17   Measure the belt deflection midway between the water pump and the camshaft pulley with a straightedge and ruler **(see illustration)**. Adjust the belt tension until the deflection is 1/4-inch.

1988 and earlier adjustment with a factory tool

18   Install the adjusting tool and gauge as described in the instructions accompanying the tools. Adjust the tension until it's within the range on the gauge.

19   After adjusting the tension, remove the gauge, then carefully turn the crankshaft clockwise (viewed from the timing belt end) with a socket and breaker bar on the crankshaft sprocket bolt. While slowly rotating the camshaft two full turns (720 degrees), feel and listen for valve-to-piston contact. Don't force the engine - if binding is felt, backup and recheck your work. When you

reach 720 degrees, check the timing marks again (they should be aligned). **Note:** *New belts should be run-in several minutes and then rechecked.*

20   Reinstall all components, then refill the cooling system and run the engine. After normal operating temperature is reached, check carefully for leaks.

Installation and adjustment - 1989 and later

21   Recheck the alignment of the crankshaft and camshaft sprockets. Install the timing belt, routing it properly around the tensioner pulley. There should be tension on the belt between the camshaft and crankshaft pulleys, with the marks on the sprockets still in alignment with the marks on the rear cover.

22   Rotate the water pump eccentric clockwise until the tensioner makes contact with the high torque stop. Tighten the water pump bolts enough to hold the pump in position.

23   Rotate the crankshaft two full revolutions, then bring the timing marks back into alignment.

24   Loosen the water pump bolts slightly, then turn the pump counterclockwise until the hole in the tensioner arm is aligned with the hole in the tensioner base.

25   Tighten the water pump bolts to the torque specified in Chapter 3, while making sure the tensioner holes are still in alignment.

26   The remainder of installation is the reverse of the removal procedure. Refill the cooling system (see Chapter 1) and check for leaks.

7   Camshaft sprocket - removal and installation

Refer to illustration 7.4

Removal

1   Remove the timing belt front cover (see Section 4).

7.4 Hold the camshaft with a large wrench at the flats provided and remove the sprocket bolt

2   Remove the timing belt (make sure the mark on the sprocket is aligned with the one on the cover) (see Section 6).

3   Remove the camshaft cover (see Section 3).

4   Hold the camshaft with a wrench on the flats located between the lobes and remove the sprocket bolt **(see illustration)**. The camshaft must not be allowed to turn.

5   Detach the sprocket and washer.

Installation

6   Align the hole in the sprocket with the pin in the end of the camshaft (make sure the mark on the sprocket is aligned with the mark on the cover).

7   Hold the camshaft with the wrench and install the washer and bolt. Tighten the bolt to the torque listed in this Chapter's Specifications.

8   Install the timing belt, cover and any other components that were removed.

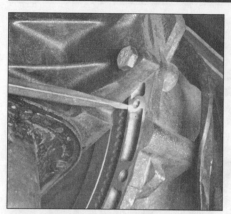

8.2 A screwdriver wedged in the starter ring-gear teeth will lock the engine so the crankshaft sprocket bolt can be loosened

9.6a A tool for installing the crankshaft front oil seal can be made from pieces of pipe, washers and a bolt

9.6b Tighten the tool bolt slowly to push the seal squarely into place in the oil pump bore

8   Crankshaft sprocket - removal and installation

Refer to illustration 8.2

Removal

1   Remove the serpentine drivebelt (see Chapter 1), crankshaft pulley, timing belt front cover (see Section 4) and timing belt (see Section 6).
2   Remove the flywheel cover and lock the flywheel by wedging a screwdriver in the starter ring-gear teeth. The screwdriver must be held against the engine block, not the transaxle **(see illustration)**.
3   Remove the bolt and washer and detach the sprocket. The bolt is usually very tight, so a 1/2-inch drive breaker bar and a six-point socket should be used.

Installation

4   Align the keyway in the sprocket with the key in the end of the crankshaft, then slide the sprocket into place. Install the washer and bolt and tighten the bolt to the torque listed in this Chapter's Specifications.
5   Remove the screwdriver and install the flywheel cover.

6   Install the timing belt, front cover, crankshaft pulley and serpentine drivebelt.

9   Crankshaft front oil seal - replacement

Refer to illustrations 9.6a and 9.6b

1   Drain the engine oil and install a new oil filter (see Chapter 1).
2   Remove the crankshaft sprocket and Woodruff key from the crankshaft nose (see Section 8). If access to the seal is restricted, you may have to remove the rear timing belt cover as well (see Section 5).
3   Pry the old oil seal out with a seal removal tool or a screwdriver. Be very careful not to nick or otherwise damage the crankshaft in the process.
4   Apply a thin coat of RTV-type sealant to the outer edge of the new seal. Lubricate the seal lip with moly-base grease or clean engine oil.
5   Place the seal squarely in position in the bore.
6   Push the seal into the bore with a special tool or one made up of a long metric coarse thread bolt, a piece of pipe and washers **(see illustrations)**. Be sure the bolt diameter and thread pitch match the sprocket bolt

and the pipe diameter matches the seal to prevent distortion. Make sure the seal is seated completely in the bore.
7   The remainder of installation is the reverse of removal.
8   Refill the engine with oil (see Chapter 1), start the engine and check for oil leaks at the seal.

10   Camshaft - removal and installation

Refer to illustrations 10.3 and 10.4

Removal

1   Refer to Section 11 and remove the camshaft carrier.
2   Remove the retainer mounting bolts (at the distributor end of the carrier). If the bolts have Allen heads, a special driver will be required for removal and installation.
3   Remove the retainer **(see illustration)**.
4   Support the camshaft at both ends and carefully withdraw it from the distributor end of the carrier (don't damage the bearing surfaces with the lobes) **(see illustration)**. Refer to Part F of this Chapter for the camshaft inspection procedure and Section 11 for the retainer and carrier inspection procedures.

10.3 Push down on the ends of the retainer (arrow) to release it from the groove in the camshaft

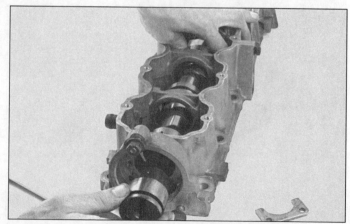

10.4 Carefully slide the camshaft out of the carrier to prevent damage to the bearing surfaces

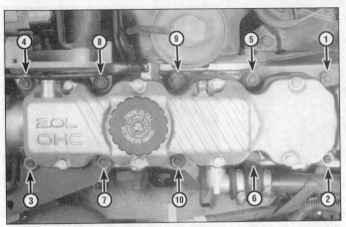

11.4 Camshaft carrier/cylinder head bolt LOOSENING sequence

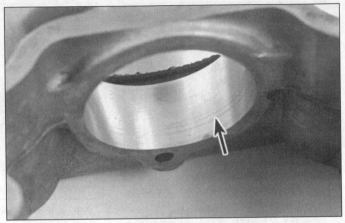

11.9 Check the camshaft carrier bearing surfaces (arrow) for wear and damage

Installation

Note: *If a new camshaft is installed, replace all rocker arms as well - don't install used rocker arms with a new camshaft.*

5   Apply engine assembly lube to the lip of the front camshaft seal, the camshaft lobes and the bearing surfaces, then carefully insert the camshaft into the carrier.

6   Install the retainer and bolts. Tighten the bolts to the torque listed in this Chapter's Specifications.

7   Check the camshaft endplay with a dial indicator and compare it to the Specifications.

8   Install the camshaft and carrier assembly as described in Section 11.

11 Camshaft carrier - removal, inspection and installation

Refer to illustrations 11.4, 11.9, 11.10, 11.16 and 11.17

Caution: *Each time the camshaft carrier and cylinder head bolts are loosened or removed, the cylinder head bolts and head gasket must be replaced with new parts. Also, the engine must be allowed to cool down completely before this procedure is started.*

Removal

1   Disconnect the cable from the negative battery terminal. Drain the cooling system (see Chapter 1).

2   Remove the air induction tube. Disconnect the PCV hose from the camshaft cover, then remove the distributor (see Chapter 5).

3   Remove the camshaft sprocket (see Section 7).

4   Loosen the cylinder head bolts 1/4-turn at a time in the correct order **(see illustration)**. As the bolts are loosened, the force exerted by the valve springs will tend to separate the carrier from the head. Remove the bolts and discard them. **Caution:** *New head bolts MUST be used when installing the cylinder head!*

5   Detach the camshaft carrier assembly from the head.

6   Refer to Section 3 and separate the cover from the carrier, then remove the camshaft from the carrier (see Section 10).

Inspection

7   Carefully pry the oil seal out of the front of the carrier.

8   Clean all parts with solvent and dry them compressed air (if available).

9   Check the bearing surfaces in the carrier for score marks and other damage **(see illustration)**. Use a telescoping gauge and micrometer to measure the camshaft bearing bores in the carrier. Measure the camshaft journal diameters with a micrometer, then subtract each journal diameter from the corresponding bore diameter to determine the oil clearances. If they're excessive, a new carrier may be required. See Part F of this Chapter for additional camshaft inspection procedures.

10   Check the camshaft retainer surface for wear, score marks and other damage. Replace it with a new one if necessary **(see illustration)**.

Installation

11   Use a hammer and a large socket or block of wood to drive the new seal into the front of the carrier. Make sure the seal is seated completely in the bore.

12   Install the camshaft in the carrier as described in Section 10.

13   Install a new cylinder head gasket (see Section 16).

14   Clean the mating surfaces of the camshaft carrier and the cylinder head with lacquer thinner or acetone, then apply a thin (1/8 inch) bead of anaerobic sealant to the

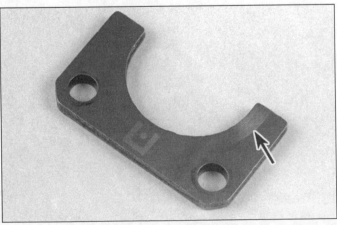

11.10 Check the camshaft retainer contact surface (arrow) for wear

11.16 Camshaft carrier/cylinder head bolt TIGHTENING sequence

carrier-to-head mating surfaces.

15 Make sure the valve lash compensators and rocker arms are in place. Position the carrier on the cylinder head and install the new bolts.

16 Tighten the bolts to 18 ft-lbs in 1/4-turn increments in the correct order **(see illustration)**. **Caution:** *Tightening in increments greater than 1/4-turn will distort the camshaft carrier.*

17 Tighten each bolt another 60-degrees, following the same sequence. This must be done three times, until each bolt has been turned an additional 180-degrees (1/2-turn) total **(see illustration)**.

18 Reinstall all components that were removed. Refill the cooling system (see Chapter 1).

19 Start the engine and run it until normal operating temperature is reached, then check for oil and coolant leaks.

20 With the engine off and still at operating temperature, tighten all of the head bolts, in sequence, an additional 30-to-50 degrees.

12 Rocker arms and valve lash compensators - removal and installation

Refer to illustrations 12.5a and 12.5b

Removal

1 Disconnect the cable from the negative battery terminal.

2 Remove the air induction tube. Disconnect the PCV valve hose from the camshaft cover.

3 Remove the camshaft cover (see Section 3).

4 Remove the camshaft carrier assembly (see Section 11).

5 Remove the rocker arms, rocker arm guides and valve lash compensators and store them in order in a numbered container **(see illustrations)**. Inspection procedures are included in Part F of this Chapter.

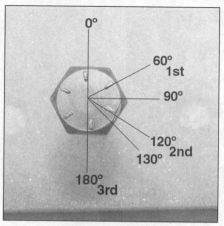

11.17 After the camshaft carrier/cylinder head bolt initial torque is reached, the bolts must be turned an additional 180-degrees in three increments

Installation

6 Install a new cylinder head gasket (see Section 16).

7 Install the valve lash compensators, followed by the rocker arms, in their original locations. Valve adjustment is not required on these models.

8 Installation is the reverse of removal.

13 Valve springs, retainers and seals - replacement

Note: *The design of the OHC engine doesn't allow for replacement of the valve stem oil seals or valve springs with the cylinder head in place. To service valve train components, the cylinder head must be removed from the engine and disassembled on a workbench. Refer to the cylinder head removal and installation procedure in Section 16 and the cylinder head overhaul procedures in Chapter 2, Part F.*

12.5a Lift the rocker arms off and keep them in order - they must be reinstalled in their original locations!

14 Intake manifold - removal and installation

Refer to illustration 14.6

Removal

1 Disconnect the cable from the negative battery terminal.

2 Remove the induction, vacuum and PCV hoses connected to the intake system.

3 Drain the coolant (see Chapter 1).

4 Remove the alternator and brackets (see Chapter 5).

5 Remove the power steering pump and brackets (see Chapter 10). Remove the cruise control cable (if equipped) from the intake manifold bracket.

6 Disconnect the throttle cable, downshift cable and TV cable from the EFI assembly **(see illustration)**. To remove the cable from the bracket, pull up while using a screwdriver to unlock tab.

7 Disconnect and label the wiring to the throttle body, MAP sensor, wastegate and ignition coil.

2A

12.5b The rocker arm guides and lash compensators (arrow) can be removed with a magnet (keep them in order as well)

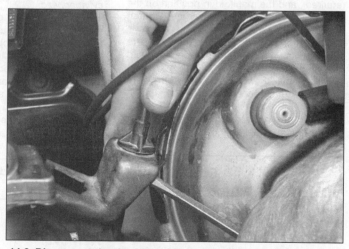

14.6 Disconnect the throttle cable from the bracket by pulling up while pushing in on the tabs with a screwdriver

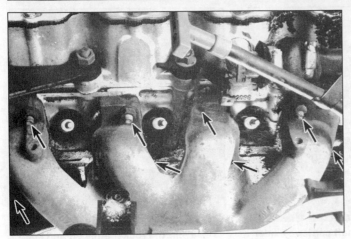

15.7 Remove the exhaust manifold mounting nuts (arrows)

16.16 Use a block of wood and a hammer to break the cylinder head gasket seal - don't strike the head directly with a metal hammer!

8   Relieve the fuel system pressure (see Chapter 4).
9   Remove the fuel lines at the fuel rail inlet and regulator outlet.
10   Detach the wires at the fuel injectors.
11   Remove the manifold support bracket.
12   Remove the manifold retaining nuts and washers.
13   Detach the intake manifold and gasket.

Installation

Note: *The mating surfaces of the head and manifold must be perfectly clean when the manifold is installed. Gasket removal solvents in aerosol cans are available at most auto parts stores. Since the components are made of aluminum, aggressive scraping can cause damage. Be sure to follow the directions printed on the container.*

14   Use a gasket scraper to remove all traces of sealant and gasket material, then clean the mating surfaces with lacquer thinner or acetone. If pieces of gasket, sealant or oil are left on the mating surfaces when the manifold is installed, vacuum leaks may develop.
15   Install a new gasket (no sealant is required), and the manifold in position on the studs and install the retaining nuts. Tighten the nuts to the torque listed in this Chapter's Specifications. Work from the center of the manifold out, in a criss-cross pattern to avoid distorting the manifold.
16   Reinstall the components that were removed to gain access to the intake manifold.
17   Start and run the engine and check for fuel and vacuum leaks.

---

15 Exhaust manifold - removal and installation

Refer to illustration 15.7

Removal

1   Disconnect the cable from the negative battery terminal.

2   Remove the air induction tube.
3   Disconnect the spark plug wires from the spark plugs and label them.
4   Unplug the oxygen sensor wire.
5   Remove the oil dipstick tube.
6   Remove the bolts and nuts holding the turbo to the manifold.
7   Remove the exhaust manifold mounting bolts and heat shield **(see illustration)**.
8   Separate the manifold from the engine.

Installation

9   Use a gasket scraper to remove all traces of carbon and old gasket material from the manifold and head mating surfaces, then clean them with lacquer thinner or acetone. Be careful not to nick or gouge the head surface.
10   It may be difficult to hold the manifold in place, position the gasket behind it and install the bolts without assistance, but it can be done. An alternative would be to attach the gasket to the manifold with sewing thread (which will hold it in place as the bolts are installed). Don't use sealant to hold the gasket in place. **Note:** *The expansion joints on the gasket must face out, away from the cylinder head.*
11   When tightening the bolts, work from the center of the manifold to the ends and use a torque wrench. Tighten the bolts in three or four equal steps to the torque listed in this Chapter's Specifications.
12   Install the components that were removed for access and connect the battery cable.
13   Start the engine and check for exhaust leaks.

---

16 Cylinder head - removal and installation

Refer to illustrations 16.16 and 16.18

Removal

1   Disconnect the cable from the negative battery terminal.

2   Remove the air induction and PCV hoses/tubes. Drain the cooling system, disconnect the upper radiator hose, unplug the connectors and remove the thermostat housing (see Chapter 1 and 3).
3   Remove the serpentine belt (see Chapter 1). Remove the alternator and bracket (see Chapter 5).
4   Remove the power steering pump and bracket assembly and lay it to one side, if necessary (see Chapter 10).
5   Disconnect the spark plug wires and distributor cap and remove them as an assembly.
6   Remove the ignition coil, distributor and wiring (see Chapter 5).
7   Disconnect the throttle cable from the intake manifold bracket.
8   Disconnect the throttle, downshift and TV cables from the EFI assembly.
9   Disconnect the ECM connectors from the EFI components.
10   Remove the vacuum hose going to the brake booster.
11   Remove the heater hose from the intake manifold fitting.
12   Disconnect the exhaust manifold from the turbo.
13   Remove the timing belt (see Section 6).
14   Refer to Section 11 and remove the camshaft carrier/cylinder head mounting bolts, then detach the carrier from the head.
15   Remove the rocker arms and valve lash compensators (see Section 12).
16   Break the gasket seal by tapping the cylinder head with a soft-face hammer or a hammer and wood block **(see illustration)**.
17   Separate the cylinder head from the engine.
18   Remove the gasket from the engine **(see illustration)**.

Installation

19   The mating surfaces of the camshaft carrier, cylinder and block must be perfectly clean when the head is installed.
20   Use a gasket scraper to remove all traces of carbon and old gasket material,

16.18 Use a scraper to remove the old head gasket

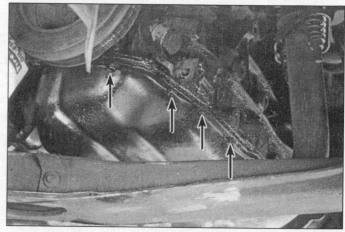

17.9 Remove the oil pan bolts and separate the oil pan from the engine

2A

then clean the mating surfaces with lacquer thinner or acetone. If there's oil on the mating surfaces when the head is installed, the gasket may not seal correctly and leaks may develop. Use a vacuum cleaner to remove any debris that falls into the cylinders.

21   Check the carrier, block and head mating surfaces for nicks, deep scratches and other damage. If damage is slight, it can be removed with a file; if it's excessive, machining may be the only alternative.

22   Use a tap of the correct size to chase the threads of the head bolt holes in the block. Dirt, corrosion, sealant and damaged threads will affect torque readings. The bolts should be discarded - new ones must be used when the head is installed.

23   Position the new gasket over the dowel pins in the block. The top of the gasket should be stamped TOP or THIS SIDE UP to ensure correct installation. Do not use sealant on the gasket.

24   Carefully position the head on the block without disturbing the gasket. Make sure it slips over the dowel pins and rests on the gasket.

25   Refer to Section 11 and install the camshaft carrier and cylinder head bolts.

26   The remaining installation is the reverse of removal.

---

17   Oil pan - removal and installation

Refer to illustration 17.9

Removal

1   Disconnect the cable from the negative battery terminal.

2   Loosen the lug nuts on the right front wheel.

3   Raise the front of the vehicle and support it securely on jackstands.

4   Remove the right front wheel.

5   Remove the right inner splash shield.

6   Disconnect the exhaust pipe at the wastegate.

7   Remove the bellhousing dust cover.

8   Drain the engine oil and replace the filter (see Chapter 1).

9   Remove the oil pan bolts and separate the oil pan from the engine **(see illustration)**. Use a hammer and a block of wood to dislodge it if it's stuck - don't pry between the sealing surfaces as damage that could lead to oil leaks may occur.

Installation

10   Use a gasket scraper to remove all traces of old gasket material and sealant from the windage tray, oil pan and block, then clean the mating surfaces with lacquer thinner or acetone.

11   Make sure the bolt holes in the block are clean. Check the oil pan and windage tray flanges for distortion, particularly around the bolt holes. If necessary, place them on a block of wood and use a hammer to flatten and restore the mating surfaces.

12   Attach the new gasket to the windage tray, then apply RTV-sealant to the oil pan flange and the upper side of the gasket.

13   Attach the oil pan, windage tray and gasket to the engine and install the bolts. Tighten the bolts to the torque listed in this Chapter's Specifications in three or four steps. Start at the center of the pan and work out toward the ends in a spiral pattern.

14   The remaining steps are in reverse of removal. **Caution:** *Don't forget to refill the engine with oil before starting it (see Chapter 1).*

15   Start the engine and check carefully for oil leaks at the oil pan-to-block junction.

---

18   Oil pump screen and pick-up tube - removal and installation

1   Remove the oil pan (see Section 17).

2   Remove the bolts and detach the pick-up tube from the block.

3   Remove the O-ring from the tube and discard it. Clean the tube and screen assem-

bly with solvent and dry it with compressed air (if available).

4   Attach a new O-ring to the tube and position the tube on the block. Install the bolts and tighten them to the torque listed in this Chapter's Specifications.

5   Install the oil pan.

---

19   Oil pump - removal and installation

Removal

1   The oil pump is mounted low on the timing belt end of the engine and is driven directly off the end of the crankshaft. Remove the timing belt, the rear timing belt cover and the crankshaft sprocket (see Sections 5, 6 and 8).

2   Unplug the wire harness from the oil pressure switch, located near the oil filter.

3   Remove the oil pan (see Section 17) and the oil filter.

4   Remove the pick-up tube assembly (see Section 18).

5   Pry out the crankshaft oil seal - be careful not to damage the crankshaft or bore in the process!

6   Remove the six bolts and separate the oil pump from the block. Refer to Section 20 for the disassembly, inspection and reassembly procedure.

Installation

7   Use a gasket scraper to remove all old gasket material from the oil pump and block, then clean them with lacquer thinner or acetone.

8   Place the pump and new gasket in position and install the bolts. Tighten the bolts to the torque listed in this Chapter's Specifications.

9   Install the pick-up tube assembly (see Section 18).

10   Install a new oil seal (see Section 9).

11   Install the oil pan (see Section 17).

12   Install a new oil filter and connect the oil

20.3 The oil pump will be easier to work on if it's mounted in a vise with padded jaws

A   Oil pressure sending unit
B   Pressure regulator valve plug

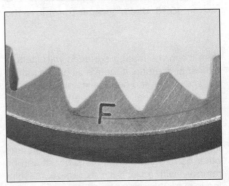

20.6 Check the idler gear-to-body clearance with a feeler gauge

20.7 Check the drive gear-to-body clearance

20.8 The gear-to-cover clearance is checked by inserting a feeler gauge between the gear and a straightedge laid across the pump body at point A

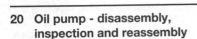

20.11 The mark (F) on the pump idler gear MUST face the cover

pressure switch harness.
13 Install the crankshaft sprocket, timing belt and covers.
14 Refill the engine with the specified oil (see Chapter 1).
15 Start the engine and check for oil leaks.

20 Oil pump - disassembly, inspection and reassembly

Refer to illustrations 20.3, 20.6, 20.7, 20.8 and 20.11

Disassembly

1   Remove the screws and detach the cover from the rear of the pump.
2   Remove the gears from the pump body.
3   Mount the pump body in a vise equipped with soft jaws and remove the oil pressure sending unit, plug, pressure regulator valve and spring (see illustration).

Inspection

4   Clean the parts with solvent and dry them with compressed air.
5   Inspect the components for wear, cracks and other damage. Replace any damaged or worn parts with new ones.
6   Check the outer (idler) gear-to-body

clearance (see illustration).
7   Check the inner (drive) gear-to-body clearance (see illustration).
8   Check the gear-to-cover clearance (see illustration).

Reassembly

9   Install the valve plunger and spring assembly.
10 Coat the plug threads with non-hardening thread locking compound, then install and tighten it to the torque listed in this Chapter's Specifications.
11 Pack all the pump cavities with petroleum jelly to ensure pump priming. Install the gears, noting that the outer gear is identified by a mark. This mark must face the cover (see illustration).
12 Install the cover and tighten the screws securely.
13 Install the oil pressure sending unit.

21 Rear main oil seal - replacement

Refer to illustrations 21.3 and 21.6
Warning: *A special tool is available to support the engine during repair operations. These fixtures are available from rental yards. Improper lifting methods or devices are haz-*

ardous and could result in severe injury or death. DO NOT place any part of your body under the engine/transaxle when it's supported only by a jack. Failure of the lifting device could result in serious injury or death.
Note: *The rear main bearing oil seal is a one piece unit that can be replaced without removing the oil pan or crankshaft. However, the transaxle must be removed and the engine must be supported as this procedure is done. A special tool is available for seal installation, but the procedure outlined here was devised to avoid using the tool.*

Removal

1   Remove the transaxle (see Chapter 7).
2   Remove the driveplate (automatic transaxle) or pressure plate, clutch disc and flywheel (manual transaxle).
3   Pry the old seal out very carefully with a seal removal tool or a screwdriver (see illustration). If the crankshaft is nicked or scratched as this is done, the new seal will be damaged when the engine is started and oil leaks will result.

Installation

4   Remove all traces of oil from the engine block seal bore and check the seal contact surface on the crankshaft for scratches and burrs that could damage the new seal. If the crankshaft is damaged, a new or different crankshaft may have to be installed.
5   Apply a thin coat of engine oil to the outer edge of the new seal and coat the seal

21.3 Pry out the rear oil seal very carefully - don't damage the surface of the crankshaft or the new seal will leak

21.6 Tap around the outer edge of the new oil seal with a hammer and a blunt punch to seat it squarely in the bore

lip with multi-purpose grease.

6   Insert the new seal squarely into the bore and tap it into place until it's completely seated **(see illustration)**. Be very careful not to damage the seal in the process and make sure it's driven squarely.

7   Install the clutch and flywheel or driveplate.

8   Reinstall the transaxle.

22 Flywheel/driveplate - removal and installation

1   Remove the transaxle (see Chapter 7). If your vehicle has a manual transaxle, the pressure plate and clutch will also have to be removed (see Chapter 8).

2   Jam a large screwdriver in the starter ring gear to keep the crankshaft from turning, then remove the mounting bolts. Since it's fairly heavy, support the flywheel as the last bolt is removed. The driveplate bolts (automatic transaxle) can be reused.

3   Pull straight back on the flywheel/driveplate to detach it from the crankshaft.

4   Installation is the reverse of removal.

When installing the flywheel on the manual transaxle equipped vehicles, be sure to use new mounting bolts. Align the hole in the flywheel/driveplate with the dowel pin in the crankshaft. Use non-hardening thread locking compound on the bolt threads and tighten them to the torque listed in this Chapter's Specifications in a criss-cross pattern. On manual transaxle equipped vehicles, after the specified torque is reached, tighten each bolt an additional 30-degrees.

23 Engine and transaxle mounts - replacement

Refer to illustrations 23.8, 23.12a and 23.12b
Warning: *A special tool is available to support the engine during repair operations. These fixtures are available from rental yards. Improper lifting methods or devices are hazardous and could result in severe injury or death. DO NOT place any part of your body under the engine/transaxle when it's supported only by a jack. Failure of the lifting device could result in serious injury or death.*
Note: *Whenever engine mount bolts are*

removed, the bolt threads must be thoroughly cleaned and new thread-locking compound applied to the threads before installing.

1   If the rubber mounts have hardened, cracked or separated from the metal backing plates, they must be replaced. This operation may be carried out with the engine/transaxle still in the vehicle.

2   Disconnect the cable from the negative battery terminal.

3   Raise the front of the vehicle and support it securely on jackstands.

4   Support the engine with a engine support fixture or jack.

Front mount

5   Remove the two mount-to-bracket bolts.

6   Remove the mount-to-frame bolts and remove the mount.

7   Installation is the reverse of removal.

Rear mount

8   Remove the two mount-to-bracket bolts **(see illustration)**.

9   Remove the lower mount nuts and reinforcement.

10   Remove the mount from the vehicle.

11   Installation is the reverse of removal.

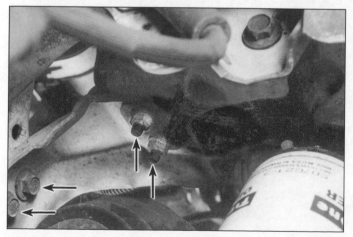

23.8 Typical engine mounts

1   *Front engine mount*   2   *Rear engine mount*

23.12a Typical rear manual transaxle mounting bolt (arrow)

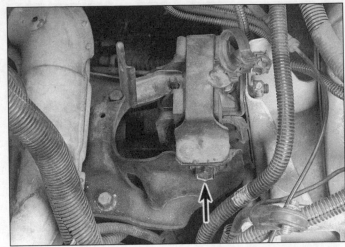

23.12b Typical rear automatic transaxle mounting bolt (arrow)

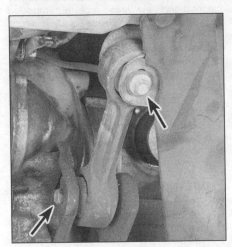

24.2 Remove the transaxle strut mounting bolts (arrows)

Transaxle mount

12   Loosen the lower mount bolt (see illustrations).
13   Remove the long bracket-to-mount bolt.
14   Remove the upper mount nuts.
15   Remove the transaxle mount.
16   Position the transaxle mount over the lower bolt.
17   Loosely attach the upper mount bolts.
18   Insert the long bracket-to-mount bolt and tighten the bolts.

All mounts

19   Gently lower the lifting device.
20   Tighten the bolts securely.
21   Reconnect the negative battery cable.

24   Transaxle strut - removal and installation

Refer to illustrations 24.2

1   The automatic transaxle is equipped with two struts. One, called a lateral strut, and a second to control fore-and-aft movement. Manual transaxles are equipped with only one strut. Disconnect the cable from the negative battery terminal.
2   Remove the strut-to-bracket bolt (see illustration).
3   Remove the strut-to-transaxle bolt.
4   Remove the strut from the vehicle.
5   Bolt the strut to the transaxle.
6   Install the strut-to-bracket bolt.
7   Tighten the fasteners securely.
8   Reconnect the battery cable.

Chapter 2 Part B
2.3L (Quad-4) four-cylinder engine

Contents

Specifications

General

Cylinder numbers (drivebelt end-to-transaxle end)	1-2-3-4
Firing order	1-3-4-2

2.3L (Quad-4) FRONT

Cylinder location

Camshaft(s) and housing(s)

Lobe lift	
1988 through 1990	
Intake	
VIN D	0.340 inch
VIN A	0.410 inch
Exhaust	
VIN D	0.350 inch
VIN A	0.410 inch
1991 through 1994	
Intake	
VIN D	0.375 inch
VIN A and 3	0.410 inch
Exhaust	
VIN D	0.375 inch
VIN A and 3	0.410 inch
Endplay	0.0009 to 0.0088 inch
Journal diameter	
Number 1	1.5728 to 1.5720 inches
Number 2 through 5	1.3751 to 1.3760 inches
Bearing oil clearance	0.0019 to 0.0043 inch
Lifters	
Bore diameter	1.3775 to 1.3787 inches
Outside diameter	1.3763 to 1.3770 inches
Lifter-to-bore clearance	0.0006 to 0.0024 inch
Camshaft housing warpage limit	0.001 inch per 3.937 inches

Balance shaft assembly

Chain tensioner groove depth	0.045 inch maximum
Chain-to-tensioner clearance	0.04 inch
Balance shaft gear backlash	0.0091 to 0.0201 inch

Oil pump

Drive gear-to-driven gear backlash	0.0091 to 0.0201 inch
Outer gerotor diameter-to-housing clearance	0.0013 to 0.0052 inch
Inner gear-to-outer gear tip clearance	0.0059 inch maximum
Gerotor pump cavity depth	0.6736 to 0.6756 inch

Torque specifications

Ft-lbs (unless otherwise indicated)

Balance assembly-to-block bolts
  Step 1
    Bolts 1, 2 and 4 18
    Bolt 3 30
    Bolt 5 39
  Step 2
    Bolts 1, 2 and 4 .... Turn an additional 70-degrees
    Bolt 3 .... Turn an additional 60-degrees
Balance shaft housing bolts
  Step 1
    Bolts 1, 2, 4, 5, 6 and 7 .... 89 inch-lbs
    Bolts 3 and 8 .... 11 inch-lbs
  Step 2 .... Turn all bolts an additional 40-degrees
Balance shaft sprocket bolt (left hand thread)
  Step 1 22
  Step 2 .... Turn an additional 45-degrees
Balance shaft chain tensioner bolt .... 115 inch-lbs
Balance shaft chain cover nut and bolt .... 115 inch-lbs
Balance shaft thrust plate bolts .... 115 inch-lbs
Camshaft housing-to-cylinder head bolts
  Step 1 .... 132 inch-lbs
  Step 2 .... Turn an additional 75-degrees
Camshaft sprocket-to-camshaft bolt 40
Cylinder head bolts*
  1991 and earlier
    Short bolts (A)
      Step 1 26
      Step 2 .... Turn an additional 100-degrees
    Long bolts (B)
      Step 1 26
      Step 2 .... Turn an additional 110-degrees
  1992
    Step 1
      Bolts 1 through 6 26
      Bolts 7 & 8 .... 180 inch-lbs
      Bolts 9 & 10 22
    Step 2 .... Turn an additional 90-degrees in sequence
    Step 3 .... Loosen each bolt 1 turn in sequence and immediately re-tighten to the torque in Step 1
    Step 4 .... Turn an additional 90-degrees in sequence
  1993
    Step 1
      DOHC
        Bolts 1 through 6 18
        Bolts 7 & 8 22
        Bolts 9 & 10 26
      SOHC
        Bolts 1 through 6 18
        Bolts 7 & 8 26
        Bolts 9 & 10 30
    Step 2 (all)
      Bolts 1 through 6 .... Turn an additional 90-degrees in sequence
      Bolts 7 & 8 .... Turn an additional 60-degrees in sequence
      Bolts 9 & 10 .... Turn an additional 60-degrees in sequence
    Step 3 (all) .... Loosen each bolt 1 turn in sequence and immediately re-tighten to the torque in Step 1
    Step 4 (all) .... Turn each bolt the specified degrees in Step 2

Torque specifications (continued)   Ft-lbs (unless otherwise indicated)

1994 and later	
Step 1	
Bolts 1 through 8	30
Bolts 9 and 10	26
Step 2	
Bolts 1 through 10	Turn an additional 90-degrees in sequence
Exhaust manifold-to-cylinder head nuts	
1990 and earlier	27
1991 and later	31
Exhaust manifold-to-cylinder head studs	106 in-lbs
Flywheel-to-crankshaft bolts	
Step 1	22
Step 2	Turn an additional 45-degrees
Intake manifold-to-cylinder head nuts/bolts	18
Oil pan baffle studs/bolts	30
Oil pan bolts	
6 mm	106 in-lbs
8 mm	17
Oil pump-to-block bolts	
1990 and earlier	33
1991 and later	40
Oil pump cover-to-oil pump body bolts	106 in-lbs
Oil pump screen assembly-to-pump bolts	
1990 and earlier	22
1991 and later	30
Oil pump screen assembly-to-brace bolts	106 in-lbs
Crankshaft rear main oil seal housing bolts	106 in-lbs
Timing chain cover-to-housing bolts	106 in-lbs
Timing chain housing bolts	19
Timing chain housing-to-block stud	19
Timing chain tensioner-to-housing and block	
1991 and earlier	115 in-lbs
1992 and later	89 in-lbs
Vibration damper-to-crankshaft bolt	
Step 1	74
Step 2	Turn an additional 90-degrees

* Follow the procedure supplied with the new head gasket, if different than listed here

1 General information

This Part of Chapter 2 is devoted to in-vehicle repair procedures for 2.3 liter four-cylinder (Quad-4) dual overhead camshaft (DOHC) and single overhead camshaft (SOHC) engines. All information concerning engine removal and installation and engine block and cylinder head overhaul can be found in Part F of this Chapter.

The following repair procedures are based on the assumption the engine is installed in the vehicle. If the engine has been removed from the vehicle and mounted on a stand, many of the steps outlined in this Part of Chapter 2 will not apply.

The Specifications included in this Part of Chapter 2 apply only to the procedures contained in this Part. Part F of Chapter 2 contains the Specifications necessary for cylinder head and engine block rebuilding.

The 2.3 liter engine utilizes a number of advanced design features to increase power output and improve durability. Both the SOHC and the DOHC models have an aluminum cylinder head. The DOHC has four valves per cylinder. and two overhead camshafts - one for intake and one for exhaust.

The SOHC has a single camshaft and only eight valves. Both engines use a double roller timing chain to drive the camshaft gear(s) and lightweight bucket-type hydraulic lifters to actuate the valves. Rotators are used on all valves for extended service life.

Both engines are essentially the same. The SOHC doesn't have a separate exhaust cam, exhaust camshaft tower or exhaust camshaft drive gear and has both intake and exhaust lobes ground onto one camshaft running in the intake side tower. Repair procedures are also the same, except as noted in the procedures.

2 Repair operations possible with the engine in the vehicle

Warning: *Before working in the vicinity of airbag components (on models so equipped) refer to Chapter 12 for the airbag disarming procedure. Use care not to damage any wiring or sensors associated with this system or the airbag may deploy when reconnecting the battery or fail to deploy in the event of an accident.*

Many major repair operations can be accomplished without removing the engine

from the vehicle.

Clean the engine compartment and the exterior of the engine with some type of degreaser before any work is done. It'll make the job easier and help keep dirt out of the internal areas of the engine.

Depending on the components involved, it may be helpful to remove the hood to improve access to the engine as repairs are performed (refer to Chapter 11 if necessary). Cover the fenders to prevent damage to the paint. Special pads are available, but an old bedspread or blanket will also work.

If vacuum, exhaust, oil or coolant leaks develop, indicating a need for gasket or seal replacement, the repairs can generally be made with the engine in the vehicle. The intake and exhaust manifold gaskets, timing chain housing gasket, oil pan gasket, crankshaft oil seals and cylinder head gasket are all accessible with the engine in place.

Exterior engine components, such as the intake and exhaust manifolds, the oil pan (and the oil pump), the water pump, the starter motor, the alternator and the fuel system components can be removed for repair with the engine in place.

Since the cylinder head can be removed without pulling the engine, camshaft and

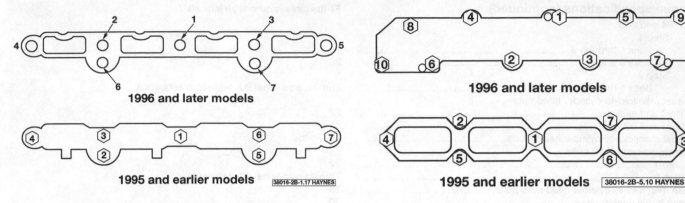

1996 and later models

1995 and earlier models   38016-2B-1.17 HAYNES

3.16 Intake manifold fastener tightening sequence

1996 and later models

1995 and earlier models   38016-2B-5.10 HAYNES

4.10 Exhaust manifold fastener tightening sequence

valve component servicing can also be accomplished with the engine in the vehicle. Replacement of the timing chain and sprockets is also possible with the engine in the vehicle.

In extreme cases caused by a lack of necessary equipment, repair or replacement of piston rings, pistons, connecting rods and rod bearings is possible with the engine in the vehicle. However, this practice is not recommended because of the cleaning and preparation work that must be done to the components involved.

3   Intake manifold - removal and installation

Removal

Warning: *Allow the engine to cool completely before performing this procedure.*
Caution: *If the vehicle is equipped with a Delco Loc II audio system, make sure you have the correct activation code before disconnecting the battery. See the information at the front of this manual for the radio re-activation procedure.*

1   Relieve the fuel system pressure as described in Chapter 4.
2   Disconnect the battery cable from the negative battery terminal, then refer to Chapter 1 and drain the cooling system.
3   Remove the throttle body (see Chapter 4).
4   Label and disconnect the vacuum and breather hoses and electrical wires.
5   Remove the oil/air separator (see Chapter 6).
6   Remove the oil fill cap and dipstick assembly.
7   Unbolt the oil fill tube and detach it from the engine block, rotating it as necessary to gain clearance between the intake tubes.
8   Remove the intake manifold brace.
9   Loosen the manifold mounting nuts/bolts in 1/4-turn increments until they can be removed by hand.
10   The manifold will probably be stuck to the cylinder head and force may be required

to break the gasket seal. If necessary, dislodge the manifold with a soft-face hammer.
Caution: *Don't pry between the head and manifold or damage to the gasket sealing surfaces will result and vacuum leaks could develop.*

Installation

Refer to illustration 3.16
Note: *The mating surfaces of the cylinder head and manifold must be perfectly clean when the manifold is installed. Gasket removal solvents in aerosol cans are available at most auto parts stores and may be helpful when removing old gasket material stuck to the head and manifold (since the components are made of aluminum, aggressive scraping can cause damage). Be sure to follow the directions printed on the container.*
11   Use a gasket scraper to remove all traces of sealant and old gasket material, then clean the mating surfaces with lacquer thinner or acetone. If there's old sealant or oil on the mating surfaces when the manifold is reinstalled, vacuum leaks may develop.
12   Use a tap of the correct size to chase the threads in the bolt holes, then use compressed air (if available) to remove the debris from the holes. **Warning:** *Wear safety glasses or a face shield to protect your eyes when using compressed air. Use a die to clean and restore the stud threads.*
13   Position the gasket on the cylinder head. Make sure all intake port openings, coolant passage holes and bolt holes are aligned correctly.
14   Install the manifold, taking care to avoid damaging the gasket.
15   Thread the nuts/bolts into place by hand.
16   Tighten the nuts/bolts to the torque listed in this Chapter's Specifications following the recommended sequence **(see illustration)**. Work up to the final torque in three steps.
17   The remaining installation steps are the reverse of removal. Start the engine and check carefully for leaks at the intake manifold joints.

4   Exhaust manifold - removal and installation

Refer to illustration 4.10

Removal

Warning: *Allow the engine to cool completely before performing this procedure.*
Caution: *If the vehicle is equipped with a Delco Loc II audio system, make sure you have the correct activation code before disconnecting the battery. See the information at the front of this manual for the radio re-activation procedure.*
1   Disconnect the battery cable from the negative battery terminal.
2   Unplug the oxygen sensor (see Chapter 6).
3   Remove the manifold heat shields as necessary to access exhaust manifold nuts.
4   Raise the vehicle and support it securely on jackstands, then remove the exhaust pipe-to-manifold nuts. The nuts are usually rusted in place, so penetrating oil should be applied to the stud threads before attempting to remove them. Loosen them a little at a time, working from side-to-side to prevent the flange from jamming.
5   Remove the exhaust manifold brace.
6   Separate the exhaust pipe flange from the manifold studs, then pull the pipe down slightly to break the seal at the manifold joint.
7   Loosen the exhaust manifold mounting nuts 1/4-turn at a time each, working from the inside out, until they can be removed by hand.
8   Separate the manifold from the head and remove it.

Installation

9   The manifold and cylinder head mating surfaces must be clean when the manifold is reinstalled. Use a gasket scraper to remove all traces of old gasket material and carbon deposits.
10   Using a new gasket, install the manifold and hand tighten the fasteners. Working from the center out following the recommended sequence **(see illustration)**, tighten the

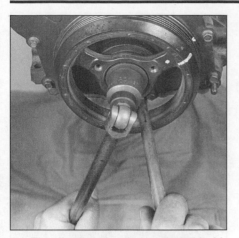

5.4 The vibration damper can be held with a bar while the bolt is loosened or tightened

5.5 Use a bolt type puller that applies force to the damper hub as shown here - don't use a jaw type puller that applies force to the outer edge or damage to the damper will occur

5.8 Align the keyway in the vibration damper hub with the Woodruff key in the crankshaft (arrow)

bolts/nuts to the torque listed in this Chapter's Specifications.
11 The remaining installation steps are the reverse of removal.

---

5 Vibration damper - removal and installation

Refer to illustrations 5.4, 5.5 and 5.8
Caution: *If the vehicle is equipped with a Delco Loc II audio system, make sure you have the correct activation code before disconnecting the battery. See the information at the front of this manual for the radio re-activation procedure.*

Removal

1 Remove the cable from the negative battery terminal.
2 Remove the drivebelt (see Chapter 1).
3 With the parking brake applied and the shifter in Park (automatic) or in gear (manual), raise the front of the vehicle and support it securely on jackstands.
4 Remove the bolt from the front of the crankshaft. A breaker bar will probably be necessary, since the bolt is very tight. Use a special tool, available at most auto parts stores, to keep the crankshaft from turning. If the special tool isn't available, insert a bar through a hole in the damper to prevent the crankshaft from turning **(see illustration)**.
5 Using a puller, remove the vibration damper from the crankshaft **(see illustration)**.
6 Check the oil seal and replace it if necessary. (see Section 6).

Installation

7 Apply a thin layer of clean multi-purpose grease to the seal contact surface of the vibration damper hub.
8 Position the damper on the crankshaft and slide it through the seal until it bottoms against the crankshaft sprocket. Note that

6.2 Pry the old seal out with a seal removal tool (shown here) or a screwdriver

the slot (keyway) in the hub must be aligned with the Woodruff key in the end of the crankshaft **(see illustration)**. The crankshaft bolt can also be used to press the damper into position.
9 Tighten the crankshaft bolt to the torque listed in this Chapter's Specifications.
10 The remaining installation steps are the reverse of removal.

---

6 Crankshaft front oil seal - replacement

Refer to illustrations 6.2 and 6.5
1 Remove the vibration damper (see Section 5).
2 Pry the old oil seal out with a seal removal tool **(see illustration)** or a screwdriver. Be very careful not to nick or otherwise damage the crankshaft in the process and don't distort the timing chain cover.
3 Apply a thin coat of RTV-type sealant to

6.5 Drive the new seal in with a large socket or section of pipe

the outer edge of the new seal. Lubricate the seal lip with multi-purpose grease or clean engine oil.
4 Place the seal squarely in position in the bore with the spring side facing in.
5 Carefully tap the seal into place with a large socket or section of pipe and a hammer **(see illustration)**. The outer diameter of the socket or pipe should be the same size as the seal outer diameter. Allow time for the RTV to cure.
6 Install the vibration damper (see Section 5).
7 Start the engine and check for oil leaks at the seal.

---

7 Timing chain and sprockets - removal, inspection and installation

Note: *Special tools are normally required to perform this operation. Read through the entire Section carefully and rent or buy the tools before beginning this procedure.*

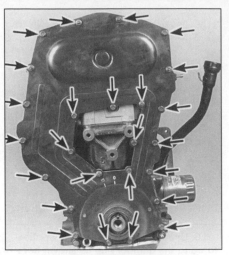

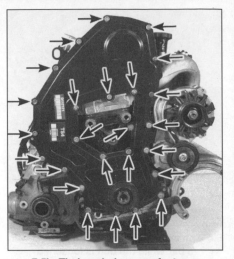

7.3 Remove the vent hose and engine lifting bracket bolts

   1   *Vent hose fitting*
   2   *Engine lifting bracket bolts*

7.5a Timing chain cover fastener locations (DOHC engine)

7.5b Timing chain cover fastener locations (SOHC engine)

Removal

Refer to illustrations 7.3, 7.5a, 7.5b, 7.8, 7.10a, 7.10b, 7.11, 7.12a, 7.12b, 7.14, 7.15, 7.17 and 7.18

Caution: *If the vehicle is equipped with a Delco Loc II audio system, make sure you have the correct activation code before disconnecting the battery. See the information at the front of this manual for the radio re-activation procedure.*

1   Disconnect the battery cable from the negative battery terminal.

2   Remove the coolant reservoir (see Chapter 3).

3   Detach the timing chain cover vent hose and unbolt the engine lifting bracket at the drivebelt end of the engine **(see illustration)**.

4   Remove the vibration damper (see Section 5).

5   Working from above, remove the upper timing chain cover fasteners **(see illustrations)**.

6   Working from below, remove the lower timing chain cover fasteners.

7   Detach the cover and gaskets from the housing.

8   Slide the oil slinger off the crankshaft **(see illustration)**.

9   Temporarily reinstall the vibration damper bolt to use when turning the crankshaft.

10   Turn the crankshaft clockwise until the camshaft sprockets' timing pin hole(s) line up with the hole(s) in the timing chain housing. Insert 8 mm bolt(s) into the hole(s) to maintain alignment **(see illustrations)**.

11   The mark on the crankshaft sprocket should line up with the mark on the engine block **(see illustration)**. The crankshaft sprocket keyway should point up and line up with the centerline of the cylinder bores.

12   Remove the timing chain guides **(see illustrations)**.

13   On 1991 and earlier models, detach the

7.8 Note how it's installed, then remove the oil slinger (arrow) from the crankshaft

7.10b Insert an 8 mm bolt as an alignment pin (arrow) to hold the camshaft sprocket (SOHC engine)

timing chain tensioner sleeve and spring.

14   On 1991 and earlier models, make sure all the slack in the timing chain is above the tensioner assembly, then remove the chain tensioner shoe **(see illustration)**. The timing

7.10a Insert 8 mm bolts as alignment pins (arrows) to hold the camshaft sprockets (DOHC engine)

chain must be disengaged from the wear grooves in the tensioner shoe in order to remove the shoe. Slide a screwdriver blade under the timing chain while pulling the shoe out. If difficulty is encountered when removing

7.11 The mark on the crankshaft sprocket must align with the mark on the block (arrows)

7.14 The timing chain tensioner shoe is held in place by a retaining clip on 1991 and earlier models

1   *Tensioner mounting bolts*
2   *E-clip*

2B

7.12a The three DOHC timing chain guides are wedged into the housing at four points (arrows) - just pull them out

7.12b The two SOHC timing chain guides slide into the housing at four points (arrows) - just pull them out

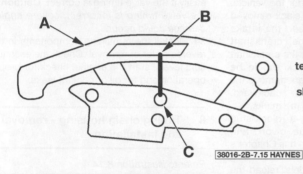

7.15 After retracting the tensioner shoe, insert a piece of wire (B) bent into a "U" shape between the tensioner shoe (A) and reset hole (C)

could come out with great force, causing personal injury. Remove the chain housing-to-block stud (timing chain tensioner shoe pivot).
17   Slip the timing chain off the sprockets **(see illustration)**.
18   To remove the camshaft sprockets (if not already done), loosen the bolts while the pins are still in place. Mark the sprockets for identification **(see illustration)**, remove the bolts and pins, then pull on the sprockets by hand until they slip off the dowels.
19   The crankshaft sprocket will slip off the crankshaft by hand.
20   The idler sprocket and bearing are pressed into place. If replacement is necessary, remove the timing chain housing (see Section 8) and take it to a dealer service department or automotive machine shop. Special tools are required and the bearing must be replaced each time it's pressed out.

Inspection

21   Visually inspect all parts for wear and damage. Look for loose pins, cracks, worn rollers and side plates. Check the sprockets for hook-shaped, chipped and broken teeth. **Note:** *Some scoring of the timing chain shoe*

the chain tensioner shoe, proceed as follows:

a) *Hold the intake camshaft sprocket with an appropriate tool and remove the sprocket bolt and washer.*
b) *Remove the washer from the bolt and thread the bolt back into the camshaft by hand.*
c) *Remove the intake camshaft sprocket, using a three-jaw puller in the three relief holes in the sprocket, if necessary. Caution: Don't try to pry the sprocket off the camshaft or damage to the sprocket could occur.*

15   On 1992 and later models, bend a piece of heavy wire into a "U", then apply light force to the tensioner shoe. While applying force, insert a small screwdriver into the reset hole **(see illustration)** and pry the ratchet pawl away from the ratchet teeth. When the shoe is fully retracted, insert the piece of bent wire as shown to hold the shoe in place.
16   On all models, remove the tensioner assembly retaining bolts and tensioner. On 1991 and earlier models, the spring can be caged with an appropriate tool. **Warning:** *The tensioner plunger is spring loaded and*

7.17 On the DOHC models, begin removing the chain at the exhaust camshaft sprocket

7.18 On DOHC models, mark the sprockets exhaust and intake (arrows), then remove the bolts and pull the sprockets off

7.22 The camshaft sprocket dowel pin(s) should be near the top (arrows) prior to sprocket installation

8.14 Position a new gasket over the dowel pins (arrows)

and guides is normal. Replace the timing chain, sprockets, chain shoe and guides as a set if the engine has high mileage or fails the visual parts inspection.

Installation

Refer to illustration 7.22

22   Turn the camshafts until the dowel pins are at the top **(see illustration)**. Install both camshaft sprockets (if removed). Apply sealant to the camshaft sprocket bolt threads and make sure the washers are in place. Keep the camshaft from turning with 8 mm bolts inserted into the alignment holes. Tighten the camshaft sprocket bolts to the torque listed in this Chapter's Specifications.

23   Recheck the positions of the camshaft and crankshaft sprockets for correct valve timing **(see illustrations 7.10a, 7.10b and 7.11)**. **Note:** *If the camshafts are out of position and must be rotated more than 1/8-turn in order to install the alignment dowel pins:*

  a) *The crankshaft must be rotated 90-degrees clockwise past Top Dead Center to give the valves adequate clearance to open.*

  b) *Once the camshafts are in position and the dowels installed, rotate the crankshaft counterclockwise back to Top Dead Center.* **Caution:** *Do not rotate the crankshaft clockwise to TDC (valve or piston damage could occur).*

24   Slip the timing chain over the exhaust camshaft sprocket, then around the idler and crankshaft sprockets.

25   Remove the alignment pin (8 mm bolt) from the intake camshaft. Using an appropriate tool, rotate the intake camshaft sprocket counterclockwise enough to mesh the timing chain with it. Release the special tool. The chain run between the two camshaft sprockets will tighten. If the valve timing is correct, the intake camshaft alignment pin (8 mm bolt) should slide in easily. If it doesn't index, the camshafts aren't timed correctly; repeat the procedure.

26   Leave the 8 mm bolt/alignment pins

installed for now. Working under the vehicle, check the timing marks. With slack removed from the timing chain between the intake camshaft sprocket and the crankshaft sprocket, the timing marks on the crankshaft sprocket and the engine block should be aligned. If the marks aren't aligned, move the chain one tooth forward or backward, remove the slack and recheck the marks.

27   Install the chain housing-to-block stud (timing chain tensioner shoe pivot), and tighten it to the torque listed in this Chapter's Specifications.

28   On 1991 and earlier models, reload the timing chain tensioner assembly to its "zero" position as follows:

  a) *Assemble the restraint cylinder, spring and nylon plug in the plunger. While rotating the restraint cylinder clockwise, push it into the plunger until it bottoms. Keep rotating the restraint cylinder clockwise, but allow the spring to push it out of the plunger. The pin in the plunger will lock the restraint cylinder in the loaded position.*

  b) *Install the plunger assembly in the tensioner body with the long end toward the crankshaft when installed.*

29   Install the tensioner assembly in the chain housing. Tighten the bolts to the torque listed in this Chapter's Specifications. **Note:** *Recheck the plunger assembly installation - it's correctly installed when the long end is toward the crankshaft.*

30   Install the tensioner shoe, spring and sleeve.

31   Remove the bent piece of wire and squeeze the plunger assembly into the tensioner body to unload the plunger assembly.

32   Remove the 8 mm bolt/alignment pins.

33   Slowly rotate the crankshaft clockwise two full turns (720-degrees). Do not force it; if resistance is felt, back up and recheck the installation procedure. Align the crankshaft timing mark with the mark on the engine block and temporarily reinstall the 8 mm bolt/alignment pins. The bolts should slide in

easily if the valve timing is correct. **Caution:** *If the valve timing is incorrect, severe engine damage could occur.*

34   Install the remaining components in the reverse order of removal. Check the essential fluid levels, start the engine, check for proper operation and for oil or coolant leaks.

8   Timing chain housing - removal and installation

Refer to illustration 8.14

1   Remove the timing chain and sprockets (see Section 7).

2   Remove the exhaust manifold (see Section 4).

3   If you're installing a replacement timing chain housing, remove the water pump (see Chapter 3).

4   Remove the timing chain housing-to-belt tensioner bracket brace.

5   Remove the four oil pan-to-timing chain housing bolts.

6   Remove the timing chain housing-to-block lower fasteners.

7   Remove the lowest cover retaining stud from the timing chain housing.

8   Remove the rear engine mount nut (see Section 17).

9   Loosen the front engine mount nut, leaving about three threads remaining in contact.

10   Remove the eight chain housing-to-camshaft housing bolts.

11   Position a floor jack under the oil pan, use a wood block on the jack pad to distribute the weight.

12   Raise the engine off the front and rear mounts until the front mount bracket contacts the nut.

13   Remove the timing chain housing and gaskets. Thoroughly clean the mating surfaces to remove any traces of old sealant or gasket material.

14   Install the timing chain housing with new gaskets **(see illustration)**. Tighten the bolts

9.7 If the center of the pulley has the groove for puller attachment a puller like this one must be used

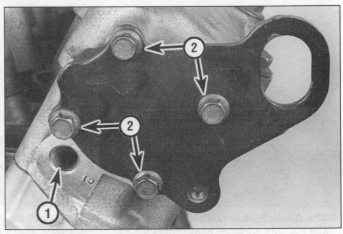

9.10 Oil pressure sending unit mounting hole (1) and engine lifting bracket bolts (2)

9.11 Gently lift the camshaft housing off the cylinder head and turn it over so the lifters don't fall out

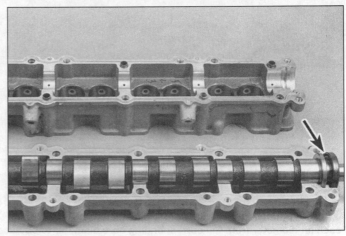

9.14 Remove the oil seal (arrow) from the intake camshaft

to the torque listed in this Chapter's Specifications.

15   The remaining steps are the reverse of removal.

9   Camshaft, lifters and housing - removal, inspection and installation

Note: *Special tools are normally required to perform this operation. Read through the entire Section carefully and rent or buy the tools before beginning this procedure.*

Removal

Refer to illustrations 9.7, 9.10, 9.11 and 9.14
Caution: *If the vehicle is equipped with a Delco Loc II audio system, make sure you have the correct activation code before disconnecting the battery. See the information at the front of this manual for the radio re-activation procedure.*

1   Disconnect the cable from the negative battery terminal.
2   Remove the timing chain and sprock-et(s) (see Section 7).
3   Remove the timing chain housing-to-camshaft housing bolts (see Section 8).
4   Remove the ignition coil and module assembly (see Chapter 5).

Front camshaft (intake - DOHC, intake/exhaust - SOHC)

5   Disconnect the electrical connector to the idle speed/power steering pressure switch.
6   Remove the power steering pump and brackets (see Chapter 10).
7   Remove the power steering pump drive pulley **(see illustration). Caution:** *The power steering pump drive pulley must be removed with the proper puller or damage to the pulley will result.*
8   Remove the oil/air separator box as an assembly, with the hoses attached.
9   Remove the fuel rail from the cylinder head and set it aside (see Chapter 4).

Rear camshaft (exhaust - DOHC only)

10   Disconnect the electrical connector to

the oil pressure sending unit and unbolt the engine lifting bracket **(see illustration)**.

Front and rear camshafts

11   Loosen the camshaft housing-to-cylinder head bolts in 1/4-turn increments, following the reverse order of the tightening sequence **(see illustration 9.28)**. Leave the two cover-to-housing bolts in place temporarily. Lift the housing off the cylinder head **(see illustration)**.
12   Remove the two camshaft cover-to-housing bolts. Push the cover off the housing by threading four of the housing-to-head bolts into the tapped holes in the cover. Carefully lift the camshaft out of the housing.
13   Remove all traces of old gasket material from the mating surfaces and clean them with lacquer thinner or acetone to remove any traces of oil.
14   Remove the oil seal from the front camshaft **(see illustration)** and discard it.
15   Remove the lifters and store them in order so they can be reinstalled in their original locations. To minimize lifter bleed-down, store the lifters valve-side up, submerged in clean engine oil.

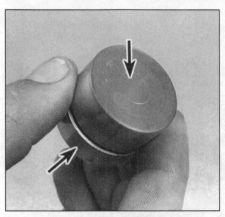

9.17a Check the camshaft lobe surfaces
and the bore surfaces of the lifters for
wear (arrows)

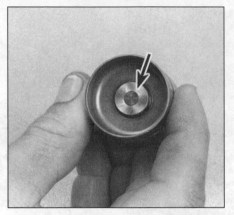

9.17b Check the valve-side of the lifters
too, especially the valve stem contact
area (arrow)

9.18 Use a telescoping gauge and
micrometer to measure the lifter bores . . .

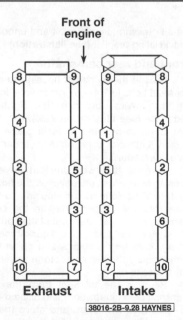

9.19 . . . then measure the lifters with a micrometer - subtract
each lift diameter from the corresponding bore diameter to obtain
the lifter-to-bore clearances

9.24 The dowel pins (arrows) should be at the top
(12 o'clock position)

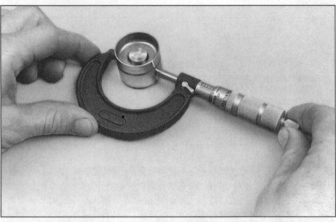

Front of
engine

Exhaust   Intake

38016-2B-9.28 HAYNES

9.28 Camshaft housing-to-cylinder head
bolt tightening sequence

Inspection

*Refer to illustrations 9.17a, 9.17b, 9.18 and
9.19*

16   Refer to Chapter 2, Part F, for camshaft
inspection procedures, but use this Chapter's
Specifications. Do not attempt to salvage
camshafts. Whenever a camshaft is replaced,
replace all the lifters actuated by the
camshaft as well.
17   Visually inspect the lifters for wear,
galling, score marks and discoloration from
overheating **(see illustrations)**.
18   Measure each lifter bore inside diameter
and record the results **(see illustration)**.
19   Measure each lifter outside diameter
and record the results **(see illustration)**.
20   Subtract the lifter outside diameter from
the corresponding bore inside diameter to
determine the clearance. Compare the
results to this Chapter's specifications and
replace parts as necessary.

Installation

Refer to illustrations 9.24, 9.28 and 9.29
21   Using a new gasket, position the
camshaft housing on the cylinder head and
temporarily hold it in place with one bolt.
22   Coat the camshaft journals and lobes

and the lifters with camshaft assembly lube
and install them in their original locations.
23   On the intake camshaft only, lubricate
the lip of the oil seal, then position the seal on
the camshaft journal with the spring side facing in.
24   Install the camshaft in the housing with
the sprocket dowel pin UP (12 o'clock position) **(see illustration)**. Position the cover on
the housing, holding it in place with the two
bolts, as described above.
25   Apply Teflon Pipe Sealant to the threads
of the camshaft housing and cover bolts.
26   Install new housing seals. **Note:** *Each
housing seal is different shape and color. The
intake seals are green with the inner seal configured differently than the outer seal. The
exhaust seals are orange and they are also
configured differently.*
27   Install the camshaft cover and bolts
while positioning the oil seal (intake side
only). Be sure the seal is installed to a precise
0.020 inch depth from the outer housing face.
28   Tighten the bolts in the sequence shown
(see illustration) to the torque listed in this
Chapter's Specifications.
29   Install the power steering pump pulley
with a pulley installation tool **(see illustration)**.

9.29 Press the power steering pump drive pulley on with a special tool

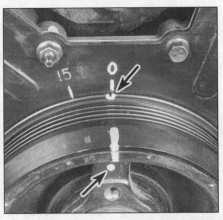

10.4 When the timing marks are aligned (arrows) number one and four cylinders are at top dead center (TDC)

10.5 This is what the air hose adapter that threads into the spark plug hole looks like - they're commonly available from auto parts stores

10.18 Apply a small dab of grease to each keeper before installation to hold it in place on the valve stem until the spring is released

2B

30   Install the remaining parts in the reverse order of removal.
31   Change the oil and filter (see Chapter 1). Add one container of engine oil supplement. **Note:** *If new lifters have been installed or the lifters bled down while the engine was disassembled, excessive lifter noise may be experienced after startup - this is normal. Use the following procedure to purge the lifters of air:*
  a) *Start the engine and allow it to warm up for five minutes.*
  b) *Increase engine speed to 2000 rpm until the lifter noise is gone.*
32   Road test the vehicle and check for oil and coolant leaks.

10   Valve springs, retainers and seals - replacement

Refer to illustrations 10.4, 10.5 and 10.18
Note: *Broken valve springs and defective valve stem seals can be replaced without removing the cylinder head. Two special tools and a compressed air source are normally required to perform this operation, so read through this Section carefully and rent or buy the tools before beginning the job. If compressed air isn't available, a length of nylon rope can be used to keep the valves from falling into the cylinder during this procedure.*
1   Refer to Chapter 5 and remove the ignition coil assembly.
2   Remove the spark plug from the cylinder which has the defective part. Due to the design of this engine, the intake and exhaust camshaft housings can be removed separately to service their respective components. If all of the valve stem seals are being replaced, all of the spark plugs and both camshaft housings should be removed.
3   Remove the camshaft(s), lifters and housing(s) as described in Section 9.
4   Turn the crankshaft until the piston in the affected cylinder is at top dead center (see Chapter 2F) **(see illustration)**. This will prevent the valves from falling into the cylinder if air pressure is lost while the valve retainers and keepers are removed. If you're

replacing all of the valve stem seals, begin with cylinder number one and work on the valves for one cylinder at a time. Move next to cylinder number four and perform repairs. Then rotate the crankshaft 180-degrees (one half turn) and repeat for cylinders number two and number three.
5   Thread an adapter into the spark plug hole **(see illustration)** and connect an air hose from a compressed air source to it. Most auto parts stores can supply the air hose adapter. **Note:** *Many cylinder compression gauges utilize a screw-in fitting that may work with your air hose quick-disconnect fitting.*
6   Apply compressed air to the cylinder. **Warning:** *The piston may be forced down by compressed air, causing the crankshaft to turn suddenly. If the wrench used when positioning the number one piston at TDC is still attached to the bolt in the crankshaft nose, it could cause damage or injury when the crankshaft moves.*
7   The valves should be held in place by the air pressure. If the valve faces or seats are in poor condition, leaks may prevent air pressure from retaining the valves - in this case a "valve job" is needed.
8   If you don't have access to compressed air, an alternative method can be used. Position the piston at a point approximately 45-degrees before TDC, then feed a long piece of nylon rope through the spark plug hole until it fills the combustion chamber. Be sure to leave the end of the rope hanging out of the engine so it can be removed easily. Use a large ratchet and socket to rotate the crankshaft in the normal direction of rotation (clockwise) until slight resistance is felt.
9   Cover the spark plug holes and the oil drain back holes next to the valves to prevent parts and tools from falling into the engine, then use a valve spring compressor to compress the spring. Remove the keepers with small needle-nose pliers or a magnet.
10   Remove the retainer and valve spring, then remove the valve guide seal and rotator. **Note:** *If air pressure fails to hold the valve in the closed position during this operation, the valve face or seat is probably damaged. If so,*

the cylinder head will have to be removed for additional repair operations.
11   Wrap a rubber band or tape around the top of the valve stem so the valve won't fall into the combustion chamber, then release the air pressure. **Note:** *If a rope was used instead of air pressure, turn the crankshaft slightly in a counterclockwise direction (opposite normal rotation).*
12   Inspect the valve stem for damage. Rotate the valve in the guide and check the end for eccentric movement, which would indicate the valve stem is bent.
13   Move the valve up-and-down in the guide and make sure it doesn't bind. If the valve stem binds, either the valve is bent or the guide is damaged. In either case, the head will have to be removed for repair.
14   Reapply air pressure to the cylinder to retain the valve in the closed position, then remove the tape or rubber band from the valve stem. If a rope was used instead of air pressure, rotate the crankshaft until slight resistance is felt.
15   Reinstall the valve rotator.
16   Lubricate the valve stem with engine oil and install a new guide seal.
17   Install the spring in position over the valve.
18   Install the valve spring retainer. Compress the valve spring and carefully install the keepers in the groove. Apply a small dab of grease to the inside of each keeper to hold it

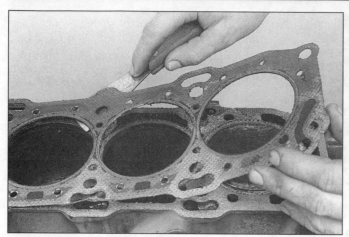

11.11 Remove the old gasket and clean the head thoroughly

11.16a Cylinder head bolt TIGHTENING sequence (1991 and earlier models)

A   *Short bolts*   B   *Long bolts*

11.16b Cylinder head bolt TIGHTENING sequence (1992 and later models)

in place if necessary **(see illustration)**. Remove the pressure from the spring tool and make sure the keepers are seated.

19 Disconnect the air hose and remove the adapter from the spark plug hole. If a rope was used in place of air pressure, rotate the crankshaft slightly and pull it out of the cylinder.

20 Refer to Section 9 and install the camshaft(s), lifters and housing(s).

21 Install the spark plugs and coil assembly.

22 Start and run the engine, then check for oil leaks and unusual sounds coming from the camshaft housings.

11   Cylinder head - removal and installation

Removal

Caution: *If the vehicle is equipped with a Delco Loc II audio system, make sure you have the correct activation code before disconnecting the battery. See the information at the front of this manual for the radio re-activation procedure.*

1 Disconnect the negative cable from the battery.

2 Refer to Section 3 and remove the intake manifold.

3 Drain the cooling system (see Chapter 3) to prevent coolant from getting into internal areas of the engine when the head is removed.

4 Refer to Section 4 and detach the exhaust manifold.

5 Remove the camshafts and housings as described in Section 9.

6 Make a holder for the head bolts. Using the new head gasket, outline the cylinders and bolt pattern on a piece of cardboard. Be sure to indicate the front of the engine for reference. Punch holes at the bolt locations.

7 Loosen the head bolts in 1/4-turn increments until they can be removed by hand, following a pattern that's the reverse of the tightening sequence **(see illustration 11.16a**

or **11.16b)**. Store the bolts in the cardboard holder as they're removed - this will ensure they are reinstalled in their original locations.

8 Lift the head off the engine. If resistance is felt, don't pry between the head and block as damage to the mating surfaces will result. To dislodge the head, place a wood block against the end of the head and strike it with a hammer. Store the head on wood blocks to prevent damage to the gasket sealing surfaces.

9 Cylinder head disassembly and inspection procedures are covered in detail in Chapter 2, Part F.

Installation

Refer to illustrations 11.11, 11.16a and 11.16b

10 The mating surfaces of the cylinder head and block must be perfectly clean when the head is installed.

11 Use a gasket scraper to remove all traces of carbon and old gasket material **(see illustration)**, then clean the mating surfaces with lacquer thinner or acetone. If there's oil on the mating surfaces when the head is installed, the gasket may not seal correctly and leaks could develop. **Note:** *Since the head is made of aluminum, aggressive scraping can cause damage. Be extra careful not to*

nick or gouge the mating surface with the scraper. If gasket material is stuck to the head surface, loosen it first with a chemical gasket remover. Use a vacuum cleaner to remove debris that falls into the cylinders.

12 Check the block and head mating surfaces for nicks, deep scratches and other damage. If damage is slight, it can be removed with a flat mill file; if it's excessive, machining may be the only alternative.

13 Use a wire brush to clean all the head bolts. Clean the head bolt holes in the block with a small round wire or nylon brush and blow them out with compressed air. Dirt, corrosion, sealant and damaged threads will affect torque readings. **Caution:** *Don't use a tap in the head bolt holes to clean them and don't use a die to chase the threads on the head bolts. If the bolt threads are damaged or corroded install new head bolts.*

14 Position the new gasket over the dowel pins in the block.

15 Carefully position the head on the block without disturbing the gasket.

16 Lubricate the bolt threads and washer with engine oil. Install them in their original locations and tighten them finger tight. Following the recommended sequence **(see illustrations)**, tighten the bolts in several steps to the torque listed in this Chapter's Specifications.

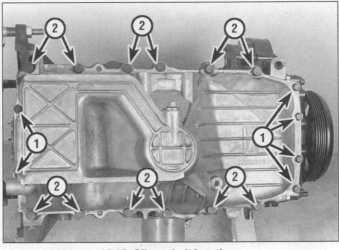

12.11 The oil pan baffle is held in place by four bolts (arrows)

12.15 Oil pan bolt locations

1   6 mm bolts   *2   8 mm bolts*

17   The remaining installation steps are the reverse of removal.
18   Refill the cooling system and change the oil and filter (see Chapter 1, if necessary).
19   Run the engine and check for leaks and proper operation.

12 Oil pan - removal and installation

Refer to illustrations 12.11 and 12.15
Note: *The following procedure is based on the assumption the engine is in place in the vehicle. If its been removed, simply unbolt the oil pan and detach it from the block.*

Removal

Caution: *If the vehicle is equipped with a Delco Loc II audio system, make sure you have the correct activation code before disconnecting the battery. See the information at the front of this manual for the radio re-activation procedure.*
1   Disconnect the cable from the negative battery terminal, then refer to Chapter 1 and drain the engine oil. On 1992 and later models, drain the coolant and remove the serpentine drivebelt.
2   Remove the lower splash shield.
3   Detach the lower transaxle bellhousing cover.
4   Unbolt the exhaust manifold brace (see Section 4). On 1992 and later models, remove the engine mount strut and the strut bracket. Remove the air-conditioning compressor from the bracket and support the compressor out of the way.
5   Remove the radiator outlet pipe-to-oil pan bolt. On 1992 and later models, remove the radiator outlet pipe from the lower radiator hose.
6   On manual transaxle equipped models, remove the transaxle-to-oil pan nut and stud with a 7 mm socket.
7   Gently pry the spacer out from between the oil pan and transaxle.

8   Remove the oil pan-to-transaxle bolt.
9   Remove the oil pan mounting bolts. On 1992 and later models, disconnect the oil level sensor electrical connector.
10   Carefully separate the pan from the block. Don't pry between the block and pan or damage to the sealing surfaces may result and oil leaks may develop. **Note:** *The crankshaft may have to be rotated to gain clearance for oil pan removal.*
11   If you need to get at the crankshaft or other lower end components, remove the oil pan baffle **(see illustration).**

Installation

12   Clean the sealing surfaces with lacquer thinner or acetone. Make sure the bolt holes in the block are clean.
13   The gasket should be checked carefully and replaced with a new one if damage is noted. Minor imperfections can be repaired with RTV sealant. **Caution:** *Use only enough sealant to restore the gasket to its original size and shape. Excess sealant may cause*

13.5 Check the oil pump drive gear (arrow) and driven gear for wear and damage

part misalignment and oil leaks.
14   Reinstall the oil pan baffle, if removed. With the gasket in position, carefully hold the pan against the block and install the bolts finger tight.
15   Tighten the bolts in three steps to the torque listed in this Chapter's Specifications **(see illustration).** Start at the center of the pan and work out toward the ends in a spiral pattern.
16   The remaining steps are the reverse of removal. **Caution:** *Don't forget to refill the engine with oil and coolant before starting it* (see Chapter 1).
17   Start the engine and check carefully for oil leaks at the oil pan.

13 Oil pump - removal, inspection and installation

Refer to illustrations 13.5 and 13.8
Note: *Two different oil pump designs are used in the Quad-4 engines. Both are mounted in the oil pan, at the rear of the crankshaft, and can be removed once the oil pan is removed. 1994 and earlier pumps are driven by the oil pump gear meshing with the gear on the crankshaft* **(see illustration 13.5).** *1995 models use a twin shaft balance system, driven by a chain from the rear of the crankshaft. The oil pump is mounted to the rear of the balancer housing and driven by the balance shafts.*

Removal

1   Remove the oil pan as described in Section 12.
2   While supporting the oil pump, remove the mounting bolts.
3   Lower the pump from the engine.

Inspection

4   Clean all parts thoroughly and remove the cover.

13.8 Shims between the oil pump and engine block allow for adjustment of gear backlash

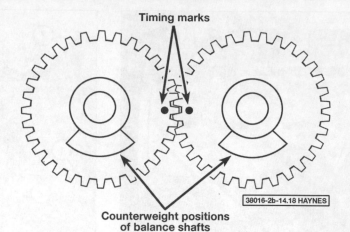

14.18 Be sure the timing marks are correctly on the balance shaft gears

Counterweight positions of balance shafts

Timing marks

5   Visually inspect all parts for wear, cracks and other damage (see illustration). Three clearances must be checked before pump assembly:

a) Outer gerotor diameter-to-housing.
b) Tip clearance of inner gear-to-outer gear.
c) Depth of the gerotor cavity (from the machined surface) in the housing.

Replace the pump if it's defective, if the engine has high mileage or if the engine is being rebuilt.

6   Lubricate the gears with clean engine oil and pack all the pump cavities with petroleum jelly prior to installation to ensure that there is oil pressure immediately on start-up. Reassemble the pump and install the cover.

Installation

7   Position the pump and shims on the engine and install the mounting bolts. Tighten them to the torque listed in this Chapter's Specifications.

8   On 1994 and earlier models, oil pump drive gear backlash must be checked whenever the oil pump, crankshaft or engine block is replaced. Mount a dial indicator on the engine with the indicator stem touching the oil pump driven gear. Check the backlash and compare it to the Specifications in this Chapter. Add or subtract shims (see illustration) to obtain the desired backlash.

9   Install the oil pan (and baffle, if removed).

10   Add oil and run the engine. Check for oil pressure and leaks.

14   Balance shaft assembly (1995 models only) - removal, inspection and installation

Note: Special tools are normally required to perform this operation. Read through the entire Section carefully and rent or buy the tools before beginning this procedure.

Removal

1   Remove the oil pan (see Section 12). Remove the balance shaft chain cover.

2   Remove the oil pump assembly (see Section 13).

3   Loosen, but don't remove, the balance shaft chain guide.

4   Remove the balance shaft driven sprocket. Caution: The bolt is a left handed thread and must be loosened in a clockwise direction. Before removal of the driven sprocket, if it is to be reused, mark the face of the sprocket so it can be installed the same way it came off. The balance shaft may try to rotate as the bolt is loosened. Wedge a screwdriver in the flywheel/driveplate ring gear teeth to hold the crankshaft still (which will also prevent the balance shafts from turning).

5   Just break loose the bolts holding the upper and lower housing halves together. DO NOT loosen or remove at this time. The bolts that retain only the balance shaft housing and do not extend into the engine block must be left alone at this time

6   Remove the balance shaft assembly-to-block bolts. Caution: Support the assembly securely before removal of the bolts. The drive chain may hang up on the driven gear.

7   Remove the balance shaft assembly and place it on a workbench for disassembly and inspection.

Inspection

8   Remove the bolts and separate the upper and lower housing.

9   Pry out the oil pump pick-up screen. Clean or replace before reassembly.

10   Remove the thrust plate bolts and plate.

11   Inspect the thrust plate for gouges or burrs.

12   Remove each balance shaft and gear assembly.

13   Inspect all parts. Look for damage such: nicks, cracks, scored bearing bores, damaged threaded holes, broken or worn guides, etc. and replace any necessary parts. Caution: If the housing is damaged in any way, replace the entire assembly.

14   Remove the bearings from the housings

and inspect the bearings for scoring, overheating, etc. in both the upper and lower housings. Replace if necessary. Caution: Balance shafts must be replaced together. Any time balance shafts are replaced, the bearings must also be replaced.

15   Inspect the chain for damaged links and measure the chain length and compare it to the specification at the beginning of this Chapter. Caution: DO NOT replace individual links in the chain. The entire chain must be replaced if any damage is found. If the chain is to be replaced, the sprockets must also be replaced.

Installation

Refer to illustrations 14.18 and 14.19

16   Assemble the thrust plate and tighten the bolts to the torque listed in this Chapter's Specifications.

17   Install the bearing halves in the upper and lower housings and lubricate the bearing faces with engine assembly lube.

18   Install the balance shafts into the housings. Align the timing marks (see illustration)

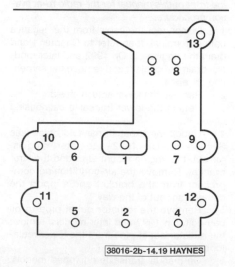

14.19 Balance shaft housing bolt tightening sequence

16.5 Remove the seal housing bolts (arrows)

16.6 After removing the housing from the engine, support it on wood blocks and drive out the old seal with a punch and hammer

as shown. **Caution:** *The engine will make noise or vibrate if the marks are not properly aligned.*

19   Assemble the upper and lower housings and tighten the bolts to 44 inch-lbs following the correct sequence **(see illustration)**. Final tightening will be done after the balance shaft assembly is installed on the block.

20   Place the number 1 piston at TDC (Top Dead Center), see Chapter 2F.

21   Rotate the crankshaft, clockwise, 90-degrees.

22   Bolt the balance assembly to the engine block. **Note:** *Use a non-hardening thread locking compound on the housing-to-block bolts.*

23   Tighten the housing-to-block bolts, in sequence, to 44 inch-lbs **(see illustration 14.19)**. Make sure the balance shafts spin freely.

24   Tighten all bolts, in sequence **(see illustration 14.19)** to the torque listed in this Chapter's Specifications.

25   Install the oil pick-up screen. **Caution:** *The screen must not be installed until all bolts have been tightened to the final specification.*

26   Assemble the driveshaft sprocket and chain and bolt the sprocket to the balance shaft. **Caution:** *If reusing the old sprocket, be sure the mark, made on disassembly, shows.*

27   Immobilize the crankshaft as described in Step 4 and tighten the bolt to the torque listed in this Chapter's Specifications. The balance shafts must not turn while the driven sprocket is being tightened. Remember, the balance shaft sprocket bolt is reverse threaded, so turn it counter-clockwise to tighten.

28   Loosely install the chain tensioner and bolts.

29   Adjust the chain tensioner by inserting a 0.040-inch brass feeler gauge between the chain and chain guide. Apply light pressure (about 3 lbs) to the chain guide and tighten the chain guide bolt to the torque listed in this Chapter's Specifications. **Caution:** *A brass feeler gauge is necessary to measure chain clearance. A steel gauge will not bend and will give an incorrect chain-to-guide clearance.*

30   The remainder is the reverse of removal procedure.

31   Add oil and a new filter, run the engine and check for leaks.

15   Flywheel/driveplate - removal and installation

1   Remove the transaxle (see Chapter 7). If your vehicle has a manual transaxle, the pressure plate and clutch will also have to be removed (see Chapter 8).

2   Jam a large screwdriver in the starter ring gear to keep the crankshaft from turning, then remove the mounting bolts. Since it's fairly heavy, support the flywheel as the last bolt is removed.

3   Pull straight back on the flywheel/drive-plate to detach it from the crankshaft.

4   Installation is the reverse of removal. When installing the flywheel on the manual transaxle equipped vehicles, be sure to use new mounting bolts. Align the hole in the flywheel/driveplate with the dowel pin in the crankshaft. Use a non-hardening thread locking compound on the bolt threads and tighten them to the torque listed in this Chapter's Specifications in a criss-cross pattern.

16   Rear main oil seal - replacement

Refer to illustrations 16.5, 16.6, 16.7 and 16.8
Warning: *A special tool is available to support the engine during repair operations. These fixtures are available from rental yards. Improper lifting methods or devices are hazardous and could result in serious injury or death. DO NOT place any part of your body under the engine/transaxle when it's supported only by a jack. Failure of the lifting device could result in serious injury or death.*

1   Remove the transaxle (see Chapter 7).

2   Remove the pressure plate and clutch disc, if equipped (see Chapter 8).

3   Remove the flywheel/driveplate (see Section 15).

4   Remove the oil pan (see Section 12).

16.7 Drive the new seal into the housing with a wood block - be careful not to cock the seal in the housing bore

5   After the oil pan has been removed, remove the bolts **(see illustration)**, detach the seal housing and peel off all the old gasket material.

6   Position the seal housing between wooden blocks on a workbench and drive the old seal out from the back side with a punch and hammer **(see illustration)**.

7   Drive the new seal into the housing with a wood block **(see illustration)**.

8   Lubricate the crankshaft seal journal

16.8 Position a new gasket over the dowel pins (arrows)

and the lip of the new seal with multi-purpose grease. Position a new gasket on the engine block **(see illustration)**.

9   Slowly and carefully push the new seal onto the crankshaft. The seal lip is stiff, so work it onto the crankshaft with a smooth object such as the end of an extension as you push the housing against the block.

10   Install and tighten the housing bolts to the torque listed in this Chapter's specifications.

11   Install the flywheel/driveplate and clutch components, if equipped.

12   Reinstall the transaxle.

---

17   Engine mounts - check and replacement

Warning: *A special tool is available to support the engine during repair operations. These fixtures are available from rental yards. Improper lifting methods or devices are hazardous and could result in severe injury or death. DO NOT place any part of your body under the engine/transaxle when it's supported only by a jack. Failure of the lifting device could result in serious injury or death.*

1   Engine mounts seldom require attention, but broken or deteriorated mounts should be replaced immediately or the added strain placed on the driveline components may cause damage or wear.

Check

2   During the check, the engine must be raised slightly to remove the weight from the mounts.

3   Raise the vehicle and support it securely on jackstands. Support the engine as described above. If the special support fixture is unavailable, position a jack under the engine oil pan. Place a large wood block between the jack head and the oil pan, then carefully raise the engine just enough to take the weight off the mounts. **Warning:** *DO NOT place any part of your body under the engine when it's supported only by a jack!*

4   Check the mounts to see if the rubber is cracked, hardened or separated from the metal plates. Sometimes the rubber will split right down the center.

5   Check for relative movement between the mount plates and the engine or frame (use a large screwdriver or pry bar to attempt to move the mounts). If movement is noted, lower the engine and tighten the mount fasteners.

6   Rubber preservative should be applied to the mounts to slow deterioration.

Replacement

Caution: *If the vehicle is equipped with a Delco Loc II audio system, make sure you have the correct activation code before disconnecting the battery. See the information at the front of this manual for the radio re-activation procedure.*

1991 and earlier models

Front mount

7   Detach the cable from the negative battery terminal. Remove the upper mount nut.

8   Raise the engine weight off the mount.

9   Remove the two lower mount nuts.

10   Remove the mount.

11   Place the new mount in position and install the nuts. Gently lower the engine and tighten the nuts securely.

Rear mount

12   Detach the cable from the negative battery terminal.

13   Raise and support the front of the vehicle. Remove the right front wheel and tire. Remove the right lower splash shield.

14   Working under the mount, remove the nut from the through-bolt.

15   Raise the engine weight off the mount.

16   Remove the four mount-to-bracket nuts.

17   Remove the mount from the vehicle.

18   Installation is the reverse of removal.

19   Gently lower the engine.

20   Tighten the nuts securely.

1992 and later models

Engine mount

21   Detach the cable from the negative battery terminal.

22   Raise and support the front of the vehicle. Remove the right front tire and wheel.

23   Working from the fender well, remove the two mount-to-chassis bolts.

24   Raise the engine weight off the mount.

25   From the engine compartment, remove the nut holding the mount to the chassis.

26   Remove the four bolts holding the engine mount to the mount bracket on the timing cover.

27   Installation is the reverse of removal.

Strut mount

28   Detach the cable from the negative battery terminal.

29   Raise and support the front of the vehicle. Remove the right front tire and wheel. Remove the right inner splash shield.

30   Raise the engine weight off the mount.

31   Note installed position of the strut and remove the strut bolts.

32   Installation is the reverse of removal. Be sure to position the front bolt of the lower strut in the correct hole of the engine mount bracket.

Chapter 2 Part C
2.5L overhead valve (OHV) four-cylinder engine

Contents

Specifications

General
Cylinder numbers (drivebelt end-to-transaxle end)	1-2-3-4
Firing order	1-3-4-2
Direction distributor rotor rotates	Clockwise

Cylinder location and distributor rotation/coil terminal positions

The blackened terminal shown on the distributor cap indicates the Number One spark plug wire position

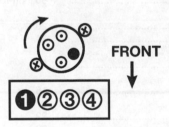

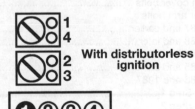

FRONT

With distributorless ignition

2.5L four-cylinder engine   24032-2c-specs HAYNES

Torque specifications

Ft-lbs (unless otherwise noted)

Oil pan bolts	90 inch-lbs
Oil screen support bolt	37
Oil pump-to-block bolt	22
Oil pump cover bolt	
1987 and earlier models	120 inch-lbs
1988 and later models	90 inch-lbs
Force balancer assembly-to-block bolts	
1988 and earlier	
Short bolts	
Step 1	108 inch-lbs
Step 2	Turn an additional 75 degrees
Long bolts	
Step 1	108 inch-lbs
Step 2	Turn an additional 90 degrees

Torque specifications (continued)   Ft-lbs (unless otherwise noted)

1989
   Short bolts
      Step 1 .... 180 inch-lbs
      Step 2 .... Turn an additional 60 degrees
   Long bolts
      Step 1 .... 132 inch-lbs
      Step 2 .... Turn an additional 90 degrees
1990
   Short bolts
      Step 1 .... 132 inch-lbs
      Step 2 .... Turn an additional 75 degrees
   Long bolts
      Step 1 .... 132 inch-lbs
      Step 2 .... Turn an additional 90 degrees
1991 and later
   Short bolts
      Step 1 .... 108 inch-lbs
      Step 2 .... 132 inch-lbs, then turn an additional 75-degrees
   Long bolts
      Step 1 .... 108 inch-lbs
      Step 2 .... 132 inch-lbs, then turn an additional 90 degrees
Pushrod cover bolts .... 90 inch-lbs
Harmonic balancer bolts
   1990 and earlier.. 200
   1991 and later 162
Driveplate-to-crankshaft bolts
   1987 and earlier.. 63
   1988 and later 55
Flywheel-to-crankshaft bolts
   1990 and earlier.. 70
   1991 and later 55
Intake manifold bolts
   1990 and earlier.. 29
   1991 and later 25
Exhaust manifold bolts
   1990 and earlier.. 44
   1991 and later **(see illustration 7.13)**
      Bolts 1, 2 and 3.. 37
      Bolts 4, 5, 6 and 7.. 28
Timing cover bolts .... 90 inch-lbs
Rocker arm bolts
   1987 and earlier.. 20
   1988 and later 24
Cylinder head bolts
   1985 and earlier.. 85
   1986 and 1987
      Step 1... 18
      Step 2
         All but bolt 9 22
         Bolt 9 29
      Step 3
         All but bolt 9 .... Turn an additional 120 degrees
         Bolt 9 .... Turn an additional 90 degrees
   1988 and later
      Step 1... 18
      Step 2
         All but bolt 9 26
         Bolt 9 18
      Step 3 (all bolts) .... Turn an additional 90 degrees
Valve cover bolts .... 60 inch-lbs
Camshaft sprocket bolt 43
Camshaft thrust plate bolts .... 90 inch-lbs

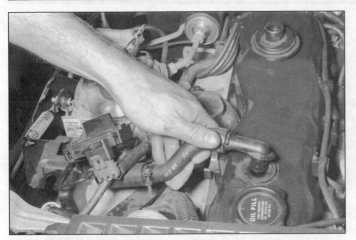

3.3 The PCV valve can be pulled out of the rubber grommet in the valve cover (leave the hose attached to the valve)

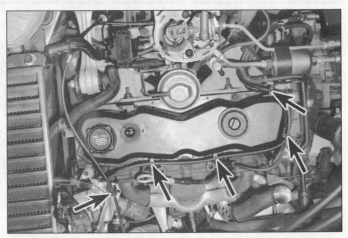

3.4 Disconnect all four spark plug wire retainer clips and detach the throttle cable from the exhaust manifold bracket (arrows)

2C

1 General information

The Sections in this Part of Chapter 2 are devoted to in-vehicle repair procedures for the 2.5 liter four-cylinder engine. Information concerning engine removal, engine block and cylinder head servicing is in Part F of this Chapter.

The repair procedures are based on the assumption that the engine is in the vehicle. Therefore, if this information is being used during a complete engine overhaul, with the engine already out of the vehicle and on a stand, many of the steps included here will not apply.

The specifications included apply only to the engine and procedures found here. For specifications regarding engines other than the 2.5 liter four-cylinder engine, see Part A, B, D or E, whichever applies. Part F contains the specifications necessary for engine block and cylinder head rebuilding. **Caution:** *On models equipped with the Delco Loc II audio system, be sure the lockout feature is turned off before performing any procedure that requires disconnecting the battery.*

2 Repair operations possible with the engine in the vehicle

Warning: *Before working in the vicinity of airbag components (on models so equipped) refer to Chapter 12 for the airbag system disarming procedure. Use care not to damage any wiring or sensors associated with this system or the airbag may deploy when reconnecting the battery or fail to deploy in the event of an accident.*

Many major repair operations can be accomplished without removing the engine from the vehicle.

Clean the engine compartment and the exterior of the engine with some type of pressure washer before any work is done. A clean engine will make the job easier and will help keep dirt out of the internal areas of the engine. **Caution:** *Don't pressure wash any electronic components or control units.* On distributorless ignition models, if any spark plug hole fills with water, it will ground the corresponding plug (on the same coil section). So if the front two plugs or wires ground, none of the spark plugs will fire. If the engine won't start after washing it, make certain ALL of the spark plugs and wires are completely dry. Water can also short the ignition module and other electronic control units causing them to completely fail.

Depending on the components involved, it may be a good idea to remove the hood to improve access to the engine (refer to Chapter 11 if necessary).

If vacuum, exhaust, oil or coolant leaks develop, indicating a need for gasket or seal replacement, the repairs can generally be made with the engine in the vehicle. The intake and exhaust manifold gaskets, oil pan gasket and cylinder head gaskets are all accessible with the engine in place.

Exterior engine components such as the intake and exhaust manifolds, the oil pan, the oil pump, the water pump, the starter motor, the alternator, the distributor and the fuel injection system can be removed for repair

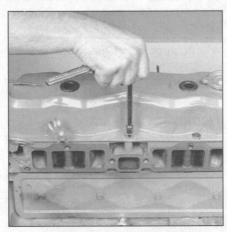

3.6 Remove the valve cover bolts (manifold removed for clarity)

with the engine in place. The timing chain and sprockets can also be replaced with the engine in the vehicle, but the camshaft cannot be removed.

Since the cylinder heads can be removed without pulling the engine, valve component servicing can also be accomplished with the engine in the vehicle.

In extreme cases caused by a lack of necessary equipment, repair or replacement of piston rings, pistons, connecting rods and rod bearings is possible with the engine in the vehicle. However, this practice is not recommended because of the cleaning and preparation work that must be done to the components involved.

3 Valve cover - removal and installation

Refer to illustrations 3.3, 3.4, 3.6, 3.7, 3.8 and 3.9

Removal

1   Remove the air cleaner assembly. Tag each hose with a piece of numbered tape to simplify installation.
2   Disconnect the throttle cable from the fuel injection assembly, making careful note of the exact locations of the cable components and hardware to ensure correct reinstallation.
3   Remove the PCV valve from the valve cover **(see illustration)**.
4   Remove the spark plug wires from the spark plugs, referring to the removal technique described in Chapter 1, then remove the wires and retaining clips from the valve cover **(see illustration)**. Be sure to label each wire before removal to ensure that all wires are reinstalled correctly.
5   Loosen the fuel injection mounting nuts and bolts to provide clearance for removal of the EGR valve, then remove the EGR valve (see Chapter 6, if necessary).
6   Remove the valve cover bolts **(see illustration)**.

3.7 The valve cover may be sealed with RTV - if you have to pry it off the head, try to avoid bending the flange

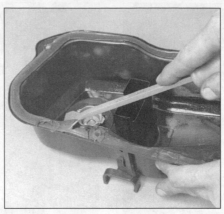

3.8 Remove the old sealant from the valve cover flange and the cylinder head with a gasket scraper, then clean the mating surfaces with lacquer thinner or acetone

3.9 On 1990 and earlier models, apply a continuous 3/16-inch bead of RTV-type sealant (arrow) to the valve cover flange (make sure it is applied to the inside of the bolt holes)

4.3 The pushrod cover is held in place with four nuts (arrows)

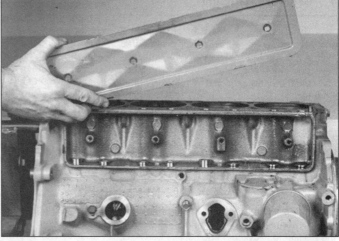

4.7a Apply a continuous 3/16-inch bead of RTV-type sealant to the pushrod cover flange

7   Remove the valve cover. **Note:** *If the cover sticks to the cylinder head, use a wood block and a hammer to dislodge it. If the cover still will not come loose, pry on it carefully, but do not distort the sealing flange surface* **(see illustration)**.

Installation

8   Clean all dirt, oil and old gasket material from the sealing surfaces of the cover and cylinder head with a scraper and a degreaser, such as acetone or lacquer thinner **(see illustration)**. **Note:** *Aerosol gasket removal solvents are available at auto parts stores and may prove helpful.*
9   If the cover was sealed with RTV (no gasket) (1990 and earlier models), apply a continuous 3/16-inch diameter bead of RTV-type sealant to the sealing flange of the cover. Be sure to apply the sealant inside of the bolt holes.**(see illustration)**.
10   If the cover was sealed with a gasket (1991 and later models), install the new gasket with no RTV sealant.
11   Place the valve cover on the cylinder

head while the sealant (if used) is still wet and install the mounting bolts. Tighten the bolts from the center out, a little at a time, to the torque listed in this Chapter's Specifications.
12   Complete installation by reversing the removal procedure.

4   Pushrod cover - removal and installation

Refer to illustrations 4.3, 4.7a, 4.7b and 4.8

Removal

1   Remove the air intake assembly. Tag each hose with a piece of numbered or colored tape to ensure correct installation.
2   Remove the intake manifold assembly (see Section 6).
3   Remove the four pushrod cover nuts **(see illustration)**.
4   To break the seal and remove the pushrod cover, flip one nut over so the washer faces out and reinstall it on the long

inner stud with the washer facing out. Put a second nut on the stud with the washer facing in and tighten them together. Put two 6 mm nuts on the shorter stud and tighten them together. Unscrew the studs by turning out on the inner nuts until the cover breaks free.
5   Remove the pushrod cover nuts and lift off the cover. Reinstall and tighten the cover studs into the engine block.

Installation

6   Using a scraper and degreaser, clean the sealing surfaces on the cover and engine block to remove all oil and old gasket material. **Note:** *Aerosol gasket removal solvents are available at auto parts stores and may prove helpful.*
7   Prior to installation of the cover apply a continuous 3/16-inch bead of RTV-type sealant to the mounting flange of the pushrod cover **(see illustrations)**. Also be sure to install new rubber sealing washers on the pushrod cover mounting studs **(see illustration)**.

4.7b Don't forget to install new rubber sealing washers around the pushrod cover mounting studs or oil will leak past the studs

4.8 Install the pushrod cover while the sealant is still tacky - be sure the semi-circular cutout (arrow) is facing down

5.4 This is what the air hose adapter that threads into the spark plug hole looks like - they're commonly available at auto parts stores

2C

8   With the sealant still wet, place the cover in position on the block and install the cover nuts **(see illustration)**. Tighten the nuts gradually, following a crisscross pattern, to the torque listed in this Chapter's Specifications.
9   The remainder of installation is the reverse of removal.

5   Valve train components - replacement

Refer to illustrations 5.4, 5.5a, 5.5b, 5.5c, 5.9a, 5.9b, 5.10, 5.17a and 5.17b
Note: *Broken valve springs and defective valve stem seals can be replaced without removing the cylinder heads. Two special tools and a compressed air source are normally required to perform this operation, so read through this Section carefully and rent or buy the tools before beginning the job. If compressed air isn't available, a length of nylon rope can be used to keep the valves from falling into the cylinder during this procedure.*
1   Refer to Section 3 and remove the valve cover from the cylinder head.
2   Remove the spark plug from the cylinder that has the defective component. If all of the valve stem seals are being replaced, all of the spark plugs should be removed.
3   Turn the crankshaft until the piston in the affected cylinder is at top dead center on the compression stroke (refer to Chapter 2 Part F). If you're replacing all of the valve stem seals, begin with cylinder number one and work on the valves for one cylinder at a time. Move from cylinder-to-cylinder, following the firing order sequence (see the Specifications).
4   Thread an adapter into the spark plug hole **(see illustration)** and connect an air hose from a compressed air source to it. Most auto parts stores can supply the air hose adapter. **Note:** *Many cylinder compres-*

5.5a Loosen the rocker arm bolt, rotate the rocker arm to one side and lift out the pushrod

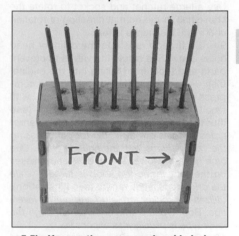

5.5b If more than one pushrod is being removed, store them in a perforated cardboard box to prevent mix-ups during installation - note the label on the box indicating the front (drivebelt end) of the engine

sion gauges utilize a screw-in fitting that may work with your air hose quick-disconnect fitting.
5   Loosen the rocker arm nut and pivot the rocker arm aside for the valve with the defective part and pull out the pushrod **(see illustration)**. If all of the valves are being worked on, all of the rocker arms and pushrods

should be removed. Store the pushrods so they can be returned to their original locations with the same end facing down **(see illustration)**. If necessary, also remove the pushrod guides **(see illustration)**.

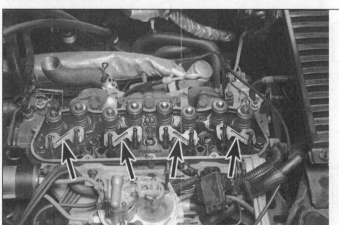

5.5c If they're removed, make sure the pushrod guides (arrows) are kept in order also

6   Apply compressed air to the cylinder. **Warning:** *The piston may be forced down by compressed air, causing the crankshaft to turn suddenly. If the wrench used when positioning the number one piston at TDC is still attached to the bolt in the crankshaft nose, it could cause damage or injury when the crankshaft moves.*

7   The valves should be held in place by the air pressure. If the valve faces or seats are in poor condition, leaks may prevent air pressure from retaining the valves - refer to the alternative procedure below.

8   If you don't have access to compressed air, an alternative method can be used. Position the piston at a point just before TDC on the compression stroke, then feed a long piece of nylon rope through the spark plug hole until it fills the combustion chamber. Be sure to leave the end of the rope hanging out of the engine so it can be removed easily. Use a large ratchet and socket to rotate the crankshaft in the normal direction of rotation until slight resistance is felt.

9   Stuff shop rags into the cylinder head holes above and below the valves to prevent parts and tools from falling into the engine, then use a valve spring compressor to compress the spring. Remove the keepers with small needle-nose pliers or a magnet **(see illustration)**. **Note:** *A couple of different types of tools are available for compressing the valve springs with the head in place. One type grips the lower spring coils and presses on the retainer as the knob is turned, while the other type, shown here* **(see illustration)**, *utilizes the rocker arm stud and nut for leverage. Both types work very well, although the lever type is usually less expensive.*

10   Remove the spring retainer, shield and valve spring, then remove the seal **(see illustration)**. **Note:** *If air pressure fails to hold the valve in the closed position during this operation, the valve face or seat is probably damaged. If so, the cylinder head will have to be removed for additional repair operations.*

11   Wrap a rubber band or tape around the top of the valve stem so the valve won't fall into the combustion chamber, then release the

5.9a After the valve spring has been compressed, the keepers can be removed with needle-nose pliers or a magnet

air pressure. **Note:** *If a rope was used instead of air pressure, turn the crankshaft slightly in the direction opposite normal rotation.*

12   Inspect the valve stem for damage. Rotate the valve in the guide and check the end for eccentric movement, which would indicate that the valve is bent.

13   Move the valve up-and-down in the guide and make sure it doesn't bind. If the valve stem binds, either the valve is bent or the guide is damaged. In either case, the head will have to be removed for repair.

14   Reapply air pressure to the cylinder to retain the valve in the closed position, then remove the tape or rubber band from the valve stem. If a rope was used instead of air pressure, rotate the crankshaft in the normal direction of rotation until slight resistance is felt.

15   Lubricate the valve stem with engine oil.

16   Install the spring and shield in position over the valve.

17   Install the valve spring retainer. Compress the valve spring and carefully install the O-ring seal **(see illustration)**, then install the keepers. Apply a small dab of grease to the inside of each keeper to hold it in place **(see illustration)**.

5.9b Using a lever-type valve spring compressor to compress a valve spring

18   Remove the pressure from the spring tool and make sure the keepers are seated.

19   Disconnect the air hose and remove the adapter from the spark plug hole. If a rope was used in place of air pressure, pull it out of the cylinder.

20   Install the rocker arm(s) and pushrod(s).

21   Install the spark plug(s) and hook up the wire(s).

22   Install the valve cover.

23   Start and run the engine, then check for oil leaks and unusual sounds coming from the valve cover area.

5.17a Make sure the O-ring seal under the retainer is seated in the groove and not twisted before installing the keepers

5.17b Put a small dab of grease on the inside of each keeper before assembly - it'll hold them in place until the spring is released

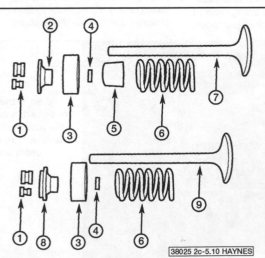

5.10 Typical engine valves and related components - exploded view

1   Keepers
2   Retainer
3   Oil shield
4   O-ring oil seal
5   Umbrella seal (if equipped)
6   Spring
7   Intake valve
8   Retainer/rotator
9   Exhaust valve

38025 2c-5.10 HAYNES

6.11 Remove the old intake manifold gasket with a scraper - don't leave any material on the mating surfaces

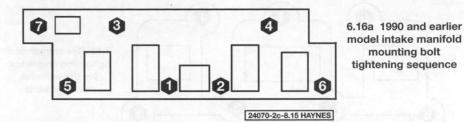

6.16a 1990 and earlier model intake manifold mounting bolt tightening sequence

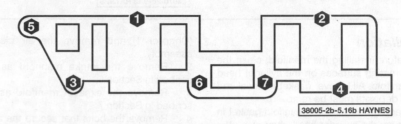

6.16b Use this intake manifold bolt tightening sequence on 1991 and later models

2C

6   Intake manifold - removal and installation

Refer to illustrations 6.11, 6.16a and 6.16b
Warning: *Gasoline is extremely flammable, so take extra precautions when you work on any part of the fuel system. Don't smoke or allow open flames or bare light bulbs near the work area, and don't work in a garage where a natural gas-type appliance (such as a water heater or clothes dryer) with a pilot light is present. Since gasoline is carcinogenic, wear latex gloves when there's a possibility of being exposed to fuel, and, if you spill any fuel on your skin, rinse it off immediately with soap and water. Mop up any spills immediately and do not store fuel-soaked rags where they could ignite. The fuel system is under constant pressure, so, if any fuel lines are to be disconnected, the fuel pressure in the system must be relieved first. When you perform any kind of work on the fuel system, wear safety glasses and have a Class B type fire extinguisher on hand.*

Removal

1   Relieve the fuel system pressure, then disconnect the cable from the negative battery terminal.
2   Remove the air cleaner assembly, tagging each hose as it is disconnected with a piece of numbered tape to simplify reinstallation.
3   Remove the PCV valve and hose.
4   Drain the cooling system (refer to Chapter 1).
5   Label and disconnect the fuel line, vacuum lines and electrical connectors from the fuel injection assembly. When disconnecting the fuel line be prepared to catch some fuel, then plug the fuel line to prevent contamination.
6   Disconnect the throttle linkage, making careful note of how it is installed.
7   Disconnect the cruise control linkage (if so equipped).
8   Disconnect the coil wire, remove the

two retaining screws and one bolt, then remove the coil.
9   Remove the coolant hoses from the manifold.
10   Remove the manifold retaining bolts and separate the manifold from the cylinder head. Do not pry between the manifold and head, as damage to the gasket sealing surfaces may result.

Installation

11   Remove the manifold gasket with a scraper **(see illustration)**.
12   If the intake manifold is to be replaced with another, transfer all components still attached to the old manifold to the new one.
13   Before installing the manifold, clean the cylinder head and manifold gasket surfaces. All gasket material and sealing compound must be removed prior to installation. Gasket removal solvents are available at auto parts stores and may prove helpful. After the gasket material and sealing compound is removed, wipe the gasket surfaces clean with a rag soaked in lacquer thinner or acetone.
14   Apply a thin bead of RTV-type sealant to the intake manifold and cylinder head mating surfaces. Make certain that the sealant will not spread into the air or coolant passages when the manifold is installed.
15   Place a new intake manifold gasket on the manifold, hold the manifold in position against the cylinder head and install the mounting bolts finger tight.
16   Tighten the mounting bolts a little at a time in the sequence shown until they are all at the torque listed in this Chapter's Specifications **(see illustrations)**.
17   Install the remaining components in the reverse order of removal.
18   Fill the radiator with coolant, start the engine and check for leaks. Adjust the ignition timing and idle speed as necessary (Chapter 1).

7   Exhaust manifold - removal and installation

Refer to illustration 7.13
Warning: *The engine must be completely cool before beginning this procedure.*

Removal

1   If the vehicle is equipped with air conditioning, carefully examine the routing of the hoses and the mounting of the compressor. You may be able to remove the exhaust manifold without disconnecting the system. If you are in doubt, take the vehicle to a dealer or automotive air conditioning shop to have the system depressurized. **Caution:** *Do not, under any circumstances, disconnect any air conditioning system lines while the system is under pressure.*
2   Remove the cable from the negative battery terminal.
3   Remove the air cleaner assembly, tagging each hose as it is disconnected with a piece of numbered tape to simplify reinstallation.
4   Disconnect and remove the torque strut located between the engine mount bracket and cylinder head.
5   Raise the vehicle and support it securely on jackstands.
6   Remove the oxygen sensor (see Chapter 6).
7   Label the spark plug wires, then disconnect them and secure them out of the way.
8   Disconnect the exhaust pipe from the exhaust manifold. You may have to apply penetrating oil to the fastener threads, as they are usually corroded. The exhaust pipe can be hung from the frame with a piece of wire.
9   Remove the exhaust manifold end bolts first, then remove the center bolts and separate the exhaust manifold from the engine.
10   Remove the exhaust manifold gasket.

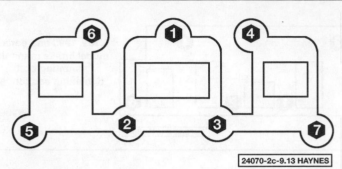

7.13 Recommended tightening sequence for the exhaust manifold bolts

24070-2c-9.13 HAYNES

8.11 Use a socket and ratchet to remove the rocker arm nuts

Installation

11   Before installing the manifold, clean the gasket mating surfaces on the cylinder head and manifold. All leftover gasket material and carbon deposits must be removed.

12   Place a new exhaust manifold gasket in position on the cylinder head, then place the manifold in position and install the mounting bolts finger tight.

13   Tighten the mounting bolts a little at a time, in the sequence shown in the accompanying illustration, until all of the bolts are at the torque listed in this Chapter's Specifications **(see illustration)**.

14   Lower the vehicle.

15   Install the remaining components in the reverse order of removal, using new gaskets wherever one has been removed.

16   Start the engine and check for exhaust leaks between the manifold and cylinder head and between the manifold and exhaust pipe.

8   Cylinder head - removal and installation

Refer to illustrations 8.11, 8.12, 8.14a, 8.14b, 8.15, 8.18, 8.23 and 8.24

Removal

1   Disconnect the cable from the negative battery terminal. Drain the cooling system

(Chapter 1) and remove the air cleaner assembly.

2   Remove the intake manifold as described in Section 6.

3   Remove the exhaust manifold as described in Section 7.

4   Remove the bolts that secure the alternator bracket to the cylinder head.

5   If so equipped, unbolt the air conditioning compressor and swing it out of the way for clearance. Normally, you won't have to disconnect any air conditioning hoses or lines. **Caution:** *Do not disconnect any of the air conditioning hoses or lines unless the system has been depressurized by a dealer service department or automotive air conditioning shop.*

6   Disconnect all electrical and vacuum lines from the cylinder head. Be sure to label the lines to simplify reinstallation.

7   Remove the upper radiator hose.

8   Disconnect the spark plug wires and remove the spark plugs. Be sure to label the plug wires to simplify reinstallation.

9   Remove the valve cover. Refer to Section 3 if necessary.

10   When disassembling the valve mechanisms, keep all of the components separate so they can be reinstalled in their original positions. A cardboard box or rack, numbered to correspond to the engine cylinders, can be used for this purpose.

11   Remove each of the rocker arm nuts and separate the rocker arms and pivots from

the cylinder head **(see illustration)**.

12   Remove the pushrods **(see illustration)**.

13   If the ignition coil is mounted separately from the distributor, disconnect the wires and remove the coil.

14   Loosen each of the cylinder head mounting bolts one turn at a time, following the reverse of the tightening sequence found in illustration 8.24, until they can be removed. Note the length and position of each bolt to ensure correct reinstallation **(see illustrations)**.

15   Lift the head off the engine. If it is stuck to the engine block, try using a hammer and wood block to tap the head and break the gasket seal. If this does not work, pry carefully at the casting overhang **(see illustration)**. Place the head on a wood block to prevent damage to the gasket surface.

16   Refer to Chapter 2 Part F for cylinder head disassembly and valve service procedures.

Installation

17   If a new cylinder head is being installed, transfer all external parts from the old cylin-

8.12 Remove the pushrods and store them in order so they can be reinstalled in the same holes with the same end facing up

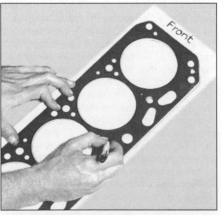

8.14a To avoid mixing up the head bolts, use a new gasket to transfer the bolt hole pattern to a piece of cardboard, then punch holes to accept the bolts . . .

8.14b . . . and push each bolt through the matching hole in the cardboard

8.15 If the head is stuck, pry it up at the overhang just behind and below the thermostat housing

8.18 Once the head is off, stuff the cylinders with clean shop rags to prevent debris from falling into them and scrape off the old gasket material with a gasket scraper

8.23 The cylinder head mounting bolts should be coated with sealant at the location shown (arrows) before installation

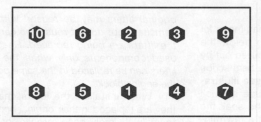

8.24 Cylinder head bolt positions and bolt tightening sequence

24070-2c-10.25 HAYNES

2C

der head to the new one.

18 Using a scraper, thoroughly clean the gasket surfaces on the cylinder head and the engine block **(see illustration)**. Do not gouge or otherwise damage the gasket surfaces. **Note:** *Aerosol gasket removal solvents are often available at auto parts stores and may prove helpful.* After all gasket material is removed, wipe the gasket surfaces clean with a rag soaked in lacquer thinner or acetone.

20 To get the proper torque readings, the threads of the head bolts must be clean. This also applies to the threaded holes in the engine block. Use a wire brush for the bolt threads and a round wire brush for the bolt holes. Don't use a tap or die to clean the head bolts or holes.

21 Place the new gasket in position over the engine block dowel pins.

22 Carefully lower the cylinder head onto the engine, over the dowel pins and the gasket.

23 Coat the threads of each cylinder head bolt and the point at which the head and the bolt meet with sealing compound and install the bolts finger tight. Do not tighten any of

the bolts at this time **(see illustration)**.
24 Tighten each of the bolts a little at a time in the proper sequence **(see illustration)**. Continue tightening in this sequence until the proper torque reading is obtained (see the Specifications). As a final check, work around the head in a front-to-rear sequence to make sure none of the bolts have been left out of the sequence. Note that later model head bolts are torqued in steps. Tighten all bolts to the torque listed in each step before proceeding to the next step **(see illustration)**.
25 The remaining steps are the reverse of the removal procedure. Run the engine and check for leaks.

9   Hydraulic lifters - removal, inspection and installation

Refer to illustrations 9.7a, 9.7b, 9.8, 9.9, 9.10a and 9.10b
1 A noisy valve lifter can be isolated when the engine is idling. Place a length of hose or tubing near the position of each valve while listening at the other end of the tube. Another method is to remove the valve cover and, with the engine idling, place a finger on each of the valve spring retainers, one at a time. If a valve lifter is defective, it will be evident from the shock felt at the retainer as the valve seats.
2 A common cause of a noisy valve lifter is dirt trapped between the plunger and the lifter body.

Removal
3 Remove the valve cover as described in Section 3.
4 Remove the intake manifold as described in Section 6.
5 Remove the pushrod cover as described in Section 4.
6 Loosen the rocker arm bolt and rotate the rocker arm away from the pushrod.
7 Remove the retainers and guides **(see illustrations)**. If the lifters are not marked to show which end faces the drivebelt end of the engine, mark them with paint. The lifters must be reinstalled so the roller rotates the same direction as originally installed.

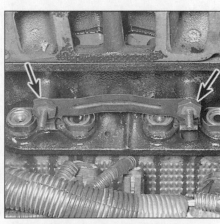

9.7a The roller lifter guides are held in place by the retainers

9.7b Remove the lifter guide - if you're removing more than one guide, keep them in order to prevent mix-ups during installation

9.8 On engines that haven't accumulated a lot of sludge and varnish, the lifters can usually be removed by hand

9.9 If you're removing more than one lifter, keep them in order in a clearly labeled box

8   If the lifters are relatively clean (not a lot of carbon and varnish build-up below the bores), they can sometimes be pulled out by hand or with the pointed end of a bent scribe hooked under the lifter retainer **(see illustration)**. If the lifters are stuck, use a small amount of carburetor cleaner and soak the lifters around the bores. Let set a few minutes, then gently work them up and down a few times. They should then pull out. Also, special tools designed to grip and remove the lifters are manufactured by many tool companies and are widely available. **Caution:** *Don't grab the outer circumference of the lifter with pliers or anything that could scratch the lifter.*

9   The lifters should be kept in order for reinstallation in their original positions **(see illustration)**.

Inspection and installation

10   Inspect each lifter to identify excessive wear and damage **(see illustrations)**. If they are worn, damaged or stuck, replace them as a set, along with a new camshaft. **Caution:** *Never replace only the lifters, since accelerated wear to the components may result. The*

original lifters may be reused with a new camshaft, but do not reuse the camshaft if the lifters are being replaced. Reassemble used components only when the original lifters can be replaced in the same position in the engine block.

11   When installing the lifters, make sure they are replaced in their original bores. Coat them with moly-base grease or engine assembly lube.

12   During installation, position the lifter guides and retainers. Tighten the retainer studs before installing the pushrods.

13   The remaining installation steps are the reverse of removal.

10 Oil pump drive assembly - removal and installation

Refer to illustration 10.3
Note: *This procedure does not apply to 1987 and later models with force balancers. These models are most easily identified by the oil filter in the bottom of the oil pan. On models without force balancers, the oil filter is on the side of the engine block.*

Removal

1   Raise the vehicle and support it securely on jackstands.
2   Remove the oil filter.
3   Remove the oil pump driveshaft cover plate bolts **(see illustration)**.
4   Remove the bearing or bushing, depending on which is used.
5   Remove the shaft and gear assembly.

Installation

6   Thoroughly clean the sealing surfaces on the engine block and cover plate.
7   Inspect the gear teeth to see if they are chipped or cracked.
8   Install the oil pump driveshaft in the block and turn it until it engages with the camshaft drive gear and the oil pump body.
9   Apply a 1/16-inch diameter bead of RTV-type sealant to the cover plate so that it completely seals around the oil pump driveshaft hole in the block.
10   Install the cover plate mounting bolts and tighten them to the torque listed in this Chapter's Specifications.
11   The remainder of installation is the reverse of the removal procedure.

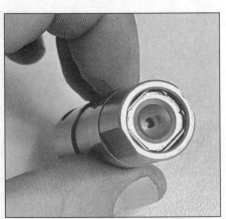

9.10a Check the pushrod seat (arrow) in the top of each lifter for wear

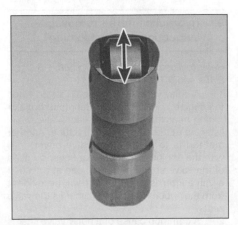

9.10b The roller on roller lifters must turn freely - check for wear and excessive play as well

10.3 The oil pump driveshaft cover is located near the oil filter

11   Oil pan - removal and installation

Removal

1   Disconnect the cable from the negative battery terminal.
2   Raise the vehicle and place it securely on jackstands.
3   Drain the engine oil and remove the oil filter. Refer to Chapter 1 if necessary
4   Disconnect the exhaust pipe at the exhaust manifold and at the hangers. Swing it down and secure it out of the way.
5   Remove the flywheel inspection covers.
6   Remove the starter (see Chapter 5).
7   Remove the oil pan bolts and separate the oil pan from the block. **Note:** *Because RTV sealant is used on the oil pan instead of a gasket, the pan may be difficult to remove. If so, try striking the side of the pan with a rubber mallet. If this does not work, try running a sharp knife between the block and pan to cut the RTV seal. Be careful not to damage the gasket mating surfaces.*

Installation

8   Clean the pan with solvent and, using a scraper, remove all old sealant and gasket material from the block and pan sealing surfaces. Gasket removal solvents are available at many auto parts stores and may prove helpful. If the flange where the pan mates to the block is bent, straighten it with a wood block and a hammer.
9   Apply a continuous bead of RTV sealant to the oil pan. Be sure to run the sealant around the inside of the bolt holes.
10   Attach the oil pan to the block. The bolts that secure the pan to the timing cover should be installed last. They are installed at an angle into holes that will line up as the rest of the pan bolts are tightened.
11   After all bolts are installed, tighten them to the torque listed in this Chapter's Specifications. Use a criss-cross pattern and work up to the final torque in three or four steps.
12   Install a new oil filter and fill the crankcase with oil (see Chapter 1). The remaining steps are the reverse of the removal procedure.

12   Oil pump (models without force balancers) - removal and installation

Refer to illustration 12.2
Note: *This procedure does not apply to 1987 and later models with force balancer assemblies (these are most easily identified by the oil filter in the oil pan, instead of on the side of the engine). See Section 13 to remove the oil pump on force balancer-equipped models.*

Removal

1   Remove the oil pan (see Section 11).
2   Remove the two oil pump flange mounting bolts and the nut from the main bearing cap bolt **(see illustration)**.

12.2 Remove the oil pump flange mounting bolts

3   Lift out the oil pump and screen as an assembly.

Installation

4   To install the pump, align the shaft so it mates with the oil pump driveshaft tang, then install the pump on the block, over the oil pump driveshaft lower bushing. No gasket is used. The oil pump should slide easily into place. If not, remove it and relocate the slot.
5   Install the mounting bolts and nut and tighten them to the torque listed in this Chapter's Specifications.
6   Reinstall the oil pan (see Section 11).

13   Force balancer/oil pump assembly - removal and installation

Removal

Note: *To remove the oil pump only, it is not necessary to remove the entire force balancer/oil pump assembly. To remove only the oil pump, see Section 14.*
1   Some 1987 and all 1988 and later model 2.5L engines are equipped with a force balancer.
2   The balancer-equipped engine can be distinguished by the element-type oil filter located in the oil pan. The assembly consists of two eccentric weighted shafts and gears that are counter-rotated by a concentric gear on the crankshaft at twice crankshaft speed, dampening engine vibration. The oil filter, a pick-up screen and gerotor type oil pump are also integral parts of the assembly, so the oil pump removal procedure in Section 12 does not apply. The oil pump is driven from the back side of one of the balancers.
3   The force balancer/oil pump assembly must be removed to disassemble the engine for overhaul.
4   Remove the oil pan (see Section 11).
5   Position the number 1 piston at TDC on the compression stroke (see Chapter 2, Part F).
6   Unbolt the balancer assembly and remove it from the engine. **Warning:** *The*

assembly is heavy, so support it carefully before removing the bolts and be careful not to drop it!

Installation

1987 through 1990 models

7   Position the crankshaft by measuring from the engine block to the first cut of the double notch on the reluctor ring. The distance should be 1-11/16-inches. If it isn't, turn the crankshaft until it is.
8   Mount the balancer with the counterweights parallel and pointing AWAY from the crankshaft. Tighten the bolts to the torque listed in this Chapter's Specifications.

1991 and later models

9   Rotate the crankshaft until the number 4 counterweight is EXACTLY at Bottom Dead Center. **Note:** *When installing the balancer, the housing end without dowel pins must continuously remain in contact with the engine block surface. If it loses contact, the gears may lose their proper engagement and damage may occur to either the crankshaft or balancer gears.*
10   Install the balancer onto the engine block with the balance weights EXACTLY at Bottom Dead Center (plus or minus 1/2 gear tooth).
11   Install the balancer bolts and hand tighten evenly.
12   Tighten all bolts in the sequence 3-1-2-4. Use the Steps and torque listed in this Chapter's Specifications.

All models

13   Rotate the crankshaft four times and check for clearance between the fourth counterweight and the balancer weights.
14   Install the oil pan.
15   Install a new oil filter and add oil (see Chapter 1). Run the engine and check for leaks.

14   Oil pump/pressure regulator valve (models with force balancers) - removal, inspection, and installation

Removal

Note: *It isn't necessary to remove the force balancer assembly to service the oil pump or pressure regulator valve.*
1   Remove the oil pan (see Section 11).
2   Remove the restrictor (if equipped).
3   Remove the oil pump cover assembly and oil pump gears or, on later models, the gerotor assembly.
4   **Warning:** *The pressure regulator valve is under pressure. Exercise caution when unscrewing the plug or removing the pin, as bodily injury may result.* Remove the pressure regulator valve plug (or pin) and spring, then remove the valve itself. If the valve is stuck, clean the valve and pump housing with carburetor cleaner or solvent.
5   Remove any sludge, oil or varnish from

2C

15.4 Remove the crankshaft hub bolt

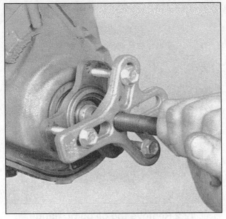

15.6 Use a puller to remove the hub from the crankshaft

15.10 Use the pulley hub bolt to press the hub onto the crankshaft

the parts with carburetor cleaner or solvent. If the varnish on any of the parts is difficult to remove, allow them to soak for a while.

Inspection

6   Inspect all parts for the presence of foreign material. If you find evidence of contamination, determine its source.
7   Inspect the oil pump pocket and oil pump cover assembly for cracks, scoring, and casting imperfections.
8   Inspect the pressure regulator valve for scoring and sticking. Remove burrs with a fine oil stone.
9   Inspect the pressure regulator valve spring for distortion and loss of tension. If you have any doubt regarding the condition of the spring, replace it.
10   Clean the screen assembly and inspect it for damage.
11   Inspect the pump gears for chipping, galling, and wear.
12   We recommend replacing the oil pump gears (or gerotor assembly on later models) whenever they are removed, since they are so critical to proper engine lubrication.

Installation

13   Lubricate all internal parts with engine oil.
14   To ensure priming and avoid engine damage, pack all pump cavities with petroleum jelly.
15   Install the oil pump gears.
16   Install the oil pump cover assembly.
17   Install the pressure regulator valve and spring.
18   Install the pressure regulator plug or pin. Make sure it's properly secured.
19   Install the oil pump cover assembly and tighten the bolts securely.
20   Install the restrictor (if equipped) and a new filter.
21   Install the oil pan.
22   Fill the crankcase to the correct level with clean engine oil.
23   Remove the oil pressure sending unit and install an oil pressure gauge in its place.
24   Start the engine and note the oil pres-

sure. If it doesn't build up quickly, remove the oil pan and examine the pump. If necessary, disassemble the pump and repack all cavities with petroleum jelly. Running the engine without oil pressure will cause extensive damage.

15 Crankshaft pulley hub and front oil seal - removal and installation

Refer to illustrations 15.4, 15.6 and 15.10

Removal

1   Remove the cable from the negative battery terminal.
2   Loosen the accessory drivebelt tension adjusting bolts, as necessary, and remove the drivebelts (see Chapter 1).
3   Remove the right front inner fender splash shield.
4   Remove the flywheel/driveplate access cover and wedge a large screwdriver into the ring gear teeth to keep the engine from turning, then loosen the hub bolt. A breaker bar will probably be necessary, since the bolt is very tight **(see illustration)**.
5   Mark the position of the pulley in relation to the hub. Remove the bolts and separate the pulley from the hub.
6   Using a puller, remove the hub from the crankshaft **(see illustration)**.
7   If you're replacing the front seal with the cover installed, carefully pry the oil seal out of the front cover with a large screwdriver. Be careful not to distort the cover.

Installation

8   Install the new seal with the helical lip toward the engine. Drive the seal into place using a seal installation tool or a large socket and hammer. If there is enough room, a wood block and hammer can also be used.
9   Apply a thin layer of multi-purpose grease to the seal contact surface of the hub.
10   Position the pulley hub on the crankshaft and slide it through the seal until it bottoms against the crankshaft gear. Note that the slot in the hub must be aligned with the

Woodruff key in the end of the crankshaft. The hub-to-crankshaft bolt can also be used to press the hub into position **(see illustration)**.
11   Install the crank pulley on the hub, noting the alignment marks made during removal. The pulley-to-hub bolts should be coated with thread locking compound whenever they are removed and installed.
12   Tighten the hub-to-crankshaft bolt to the torque listed in this Chapter's Specifications.
13   The remaining installation steps are the reverse of removal. Tighten the drivebelts to the proper tension (see Chapter 1).

16 Timing gear cover- removal and installation

Refer to illustrations 16.3, 16.7 and 16.9

Removal

1   Remove the crankshaft pulley hub as described in Section 15.
2   Remove the oil pan-to-timing gear cover bolts.
3   Remove the timing cover-to-block bolts **(see illustration)**.

16.3 Remove the timing gear cover mounting bolts

2C

16.7 Use a wood block and hammer to install the oil seal

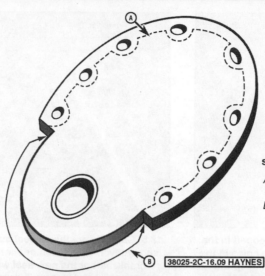

16.9 Timing gear cover sealant application details

A 1/4-inch by 1/8-inch bead of RTV sealant
B 3/8-inch by 3/16-inch bead of RTV sealant

38025-2C-16.09 HAYNES

4   Remove the timing cover by prying it off at the top edge first and then twisting it down to break the seal at the oil pan. The cover is sealed with RTV, so it may be stuck to the block. Use care not to distort the cover too much that it can't be straightened.

5   Using a scraper and degreaser, remove all dirt and old gasket material from the sealing surfaces of the timing gear cover, engine block and oil pan. Gasket removal solvents are available at auto parts stores and may prove helpful.

6   Remove the front oil seal by carefully prying it out of the timing gear cover with a large screwdriver. Do not distort the cover.

Installation

7   Install the new seal with the helical lip toward the inside of the cover. Drive the seal into place using a seal installation tool or a large socket and hammer. A wood block will also work **(see illustration)**.

8   Apply a bead of RTV-type sealant to the joint between the oil pan and engine block.

9   Apply a 3/8-inch (wide) by 3/16-inch (thick) bead of RTV sealant to the joint at the oil pan and timing gear cover **(see illustration)**.

10   Apply a 1/4-inch (wide) by 1/8-inch (thick) bead of RTV sealant to the timing gear cover at the block mating surfaces.

11   Lubricate the pulley hub seal with clean engine oil.

12   Insert the hub through the cover seal and place the cover in position on the block as the hub slides onto the crankshaft. This will ensure that the seal is centered evenly on the hub.

13   Install the oil pan-to-cover bolts and partially tighten them.

14   Install the bolts that secure the cover to the block, then tighten all of the mounting bolts to the torque listed in this Chapter's Specifications.

15   The remainder of installation is the reverse of removal.

17.2 Temporarily reinstall the crankshaft pulley hub, thread two bolts into it and use a large prybar to prevent it from turning while loosening the camshaft sprocket bolt

17   Timing chain - replacement

Refer to illustrations 17.2 and 17.6

Note: *This procedure is for 1990 and later models only. 1989 and earlier models use timing gears instead of a chain. The camshaft gear is pressed on the camshaft and normally can't be removed without first removing the camshaft from the engine (see Chapter 2F).*

1   Remove the front cover (see Section 15).

2   Loosen, but do not remove, the camshaft sprocket bolt **(see illustration)**.

3   Align the timing marks on the camshaft sprocket and the crankshaft sprocket, with the engine at Top Dead Center (TDC) for number one cylinder. This can be confirmed by removing the spark plug from the number one cylinder and turning the engine in the normal direction of rotation while holding your finger over the spark plug hole. When you feel compression building up, the number one cylinder is approaching TDC. Continue turning the engine until the timing marks are aligned.

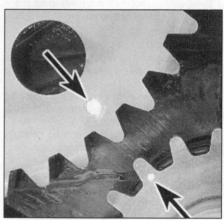

17.6 Proper positioning of the timing marks - 2.5L OHV engine with a timing chain

4   Remove the camshaft sprocket bolt, then slip the timing chain and camshaft sprocket off the camshaft. **Note:** *If the timing chain is to be replaced, also replace the camshaft sprocket and the crankshaft sprocket.*

5   Check the tensioner for signs of wear and replace it if necessary. The tensioner is retained by a single bolt.

6   Installation is the reverse of the removal procedure, but make sure the timing marks are in alignment **(see illustration)** and tighten the camshaft sprocket bolt to the torque listed in this Chapter's Specifications.

18   Flywheel/driveplate and rear main bearing oil seal - removal and installation

Refer to illustrations 18.4, 18.5 and 18.8

Removal

1   The rear main bearing oil seal can be replaced without removal of the oil pan or crankshaft.

2   Refer to Chapter 7, follow all precaution-

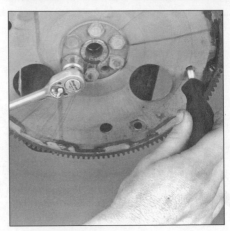

18.4 A large screwdriver wedged in the ring gear teeth or one of the holes in the driveplate can be used to keep the flywheel/driveplate from turning as the bolts are removed

18.5 Carefully pry the oil seal out with a screwdriver - don't nick or scratch the crankshaft or the new seal will be damaged and leaks will develop

18.8 Tap around the outer edge of the new seal with a hammer and the blunt end of a punch to seat it squarely in the bore

ary notes and remove the transaxle.

3   If equipped with a manual transmission, remove the pressure plate and clutch disc (see Chapter 8).

4   Remove the flywheel or driveplate mounting bolts and separate it from the crankshaft **(see illustration)**.

5   Using a screwdriver or prybar, carefully remove the oil seal from the block **(see illustration)**.

Installation

6   Using solvent, thoroughly clean the block-to-seal mating surfaces, then dry them with compressed air. **Warning:** *Wear eye protection when using compressed air.*

7   Apply a light coat of engine oil to the lip and outside surface of the new seal.

8   Carefully work the lip of the new seal over the crankshaft, then gently tap the seal into place with a hammer and the blunt end of a punch or other suitable tool **(see illustration)**.

9   Install the flywheel or driveplate and tighten the bolts to the torque listed in this Chapter's Specifications.

10   If equipped with a manual transaxle, reinstall the clutch disc and pressure plate.

11   Reinstall the transaxle as described in Chapter 7.

---

19   Engine mounts - check and replacement

Refer to illustration 19.4

Warning: *A special tool is available to support the engine during repair operations. These fixtures are available from rental yards. Improper lifting methods or devices are hazardous and could result in severe injury or death. DO NOT place any part of your body under the engine/transaxle when it's supported only by a jack. Failure of the lifting device could result in serious injury or death.*

19.4 Typical engine mount details (arrows)

1   Front engine mount   2   Rear engine mount

Note: *Whenever engine mount bolts are removed, the bolt threads must be thoroughly cleaned and new thread-locking compound applied to the threads before installing.*

Check

1   If the rubber mounts have become hard, split or separated from the metal backing, they must be replaced. Applying rubber preservative to the mounts will help slow deterioration. To check the mounts, raise the vehicle, place it securely on jackstands, then raise the engine slightly with an engine support or jack (just enough to take the weight off the mount) - see Step 3. Check the following:

a) Check the mounts to see if the rubber is cracked, hardened or separated from the metal plates. Sometimes the rubber will split right down the center.

b) Check for relative movement between the mount plates and the engine or frame (use a large screwdriver or prybar to attempt to move the mounts). If movement is noted, lower the engine and tighten the mount fasteners.

Engine mount removal and installation

2   Raise the vehicle and support it securely on jackstands.

3   Support the engine with an engine support fixture, engine hoist or a jack. If you must use a jack, position the jack head under the oil pan and place a large wood block between the jack head and oil pan to prevent pan dents and possible oil starvation. **Warning:** *Never position any part of your body under the engine when it's supported only by a jack.*

Front engine mount

4   Remove the two mount-to-engine bracket bolts **(see illustration)**.

5   Remove the mount-to-chassis bolts and remove the mount from the vehicle.

6   Installation is the reverse of removal.

Rear engine mount

7   Remove the mount-to-chassis nuts.

8   Remove the mount-to-engine bracket bolts and remove the mount from the vehicle.

9   Installation is the reverse of removal.

Chapter 2 Part D
3.1L V6 engine

Contents

2D

Specifications

General

Cylinder numbers (drivebelt end-to-transaxle end)
Front bank (radiator side)	2-4-6
Rear bank	1-3-5
Firing order	1-2-3-4-5-6

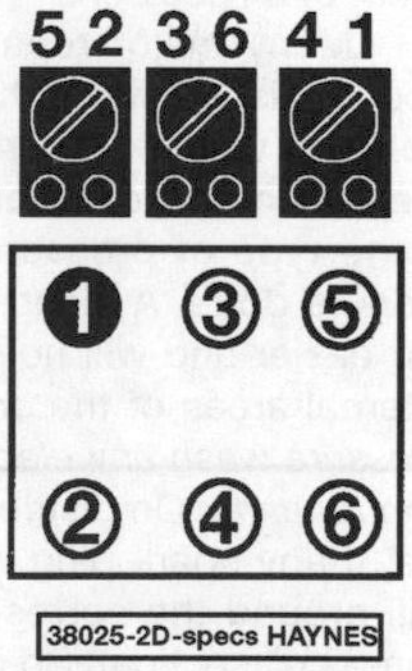

Torque specifications

Ft-lbs (unless otherwise indicated)

Camshaft sprocket bolt	74
Camshaft retainer (thrust) plate	96 inch-lbs
Rear camshaft cover plate bolts	84 inch-lbs
Cylinder head bolts	
Step 1	33
Step 2	Turn an additional 90-degrees
Vibration damper bolt	76
Exhaust manifold nuts	144 inch-lbs
Flywheel/driveplate mounting bolts	61
Front cover mounting bolts	
Small bolts	180 inch-lbs
Large bolts	35
Hydraulic lifter guide bolts	96 inch-lbs
Intake manifold mounting bolts	
Lower bolts	120 inch-lbs
Upper plenum bolts	18
Oil pan mounting bolts	18
Oil pan side bolts	37
Oil pump mounting bolt	27
Oil pump cover bolts	96 inch-lbs
Oil pump drive hold-down bolt	27
Rocker arm nuts	18
Spark plug	132 inch-lbs
Timing chain damper bolts	18
Valve cover bolts	96 inch-lbs

```
5 2   3 6   4 1
```

```
①   ③   ⑤

②   ④   ⑥
```

38025-2D-specs HAYNES

Cylinder and coil terminal location

1   General information

The following Sections in this Part of Chapter 2 are devoted to in vehicle repair procedures for the 3.1 liter (3100) V6 engine. All information concerning engine removal and installation and cylinder block and cylinder head servicing can be found in Part F of this Chapter.

The repair procedures are based on the assumption that the engine is still installed in the vehicle. Therefore, if this information is being used during a complete engine overhaul - with the engine already out of the vehicle and on a stand - many of the Steps included here will not apply.

The Specifications included in this Part of Chapter 2 apply only to the engines and procedures found here. For specifications regarding engines other than the 3.1 liter V6, see Part A, B, C or E, whichever applies. Part F of Chapter 2 contains the specifications necessary for engine block and cylinder head rebuilding procedures.

2   Repair operations possible with the engine in the vehicle

Warning: *Before working in the vicinity of airbag components (on models so equipped) refer to Chapter 12 for the airbag system disarming procedure. Use care not to damage any wiring or sensors associated with this system or the airbag may deploy when reconnecting the battery or fail to deploy in the event of an accident.*

Many major repair operations can be accomplished without removing the engine from the vehicle. Clean the engine compartment and the exterior of the engine with some type of pressure washer before any work is done. A clean engine will make the job easier and will help keep dirt out of the internal areas of the engine. **Caution:** *Don't pressure wash any electronic components or control units.* On distributorless ignition models, if any spark plug hole fills with water, it will ground the corresponding plug (on the same coil section). So if the front three plugs or wires ground, none of the spark plugs will fire. If the engine won't start after washing it, make certain ALL of the spark plugs and wires are completely dry. Water can also short the ignition module and other electronic control units causing them to completely fail.

Depending on the components involved, it may be a good idea to remove the hood to improve access to the engine (refer to Chapter 11 if necessary).

If vacuum, exhaust, oil or coolant leaks develop, indicating a need for gasket or seal replacement, the repairs can generally be made with the engine in the vehicle. The intake and exhaust manifold gaskets, oil pan gasket and cylinder head gaskets are all accessible with the engine in place. Exterior engine components such as the

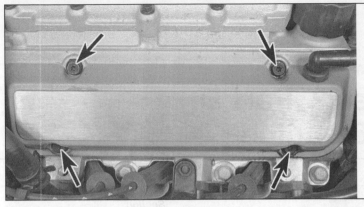

3.16 Valve cover mounting bolt locations

intake and exhaust manifolds, the oil pan, the oil pump, the water pump, the starter motor, the alternator, the distributor and the fuel injection system can be removed for repair with the engine in place. The timing chain and sprockets can also be replaced with the engine in the vehicle, but the camshaft cannot be removed.

Since the cylinder heads can be removed without pulling the engine, valve component servicing can also be accomplished with the engine in the vehicle.

In extreme cases caused by a lack of necessary equipment, repair or replacement of piston rings, pistons, connecting rods and rod bearings is possible with the engine in the vehicle. However, this practice is not recommended because of the cleaning and preparation work that must be done to the components involved.

3   Valve covers - removal and installation

Removal

1   Disconnect the cable from the negative battery terminal. **Caution:** *If the vehicle is equipped with a Delco Loc II audio system, make sure you have the correct activation code before disconnecting the battery. See the information at the front of this manual for the radio re-activation procedure.*
2   Disconnect any wires and hoses that would interfere with the removal of the valve cover, labeling them as they are disconnected.

Front cover

3   Detach the PCV valve from the valve cover.
4   Remove any fuel injection (air induction) parts necessary to gain access to the valve cover bolts and cover.
5   Partially drain the cooling system (see Chapter 1).
6   Loosen the coolant tube hose clamp below the thermostat housing, then disconnect the other end of the hose at the water pump.
7   Unbolt the coolant tube bracket from the exhaust and move it aside.

8   Remove the vent tube from the valve cover to the air inlet hose

Rear cover

9   On automatic transaxle-equipped models, disconnect the Throttle Valve (TV) cable.
10   Detach the brake booster vacuum line from the bracket.
11   Remove the serpentine drivebelt (see Chapter 1).
12   Mark the wires to the alternator with pieces of numbered tape, then disconnect the wires. Remove the rear alternator brace and detach the alternator.
13   Remove the alternator bracket.

Both covers

Refer to illustration 3.16

14   Mark the spark plug wires with tape to facilitate reassembly, then disconnect the wires and lay them out of the way.
15   Move aside any wires and hoses that may interfere with valve cover removal.
16   Remove the valve cover bolts **(see illustration)**.
17   Remove the valve cover(s). **Note:** *If the cover sticks to the cylinder head, use a block of wood and a hammer to dislodge it. If the cover still will not come loose, pry on it carefully, but do not damage or distort the sealing flange surface.*

Installation

18   Clean the valve cover and cylinder head mating surfaces with a scraper and solvent or degreaser. Be sure to remove all traces of old gasket material and sealant.
19   Apply a 1/8-inch dab of RTV sealant to the intake manifold-to-cylinder head notch at each end of the engine.
20   Install a new valve cover gasket. It may be helpful to "glue" the gasket to the valve cover using a small amount of sealant. Make sure the bolt holes in the gasket line up with the holes in the cover.
21   Place the valve cover on the cylinder head while the sealant is still wet and install the mounting bolts. Tighten the bolts a little at a time to the torque listed in this Chapter's Specifications.
22   Complete the job by reversing the removal procedure. Run the engine and check for leaks.

4   Valve train components - replacement (cylinder head installed)

This procedure is essentially the same as for the 2.5L four-cylinder engine. Follow the procedure in Chapter 2, Part C, except note that the valve seals, which are pressed onto the valve guide protrusion on the cylinder head, are removed differently. GM recommends using a special valve seal removal tool to avoid seal damage, although a pair of pliers will work, since the old seal is always discarded. Install the new seal before installing the spring and retainer, and note that intake and exhaust valve seals are different.

5   Intake manifold - removal and installation

Warning: *Gasoline is extremely flammable, so take extra precautions when you work on any part of the fuel system. Don't smoke or allow open flames or bare light bulbs near the work area, and don't work in a garage where a natural gas-type appliance (such as a water heater or clothes dryer) with a pilot light is present. Since gasoline is carcinogenic, wear latex gloves when there's a possibility of being exposed to fuel, and, if you spill any fuel on your skin, rinse it off immediately with soap and water. Mop up any spills immediately and do not store fuel-soaked rags where they could ignite. The fuel system is under constant pressure, so, if any fuel lines are to be disconnected, the fuel pressure in the system must be relieved first (see Chapter 4 for more information). When you perform any kind of work on the fuel system, wear safety glasses and have a Class B type fire extinguisher on hand.*

Removal

Refer to illustrations 5.16 and 5.18

1   If the vehicle is equipped with air conditioning, carefully examine the routing of the hoses and the mounting of the compressor. You may be able to remove the intake manifold without disconnecting the system (this may involve unbolting the air conditioning compressor and setting it aside, without disconnecting the lines). If you are in doubt, take the vehicle to a dealer service department or automotive air conditioning shop to have the system depressurized. Do not, under any circumstances, disconnect the hoses while the system is under pressure.

2   Relieve the fuel system pressure (see Chapter 4).

3   Disconnect the cable from the negative battery terminal. **Caution:** *If the vehicle is equipped with a Delco Loc II audio system, make sure you have the correct activation code before disconnecting the battery. See the information at the front of this manual for the radio re-activation procedure.*

4   Drain the coolant from the radiator (see

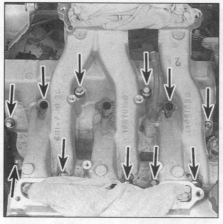

5.16 Intake manifold mounting bolt/nut locations (arrows)

Chapter 1).

5   Remove the air intake plenum (upper intake manifold) (see Chapter 4, Section 15).

6   Place a jack, with a wood block on the jack head to serve as a cushion, under the oil pan to support the engine weight. Remove the right (passenger's side) engine mount (see Section 17).

7   Remove the serpentine drivebelt (see Chapter 1), then remove the power steering pump without disconnecting the hoses and set it aside, being careful not to spill any fluid (see Chapter 10).

8   Remove the alternator and bracket (see Chapter 5).

9   Remove the EGR valve.

10   Disconnect the fuel lines and remove the fuel rail (see Chapter 4).

11   Remove the valve covers (see Section 3).

12   Remove the upper radiator hose from the thermostat housing on the manifold.

13   Disconnect the heater hose at the manifold.

14   Make sure that all wires, vacuum hoses and coolant hoses that would interfere with manifold removal have been disconnected.

16   Remove the lower intake manifold mounting bolts **(see illustration)**.

17   Separate the manifold from the engine by prying with a suitable bar (do not pry

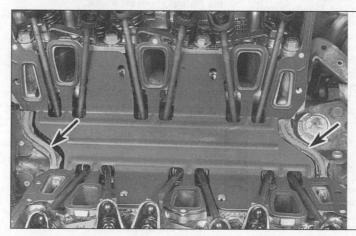

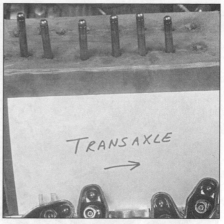

5.18 A perforated cardboard box can be used to store the pushrods to ensure they are reinstalled in their original locations - note the label indicating the transaxle end of the engine

between the mating surfaces) or tapping the manifold with a hammer and wooden block to loosen it.

18   Loosen the rocker arm nuts, rotate the rocker arms out of the way and remove the pushrods that go through the manifold gasket. Store the pushrods separately to ensure reinstallation in the same positions **(see illustration)**.

Installation

Refer to illustration 5.21

19   If a new manifold is being installed, transfer the external components from the old manifold to the new one.

20   Before installing the manifold, place clean, lint-free rags in the engine cavity and clean the engine block, cylinder head and manifold gasket surfaces. All gasket material and sealant must be removed prior to installation (a gasket scraper is very helpful). Remove all dirt and gasket remnants from the engine cavity.

21   Clean the gasket sealing surfaces with degreaser, then apply a 3/16-inch diameter bead of RTV sealant to the engine block end ridges only **(see illustration)**.

22   Install the new intake gaskets on the

5.21 Apply a 3/16-inch bead of RTV sealant (arrows) to the front and rear ridges of the engine block

2D

7.1 Remove the bolts (A) and pull up the roller lifter guides (B)

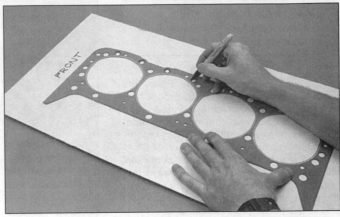

8.7 To avoid mixing up the head bolts, use the new gasket to transfer the bolt hole pattern to a piece of cardboard, then punch holes in the cardboard to accept the bolts

cylinder heads. Notice that the gaskets are normally marked Right and Left. Be sure to use the correct gasket on each cylinder head.

23   Install the pushrods in their original locations and reposition the rocker arms on the pushrods. Tighten the rocker arm nuts to the torque listed in this Chapter's Specifications.

24   Hold the gaskets in place by extending the bead of RTV 1/4-inch onto the gasket ends.

25   Carefully lower the intake manifold into position, making sure that you do not disturb the gaskets.

26   Install the intake manifold mounting bolts and tighten them a little at a time until they are all at the torque listed in this Chapter's Specifications.

27   Install the remaining components in the reverse order of removal.

28   Fill the radiator with coolant (see Chapter 1), start the engine and check for leaks.

6   Exhaust manifolds - removal and installation

Warning: *The engine must be completely cool before beginning this procedure.*

1   Remove the cable from the negative battery terminal. **Caution:** *If the vehicle is equipped with a Delco Loc II audio system, make sure you have the correct activation code before disconnecting the battery. See the information at the front of this manual for the radio re-activation procedure.*

2   Disconnect the top half of the air intake duct at the throttle body.

3   Remove the EGR pipe. Remove the bolts retaining the crossover pipe to the manifolds, then disconnect the pipe from the manifolds.

Rear manifold

4   Raise the front of the vehicle and support it securely on jackstands. Block the rear wheels to keep the vehicle from rolling.

5   Remove the bolts attaching the exhaust pipe to the exhaust manifold, then separate

the pipe from the manifold.

6   Remove the catalytic converter heat shield.

7   Disconnect the oxygen sensor electrical connector.

8   Remove the transaxle dipstick and fill tube.

9   Disconnect the spark plug wires from the spark plugs, labeling them as they are disconnected to simplify installation.

10   Remove the exhaust manifold mounting nuts, separate the manifold from the engine and remove from under the vehicle.

11   Installation is the reverse of the removal procedure. Before installing the manifold, be sure to thoroughly clean the mating surfaces on the manifold and cylinder head. Tighten the fasteners to the torque listed in this Chapter's Specifications.

Front manifold

12   Remove the radiator cooling fans (see Chapter 3).

13   Remove the engine oil dipstick and dipstick tube.

14   Remove the exhaust manifold heat shields (upper and lower).

15   Disconnect and label any wires that will interfere with the removal of the manifold.

16   Remove the manifold nuts and separate the manifold from the engine.

17   Installation is the reverse of the removal procedure. Be sure to thoroughly clean the cylinder head and manifold surfaces before installing the manifold. Tighten the fasteners to the torque listed in this Chapter's Specifications.

7   Hydraulic lifters - removal, inspection and installation

Refer to illustration 7.1

This procedure is essentially the same as for the 2.5L four-cylinder engine with roller lifters. Refer to Chapter 2, Part C for the procedure, but follow the procedures in this Part for valve cover and intake manifold removal

and installation. Also refer to the accompanying illustration of the lifter guides **(see illustration)**.

8   Cylinder heads - removal and installation

Removal

Refer to illustrations 8.7 and 8.9

1   Remove the intake manifold (see Section 5).

2   Remove the exhaust manifolds (see Section 6).

3   If the front cylinder head is being taken off, remove the dipstick tube mounting bolt.

4   Raise the vehicle and place it securely on jackstands.

5   Locate the engine block drain plugs, remove them and drain the coolant.

6   Loosen the rocker arm nuts enough to allow removal of the pushrods, then remove the pushrods.

8.9 Use a tool such as a breaker bar inserted into an exhaust port to break the gasket seal on the cylinder head - since the head is aluminum, use care not to damage the port

8.10a Remove the old gasket and carefully scrape off all old gasket material and sealant

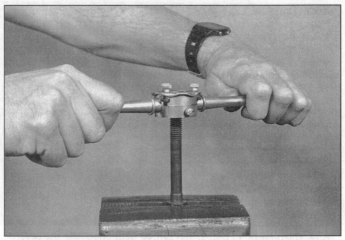

8.10b Use the correct die to clean the cylinder head bolt threads prior to installation

2D

8.11a Position the new gasket over the dowel pins (arrows) . . .

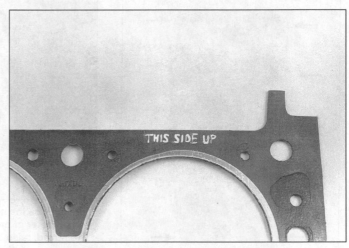

8.11b . . . with the correct side facing up

7   Using a new head gasket, outline the cylinders and bolt pattern on a piece of cardboard **(see illustration)**. Be sure to indicate the front (timing chain end) of the engine for reference. Punch holes at the bolt locations.

8   Loosen the head bolts in a sequence opposite to the one used for tightening **(see illustration 8.14)**. Remove and store the bolts in the cardboard holder as they're removed.

9   Remove the cylinder heads. To break the gasket seal, insert a bar into one of the exhaust ports, then carefully lift on the tool **(see illustration)**. If this is not possible, pry between the cylinder block and a casting protrusion on the cylinder head - NOT between the block and head mating surfaces.

Installation

Refer to illustrations 8.10a, 8.10b, 8.11a, 8.11b, 8.13 and 8.14

10   If a new cylinder head is being installed, transfer the various components, such as the manifold, brackets and coolant temperature sensor, from the old head. Before installing the new head, use a gasket scraper to clean

the gasket surfaces of both the head and the engine block **(see illustration)** and make sure they're free of nicks and scratches. Also, the threads in the block and on the head bolts must be completely clean, as any dirt or sealant in the threads will affect bolt torque. Taps and dies can be used to clean the bolt holes and bolts **(see illustration)**. Gasket removal solvents are commonly available at

auto parts stores and may prove helpful.

11   Place the gaskets in position over the locating dowels, with the note *This Side Up* visible **(see illustrations)**.

12   Position the cylinder heads over the gaskets.

13   Coat the cylinder head bolts with an appropriate sealant and install the bolts **(see illustration)**.

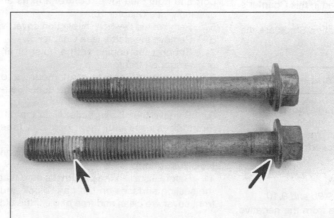

8.13 Two different length cylinder head bolts are used - apply sealant to the threads and the underside of the bolt heads (arrows)

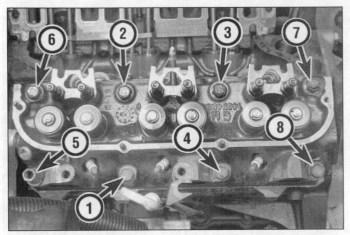

8.14 Cylinder head bolt TIGHTENING sequence (use the reverse of this order for removing the bolts)

9.9a Remove the oil pan side bolts (arrows A indicate three on the radiator side) - also remove the oil filter bolts (B), if equipped

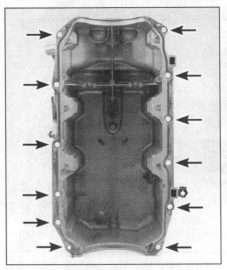

9.9b Remove the 12 oil pan-to-block bolts (arrows) - pan remove for clarity

9.10 Once the nuts/bolts around the perimeter of the oil pan have been removed, raise the engine and lower the oil pan

9.12 Apply a bead of RTV sealant on either side of the rear main cap, where the pan gasket will meet it (arrow)

14   Tighten the bolts in the proper sequence **(see illustration)** to the torque listed in this Chapter's Specifications. Work up to the final torque in two steps.

15   Install the pushrods, making sure the lower ends are in the lifter seats, place the rocker arm ends over the pushrods and install the rocker arms. Tighten the rocker arm nuts to the torque listed in this Chapter's Specifications.

16   The remaining installation Steps are the reverse of those for removal.

***

9   Oil pan - removal and installation

Note: *Most of the Steps in this procedure will not be required if the engine has been removed from the vehicle. The pan can simply be unbolted and removed, cleaned and installed as indicated.*

Removal

Refer to illustrations 9.9a, 9.9b and 9.10

1   Disconnect the cable from the negative battery terminal. **Caution:** *If the vehicle is equipped with a Delco Loc II audio system, make sure you have the correct activation code before disconnecting the battery. See the information at the front of this manual for the radio re-activation procedure.*

2   Raise the vehicle and support it on jackstands.

3   Drain the engine oil (see Chapter 1).

4   Remove the right side suspension support and right side lower control arm as an assembly (see Chapter 10).

5   Remove the flywheel inspection cover.

6   Remove the starter (see Chapter 5).

7   Support the engine with a hoist or an engine support fixture.

8   Remove the engine strut mount and mount bracket-to-engine bolts (see Section 17).

9   Remove the oil pan bolts. Note the different sizes used and their locations **(see illustrations)**.

10   Raise the engine and remove the oil pan **(see illustration)**.

11   Before installing the pan, make sure that the sealing surfaces on the pan, block and front cover are clean and free of oil. If the old pan is being reinstalled, make sure that all sealant has been removed from the pan sealing flange and from the blind attaching holes. Gasket removal solvents are available at auto parts stores and may be helpful. Make sure all of the bolts are clean and that the pan sealing flanges are straight.

Installation

Refer to installation 9.12

12   Apply a bead of RTV sealant to the front of the gasket, where it contacts the front cover and also to the rear of the gasket, where the rear main bearing cap meets the engine block **(see illustration)**, then install the new gasket on the pan carefully so it does not fall out of position when installed.

13   Lift the pan into position and install all bolts finger tight. Tighten the mounting bolts, working from the center out, to the torque listed in this Chapter's Specifications. Then tighten the side bolts, working from the center out, to the torque listed in this Chapter's Specifications.

14   Follow the removal steps in reverse order. Fill the crankcase with the correct grade and quantity of oil (see Chapter 1), start the engine and check for leaks.

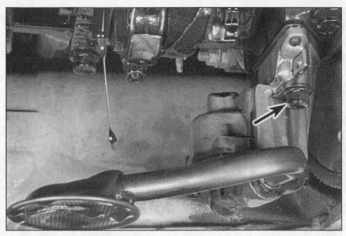

10.2 Remove the oil pump-to-rear main bearing cap bolt (arrow)

11.3 Use a screwdriver to pry the rear main oil seal from the bore (be careful not to scratch the crankshaft sealing surface or the edge of the bore)

10 Oil pump - removal and installation

Refer to illustration 10.2

1   Remove the oil pan (see Section 9).
2   Remove the pump-to-rear main bearing cap bolt and separate the pump and pump driveshaft from the engine **(see illustration)**.
3   Considering the relatively reasonable cost of a new oil pump compared with the potential of major engine damage if the oil pump malfunctions, we recommend replacing the oil pump any time it's removed. Inspect the driveshaft for any wear in the areas where it fits into the drive gear and oil pump. Also inspect the shaft for twisting damage. Replace it if there's any wear or damage. Again, we recommend replacing the shaft as a matter of course whenever it's removed, since shaft failure means a complete loss in oil pressure.
4   To install the pump, move it into position and align the top end of the driveshaft with the hexagonal socket in the lower end of the drive gear.
5   Install the oil pump-to-rear main bearing cap bolt and tighten it to the torque listed in this Chapter's Specifications.
6   Reinstall the oil pan.

11 Rear main oil seal - replacement (engine in vehicle)

Warning: *A special tool is available to support the engine during repair operations. Similar fixtures are available from rental yards. Improper lifting methods or devices are hazardous and could result in severe injury or death. DO NOT place any part of your body under the engine/transaxle when it's supported only by a jack. Failure of the lifting device could result in serious injury or death.*
Note: *The rear main bearing oil seal is a one piece unit that can be replaced without removing the oil pan or crankshaft. However, the transaxle must be removed and the*

engine must be supported as this procedure is done. A special tool is available for the seal installation, but the procedures are also outlined here to avoid having to use the tool.

Removal

Refer to illustration 11.3

1   Remove the transaxle (see Chapter 7).
2   Remove the flywheel/driveplate (see Chapter 2, Part A, Section 22).
3   Pry out the old seal **(see illustration)**, taking care not to mar the crankshaft or seal bore surfaces. Inspect the crankshaft for scratches, burrs and nicks on the sealing surface.

Installation

With a seal driver

4   Lubricate the seal bore, seal lip and sealing surface on the crankshaft with engine oil. Slide the seal over the mandrel on the tool until the dust lip on the seal bottoms squarely against the collar on the tool.
5   Position the dowel pin on the tool in the alignment hole in the crankshaft and secure the tool to the crankshaft.
6   Turn the T-handle of the tool until the collar pushes the seal completely into the bore. Make sure the seal is installed squarely.
7   To complete the operation, install the flywheel (or driveplate) and transaxle, then start the engine and check for leaks.

Without a seal driver

Refer to illustration 11.10

8   Remove all traces of oil from the engine block seal bore and check the seal contact surface on the crankshaft for scratches and burrs that could damage the new seal. If the crankshaft is damaged, a new or different crankshaft may have to be installed.
9   Lubricate the seal bore, seal lip and sealing surface on the crankshaft with engine oil.
10   Insert the new seal squarely into the bore and tap it into place until it's completely seated **(see illustration)**. Be very careful not to damage the seal in the process and make sure it's driven in squarely.

11.10 Tap around the outer edge of the new seal with a hammer and a blunt drift to seat it squarely in the bore

11   To complete the operation, install the flywheel (or driveplate) and transaxle, then start the engine and check for leaks.

12 Vibration damper - removal and installation

Refer to illustrations 12.6 and 12.7

Removal

1   Disconnect the negative cable at the battery. **Caution:** *If the vehicle is equipped with a Delco Loc II audio system, make sure you have the correct activation code before disconnecting the battery. See the information at the front of this manual for the radio re-activation procedure.*
2   Loosen the accessory drivebelt adjusting bolts as necessary, then remove the drivebelts, tagging each one as it is removed to simplify reinstallation.
3   Loosen the lug nuts on the right front wheel, then raise the vehicle and support it securely on jackstands.
4   Remove the right front wheel and the

right inner fender splash shield for access to the damper.

5   Remove the serpentine belt.

6   Remove the center bolt from the vibration damper **(see illustration)**. The crankshaft will probably rotate, since the bolt is very tight. Wedge a large screwdriver into the ring gear teeth on the flywheel/driveplate to keep the crankshaft from rotating.

7   Attach a puller to the damper. Draw the damper off the crankshaft, being careful not to drop it as it breaks free **(see illustration)**. A common gear puller should not be used to draw the damper off, as it may separate the outer portion of the damper from the hub. Use only a puller that bolts to the hub.

Installation

8   Before installing the damper, coat the front cover seal area on the damper with clean engine oil.

9   Place the damper in position over the key on the crankshaft. Make sure the damper keyway lines up with the key.

10   Using a damper installation tool push the damper onto the crankshaft. The special tool distributes the pressure evenly around the hub.

11   Remove the installation tool and install the damper retaining bolt. Tighten the bolt to the torque listed in this Chapter's Specifications.

12   Follow the removal procedure in the reverse order for the remaining components.

---

13   Crankcase front cover - removal and installation

Refer to illustrations 13.4 and 13.14

Removal

1   Disconnect the cable from the negative battery terminal. **Caution:** *If the vehicle is equipped with a Delco Loc II audio system, make sure you have the correct activation code before disconnecting the battery. See the information at the front of this manual for*

12.6 Remove the vibration damper-to-crankshaft bolt (arrow) - it's very tight, so use a six-point socket and a breaker bar

12.7 Use a puller that bolts to the vibration damper hub; jaw-type pullers will damage the vibration damper

the radio re-activation procedure.

2   Drain the cooling system (see Chapter 1).

3   Remove the serpentine belt (see Chapter 1).

4   Remove the serpentine belt tensioner **(see illustration)**.

5   Unbolt the alternator and position it aside.

6   Unbolt the power steering pump and move it aside. It is not necessary to disconnect the power steering hoses.

7   Using a suitable support fixture, support the engine from above and remove the front engine mount bracket (see Section 17). Raise the vehicle and support it on jackstands.

8   Remove the vibration damper (see Section 12).

9   Drain the engine oil and remove the oil pan (see Section 9).

10   Remove the lower front cover bolts.

11   Lower the vehicle.

12   Disconnect the radiator hose at the water pump.

13   Disconnect the heater hose, bypass and overflow hoses, and position them aside.

14   Remove the remaining front cover bolts

and separate the cover from the engine block **(see illustration)**. If the cover sticks, break it loose with a soft-face hammer, but do not pry between the sealing surfaces.

Installation

15   Clean all traces of old gasket material from the front cover and engine block mating surfaces.

16   Install a new front cover gasket and apply RTV sealant to the bottom ends of the gasket.

17   Place the front cover in position and install the upper mounting bolts.

18   Once again, raise the vehicle and support it on jackstands.

19   Install the lower cover mounting bolts and tighten them to the torque listed in this Chapter's Specifications.

20   Tighten the upper bolts to the torque listed in this Chapter's Specifications.

21   Install the crankshaft damper pulley.

22   Lower the vehicle. Install the engine support bracket.

23   Reconnect the heater hose, radiator hose, and bypass and overflow hoses.

24   Install the power steering pump.

13.4 The drivebelt tensioner retaining bolt

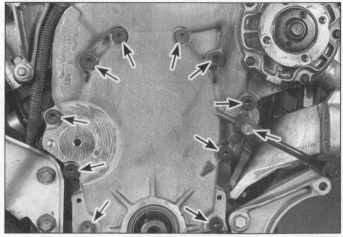

13.14 Front cover bolt locations

14.1 Carefully pry the old seal out of the front cover - don't damage the crankshaft

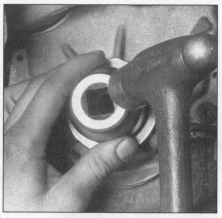

14.3 Drive the new seal into place with a large socket and hammer

14.7 Support the front cover properly, and drive the seal out of the front cover

14.9 Install the front oil seal with a wood block and hammer

25   Install the alternator.

26   Install the belt tensioner and serpentine belt.

27   Fill the cooling system with the proper antifreeze solution (see Chapter 1). Do not install the cooling system pressure cap at this time

28   Reconnect the battery cable and start the engine. Allow it to run until the upper radiator hose becomes warm to the touch, indicating that the thermostat has opened.

29   Stop the engine and check the coolant level. Add coolant as necessary, install the pressure cap and check for leaks.

14   Front cover oil seal - replacement

Note: *Always inspect the seal contact area on the vibration damper as part of this procedure. If there is a groove on the damper (caused by wear from contacting the seal), the new seal will probably leak. Auto parts stores may stock sleeves to fit over the damaged area, restoring a flat contact surface. If a sleeve is not available, the only alternative is a new vibration damper.*

With front cover installed

Refer to illustrations 14.1 and 14.3

Note: *This method is not preferred, since it's more difficult to perform. However, it saves much time and effort if the front cover does not need to be removed.*

1   With the vibration damper removed (see Section 12), pry the old seal out of the crankcase front cover with a seal removal tool or screwdriver **(see illustration)**. Be careful not to damage the surface of the crankshaft or the seal bore. If you're using a screwdriver, it's a good idea to wrap the tip with tape to prevent damaging the crankshaft or seal bore.

2   Coat the inside and outside diameter of the new seal with engine oil. Place the new seal in position with the open end of the seal (seal lip) toward the engine.

3   Drive the seal into the cover until it is

seated. A section of large-diameter pipe or a large socket can be used if a proper seal driver is not available. Be careful not to distort the front cover **(see illustration)**.

4   Install all components previously removed. Run the engine and check for leaks.

With front cover removed

Refer to illustrations 14.7 and 14.9

5   This is preferred, as the cover can be supported while the old seal is removed and the new one is installed.

6   Remove the front cover (see Section 13).

7   Using a large screwdriver, pry the old seal out of the front cover. Alternatively, support the cover and drive the seal out from the rear **(see illustration)**. Be careful not to damage the cover.

8   Coat the inside lip and the outside circumference of the new seal with engine oil. With the front of the cover facing up, place the new seal in position with the open end (lip) of the seal toward the inside of the cover.

9   Using a wooden block and hammer, drive the new seal into the cover until it's completely seated **(see illustration)**.

10   Install the cover by reversing the removal procedure. Run the engine and check for leaks.

15   Timing chain and sprockets - inspection, removal and installation

Refer to illustrations 15.9 and 15.10

1   Disconnect the cable from the negative battery terminal. **Caution:** *If the vehicle is equipped with a Delco Loc II audio system, make sure you have the correct activation code before disconnecting the battery. See the information at the front of this manual for the radio re-activation procedure.*

2   Remove the vibration damper (see Section 12).

3   Remove the crankcase front cover (see Section 13).

Inspection

4   Before removing the chain and sprockets, visually inspect the teeth on the sprockets for signs of wear and the chain for looseness. Check the condition of the timing chain damper.

5   It either or both sprockets show any signs of wear (edges on the teeth of the camshaft sprocket not "square," bright blue areas on the teeth of either sprocket, chipping, pitting, etc.), they should be replaced with new ones. Wear in these areas is very common.

6   Failure to replace a worn timing chain may result in erratic engine performance, loss of power and lowered gas mileage.

7   If any one component requires replacement, all related components, including the damper, should be replaced as well.

8   If it is determined that the timing components require replacement, proceed as follows. **Note:** *Considering how time consuming it is to change the chain and sprockets, we recommend doing so whenever they are removed.*

2D

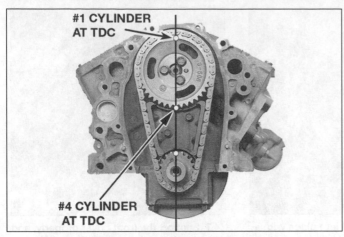

15.9 Proper alignment of the camshaft and crankshaft timing marks

15.10 Remove the three camshaft gear retaining bolts

Removal

9   Rotate the crankshaft until the marks on the camshaft and crankshaft are in exact alignment (this can be done by re-installing the vibration damper bolt into the end of the crankshaft and using a socket and breaker bar to turn it). At this point the number one and four pistons will be at top dead center with the number four piston in the firing position (this can be verified by removing the number four spark plug and feeling for compression at the spark plug hole as the crankshaft is rotated). Do not attempt to remove either sprocket or the timing chain until this is done and do not turn the crankshaft or camshaft after the sprockets and chain are removed **(see illustration)**.

10   Remove the three camshaft sprocket retaining bolts and lift the camshaft sprocket and timing chain off the front of the engine. It may be necessary to tap the sprocket with a soft-face hammer to dislodge it **(see illustration)**.

11   If it is necessary to remove the crankshaft sprocket, it can be withdrawn from the crankshaft with a puller.

Installation

12   Push the crankshaft sprocket onto the nose of the crankshaft, aligning it with the key, until it seats against the shoulder.

13   Install the timing chain over the camshaft sprocket with the slack in the chain hanging down over the crankshaft sprocket. Draw the camshaft sprocket up to engage the crankshaft sprocket with the chain. The timing marks should be aligned for number four TDC, as shown in illustration 15.9.

14   Install the camshaft sprocket draw it into place with the three retaining bolts. Do not hammer or attempt to drive the camshaft sprocket into place, as it could damage the cam plate at the rear of the engine.

15   With the chain and both sprockets in place, check again to ensure that the timing marks on the two sprockets are properly aligned. If not, remove the timing chain and cam sprocket, turn the camshaft enough to change the chain position on the crankshaft sprocket one tooth, reinstall the chain and camshaft sprocket and check the timing mark alignment. Repeat as necessary until the marks are in alignment.

16   Lubricate the chain with engine oil and install the remaining components in the reverse order of removal.

16   Camshaft - removal and installation

Since the engine must be removed from the vehicle for this procedure, the procedure is covered in Chapter 2, Part F.

17   Engine mounts - check and replacement

Refer to Chapter 2, Part B for the engine mount check and replacement procedure.

Chapter 2 Part E
3.0 and 3.3L V6 engines

Contents

2E

Specifications

General

Firing order	1-6-5-4-3-2
Cylinder numbers (drivebelt end-to-transaxle end)	
Front bank	1-3-5
Rear bank	2-4-6

Oil pump service limits

Outer gear diameter	3.497 to 3.500 inches
Outer gear-to-housing clearance	0.008 to 0.015 inch
Inner gear diameter	2.839 inches
Inner gear tip clearance	0.006 inch
Gear pocket depth	0.461 to 0.4625 inch
Gear pocket diameter	3.508 to 3.512 inches
Gear end clearance	0.001 to 0.0035 inch
Pump cover warpage limit	0.002 inch

3.0L V6 engine

38025-2E-specs HAYNES

Torque specifications

	Ft-lbs (unless otherwise indicated)
Camshaft sprocket-to-camshaft bolts	
1990 and earlier	26
1991 and later	74 plus an additional 105-degrees rotation
Crankshaft balancer bolt	
1991 and earlier	200 to 225
1992 and later	110 plus an additional 76-degrees rotation
Cylinder head bolts	
3.0L engine	
Step 1	25
Step 2	Turn an additional 90-degrees
Step 3	Turn an additional 90-degrees
(**Caution:** *If a torque value of 60 ft-lbs is attained during step 2 or 3, stop at this point. Do not continue to tighten the bolt*)	
3.3L engine	
Step 1	35
Step 2	Turn an additional 130-degrees
Step 3 (four center bolts only)	Turn an additional 30-degrees

FRONT
↓

38025-2E-specs HAYNES

3.3L V6 engine

Cylinder number locations and coil terminal positions

Torque specifications (continued)

	Ft-lbs (unless otherwise indicated)
Driveplate or flywheel-to-crankshaft bolts	
1989 and earlier	60
1990 and 1991	84 inch-lbs plus an additional 90-degrees rotation
1992 and later	132 inch-lbs plus an additional 50-degrees rotation
Intake manifold bolts	
1988 and earlier	32
1989 and later	88 in-lbs (tighten twice in the proper sequence)
Exhaust manifold bolts	
1988 and earlier	37
1989 and later	30
Oil pan bolts	144 inch-lbs
Oil pump	
Cover bolts	120 inch-lbs
Pressure regulator retainer bolt	35
Rocker arm pedestal bolts	
1988 and earlier	43
1989 through 1992	28
1993 and later	18 plus an additional 70-degrees of rotation
Timing chain cover bolts	22
Timing chain dampener bolt	
1988 and earlier	168 inch-lbs
1999 and later	16
Valve cover-to-cylinder head (nuts/bolts)	88 inch-lbs

1   General information

This Part of Chapter 2 covers in-vehicle repair procedures for the 3.0 and 3.3 liter V6 engines.

Information concerning engine removal and installation, as well as engine block and cylinder head overhaul, is in Part F of this Chapter.

The following repair procedures are based on the assumption that the engine is installed in the vehicle. If the engine has been removed from the vehicle and mounted on a stand, many of the steps included in this Part of Chapter 2 will not apply.

The Specifications included in this Part of Chapter 2 apply only to the engine and procedures in this Part. The Specifications necessary for rebuilding the block and cylinder heads are found in Part F.

2   Repair operations possible with the engine in the vehicle

Warning: *Before working in the vicinity of airbag components (on models so equipped) refer to Chapter 12 for the airbag system disarming procedure. Use care not to damage any wiring or sensors associated with this system or the airbag may deploy when reconnecting the battery or fail to deploy in the event of an accident.*

Many major repair operations can be accomplished without removing the engine from the vehicle.

Clean the engine compartment and the exterior of the engine with some type of pressure washer before any work is done. A clean engine will make the job easier and will help keep dirt out of the internal areas of the engine. **Caution:** *Don't pressure wash any*

electronic components or control units. On distributorless ignition models, if any spark plug hole fills with water, it will ground the corresponding plug (on the same coil section). So if the front three plugs or wires ground, none of the spark plugs will fire. If the engine won't start after washing it, make certain ALL of the spark plugs and wires are completely dry. Water can also short the ignition module and other electronic control units causing them to completely fail.

Depending on the components involved, it may be a good idea to remove the hood to improve access to the engine (refer to Chapter 11 if necessary).

If vacuum, exhaust, oil or coolant leaks develop, indicating a need for gasket or seal replacement, the repairs can generally be made with the engine in the vehicle. The intake and exhaust manifold gaskets, oil pan gasket and cylinder head gaskets are all accessible with the engine in place.

Exterior engine components such as the intake and exhaust manifolds, the oil pan, the oil pump, the water pump, the starter motor, the alternator, the distributor and the fuel injection system can be removed for repair with the engine in place. The timing chain and sprockets can also be replaced with the engine in the vehicle, but the camshaft cannot be removed.

Since the cylinder heads can be removed without pulling the engine, valve component servicing can also be accomplished with the engine in the vehicle.

In extreme cases caused by a lack of necessary equipment, repair or replacement of piston rings, pistons, connecting rods and rod bearings is possible with the engine in the vehicle. However, this practice is not recommended because of the cleaning and preparation work that must be done to the components involved.

3   Valve covers - removal and installation

Refer to illustrations 3.8 and 3.16

1   Disconnect the cable from the negative battery terminal. **Caution:** *If the vehicle is equipped with a Delco Loc II audio system, make sure you have the correct activation code before disconnecting the battery. See the information at the front of this manual for the radio re-activation procedure.*

Removal - right side (rear) cover

2   Remove the serpentine drivebelt (see Chapter 1).

3   On 1988 and earlier models, remove the ignition coil module and wiring (see Chapter 5) and the EGR solenoid, wiring and vacuum hoses (see Chapter 6).

4   On 1988 and earlier models, remove the rear alternator mount bolt, rotate the alternator toward the front of the vehicle and remove the engine lift bracket and rear alternator brace.

5   On 1988 and earlier models, remove the drivebelt tensioner assembly.

6   On 1989 and later models, loosen the power steering pump bolts, slide the pump forward and remove the power steering pump braces.

7   Remove the spark plug wires from the spark plugs (see Chapter 1). Be sure to label each wire before removal to ensure correct reinstallation. Remove the spark plug wire cover and position the harness out of the way.

8   On 1988 and earlier models, drain at least three quarts of coolant from the radiator (see Chapter 1) and disconnect the coolant hoses at the throttle body **(see illustration)**.

3.8 On 1988 and earlier models, you may have to remove the throttle body to gain access to the hose clamp screws (arrows)

3.16 Tighten the valve cover retaining nuts evenly and in several steps (arrows)

2E

Note: *You may have to remove the throttle body to gain access to the hose clamp screws (see Chapter 4).*

9   Remove the valve cover mounting nuts or bolts and remove the valve cover. **Note:** *If the cover sticks to the cylinder head, use a wood block and a hammer to dislodge it. If the cover still won't come loose, pry on it carefully, but don't distort the sealing flange.*

Removal - left-side (front) cover

10   On 1988 and earlier models, remove the PCV pipe.
11   On 1989 and later models, remove the serpentine drivebelt and the alternator brace.
12   Remove the spark plug wires from the spark plugs (see Chapter 1). Be sure to label each wire before removal to ensure correct reinstallation. Remove the spark plug wire cover and position the harness out of the way.
13   Remove the valve cover mounting nuts and remove the valve cover. **Note:** *If the cover sticks to the cylinder head, use a wood block and a hammer to dislodge it. If the cover still won't come loose, pry on it carefully, but don't distort the sealing flange.*

Installation - both covers

14   The mating surfaces of each cylinder head and valve cover must be perfectly clean when the covers are installed. Use a gasket scraper to remove all traces of sealant or old gasket, then clean the mating surfaces with lacquer thinner or acetone (if there's sealant or oil on the mating surfaces when the cover is installed, oil leaks may develop). Most valve covers are made of aluminum, so be extra careful not to nick or gouge the mating surfaces with the scraper.
15   Clean the mounting bolt/nut threads with a die to remove any corrosion or sealer and restore damaged threads.
16   Place the valve cover and new gasket in position, then install the bolts or the new rubber grommets, washers and mounting nuts **(see illustration)**. Tighten the bolt/nuts in

5.2 Loosen the rocker arm bolts

several steps to the torque listed in this Chapter's Specifications.
17   The remainder of installation is the reverse of the removal procedure. Start the engine and check carefully for oil leaks at the valve cover-to-head joints.

---

4   Valve springs, retainers and seals - replacement

This procedure is essentially the same as for the 2.5L four-cylinder engine. Refer to Chapter 2, Part C, except note that many models use a valve seal only on the intake valve. Also note that the rocker arms must be removed (see Section 5) before the springs can be compressed.

---

5   Rocker arms and pushrods - removal, inspection and installation

Removal

Refer to illustrations 5.2 and 5.3
1   Refer to Section 3 and detach the valve

5.3 A perforated cardboard box can be used to store the pushrods to ensure that they're reinstalled in their original locations - note the label indicating the front (drivebelt end) of the engine

covers from the cylinder heads.
2   Loosen the rocker arm pedestal bolts and remove the bolts, pedestals, rocker arms and pedestal retainers **(see illustration)**. Store each set of valve components separately in a marked plastic bag to ensure that they're reinstalled in their original locations.
3   Remove the pushrods and store them separately to make sure they don't get mixed up during installation **(see illustration)**. Also keep track of which end of the pushrod faces up, since the wear patterns at the pushrod ends must match their respective lifter and rocker arm.

Inspection

4   Check each rocker arm for wear, cracks and other damage, especially where the pushrods and valve stems contact the rocker arm. Keep track of the rocker arm positions, since they must be returned to the same locations. Put the rocker arms (along with their pedestals) in separate labeled bags.

6.13a Remove the vacuum line bracket nut . . .

6.13b . . . and remove the vacuum hoses from the fitting

6.15 Note the locations of the mounting studs prior to manifold removal

5   Check the pedestal seat in each rocker arm and the pedestal faces. Look for galling, stress cracks and unusual wear patterns. If the rocker arms are worn or damaged, replace the rocker arm and pedestal as an assembly.

6   Make sure the hole at the pushrod end of each rocker arm is open.

7   Inspect the pushrods for cracks and excessive wear at the ends. Roll each pushrod across a piece of plate glass to see if it's bent (if it wobbles, it's bent).

Installation

8   Lubricate the lower end of each pushrod with clean engine oil or moly-base grease and install them in their original locations. Make sure each pushrod seats completely in the lifter socket.

9   Apply moly-base grease to the ends of the valve stems and the upper ends of the pushrods.

10   Apply moly-base grease to the pedestal faces to prevent damage to the mating surfaces before the engine has oil pressure. Install the rocker arm components. Tighten the bolts to the torque listed in this Chapter's Specifications. As the bolts are tightened, make sure the pushrods engage properly in the rocker arms.

11   Install the valve covers.

6   Intake manifold - removal and installation

Warning: *Gasoline is extremely flammable, so take extra precautions when you work on any part of the fuel system. Don't smoke or allow open flames or bare light bulbs near the work area, and don't work in a garage where a natural gas-type appliance (such as a water heater or clothes dryer) with a pilot light is present. If you spill any fuel on your skin, rinse it off immediately with soap and water. When you perform any kind of work on the fuel system, wear safety glasses and have a Class B type fire extinguisher on hand.*

Removal

Refer to illustrations 6.13a, 6.13b and 6.15

1   Relieve the fuel system pressure (see Chapter 4).

2   Disconnect the cable from the negative battery terminal. **Caution:** *If the vehicle is equipped with a Delco Loc II audio system, make sure you have the correct activation code before disconnecting the battery. See the information at the front of this manual for the radio re-activation procedure.*

3   Remove the serpentine drivebelt (see Chapter 1).

4   Remove the mass airflow sensor and the air intake duct (see Chapter 4).

5   Remove the PCV valve from the intake manifold.

6   Remove the throttle and cruise control (if equipped) cable(s) from the manifold bracket.

7   Remove the transaxle throttle valve (TV) cable from the manifold bracket (automatic transaxle only) (see Chapter 7).

8   If it will interfere with manifold removal, remove the alternator and brackets (see Chapter 5).

9   Drain the cooling system (see Chapter 1).

10   Remove the spark plug wires that will interfere with manifold removal.

11   On 1988 and earlier models, disconnect the ignition module assembly (see Chapter 5) and set it aside.

12   Disconnect the upper radiator and coolant hoses at the manifold and throttle body.

13   Label and disconnect the fuel and vacuum lines **(see illustrations)** and electrical connectors at the manifold and throttle body. When disconnecting fuel line fittings, be prepared to catch some fuel, then cap the fittings to prevent contamination.

14   Remove the fuel rail and injectors (see Chapter 4).

15   Remove the manifold mounting bolts and separate the manifold from the engine **(see illustration)**. Do not pry between the manifold and heads, as damage to the gasket sealing surfaces may result. If a new manifold

6.16 Use a gasket scraper to remove all traces of sealant and old gasket material from the head and manifold mating surfaces

is being installed, transfer the EGR valve and all fittings and sensors to the new manifold.

Installation

Refer to illustrations 6.16 and 6.20

Note: *The mating surfaces of the cylinder heads, block and manifold must be perfectly clean when the manifold is installed. Gasket removal solvents in aerosol cans are available at most auto parts stores and may be helpful when removing old gasket material that's stuck to the heads and manifold (since the manifold is made of aluminum, aggressive scraping can cause damage). Be sure to follow the directions printed on the container.*

16   Use a gasket scraper to remove all traces of sealant and old gasket material **(see illustration)**, then clean the mating surfaces with lacquer thinner or acetone. If there is old sealant or oil on the mating surfaces when the manifold is installed, oil or vacuum leaks may develop. Use a vacuum cleaner to remove any gasket material that falls into the intake ports or the lifter valley.

17   Use a tap of the correct size to chase the threads in the bolt holes, then use com-

6.20 Intake manifold bolt tightening sequence

7.8 Exhaust manifold mounting details (engine removed for clarity) - note the oxygen sensor wire connector (arrow)

pressed air (if available) to remove the debris from the holes. **Warning:** *Wear safety glasses or a face shield to protect your eyes when using compressed air.*

18   If steel manifold gaskets are used, apply RTV sealant to both sides of the gaskets before positioning them on the heads. Apply RTV sealant to the ends of the new manifold-to-block seals, then install them. Make sure the pointed end of the seal fits snugly against both the head and block.

19   Carefully lower the manifold into place and install the mounting bolts finger tight. **Caution:** *Apply thread-locking compound to the intake manifold bolts before installation.*

20   Tighten the mounting bolts following the recommended sequence **(see illustration)**, to the torque listed in this Chapter's Specifications.

21   Install the remaining components in the reverse order of removal.

22   Change the oil and filter (see Chapter 1).

23   Fill the cooling system (see Chapter 1), start the engine and check for leaks.

---

7   Exhaust manifolds - removal and installation

---

1   Disconnect the negative battery cable. **Caution:** *If the vehicle is equipped with a Delco Loc II audio system, make sure you have the correct activation code before disconnecting the battery. See the information at the front of this manual for the radio re-activation procedure.*

Right (rear) manifold

Refer to illustration 7.8

2   On 1988 and earlier models, allow the engine to cool completely, then drain the coolant and remove the heater hoses and tubing above the exhaust manifold.

3   Remove the two nuts attaching the crossover pipe to the rear exhaust manifold.

4   Disconnect the spark plug wires from the rear plugs (see Chapter 1).

5   If necessary for clearance, remove the alternator (see Chapter 5).

6   If necessary for clearance, unbolt the power steering pump without removing the hoses and secure it to one side with a wire (see Chapter 10).

7   On 1988 and earlier models, remove the ignition module bracket nuts.

8   Remove the manifold heat shield and coolant tube brackets **(see illustration)**.

9   Set the parking brake, block the rear wheels and raise the front of the vehicle, supporting it securely on jackstands.

10   Working under the vehicle, remove the two exhaust pipe-to-manifold bolts. You may have to apply penetrating oil to the fastener threads - they're usually corroded.

11   Disconnect the oxygen sensor electrical connector, then lower the vehicle.

12   Remove the bolts and detach the manifold from the head.

13   Clean the mating surfaces to remove all traces of old sealant, then check for warpage and cracks. Warpage can be checked with a precision straightedge held against the mating flange. If a feeler gauge thicker than 0.030-inch can be inserted between the straightedge and flange surface, take the manifold to an automotive machine shop for resurfacing.

14   Place the manifold in position and install the bolts finger tight.

15   Starting in the middle and working out toward the ends, tighten the mounting bolts a little at a time until all of them are at the torque listed in this Chapter's Specifications.

16   Install the remaining components in the reverse order of removal.

17   Start the engine and check for exhaust leaks between the manifold and cylinder head and between the manifold and exhaust pipe.

Left (front) manifold

Refer to illustrations 7.24a and 7.24b

18   Remove the air cleaner duct.

19   Remove the cooling fan (see Chapter 3).

20   Unbolt the crossover pipe from the manifold.

21   Remove the dipstick tube hold-down nut and remove the dipstick tube out of the block.

22   Remove the spark plug wire cover and wires (see Chapter 1).

23   Remove the spark plugs to prevent breaking them.

24   Unbolt the heat shield. If turning the nuts causes the studs to turn and bend the shield **(see illustration)**, keep the stud from turning with a thin 14 mm open-end wrench or a pair of locking pliers **(see illustration)**.

7.24a When removing the nut, the stud may turn and distort the heat shield, so ...

7.24b ... hold the stud with a pair of pliers while loosening the nut

8.3 Remove the bolts holding the brackets to the cylinder head (arrows)

8.11 Pry the cylinder head loose at the rear corner to avoid damage to the gasket sealing surfaces

8.14 The cylinder head and block mating surfaces must be perfectly clean to ensure a good gasket seal

25   Unbolt and remove the exhaust manifold.
26   Follow Steps 13 through 17 above.

8   Cylinder heads - removal and installation

Removal

Refer to illustrations 8.3 and 8.11

1   Disconnect the cable from the negative battery terminal. **Caution:** *If the vehicle is equipped with a Delco Loc II audio system, make sure you have the correct activation code before disconnecting the battery. See the information at the front of this manual for the radio re-activation procedure.*
2   Remove the intake manifold as described in Section 6.
3   When removing the left (front) cylinder head, remove the dipstick tube retaining nut and remove the tube out of the block. Remove the alternator and the support brackets **(see illustration)**.
4   When removing the right cylinder head, remove the power steering pump and brackets (see Chapter 10). Remove the drivebelt tensioner.

5   Disconnect all wires and vacuum hoses from the cylinder head(s). Be sure to label them to simplify reinstallation.
6   Disconnect the spark plug wires and remove the spark plugs (see Chapter 1). Be sure to label the plug wires to simplify reinstallation.
7   Detach the exhaust manifolds from the cylinder heads (see Section 7).
8   Remove the valve covers (see Section 3).
9   Remove the rocker arms and pushrods (see Section 5).
10   Loosen the head bolts in 1/4-turn increments until they can be removed by hand. Work from bolt-to-bolt in a pattern that's the reverse of the tightening sequence shown in illustration 8.20. Remove the bolts.
11   Lift the head(s) off the engine. If resistance is felt, don't pry between the head(s) and block as damage to the mating surfaces will result. Recheck for head bolts that may have been overlooked, then use a hammer and wood block to tap the head(s) and break the gasket seal. Be careful because there are locating dowels in the block that position each head. As a last resort, pry each head up at the rear corner only and be careful not to damage anything **(see illustration)**. After

removal, place the head(s) on wood blocks to prevent damage to the gasket surfaces.
12   Refer to Chapter 2, Part F, for cylinder head disassembly, inspection and valve service procedures.

Installation

Refer to illustrations 8.14, 8.19 and 8.20

13   The mating surfaces of the cylinder heads and block must be perfectly clean when the heads are installed.
14   Use a gasket scraper to remove all traces of carbon and old gasket material, then clean the mating surfaces with lacquer thinner or acetone. If there's oil on the mating surfaces when the heads are installed, the gaskets may not seal correctly and leaks may develop. When working on the block, it's a real good idea to cover the lifter valley with shop rags to keep debris out of the engine. Use a shop rag or vacuum cleaner to remove any debris that falls into the cylinders **(see illustration)**.
15   Check the block and head mating surfaces for nicks, deep scratches and other damage. If damage is slight, it can be removed with a file; if it's excessive, machining may be the only alternative.

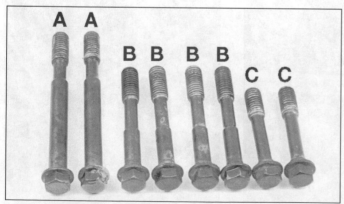

8.19 Head bolt locations (refer to illustration 8.20)

A   1 and 3   C   5 and 8
B   2, 4, 6 and 7

8.20 Cylinder head bolt tightening sequence

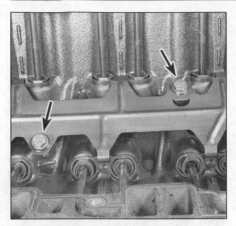

9.1 The guide retainer is held in place by two bolts (arrows)

10.7 The crankshaft balancer is attached to the end of the crankshaft - the bolt is very tight, so use a large breaker bar and six-point socket to remove it

11.9 Typical timing chain cover bolt locations

16 Use a tap of the correct size to chase the threads in the head bolt holes. Dirt, corrosion, sealant and damaged threads will affect torque readings.

17 Position the new gaskets over the dowel pins in the block. Some gaskets are marked TOP or THIS SIDE UP, make certain they are installed properly.

18 Carefully position the heads on the block without disturbing the gaskets.

19 Use NEW head bolts - don't reinstall the old ones - and apply sealant to the threads and the undersides of the bolt heads. Install the bolts in the correct locations - three different lengths are used **(see illustration)**.

20 Tighten the bolts in the sequence shown **(see illustration)** to the torque listed in this Chapter's Specifications. **Note:** *First tighten all bolts to Step 1 in the Specifications, then complete the procedure by tightening the bolts the specified number of degrees of rotation listed in the subsequent Step(s). To obtain accurate results, we recommend using a special torque angle meter.*

21 The remaining installation steps are the reverse of removal.

22 Change the oil and filter (see Chapter 1).

9 Hydraulic lifters - removal, inspection and installation

Refer to illustration 9.1

This procedure is essentially the same as for the 2.5L four-cylinder engine. Follow the procedure in Chapter 2, Part C, but follow the procedures in this Chapter for valve cover and intake manifold removal and installation. Note that models with roller lifters have lifter guides and a guide retainer that must be removed before the lifters can be removed **(see illustration)**.

10 Crankshaft balancer - removal and installation

Refer to illustration 10.7
Note: *The engine balancer, which is essen-*

tially the same as a vibration dampener, is serviced as an assembly. Do not attempt to separate the pulley from the balancer hub.

1 Disconnect the negative cable from the battery. **Caution:** *If the vehicle is equipped with a Delco Loc II audio system, make sure you have the correct activation code before disconnecting the battery. See the information at the front of this manual for the radio re-activation procedure.*

2 Loosen the lug nuts on the right front wheel.

3 Raise the vehicle and support it securely on jackstands.

4 Remove the right front wheel.

5 Remove the right front fender liner (see Chapter 11).

6 Remove the drivebelt(s) (see Chapter 1).

7 Remove the flywheel cover plate and position a large screwdriver in the ring gear teeth to keep the crankshaft from turning while an assistant removes the crankshaft balancer bolt **(see illustration)**. The bolt is normally quite tight, so use a large breaker bar and a six-point socket.

8 Pull the balancer off the crankshaft by hand. Leave the Woodruff key in place in the end of the crankshaft.

9 Installation is the reverse of removal. Be sure to apply multi-purpose grease to the seal contact surface on the back side of the balancer (if it isn't lubricated, the seal lip could be damaged and oil leakage would result).

10 Tighten the crankshaft bolt to the torque listed in this Chapter's Specifications.

11 Timing chain cover - removal and installation

Refer to illustrations 11.9, 11.10 and 11.12

Removal

1 Disconnect the cable from the negative battery terminal. **Caution:** *If the vehicle is equipped with a Delco Loc II audio system,*

make sure you have the correct activation code before disconnecting the battery. See the information at the front of this manual for the radio re-activation procedure.

2 Drain the coolant (see Chapter 1).

3 Drain the oil and replace the oil filter (see Chapter 1).

4 Remove the lower radiator hose and the heater return hose at the timing chain cover.

5 Remove the water pump (see Chapter 3).

6 Remove the crankshaft balancer from the front of the crankshaft (see Section 10).

7 Remove the crankshaft sensor (see Chapter 5).

8 Remove the timing chain cover-to-oil pan bolts.

9 Remove the timing chain cover-to-engine block bolts **(see illustration)**.

10 Separate the cover from the front of the engine. On early models, inside the cover is a spring and button that controls camshaft endplay. If it's missing, look for it in the oil pan **(see illustration)**.

Installation

11 Use a gasket scraper to remove all traces of old gasket material and sealant from the cover and engine block. The cover is

11.10 Once the timing cover has been removed, remove the camshaft button from the end of the camshaft

2E

11.12 The camshaft thrust surface on this cover is worn away (arrow), which means that a new cover must be installed

12.6 Use a cold chisel and hammer to separate the seal from the cover - drive the chisel into the joint, but don't distort the cover

12.7a Clean the bore, then apply grease or oil to the outer edge of the new seal and drive it squarely into the cover with a large socket . . .

12.7b . . . or a wood block and hammer - DO NOT damage the seal in the process!

made of aluminum, so be careful not to nick or gouge it. Clean the gasket sealing surfaces with lacquer thinner or acetone.

12   Check the camshaft thrust surface in the cover for excessive wear (see illustration). If it's worn, a new cover will be required.

13   The oil pump is mounted to the back of the front cover. The oil pump cover must be removed and the cavity packed with petroleum jelly (see Section 13) before the cover is installed.

14   Apply a thin layer of RTV sealant to both sides of the new gasket, then position the gasket on the engine block (the dowel pins should keep it in place). Make sure the spring and button (if equipped) are in place in the end of the camshaft, then attach the cover to the engine. The oil pump drive must engage with the distributor gear.

15   Apply thread sealant to the bolt threads, then install them finger tight. On models so equipped, install the crankshaft position sensor, but leave the bolts finger tight until Step 16. Tighten the other bolts, following a criss-cross pattern when tightening them and working up to the torque listed in this Chapter's Specifications in three steps to avoid warping the cover.

16   On 1992 and earlier models, position the sensor as described in Chapter 5, Section 10, Step 66. Tighten the bolts to the torque listed in this Chapter's Specifications for the timing chain cover. Note: The crankshaft sensor on 1993 and later models requires no adjustment.

17   The remainder of installation is the reverse of removal.

18   Add oil and coolant, start the engine and check for leaks.

12   Crankshaft front oil seal - replacement

Note: The crankshaft front oil seal can be replaced with the timing chain cover in place.

However, due to the limited amount of room available, you may conclude that the procedure would be easier if the cover were removed from the engine first. If so, refer to Section 11 for the cover removal and installation procedure.

Timing chain cover in place

1   Remove the crankshaft balancer (see Section 10).

2   Use a small chisel and a hammer to remove the seal from the cover. Carefully drive the chisel under the outer flange of the seal at several points until the seal can be pried out. Be very careful not to distort the cover!

3   Apply clean engine oil or multi-purpose grease to the outer edge of the new seal, then install it in the cover. Drive the seal into place with a large socket and a hammer (if a large socket isn't available, a piece of pipe will also work). Make sure the seal enters the bore squarely and seats completely.

4   Install the crankshaft balancer (see Section 10).

Timing chain cover removed

Refer to illustrations 12.6, 12.7a and 12.7b

5   Remove the timing chain cover as described in Section 11.

6   Use a small chisel and a hammer to remove the seal from the cover. Carefully drive the chisel under the outer flange of the seal at several points until the seal can be pried out (see illustration). Be very careful not to distort the cover!

7   Apply clean engine oil or multi-purpose grease to the outer edge of the new seal, then install it in the cover. Drive the seal into place with a large socket and a hammer (if a large socket isn't available, a piece of pipe or even a large wood block will also work) (see illustrations). Make sure the seal enters the bore squarely and seats completely.

8   Reinstall the timing chain cover.

13   Oil pump - removal, inspection and installation

Refer to illustrations 13.4, 13.10 and 13.11

Removal

1   Remove the oil filter (see Chapter 1).

2   Remove the oil filter adapter, pressure regulator valve and spring (see Section 14).

3   Remove the timing chain cover (see Section 11).

4   Remove the oil pump cover-to-timing chain cover bolts with a T-30 Torx bit (see illustration).

5   Lift out the cover and oil pump gears as an assembly.

Inspection

6   Clean the parts with solvent and dry them with compressed air (if available).

7   Inspect all components for wear and score marks. Replace any worn out or damaged parts.

8   Refer to Section 14 for pressure regulator valve information.

13.4 The oil pump cover is attached to the inside of the timing chain cover - a T-30 Torx driver is required for removal of the screws

13.10 Measure the outer gear-to-housing clearance with a feeler gauge

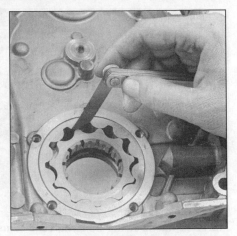

13.11 Measure the inner gear tip clearance with a feeler gauge

14.3 Carefully pull the oil filter adapter away from the timing chain cover; the pressure regulator (arrow) is spring loaded and may spring out when the adapter is removed

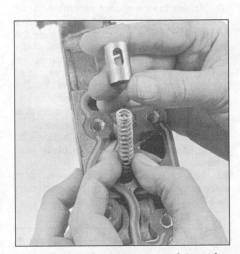

14.4 Remove the pressure regulator valve and spring, then check the valve for wear and damage

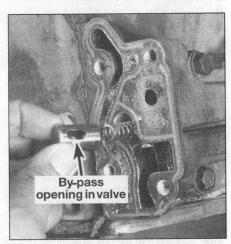

14.6 If the timing chain cover is replaced with a new one, be sure to use the correct pressure relief valve - an early valve will not work in a later model timing chain cover! (early model shown; later models use a solid valve)

2E

9   Reinstall the gears in the timing chain cover.

10   Measure the outer gear-to-housing clearance with a feeler gauge **(see illustration)**.

11   Measure the inner gear tip gear clearance at several points **(see illustration)**.

12   Use a dial indicator or straightedge and feeler gauges to measure the gear end clearance (distance from the gear to the gasket surface of the cover).

13   Check for pump cover warpage by laying a precision straightedge across the cover and trying to slip a feeler gauge between the cover and straightedge.

14   Compare the measurements to the Specifications. Replace all worn or damaged components with new ones.

Installation

15   Remove the gears and pack the pump cavity with petroleum jelly.

16   Install the gears - make sure petroleum jelly is forced into every cavity. Failure to do

so could cause the pump to lose its prime when the engine is started, causing damage from lack of oil pressure.

17   Install the pump cover, using a new gasket only - its thickness is critical for maintaining the correct clearances.

18   Install the pressure regulator spring and valve.

19   Install the timing chain cover.

20   Install the oil filter and check the oil level. Start and run the engine and check for correct oil pressure, then look carefully for oil leaks at the timing chain cover.

14   Oil filter adapter and pressure regulator valve - removal and installation

Refer to illustrations 14.3, 14.4 and 14.6

1   Remove the oil filter (see Chapter 1).

2   Remove the timing chain cover (see Section 11).

3   Remove the four bolts holding the oil filter adapter to the timing chain cover **(see**

illustration). The cover is spring loaded, so remove the bolts while keeping pressure on the cover, then release the spring pressure carefully.

4   Remove the pressure regulator valve and spring **(see illustration)**. Use a gasket scraper to remove all traces of the old gasket.

5   Clean all parts with solvent and dry them with compressed air (if available). Check for wear, score marks and valve binding.

6   Installation is the reverse of removal. Be sure to use a new gasket. **Caution:** *If a new timing chain cover is being installed on the engine, make sure the oil pressure relief valve supplied with the new cover is used. If the old style relief valve is installed in a new cover, oil pressure problems will result* **(see illustration)**.

7   Tighten the bolts to the torque listed in this Chapter's Specifications.

8   Run the engine and check for oil leaks.

15.1 The marks on the crankshaft and camshaft sprockets must be aligned opposite each other as shown

15.4 Remove the camshaft sprocket retaining bolts (arrows)

15 Timing chain and sprockets - removal and installation

Refer to illustrations 15.1 and 15.4

Removal

1   Remove the timing chain cover (see Section 11), then slide the shim or oil slinger off the nose of the crankshaft **(see illustration)**.
2   The timing chain should be replaced with a new one if the total freeplay midway between the sprockets exceeds one inch. Failure to replace the timing chain may result in erratic engine performance, loss of power and lowered gas mileage.
3   Temporarily install the crankshaft balancer bolt and turn the bolt to align the timing marks on the crankshaft and camshaft sprockets directly opposite each other **(see illustration 15.1)**.
4   Remove the camshaft sprocket bolts **(see illustration)**. Try not to turn the camshaft in the process (if you do, realign the timing marks after the bolts are out).
5   Use two large screwdrivers to alternately pry the camshaft sprocket and then the crankshaft sprocket forward and remove the camshaft sprocket and timing chain.
6   Remove the crankshaft sprocket.
7   Detach the spring, then remove the bolt and separate the timing chain dampener from the block.
8   Clean the timing chain and sprockets with solvent and dry them with compressed air (if available).
9   Inspect the components for wear and damage. Look for teeth that are deformed, chipped, pitted, polished or discolored.

Installation

Note: *If the crankshaft has been disturbed, turn it until the O stamped on the crank sprocket is exactly at the top. If the camshaft was turned, install the sprocket temporarily and turn the camshaft until the timing mark is at the bottom, opposite the mark on the crank sprocket* **(see illustration 15.1)**.

10   Attach the dampener assembly to the block and install the spring. Assemble the timing chain on the sprockets, then slide the sprocket and chain assembly onto the shafts with the timing marks aligned as shown in illustration 15.1. Hold the dampener out of the way, against spring pressure, as the chain/sprocket assembly is installed.
11   Install the camshaft sprocket bolts and tighten them to the specified torque.
12   Install the camshaft thrust button and spring, if equipped. Hold it in place with grease.
13   Lubricate the chain and sprocket with clean engine oil. Install the timing chain cover (see Section 11).

16 Oil pan - removal and installation

Removal

1   Disconnect the cable from the negative battery terminal. **Caution:** *If the vehicle is equipped with a Delco Loc II audio system, make sure you have the correct activation code before disconnecting the battery. See the information at the front of this manual for the radio re-activation procedure.*
2   Raise the vehicle, place it securely on jackstands and drain the engine oil and remove the oil filter (refer to Chapter 1 if necessary).
3   Remove the flywheel inspection cover. Remove the starter motor (see Chapter 5).
4   On 1992 and later models, remove the drivebelt, the crankshaft balancer/pulley, and the crankshaft sensor shield. Remove the air-conditioning compressor from the brackets, but do not disconnect the hoses. Support the compressor, out of the way. Remove the right front suspension support bolts and loosen the remainder of the support bolts, allowing the suspension to drop at least 1-1/2 inch. Remove the oil level sensor electrical connector.
5   Remove the bolts and stiffener plates (if equipped) and carefully separate the oil pan from the block. Don't pry between the block

and the pan or damage to the sealing surfaces may result and oil leaks may develop. Instead, tap the pan with a soft-face hammer to break the gasket seal.

Installation

6   Clean the pan with solvent and remove all old sealant and gasket material from the block and pan mating surfaces. Gasket removal solvents are available at auto parts stores and may prove helpful. Clean the mating surfaces with lacquer thinner or acetone and make sure the bolt holes in the block are clear. Check the oil pan flange for distortion, particularly around the bolt holes. If necessary, place the pan on a wood block and use a hammer to flatten and restore the gasket surface.
7   Some models have a gasket, while others use RTV sealant to seal the oil pan. On models that have a gasket, always use a new gasket whenever the oil pan is installed. On models that use RTV sealant, apply a 1/8-inch diameter bead of sealant to the oil pan flange, inboard of the bolt holes.
8   Place the oil pan in position on the block and install the bolts. Don't forget the stiffener plates (if used).
9   After the bolts are installed, tighten them to the torque listed in this Chapter's Specifications. Starting at the center, follow a criss-cross pattern and work up to the final torque in three steps.
10   The remaining steps are the reverse of the removal procedure.
11   Refill the engine with oil, run it until normal operating temperature is reached and check for leaks.

17 Oil pump pipe and screen assembly - removal and installation

1   Remove the oil pan (see Section 16).
2   Unbolt the oil pump pipe and screen assembly and detach it from the engine.
3   Clean the screen and housing assembly with solvent and dry it with compressed air, if

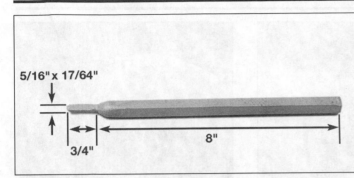

18.3a Grind a piece of 1/2-inch diameter brass or aluminum rod to these dimensions as a rear seal driver

5/16" x 17/64"

3/4"

8"

available. **Note:** *If the oil screen is damaged or has metal chips in it, replace it. An abundance of metal chips indicates a major engine problem that must be corrected.*

4   Make sure the mating surfaces of the pipe flange and the engine block are clean and free of nicks and install the pump and screen assembly with a new gasket.

5   Install the oil pan (see Section 16).

6   Refill the engine with oil before running it.

18   Rear main bearing oil seal - replacement

1990 and earlier models

Refer to illustrations 18.3a, 18.3b, 18.6, 18.9 and 18.12

Note: *Braided fabric seals inserted into grooves in the engine block and main bearing cap are used to seal against oil leakage around the crankshaft. The upper rear main bearing oil seal can be replaced only with the crankshaft removed (see Chapter 2, Part D) but it can be repaired with the crankshaft in place. Two piece rubber seals are available from aftermarket suppliers. Several special tools are required for this procedure.*

1   Remove the oil pan (see Section 16).

2   Remove the rear main bearing cap.

3   Using a special tool, (available at most auto parts stores) or a homemade equivalent, drive the upper seal gently back into the

groove in the engine block, packing it tight. It will pack in to a depth of between 1/4-inch and 3/4-inch **(see illustrations)**.

4   Repeat the procedure on the other end of the seal.

5   Measure how far the seal was driven up in the groove on each side and add 1/16-inch. Remove the old seal from the main bearing cap. Use the main bearing cap as a fixture and cut two pieces of the old seal to the predetermined lengths.

6   Using the packing tool, work the short pieces of the previously cut seal into the engine block groove. Lubricate the seal with oil to ease installation **(see illustration)**.

7   Remove the guide tool.

8   Place a new seal in the main bearing cap groove with both ends projecting above the parting surface of the cap.

9   Use the handle of a hammer or similar tool to force the seal into the groove until it projects no more than 1/16-inch. Cut the ends of the seal flush with the surface of the cap with a single-edge razor blade **(see illustration)**.

10   Soak the neoprene seals that fit into the side grooves in the bearing cap in light oil or kerosene for one or two minutes.

11   Install the neoprene seals in the groove between the bearing cap and the block. The seals are slightly undersize and swell in the presence of heat and oil. They are slightly longer than the groove in the bearing cap and must be cut to fit.

12   Apply a small amount of RTV sealant to the joint where the bearing cap meets the block to help eliminate oil leakage. A very thin coat is all that's necessary **(see illustration)**.

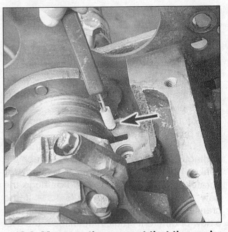

18.3b Pack the seal into the engine block groove with the special tool (arrow)

18.6 Measure the amount that the seal has been driven into the groove - here a small screwdriver was used with a sleeve of masking tape (arrow) to serve as a depth indicator

13   Install the main bearing cap on the block. Force the seals up into the bearing cap with a blunt instrument to be sure of a good seal at the upper parting line. Install the bolts and tighten them to the torque listed in the Part F Specifications.

14   Install the oil pan.

2E

18.9 Press the seal into the cap with a hammer handle or a wood dowel

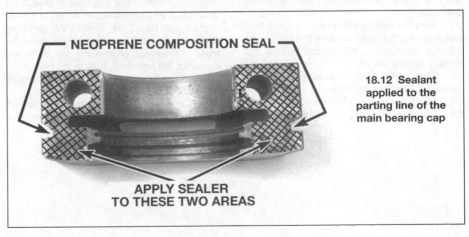

NEOPRENE COMPOSITION SEAL

APPLY SEALER TO THESE TWO AREAS

18.12 Sealant applied to the parting line of the main bearing cap

18.17 Carefully pry the old oil seal out

20.1 Here's what a broken engine mount looks like

20.4 Remove the front engine mount-to-engine bracket bolts (arrows)

1991 and later models

Refer to illustration 18.17

15   Remove the transaxle (see Chapter 7).
16   Remove the flywheel or driveplate (see Section 19).
17   Using a thin screwdriver or seal removal tool, carefully remove the oil seal from the engine block **(see illustration)**. Be very careful not to damage the crankshaft surface while prying the seal out.
18   Clean the bore in the block and the seal contact surface on the crankshaft. Check the seal contact surface on the crankshaft for scratches and nicks that could damage the new seal lip and cause oil leaks - if the crankshaft is damaged, the only alternative is a new or different crankshaft. Inspect the seal bore for nicks and scratches. Carefully smooth it with a fine file if necessary, but don't nick the crankshaft in the process.
19   A special tool is recommended to install the new oil seal. Lubricate the lips of the seal with clean engine oil. Slide the seal onto the mandrel until the dust lip bottoms squarely against the collar of the tool. **Note:** *If the special tool isn't available, carefully work the seal lip over the crankshaft and tap it into place with a hammer and blunt punch.*
20   Align the dowel pin on the tool with the dowel pin hole in the crankshaft and attach the tool to the crankshaft by hand-tightening the bolts.
21   Turn the tool handle until the collar bottoms against the case, seating the seal.
22   Loosen the tool handle and remove the bolts. Remove the tool.
23   Check the seal and make sure it's seated squarely in the bore.
24   Install the flywheel or driveplate.
25   Install the transaxle (see Chapter 7).

19   Flywheel/driveplate - removal and installation

1   Refer to Chapter 7, follow all precautionary notes and remove the transaxle.
2   If equipped with a manual transmission, remove the pressure plate and clutch disc (see Chapter 8).
3   Remove the flywheel or driveplate mounting bolts and separate it from the crankshaft.
4   Install the flywheel or driveplate and tighten the bolts to the torque listed in this Chapter's Specifications.
5   If equipped with a manual transaxle, reinstall the clutch disc and pressure plate.
6   Reinstall the transaxle as described in Chapter 7.

20   Engine and transaxle mounts - replacement

Refer to illustrations 20.1, 20.4 and 20.9
Warning: *A special tool is available to support the engine during repair operations. These fixtures are available from rental yards. Improper lifting methods or devices are hazardous and could result in severe injury or death. DO NOT place any part of your body under the engine/transaxle when it's supported only by a jack. Failure of the lifting device could result in serious injury or death.*
Note: *Whenever engine mount bolts are removed, the bolt threads must be thoroughly cleaned and new thread-locking compound applied to the threads before installing.*
1   If the rubber mounts have hardened, cracked or separated from the metal backing

plates, they must be replaced **(see illustration)**. This operation may be carried out with the engine/transaxle still in the vehicle.

Front engine mount

2   Raise the front of the vehicle and support it securely on jackstands.
3   Support the engine.
4   Remove the mount-to-engine bracket bolts **(see illustration)**.
5   Raise the engine slightly, remove the mount-to-frame bolts and remove the mount.
6   Installation is the reverse of removal.

Rear engine mount

7   Raise the vehicle and support it securely on jackstands.
8   Support the engine.
9   Remove the mount-to-frame bracket nuts **(see illustration)**.
10   Remove the mount-to-engine bracket bolts and remove the mount.
11   Installation is the reverse of removal.

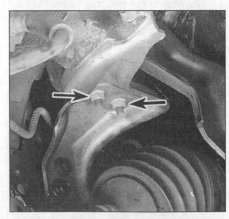

20.9 Remove the rear engine mount-to-frame bracket nuts (arrows)

Chapter 2 Part F
General engine overhaul procedures

Contents

2F

Specifications

2.0 liter OHC four-cylinder engine

General

Displacement	122 cubic inches
Cylinder compression	
Minimum	100 psi
Maximum variation between cylinders	25 percent
Oil pressure	
At 1000 rpm	15 psi minimum
At 2500 rpm	45 psi minimum

Cylinder head

Warpage limit	0.005 inch

Valves and related components

Valve face angle	46-degrees
Valve seat angle	45-degrees
Stem-to-guide clearance	
Intake	0.0006 to 0.002 inch
Exhaust	0.001 to 0.0024 inch
Valve seat runout limit	0.002 inch

Crankshaft and connecting rods

Crankshaft endplay	0.003 to 0.012 inch
Connecting rod side clearance	0.0027 to 0.0095 inch

Crankshaft and connecting rods (continued)

Main bearing journal
    Diameter
        Coded brown .... 2.2830 to 2.2833 inches
        Coded green .... 2.2827 to 2.2830 inches
    Taper limit.. 0.0002 inch
    Out-of-round limit... 0.0002 inch
Main bearing oil clearance.. 0.0006 to 0.0016 inch
Connecting rod bearing journal
    Diameter... 1.9278 to 1.9286 inches
    Taper limit.. 0.0002 inch
    Out-of-round limit... 0.0002 inch
Connecting rod bearing oil clearance... 0.0007 to 0.0024 inch

Engine block

Cylinder bore
    Diameter... 3.385 to 3.387 inches
    Out-of-round limit... 0.005 inch
    Taper limit.. 0.005 inch

Pistons and rings

Piston-to-bore clearance
    VIN K .... 0.0004 to 0.0012 inch
    VIN M .... 0.0012 to 0.0020 inch
Piston ring end gap
    Top compression ring .... 0.012 to 0.020 inch
    2nd compression ring .... 0.012 to 0.020 inch
    Oil control ring .... 0.016 to 0.055 inch
Piston ring side clearance
    Top compression ring .... 0.002 to 0.003 inch
    2nd compression ring .... 0.001 to 0.0024 inch

Camshaft

Lobe lift (intake and exhaust).. 0.241 inch
Endplay .... 0.016 to 0.064 inch
Journal diameters
    No. 1
        1988 .... 1.6714 to 1.6720 inches
        1989 .... 1.6712 to 1.6707 inches
    No. 2
        1988 .... 1.6812 to 1.6816 inches
        1989 .... 1.6812 to 1.6818 inches
    No. 3 .... 1.6911 to 1.6917 inches
    No. 4 .... 1.7009 to 1.7015 inches
    No. 5
        1988 .... 1.7108 to 1.7114 inches
        1989 .... 1.7100 to 1.7106 inches
Bearing oil clearance .... 0.0008 inch

Torque specifications*

Ft-lbs (unless otherwise indicated)

Main bearing cap bolts
    Step 1 44
    Step 2 .... Turn an additional 40 to 50-degrees
Connecting rod cap bolts**
    Step 1 26
    Step 2 .... Turn an additional 40 to 45-degrees

* Note: Refer to Part A for additional torque specifications.
** Use new bolts during final engine assembly (use the old ones when checking bearing oil clearance).

2.3 liter four-cylinder engines

General

Displacement... 138 cubic inches
Cylinder compression pressure
    Minimum.. 100 psi
    Maximum variation between cylinders... 30 percent
Oil pressure
    At 900 rpm.. 15 psi minimum
    At 2000 rpm.. 30 psi minimum

Camshafts and housings

Lobe lift
  Intake
    VIN D
      1989 and earlier .... 0.340 inch
      1990 on .... 0.375 inch
      VIN A and 3 .... 0.410 inch
  Exhaust
    VIN D
      1989 and earlier .... 0.350 inch
      1990 on .... 0.375 inch
      VIN A and 3 .... 0.410 inch
Lobe taper limit .... 0.0018 to 0.0033 inch per 0.5512 inch
Endplay .... 0.0009 to 0.0088 inch
Journal diameter
  1989 and earlier VIN A and all 1990 and later models
    No. 1 .... 1.5728 to 1.5720 inches
    All others .... 1.3751 to 1.3760 inches
  1989 and earlier VIN D (all) .... 1.3751 to 1.3760 inches
Bearing oil clearance
  1989 and earlier .... 0.006 to 0.014 inch
  1990 on .... 0.0009 to 0.0088 inch
Lifters
  Bore diameter .... 1.3775 to 1.3787 inches
  Outside diameter .... 1.3763 to 1.3770 inches
  Lifter-to-bore clearance .... 0.0006 to 0.0024 inch
Camshaft housing warpage limit .... 0.001 inch per 3.937 inches

Cylinder head

Warpage limit .... 0.008 inch

Valves and related components

Valve face
  Angle
    Intake 44-degrees
    Exhaust 44.5-degrees
Runout limit .... 0.0015 inch
Valve seats
  Angle (intake and exhaust) 45-degrees
  Width (intake and exhaust) .... 0.0370 to 0.0748 inch
Valve margin width .... 1/32 inch minimum
Valve stem diameter
  Intake .... 0.27512 to 0.27445 inch
  Exhaust .... 0.2740 to 0.2747 inch
Valve stem-to-guide clearance
  Intake .... 0.0010 to 0.0027 inch
  Exhaust .... 0.0015 to 0.0032 inch
Valves
  Length
    Intake .... 4.3300 inches
    Exhaust .... 4.3103 inches
Installed height*
  1989 and earlier .... 1.4232 to 1.4429 inches
  1990 on .... 0.9840 to 1.0040 inches
Stem length exposed beyond retainer
  1989 and earlier .... 0.0394 to 0.0787 inch
  1990 on .... 0.1190 to 0.1367 inch
* Measured from tip of stem to top of camshaft housing mounting surface

Oil pump

Gear backlash .... 0.0091 to 0.0201 inch

Crankshaft and connecting rods

Crankshaft
  Endplay .... 0.0034 to 0.0095 inch
  Runout
    At center main journal .... 0.00098 inch
    At flywheel flange .... 0.00098 inch

Crankshaft and connecting rods (continued)

Main bearing journal
    Diameter .... 2.0470 to 2.0480 inches
    Out-of-round/taper limits .... 0.0005 inch
Main bearing oil clearance .... 0.0005 to 0.0023 inch
Connecting rod bearing journal
    Diameter .... 1.8887 to 1.8897 inches
    Out-of-round/taper limits .... 0.0005 inch
Connecting rod bearing oil clearance .... 0.0005 to 0.0020 inch
Seal journal
    Diameter .... 3.2210 to 3.2299 inches
    Runout limit .... 0.0012 inch
Connecting rod side clearance (endplay) .... 0.0059 to 0.0177 inch

Engine block

Cylinder bore
    Diameter .... 3.6217 to 3.6223 inches
    Out-of-round limit .... 0.0004 inch
    Taper limit (thrust side) .... 0.0003 inch measured 4.173 inches down the bore
Block deck warpage limit .... If more than 0.010 inch must be removed, replace the block
Transaxle mounting bolt boss runout
    limit (rear face-to-crankshaft flange) .... 0.008 inch

Pistons and rings

Piston diameter .... 3.6203 to 3.6210
Piston-to-bore clearance .... 0.0007 to 0.0020 inch
Piston ring end gap
    Top compression ring .... 0.0138 to 0.0236 inch
    Second compression ring .... 0.0157 to 0.0256 inch
    Oil control ring .... 0.0157 to 0.0551 inch
Piston ring side clearance
    Top compression ring .... 0.0027 to 0.0047 inch
    Second compression ring .... 0.00157 to 0.00315 inch

Torque specifications
Ft-lbs (unless otherwise indicated)

Main bearing cap bolts
    Step 1 15
    Step 2 .... Turn an additional 90-degrees
Connecting rod cap nuts
    1988
        Step 1 15
        Step 2 .... Turn nuts an additional 75-degrees
    1989 on
        Step 1 18
        Step 2 .... Turn bolts an additional 80-degrees
Oil pan baffle studs/bolts 30

Note: *Refer to Part B for additional torque specifications.*

2.5 liter OHV four-cylinder engine

General

Displacement .... 151 cubic inches
Cylinder compression
    Minimum .... 100 psi
    Maximum variation between cylinders .... 25 percent
Oil pressure
    1987 and earlier .... 36 to 41 psi at 2000 rpm
    1988 through 1990 .... 50 psi at 2000 rpm
    1991 on .... 26 psi at 800 rpm

Cylinder head

Warpage limit .... 0.006 inch

Valves and related components

Valve face angle 45-degrees
Valve seat angle
    1985 and 1986 .... 45-degrees
    1985 on 46-degrees
Valve margin width .... 1/32 inch minimum

Stem-to-guide clearance
    Intake .... 0.0006 to 0.002 inch
    Exhaust.. 0.001 to 0.0027 inch
Valve seat width
    Intake .... 0.035 to 0.075 inch
    Exhaust.. 0.058 to 0.105 inch
Valve seat runout limit .... 0.002 inch
Valve spring installed height
    1985 and 1986 .... 1.690 inches
    1987 .... 1.440 inches
    1988 on .... 1.679 inches
Valve spring pressure - at height
    1985 and 1986
        At 1.660 inches .... 78 to 86 lbs
        At 1.260 inches .... 170 to 180 lbs
    1987
        At 1.440 inches .... 71 to 78 lbs
        At 1.040 inches .... 158 to 170 lbs
    1988 on
        At 1.680 inches .... 70 to 78 lbs
        At 1.239 inches .... 169 to 181 lbs

Crankshaft and connecting rods

Crankshaft endplay.. 0.005 to 0.010 inch
Connecting rod side clearance... 0.006 to 0.024 inch
Main bearing journal
    Diameter.. 2.300 inches
    Taper limit... 0.0005 inch
    Out-of-round limit... 0.0005 inch
Main bearing oil clearance... 0.0006 to 0.0011 inch
Connecting rod bearing journal
    Diameter.. 2.000 inches
    Taper limit... 0.0005 inch
    Out-of-round limit... 0.0005 inch
Connecting rod bearing oil clearance... 0.0005 to 0.003 inch

Engine block

Cylinder bore
    Diameter.. 4.000 inches
    Out-of-round limit... 0.0015 inch
    Taper limit... 0.005 inch

Pistons and rings

Piston diameter (measured 1.125 inches down
    from the piston top).. 3.9971 to 3.9975 inches
Piston-to-bore clearance
    Top .... 0.0025 to 0.0033 inch
    Bottom.. 0.0017 to 0.0041 inch
Piston ring end gap
    Top compression ring .... 0.010 to 0.025 inch
    2nd compression ring .... 0.009 to 0.019 inch
    Oil control ring... 0.016 to 0.055 inch
Piston ring side clearance
    Top compression ring .... 0.002 to 0.003 inch
    2nd compression ring .... 0.001 to 0.0024 inch
Piston pin diameter... 0.938 to 0.942 inch

Camshaft

Lobe lift (intake and exhaust)
    1985 .... 0.398 inch
    1986 through 1989 .... 0.232 inch
    1990 on .... 0.248 inch
Bearing journal diameter.. 1.869 inches
Bearing oil clearance .... 0.0007 to 0.0027 inch
Camshaft thrust plate (end) clearance.. 0.015 to 0.050 inch

Torque specifications*

                                                            Ft-lbs (unless otherwise indicated)
Main bearing cap bolts 70
Connecting rod cap nuts 32
Camshaft thrust plate .... 90 inch-lbs

* **Note:** *Refer to Part C for additional torque specifications.*

3.0 and 3.3 liter V6 engines

General

Displacement
    3.0L .... 181 cubic inches
    3.3L .... 204 cubic inches
Cylinder compression pressure
    Minimum.. 100 psi
    Maximum variation between cylinders...................................... 25 percent
Oil pressure
    At 900 rpm.. 19 psi minimum
    At 2000 rpm.. 36 psi minimum

Cylinder head

Warpage limit.. 0.005 inch maximum

Valves and related components

Valve face
    Angle
        Intake .... 45 degrees
        Exhaust .... 45 degrees
        Runout limit .... 0.0015 inch
Valve seats
    Angle (intake and exhaust)
        1985 .... 46 degrees
        1986 on .... 45 degrees
    Width
        3.0L
            Intake .... 0.062 to 0.094 inch
            Exhaust... 0.0074 to 0.0104 inch
        3.3L
            Intake .... 0.060 to 0.080 inch
            Exhaust... 0.090 to 0.110 inch
Valve margin width .... 1/32 inch minimum
Valve stem diameter
    Intake .... 0.3405 to 0.3412 inch
    Exhaust.. 0.3401 to 0.3412 inch
Valve stem-to-guide clearance
    Intake .... 0.0015 to 0.0035 inch
    Exhaust.. 0.0015 to 0.0032 inch
Valve spring free length
    3.0L .... 2.030 inches
    3.3L .... 1.981 inches
Valve spring installed height .... 1.690 to 1.720 inches
Valve spring pressure - at height
    3.0L
        1985
            At 1.730 inches.. 93 +/- 5 lbs
            At 1.340 inches.. 220 +/- 10 lbs
        1986 on
            At 1.727 inches.. 90 +/- 5 lbs
            At 1.340 inches.. 185 +/- 10 lbs
    3.3L
        At 1.750 inches... 76 to 84 lbs
        At 1.315 inches... 200 to 220 lbs

Oil pump

Gear backlash.. 0.0091 to 0.0201 inch

Crankshaft and connecting rods

Crankshaft
    Endplay .... 0.0034 to 0.0105 inch
    Runout
        At center main journal.. 0.00098 inch
        At flywheel flange.. 0.00098 inch
Main bearing journal
    Diameter
        3.0L
            1985... 2.4995 inches
            1986 on.. 2.4988 to 2.4998 inches
        3.3L.. 2.4988 to 2.4998 inches

Out-of-round/taper limits...	0.0003 inch
Main bearing oil clearance	
3.0L	0.0003 to 0.0018inch
3.3L	
1992 and earlier	0.0003 to 0.0018 inch
1993	0.0008 to 0.0022 inch
Connecting rod bearing journal	
Diameter...	2.2487 to 2.2495 inches
Out-of-round/taper limits	0.0003 inch
Connecting rod bearing oil clearance	
3.0L	0.0005 to 0.0026
3.3L	
1992 and earlier	0.0003 to 0.0026
1993	0.0008 to 0.0022 inch
Connecting rod side clearance (endplay)	
3.0L	
1985	0.005 to 0.026 inch
1986 on	0.003 to 0.015 inch
3.3L	0.003 to 0.015 inch

Engine block

Cylinder bore	
Diameter	
3.0L	3.80 inches
3.3L	3.70 inches
Out-of-round limit..	0.0004 inch
Taper limit (thrust side)...	0.0008 inch

Pistons and rings

Piston-to-bore clearance...	0.0007 to 0.0022 inch
Piston ring end gap	
Top compression ring	0.013 to 0.023 inch
Second compression ring	0.015 to 0.025 inch
Oil control ring...	0.0157 to 0.0551 inch
Piston ring side clearance	
Top compression ring	0.0013 to 0.0031 inch
Second compression ring	0.0013 to 0.0031 inch
Oil control ring...	0.0081 to 0.011 inch
Piston pin	
Diameter..	0.9053 to 0.9055 inch
Fit in piston (clearance)	0.0004 to 0.0008 inch
Fit in connecting rod (press fit)..	-0.0007 to -0.0017 inch

Camshaft

Lobe lift	
Intake	
1985	0.210 inch
1986 on	0.250 inch
Exhaust	
1985	0.240 inch
1986 on	0.255 inch
Journal diameter...	1.785 to 1.786 inches
Bearing oil clearance	0.0005 to 0.0035 inch

Torque specifications*

	Ft-lbs (unless otherwise indicated)
Main bearing cap bolts	
3.0L	100
3.3L	
1989 and 1990	90
1991	
Step 1	26
Step 2	Rotate an additional 45-degrees
1992 and 1993	
Step 1	26
Step 2	Rotate an additional 50-degrees
Connecting rod cap nuts	
3.0L	
1985 and 1986	40
1987 and 1988	45

2F

Torque specifications*(continued)

Ft-lbs (unless otherwise indicated)

3.3L
Step 1.. 20
Step 2.. Rotate an additional 50-degrees

* **Note:** *Refer to Part E for additional torque specifications.*

3.1 liter V6 engine

General

Displacement...	192 cubic inches
Cylinder compression pressure	
Minimum...	100 psi
Maximum variation between cylinders...........................	30 percent
Oil pressure	
At 1100 rpm...	15 psi minimum
At 2500 rpm...	42 psi minimum

Cylinder head

Warpage limit..	0.005 inch

Valves and related components

Valve face angle (intake and exhaust)	45-degrees
Runout limit...	0.001 inch
Valve seats	
Angle (intake and exhaust).......................................	45-degrees
Width	
Intake	0.061 to 0.073 inch
Exhaust	0.067 to 0.079 inch
Valve margin width	
Intake	0.083 inch minimum
Exhaust	0.106 inch minimum
Valve stem diameter	0.0010 to 0.0027 inch
Valve stem-to-guide clearance (all)	0.001 to 0.0027 inch
Valve spring free length	1.890 inches
Valve spring installed height	1.710 inches
Valve spring pressure - at height	
At 1.710 inches..	80 lbs
At 1.239 inches..	250 lbs

Oil pump

Gear backlash...	0.0037 to 0.0077 inch

Crankshaft and connecting rods

Crankshaft	
Endplay	0.0024 to 0.0083 inch
Runout	
At center main journal	0.0002 inch
At flywheel flange	0.0016 inch
Main bearing journal	
Diameter..	2.6473 to 2.6483 inches
Out-of-round/taper limits	0.0002 inch
Main bearing oil clearance	0.0012 to 0.0030 inch
Connecting rod bearing journal	
Diameter..	1.9982 to 1.9984 inches
Out-of-round/taper limits	0.0002 inch
Connecting rod bearing oil clearance.............................	0.0011 to 0.0037 inch
Connecting rod side clearance (endplay)	0.0071 to 0.0173 inch

Engine block

Cylinder bore	
Diameter..	3.505 inches
Out-of-round limit..	0.0005 inch
Taper limit (thrust side)..	0.0008 inch

Pistons and rings

Piston-to-bore clearance...	0.0013 to 0.0027 inch
Piston ring end gap	
Top compression ring	0.007 to 0.016 inch
Second compression ring	0.020 to 0.028 inch
Oil control ring	0.010 to 0.030 inch

Piston ring side clearance
    Top compression ring .... 0.0020 to 0.0035 inch
    Second compression ring .... 0.0020 to 0.0035 inch
    Oil control ring .... 0.0081 to 0.011 inch
Piston pin
    Diameter .... 0.9052 to 0.9054 inch
    Fit in piston (clearance) .... 0.0004 to 0.0008 inch
    Fit in connecting rod .... Press fit

Camshaft

Lobe lift (intake and exhaust) .... 0.2727 inch
Journal diameter .... 1.868 to 1.869 inches
Bearing inside diameter .... 1.871 to 1.872 inches
Bearing oil clearance .... 0.001 to 0.004 inch

Torque specifications*

Ft-lbs

Main bearing cap bolts
    Step 1 37
    Step 2 .... Turn an additional 77-degrees
Connecting rod cap nuts
    Step 1 15
    Step 2 .... Turn an additional 75-degrees

* **Note:** *Refer to Part D for additional torque specifications.*

1 General information

Included in this portion of Chapter 2 are the general overhaul procedures for the cylinder head(s) and internal engine components. The information ranges from advice concerning preparation for an overhaul and the purchase of replacement parts to detailed, step-by-step procedures covering removal and installation of internal engine components and the inspection of parts. Engine removal and installation procedures are also included.

The following Sections have been written based on the assumption that the engine has been removed from the vehicle. For information concerning in-vehicle engine repair, as well removal and installation of the external components necessary for the overhaul, see Part A, B, C, D or E of this Chapter and Section 7 of this Part.

The Specifications included here in Part F are only those necessary for the inspection and overhaul procedures that follow. Refer to Part A, B, C, D or E for additional Specifications.

2 Engine overhaul - general information

Refer to illustrations 2.4a through 2.4c

It's not always easy to determine when, or if, an engine should be completely overhauled, as a number of factors should be considered.

High mileage isn't necessarily an indication that an overhaul is needed, while low mileage doesn't preclude the need for an overhaul. Frequency of servicing is probably the most important consideration. An engine that's had regular and frequent oil and filter changes, as well as other required maintenance, will most likely give many thousands of miles of reliable service. Conversely, a

neglected engine may require an overhaul very early in its life.

Excessive oil consumption is an indication that cylinder walls, pistons, rings and/or valve guides are in need of attention. Make sure that oil leaks aren't responsible before deciding that the rings and/or guides are bad. Perform a cylinder compression check (see Section 3) or leakdown test and a vacuum diagnostic check (see Section 4) to determine the extent of the work required.

If the engine is making obvious knocking or rumbling noises, the connecting rod and/or main bearings may be at fault. Check the oil pressure with a gauge installed in place of the oil pressure sending unit **(see illustrations)** and compare it to the Specifications. If it's extremely low, the bearings and oil pump are probably worn.

Loss of power, rough running, excessive valve train noise and high fuel consumption rates may also point to the need for an overhaul, especially if they're all present at the same time. If a complete tune-up doesn't

2.4a On the 2.3L four-cylinder engine, the oil pressure sending unit is located in the transaxle end of the camshaft housing

2.4b On 3.1L V6 engines, the oil pressure sending unit is located next to the oil filter housing (arrow)

2.4c On 3.0L and 3.3L V6 engines, the oil pressure sending unit is located just above the oil filter (arrow)

remedy the situation, major mechanical work is the only solution.

An engine overhaul involves restoring the internal parts to the specifications of a new engine. During an overhaul, the piston rings

2F

are replaced and the cylinder walls are reconditioned (rebored and/or honed). If a rebore is done, new pistons are required. The main bearings, connecting rod bearings and the camshaft bearings are generally replaced with new ones and, if necessary, the crankshaft may be reground to restore the journals. Generally, the valves are serviced as well, since they're usually in less-than-perfect condition at this point. While the engine is being overhauled, other components, such as the distributor, starter and alternator, can be rebuilt as well. The end result should be a like new engine that will give many trouble free miles. **Note:** *Critical cooling system components such as the hoses, drivebelts, thermostat and water pump MUST be replaced with new parts when an engine is overhauled. The radiator should be checked carefully to ensure that it isn't clogged or leaking; if in doubt, replace it with a new one. Also, we don't recommend overhauling the oil pump - always install a new one when an engine is rebuilt.*

Before beginning an engine overhaul, read through the entire procedure to familiarize yourself with the scope and requirements of the job. Overhauling an engine is not extremely difficult, but it is time consuming. Plan on the vehicle being tied up for a minimum of two weeks, especially if parts must be taken to an automotive machine shop for repair or reconditioning. Check on availability of parts and make sure that any necessary special tools and equipment are obtained in advance. Most work can be done with typical hand tools, although a number of precision measuring tools are required for inspecting parts to determine if they must be replaced. Often an automotive machine shop will handle the inspection of parts and offer advice concerning reconditioning and replacement. **Note:** *Always wait until the engine has been completely disassembled and all components, especially the engine block, have been inspected before deciding which service and repair operations must be performed by an automotive machine shop. Since the block's condition will be the major factor to consider when determining whether to overhaul the original engine or buy a rebuilt one, never purchase parts or have the machine work done on other components until the block has been thoroughly inspected. Since an overhaul requires so much labor, it doesn't pay to cut corners or install worn or substandard parts.*

To ensure maximum life and minimum trouble from a rebuilt engine, everything must be assembled with care in a spotlessly clean environment.

3   Cylinder compression check

Refer to illustration 3.4

1   A compression check will tell you the mechanical condition of the engine (pistons, rings, valves and head gaskets). Specifically, it can tell you if the compression is down due to leakage caused by worn piston rings,

3.4 A compression gauge with a threaded fitting for the spark plug hole is preferred over the type that requires hand pressure to maintain the seal

defective valves and seats or a blown head gasket. **Note:** *The engine must be at normal operating temperature for this check and the battery must be fully charged.*

2   Begin by cleaning the area around the spark plugs before you remove them (compressed air should be used, if available, otherwise a small brush or even a bicycle tire pump will work). This will prevent dirt from getting into the cylinders as the compression check is being done. Remove all of the spark plugs from the engine. Be careful not to burn yourself.

3   Block the throttle wide open. On models with distributorless ignition systems remove the ERLS or IGN ECM fuse to disable the ignition. On models with HEI (distributor) ignition, unplug the primary (low voltage) electrical connectors from the ignition coil.

4   With the compression gauge in the number one spark plug hole **(see illustration)**, crank the engine over at least four compression strokes while watching the gauge. The compression should build up quickly in a healthy engine. Low compression on the first stroke, followed by a gradually increasing pressure on successive strokes, indicates worn piston rings. A low compression reading on the first stroke, which doesn't build up during successive strokes, indicates leaking valves or a blown head gasket (a cracked head could be the cause). Record the highest gauge reading obtained.

5   Repeat the procedure for the remaining cylinders and compare the results to the Specifications.

6   Add some engine oil (about three squirts from a plunger-type oil can) to each cylinder, through the spark plug hole, and repeat the test.

7   If the compression increases significantly after the oil is added, the piston rings are definitely worn. If the compression doesn't increase significantly, the leakage is occurring at the valves or head gasket. Leakage past the valves may be caused by burned valve seats and/or faces or warped, cracked or bent valves.

8   If two adjacent cylinders have equally

low compression, there's a strong possibility that the head gasket between them is blown. The appearance of coolant in the combustion chambers or the crankcase would verify this condition.

9   If the compression is unusually high, the combustion chambers are probably coated with carbon deposits. If that's the case, the cylinder head(s) should be removed and decarbonized.

10   If compression is way down or varies greatly between cylinders, it would be a good idea to have a leak-down test performed by an automotive repair shop. This test will pinpoint exactly where the leakage is occurring and how severe it is.

4   Vacuum gauge diagnostic checks

Refer to illustrations 4.1, 4.2, 4.3, 4.4, 4.5, 4.7 and 4.9

A vacuum gauge provides valuable information about what is going on in the engine at a low-cost. You can check for worn rings or cylinder walls, leaking head or intake manifold gaskets, restricted exhaust, stuck or burned valves, weak valve springs, improper ignition or valve timing and ignition problems.

Unfortunately, vacuum gauge readings are easy to misinterpret, so they should be used in conjunction with other tests to confirm the diagnosis.

Both the absolute readings and the rate of needle movement are important for accurate interpretation. Most gauges measure vacuum in inches of mercury (in-Hg). As vacuum increases (or atmospheric pressure decreases), the reading will decrease. Also, for every 1,000 foot increase in elevation above approximately 2000 feet, the gauge readings will decrease about one inch of mercury.

Connect the vacuum gauge directly to intake manifold vacuum, not to ported (above the throttle plate) vacuum. Be sure no hoses are left disconnected during the test or false readings will result.

Before you begin the test, allow the engine to warm up completely. Block the wheels and set the parking brake. With the transmission in neutral (or Park, on automatics), start the engine and allow it to run at normal idle speed. **Warning:** *Carefully inspect the fan blades for cracks or damage before starting the engine. Keep your hands and the vacuum tester clear of the fan and do not stand in front of the vehicle or in line with the fan when the engine is running.*

Read the vacuum gauge; an average, healthy engine should normally produce about 17 to 22 inches of vacuum with a fairly steady needle. Refer to the following vacuum gauge readings and what they indicate about the engines condition:

1   A low steady reading usually indicates a leaking gasket between the intake manifold and throttle body, a leaky vacuum hose, late ignition timing or incorrect camshaft timing

4.1 Low, steady reading

4.2 Low, fluctuating needle

4.3 Regular drops

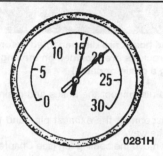

4.4 Irregular drops

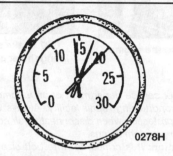

4.5 Rapid vibration

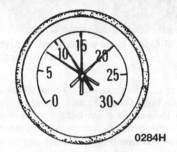

4.7 Large fluctuation

2F

(see illustration). Check ignition timing with a timing light and eliminate all other possible causes, utilizing the tests provided in this Chapter before you remove the timing chain cover to check the timing marks.

2 If the reading is three to eight inches below normal and it fluctuates at that low reading, suspect an intake manifold gasket leak at an intake port **(see illustration).**

3 If the needle has regular drops of about two to four inches at a steady rate the valves are probably leaking. Perform a compression or leak-down test to confirm this **(see illustration).**

4 An irregular drop or down-flick of the needle can be caused by a sticking valve or an ignition misfire. Perform a compression or leak-down test and read the spark plugs **(see illustration).**

5 A rapid vibration of about four in.-Hg vibration at idle combined with exhaust smoke indicates worn valve guides **(see illustration).** Perform a leak-down test to confirm this. If the rapid vibration occurs with an increase in engine speed, check for a leaking intake manifold gasket or head gasket, weak valve springs, burned valves or ignition misfire.

6 A slight fluctuation, say one inch up and down, may mean ignition problems. Check all the usual tune-up items and, if necessary, run the engine on an ignition analyzer.

7 If there is a large fluctuation, perform a compression or leak-down test to look for a weak or dead cylinder or a blown head gasket **(see illustration).**

8 If the needle moves slowly through a wide range, check for a clogged PCV system or throttle body or intake manifold gasket leaks.

9 Check for a slow return after revving the engine by quickly snapping the throttle open until the engine reaches about 2,500 rpm and let it shut **(see illustration).** Normally the reading should drop to near zero, rise above normal idle reading (about 5 in.-Hg over) and then return to the previous idle reading. If the vacuum returns slowly and doesn't peak when the throttle is snapped shut, the rings may be worn. If there is a long delay, look for a restricted exhaust system (often the muffler or catalytic converter). An easy way to check this is to temporarily disconnect the exhaust ahead of the suspected part and redo the test.

5 Engine removal - methods and precautions

If you've decided that the engine must be removed for overhaul or major repair work, several preliminary steps should be taken.

Choosing a work area is the first step. A shop, obviously, is the most desirable place to work. Adequate work space, along with storage space for the vehicle, will be needed. If a shop or garage isn't available, try to find a flat, level, clean work surface made of concrete or asphalt.

Cleaning the engine compartment and engine before beginning the removal procedure will help keep you and your tools clean.

An engine hoist or A-frame will also be needed. Make sure the equipment is load rated in excess of the combined weight of the engine and transaxle. Safety is the most important item, considering the potential hazards involved in lifting the engine out of the vehicle.

4.9 Slow return after revving

If the engine is being removed by a novice, a helper should be available. Advice and aid from someone more experienced would also be helpful. There are many times when one person can't do everything required at one time when lifting the engine out of the vehicle.

Plan the operation ahead of time. Arrange for or obtain all the tools and equipment you'll need before beginning the job. Some of the equipment necessary to perform engine removal and installation safely and easily are an engine hoist, a heavy duty floor jack, complete sets of wrenches and sockets described in the front of this manual, drain pans for coolant and oil, wooden blocks and plenty of rags and cleaning solvent for mopping spills. If the hoist must be rented, make sure that you arrange for it in advance and perform beforehand all of the operations possible without it. This will save you money and time.

Plan for the vehicle to be out of use for quite a while. A machine shop will be required to perform some of the work that the do-it-yourselfer cannot accomplish due to a

6.36 Use a large screwdriver or prybar to separate the engine from the transaxle

6.37 Make sure all wires and hoses are disconnected before lifting the engine out (lifting brackets are provided on the engine for attaching a chain or cable)

lack of special equipment. These shops often have a busy schedule, so it would be a good idea to consult them before removing the engine in order to accurately estimate the amount of time required to rebuild or repair components that may need work.

Always be very careful when removing and installing the engine. Serious injury can result from careless actions. Plan ahead, take your time and a job of this nature, although major, can be accomplished successfully.

6   Engine - removal and installation

Refer to illustrations 6.36 and 6.37
Warning 1: *The engine and transaxle are very heavy. Use suitable lifting equipment. Never place any part of your body under the engine/transaxle when it's supported only by lifting equipment. It could shift or fall, causing serious injury or death!*
Warning 2: *Gasoline is extremely flammable, so take extra precautions when you work on any part of the fuel system. Don't smoke or allow open flames or bare light bulbs near the work area, and don't work in a garage where a natural gas-type appliance (such as a water heater or clothes dryer) with a pilot light is present. Since gasoline is carcinogenic, wear latex gloves when there's a possibility of being exposed to fuel, and, if you spill any fuel on your skin, rinse it off immediately with soap and water. Mop up any spills immediately and do not store fuel-soaked rags where they could ignite. The fuel system is under constant pressure, so, if any fuel lines are to be disconnected, the fuel pressure in the system must be relieved first. When you perform any kind of work on the fuel system, wear safety glasses and have a Class B type fire extinguisher on hand.*
Warning 3: *The air conditioning system is under high pressure. Do not loosen any fittings or remove any components until after the system has been discharged. Air conditioning refrigerant should be properly discharged into an EPA-approved container at a*

dealer service department or an automotive air conditioning repair facility. Always wear eye protection when disconnecting air conditioning system fittings.
Caution: *It is critical to note bolt size and location during ALL disassembly procedures so that they are reinstalled in their original position. If a bolt is misplaced or needs replacement, use the exact size of the original by either measurement or by ordering a new one by part number. If an incorrect size is used, it may bottom and crack or ruin the component it is being tightened into or register a false torque reading.*
Note: *On 2.0L OHC and 2.5L OHV engines with a low mount air conditioning compressor, have the air conditioning system discharged by a professional before proceeding with engine removal.*

Removal
All models
1   Disconnect the battery and remove the ground straps. **Caution:** *If the vehicle is equipped with a Delco Loc II audio system, make sure you have the correct activation code before disconnecting the battery. See the information at the front of this manual for the radio re-activation procedure.* Refer to Chapter 11 and remove the hood.
2   Drain the coolant (see Chapter 1).
3   Drain the engine oil (see Chapter 1).
4   Remove the air cleaner assembly (see Chapter 4).
5   Relieve the fuel pressure and disconnect the fuel lines at the engine (see Chapter 4).
6   Disconnect the engine wiring harness at the bulkhead connector and lay it on the engine.
7   Tag and disconnect all other wires and vacuum hoses attached to the engine.
8   Detach the radiator and heater hoses connected to the engine.
9   Disconnect the shift, throttle, TV and cruise control cables as applicable.
10   Unbolt the power steering pump and tie it aside. On 2.0L turbocharged engines you'll

have to disconnect the hoses and drain the pump.
11   Disconnect the exhaust pipe and tie it out of the way.
12   Remove the cooling fan (see Chapter 3).
13   Remove the front fender liners (see Chapter 11).
14   The following items apply to specific models. On manual transaxle equipped vehicles only, remove the clutch slave cylinder (see Chapter 8).
15   If your vehicle has a four-cylinder engine and an automatic transaxle, disconnect the transmission oil cooler lines. Catch the fluid in a drain pan.
16   On 2.5L four-cylinder engines, remove the multi-relay bracket and power steering bracket.
17   To remove the air conditioning compressor on four-cylinder engines with a low mount compressor, disconnect the refrigerant hoses from the compressor and cap the ends (after system discharge). On 2.5L four-cylinder engines with a top-mounted compressor and all V6 engines, leave the hoses connected and unbolt the compressor from the engine, then tie it aside.
18   Recheck to be sure all wires, hoses and linkages are disconnected.

Four-cylinder models
19   Remove the front wheels.
20   Remove front brake calipers and discs (see Chapter 9).
21   Remove the two steering knuckle-to-strut bolts on each side of the vehicle. Be sure to mark their positions before disassembly (see Chapter 10).
22   Unbolt the two body-to-cradle bolts at the lower control arm on each side.
23   Loosen the eight remaining body-to-cradle bolts at the ends.
24   Remove one bolt at each end of each side, leaving one bolt per corner.
25   Support the body using a floor jack and a six foot long 4x4 timber placed crosswise under the firewall. Keep jackstands under the vehicle for safety.
26   Place a strong four wheel dolly under

the engine/transaxle assembly. Use wooden blocks to position the engine/transaxle on the dolly.

27 Lower the vehicle gently until the engine rests on the dolly.

28 Disconnect the engine/transaxle and strut mounting bolts.

29 Remove the four remaining cradle-to-body bolts.

30 Lift the body up, leaving the engine/transaxle on the dolly.

V6 models

31 Remove the mass airflow sensor (see Chapter 4).

32 Remove the radiator (see Chapter 3).

33 Attach an engine hoist to the engine. Make sure the cable or chains are securely bolted to the engine.

34 Unbolt the torque converter from the driveplate (see Chapter 7).

35 Unbolt the engine mounts.

36 Unbolt and separate the transaxle from the engine **(see illustration)**.

37 Lift the engine out through the top of the engine compartment **(see illustration)**.

Installation

38 Installation is the reverse of removal.

39 On automatic transaxle equipped models, be sure the torque converter is completely seated in the transaxle before installation of the engine.

40 Keep the hoist hooked up until all mounts are connected. On automatic transaxle equipped models, install the torque converter-to-driveplate fasteners and tighten them to the torque listed in the Chapter 7 Part B Specifications.

41 Add coolant, transaxle oil and engine oil as needed.

42 Adjust the drivebelt(s).

43 Check all cables and linkages for proper adjustment.

44 Run the engine, check for leaks and proper operation of all systems.

45 Recheck all fluid levels.

46 Where applicable, have the air conditioning system evacuated, charged and leak tested by a professional.

47 On four-cylinder models, have the front end alignment checked.

7 Engine rebuilding alternatives

The do-it-yourselfer is faced with a number of options when performing an engine overhaul. The decision to replace the engine block, piston/connecting rod assemblies and crankshaft depends on a number of factors, with the number one consideration being the condition of the block. Other considerations are cost, access to machine shop facilities, parts availability, time required to complete the project and the extent of prior mechanical experience on the part of the do-it-yourselfer.

Some of the rebuilding alternatives include:

Individual parts - If the inspection procedures reveal that the engine block and most engine components are in reusable condition, purchasing individual parts may be the most economical alternative. The block, crankshaft and piston/connecting rod assemblies should all be inspected carefully. Even if the block shows little wear, the cylinder bores should be surface honed.

Crankshaft kit - This rebuild package consists of a reground crankshaft and a matched set of pistons and connecting rods. The pistons will already be installed on the connecting rods. Piston rings and the necessary bearings will be included in the kit. These kits are commonly available for standard cylinder bores, as well as for engine blocks that have been bored to a regular oversize.

Short block - A short block consists of an engine block with a crankshaft and piston/connecting rod assemblies already installed. All new bearings are incorporated and all clearances will be correct. The existing camshaft, valve train components, cylinder head(s) and external parts can be bolted to the short block with little or no machine shop work necessary.

Long block - A long block consists of a short block plus an oil pump, oil pan, cylinder head(s), rocker arm cover(s), camshaft and valve train components, timing sprockets and chain or gears and timing cover. All components are installed with new bearings, seals and gaskets incorporated throughout. The installation of manifolds and extreme parts is all that is necessary.

Give careful thought to which alternative is best for you and discuss the situation with local automotive machine shops, auto parts dealers and experienced rebuilders before ordering or purchasing replacement parts.

8 Engine overhaul - disassembly sequence

1 It's much easier to disassemble and work on the engine if it's mounted on a portable engine stand. These stands can often be rented quite cheaply from an equipment rental yard. Before the engine is mounted on a stand, the flywheel/driveplate should be removed from the crankshaft.

2 If a stand isn't available, it's possible to disassemble the engine with it blocked up on a sturdy workbench or on the floor. Be extra careful not to tip or drop the engine when working without a stand.

3 If you're going to buy a rebuilt engine, all external components must come off first, to be transferred to the replacement engine, just as they will if you're doing a complete engine overhaul yourself. They include:

Alternator and brackets
Emissions control components
Distributor (if equipped), coil pack, spark plug wires and spark plugs
Thermostat and housing cover

Water pump
EFI components
Intake/exhaust manifolds
Oil filter
Engine mounts
Clutch and flywheel or driveplate

Caution: *It is critical to note bolt size and location during ALL disassembly procedures so that they are reinstalled in their original position. If a bolt is misplaced or needs replacement, use the exact size of the original by either measurement or by ordering a new one by part number. If an incorrect size is used, it may bottom and crack or ruin the component it is being tightened into or register a false torque reading.*

Note: *When removing the external components from the engine, pay close attention to details that may be helpful or important during reassembly. Note the installed position of gaskets, seals, spacers, pins, washers, bolts and other small items.*

4 If you're installing a short block, which consists of the engine block, crankshaft, pistons and connecting rods all assembled, then the cylinder head(s), oil pan and oil pump will have to be removed as well. See *Engine rebuilding alternatives* for additional information regarding the different possibilities to be considered.

5 If you're planning a complete overhaul, the engine must be disassembled and the internal components removed in the following general order:

2.0L OHC four-cylinder engine

Clutch and flywheel or driveplate
Camshaft cover
Intake and exhaust manifolds
Timing belt/sprockets
Camshaft carrier and camshaft
Cylinder head
Oil pan
Oil pump
Piston/connecting rod assemblies
Crankshaft and main bearings

2.3 liter four-cylinder engines

Timing chain and sprockets
Timing chain housing
Cylinder head and camshafts
Oil pan
Oil pump
Balance shaft assembly (if equipped)
Piston/connecting rod assemblies
Rear main oil seal housing
Crankshaft and main bearings

2.5L OHV four-cylinder and V6 engines

Clutch and flywheel or driveplate
Rocker arm cover(s)
Intake and exhaust manifolds
Rocker arms and pushrods
Valve lifters
Cylinder head(s)
Front cover
Timing chain and sprockets or timing gears

2F

9.1 A small plastic bag, with an appropriate label, can be used to store the valve train components so they can be kept together and reinstalled in the correct guide

9.2 Be sure to check the valve spring installed height (the distance from the top of the seat/shims to the underside of the retainer)

9.3a Use a valve spring compressor to compress the spring, then remove the keepers from the valve stem

9.3b If the valve won't pull through the guide, deburr the edge of the stem end and the area around the top of the keeper groove with a file or whetstone

Camshaft
Oil pan
Oil pump (2.5L four-cylinder only)
Engine force balancer assembly
   (some 2.5L four-cylinder engines)
Piston/connecting rod assemblies
Crankshaft and main bearings

6   Critical cooling system components such as the hoses, drivebelts, thermostat and water pump MUST be replaced with new parts when an engine is overhauled. Also, we don't recommend overhauling the oil pump - always install a new one when an engine is rebuilt.

7   Before beginning the disassembly and overhaul procedures, make sure the following items are available:

Common hand tools
Small cardboard boxes or plastic bags for
   storing parts
Gasket scraper
Ridge reamer
Vibration damper puller
Micrometers
Telescoping gauges
Dial indicator set
Valve spring compressor
Cylinder surfacing hone
Piston ring groove cleaning tool
Electric drill motor
Tap and die set
Wire brushes
Oil gallery brushes
Cleaning solvent

9   Cylinder head - disassembly

Refer to illustrations 9.1, 9.2, 9.3a and 9.3b
Note: *New and rebuilt cylinder heads are commonly available for most engines at dealerships, automotive machine shops and auto parts stores. Due to the fact that some specialized tools are necessary for the disassembly and inspection procedures, and replacement parts may not be readily available, it*

may be more practical and economical to purchase exchange replacement head(s) rather than taking the time to disassemble, inspect and recondition the original(s).

1   Cylinder head disassembly involves removal of the intake and exhaust valves and related components. If they're still in place, remove the rocker arms before proceeding (2.5L four-cylinder and V6 engines). On 2.3 liter OHC engines, remove the camshaft(s) and housing(s) before beginning the cylinder head disassembly procedure (see Part B of this Chapter). Before the valves are removed, arrange to label and store them, along with their related components, so they can be kept separated and be reinstalled in their original locations **(see illustration)**.

2   Measure the valve spring installed height for each valve and compare it to the Specifications. The measurement is taken from the bottom of the spring to the underside of the retainer **(see illustration)**.

3   Compress the springs on the first valve with a spring compressor and remove the keepers (see illustration). Carefully release the valve spring compressor and remove the retainer, the springs and the spring seat. **Note:** *On the 2.3 liter OHC engines, the valve rotators are located under the valve springs.* Next, remove the O-ring seal from the upper end of the valve stem and the umbrella-type (PC) seal (if used) from the guide, then pull the valve out of the head. If the valve binds in the guide (won't pull through), push it back into the head and deburr the area around the keeper groove with a fine file or whetstone **(see illustration)**.

4   Repeat the procedure for the remaining valves. Remember to keep all the parts for each valve together so they can be reinstalled in the same location.

5   Once the valves and related components have been removed, the head should be thoroughly cleaned and inspected. If a complete engine overhaul is being done, finish the engine disassembly procedures before beginning the cylinder head cleaning and inspection process.

10   Cylinder head - cleaning and inspection

Refer to illustrations 10.11a, 10.11b, 10.13, 10.14, 10.15, 10.16, 10.17 and 10.18
1   Thorough cleaning of the cylinder head(s) and related valve train components, followed by a detailed inspection, will enable you to decide how much valve service work must be done during the engine overhaul.

Cleaning

2   Remove all traces of old gasket material and sealing compound from the head gasket, intake manifold and exhaust manifold sealing surfaces with a gasket scraper. Be very careful not to gouge the cylinder head, particularly if it's made of aluminum. Special gasket removal solvents, which soften gaskets and make removal much easier, are available at auto parts stores.

3   Remove any built up scale from the coolant passages.

4   Run a stiff wire brush through the various holes to remove any deposits that may have formed in them.

5   Run an appropriate size tap into each of

10.11a Check the cylinder head gasket surface for warpage by trying to slip a feeler gauge under the straightedge (see the Specifications for the maximum warpage allowed and use a feeler gauge of that thickness)

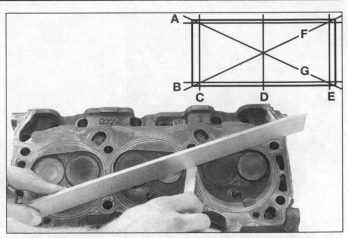

10.11b Make the check with the straightedge positioned diagonally, lengthwise and across the head as shown in the inset (upper right corner)

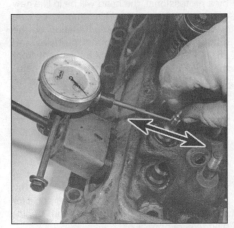

10.13 A dial indicator can be used to determine the valve stem-to-guide clearance (move the valve stem as indicated by the arrows)

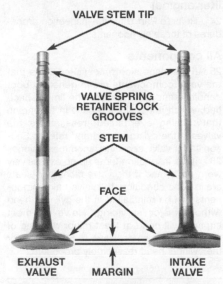

10.14 Check for valve wear at the points shown here

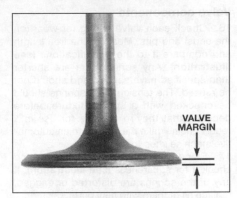

10.15 The margin width on each valve must be as specified (if no margin exists, the valve cannot be reused)

2F

the threaded holes to remove corrosion and thread sealant that may be present. If compressed air is available, use it to clear the holes of debris produced by this operation.

6   On overhead valve models, clean the rocker arm pivot bolt threads with a wire brush.

7   Clean the cylinder head with solvent and dry it thoroughly. Compressed air will speed the drying process and ensure that all holes and recessed areas are clean. **Note:** *Decarbonizing chemicals are available and may prove very useful when cleaning cylinder heads and valve train components. They are very caustic and should be used with caution. Wear eye protection and solvent proof gloves. Be sure to follow the instructions on the container.*

8   Clean the valve train parts with solvent and dry them thoroughly. Do the components from one valve at a time to avoid mixing up the parts.

9   Scrape off any heavy deposits that may have formed on the valves. Use a motorized wire brush to remove deposits from the valve heads and stems (be sure to wear eye pro-

tection). Again, make sure the valves don't become mixed.

Inspection

10   Inspect the head very carefully for cracks, evidence of coolant leakage and other damage. If cracks are found, a replacement cylinder head should be obtained.

11   Using a straightedge and feeler gauge, check the head gasket mating surface for warpage **(see illustrations)**. If the warpage exceeds the specified limit, it can be resurfaced at an automotive machine shop. **Note:** *On V6 engines, if the heads are resurfaced, the intake manifold flanges will also require machining. If more than 0.010-inch must be removed, a new head will be required.*

12   Examine the valve seats in each of the combustion chambers. If they're pitted, cracked or burned, the head will require valve service that's beyond the scope of the home mechanic.

13   Check the valve stem-to-guide clearance by measuring the lateral movement of the valve stem using a dial indicator attached securely to the head **(see illustration)**. The valve must be in the guide and approximately 1/16-inch off the seat. The total valve stem movement indicated by the gauge needle must be divided by two to obtain the actual clearance. After this is done, if there is still some doubt regarding the condition of the valve guides they should be checked by an automotive machine shop (the cost should be minimal).

Valves

14   Carefully inspect each valve face for uneven wear, deformation, cracks, pits and burned spots. Check the valve stem for scuffing and galling and the neck for cracks. Rotate the valve and check for any obvious indication that it's bent. Look for pits and excessive wear on the end of the stem **(see illustration)**. The presence of any of these conditions indicates the need for valve service by an automotive machine shop.

15   Measure the margin width on each valve **(see illustration)**. Any valve with a margin narrower than 1/32-inch will have to be replaced with a new one.

10.16 Measure the free length of each valve spring with a dial or vernier caliper

10.17 Check each valve spring for squareness

10.18 The valve rotators can be checked by turning the inner and outer sections in opposite directions, feeling for smooth movement and excessive play

Valve components

16   Check each valve spring for wear (on the ends) and pits. Measure the free length and compare it to the Specifications **(see illustration)**. Any springs that are shorter than specified have sagged and should not be reused. The tension of all springs should be checked with a special fixture before deciding that they're suitable for use in a rebuilt engine (take the springs to an automotive machine shop for this check).

17   Stand each spring on a flat surface and check it for squareness **(see illustration)**. If any of the springs are distorted or sagged, replace all of them with new parts.

18   Check the spring retainers and keepers for obvious wear and cracks. Any questionable parts should be replaced with new ones, as extensive damage will occur if they fail during engine operation. Make sure the valve rotators (if used) operate smoothly with no binding or excessive play **(see illustration)**.

Valve actuators

19   Check the rocker arm faces (the areas that contact the pushrod ends and valve stems or, in the case of OHC four-cylinder engines, the areas that contact the lash compensators, rocker arm guides and camshaft lobes) for pits, wear, galling, score marks and rough spots.

20   Check the rocker arm pivot contact areas and pedestals/pivot balls as well. Look for cracks in each rocker arm. Check the rocker arm bolts to make sure they're in good condition.

21   On overhead valve models, check the pushrod ends for scuffing and excessive wear. Roll each pushrod on a flat surface, such as a piece of plate glass, to determine if it's bent.

22   If you're working on an OHC four-cylinder engine, check the valve lash compensators and bores for wear and damage. Look for score marks, galling and pits.

23   Any damaged or excessively worn parts must be replaced with new ones.

Camshafts, lifters and housings (2.3 liter engine)

24   Refer to Part B for the inspection procedures of these components.

All components

25   If the inspection process indicates that the valve components are in generally poor condition and worn beyond the limits specified, which is usually the case in an engine that's being overhauled, reassemble the valves in the cylinder head and refer to Section 11 for valve servicing recommendations.

26   If the inspection turns up no excessively worn parts, and if the valve faces and seats are in good condition, the valve train components can be reinstalled in the cylinder head without major servicing. However, most engines will need at least minor refacing of the valves and seats. Refer to Section 12 for the cylinder head reassembly procedure.

11   Valves - servicing

1   Because of the complex nature of the job and the special tools and equipment needed, servicing of the valves, the valve seats and the valve guides, commonly known as a valve job, is best left to a professional.

2   The home mechanic can remove and disassemble the head(s), do the initial cleaning and inspection, then reassemble and deliver the head(s) to a dealer service department or an automotive machine shop for the actual valve servicing.

3   The dealer service department, or automotive machine shop, will remove the valves and springs, recondition or replace the valves and valve seats, recondition the valve guides, check and replace the valve springs, spring retainers or rotators and keepers (as necessary), replace the valve seals with new ones, reassemble the valve components and make sure the installed spring and stem height is correct. The cylinder head gasket surface will also be resurfaced if it's warped.

4   After the valve job has been performed

by a professional, the head will be in like new condition. When the head is returned, be sure to clean it again before installation on the engine to remove any metal particles and abrasive grit that may still be present from the valve service or head resurfacing operations. Use compressed air, if available, to blow out all the oil holes and passages.

12   Cylinder head-reassembly

Refer to illustrations 12.4, 12.7, 12.8 and 12.10

1   Regardless of whether or not a cylinder head is sent to an automotive repair shop for resurfacing, it must be clean before beginning reassembly.

2   If the head was sent out for valve servicing, the valves and related components will already be in place. Begin the reassembly procedure with Step 8.

3   Drop the spring seat or shim(s) over the valve guide.

4   Install new seals on each of the intake valve guides. Using a deep socket **(see illustration)**, gently tap PC-type seals into place until it's completely seated on the guide, or

12.4 Make sure the valve stem seals are seated against the tops of the valve guides

12.7 Make sure the O-ring seal under the retainer is seated in the groove and not twisted before installing the keepers

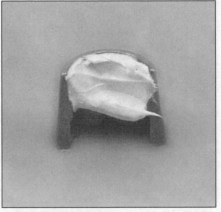

12.8 Apply a small dab of grease to each keeper as shown here before installation - it will hold them in place on the valve stem as the spring is released

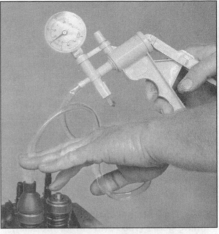

12.10 A special adapter and vacuum pump are required to check the O-ring valve stem seals for leaks (not all engines)

13.4 When checking the camshaft lobe lift (OHV engines only), the dial indicator plunger must be positioned directly in line with the pushrod (use a short length of vacuum hose to hold the plunger over the pushrod end, if you encounter difficulty keeping the plunger on the pushrod)

push umbrella-type seals until they've bottomed on the valve spring shim. Don't twist or cock the seals during installation or they won't seal properly on the valve stems. The umbrella-type seals are installed over the exhaust valves after the valves are in place.

5   Beginning at one end of the head, lubricate and install the first valve. Apply moly-base grease or clean engine oil to the valve stem.

6   Set the valve springs, shield and retainer (or rotator) in place.

7   On earlier model engines, using an O-ring type valve stem seal, compress the springs with a valve spring compressor and carefully install the O-ring in the lower groove of the valve stem (not used on all engines). Make sure the seal is not twisted - it must lie perfectly flat in the groove **(see illustration)**.

8   On all engines, position the keepers in the upper groove, then slowly release the compressor and make sure the keepers seat properly. Apply a small dab of grease to each keeper to hold it in place if necessary **(see illustration)**.

9   Repeat the procedure for the remaining valves. Be sure to return the components to their original locations - don't mix them!

10   Once all the valves are in place, valve stem O-ring seals (on models so equipped) must be checked to make sure they don't leak. This procedure requires a vacuum pump and a special adapter, so it may be a good idea to have it done by a dealer service department, repair shop or automotive machine shop. The adapter is positioned on each valve retainer or rotator and vacuum is applied with the hand pump **(see illustration)**. If the vacuum cannot be maintained, the seal is leaking and must be checked/replaced before the head is installed on the engine.

11   Check the installed valve spring height with a ruler graduated in 1/32-inch increments or a dial caliper. If the head was sent out for service work, the installed height should be correct (but don't automatically assume that it is). The measurement is taken from the top of each spring seat or shim(s) to

the top of the oil shield (or bottom of the retainer/rotator - the two points are the same) **(see illustration 9.2)**. If the height is greater than specified, shims can be added under the springs to correct it. **Caution:** *Do not, under any circumstances, shim the springs to a point where the installed height is less than specified.*

12   On overhead valve models, apply moly-base grease to the rocker arm faces and pilot balls or pedestals, then install the rocker arms, but don't tighten the bolts completely.

13   On 2.3 liter OHC engines, refer to Part B and install the camshaft(s), lifter(s) and the camshaft housing(s) onto the head.

13 Camshaft, bearings and lifters - removal, inspection and installation

Removal

2.0L and 2.3L OHC four-cylinder engines

1   These parts can be removed with the engine installed in the vehicle. Refer to specific engine section of this Chapter for removal procedures.

2.5L OHV four-cylinder engine

Refer to illustrations 13.4, 13.10a and 13.10b

Note: *It's assumed that the engine is already out of the vehicle and the valve cover has been removed. This procedure is not possible with the engine in the vehicle.*

2   In order to determine the extent of cam lobe wear, the lobe lift should be checked prior to camshaft removal.

3   Position the number one piston at TDC on the compression stroke (see Section 23).

4   Beginning with the number one cylinder valves, loosen the rocker arms nuts and pivot the rocker arms sideways. Mount a dial indicator on the engine and position the plunger against the top of the first pushrod **(see illustration)**.

5   Zero the dial indicator, then very slowly turn the crankshaft in the normal direction of rotation until the indicator needle stops and begins to move in the opposite direction. The point at which it stops indicates maximum cam lobe lift.

6   Record this figure for future reference, then reposition the piston at TDC on the compression stroke.

7   Move the dial indicator to the remaining number one cylinder rocker arm and repeat the check. Be sure to record the result for each valve.

8   Repeat the check for the remaining valves. Since each piston must be at TDC on the compression stroke for this procedure, work from cylinder-to-cylinder following the firing order sequence.

9   After the check is complete, compare the results to the Specifications. If camshaft lobe lift is less than specified, cam lobe wear

2F

13.10a On 2.5L four-cylinder engines with timing gears (1989 and earlier models), turn the camshaft until the holes in the gear are aligned with the thrust plate bolts, then remove them with a ratchet and socket

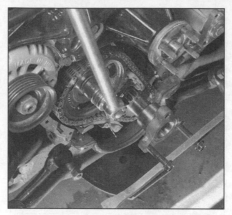

13.10b Use a prybar against two bolts in the temporarily installed crankshaft hub to hold the engine while a breaker bar is used on the camshaft bolt

13.12 Support the camshaft near the block to prevent damage to the bearings (V6 engine shown)

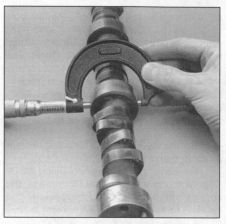

13.14 The camshaft bearing journal diameters are checked to pinpoint excessive wear and out-of-round conditions

has occurred and a new camshaft should be installed. Once lobe lift has been determined, the pushrods, pushrod cover, hydraulic lifters, distributor, oil pump driveshaft, crankshaft pulley and hub and timing gear cover must be removed (see Part C) before the camshaft can be removed from the block.

10   Turn the crankshaft until the holes in the camshaft gear are aligned with the thrust plate bolts and remove the bolts through the holes in the cam gear. On chain driven gears, remove the center camshaft sprocket bolt and remove the chain and gear set (**see illustrations**).

11   Carefully pull the camshaft out of the block. **Caution:** *To avoid damage to the camshaft bearings as the lobes pass over them, support the camshaft near the block as it's withdrawn.*

V6 engines

Refer to illustration 13.12

Note: *It's assumed that the engine is already out of the vehicle and the valve covers have been removed. This procedure is not possible with the engine in the vehicle. The pushrods, distributor, oil pump driveshaft, intake manifold, hydraulic lifters, crankshaft balancer, timing chain cover, timing chain and camshaft sprocket must be removed (see Part D and E) before the camshaft can be removed from the block.*

12   Carefully pull the camshaft out of the block. **Caution:** *To avoid damage to the camshaft bearings as the lobes pass over them, support the camshaft near the block as it's withdrawn* (**see illustration**).

Inspection

Refer to illustrations 13.14, 13.19a, 13.19b, 13.19c and 13.21

Camshaft

13   After the camshaft has been removed from the engine, cleaned with solvent and dried, inspect the bearing journals for uneven

wear, pitting and evidence of seizure. If the journals are damaged, the bearing inserts in the block (or the bearing surfaces in the camshaft carrier on the OHC four-cylinder engine) are probably damaged as well. Both the camshaft and bearings will have to be replaced. If the bearing surfaces in the camshaft carrier on the OHC engine are worn or damaged, a new carrier will be required.

14   If the journals are in good condition, measure the bearing journals with a micrometer (**see illustration**) to determine their sizes and whether or not they're out-of-round. The inside diameter of each bearing can be measured with a telescoping gauge and micrometer. Subtract each cam journal diameter from the corresponding bearing inside diameter to obtain the bearing oil clearance. Compare the clearance for each bearing to the Specifications. If it's excessive for any of the bearings, have new bearings installed by an automotive machine shop.

15   Check the camshaft lobes for heat discoloration, score marks, chipped areas, pitting and uneven wear. If the lobes are in good condition and if the lobe lift measurements are as specified, the camshaft can be reused.

Gears (1989 and earlier 2.5L four-cylinder engine only)

16   Check the camshaft drive and driven gears for cracks, missing teeth and excessive wear. If the teeth are highly polished, pitted and galled, or if the outer hardened surface of the teeth is flaking off, new parts will be required. If one gear is worn or damaged, replace both gears as a set. Never install one new and one used gear.

17   Check the gear end clearance with a feeler gauge and compare it to the Specifications. If it's less than the minimum specified, the spacer ring should be replaced. If it's excessive, the thrust plate must be replaced. In either case, the gear will have to be pressed off the camshaft, so take the parts to an automotive machine shop.

Conventional lifters

18   Clean the lifters with solvent and dry

them thoroughly without mixing them up.

19   Check each lifter wall, pushrod seat and foot for scuffing, score marks and uneven wear. Each lifter foot (the surface that rides on the cam lobe) must be slightly convex, although this can be difficult to determine by eye. If the base of the lifter is concave (**see illustrations**), the lifters and camshaft must be replaced. If the lifter walls are damaged or worn (which isn't very likely), inspect the lifter bores in the engine block as well. If the pushrod seats (**see illustration**) are worn, check the pushrod ends.

20   If new lifters are being installed, a new camshaft must also be installed. If a new camshaft is installed, then use new lifters as well. Never install used lifters unless the original camshaft is used and the lifters can be installed in their original location!

Roller lifters

21   Check the rollers carefully for wear and damage and make sure they turn freely without excessive play (**see illustration**). The inspection procedure for conventional lifters also applies to roller lifters.

22   Used roller lifters can be reinstalled with a new camshaft if they are in good condition,

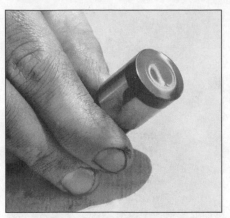

13.19a If the bottom (foot) of any lifter is worn concave, scratched or pitted, replace the entire set with new lifters

13.19b The bottom (foot) of each lifter should be slightly convex - the side of another lifter can be used as a straightedge to check it (if it appears flat, it's worn and should be discarded)

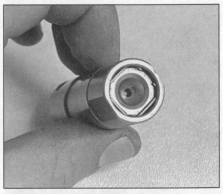

13.19c Check the pushrod seat (arrow) in the top of each lifter for wear

13.21 The roller on roller lifters must turn freely - check for wear, roller pitting and excessive play as well

13.25 Be sure to prelube the camshaft bearing journals and lobes before installation

13.27a Align the timing marks as shown here when installing the camshaft on the 2.5L OHV four-cylinder engine with timing gears

2F

13.27b Proper positioning of the timing marks - 2.5L OHV engine with a timing chain

but don't use the original camshaft if new lifters are installed.

Bearing replacement

23   Camshaft bearing replacement requires special tools and expertise that places it outside the scope of the home mechanic. Take the block to an automotive machine shop to ensure that the job is done correctly. The OHC four-cylinder engine doesn't have bearing inserts - if the bearing surfaces are damaged or excessively worn, a new camshaft carrier will have to be installed.

Installation

2.0L and 2.3L OHC four-cylinder engines

24   Since it's part of the cylinder head installation procedure and can be done with the engine in the vehicle, camshaft installation is covered in Chapter 2, Part A (2.0L engine) or Part B (2.3L engine).

2.5L OHV four-cylinder engine

Refer to illustrations 13.25, 13.27a and 13.27b
25   Lubricate the camshaft bearing journals and cam lobes with camshaft and lifter pre-

lube **(see illustration)**.
26   Slide the camshaft into the engine. Support the cam near the block and be careful not to scrape or nick the bearings.
27   Install the gear on the end of the crankshaft (if not already done). Don't forget the Woodruff key and don't hammer the gear onto the shaft. On gear-driven camshafts, align the timing marks on the gears as the gears mesh **(see illustration)**. On chain-driven camshafts, install the camshaft into the engine block first, then install the timing gears and chain, making sure the timing marks are properly aligned **(see illustration)**.
28   Line up the access holes in the gear with the thrust plate holes and the bolt holes in the block. Apply a non-hardening thread-locking compound to the threads, then install the thrust plate bolts and tighten them to the torque listed in this Chapter's Specifications.

V6 engines

29   Lubricate the camshaft bearing journals and cam lobes with camshaft and lifter prelube **(see illustration 13.25)**.
30   Slide the camshaft into the engine. Support the cam near the block and be careful not to scrape or nick the bearings.

14   Piston/connecting rod assembly - removal

Refer to illustrations 14.1, 14.3 and 14.5
Note: *Prior to removing the piston/connecting rod assemblies, remove the cylinder head(s), the oil pan and the oil pump by referring to the appropriate Parts of Chapter 2. If your engine is a later model four-cylinder with*

14.1 A ridge reamer is required to remove the ridge from the top of the cylinder - do this before removing the pistons!

14.3 Check the connecting rod side clearance with a feeler gauge as shown

14.5 To prevent damage to the crankshaft journals and cylinder walls, slip sections of hose over the rod bolts before removing the pistons

a balancer assembly, remove it as well.

1   Completely remove the ridge at the top of each cylinder with a ridge reaming tool **(see illustration)**. Follow the manufacturer's instructions provided with the tool. Failure to remove the ridge before attempting to remove the piston/connecting rod assemblies may result in piston breakage.

2   After the cylinder ridges have been removed, turn the engine upside-down so the crankshaft is facing up.

3   Before the connecting rods are removed, check the side clearance with feeler gauges. Slide them between the first connecting rod and the crankshaft throw until the play is removed **(see illustration)**. The clearance is equal to the thickness of the feeler gauge(s). If it exceeds the service limit, new connecting rods will be required. If new rods (or a new crankshaft) are installed, the clearance may fall under the specified minimum (if it does, the rods will have to be machined to restore it - consult an automotive machine shop for advice if necessary). Repeat the procedure for the remaining connecting rods.

4   Check the connecting rods and caps for identification marks. If they're not plainly marked, use a small center punch to make the appropriate number of identifications on each rod and cap to match the cylinder they're associated with.

5   Loosen each of the connecting rod cap nuts or bolts 1/2-turn at a time until they can be removed by hand. Remove the number one connecting rod cap and bearing insert. Don't drop the bearing insert out of the cap. Slip a short length of plastic or rubber hose over each connecting rod cap bolt (only on models where the bolt is pressed into the connecting rod) to protect the crankshaft journal and cylinder wall when the piston is removed **(see illustration)**. Push the connecting rod/piston assembly out through the top of the engine. Use a wooden hammer handle to push on the upper bearing insert in the connecting rod. If resistance is felt, double-check to make sure all of the ridge was removed from the cylinder.

6   Repeat the procedure for the remaining cylinders. After removal, reassemble the connecting rod caps and bearing inserts in their respective connecting rods and install the cap nuts or bolts finger tight. Leaving the old bearing inserts in place until reassembly will help prevent the connecting rod bearing surfaces from being accidentally nicked or gouged. **Note:** *On 2.0L OHC engines new rod bolts must be installed when the engine is reassembled. However, save the old bolts for use when checking the rod bearing oil clearance (as described in Section 27).*

15 Crankshaft - removal

Refer to illustrations 15.1, 15.3, 15.4a, 15.4b and 15.4c

Note: *The crankshaft can be removed only after the engine has been removed from the vehicle. It's assumed that the flywheel or drivebelt, crankshaft balancer/pulley hub, timing chain or gears, oil pan, oil pump and piston/connecting rod assemblies have already been removed. If your engine is equipped with a one-piece rear main oil seal, the seal (and housing, on engines so equipped) must*

be removed from the block before proceeding with crankshaft removal.

1   Before the crankshaft is removed, check the endplay. Mount a dial indicator with the stem in-line with the crankshaft and just touching one of the crank throws **(see illustration)**.

2   Push the crankshaft all the way to the rear and zero the dial indicator. Next, pry the crankshaft to the front as far as possible and check the reading on the dial indicator. The distance that it moves is the endplay. If it's greater than specified, check the crankshaft thrust surfaces for wear. If no wear is evident, new main bearings should correct the endplay.

3   If a dial indicator isn't available, feeler gauges can be used. Gently pry or push the crankshaft all the way to the front of the engine. Slip feeler gauges between the crankshaft and the front face of the thrust main bearing to determine the clearance **(see illustration)**.

4   Check the main bearing caps to see if they're marked to indicate their locations. They should be numbered consecutively

15.1 Checking crankshaft endplay with a dial indicator

15.3 Checking crankshaft endplay with a feeler gauge (this must be done at the thrust bearing)

15.4a Use a center punch or number stamping dies to mark the main bearing caps to ensure that they're reinstalled in their original locations on the block (make the punch marks near one of the bolt heads)

15.4b Mark the caps in order from the front of the engine to the rear (one mark for the front cap, two for the second one and so on) - the rear cap doesn't have to be marked since it usually can't be installed in any other location

15.4c The arrow on the main bearing cap indicates the front of the engine

from the front of the engine to the rear. If they aren't, mark them with number stamping dies or a center punch **(see illustrations)**. Main bearing caps generally have a cast-in arrow, which points to the front of the engine **(see illustration)**. Loosen each of the main bearing cap bolts 1/4-turn at a time each, until they can be removed by hand.

5   Gently tap the caps with a soft-face hammer, then separate them from the engine block. If necessary, use the bolts as levers to remove the caps. Try not to drop the bearing inserts if they come out with the caps.

6   Carefully lift the crankshaft out of the engine. **Caution:** *On 1995 2.3L engines, the balance shaft drive chain will be around the transaxle end of the crankshaft. Lift it out with the crankshaft and remove it once clear of the engine block. For information on balance shaft assembly removal and installation, refer to Chapter 2, Part B. Keep the bearing inserts in place in the engine block and main bearing caps, return the caps to their respective locations on the engine block and tighten the bolts finger tight.*

16   Engine block - cleaning

Refer to illustrations 16.1a, 16.1b, 16.8 and 16.10

Note: *The core plugs (also known as freeze or soft plugs) may be difficult or impossible to retrieve if they're driven into the block coolant passages.*

1   Remove the core plugs from the engine block. To do this, knock the plugs sideways into the block using a hammer and punch, then grasp them with large pliers and pull them back through the holes **(see illustrations)**.

2   Using a gasket scraper, remove all traces of gasket material from the engine block. Be very careful not to nick or gouge the gasket sealing surfaces.

3   Remove the main bearing caps and separate the bearing inserts from the caps and the engine block. Tag the bearings, indicating which cylinder they were removed from and whether they were in the cap or the block, then set them aside.

4   Unscrew and remove all of the threaded oil gallery plugs from the rear of the block.

Use new plugs when the engine is reassembled.

5   If the engine is extremely dirty it should be taken to an automotive machine shop to be cleaned.

6   After the block is returned, clean all oil holes and oil galleries one more time. Brushes specifically designed for this purpose are available at most auto parts stores. Flush the passages with hot soapy water until the water runs clear, dry the block thoroughly and wipe all machined surfaces with a light, rust preventative oil. If you have access to compressed air, use it to speed the drying process and to blow out all the oil holes and galleries.

7   If the block isn't extremely dirty or sludged up, you can do an adequate cleaning job with hot soapy water and a stiff brush. Take plenty of time and do a thorough job. Regardless of the cleaning method used, be sure to clean all oil holes and galleries very thoroughly, dry the block completely and coat all machined surfaces with light oil.

8   The threaded holes in the block must be clean to ensure accurate torque readings during reassembly. Run the proper size tap into each of the holes to remove any rust, corrosion, thread sealant or sludge and to restore any damaged threads **(see illustra-**

2F

16.1a A hammer and large punch can be used to knock the core plugs sideways

16.1b Use pliers to remove the core plugs from the block

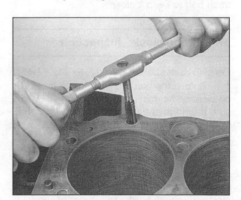

16.8 All bolt holes in the block - particularly the main bearing cap and head bolt holes - should be cleaned and restored with a tap (be sure to remove debris from the holes after this is done)

16.10 A large socket on an extension can be used to drive the new core plugs into the block holes

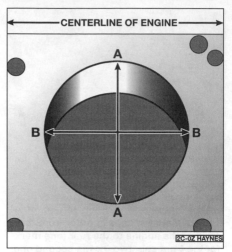

17.4a Measure the diameter of each cylinder at a right angle to engine centerline (A), and parallel to the engine centerline (B) - out-of-round is the difference between A and B; taper is the difference between A and B at the top of the cylinder and A and B at the bottom of the cylinder

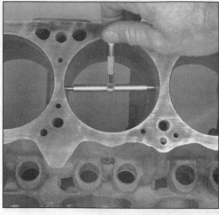

17.4b The ability to "feel" when the telescoping gauge is at the correct point will be developed over time, so work slowly and repeat the check until you're satisfied the bore measurement is accurate

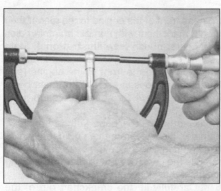

17.4c The gauge is then measured with a micrometer to determine the bore size

tion). **Caution:** *The manufacturer recommends that on the 2.3L four-cylinder engines, a tap should not be used to clean the bolt holes. If possible, use compressed air to clear the holes of debris produced by this operation. Now is a good time to clean the threads on the head bolts and main bearing cap bolts as well.*

9   Reinstall the main bearing caps and tighten the bolts finger tight.

10   After coating the sealing surfaces of the new core plugs with a hardening-type sealant (such as Permatex no. 1), install them in the engine block **(see illustration)**. Make sure they're driven straight and seated properly or leakage could result. Special tools are available for this purpose, but equally good results can be obtained using a large socket, with an outside diameter that will just slip into the core plug, a 1/2-inch drive extension and a hammer.

11   Apply a non-hardening sealant (such as Permatex number 2 or Teflon tape) to the new oil gallery plugs and thread them into the holes at the rear of the block. Make sure they're tightened securely.

12   If the engine isn't going to be reassembled right away, cover with a large plastic trash bag to keep it clean.

17 Engine block - inspection

Refer to illustrations 17.4a, 17.4b and 17.4c

1   Before the block is inspected, it should be cleaned as described in Section 16. Make sure the ridge at the top of each cylinder has been completely removed.

2   Visually check the block for cracks, rust and corrosion. Look for stripped threads in the bolt holes. It's also a good idea to have the block checked for hidden cracks by an automotive machine shop that has the special equipment to do this type of work. If defects are found, have the block repaired, if possible, or replaced.

3   On 2.3L OHC engines, check the oil flow check valve located in the oil passage in the right front corner of the block.

4   Measure the diameter of each cylinder at the top (just under the ridge area), center and bottom of the cylinder bore, parallel to the crankshaft axis **(see illustration)**. Next, measure each cylinder's diameter at the same three locations **(see illustrations)** across the crankshaft axis. Compare the results with the Specifications. If the cylinder walls are badly scuffed or scored, or if they're out-of-round or tapered beyond the limits given in the Specifications, have the engine block rebored and honed at an automotive machine shop. If you don't have the necessary measuring tools, the machine shop will also check the cylinder bores. If a rebore is done, oversize pistons and rings will be required.

5   If the cylinders are in good condition and not worn beyond specified limits, and if the piston-to-cylinder clearances can be maintained properly, then they don't have to be rebored. Honing is all that is necessary (see Section 18).

18 Cylinder honing

Refer to illustrations 18.3 and 18.3b

1   Prior to engine reassembly, the cylinder bores must be honed so the new piston rings will seat correctly and provide the best possible combustion chamber seal. **Note:** *If you don't have the tools or don't want to tackle the honing operation, most automotive machine shops will do it for a reasonable fee.*

2   Before honing the cylinders, install the main bearing caps and tighten the bolts to the torque listed in this Chapter's Specifications.

3   Two types of cylinder hones are com-

monly available - the flex hone or "bottle brush" type and the more traditional surfacing hone with spring loaded stones. Both will do the job, but for the less experienced mechanic the "bottle brush" hone will probably be easier to use. You'll also need plenty of light oil or honing oil, some rags and an electric drill motor. Proceed as follows:

a) *Mount the hone in the drill motor, compress the stones and slip it into the first cylinder* **(see illustration)**. *Be sure to wear eye protection!*

b) *Lubricate the cylinder with plenty of oil, turn on the drill and move the hone up-and-down in the cylinder at a pace that will produce a fine cross-hatch pattern on the cylinder walls. Ideally, the cross-hatch lines should intersect at approximately a 60-degree angle* **(see illustration)**. *Be sure to use plenty of lubricant and don't take off any more material than is absolutely necessary to produce the desired finish.* **Note:** *Piston ring manufacturers may specify a smaller cross-hatch angle than the traditional 60-degree - read and follow any instructions printed on the piston ring packages.*

18.3a A "bottle brush" hone will produce better results if you've never done cylinder honing before

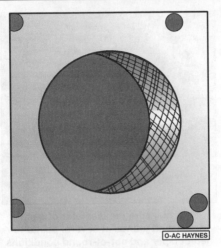

18.3b The cylinder hone should leave a smooth cross-hatch pattern with the lines intersecting at approximately a 60-degree angle

19.4a The piston ring grooves can be cleaned with a special tool . . .

19.4b . . . or a section of a broken ring

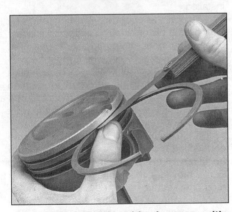

19.10 Check the ring side clearance with a feeler gauge at several points around the groove

c) *Don't withdraw the hone from the cylinder while it's running. Instead shut off the drill and continue moving the hone up-and down the cylinder until it comes to a complete stop, then compress the stones and withdraw the hone. If you're using a "bottle brush" type hone, stop the drill motor, then turn the chuck in the normal direction of the rotation while withdrawing the hone from the cylinder.*

d) *Wipe the oil out of the cylinder and repeat the procedure for the remaining cylinders.*

4   After the honing job is complete, chamfer the top edges of the cylinder bores with a small file so the rings won't catch when the pistons are installed. Be very careful not to nick the cylinder walls with the end of the file.

5   The entire engine block must be washed again very thoroughly with warm, soapy water to remove all traces of the abrasive grit produced during the honing operation. **Note:** *The bores can be considered clean when a white cloth - dampened with clean engine oil - used to wipe down the bores doesn't pickup any more honing residue, which will show up as gray areas on the cloth.* Be sure to run a brush through all oil holes and galleries and flush them with running water.

6   After rinsing, dry the block and apply a coat of light rust preventative oil to all machined surfaces. Wrap the block in a plastic bag to keep it clean and set it aside until reassembly.

19 Piston/connecting rod assembly - inspection

Refer to illustrations 19.4a, 19.4b, 19.10 and 19.11

1   Before the inspection process can be carried out, the piston/connecting rod assemblies must be cleaned and the original piston rings removed from the pistons. **Note:** *Always use new piston rings when the engine is reassembled.*

2   Using a piston ring installation tool, remove the rings from the pistons. Be careful not to nick or gouge the pistons in the process.

3   Scrape all traces of carbon from the tops of the pistons. A hand-held wire brush or a piece of fine emery cloth can be used once the majority of the deposits have been scraped away. Do not, under any circumstances, use a wire brush mounted on a drill motor to remove deposits from the pistons. The piston material is soft and may be eroded away by the wire brush.

4   Use a piston ring groove cleaning tool to remove carbon deposits from the ring grooves. If the tool isn't available, a piece broken off the old ring will do the job. Be very careful to remove only the carbon deposits - don't remove any metal and don't nick or scratch the sides of the ring grooves **(see illustrations)**.

5   Once the deposits have been removed, clean the piston/rod assemblies with solvent and dry them with compressed air (if available). Make sure the oil return holes in the back sides of the ring grooves are clear.

6   If the pistons aren't damaged or worn excessively, and if the engine block isn't rebored, new pistons won't be necessary. Normal piston wear appears as even vertical wear on the piston thrust surfaces and slight looseness of the top ring in it's groove.

7   Carefully inspect each piston for cracks, especially around the skirt, at the pin bosses and the ring lands.

8   Look for scoring and scuffing on the thrust faces of the skirt, holes in the piston crown and burned areas at the edge of the crown. If the skirt is scored or scuffed, the engine may have been suffering from overheating and/or abnormal combustion, which caused excessively high operating temperatures. The cooling and lubricating systems should be checked thoroughly. A hole in the top of the piston is an indication that abnormal combustion (preignition) was occurring. Burned areas at the edge of the piston crown

are usually evidence of spark knock (detonation). If any of the above problems exist, the causes must be corrected or the damage will occur again.

9   Small pits in the piston top indicate that coolant has leaked into the combustion chamber. Again, the cause must be corrected or the problem may persist in the rebuilt engine.

10   Measure the piston ring side clearance by laying a new piston ring in each ring groove and slipping a feeler gauge in beside it **(see illustration)**. Check the clearance at three or four locations around each groove.

19.11 Measure the piston diameter at a 90-degree angle to the piston pin and in line with it

Be sure to use the correct ring for each groove; they are different. If the side clearance is greater than specified, new pistons will have to be used.

11   Check the piston-to-bore clearance by measuring the bore (see Section 17) and the piston diameter. Make sure the pistons and bores are correctly matched. Measure the piston across the skirt, at a 90-degree angle to and in-line with the piston pin (see illustration). Subtract the piston diameter from the bore diameter to obtain the clearance. If it's greater than specified, the block will have to be rebored and new pistons and rings installed.

12   Check the piston-to-rod clearance by twisting the piston and rod in opposite directions. Any noticeable play indicates that there's excessive wear, which must be corrected. The piston/connecting rod assemblies should be taken to an automotive machine shop to have the pistons and rods rebored and new pins installed. Usually when the wrist pins are loose the pistons are worn out also.

13   If the pistons must be removed from the connecting rods for any reason, they should be taken to an automotive machine shop. While they are there have the connecting rods checked for bend and twist, since automotive machine shops have special equipment for this purpose. Note: *Unless new pistons and/or connecting rods must be installed, don't disassemble the pistons and connecting rods.*

14   Check the connecting rods for cracks and other damage. Temporarily remove the rod caps, lift out the old bearing inserts, wipe the rod and cap bearing surfaces clean and inspect them for nicks, gouges and scratches. After checking the rods, replace the old bearings, slip the caps into place and tighten the nuts or bolts finger tight.

20   Crankshaft - inspection

Refer to illustration 20.2
Note: *On 1995 engines with the balance shaft*

20.2 Measure the diameter of each crankshaft journal at several points to detect taper and out-of-round conditions

assembly drive gear, if inspection or chain replacement require gear replacement, an automotive machine shop will have to install the new gear. An oven and special heat indicator material is used to heat up the gear to the correct temperature in order to slip it over the crankshaft. The gear becomes fixed in place as it cools and contracts on the crankshaft.

1   Clean the crankshaft with solvents and dry it with compressed air (if available). Be sure to clean the oil holes with a stiff brush and flush them with solvent. Check the main and connecting rod bearing journals for uneven wear, scoring, pits and cracks. Check

the rest of the crankshaft for cracks and other damage.

2   Using a micrometer, measure the diameter of the main and connecting rod journals and compare the results to the Specifications (see illustration). By measuring the diameter at a number of points around each journal's circumference, you'll be able to determine whether or not the journal is out of round. Take the measurement at each end of the journal, near the crank throws, to determine if the journal is tapered.

3   If the crankshaft journals are damaged, tapered, out-of-round or worn beyond the limits given in the specifications, have the crankshaft reground by an automotive machine shop. Be sure to use the correct size bearing inserts if the crankshaft is reconditioned.

4   Crankshafts damaged by spun bearings, etc., can sometimes be repaired by shops specializing in crankshaft welding.

5   Refer to Section 21 and examine the main and rod bearing inserts.

21   Main and connecting rod bearings - inspection

Refer to illustration 21.1
1   Even though the main and connecting rod bearings should be replaced with new ones during the engine overhaul, the old bearings should be retained for close exami-

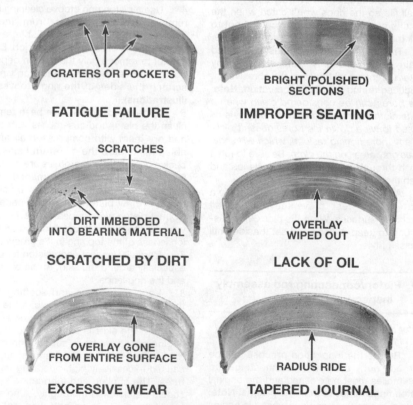

21.1 Typical bearing failures

CRATERS OR POCKETS
FATIGUE FAILURE

BRIGHT (POLISHED) SECTIONS
IMPROPER SEATING

SCRATCHES
DIRT IMBEDDED INTO BEARING MATERIAL
SCRATCHED BY DIRT

OVERLAY WIPED OUT
LACK OF OIL

OVERLAY GONE FROM ENTIRE SURFACE
EXCESSIVE WEAR

RADIUS RIDE
TAPERED JOURNAL

nation, as they may reveal valuable information about the condition of the engine **(see illustration)**.

2   Bearing failure occurs from age or because of lack of lubrication, the presence of dirt or other foreign particles, fuel and coolant contamination, over stressing the engine and corrosion. Regardless of the cause of bearing failure, it must be corrected before the engine is reassembled to prevent it from reoccurring.

3   When examining the bearings, remove them from the engine block, the main bearing caps, the connecting rods and the rod caps and lay them out on a clean surface in the same general position as their location in the engine. This will enable you to match any bearing problems with the crankshaft journal. Be sure to note the position of the thrust bearing!

4   Dirt and other foreign particles get into the engine in a variety of ways. It may be left in the engine during assembly, or it may pass through filters of the PCV system. It may get into the oil, and from there into the bearings. Metal chips from machining operations and normal engine wear are often present. Abrasives are sometimes left in engine components after reconditioning, especially when parts are not thoroughly cleaned using the proper cleaning methods. Whatever the source, these foreign objects often end up embedded in the soft bearing material and are easily recognized. Large particles will not embed in the bearing and will score or gouge the bearing and journal. The best prevention for this cause of bearing failure is to clean all parts thoroughly and keep everything spotlessly clean during engine assembly. Frequent and regular engine oil and filter changes are also recommended.

5   Lack of lubrication (or lubrication breakdown) has a number of interrelated causes. Excessive heat (which thins the oil), overloading (which squeezes the oil from the bearing face) and oil leakage or throw off (from excessive bearing clearances, worn oil pump or high engine speeds) all contribute to lubrication breakdown. Blocked oil passages, which usually are the result of misaligned oil holes in a bearing shell or foreign matter, will also oil starve a bearing and destroy it. When lack of lubrication is the cause of bearing failure, the bearing material is wiped or extruded from the steel backing of the bearing. Temperatures may increase to the point where the steel backing turns blue from overheating.

6   Driving habits can have a definite effect on bearing life. Full throttle, low speed operation (lugging the engine) puts very high loads on bearings, which tends to squeeze out the oil film. These loads cause the bearings to flex, which produces fine cracks in the bearing face (fatigue failure). Eventually the bearing material will loosen in pieces and tear away from the steel backing. Short-trip driving leads to corrosion of bearings because insufficient engine heat is produced to drive off the condensed water and corrosive

gases. These products collect in the engine oil, forming acids and sludge. As the oil is carried to the engine bearings, the acid attacks and corrodes the bearing material.

7   Incorrect bearing installation during engine reassembly will lead to bearing failure as well. Tight fitting bearings leave insufficient bearing oil clearance and will result in oil starvation. Dirt or foreign particles trapped behind a bearing insert result in high spots on the bearing that lead to failure.

8   Determine the cause of any unusual wear before reassembling the engine. Any good automotive machine shop should be able to assist in determining the reason for bearing damage.

22 Engine overhaul - reassembly sequence

1   Before beginning engine reassembly, make sure you have all the necessary new parts, gaskets and seals as well as the following items on hand:

   Common hand tools
   1/2-inch drive torque wrench
   Piston ring installation tool
   Piston ring compressor
   Short lengths of rubber or plastic hose to fit over connecting rod bolts
   Plastigage
   Feeler gauges
   A fine-tooth file
   New engine oil
   Engine assembly lube or moly-base grease
   RTV gasket sealant
   Thread locking compound (Loctite)

2   In order to save time and avoid problems, engine reassembly should be done in the following general order:

2.0L OHC four-cylinder engine

   Crankshaft and main bearings
   Piston rings
   Piston/connecting rod assemblies
   Oil pump/front crankshaft oil seal
   Rear main oil seal
   Oil pan
   Cylinder head
   Camshaft/camshaft carrier
   Timing belt/sprockets and covers
   Intake and exhaust manifolds
   Camshaft cover
   Flywheel or driveplate

2.3L OHC (Quad-4) four-cylinder engines

   Crankshaft and main bearings
   Rear main oil seal housing
   Piston/connecting rod assemblies
   Balance shafts (if equipped)
   Oil pump
   Oil pan
   Cylinder head and camshaft(s)
   Timing chain housing
   Timing chain and sprockets

2.5L OHV four-cylinder and V6 engines

   New camshaft bearings (must be done by an automotive machine shop)
   Crankshaft, main bearings and rear main oil seal
   Piston rings
   Piston/connecting rod assemblies
   Oil pump (2.5L four-cylinder only)
   Engine force balancer assembly (not all models)
   Camshaft
   Timing chain and sprockets (V6 engines and 1990 and later four-cylinder engines)
   Timing cover/crankshaft front oil seal
   Oil pan
   Valve lifters
   Cylinder head(s)
   Pushrod cover (2.5L four-cylinder only)
   Intake and exhaust manifolds
   Valve cover(s)
   Flywheel or driveplate

23 Top dead center (TDC) for number 1 piston - locating

Refer to illustration 23.6
Note: *The following procedure is based on the assumption that the distributor is correctly installed. If you are trying to locate TDC to install the distributor correctly, piston position must be determined by feeling for compression at the number one spark plug hole, then aligning the ignition timing marks as described in Step 8.*

1   Top Dead Center (TDC) is the highest point in the cylinder that each piston reaches as it travels up-and-down when the crankshaft turns. Each piston reaches TDC on the compression stroke and again on the exhaust stroke, but TDC generally refers to piston position on the compression stroke.

2   Positioning the piston(s) at TDC on the compression stroke is an essential part of many procedures such as valve train component removal and distributor removal.

3   Before beginning this procedure, be sure to place the transaxle in Neutral and apply the parking brake or block the rear wheels. Also, disable the ignition system by detaching the coil wire from the center terminal of the distributor cap and grounding it on the block with a jumper wire (models with a distributor) or disconnecting the small-wire (primary) electrical connector from the coil pack (models with distributorless ignition). Remove the spark plugs (see Chapter 1).

4   When looking at the drivebelt end of the engine, normal crankshaft rotation is clockwise. In order to bring any piston to TDC, the crankshaft must be turned with a socket and ratchet attached to the bolt threaded into the center of the lower drivebelt pulley (vibration damper) on the crankshaft.

5   Have an assistant turn the crankshaft with a socket and ratchet as described above

2F

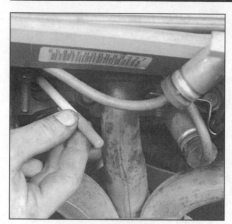

23.6 On engines with distributorless ignition and no timing marks, a plastic pen inserted into the spark plug hole can be used to find TDC

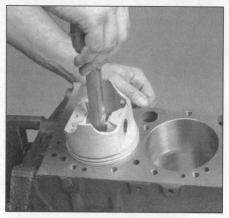

24.3 When checking piston ring end gap, the ring must be square in the cylinder bore (this is done by pushing the ring down with the top of a piston as shown)

24.4 With the ring square in the cylinder, measure the end gap with a feeler gauge

24.8a Installing the spacer/expander in the oil control ring groove

24.8b DO NOT use a piston ring installation tool when installing the oil ring side rails

while you hold a finger over the number one spark plug hole. **Note:** *See the Specifications for the engine you are working on for the number one cylinder location.*

6   When the piston approaches TDC on the compression stroke, air pressure will be felt exiting the spark plug hole. Have your assistant stop turning the crankshaft when the timing marks at the crankshaft pulley are aligned. **Note:** *On models with distributorless ignition systems, there may be no timing marks. After you feel pressure on these models, stop turning the crankshaft, then insert a plastic pen into the spark plug hole (see illustration). As the piston rises, the pen will be pushed out. Note the point where the pen stops moving out - this is TDC.*

7   If the timing marks are bypassed, turn the crankshaft two complete revolutions clockwise until the timing marks are properly aligned again.

8   After the number one piston has been positioned at TDC on the compression stroke, TDC for any of the remaining pistons can be located by turning the crankshaft one-half turn (180-degrees) on four-cylinder engines or one-third turn (120-degrees) on V6 engines to get to TDC for the next cylinder in the firing order.

24 Piston rings - installation

Refer to illustrations 24.3, 24.4, 24.8a, 24.8b and 24.11

1   Before installing the new piston rings, the ring and gaps must be checked. It's assumed that the piston ring side clearance has been checked and verified correct (see Section 19).

2   Lay out the piston/connecting rod assemblies and the new ring sets so the rings will be matched with the same piston and cylinder during the end gap measurement and engine assembly.

3   Insert the top (number one) ring into the first cylinder and square it up with the cylinder walls by pushing it in with the top of the

piston **(see illustration)**. The ring should be near the bottom of the cylinder, at the lower limit of ring travel.

4   To measure the end gap, slip feeler gauges between the ends of the ring until a gauge equal to the gap width is found **(see illustration)**. The feeler gauge should slide between the ring ends with slight amount of drag. Compare the measurement to the Specifications. If the gap is larger or smaller than specified, double check to make sure you have the correct rings before proceeding. **Note:** *Piston rings manufactured today shouldn't require filing of the end gaps. If the the set has end gaps that are to tight, first check with the auto parts store to be sure they are the correct size or consult an auto-motive machine shop.*

5   Excess end gap is not critical unless it's greater than 0.040-inch. Again, double check to make sure you have the correct rings for your engine.

6   Repeat the procedure for every ring in the engine. Remember to keep rings, pistons and cylinders matched up.

7   Once the ring end gaps have been checked/corrected, the rings can be installed on the engine.

8   The oil control ring (lowest one on the piston) is installed first. It's composed of three separate components. Slip the spacer/expander into the groove **(see illustration)**. If an anti-rotation tang is used, make sure it's inserted into the drilled hole in the ring groove. Next, install the lower side rails. Don't use a piston ring installation tool on the oil ring side rails, as they may be damaged. Instead, place one end of the side rail into the groove between the spacer/expander and the ring land, hold it firmly in place and slide a finger around the piston while pushing the rail into the groove **(see illustration)**. Next, install the upper side rail in this same manner.

9   After the three oil ring components have been installed, check to make sure both the upper and lower side rails can be turned smoothly in the ring groove.

10   The number two (middle) ring is installed next. It may be stamped with a mark that must face up, toward the top of the piston. **Note:** *Always follow the instructions printed on the ring package or box - different manu-facturers may require different approaches. Don't mix up the top and middle rings, as they have different cross sections.*

24.11 Installing the compression rings with a ring expander - the mark (arrow) must face up

25.5 Remove the seal housing bolts (arrows)

25.6 After removing the housing from the engine, support it on wood blocks and drive out the old seal with a punch and hammer

25.8 Drive the new seal into the housing with a block of wood or a section of pipe, if you have one large enough - don't cock the seal in the housing bore

25.9 Lubricate the seal journal and lip, then position a new gasket over the dowel pins (arrows)

2F

11   Use a piston ring installation tool and make sure the identification mark is facing the top of the piston, then slip the ring into the middle groove on the piston (see illustration). Don't expand the ring any more than necessary to slide it over the piston.

12   Install the number one (top) ring in the same manner. Make sure the mark, if any, is facing up. Be careful not to confuse the number one and number two rings.

13   Repeat the procedure for the remaining pistons and rings.

25   Rear main oil seal - installation

One piece seal

Note: *There are several different seal arrangements used in the vehicles covered by this manual. Individual engine Chapters, 2A through 2E, cover seal replacement without removal of the crankshaft or seal retainer.*

One-piece seal - with bolt-on seal retainer

Refer to illustrations 25.5, 25.6, 25.8 and 25.9

1   The rear main oil seal is installed after the crankshaft is in place and the main bearing caps have been installed.

2   The transmission must be removed from the vehicle for this procedure (see Chapter 7).

3   Remove the flywheel/driveplate (see the appropriate chapter for your engine).

4   The seal can be replaced without removing the oil pan.

5   Unbolt and remove the rear seal retainer, if it's still on the engine block (see illustration). Note: *Alternative in-vehicle replacement procedures are shown in each specific engine Chapter.*

6   The old seal can be removed from the retainer by driving it out from the back side with a hammer and punch (see illustration). Be sure sure to note how far it's recessed into the bore before removing it; the new seal will have to be recessed an equal amount. Be very careful not to scratch or otherwise damage the bore in the retainer or oil leaks could develop.

7   Make sure the retainer is clean, then apply a thin coat of engine oil to the outer edge of the new seal. The seal must be pressed squarely into the bore, so hammering it into place isn't recommended. If you

don't have access to a press, sandwich the housing and seal between two smooth pieces of wood and press the seal into place with the jaws of a large vise. The pieces of wood must be thick enough to distribute the force evenly around the entire circumference of the seal. Work slowly and make sure the seal enters the bore squarely.

8   As a last resort, the seal can be tapped into the retainer with a hammer and block of wood. Be sure to distribute the force evenly and make sure the seal is driven in squarely (see illustration).

9   The seal lip must be lubricated with clean engine oil or multi-purpose grease before the seal/retainer is slipped over the crankshaft and bolted to the block. Use a new gasket or RTV sealant, whichever is used, and make sure the dowel pins are in place before installing the retainer.

10   Tighten the bolts a little at a time until they're all at the torque listed in this Chapter's Specifications.

One-piece seal - installed in crankshaft rear main bearing cap

Refer to illustrations 25.13, 25.14 and 25.16

11   The recommended replacement procedure is after the crankshaft has been

25.13 Apply multi-purpose grease to the lip of the new seal and slide it carefully over the rear end of the crankshaft

25.14 Make sure the rear main oil seal is seated in the recess in the block

25.16 Fill the groove at each side of the rear main bearing cap with RTV sealant, then remove the excess sealant from the oil pan mating surface

25.17 When correctly installed, the ends of the rope-type seal should extend out of the block slightly

25.18 Seat the seal in the groove, but don't depress it below the bearing surface (the seal must contact the crankshaft journal)

removed from the engine block. **Note:** *Alternative in-vehicle replacement procedures are shown in each specific engine Chapter.*

12   Clean the bearing cap and the block and inspect the crankshaft seal surface for excessive wear, nicks and scratches.

13   Apply multi-purpose grease to the lip of the seal, then slide it onto the crankshaft with the lip facing IN **(see illustration)**.

14   Install the crankshaft in the block **(see illustration)**. Tap the seal lightly to seat it against the rear main bearing.

15   Coat the horizontal parting line surface of the bearing cap with RTV sealant and, while the sealant is still wet, install the bearing cap. Tighten the bolts to 10-to-12 ft lbs. Tap the crankshaft forward and backward with a brass or lead hammer, then retighten the rear main bearing cap bolts to the final

torque listed in this Chapter's Specifications.

16   Inject RTV sealant into the vertical grooves between the rear main bearing cap and the block **(see illustration)**. Clean off excess sealant.

Two piece seals

Refer to illustrations 25.17, 25.18, 25.19a, 25.19b, 25.20 and 25.23

Note: *The rear main oil seal must be in place prior to crankshaft installation. An aftermarket neoprene lip type seal (manufactured by Fel-pro) is available for early V6 engines. Follow the instructions included with the new seal if you decide to install one.*

17   Lay one seal section on edge in the seal groove in the block and push it into place with your thumbs. Both ends of the seal should extend out of the block slightly **(see illustration)**.

18   Seat it in the groove by rolling a large socket or piece of bar stock along the entire length of the seal **(see illustration)**. As an alternative, roll the seal very carefully into place with a wooden hammer handle.

19   Once the seal is completely seated in the groove, trim off the excess on the ends with a single-edge razor blade or razor knife

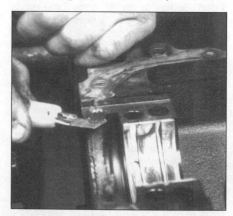

25.19a Trim the seal ends flush with the block . . .

25.19b . . . but leave the inner edges (arrow) protruding slightly

25.20 Lubricate the seal with assembly lube or multi-purpose grease

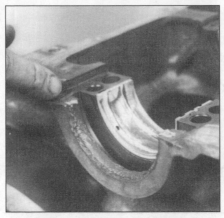

25.23 When applying sealant, be sure it gets into each corner and onto the vertical cap-to-block mating surfaces or oil leaks will result

26.10 Lay the Plastigage strips on the main bearing journals, parallel to the crankshaft centerline

2F

(see illustrations). The seal ends must be flush with the block-to-cap mating surfaces. Make sure the cut is clean so no seal fibers become caught between the block and the cap.

20   Repeat the entire procedure to install the other half of the seal in the bearing cap. Apply a thin film of assembly lube or multi-purpose grease to the edge of the seal where it contacts the crankshaft (see illustration).

21   Soak the bearing cap side seals in kerosene or light oil prior to installation. They swell in the presence of oil and heat. The seals are slightly longer than the bearing cap grooves and must be cut to length.

22   Lightly coat the crankshaft journal with assembly lube or moly-base grease, then refer to Section 26 and install the crankshaft.

23   During the final installation of the crankshaft (after the main bearing oil clearances have been checked with Plastigage), apply a thin, even coat of anaerobic gasket sealant to the parting surfaces of the bearing cap or block (see illustration). Don't get any sealant on the bearing or seal faces.

24   Install the cap, bearing and oil seal assembly and tighten the cap bolts to the torque listed in this Chapter's Specifications. After the cap is bolted in place, insert the side seals into the grooves and make sure they're seated. As an alternative, you can inject RTV sealant into the grooves.

26   Crankshaft - installation and main bearing oil clearance check

Refer to illustrations 26.10 and 26.14

1   Crankshaft installation is the first step in engine reassembly. It's assumed at this point that the engine block and crankshaft have been cleaned, inspected and repaired or reconditioned.

2   Position the engine with the bottom facing up.

3   Remove the main bearing cap bolts and lift out the caps. Lay them out in the proper order to ensure correct installation.

4   Wipe the main bearing surfaces of the block and caps with a clean, lint free cloth. They must be kept spotlessly clean.

5   Clean the back sides of the new main bearing inserts and lay one bearing half in each main bearing saddle in the block. Install the other bearing half from each bearing set in the corresponding main bearing cap. Make sure the tab on the bearing insert fits into the recess in the block or cap. Also, the oil holes in the block must line up with the oil holes in the bearing insert. Do not hammer the bearing into place and don't nick or gouge the bearing faces. No lubrication should be used at this time.

6   The flanged thrust bearing is the (number three) bearing on the OHC four-cylinder engine and the 60-degree (3.1L) V6 engine, the rear (number five) bearing on the OHV four-cylinder engine, and the number two bearing on 90-degree (3.0L and 3.3L) V6 engines (number one bearing is in front on all engines).

7   Clean the faces of the bearings in the block and the crankshaft main bearing journals with a clean, lint free cloth. Check or clean the oil holes in the crankshaft, as any dirt here will go straight through the new bearings.

8   Once you're certain the crankshaft is clean, carefully lay it in position in the main bearings.

9   Before the crankshaft can be permanently installed, the main bearing oil clearance must be checked.

10   Trim several pieces of the appropriate size Plastigage (they must be slightly shorter than the width of the main bearings) and place one piece on each crankshaft main bearing journal, parallel with the journal axis (see illustration).

11   Clean the faces of the bearings in the caps and install the caps in their respective positions (don't mix them up) with the arrows pointing toward the front of the engine. Don't disturb the Plastigage.

12   Starting with the center main and working out toward the ends, tighten the main

bearing cap bolts, in three steps, to the torque listed in this Chapter's Specifications. Don't rotate the crankshaft at any time during this operation.

13   Remove the bolts and carefully lift off the main bearing caps. Keep them in order. Don't disturb the Plastigage or rotate the crankshaft. If any of the main bearing caps are difficult to remove, tap them gently from side-to-side with a soft-face hammer to loosen them.

14   Compare the width of the crushed Plastigage on each journal to the scale printed on the Plastigage container to obtain the main bearing oil clearance (see illustration). Check the Specifications to make sure it's correct.

15   If the clearance isn't as specified, the bearing inserts may be the wrong size (which means different ones will be required). Before deciding that different inserts are needed, make sure that no dirt or oil was between the bearing inserts and the caps or block when the clearance was measured. If the Plasti-

26.14 Compare the width of the crushed Plastigage to the scale on the container to determine the main bearing oil clearance (always take the measurement at the widest point of the Plastigage); be sure to use the correct scale - standard and metric scales are included

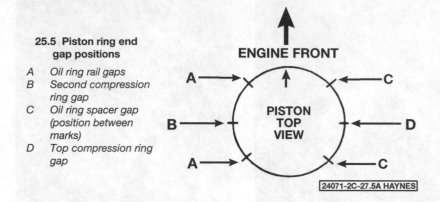

25.5 Piston ring end gap positions

A   *Oil ring rail gaps*
B   *Second compression ring gap*
C   *Oil ring spacer gap (position between marks)*
D   *Top compression ring gap*

ENGINE FRONT

A → ← C
B → **PISTON TOP VIEW** ← D
A → ← C

24071-2C-27.5A HAYNES

27.8 The notch in each piston must face the FRONT of the engine as the pistons are installed

gage was wider at one end than the other, the journal may be tapered (refer to Section 20).

16   Carefully clean all traces of plastigage material off the main bearing journals and/or the bearing faces with your fingernails or a piece of wood. Don't nick or scratch the bearing faces.

17   Carefully lift the crankshaft out of the engine. Clean the bearing faces in the block, then apply a thin, uniform layer of clean moly-base grease or engine assembly lube to each of the bearing surfaces. Be sure to coat the thrust faces as well as the journal face of the thrust bearing.

18   If you're working on an engine with a two piece rear main seal, refer to Section 25 and install the rear main oil seal sections to the block and bearing cap. Lubricate the seal faces with multi-purpose grease or engine assembly lube. If you're working on an engine with a one-piece seal without a retainer (held in place by the rear main bearing cap), also refer to Section 25 and install it.

19   Make sure the crankshaft journals are clean, then lay the crankshaft back in place in the block. Clean the faces of the bearings in the caps, then apply lubricant to them. Install the caps in their respective positions with the arrows pointing toward the front of the engine. Install the bolts finger tight.

20   Tighten all but the thrust bearing cap bolts to the torque listed in this Chapter's Specifications (work from the center out and approach the final torque in three steps). Tighten the thrust bearing cap bolts to 10 to 12 ft-lbs. Tap the ends of the crankshaft forward and backward with a block of wood and a hammer to line up the main bearing and crankshaft thrust surfaces. Retighten all main bearing cap bolts to the specified torque, starting with the center main and working out toward the ends.

21   Rotate the crankshaft a number of times by hand to check for any obvious binding (if the crankshaft binds, correct before proceeding).

22   The final step is to check the crankshaft endplay as described in Section 15. The endplay should be correct if the crankshaft thrust faces are not worn or damaged and new bearings have been installed.

23   If your engine has a one-piece rear main oil seal mounted in a retainer, refer to Section 25 and install a new seal.

24   If you're working on a 2.0L OHC four-cylinder engine, inject RTV sealant into the rear main bearing cap-to-block parting line holes until it runs out of the joint at the base of the cap (where it meets the block horizontally).

25   If you're working on a V6 engine, don't forget to install the rear main bearing cap side seals, if required (see Section 25).

27   Piston/connecting rod assembly - installation and rod bearing oil clearance check.

Refer to illustrations 27.5, 27.8, 27.9, 27.11 and 27.13

1   Before installing the piston/connecting rod assemblies, the cylinder walls must be perfectly clean, the top edge of each cylinder must be chamfered, and the crankshaft must be in place.

2   Remove the connecting rod cap from the end of the number one connecting rod. Remove the old bearing inserts and wipe the bearing surfaces of the connecting rod and cap with a clean, lint free cloth. They must be kept spotlessly clean.

3   Clean the back side of the new upper bearing half, then lay it in place in the connecting rod. Make sure the tab on the bearing fits into the recess in the rod. Don't hammer the bearing insert into place and be very careful not to nick or gouge the bearing face. Don't lubricate the bearing at this time.

4   Clean the back side of the other bearing insert and install it in the rod cap. Again, make sure the tab on the bearing fits into the recess in the cap and don't apply any lubricant. It's critically important that the mating surfaces of the bearing and connecting rod are perfectly clean and oil free when they're assembled.

5   Stagger the piston ring gaps around the piston **(see illustration)**, then slip a section of plastic or rubber hose over each connecting rod cap bolt.

6   Lubricate the piston and rings with clean engine oil and attach a piston ring compres-

sor to the piston. Leave the skirt protruding about 1/4-inch to guide the piston into the cylinder. The rings must be compressed until they're flush with the piston.

7   Rotate the crankshaft until the number one connecting rod journal is at BDC (bottom dead center) and apply a coat of engine oil to the cylinder walls.

8   With the notch on top of the piston **(see illustration)** facing the front of the engine, gently insert the piston/connecting rod assembly into the number one cylinder bore and rest the bottom edge of the ring compressor on the engine block. Tap the top edge of the ring compressor to make sure it's contacting the block around its entire circumference.

9   Carefully tap on top of the piston with the end of a wooden hammer handle **(see illustration)** while guiding the end of the connecting rod into place on the crankshaft journal. The piston rings may try to pop out of the ring compressor just before entering the cylinder bore, so keep some down pressure on the ring compressor. Work slowly, and if any resistance is felt as the piston enters the cylinder, stop immediately. Find out what's

27.9 The piston can be driven (gently) into the cylinder bore with the end of a wooden hammer handle

27.11 Lay the Plastigage strips on each rod bearing journal, parallel to the crankshaft centerline

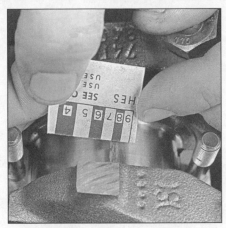

27.13 Measuring the width of the crushed Plastigage to determine the rod bearing oil clearance (be sure to use the correct scale - standard and metric scales are included)

hanging up and fix it before proceeding. Do not, for any reason, force the piston into the cylinder - you'll break a ring and/or a piston.

10   Once the piston/connecting rod assembly is installed, the connecting rod bearing oil clearance must be checked before the rod cap is permanently bolted in place.

11   Cut a piece of the appropriate size Plastigage slightly shorter than the width of the connecting rod bearing and lay it in place on the number one connecting rod journal, parallel with the journal axis **(see illustration)**.

12   Clean the connecting rod cap bearing face, remove the protective hoses from the connecting rod bolts and install the rod cap. Make sure the mating mark on the cap is on the same side as the mark on the connecting rod. Install the nuts or bolts and tighten them to the torque listed in this Chapter's Specifications, working up to it in two steps. **Caution:** *If you're working on a 2.0L OHC four-cylinder engine, use the old bolts for this procedure. New ones must be used after the oil clearance has been checked and verified to be correct, when final assembly is performed.* **Note:** *Use a thin-wall socket to avoid erroneous torque readings that can result if the socket becomes wedged between the rod cap and nut. Don't rotate the crankshaft at any time during this operation.*

13   Remove the rod cap, being very careful not to disturb the Plastigage. Compare the width of the crushed Plastigage to the scale printed on the Plastigage container to obtain the oil clearance **(see illustration)**. Compare it to the Specifications to make sure the clearance is correct. If the clearance isn't as specified, the bearing inserts may be the wrong size (which means different ones will be required). Before deciding that different inserts are needed, make sure that no dirt or oil was between the bearing inserts and the

connecting rod or cap when the clearance was measured. Also, recheck the journal diameter. If the Plastigage was wider at one end than the other, the journal may be tapered (refer to Section 20).

14   Carefully scrape all traces of the Plastigage material off the rod journal and/or bearing face. Be very careful not to scratch the bearing - use your fingernail or a piece of wood. Make sure the bearing faces are perfectly clean, then apply a uniform layer of clean moly-base grease or engine assembly lube to both of them. You'll have to push the piston into the cylinder to expose the face of the bearing insert in the connecting rod - be sure to slip the protective hoses over the rod bolts first.

15   Slide the connecting rod back into place on the journal, remove the protective hoses from the rod cap bolts (if applicable), install the rod cap with the marks properly aligned and install and tighten the nuts or bolts to the torque listed in this Chapter's Specifications. Again, work up to the torque in two steps.

16   Repeat the entire procedure for the remaining piston/connecting rod assemblies. Keep the back sides of the bearing inserts and the inside of the connecting rod and cap perfectly clean when assembling them. Make sure you have the correct piston for the cylinder and that the notch on the piston faces to the front of the engine when the piston is installed. Remember, use plenty of oil to lubricate the piston before installing the ring compressor. Also, when installing the rod caps for the final time, be sure to lubricate the bearing faces adequately.

17   After all the piston/connecting rod assemblies have been properly installed, rotate the crankshaft a number of times by

hand to check for any obvious binding.

18   As a final step, the connecting rod side clearance must be checked. Refer to Section 14 for this procedure. Compare the measured clearance to the Specifications to make sure it's correct. If it was correct before disassembly and the original crankshaft and rods were reinstalled, it should still be right. If new rods or a new crankshaft were installed, the clearance may be too small. If so, the rods will have to be removed and taken to an automotive machine shop for resizing.

19   If you're working on a later model 2.5L OHV four-cylinder engine, be sure to install the engine force balancer.

28   Initial start-up and break-in after overhaul

Warning: *Have a fire extinguisher handy when starting the engine for the first time.*

1   Once the engine has been installed in the vehicle, double check the engine oil and coolant levels.

2   With the spark plugs out of the engine and the ignition system disabled (see Section 3), crank the engine until oil pressure registers on the gauge or the oil light goes out.

3   Install the spark plugs, hook up the plug wires and restore power to the ignition system.

4   Start the engine. It may take a few moments for the gasoline to reach the injectors, but the engine should start without a great deal of effort.

5   After the engine starts, it should be allowed to warm up to normal operating temperature. While the engine is warming up, make a thorough check for oil and coolant leaks.

6   Shut the engine off and recheck the engine oil and coolant levels.

7   Drive the vehicle to an area with minimum traffic, accelerate at full throttle from 30 to 50 mph, then allow the vehicle to slow to 30 mph with the throttle closed. Repeat the procedure 10 or 12 times. This will load the piston rings and cause them to seat properly against the cylinder walls. Check again for oil and coolant leaks.

8   Drive the vehicle gently for the first 500 miles (no sustained high speeds) and keep a constant check on the oil level. It isn't unusual for an engine to use oil during the break-in period.

9   At approximately 500 to 600 miles, change the oil and filter.

10   For the next few hundred miles, drive the vehicle normally. Don't pamper or abuse it.

11   After 2000 miles, change the oil and filter again and consider the engine fully broken in.

2F

Notes

Chapter 3
Cooling, heating and air conditioning systems

Contents

Specifications

General

Coolant capacity	See Chapter 1
Radiator cap pressure cap rating	15 psi
Thermostat rating	195-degrees F

Torque specifications

Ft-lbs (unless otherwise indicated)

Thermostat housing bolts
  2.0/2.5L four-cylinder engines
    Steel housing .... 156 in-lbs
    Cast housing 19
  2.3L four-cylinder (Quad-4) engine
    1993 and earlier models (at cylinder head) 19
    1994 and later (at pump cover) .... 124 in-lbs
  V6 engines
    Steel housing .... 88 in-lbs
    Cast housing 20
Water pump mounting bolts
  2.0L four-cylinder engine 18
  2.3L four-cylinder (Quad-4) engines
    Pump-to-timing chain housing 19
    Pump cover-to-pump .... 124 in-lbs
    Pump cover-to-block 19
  2.5L four-cylinder engine
    1986 and earlier 21
    1987 and later 24
  V6 engines
    Long bolts 22
    Short bolts .... 89 in-lbs
Water pump pulley bolts
  2.0/2.5L four-cylinder engines 22
  V6 engines .... 115 in-lbs

3

Component location

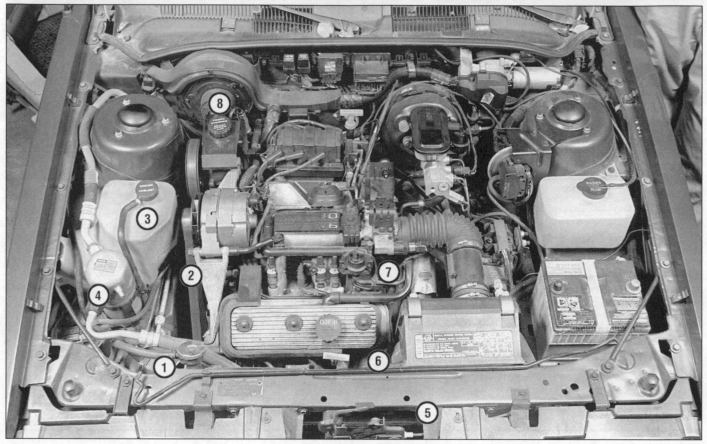

Typical 3.0L V6 engine cooling, heating and air conditioning system

1	Radiator cap	4	Air conditioning accumulator	7	Thermostat housing
2	Water pump	5	Air conditioning condenser	8	Blower motor
3	Coolant reservoir	6	Radiator		

1   General information

Engine cooling system

All vehicles covered by this manual employ a pressurized engine cooling system with thermostatically controlled coolant circulation. An impeller type water pump circulates coolant through the engine. The coolant flows around each cylinder and toward the rear of the engine, up into the cylinder head and back to the radiator. Cast-in coolant passages direct coolant around the intake and exhaust ports, near the spark plug areas and in close proximity to the exhaust valve guide inserts.

During warm up, the closed thermostat prevents coolant from circulating through the radiator. When the engine reaches normal operating temperature, the thermostat opens and allows hot coolant to travel through the radiator, where it is cooled before returning to the engine.

The aluminum radiator is of the cross-flow type, with plastic tanks on either side of the core.

The cooling system is sealed by a pressure type cap. This raises the boiling point of the coolant and the higher boiling point of the coolant increases the cooling efficiency of the radiator. On most models this cap is located on the radiator, but on later models it's located on a translucent surge tank mounted along the right front side of the engine compartment. If the system pressure exceeds the cap pressure relief value, the excess pressure in the system forces the spring-loaded valve inside the cap off its seat and allows the coolant to escape through the overflow tube into a coolant reservoir. When the system cools, the excess coolant is automatically drawn from the reservoir back into the radiator.

Heating system

The heating system consists of a blower fan and heater core located under the dashboard, the inlet and outlet hoses connecting the heater core to the engine cooling system and the heater/air conditioning control head on the dashboard. Hot engine coolant is circulated through the heater core at all times. When the heater mode is activated, a flap opens to expose the heater box to the passenger compartment. A fan switch on the control head activates the blower motor, which forces air through the core, heating the air.

Air conditioning system

The air conditioning system consists of a condenser mounted in front of the radiator, an evaporator mounted under the dash, a compressor mounted on the engine, a filter-drier (accumulator) which contains a high pressure relief valve and the plumbing connecting all of the above.

A blower fan forces the warmer air of the passenger compartment through the evaporator core (sort of a radiator-in-reverse), transferring the heat from the air to the refrigerant. The liquid refrigerant boils off into low pressure vapor, taking the heat with it when it leaves the evaporator.

2   Antifreeze – general information

Warning: *Do not allow antifreeze to come in contact with your skin or painted surfaces of the vehicle. Rinse off spills immediately with plenty of water. Antifreeze is highly toxic if ingested (non-toxic coolant is available at most auto parts stores). Never leave anti-freeze lying around in an open container or in puddles on the floor; children and pets are attracted by it's sweet smell and may drink it. Check with local authorities about disposing of used antifreeze. Many communities have collection centers which will see that antifreeze is disposed of safely.*

The cooling system should be filled with a water/ethylene glycol based antifreeze solution which will prevent system from freezing down to at least -20-degrees F. It also provides protection against corrosion and increases the coolant boiling point.

The cooling system should be drained, flushed and refilled at least every other year (see Chapter 1). The use of antifreeze solutions for periods of longer than two years is likely to cause damage and encourage the formation of rust and scale in the system. If your tap water is "hard", use distilled water with the antifreeze.

Before adding antifreeze to the system, check all hose connections, because antifreeze tends to leak through very minute openings. Engines don't normally consume coolant, so if the level goes down, find the cause and correct it.

The exact mixture of antifreeze-to-water which you should use depends on the relative weather conditions The mixture should contain at least 50-percent antifreeze, but should never contain more than 70-percent antifreeze. Consult the mixture ratio chart on the antifreeze container before adding coolant. Hydrometers are available at most auto parts stores to test the ratio of antifreeze to water.

Antifreeze/coolant testing

Warning: *Do not remove the radiator cap to take a sample until the engine has cooled completely. The system is under pressure and extremely hot, during and after running the engine, and will severely scald skin it comes in contact with.*

Hydrometers are available at most auto parts stores. They are inexpensive and are very easy to use. To test coolant, use the hydrometer to draw a small amount from the radiator, or coolant reservoir, until all the balls (most have five small colored balls) are submerged. **Note:** *It is preferable to take the coolant sample from the radiator. The mixture in the coolant reservoir may be slightly diluted if any water has recently been added.* The strength of the mixture is shown by the number of balls that are floating. Exact temperature protection indicated by the hydrometer is clearly described on the package instructions. Always use antifreeze which meets the vehicle manufacturer's specifications.

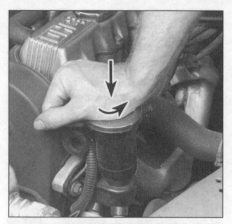

3.7 Push down while rotating to remove the thermostat cap

3   Thermostat - check and replacement

Warning: *DO NOT remove the pressure cap, drain the coolant or replace the thermostat until the engine has cooled completely. Also, when working in the vicinity of the electric cooling fan, disconnect the battery cable from the negative battery terminal to prevent the fan from coming on accidentally.*
Caution: *If the vehicle is equipped with a Delco Loc II audio system, make sure you have the correct activation code before disconnecting the battery. See the information at the front of this manual for the radio re-activation procedure.*

Check

1   Before assuming the thermostat is to blame for a cooling system problem, check the coolant level (see Chapter 1), drivebelt tension (see Chapter 1) and temperature gauge (or light) operation.
2   If the engine seems to be taking a long time to warm up (based on heater output or temperature gauge operation), the thermostat is probably stuck open. Replace the thermostat with a new one.
3   If the engine runs hot, use your hand to check the temperature of the upper radiator hose. If the hose isn't hot, but the engine is, the thermostat is probably stuck closed, preventing the coolant inside the engine from escaping to the radiator. Replace the thermostat. **Caution:** *Don't drive the vehicle without a thermostat. The computer may stay in open loop causing the emissions and fuel economy to suffer.*
4   If the upper radiator hose is hot, it means the coolant is flowing and the thermostat is open. Consult the *Troubleshooting* section at the front of this manual for cooling system diagnosis.

Replacement

Note: *The thermostat on the 1994 and later 2.3 liter four cylinder (Quad-4) engine is located above the radiator outlet pipe in the*

3.8 Removing the thermostat

water pump cover. On all other engines the thermostat is located in the coolant outlet housing on the cylinder head. Some 2.0 liter OHC and 2.5 liter OHV four-cylinder engines are equipped a with drop-in style thermostat located in a stamped steel housing mounted on the cylinder head. These models can be identified by a large cap that seals the thermostat housing.

5   Refer to the Warning and Cautions in the beginning of this Section.
6   Disconnect the cable from the negative battery terminal.

Drop-in thermostat models

Refer to illustrations 3.7, 3.8 and 3.9

7   Remove the thermostat housing cap by pushing it down and turning it in a counter-clockwise direction **(see illustration)**. Be prepared for a small amount of coolant to spill as the cap is removed.
8   Carefully pry up on the thermostat handle to loosen it. Grasp the handle and pull the thermostat from the housing **(see illustration)**.
9   If the old thermostat is to be reinstalled, inspect the rubber O-ring for cuts or damage **(see illustration)**. Inspect the cap rubber gasket for cuts and damage from corrosion.

3.9 Whenever the thermostat is removed, make sure the O-ring (arrow) is not damaged

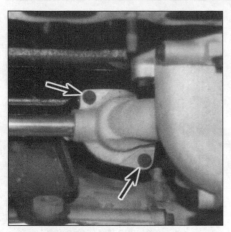

3.15 Radiator outlet pipe bolts (arrows) (exhaust manifold removed for clarity)

3.17 Radiator outlet pipe-to-oil pan stud (arrow)

3.28 Some thermostat covers are secured by two fasteners (arrows), others by three

10   If the cooling system is low or was previously drained, refill the cooling system to the top edge of the housing before installing thermostat.
11   To install, lightly lubricate thermostat O-ring with clean engine oil and insert the thermostat fully into the housing until it is seated. Replace the housing cap, making sure it seats properly.
12   Reconnect the cable from the negative battery terminal.
13   Start the engine and check for leaks. Check for proper thermostat operation (as described in Steps 2 and 3).

1994 and later 2.3 liter (Quad-4)

Refer to illustrations 3.15 and 3.17
14   Drain the cooling system (see Chapter 1). If the coolant is relatively new or in good condition, save it and reuse it.
15   Remove the radiator outlet pipe bolts from the water pump cover. **Note:** *The bolts are accessible from the top of the engine down between no. 2 and 3 exhaust manifold runners* **(see illustration)**.
16   Raise the vehicle and support it securely on jackstands.
17   Remove the stud securing the radiator outlet pipe **(see illustration)**.
18   Pull down on the radiator outlet pipe to disengage it from the water pump cover. Remove the thermostat from the water pump cover.
19   Thoroughly clean any corrosion from the mating surfaces of the water pump cover and the radiator outlet pipe.
20   Apply a small bead of RTV to the mating surface of the water pump cover. Install the thermostat with a new rubber seal into the radiator outlet pipe. Make sure the thermostat is installed with the spring end pointing up into the water pump cover. Install the radiator outlet pipe and tighten the bolts to the torque listed in this Chapter's Specifications.
21   The remaining steps are the reverse of removal.
22   Refill the cooling system (see Chapter 1).
23   Start the engine and allow it to reach

normal operating temperature, then check for leaks and proper thermostat operation (as described in Steps 2 and 3).

All other models

Refer to illustrations 3.28, 3.30 and 3.31
24   Drain the cooling system (see Chapter 1). If the coolant is relatively new or in good condition, save it and reuse it.
25   Follow the upper radiator hose to the engine and locate the thermostat cover.
26   Loosen the hose clamp, then detach the hose from the fitting. If the hose sticks, grasp it near the end with a pair of large adjustable pliers and twist it to break the seal, then pull it off. If the hose is old or deteriorated, cut it off and install a new one.
27   If the outer surface of the large fitting that mates with the hose is severely deteriorated (corroded, pitted, etc.) it may be damaged further by hose removal. If it is, the thermostat cover will have to be replaced.
28   Detach any hoses or electrical connectors that may interfere with removal of the thermostat cover. Remove the bolts/nuts and detach the thermostat cover **(see illustration)**. If the cover is stuck, tap it with a soft-face hammer to jar it loose. Be prepared for

some coolant to spill as the gasket seal is broken.
29   Note how it's installed (direction of the housing), then remove the thermostat. Clean all gasket material from the mating surfaces of the thermostat housing and cover. Clean both mating surfaces with lacquer thinner or acetone.
30   Some models are equipped with a rubber gasket around the circumference of the thermostat **(see illustration)**. If the vehicle you are working on is equipped with this type of thermostat, replace the rubber gasket.
31   Install the new thermostat in the housing **(see illustration)**. Make sure the thermostat is installed the correct way - the spring end is normally directed into the engine.
32   If there was a gasket under the thermostat cover, install a new one. If the thermostat was equipped with a rubber gasket, apply a bead of RTV sealant to the mating flange of the cover. Install the cover and tighten the bolts to the torque listed in this Chapter's Specifications.
33   The remaining steps are the reverse of removal.
34   Refill the cooling system (see Chapter 1).

3.30 Some models use a rubber gasket around the circumference of the thermostat

3.31 When installing the thermostat, make sure the spring end (arrow) is directed into the engine

4.1 The fan motor can be tested by running fused jumper wires directly from the battery to the motor terminals

35   Start the engine and allow it to reach normal operating temperature, then check for leaks and proper thermostat operation (as described in Steps 2 and 3).

4   Engine cooling fan - check, removal and installation

Refer to illustration 4.1
Warning: *When working in the vicinity of the electric fan, disconnect the cable from the negative battery terminal to prevent the fan from coming on accidentally.*
Caution: *If the vehicle is equipped with a Delco Loc II audio system, make sure you have the correct activation code before disconnecting the battery. See the information at the front of this manual for the radio re-activation procedure.*

Check

1   To test the fan motor, unplug the electrical connector at the motor and use jumper wires to connect the fan directly to the battery **(see illustration)**. If the fan still doesn't work, replace the motor.

1986 and earlier models

2   If the motor tested OK, the fault lies in the coolant fan switch, the relay or the wiring which connects the components. Plug in the electrical connector.
3   On four-cylinder models the cooling fan switch is mounted on the left end (driver's side) of the cylinder head. On V6 models it's mounted on the intake manifold, just above the water pump **(see illustration 8.1c)**. Unplug the electrical connector from the switch and, using a jumper wire, connect it to a good ground. If the fan now works, the fan switch is defective.
4   If it still doesn't work, the relay or the wiring that connects the components is defective. Carefully check all wiring and connections. If no obvious problems are found, further diagnosis should be done by a dealer service department or other repair shop.

1987 and later models

5   The electric cooling fan on these models is controlled by the Electronic Control Module (ECM) and the coolant sensor. If the fan is inoperative, check to see if any trouble codes are stored in the computer. If a problem with the coolant temperature sensor is indicated, check the sensor and its circuit. If no trouble codes are stored, have the diagnosis performed by a dealer service department or other qualified repair shop.

Removal and installation

6   Remove intake air ducting, as necessary to access fan housing.
7   Disconnect the fan connector from the fan motor.
8   Remove the fan frame-to-radiator bolts and lift the fan assembly from the engine compartment. **Note:** *On 1992 and later models equipped with 2.3 liter four cylinder (Quad-4) engines, the fan is removed from the bottom and has only one frame bolt.*
9   If you're installing a new fan or fan motor, remove the nut that retains the fan to the motor. **Note:** *This nut may have left-hand threads. Check the hub of the fan for marks that indicate which way to loosen the nut.*
10   Installation is the reverse of removal.

5   Radiator - removal, servicing and installation

Warning: *The engine must be completely cool before beginning this procedure. Also, when working in the vicinity of the electric fan, disconnect the cable from the negative battery terminal to prevent the fan from coming on accidentally.*
Caution: *If the vehicle is equipped with a Delco Loc II audio system, make sure you have the correct activation code before disconnecting the battery. See the information at the front of this manual for the radio re-activation procedure.*
Note: *Radiators used on later models are aluminum and plastic (an aluminum core with plastic side tanks). The drain fitting is located on the lower part of one of the tanks and can be repaired. Radiator repairs should be performed by a dealer service department or radiator repair shop.*

Removal

1   Refer to the Warning in Section 2.

2   Disconnect the cable from the negative battery terminal.
3   Drain the cooling system (see Chapter 1).
4   Remove the cooling fan assembly (see Section 4).
5   Detach the radiator hoses from the radiator, disconnect the coolant recovery hose, oil cooler lines and on automatic transaxle models, disconnect and plug the fluid cooler lines.
6   On air-conditioned models, remove the condenser line retaining clips and the condenser-to-radiator mounting bolts.
7   Remove the radiator mounting bolts and lift the radiator from the engine compartment.

Servicing

8   Carefully examine the radiator for evidence of leaks and damage. It is recommended that any necessary repairs be performed by a radiator repair shop.
9   With the radiator removed, brush accumulations of insects and leaves from the fins. Examine and replace any hoses or clamps which have deteriorated or been damaged.
10   The radiator can be flushed as described in Chapter 1.
11   Replace the radiator cap with a new one of the same rating, or if the cap is relatively new, have it tested by a service station.

Installation

12   If you are installing a new radiator, transfer the fittings from the old unit to the new one.
13   Installation is the reverse of removal. When setting the radiator in the chassis, make sure that it seats securely in the lower rubber mounting pads.
14   After installing the radiator, reconnect all hoses and lines, refill it with the proper coolant mixture (see Chapter 1), then start the engine and check for leaks.

6   Water pump - check

1   A failure in the water pump can cause overheating and serious engine damage, as a defective pump will not circulate coolant through the engine.
2   There are two ways to check the operation of the water pump while it is installed on the engine. If the pump is defective, it should be replaced with a new or rebuilt unit.
3   Water pumps are equipped with weep or vent holes. If a pump seal failure occurs, coolant will leak from the weep holes. In most cases it will be necessary to use a flashlight from under the vehicle to see evidence of leakage from this point on the pump body.
4   If the water pump shaft bearings fail, there may be a squealing sound emitted from the front of the engine while it is running. Shaft wear can be felt if the water pump pulley is forced up and down. Do not mistake drivebelt slippage, which also causes a squealing sound, for water pump failure.

3

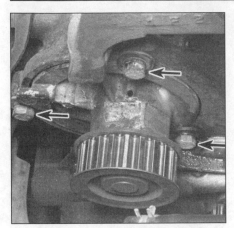

7.4 2.0L OHC water pump retaining bolts (arrows)

7.19 Lubricate the splines of the water pump drive with grease

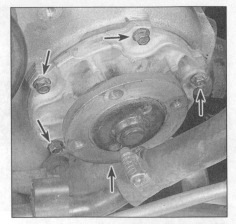

7.33 Remove the mounting bolts, located around the perimeter of the pump (arrows) 3.1L V6 shown

7   Water pump - removal and installation

Warning: *The engine must be completely cool before beginning this procedure. Also, when working in the vicinity of the electric cooling fan, disconnect the cable from the negative battery terminal to prevent the fan from coming on accidentally.*

1   Refer to the Warning in Section 2. Disconnect the cable from the negative terminal of the battery. **Caution:** *If the vehicle is equipped with a Delco Loc II audio system, make sure you have the correct activation code before disconnecting the battery. See the information at the front of this manual for the radio re-activation procedure.*

2   Drain the cooling system (see Chapter 1) and place a large plastic drain pan under the water pump.

2.0L OHC engine

Refer to illustration 7.4

3   Remove the timing belt and inner belt cover (see Chapter 2A).

4   Remove the three pump mounting bolts **(see illustration).**

5   Remove the pump and O-ring. Discard the O-ring.

6   Carefully clean the water pump bore in the block. Lubricate the new O-ring with silicone grease, position it in the groove on the pump and install the pump. Don't tighten the pump bolts all the way until the timing belt has been installed and adjusted.

7   The remainder of installation is the reverse order of removal.

8   Refill the cooling system (see Chapter 1). Run the engine and check for leaks.

2.3L (Quad-4) engine

Refer to illustration 7.19

9   Remove the exhaust manifold (see Chapter 2B).

10   Remove the radiator outlet pipe bolts from the water pump cover. **Note:** *The bolts are accessible from the top of the engine*

down between no. 2 and 3 exhaust manifold runners. Raise the vehicle and support it securely on jackstands. Remove the stud securing the radiator outlet pipe. Pull down on the pipe to disengage it from the water pump cover.

11   Remove the three water pump cover-to-block bolts.

12   Remove the bolts/nuts and detach the water pump from the engine.

13   Clean the fastener threads and any threaded holes in the engine to remove corrosion and sealant.

14   Compare the new pump to the old one to make sure they're identical.

15   Remove all traces of old gasket material from the engine.

16   Clean the engine and water pump mating surfaces with lacquer thinner or acetone.

17   Apply a thin coat of RTV sealant to the engine side of the new gasket.

18   Apply a thin layer of RTV sealant to the gasket mating surface of the new pump, then carefully mate the gasket and the pump.

19   Lubricate the splines of the water pump drive with chassis grease prior to installation **(see illustration).** Carefully attach the pump and gasket to the engine and start the bolts/nuts finger tight.

20   Tighten the fasteners in 1/4-turn increments to the torque figure listed in this Chapter's Specifications. Don't overtighten them or the pump may be damaged. Tighten the bolts in this sequence:

> *Pump-to-chain housing*
> *Pump cover-to-pump assembly*
> *Cover-to-block, bottom bolt first*

21   The remainder of installation is the reverse of removal.

22   Refill the cooling system (see Chapter 1). Run the engine and check for leaks.

2.5L OHV engine

23   Remove the accessory drivebelts (see Chapter 1).

24   Remove the water pump attaching bolts and lift the pump out. The water pump can be removed as a unit from the housing for

replacement, or the entire assembly can be unbolted from the engine block **(see illustration).**

25   Clean the pump mating surfaces.

26   If the pump is being replaced, and the new pump is not equipped with a pulley, transfer the pulley from the old pump to the new one. This will require a pulley removal tool and an installer tool, available at most auto parts stores (they are the same tools used for removing and installing the pulley on a power steering pump). **Caution:** *Do not use a press to remove or install the pulley. Do not hammer the pulley onto the pump.*

27   Apply a 3 mm (1/8-inch) bead of RTV sealant to the mating surface.

28   Coat the bolts with RTV sealant.

29   Install the pump and tighten the bolt to the torque listed in this Chapters Specifications. Reinstall accessory drivebelts.

30   Refill the cooling system (see Chapter 1). Run the engine and check for leaks.

V6 engines

Refer to illustration 7.33

31   Remove the accessory drivebelts, alternator, air conditioning compressor and other components which could interfere with removal.

32   On models that have hoses attached to the water pump, loosen the hose clamps and disconnect the hoses from the pump. Remove the water pump pulley bolts. Wedge a screwdriver between two bolts to prevent the pulley from turning as the bolts are loosened. Loosen all of the bolts before removing any of them. **Note:** *On some 3.0/3.3L engines the pulley won't clear the frame for removal until the pump is removed. If the pulley won't clear, move the pulley aside to gain access to the water pump bolts and remove the pump and pulley together.*

33   Remove the retaining bolts/nuts and lift the water pump from the engine **(see illustration).** If the pump is stuck, jar it loose with a soft-faced hammer or a block of wood. Don't pry between the pump and the engine, as damage to the sealing surfaces may

8.1a On OHC four-cylinder engines, the coolant temperature sending (arrow) is located in the thermostat housing

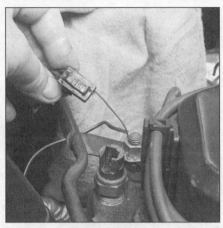

8.1b The coolant temperature sending unit on 2.5L four-cylinder engines is located at the rear of the cylinder head

8.1c On 3.0L and 3.3L V6 engines, the coolant temperature sending unit (arrow) is located on the intake manifold, just above the water pump (the sensor in the middle is the Coolant Temperature Sensor, the one on the left of the photo is the cooling fan switch)

8.1d On 3.1L V6 engines, the coolant temperature sending unit is located at the left end (driver's side) of the rear cylinder head

result. On some models it may be necessary to unbolt the right side engine mount from the cradle (subframe) and raise the engine slightly to obtain enough clearance to remove the water pump.

34 Remove all traces of old gasket material and sealant from the water pump mating surface on the engine (and on the water pump if the same one is to be reinstalled).

35 Install a new gasket and position the water pump on the engine. Coat the threads of the retaining bolts with a thin film of RTV sealant to prevent leaks. Install the bolts and tighten them to the torque listed in this Chapter's Specifications in a criss-cross pattern. If you're working on a 3.1L V6 engine, be sure the locators on the pump and gasket are vertical.

36 Install the pulley and tighten the bolts to the torque listed in this Chapter's Specifications.

37 Connect the hoses to the water pump (where applicable) and tighten the hose clamps securely.

38 The remainder of installation is the reverse of the removal procedure. Refill the cooling system with the proper coolant mixture (see Chapter 1).

39 Connect the negative battery cable, start the engine and run it until normal operating temperature is reached, then check for leaks.

8 Coolant temperature sending unit - check and replacement

Refer to illustrations 8.1a through 8.1d

1 The coolant temperature indicator system is composed of a light mounted in the instrument panel and a coolant temperature sending unit located in a water passage, usually in the cylinder head or engine block **(see illustrations)**. If a temperature gauge is included in the instrument cluster, the temperature sending unit is replaced by a transducer. **Caution:** *Since the ignition key will be in the On position for some of the diagnostic*

steps, be especially careful to stay clear of the electric cooling fan blades.

2 If overheating occurs, check the coolant level in the system and then make sure that the wiring between the light or gauge and the sending unit is secure.

3 When the ignition switch is turned on and the starter motor is turning, the indicator light should be on (overheated engine indication). If the light is not on, the bulb may be burned out, the ignition switch may be faulty or the circuit may be open.

4 As soon as the engine starts, the light should go out and remain out unless the engine overheats. Failure of the light to go out may be due to grounded wiring between the light and the sending unit, a defective sending unit or a faulty ignition switch.

5 To test the circuit, unplug the electrical connector and, using a jumper wire, connect the wiring harness to a good ground. With the ignition On, the indicator light should be glowing. If it does but the engine has been overheating and the light hasn't been coming on, replace the sending unit. If the light does not glow, there is an opening in the circuit or a burned-out bulb.

6 If the sending unit is to be replaced, it is simply unscrewed and a replacement installed. Make sure that the engine is cool before removing the defective sending unit, and prepare the new sending unit for installation by wrapping the threads with Teflon sealing tape. There will be some coolant loss, so check the level after the sending unit has been installed.

9 Heater core - replacement

Refer to illustration 9.3

Warning 1: *Before working in the vicinity of airbag components (on models so equipped) refer to Chapter 12 for the airbag system disarming procedure. Use care not to damage any wiring or sensors associated with this system or the airbag may deploy when reconnecting the battery or fail to deploy in the*

event of an accident.

Warning 2: *The engine must be completely cool before beginning this procedure. Also, when working in the vicinity of the electric cooling fan, disconnect the cable from the negative battery terminal to prevent the fan from coming on accidentally.*

1 Disconnect the cable from the negative battery terminal. **Caution:** *If the vehicle is equipped with a Delco Loc II audio system, make sure you have the correct activation code before disconnecting the battery. See the information at the front of this manual for the radio re-activation procedure.*

2 Drain the cooling system (see Chapter 1). **Warning:** *Do not allow antifreeze to come in contact with your skin or painted surfaces of the vehicle. Rinse off spills immediately with plenty of water. Antifreeze is highly toxic if ingested (non-toxic coolant is available at most auto parts stores). Never leave antifreeze lying around in an open container*

3

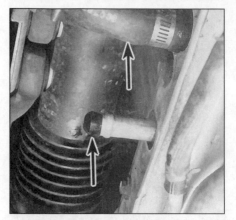

9.3 Remove the heater hoses from the heater core tubes and plug the tubes (arrows)

10.3 The air conditioner/heater control panel is retained by four screws (arrows)

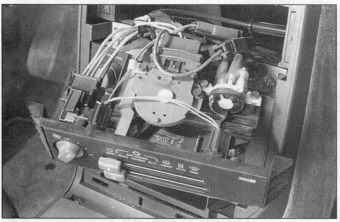

10.4 Unplug the electrical and vacuum connectors from the back of the control panel. Be sure to unplug the entire vacuum connector - not the individual hoses

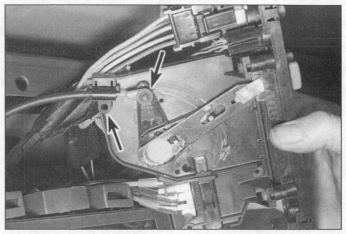

10.5 Two mounting clips (arrows) attach the temperature control cable and cable housing to the control assembly

or in puddles on the floor; children and pets are attracted by it's sweet smell and may drink it. Check with local authorities about disposing of used antifreeze. Many communities have collection centers which will see that antifreeze is disposed of safely.

3   Working in the engine compartment, loosen the hose clamps and disconnect the heater hoses from the heater core tubes at the firewall **(see illustration)**. Plug the tubes to prevent spillage when the heater core is removed. **Note:** *On some model years, it may be easier to reach the heater core hoses from under the vehicle. If the vehicle is raised, be sure to support it securely on jackstands.*

4   Working inside the vehicle, remove the console, console extensions and the sound insulators from above the footwells (see Chapter 11).

5   Remove the steering column trim panel, side and floor heater air outlet ducts.

6   Remove the screws and clips that secure the heater core cover.

7   Remove the heater core retaining straps and remove the heater core from the housing. Be careful not to spill any coolant as this is done.

8   Installation is the reverse of the removal

procedure. Refill the cooling system with the proper coolant mixture (see Chapter 1). Run the engine and check for leaks.

10 Heater and air conditioner control assembly - removal and installation

Refer to illustrations 10.3, 10.4 and 10.5
Warning: *Before working in the vicinity of airbag components (on models so equipped) refer to Chapter 12 for the airbag system disarming procedure. Use care not to damage any wiring or sensors associated with this system or the airbag may deploy when reconnecting the battery or fail to deploy in the event of an accident.*

1   Disconnect the cable from the negative battery terminal. **Caution:** *If the vehicle is equipped with a Delco Loc II audio system, make sure you have the correct activation code before disconnecting the battery. See the information at the front of this manual for the radio re-activation procedure.*

2   Remove the instrument panel center trim plate (see Chapter 11).

3   Remove the control assembly mounting screws **(see illustration)**.

4   Pull the control out of the dash, then label and unplug the vacuum and electrical connectors **(see illustration)**. **Note:** *Do not disconnect the individual vacuum lines - disconnect the entire vacuum connector.*

5   Carefully pry the cable housing and cable retaining clips off with a small screwdriver **(see illustration)**.

6   Installation is the reverse of removal.

11 Heater and air conditioner blower motor - removal and installation

Refer to illustrations 11.1, 11.2 and 11.3

1   Working in the engine compartment, disconnect the wires from the blower motor **(see illustration)**. **Note:** *On some models with 2.5 liter OHV or V6 engines it is necessary to remove the power steering pump and pump mounting bracket and set the power steering pump aside to provide clearance for blower motor removal.*

2   On 1992 and later models, partially cut the blower motor case cover as indicated by

11.1 Blower motor electrical connectors (arrows)

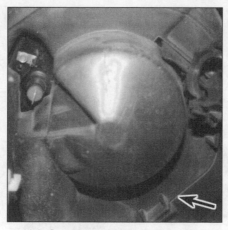

11.2 On 1992 and later models, cut a groove in the case cover (arrow) (see text)

11.3 Be careful not to damage the fan when removing the blower motor

a groove molded in the cover **(see illustration)**. Don't cut the bottom two inches of the groove and don't cut more than 1/8-inch deep. Fold the cut portion of the cover down.

3 Disconnect the fan motor cooling hose. Remove the screws and separate the motor/fan assembly from the housing **(see illustration)**.

4 Remove the retaining nut and slide the fan off the motor shaft.

5 Before installing the blower motor, apply a strip of weatherstrip caulking compound to the perimeter of the opening in the blower motor housing.

6 Installation is the reverse of removal. Be sure to attach the cooling hose to the motor. If the blower case was cut, obtain three retaining clips from a GM dealer parts department and install on posts molded on case to hold cut portion closed.

12 Air conditioning system - check and maintenance

Warning: *The air conditioning system is under high pressure. Do not loosen any fittings or remove any components until after the system has been discharged. Air conditioning refrigerant should be properly discharged into an EPA-approved container at a dealer service department or an automotive air conditioning repair facility. Always wear eye protection when disconnecting air conditioning system fittings.*

Caution: *Some 1994 and later models use a new refrigerant, R-134a, which is "environmentally friendly". Refrigerant, refrigerant oil, components and service equipment are NOT compatible and will not connect to systems using R-12 refrigerant. The air conditioning system is still under high pressure. DO NOT loosen any hose or line fittings or remove any components until after the system has been depressurized by a dealer service department or other repair shop. Always wear eye protection when disconnecting air conditioning system fittings.*

1 The following maintenance checks should be performed on a regular basis to ensure that the air conditioner continues to operate at peak efficiency. **Note:** *Long term non-use can cause hardening, and subsequent failure, of the seals.*

a) *Check the compressor drivebelt. If it's worn or deteriorated, replace it (see Chapter 1).*

b) *Check the drivebelt tension and, if necessary, adjust it (see Chapter 1).*

c) *Check the system hoses. Look for cracks, bubbles, hard spots and deterioration. Inspect the hoses and all fittings for oil bubbles and seepage. If there's any evidence of wear, damage or leaks, replace the hose(s).*

d) *Inspect the condenser fins for leaves, bugs and other debris. Use a "fin comb" or compressed air to clean the condenser.*

e) *Make sure the system has the correct refrigerant charge.*

f) *Check the evaporator housing drain tube for blockage.*

2 Because of the complexity of the air conditioning system and the special equipment necessary to service it, in-depth troubleshooting and repairs are not included in this manual. However, simple checks and component replacement procedures are provided in this Chapter. For more complete information on the air conditioning system, refer to the *Haynes Automotive Heating and Air Conditioning Manual.*

3 The most common cause of poor cooling is simply a low system refrigerant charge. If a noticeable drop in cool air output occurs, one of the following quick checks will help you determine if the refrigerant level is low.

4 Warm the engine up to normal operating temperature.

5 Place the air conditioning temperature selector at the coldest setting and put the blower at the highest setting. Open the doors (to make sure the air conditioning system doesn't cycle off as soon as it cools the passenger compartment).

6 With the compressor engaged - the

clutch will make an audible click and the center of the clutch will rotate - inspect the sight glass, if equipped. If the refrigerant looks foamy, it's low. Have the system charged by a dealer service department or other qualified repair shop.

7 If there's no sight glass, feel the inlet and outlet pipes at the compressor. One side should be much colder than the other. If there's no perceptible difference between the two pipes, there's something wrong with the compressor or the system. It might be a low charge - it might be something else. Take the vehicle to a dealer service department or other qualified repair shop.

13 Air conditioning compressor - removal and installation

Removal

Refer to illustration 13.8

Warning: *The air conditioning system is under high pressure. DO NOT loosen any hose or line fittings or remove any components until after the system has been depressurized by a dealer service department or other repair shop. Always wear eye protection when disconnecting air conditioning system fittings.*

Caution: *It is important to reinstall the compressor bolts into their original locations. If any bolt needs replacement, it should be ordered and replaced with the correct GM part number.*

1 Have the system discharged (see the Warning above).

2 Disconnect the cable from the negative battery terminal. **Caution:** *If the vehicle is equipped with a Delco Loc II audio system, make sure you have the correct activation code before disconnecting the battery. See the information at the front of this manual for the radio re-activation procedure.*

3 Set the parking brake and block the rear wheels. Raise the front of the vehicle and support it securely on jackstands.

4 Remove the right under-vehicle splash shield.

3

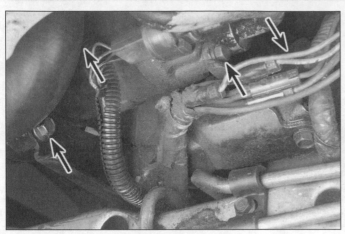

13.8 Remove the air conditioning compressor mounting bolts (arrows)

14.4 Air conditioning accumulator line fittings (arrows)

5   Remove the drivebelt (see Chapter 1). On some models it may also be necessary to remove the oil filter to provide clearance for compressor removal.
6   Disconnect the compressor clutch electrical connector.
7   Disconnect the refrigerant lines from the rear of the compressor. Plug the open fittings to prevent entry of dirt and moisture.
8   Unbolt the compressor from its mounting brackets and lower it from the vehicle **(see illustration)**.

Installation

9   If a new compressor is being installed, follow the directions with the new compressor regarding the draining of excess oil prior to installation.
10   The clutch may have to be transferred from the original to the new compressor.
11   Installation is the reverse of removal. Replace all O-rings with new ones made specifically for air conditioning system use and lubricate them with refrigerant oil.
12   Have the system evacuated, recharged and leak tested by the shop that discharged it.

14 Air conditioning accumulator - removal and installation

Refer to illustration 14.4
Warning: *The air conditioning system is under high pressure. DO NOT loosen any hose or line fittings or remove any components until after the system has been depressurized by a dealer service department or other repair shop. Always wear eye protection when disconnecting air conditioning system fittings.*
Note: *Accumulators (installed in the low-pressure side of the system) were used through the 1991 model year. 1992 and later models changed to a receiver/drier and thermal expansion valve system (installed in the high-pressure side of the system).*

Removal

1   Have the system discharged (see the Warning above).
2   Disconnect the cable from the negative battery terminal. **Caution:** *If the vehicle is equipped with a Delco Loc II audio system, make sure you have the correct activation code before disconnecting the battery. See the information at the front of this manual for the radio re-activation procedure.*
3   On some models it may be necessary to remove the air cleaner housing for access to the accumulator.
4   Disconnect the refrigerant lines from the accumulator **(see illustration)**. Use a back-up wrench to avoid twisting the tubing. Plug the open fittings to prevent the entry of dirt and moisture.
5   Loosen the mounting bracket bolts and remove the accumulator.

Installation

6   If a new accumulator is being installed, remove the Schrader valve and pour the oil out into a measuring cup, noting the amount. Add fresh refrigerant oil to the new accumulator equal to the amount removed from the old unit, plus one ounce.
7   The remainder of installation is the reverse of removal.
8   Have the system evacuated, recharged and leak tested by the shop that discharged it.

15 Air conditioning receiver/drier - removal and installation

Warning: *The air conditioning system is under high pressure. Do not loosen any fittings or remove any components until after the system has been discharged. Air conditioning refrigerant should be properly discharged into an EPA-approved container at a dealer service department or an automotive air conditioning repair facility. Always wear eye protection when disconnecting air condi-*

tioning system fittings.
Note: *1992 and later models use a receiver/drier and expansion valve system (installed in the high-pressure side of the system). 1991 and earlier systems use an accumulator (installed in the low-pressure side of the system).*

Removal

1   Have the refrigerant discharged at a dealer service department or an automotive air conditioning repair facility.
2   Disconnect the cable from the negative battery terminal. **Caution:** *If the vehicle is equipped with a Delco Loc II audio system, make sure you have the correct activation code before disconnecting the battery. See the information at the front of this manual for the radio re-activation procedure.* Raise the vehicle and support it securely on jackstands.
3   Remove the right front wheel.
4   Partially remove the splash shield from under the right side of the vehicle (enough to gain access to the receiver/drier).
5   Disconnect the refrigerant lines from the receiver/drier and discard the O-ring seals. **Caution:** *Immediately cap the open fittings to prevent the entry of dirt and moisture.*
6   Remove the receiver/drier mounting bracket-to-chassis bolts.
7   Remove the receiver/drier and bracket from the vehicle.
8   Separate the receiver/drier from the bracket.

Installation

9   Install new O-rings on the lines and lubricate them with clean refrigerant oil.
10   Installation is the reverse of removal. **Note:** *Do not remove the sealing caps until you are ready to reconnect the lines.*
11   If a new receiver/drier is installed, add one fluid ounce of refrigerant oil to the system. **Caution:** *Due to the tight fit of the receiver/drier to the surrounding sheet metal and engine components, make sure that none of the refrigerant lines rub on anything or a refrigerant leak could develop.*

12   Have the system evacuated, charged and leak tested by the shop that discharged it.

16   Air conditioning evaporator core and thermal expansion valve - removal and installation

Warning 1: *The air conditioning system is under high pressure. DO NOT loosen any hose or line fittings or remove any components until after the system has been depressurized by a dealer service department or other repair shop. Always wear eye protection when disconnecting air conditioning system fittings.*

Warning 2: *Before working in the vicinity of airbag components (on models so equipped) refer to Chapter 12 for the airbag system disarming procedure. Use care not to damage any wiring or sensors associated with this system or the airbag may deploy when reconnecting the battery or fail to deploy in the event of an accident.*

Note: *1992 and later models use a receiver/drier and expansion valve system (installed in the high-pressure side of the system) 1991 and earlier systems use an accumulator (installed in the low-pressure side of the system).*

Evaporator core
Removal

1   Have the refrigerant discharged at a dealer service department or an automotive air conditioning repair facility.
2   Disconnect the cable from the negative battery terminal. **Caution:** *If the vehicle is equipped with a Delco Loc II audio system, make sure you have the correct activation code before disconnecting the battery. See the information at the front of this manual for the radio re-activation procedure.*
3   Raise the vehicle and support it on jackstands (see Chapter 1).
4   Drain the cooling system (see Chapter 1).
5   Disconnect the hoses from the heater core tubes **(see illustration 9.3)**.
6   Remove the front exhaust shield.
7   Remove three of the bolts on the engine cradle cross-brace and swing the brace out of the way.
8   Disconnect the lines from the evaporator core at the firewall.
9   Remove the bolts from behind the steering gear on both sides of the heater core inlet/outlet area.
10   Lower the vehicle.
11   Remove the under dash insulator panel on both the left and right side (see Chapter 11).
12   Remove the steering column trim panel.
13   Remove the shift console to gain access to the floor duct and the heater core cover (see Chapter 11).
14   Remove the floor duct.
15   Disconnect the electrical connector at the heater core cover.

16   Remove the bolts from the driver's side of the housing.
17   Remove the screws and the floor outlet.
18   Remove the screws, clips and windshield defroster duct.
19   Disconnect the vacuum harness from all actuators.
20   Remove the nuts attaching the heater module to the firewall.
21   Remove the heater/air-conditioning evaporator housing.
22   Remove the heater core cover shroud and straps. **Caution:** *DO NOT apply any pressure to the heater core. It is suspended by the inlet and outlet pipes, and can be easily damaged.*
23   Remove the air conditioning evaporator assembly with the expansion valve assembly attached.
24   Separate the expansion valve from the evaporator. **Note:** *If a new evaporator is being installed, add the same amount of new refrigerant oil that was removed with the old evaporator.*

Installation
25   Installation is the reverse of removal.
26   Have the system evacuated, recharged and leak tested by the shop that discharged it.

Thermal expansion valve
Removal
Note: *The thermal expansion valve can be removed without the removal of the evaporator core.*
27   Have the refrigerant discharged at a dealer service department or an automotive air conditioning repair facility.
28   Remove the heater core cover shroud and straps (see Section 9).
29   Remove the insulation from the expansion valve assembly. **Note:** *The insulation must be put back in place after repair.*
30   Unscrew the fittings and separate the thermal expansion valve from the evaporator. Be sure to use a back-up wrench on the fittings to prevent twisting the refrigerant lines.

Installation
31   Installation is the reverse of removal.
32   Have the system evacuated, recharged and leak tested by the shop that discharged it.

17   Air conditioning expansion (orifice) tube - replacement

Note: *This procedures applies to 1991 and earlier models.*

Replacement
Refer to illustration 17.3
Warning: *The air conditioning system is under high pressure. DO NOT loosen any hose or line fittings or remove any components until after the system has been depressurized by a dealer service department or other repair shop. Always wear eye protection when disconnecting air conditioning system fittings.*
Note: *Whenever the expansion tube is replaced, the accumulator should also be replaced (see Section 14).*
1   Have the refrigerant discharged at a dealer service department or an automotive air conditioning repair facility.
2   Disconnect the cable from the negative battery terminal. **Caution:** *If the vehicle is equipped with a Delco Loc II audio system, make sure you have the correct activation code before disconnecting the battery. See the information at the front of this manual for the radio re-activation procedure.*
3   The expansion tube is a tube with a fixed diameter orifice and a mesh filter at each end **(see illustration)**. It is located in the condenser outlet pipe.
4   Unscrew the refrigerant line fitting at the condenser outlet pipe.
5   Using needle-nose pliers, remove the expansion tube.
6   The expansion tube may be reused if:
a   The screen isn't plugged with fine, gritty material
b   The screen isn't broken or torn
c   The plastic frame isn't broken
d   The brass expansion tube isn't plugged or damaged
7   Installation is the reverse of removal. Be sure to insert the expansion tube with the shorter screen end in first, towards the evaporator. **Caution:** *Always use a new O-ring when installing the expansion tube.*
8   Have the system evacuated, recharged and leak tested by the shop that discharged it.

3

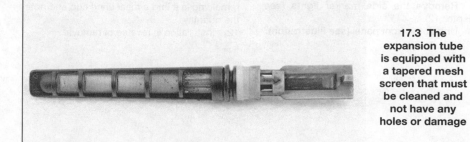

17.3 The expansion tube is equipped with a tapered mesh screen that must be cleaned and not have any holes or damage

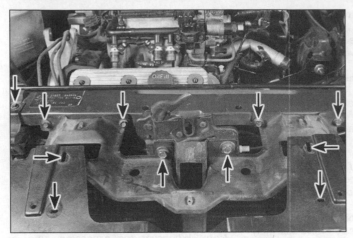

18.5 Front panel mounting bolt locations (arrows)

18.7 Bolt locations for the vertical hood latch brace (arrows)

18 Air conditioning condenser - removal and installation

Warning 1: *The air conditioning system is under high pressure. DO NOT loosen any hose or line fittings or remove any components until after the system has been depressurized by a dealer service department or other repair shop. Always wear eye protection when disconnecting air conditioning system fittings.*

Warning 2: *Before working in the vicinity of airbag components (on models so equipped) refer to Chapter 12 for the airbag system disarming procedure. Use care not to damage any wiring or sensors associated with this system or the airbag may deploy when reconnecting the battery or fail to deploy in the event of an accident.*

1   Have the refrigerant discharged at a dealer service department or an automotive air conditioning repair facility.

2   Disconnect the cable from the negative battery terminal. **Caution:** *If the vehicle is equipped with a Delco Loc II audio system, make sure you have the correct activation code before disconnecting the battery. See the information at the front of this manual for the radio re-activation procedure.*

1991 and earlier models

Refer to illustrations 18.5, 18.7 and 18.10

3   Remove the grill and headlight bezels (see Chapter 11).

4   Remove the side marker lights (see Chapter 12).

5   Unbolt the front panel **(see illustration)**.

18.10 Pull the condenser core carefully until it is free of the rubber insulators (arrows)

6   Unbolt the plastic panel which holds the headlights.

7   From beneath the vehicle, unbolt the lower spoiler to gain access to the vertical hood latch brace and remove the bolts **(see illustration)**.

8   Lift the hood latch brackets out and pull the headlight panel away from the radiator support.

9   Disconnect the refrigerant lines from the condenser. Be sure to use a backup wrench on the condenser fittings to avoid twisting the line.

10   Unbolt the condenser hold-down brackets, tilt the condenser forward and carefully lift out the condenser **(see illustration)**.

11   Tilt the condenser to pour any oil remaining in it into a measuring cup and note the quantity.

12   Installation is reverse of removal.

13   Have the system evacuated, recharged and leak tested by the shop that discharged it. Advise the technician of what was done and the quantity of oil recovered in Step 11.

1992 and later models

14   Disconnect the refrigerant lines from the condenser. Be sure to use a back-up wrench on the condenser fittings to avoid twisting the line.

15   Remove the radiator (see Section 5).

16   Remove the condenser mounting bolts.

17   If a new condenser is being installed, pour one ounce of fresh refrigerant oil into it prior to installation.

18   Reinstall the components in the reverse order of removal.

19   Have the system evacuated, recharged and leak tested by the shop that discharged it.

Chapter 4
Fuel and exhaust systems

Contents

Specifications

General

Minimum idle speed adjustment
Throttle Body Injection
Model 300 TBI
Automatic transaxle .... 500 +/- 25 rpm
Manual transaxle .... 775 +/- 25 rpm
Model 700 TBI .... 600 +/- 25 rpm
Multi Port Fuel Injection .... 500 +/- 50 rpm

Fuel pressure (at idle)

Throttle Body Injection (TBI) .... 9 to 13 psi
Multi-Port Fuel Injection (MPFI)
2.0L OHC four-cylinder engine
Key On, engine stopped .... Approximately 35 to 38 psi
Engine running .... Pressure should decrease by 5 to 10 psi
All others
Key On, engine stopped .... Approximately 41 to 47 psi
Engine running .... Pressure should decrease by 3 to 10 psi

Fuel injector resistance

Throttle Body Injection (TBI)	1.2 to 1.6 ohms
Multi-Port Fuel Injection	
Four-cylinder engines	1.9 to 2.3 ohms
V6 engines	11.8 to 12.6 ohms

Torque specifications

	Ft-lbs (unless otherwise indicated)
TBI unit mounting bolts/nuts	156 in-lbs
Throttle body (MPFI) mounting bolts/nuts	120 to 216 in-lbs
Air intake plenum mounting bolts/nuts	18
Fuel rail mounting bolts	14 to 19
Exhaust pipe-to-manifold nuts	15 to 22
Turbocharger-to-exhaust manifold nuts	18
Outlet elbow-to-turbocharger bolts	18
Turbocharger support bracket	
Lower bolt	37
Upper nut	18
Exhaust pipe-to-outlet elbow bolts	18

Component location

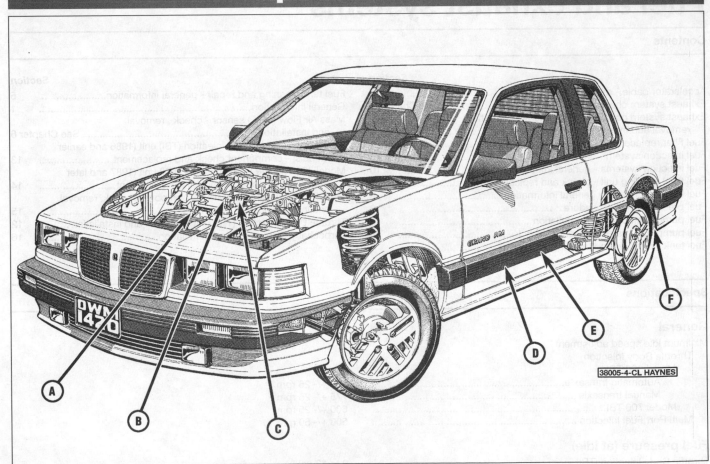

Typical fuel and exhaust system components

Component location

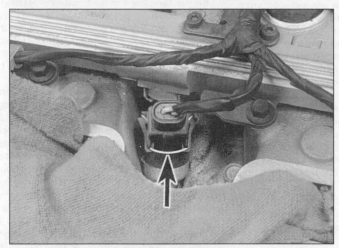

A Multi-Port fuel injector and electrical connector

B Throttle Body injection unit (TBI)

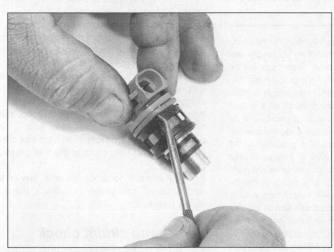

C TBI fuel injector and injector O-ring

D Fuel filter location

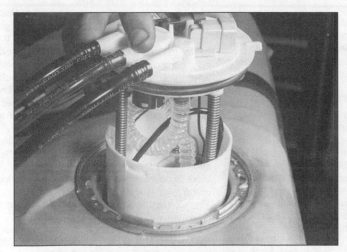

E Fuel pump and sending unit located in the fuel tank

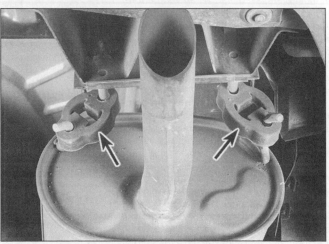

F Exhaust system rubber hangers

4

1   General information

The fuel system consists of a rear mounted fuel tank, an electric fuel pump, fuel injection system and an air cleaner.

Models equipped with Throttle Body Injection utilize one injector, centrally mounted in a carburetor-like housing. The injector is an electric solenoid, with fuel delivered to the injector at a constant pressure level. To maintain the fuel pressure at a constant level, excess fuel is returned to the fuel tank.

Models equipped with Multi-Port Fuel Injection utilize one injector per cylinder. The injectors are mounted on the intake manifold, above each intake port. The throttle body serves only to control the amount of air entering the engine. Because each cylinder is equipped with an injector mounted immediately adjacent to the intake valve, much better control of the fuel/air mixture is possible.

The exhaust system includes a catalytic converter, muffler, related emissions equipment and associated pipes and hardware.

2   Fuel pressure relief procedure

Warning: *Gasoline is extremely flammable, so take extra precautions when you work on any part of the fuel system. Don't smoke or allow open flames or bare light bulbs near the work area, and don't work in a garage where a natural gas-type appliance (such as a water heater or clothes dryer) with a pilot light is present. Since gasoline is carcinogenic, wear latex gloves when there's a possibility of being exposed to fuel, and, if you spill any fuel on your skin, rinse it off immediately with soap and water. Mop up any spills immediately and do not store fuel-soaked rags where they could ignite. The fuel system is under constant pressure, so, if any fuel lines are to be disconnected, the fuel pressure in the system must be relieved first. When you perform any kind of work on the fuel system, wear safety glasses and have a Class B type fire extinguisher on hand.*
Note: *After the fuel pressure has been relieved, it's a good idea to lay a shop towel over any fuel connection to be disassembled, to absorb the residual fuel that may leak out.*

1   Before servicing any fuel system component, you must relieve the fuel pressure to minimize the risk of fire or personal injury.
2   Remove the fuel filler cap - this will relieve any pressure built up in the tank.
3   On models with Throttle Body Injection, remove the fuel pump fuse and run the engine until it stalls, then crank the engine for three seconds. Disconnect the cable from the negative terminal of the battery. **Caution:** *If the vehicle is equipped with a Delco Loc II audio system, make sure you have the correct activation code before disconnecting the battery. See the information at the front of this manual for the radio re-activation procedure.*

4   On models with Multi-Port Fuel Injection, use one of the two following methods:
  a) *Disconnect the fuel pump electrical connector at the fuel tank (lower the tank if necessary). Run the engine until it stops, then engage the starter again for another three seconds. With the ignition turned Off, reconnect the fuel tank electrical connector, then disconnect the cable from the negative terminal of the battery (read the Caution in Step 3).*
  b) *Attach a fuel pressure gauge with a bleed-off valve to the Schrader valve on the fuel rail. Place the gauge bleeder hose in an approved fuel container. Open the valve on the gauge to relieve pressure, then disconnect the cable from the negative terminal of the battery (read the Caution in Step 3).*
5   Unless this procedure is followed before servicing fuel lines or connections, fuel spray (and possible injury) may occur

3   Fuel pump/fuel system pressure - check

Warning: *Gasoline is extremely flammable, so take extra precautions when you work on any part of the fuel system. Don't smoke or allow open flames or bare light bulbs near the work area, and don't work in a garage where a natural gas-type appliance (such as a water heater or clothes dryer) with a pilot light is present. Since gasoline is carcinogenic, wear latex gloves when there's a possibility of being exposed to fuel, and, if you spill any fuel on your skin, rinse it off immediately with soap and water. Mop up any spills immediately and do not store fuel-soaked rags where they could ignite. The fuel system is under constant pressure, so, if any fuel lines are to be disconnected, the fuel pressure in the system must be relieved first. When you perform any kind of work on the fuel system, wear safety glasses and have a Class B type fire extinguisher on hand.*
Note: *The following checks assume the fuel filter is in good condition. If you doubt its condition, install a new one (see Chapter 1). Check that there is adequate fuel in the fuel tank.*

Fuel pump operational check

1   Set the parking brake and have an assistant turn the ignition switch to the On position while you listen at the fuel pump. You should hear a whirring sound, lasting for a couple of seconds. Start the engine (if possible). The whirring sound should now be continuous (although harder to hear with the engine running). If there is no whirring sound, either the fuel pump or the fuel pump circuit is defective. Proceed to Step 10.

Pressure check

2   Relieve the fuel pressure (see Section 2).
3   If you're working on a TBI-equipped

model, remove the air cleaner assembly.
4   If you're working on a TBI-equipped model, remove the fuel line from the TBI unit and attach a fuel pressure gauge between the fuel feed line and the throttle body using a T-fitting. To do this you'll need a short section of metal fuel line with a fitting just like the one you unscrewed from the TBI unit, which must be threaded into the TBI unit. Clamp the lines securely to make sure there will not be any leaks.
5   If you're working on a model with port fuel injection, connect a fuel pressure gauge to the Schrader valve on the fuel rail.
6   Turn the ignition switch to On and measure the fuel pressure. It should be as listed in this Chapter's Specifications. Now start the engine and note the pressure - it should drop by 3 to 10 psi. With the engine running, detach the vacuum hose from the fuel pressure regulator - the fuel pressure reading should immediately increase between 3 to 10 psi. Compare the readings with the values listed in this Chapter's Specifications. If the pressure doesn't rise when the hose is disconnected, the fuel pressure regulator is faulty. Reconnect the vacuum hose.
7   If the fuel pressure is too high, check for a pinched or clogged fuel return hose or pipe. If the fuel return line is not obstructed, replace the fuel pressure regulator.
8   If the pressure is lower than specified, inspect the fuel filter - make sure it's not clogged. Look for a pinched or clogged fuel hose between the fuel tank and the fuel injection assembly. If the fuel feed line is OK, pinch the fuel return hose with a pair of pliers. If the pressure rises, replace the fuel pressure regulator.
9   If there are no problems with any of the above listed components, check the fuel pump (see below).

Fuel pump circuit check

10   If the pump does not come on (makes no sound), check the fuses. If the fuses are OK, proceed to the next step.
11   Locate the fuel pump relay. On 1993 and earlier models it's located on the far right (passenger's side) of the relay panel on the center of the firewall. On 1994 and later models it's the center relay on the right front strut tower. With the ignition "on", check for voltage at the fuel pump relay terminal "A". The light should light. If it does not light, check the wire from the fuel pump relay to the fuel pump fuse.
12   Check for voltage at fuel pump relay terminal "D". Voltage should be present for two seconds as the ignition key is cycled "on". If there is no voltage, check the wire from fuel pump relay terminal "D" to the ECM.
13   Check for a good ground at fuel pump relay terminal "F".
14   If checks 11 through 13 are OK, check for voltage at fuel pump terminal "E" as the ignition switch is cycled "on". Voltage should be present for two seconds. If there is no voltage, replace the relay and recheck. If

there is voltage at terminal "E" and no voltage at the fuel pump connector by the tank, the wire from the relay to the fuel tank should be checked.

15   Raise the rear of the vehicle and support it securely on jackstands. Disable the ignition system by disconnecting the primary wires from the ignition coil (HEI models) or by removing the ERLS or IGN ECM fuse (distributorless ignition models).

16   Locate the electrical connector to the fuel pump. It may be necessary to lower the tank slightly to provide access to the connector.

17   Unplug the electrical connector and probe the fuel pump feed wire with a test light. Have an assistant turn the ignition key to On - the test light should glow for about two seconds, then go off.

18   Have the assistant turn the ignition key to Start - the test light should glow as long as the engine is cranking.

19   If voltage is available, replace the fuel pump (see Section 6).

20   If no voltage is available, trace the fuel pump harness back and look for an open or short circuit condition. If no problem is found with the wiring harness, have the problem diagnosed by a dealer service department or other repair shop.

4   Fuel tank - removal and installation

Refer to illustration 4.9

Warning: *Gasoline is extremely flammable, so take extra precautions when you work on any part of the fuel system. Don't smoke or allow open flames or bare light bulbs near the work area, and don't work in a garage where a natural gas-type appliance (such as a water heater or clothes dryer) with a pilot light is present. Since gasoline is carcinogenic, wear latex gloves when there's a possibility of being exposed to fuel, and, if you spill any fuel on your skin, rinse it off immediately with soap and water. Mop up any spills immediately and do not store fuel-soaked rags where they could ignite. The fuel system is under constant pressure, so, if any fuel lines are to be disconnected, the fuel pressure in the system must be relieved first. When you perform any kind of work on the fuel system, wear safety glasses and have a Class B type fire extinguisher on hand.*

Note: *Don't begin this procedure until the fuel gauge indicates the tank is empty or nearly empty. If the tank must be removed when it's full (for example, if the fuel pump malfunctions), siphon any remaining fuel from the tank prior to removal.*

1   Unless the vehicle has been driven far enough to completely empty the tank, it's a good idea to siphon the residual fuel out before removing the tank from the vehicle. **Warning:** *DO NOT start the siphoning action by mouth! Use a siphoning kit, available at most auto parts stores.*

2   Relieve the fuel pressure (see Section 2).

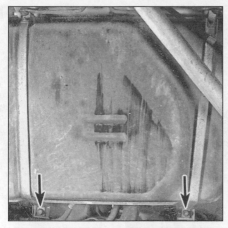

4.9 Remove the fuel tank strap retaining bolts (arrows)

3   Detach the cable from the negative terminal of the battery. **Caution:** *If the vehicle is equipped with a Delco Loc II audio system, make sure you have the correct activation code before disconnecting the battery. See the information at the front of this manual for the radio re-activation procedure.*

4   Raise the vehicle and place it securely on jackstands.

5   Locate the electrical connector for the electric fuel pump and fuel gauge sending unit in front of the tank, and unplug it. If the vehicle doesn't have a connector, see Step 9.

6   Disconnect the fuel feed and return lines, the vapor return line and the filler neck and vent tubes.

7   Support the fuel tank with a floor jack. Be sure to place a wood block on the head of the jack to protect the tank.

8   On some models, it may be necessary to lower the exhaust system to ease fuel tank removal.

9   Disconnect both fuel tank retaining straps **(see illustration)**.

10   Lower the tank enough to disconnect the wires and ground strap from the fuel pump/fuel gauge sending unit, if you haven't already done so.

11   Remove the tank from the vehicle.

12   Installation is the reverse of removal.

5   Fuel tank cleaning and repair - general information

All repairs to the fuel tank or filler neck should be carried out by a professional who has experience in this critical and potentially dangerous work. Even after cleaning and flushing of the fuel tank, explosive fumes can remain and ignite during repair of the tank.

If the fuel tank is removed from the vehicle, it should not be placed in an area where sparks or open flames could ignite the fumes coming from the tank. Be especially careful inside garages where a natural gas-type appliance is located, because the pilot light could cause an explosion.

6   Fuel pump - removal and installation

Refer to illustrations 6.5a, 6.5b, 6.8, 6.11, 6.12a, 6.12b, 6.12c, 6.12d and 6.14

Warning: *Gasoline is extremely flammable, so take extra precautions when you work on any part of the fuel system. Don't smoke or allow open flames or bare light bulbs near the work area, and don't work in a garage where a natural gas-type appliance (such as a water heater or clothes dryer) with a pilot light is present. Since gasoline is carcinogenic, wear latex gloves when there's a possibility of being exposed to fuel, and, if you spill any fuel on your skin, rinse it off immediately with soap and water. Mop up any spills immediately and do not store fuel-soaked rags where they could ignite. The fuel system is under constant pressure, so, if any fuel lines are to be disconnected, the fuel pressure in the system must be relieved first. When you perform any kind of work on the fuel system, wear safety glasses and have a Class B type fire extinguisher on hand.*

1   Relieve the fuel pressure (see Section 2).

2   Disconnect the cable from the negative battery terminal. **Caution:** *If the vehicle is equipped with a Delco Loc II audio system, make sure you have the correct activation code before disconnecting the battery. See the information at the front of this manual for the radio re-activation procedure.*

3   Remove the fuel tank (see Section 4).

4   The fuel pump/sending unit assembly is located inside the fuel tank. On 1991 and earlier models it is held in place by a cam lock ring mechanism consisting of an inner ring with three locking cams and an outer ring with three tangs. The outer ring is welded to the tank and can't be turned. On 1992 and later models it is held in place by a large snap-ring.

5   To unlock the fuel pump/sending unit assembly on a 1991 or earlier model, turn the

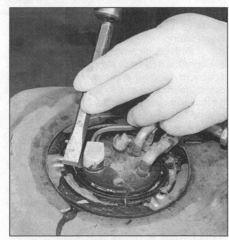

6.5a On early models, carefully tap the lock ring counterclockwise until the locking tabs align with the slots in the fuel tank

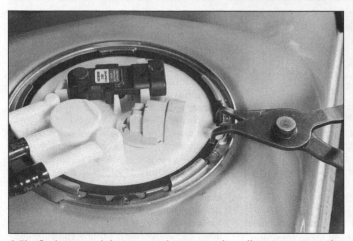

6.5b On later models, use a pair or snap-ring pliers to remove the retaining collar from the fuel pump assembly

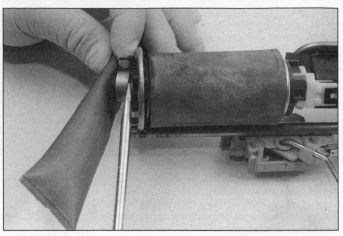

6.8 Inspect the fuel strainer for dirt; if too dirty to be cleaned carefully pry the fuel strainer from the inlet pipe

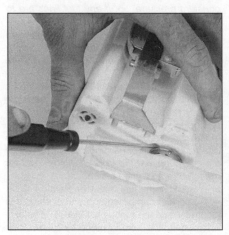

6.11 Carefully pry the fuel strainer from the inlet pipe

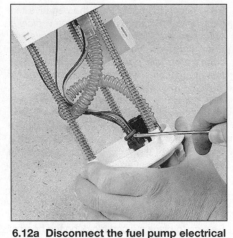

6.12a Disconnect the fuel pump electrical connections with a small screwdriver

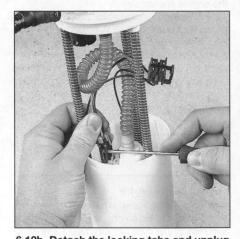

6.12b Detach the locking tabs and unplug the wiring harness from the pump

inner ring counterclockwise using a hammer and a BRASS punch or hardwood dowel until the locking cams are free of the tangs **(see illustration)**. **Warning:** *Do not use a steel punch to knock the lock rings loose - a spark could cause an explosion!* On 1992 and later models, remove the large snap-ring **(see illustration)**.

6   Lift the fuel pump/sending unit assembly from the fuel tank. **Caution:** *The fuel level float and sending unit are delicate. Do not bump them against the tank during removal or the accuracy of the sending unit may be affected.*

7   Inspect the condition of the rubber gasket around the fuel tank opening. If it is dried, cracked or deteriorated, replace it.

8   Inspect the strainer on the lower end of the fuel pump **(see illustration)**. If it is dirty, remove it, clean it with a suitable solvent and blow it out with compressed air. If it is too dirty to be cleaned, replace it.

1991 and earlier models

9   If it is necessary to separate the fuel pump and sending unit (as for pump or sending unit replacement), remove the pump from

the sending unit by pulling the fuel pump assembly into the rubber connector and sliding the pump away from the bottom support. Care should be taken to prevent damage to the rubber insulator and fuel strainer during removal. After the pump assembly is clear of

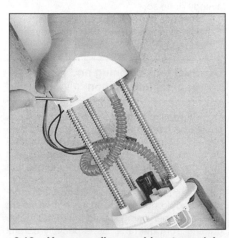

6.12c Use a small screwdriver to push in on the two tangs to release the outer reservoir . . .

the bottom support, pull it out of the rubber connector. Reconnect the pump to the sending unit by reversing the removal steps.

10   Insert the fuel pump/sending unit assembly into the fuel tank. Turn the inner lock ring clockwise until the locking cams are

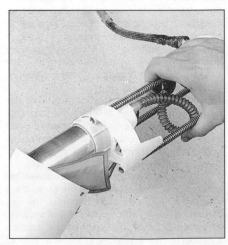

6.12d . . . and remove the outer reservoir

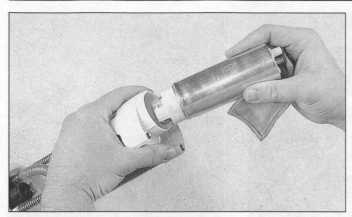

6.14 Twist the fuel pump and detach it from the retainer

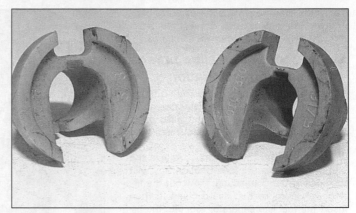

8.8 3/8 and 5/16-inch fuel line disconnect tools are available at most auto part stores

fully engaged with the retaining tangs. **Note:** *If you have installed a new O-ring type rubber gasket, it may be necessary to push down on the inner lock ring until the locking cams slide under the retaining tangs.*

1992 and later models

11   Remove the fuel strainer from the bottom of the unit **(see illustration)**.
12   Disconnect the electrical connector from the fuel pump. Gently release the fuel sender-to-cover assembly tabs by squeezing the sides of the reservoir housing and releasing the tab on the opposite side, moving clockwise to release the second and third locking tabs in the same manner **(see illustrations)**.
13   Separate the cover and reservoir assembly enough to disconnect the lower fuel pump connector.
14   Rotate the fuel pump baffle counterclockwise and separate the baffle and pump assembly from the retainer **(see illustration)**.
15   Slide the fuel pump out of the slot.
16   Installation is the reverse of removal.
17   Insert the modular sending unit into the fuel tank. Be sure to use a new O-ring if the old one is deteriorated.
18   Install the snap-ring.
19   Install the fuel tank (see Section 4).

---

7   Fuel level sending unit - check and replacement

Warning: *Gasoline is extremely flammable, so take extra precautions when you work on any part of the fuel system. Don't smoke or allow open flames or bare light bulbs near the work area, and don't work in a garage where a natural gas-type appliance (such as a water heater or clothes dryer) with a pilot light is present. Since gasoline is carcinogenic, wear latex gloves when there's a possibility of being exposed to fuel, and, if you spill any fuel on your skin, rinse it off immediately with soap and water. Mop up any spills immediately and do not store fuel-soaked rags where they could ignite. The fuel system is under*

constant pressure, so, if any fuel lines are to be disconnected, the fuel pressure in the system must be relieved first. When you perform any kind of work on the fuel system, wear safety glasses and have a Class B type fire extinguisher on hand.*

Check

1   Raise the vehicle and support it securely on jackstands.
2   Disconnect the electrical connector for the fuel pump/level sending unit. With the ignition key in the On position, the needle on the fuel level gauge should deflect to the maximum full position.
3   Using a jumper wire, ground the wire to the fuel level sending unit (it's usually the pink or purple wire). The needle on the gauge should now read empty.
4   If the gauge responds properly to these checks, the harness and gauge are OK. Replace the fuel level sending unit. If the gauge does not operate as described, the problem lies in the wiring harness to the gauge, or the gauge itself.

Replacement

5   Follow the procedure described in Section 6 to remove the fuel level sending unit (and the fuel pump). Transfer the fuel pump to the new sending unit.

---

8   Fuel lines and fittings - general information

Refer to illustration 8.8
Warning: *Gasoline is extremely flammable, so take extra precautions when you work on any part of the fuel system. Don't smoke or allow open flames or bare light bulbs near the work area, and don't work in a garage where a natural gas-type appliance (such as a water heater or clothes dryer) with a pilot light is present. Since gasoline is carcinogenic, wear latex gloves when there's a possibility of being exposed to fuel, and, if you spill any fuel on your skin, rinse it off immediately with*

soap and water. Mop up any spills immediately and do not store fuel-soaked rags where they could ignite. The fuel system is under constant pressure, so, if any fuel lines are to be disconnected, the fuel pressure in the system must be relieved first. When you perform any kind of work on the fuel system, wear safety glasses and have a Class B type fire extinguisher on hand.*

1   Always relieve the fuel pressure before servicing fuel lines or fittings (see Section 2), and be sure to disconnect the cable from the negative terminal of the battery. **Caution:** *If the vehicle is equipped with a Delco Loc II audio system, make sure you have the correct activation code before disconnecting the battery. See the information at the front of this manual for the radio re-activation procedure.*
2   The fuel feed and return lines extend from the fuel tank to the engine compartment. The lines are secured to the underbody with clip and screw assemblies. The lines must be occasionally inspected for leaks, kinks and dents.
3   If evidence of dirt is found in the system or fuel filter during disassembly, the lines should be disconnected and blown out. Check the fuel strainer on the fuel gauge sending unit (see Section 6) for damage and deterioration.

Steel tubing

4   If replacement of a fuel line or emission line is called for, use welded steel tubing meeting original equipment specifications.
5   Don't use copper or aluminum tubing to replace steel tubing. These materials cannot withstand normal vehicle vibration.
6   Because fuel lines used on fuel-injected models are under high pressure, they require special consideration.
7   Most fuel lines have threaded fittings with O-rings. Any time the fittings are loosened to service or replace components:

a)   Use a back-up wrench while loosening and tightening the fittings.
b)   Check all O-rings for cuts, cracks and deterioration. Replace any that appear worn or damaged.

4

c) *If the lines are replaced, always use orig-inal equipment parts, or parts that meet the vehicle manufacturer's standards.*

Quick-connect fuel line fittings - removal and installation

8   New quick-connect fuel line fittings were introduced on 1989 and later models. A special tool, available at most auto parts stores, is required to disconnect them **(see illustration)**.

9   To separate the fuel lines, relieve the fuel system pressure (see Section 2). Twist the lines at the connection, blow out the fit-ting with compressed air to clean it, then insert the fuel line separator tool into the fit-ting and pull the lines apart.

10   To reattach quick-connect fittings, push the line into the fitting as far as possible, then pull back on it to verify that the connection is secure. **Warning:** *The line must be pushed in and pulled back to verify proper connector engagement - DO NOT rely on an audible click or visual verification to check the assem-bly of the quick-connect fittings.*

Flexible hose

Warning: *Never use rubber hose to replace metal line on a fuel-injected vehicle - use original equipment fuel line (or equivalent line meeting original equipment specifications) only!*

11   When flexible hose is used to replace a metal line, use reinforced, fuel resistant hose with the word *Fluoroelastomer* imprinted on it. Hose(s) not clearly marked like this could fail prematurely and could fail to meet Federal emission standards. Hose inside diameter must match line outside diameter.

12   Don't use flexible hose within four inches of any part of the exhaust system or within ten inches of the catalytic converter. Metal lines and flexible hoses must never be allowed to chafe against the frame. A mini-mum of 1/4-inch clearance must be main-tained around a line or hose to prevent con-tact with the frame or other components.

9   Accelerator cable - removal and installation

Refer to illustrations 9.2, 9.6a, 9.6b and 9.7

Removal

1   Detach the screws and the clip retaining the lower instrument panel trim and lower the trim (if necessary).

2   Detach the accelerator cable from the accelerator pedal **(see illustration)**.

3   Squeeze the accelerator cable casing tangs and push the cable through the firewall into the engine compartment.

4   Remove the cable clamp attaching screws and the cable clamp (if equipped).

5   Detach the routing clip (if equipped) and the accelerator cable.

6   Detach the accelerator cable-to-throttle lever retainer and detach the accelerator

9.2 Pull the end of the accelerator cable toward you and slide it out of the slot in the pedal lever

9.6b On MPFI-equipped vehicles, you'll need to pop off the retaining clip to detach the cruise control cable from the throttle lever arm

cable from the throttle body lever **(see illus-trations)**.

7   Squeeze the accelerator cable retaining tangs and push the cable through the accel-erator cable bracket **(see illustration)**.

Installation

8   Installation is the reverse of removal. **Note:** *To prevent possible interference, flexi-ble components (hoses, wires, etc.) must not be routed within two inches of moving parts, unless routing is controlled.*

9   Operate the accelerator pedal and check for any binding condition by com-pletely opening and closing the throttle.

10   At the engine compartment side of the firewall, apply sealant around the accelerator cable casing.

10   Fuel injection systems - general information

Two types of fuel injection systems are used in the models covered by this manual.

9.6a On MPFI-equipped vehicles, push the cable end forward and lift up to detach the cable from the post on the throttle lever arm

9.7 On MPFI-equipped vehicles, the throttle and cruise control cable retainers can be detached from the cable bracket by squeezing the locking tabs on the top and bottom of the retainer with a pair of needle-nose pliers

Throttle Body Injection (TBI) and Multi-Port Fuel Injection (MPFI). Fuel injection provides optimum mixture ratios at all stages of com-bustion. Combined with its immediate response characteristics, fuel injection per-mits the engine to run on the leanest possible air/fuel mixture, which greatly reduces exhaust gas emissions.

The fuel injection system is controlled directly by the vehicle's Electronic Control Module (ECM), which automatically adjusts the air/fuel mixture in accordance with engine load and performance.

Throttle Body Injection (TBI)

The main component of the TBI system is the Throttle Body Injection (TBI) unit, which is mounted on the intake manifold just like a carburetor. The TBI unit is made up of two major assemblies: the throttle body and the fuel metering assembly.

The throttle body contains a single throttle valve, controlled by the accelerator pedal, similar to a carburetor. Attached to the exterior of the body are the Throttle Position Sensor (TPS), which sends throttle position information to the ECM, and the Idle Air Control (IAC) assembly, which is used by the ECM to maintain a constant idle speed during normal engine operation.

The fuel metering assembly contains the fuel pressure regulator and the single fuel injector. The regulator dampens the pulsations of the fuel pump and maintains a steady pressure at the injector. The fuel injector is controlled by the ECM through an electrically operated solenoid. The amount of fuel injected into the intake manifold is varied by the length of time the injector plunger is held open.

Multi-Port Fuel Injection (MPFI)

Multi-Port Fuel Injection (MPFI) consists of an air intake manifold, the throttle body, the injectors, the fuel rail assembly, an electric fuel pump and attendant plumbing.

Air is drawn through the air cleaner and throttle body. A Mass Air Flow (MAF) sensor mounted between the air cleaner and the throttle body measures the mass (weight) of air passing through the manifold and compensates for temperature and pressure variations.

While the engine is running, the fuel constantly circulates through the fuel rail, which removes vapors and keeps the fuel cool while maintaining sufficient pressure to the injectors under all running conditions.

As with TBI, the operation of the MPFI injection system is controlled by the ECM so that it works in conjunction with the rest of the vehicle functions to provide optimum driveability and emissions control.

Because the MPFI system meters fuel and air precisely, it is important to the proper operation of the vehicle that the fuel and air filters be changed at the specified intervals.

Both systems

The ECM controlling both types of fuel injection systems has a learning capability for certain performance conditions. If the battery is disconnected, part of the ECM memory is erased, which makes it necessary to "re-teach" the computer. This is done by thoroughly warming up the engine and operating the vehicle at part throttle, stop and go and idle conditions.

A fuel pump relay is used to control the electric fuel pump operation. When the ignition is turned on, the fuel pump relay immediately supplies current to the fuel pump to pressurize the fuel system. If the engine doesn't start after two seconds, the fuel pump will automatically shut off. If the fuel pump relay fails, the fuel pump will still operate after the ECM receives pulses from the distributor or about four pounds of oil pressure has built up, depending on the model.

The throttle stop screw, used to regulate the minimum idle speed, is adjusted at the factory and sealed with a plug to discourage unnecessary readjustment.

11   Fuel injection system - check

Warning: *Gasoline is extremely flammable, so take extra precautions when you work on any part of the fuel system. Don't smoke or allow open flames or bare light bulbs near the work area, and don't work in a garage where a natural gas-type appliance (such as a water heater or clothes dryer) with a pilot light is present. Since gasoline is carcinogenic, wear latex gloves when there's a possibility of being exposed to fuel, and, if you spill any fuel on your skin, rinse it off immediately with soap and water. Mop up any spills immediately and do not store fuel-soaked rags where they could ignite. The fuel system is under constant pressure, so, if any fuel lines are to be disconnected, the fuel pressure in the system must be relieved first. When you perform any kind of work on the fuel system, wear safety glasses and have a Class B type fire extinguisher on hand.*
Note: *The following procedure is based on the assumption that the fuel pump is working and the fuel pressure is adequate (see Section 3).*

Preliminary checks

1   Check all electrical connectors that are related to the system. Loose electrical connectors and poor grounds can cause many problems that resemble more serious malfunctions.
2   Check to see that the battery is fully charged, as the control unit and sensors depend on an accurate supply voltage in order to properly meter the fuel.
3   Check the air filter element - a dirty or partially blocked filter will severely impede performance and economy (see Chapter 1).
4   If a blown fuse is found, replace it and see if it blows again. If it does, search for a grounded wire in the harness to the fuel pump.

Multi-Port Fuel Injection systems

Refer to illustration 11.9
5   Check the air intake duct from the Mass Air Flow (MAF) sensor (if equipped) to the intake manifold for leaks, which will result in an excessively lean mixture. Also check the condition of the vacuum hoses connected to the intake manifold.
6   Remove the air intake duct from the throttle body and check for dirt, carbon or other residue build-up in the throttle body, particularly around the throttle plate. If it's dirty, clean it with carburetor cleaner and a toothbrush.
7   With the engine running, place a screw-driver (or stethoscope) against each injector,

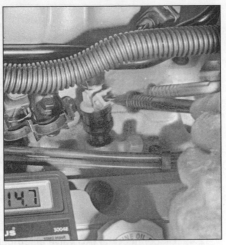

11.9 Measure the resistance of the injectors with an ohmmeter

one at a time, and listen through the handle for a clicking sound, indicating operation.
8   If an injector isn't functioning (not clicking), purchase a special injector test light (sometimes called a "noid" light) and plug it into the injector electrical connector. Crank the engine and check to see if the noid light flashes. If it does, the injector is receiving proper voltage. If it doesn't flash, further diagnosis should be performed by a dealer service department or other repair shop.
9   With the engine OFF and the fuel injector electrical connectors disconnected, measure the resistance of each injector **(see illustration)**. Compare your findings with the values listed in this Chapter's Specifications.
10   The remainder of the system checks can be found in Section 15 and Chapter 6.

TBI systems

11   Set the parking brake, remove the air cleaner top plate and, with the engine idling in Park, observe the operating fuel injector. The spray pattern should be even and conical in shape. The spray should touch the throttle body bore.

a) *If the spray is weak or uneven, the injector is clogged or faulty. Gasoline additives designed to clean fuel injectors can sometimes clear a clogged injector. If not, a dealer service department or other qualified shop has more effective cleaning equipment.*

b) *If an injector is not operating at all, check its electrical connector. If the connection is good and the injector is receiving voltage (see Step 8), but the injector still doesn't work, the injector is faulty.*

12   Turn the engine off and observe the injector. There shouldn't be any leakage or dripping. If the injector does drip, either the injector seals are faulty or the injector itself is defective. Usually a problem like this will result in a hard-starting condition and/or a puff of smoke as the engine is started.

12.4a Disconnect the IAC valve electrical connection (arrow) - Model 300 TBI unit shown

12.4b Disconnect the TPS electrical connection (arrow) - Model 700 TBI unit shown

12 Throttle Body Injection (TBI) unit - removal and installation

Refer to illustrations 12.4a and 12.4b
Warning: *Gasoline is extremely flammable, so take extra precautions when you work on any part of the fuel system. Don't smoke or allow open flames or bare light bulbs near the work area, and don't work in a garage where a natural gas-type appliance (such as a water heater or clothes dryer) with a pilot light is present. Since gasoline is carcinogenic, wear latex gloves when there's a possibility of being exposed to fuel, and, if you spill any fuel on your skin, rinse it off immediately with soap and water. Mop up any spills immediately and do not store fuel-soaked rags where they could ignite. The fuel system is under constant pressure, so, if any fuel lines are to be disconnected, the fuel pressure in the system must be relieved first. When you perform any kind of work on the fuel system, wear safety glasses and have a Class B type fire extinguisher on hand.*
Note: *The fuel injector, fuel meter assembly, throttle position sensor and the idle air control valve can be replaced without removing the throttle body assembly.*

Removal

1   Relieve the fuel system pressure (see Section 2).
2   Disconnect the cable from the negative terminal of the battery. **Caution:** *If the vehicle is equipped with a Delco Loc II audio system, make sure you have the correct activation code before disconnecting the battery. See the information at the front of this manual for the radio re-activation procedure.*
3   Remove the air cleaner housing.
4   Unplug the electrical connectors from the idle air control valve, throttle position sensor and the fuel injector **(see illustrations)**.
5   Remove the wiring harness and insulating grommet from the throttle body.
6   Disconnect the accelerator cable and

return spring, transmission control and cruise control cables, if equipped.
7   Using pieces of numbered tape, mark all of the vacuum hoses to the throttle body and disconnect them.
8   Disconnect the fuel inlet and return lines. Use a back-up wrench on the inlet and return fitting nuts to prevent damage to the throttle body and fuel lines. Remove the O-rings on the ends of the fuel lines and discard them (be sure to install new ones during reassembly). Later models use quick-connect fuel lines - refer to Section 8 for the disconnection procedure.
9   Remove the TBI assembly mounting bolts/nuts and lift the unit from the intake manifold. It's a good idea to stuff a rag into the intake manifold opening to prevent foreign matter from falling in. Remove all old gasket material from the intake manifold and the underside of the throttle body unit.

Installation

10   Installation is the reverse of the removal procedure. Be sure to install a new throttle body-to-intake manifold gasket, new fuel line O-rings and tighten the mounting bolts/nuts to the torque listed in this Chapter's Specifications.
11   Turn the ignition switch to the On position (don't start the engine) and check for fuel leaks.
12   Check to see if the accelerator pedal is free by depressing the pedal to the floor and releasing it with the ignition switch off.

13 Model 300 Throttle Body Injection (TBI) unit (1986 and earlier models) - component check and replacement

Warning: *Gasoline is extremely flammable, so take extra precautions when you work on any part of the fuel system. Don't smoke or allow open flames or bare light bulbs near the work area, and don't work in a garage where*

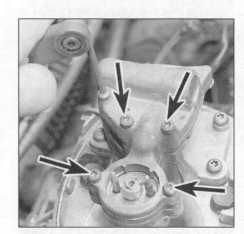

13.6 Fuel meter cover-to-fuel meter body screw locations

a natural gas-type appliance (such as a water heater or clothes dryer) with a pilot light is present. Since gasoline is carcinogenic, wear latex gloves when there's a possibility of being exposed to fuel, and, if you spill any fuel on your skin, rinse it off immediately with soap and water. Mop up any spills immediately and do not store fuel-soaked rags where they could ignite. The fuel system is under constant pressure, so, if any fuel lines are to be disconnected, the fuel pressure in the system must be relieved first. When you perform any kind of work on the fuel system, wear safety glasses and have a Class B type fire extinguisher on hand.
Note: *Because of its relative simplicity, a throttle body assembly does not need to be removed from the intake manifold nor completely disassembled for component replacement. However, for the sake of clarity, the following procedures are shown with the TBI unit removed from the vehicle.*
1   Relieve the fuel pressure (see Section 2).
2   Detach the cable from the negative terminal of the battery.
3   Remove the air cleaner housing assembly, adapter and gaskets.

13.8 The fuel pressure regulator is installed in the fuel meter cover and pre-adjusted at the factory - don't remove the four retaining screw (arrows) or you may damage the regulator

13.9a The best way to remove the fuel injector is to pry on it with a screwdriver, using a second screwdriver as a fulcrum

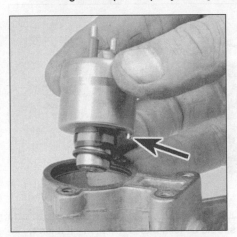

13.9b Note the position of the terminals on top and the dowel pin on the bottom of the injector in relation to the fuel meter body when you lift the injector out of the throttle body

13.11 Carefully peel away the old fuel meter outlet passage gasket and fuel meter cover gasket with razor blade

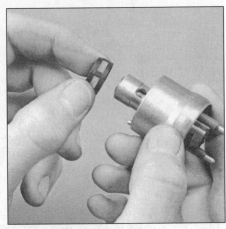

13.12 Gently rotate the fuel injector filter back and forth and pull it off the nozzle

Fuel meter cover and fuel injector

Refer to illustrations 13.6, 13.8, 13.9a, 13.9b, 13.11, 13.12, 13.18, 13.19 and 13.20

Check

4   Refer to Section 11 for the fuel injector checking procedure. Also check for stored trouble codes in the ECM (see Chapter 6).

Disassembly

5   Remove the injector electrical connector (on top of the TBI unit) by squeezing the two tabs together and pulling straight up.

6   Unscrew the five fuel meter cover retaining screws and lockwashers securing the fuel meter cover to the fuel meter body. Note the location of the two short screws **(see illustration)**.

7   Remove the fuel meter cover. **Caution:** *Do not immerse the fuel meter cover in solvent. It might damage the pressure regulator diaphragm and gasket.*

8   The fuel meter cover contains the fuel pressure regulator, which is pre-set and plugged at the factory. If a malfunction occurs, it cannot be serviced, and must be replaced as a complete assembly. **Warning:** *Do not remove the screws securing the pressure regulator to the fuel meter cover* **(see illustration)**. *It has a large spring under heavy compression inside.*

9   With the old fuel meter cover gasket in place to prevent damage to the casting, carefully pry the injector from the fuel meter body with a screwdriver until it can be lifted free **(see illustrations)**. **Caution:** *Use care in removing the injector to prevent damage to the electrical connector terminals, the injector fuel filter, the O-ring and the nozzle.*

10   The fuel meter body should be removed from the throttle body if it needs to be cleaned. To remove it, remove the fuel feed and return line fittings and the Torx screws that attach the fuel meter body to the throttle body.

11   Remove the old gasket from the fuel meter cover and discard it. Remove the large O-ring and steel back-up washer from the upper counterbore of the fuel meter body

injector cavity **(see illustration)**. Clean the fuel meter body thoroughly in carburetor cleaner and blow it dry.

12   Remove the small O-ring from the nozzle end of the injector. Carefully rotate the injector fuel filter back and forth and remove the filter from the base of the injector **(see illustration)**. Gently clean the filter in solvent and allow it to drip dry. It is too small and delicate to dry with compressed air. **Caution:** *The fuel injector itself is an electrical component. Do not immerse it in any type of cleaning solvent.*

13   The fuel injector is not serviceable. If it is malfunctioning, replace it as an assembly.

Reassembly

14   Install the clean fuel injector nozzle filter on the end of the fuel injector with the larger end of the filter facing the injector so that the filter covers the raised rib at the base of the injector. Use a twisting motion to position the filter against the base of the injector.

15   Lubricate a new small O-ring with automatic transmission fluid. Push the O-ring onto the nozzle end of the injector until it presses against the injector fuel filter.

4

13.18 Make sure that the lug is aligned with the notch in the bottom of the fuel injector cavity

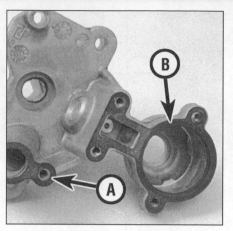

13.19 Position the fuel outlet passage gasket (A) and the fuel meter cover gasket (B) properly

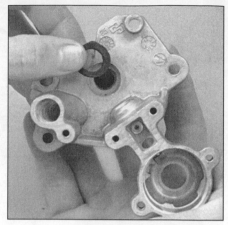

13.20 Install a new dust seal into the recess of the fuel meter body

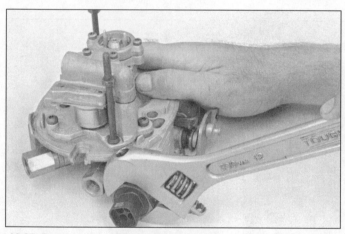

13.27 Remove the IAC valve with a large wrench, but be careful - it's a delicate device

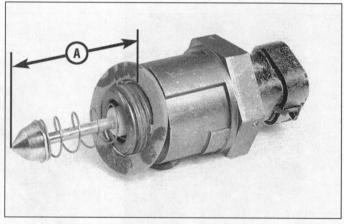

13.28 Distance A should be less than 1-1/8 inch - if it isn't, determine which kind of valve you have and adjust it accordingly

16   Insert the steel back-up washer in the top counterbore of the fuel meter body injector cavity.

17   Lubricate a new large O-ring with automatic transmission fluid and install it directly over the backup washer. Be sure the O-ring is seated properly in the cavity and is flush with the top of the fuel meter body casting surface. **Caution:** *The back-up washer and large O-ring must be installed before the injector or improper seating of the large O-ring could cause fuel to leak.* .

18   Install the injector in the cavity in the fuel meter body, aligning the raised lug on the injector base with the cast-in notch in fuel meter body cavity. Push straight down on the injector with both thumbs **(see illustration)** until it is fully seated in the cavity. **Note:** *The electrical terminals of the injector should be approximately parallel to the throttle shaft.*

19   Install a new fuel outlet passage gasket on the fuel meter cover and a new fuel meter cover gasket on the fuel meter body **(see illustration)**.

20   Install a new dust seal into the recess on the fuel meter body **(see illustration)**.

21   Install the fuel meter cover onto the fuel meter body, making sure that the pressure regulator dust seal and cover gaskets are in place.

22   Apply a thread locking compound to the threads of the fuel meter cover attaching screws. Install the screws (the two short screws go next to the injector) and tighten them securely. **Note:** *Service repair kits include a small vial of thread locking compound with directions for use. If this material is not available, use a non-hardening thread locking compound. Do not use a higher strength locking compound than recommended, as this may prevent subsequent removal of the attaching screws or cause breakage of the screw head if removal becomes necessary.*

23   Plug in the electrical connector to the injector.

24   Install the air cleaner.

Idle Air Control (IAC) valve

Refer to illustrations 13.27 and 13.28

Check

25   Refer to Chapter 6 and check for trouble codes stored in the ECM. If the IAC valve is malfunctioning, a trouble code indicating this condition would most likely have been set.

Removal

26   Unplug the electrical connector at the IAC valve.

27   Remove the IAC valve with a wrench on the hex surface only **(see illustration)**.

Installation

28   Before installing a new IAC valve, measure the distance the valve is extended **(see illustration)**. The measurement should be made from the motor housing to the end of the cone. The distance should be no greater than 1-1/8 inch. If the cone is extended too far, damage may occur to the valve when it is installed.

29   Identify the replacement IAC valve as either a Type I (with a collar at the electrical connector end) or a Type II (without a collar). If the measured dimension "A" is greater than 1-1/8 inch, the distance must be reduced as follows:

Type I -Exert firm pressure on the valve to retract it (a slight side-to-side movement may be helpful).

Type II - Compress the retaining spring of the valve while turning the valve in a clockwise direction. Return the spring to its original position with the straight portion of the spring

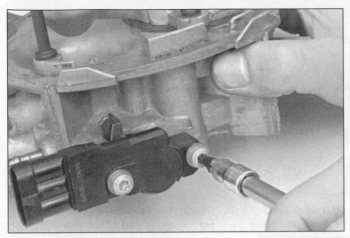

13.48 The Throttle Position Sensor (TPS) is mounted to the side of the TBI with two Torx screws

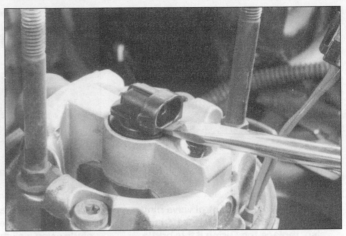

14.5 Carefully pry the injector out of the fuel meter body

aligned with the flat surface of the valve.

30   Install the new IAC valve to the throttle body. Use the new gasket supplied with the assembly.

31   Plug in the electrical connector.

32   Install the air cleaner.

33   Start the engine and allow it to reach normal operating temperature. The Electronic Control Module (ECM) will reset the idle speed when the vehicle is driven above 35 mph.

Minimum idle speed adjustment

Note: *This adjustment should be performed only when the throttle body has been replaced or if the vehicle is experiencing a stalling condition at idle. The engine should be at normal operating temperature before making the adjustment.*

34   Remove the air cleaner housing.

35   Remove the plug covering the idle stop screw by piercing it with an awl, then applying leverage.

36   Plug any vacuum ports as required by the VECI label. Also plug the idle air passage in the throttle body, adjacent to the fuel meter cover.

37   With the IAC valve connected, ground the diagnostic terminal of the ALDL connector (see Chapter 6). Turn the ignition to On but don't start the engine. Wait at least 30 seconds to allow the IAC pintle to extend and seat in the throttle body. Disconnect the IAC valve electrical connector. Remove the jumper wire from the ALDL connector and start the engine.

38   Adjust the idle stop screw to obtain the specified minimum idle speed in Park.

39   Turn the ignition off and reconnect the IAC valve electrical connector.

40   Unplug any plugged vacuum ports and reconnect the hoses.

41   Install the air cleaner housing.

42   Disconnect the cable from the negative terminal of the battery for at least ten seconds. This will erase any stored trouble codes that may have been set by unplugging the IAC valve and running the engine. **Caution:** *If the*

vehicle is equipped with a Delco Loc II audio system, make sure you have the correct activation code before disconnecting the battery. See the information at the front of this manual for the radio re-activation procedure.

Throttle Position Sensor (TPS)

Refer to illustration 13.48

General information and check

43   The Throttle Position Sensor (TPS) is connected to the throttle shaft on the TBI unit. As the throttle valve angle is changed (as the accelerator pedal is moved), the output of the TPS also changes. At a closed throttle position, the output of the TPS is below 1.25-volts. As the throttle valve opens, the output increases so that, at wide-open throttle, the output voltage is approximately 5-volts.

44   A broken or loose TPS can cause intermittent bursts of fuel from the injector and an unstable idle, because the ECM thinks the throttle is moving. If a problem with the TPS sensor or circuit develops, a trouble code most likely will be set (see Chapter 6).

45   Connect a digital voltmeter from the TPS electrical connector center terminal "B" to outside terminal "A" (you'll have to fabricate jumper wires for terminal access).

46   With the ignition on and the engine off, TPS voltage should be less than 1.25 volts. If it's more than specified, check and, if necessary, adjust the minimum idle speed before condemning the TPS.

47   The TPS is not adjustable. If the TPS malfunctions, it must be replaced as a unit.

Replacement

48   Unscrew the two Torx screws **(see illustration)** and remove the TPS.

49   Install the new TPS and tighten the screws securely. **Note:** *Make sure the tang on the lever is properly engaged with the stop on the TBI unit.*

50   Install the air cleaner assembly.

51   Attach the cable to the negative terminal of the battery.

14   Model 700 Throttle Body Injection (TBI) unit (1987 and later models - component check and replacement)

Warning: *Gasoline is extremely flammable, so take extra precautions when you work on any part of the fuel system. Don't smoke or allow open flames or bare light bulbs near the work area, and don't work in a garage where a natural gas-type appliance (such as a water heater or clothes dryer) with a pilot light is present. Since gasoline is carcinogenic, wear latex gloves when there's a possibility of being exposed to fuel, and, if you spill any fuel on your skin, rinse it off immediately with soap and water. Mop up any spills immediately and do not store fuel-soaked rags where they could ignite. The fuel system is under constant pressure, so, if any fuel lines are to be disconnected, the fuel pressure in the system must be relieved first. When you perform any kind of work on the fuel system, wear safety glasses and have a Class B type fire extinguisher on hand.*

Fuel injector

Check

1   Refer to Section 11 for the fuel injector checking procedure. Also check for stored trouble codes in the ECM (see Chapter 6).

Replacement

Refer to illustration 14.5

2   Disconnect the negative battery cable. **Caution:** *If the vehicle is equipped with a Delco Loc II audio system, make sure you have the correct activation code before disconnecting the battery. See the information at the front of this manual for the radio re-activation procedure.*

3   Unplug the electrical connector from the fuel injector.

4   Remove the injector retainer screw and the retainer.

5   Using one screwdriver as a fulcrum on the fuel meter body, place another screw-

4

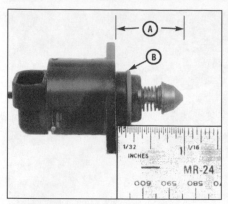

14.18a The Idle Air Control valve pintle must not extend more than 1-1/8 inch - also, replace the O-ring if it is brittle

A   *Distance of pintle extension*
B   *O-ring*

14.18b To reduce the IAC valve pintle extension, grasp the valve and depress the pintle using a slight side-to-side motion

14.30 The Throttle Position Sensor mounts to the side of the throttle body and is not adjustable

driver tip under the ridge on the fuel injector opposite the electrical connector end and gently pry the injector out **(see illustration)**.

6   If the injector is to be reused, replace the upper and lower O-rings on the injector and in the fuel injector cavity. Install the upper O-ring in the groove on the injector and the lower O-ring flush against the filter element.

7   Install the injector assembly in the fuel meter body by pushing it straight down. Make sure the connector end is facing in the direction of the opening in the fuel meter body for the wire harness grommet.

8   Install injector retainer and screw. Use a non-hardening thread locking compound on the retainer screw.

9   Reconnect the negative battery cable. Pressurize the fuel system by turning the ignition key to the On position, then inspect the area around the injector for leaks.

10   Plug the electrical connector into the injector and start the engine to check for correct operation.

Pressure regulator assembly

Check

11   Refer to Section 3 and perform the fuel pressure checks, which will diagnose a malfunctioning fuel pressure regulator.

Replacement

12   Underneath the pressure regulator cover assembly is a large spring which is highly compressed. Repairs to this component should be performed by a dealer service department or other repair shop due to the possibility of personal injury. Also, the tension on this spring affects fuel pressure and is set at the factory - any tampering with this component would be in violation of Federal law.

Idle Air Control valve

Check

13   Refer to Chapter 6 and check for trouble codes stored in the ECM. If the IAC valve is malfunctioning, a trouble code indicating this condition would most likely have been set.

Replacement

Refer to illustrations 14.18a and 14.18b

14   Disconnect the negative battery cable. **Caution:** *If the vehicle is equipped with a Delco Loc II audio system, make sure you have the correct activation code before disconnecting the battery. See the information at the front of this manual for the radio re-activation procedure.*

15   Remove the air cleaner and unplug the electrical connector from the IAC valve.

16   Remove the two valve retaining screws and pull the valve out of the throttle body.

17   If the same valve is to be reinstalled, be sure to use a new O-ring.

18   Before installing the valve, measure the distance from the end of the pintle to the mounting flange **(see illustration)**. If the distance exceeds 1-1/8 inch, reduce that distance by pushing the pintle into the valve assembly with a slight side-to-side motion **(see illustration)**. If this is not done, the valve will be damaged during installation.

19   Position the valve on the throttle body and install the screws. Plug in the electrical connector to the valve.

20   No adjustment of the IAC valve is necessary, as it is automatically reset by the ECM.

Minimum idle speed adjustment

21   Refer to Section 13, Steps 34 through 42 for this adjustment.

Throttle Position Sensor (TPS)

General information and check

22   The Throttle Position Sensor (TPS) is connected to the throttle shaft on the TBI unit. As the throttle valve angle is changed (as the accelerator pedal is moved), the output of the TPS also changes. At a closed throttle position, the output of the TPS is below 1.25-volts. As the throttle valve opens, the output increases so that, at wide-open throttle, the output voltage is approximately 5-volts.

23   A broken or loose TPS can cause intermittent bursts of fuel from the injector and an unstable idle, because the ECM thinks the throttle is moving. If a problem with the TPS

sensor or circuit develops, a trouble code most likely will be set (see Chapter 6).

24   Connect a digital voltmeter from the TPS electrical connector terminal "C" (dark blue wire) to terminal "B" (black wire) (you'll have to fabricate jumper wires for terminal access).

25   With the ignition on and the engine off, TPS voltage should be less than 1.25 volts. If it's more than specified, check and, if necessary, adjust the minimum idle speed before condemning the TPS.

26   The TPS is not adjustable. If the TPS malfunctions, it must be replaced as a unit.

Replacement

Refer to illustration 14.30

27   Disconnect the cable from the negative battery terminal. **Caution:** *If the vehicle is equipped with a Delco Loc II audio system, make sure you have the correct activation code before disconnecting the battery. See the information at the front of this manual for the radio re-activation procedure.*

28   Remove the air cleaner housing.

29   Unplug the electrical connector from the throttle position sensor.

30   Remove the two sensor mounting screws and pull the sensor from the throttle body **(see illustration)**.

31   To install the TPS, align the slot in the rear of the sensor with the throttle shaft and insert the sensor into the throttle body. Install the mounting screws and tighten them securely. This style TPS is not adjustable.

32   The remainder of installation is the reverse of the removal procedure.

---

15   Multi-Port Fuel Injection (MPFI) - component check, removal and installation

---

Warning: *Gasoline is extremely flammable, so take extra precautions when you work on any part of the fuel system. Don't smoke or allow open flames or bare light bulbs near the work area, and don't work in a garage where a natural gas-type appliance (such as a water heater or clothes dryer) with a pilot light is present. Since gasoline is carcinogenic, wear*

15.2 There are two electrical connectors plugged into the MFI type throttle body - the IAC valve (A) and the TPS (B). The connector below the throttle body is for the knock sensor (C)

15.3 To remove the IAC valve from the throttle body, use a large adjustable wrench - if there is thread locking compound on the threads and you are going to install the same IAC, don't remove the thread compound

latex gloves when there's a possibility of being exposed to fuel, and, if you spill any fuel on your skin, rinse it off immediately with soap and water. Mop up any spills immediately and do not store fuel-soaked rags where they could ignite. The fuel system is under constant pressure, so, if any fuel lines are to be disconnected, the fuel pressure in the system must be relieved first. When you perform any kind of work on the fuel system, wear safety glasses and have a Class B type fire extinguisher on hand. After servicing the system, always cycle the ignition on and off several times (wait 10 seconds between cycles) and check the system for leaks.

15.14 To detach the throttle body from the plenum/intake manifold assembly, remove these two nuts (arrows)

15.15 You can't see the two coolant hoses attached to the throttle body until you unbolt the throttle body from the plenum and turn it over

Idle Air Control (IAC) valve

Refer to illustrations 15.2 and 15.3

1   Detach the cable from the negative terminal of the battery. **Caution:** *If the vehicle is equipped with a Delco Loc II audio system, make sure you have the correct activation code before disconnecting the battery. See the information at the front of this manual for the radio re-activation procedure.*
2   Unplug the electrical connector from the IAC valve assembly **(see illustration)**.
3   Remove the IAC valve assembly from the idle air/vacuum signal housing assembly **(see illustration)**. **Caution:** *Do not remove any thread locking compound from the threads.*
4   Remove the IAC valve assembly gasket and discard it.
5   Clean the gasket mounting surface of the idle air/vacuum signal housing assembly to ensure a good seal. **Caution:** *The IAC valve assembly itself is an electrical component, and must not be soaked in any liquid cleaner or solvent, as damage may result.*
6   Before installing the IAC valve assembly, the position of the pintle must be checked. If the pintle is extended too far, damage to the assembly may occur.
7   Measure the distance from the gasket mounting surface of the IAC valve assembly to the tip of the pintle **(see illustration 13.28)**.

8   If the distance is greater than 1-1/8 inch, reduce it as follows:
  a) *If the IAC valve assembly has a collar around its electrical connector end, use firm hand pressure on the pintle to retract it (a slight side-to-side motion may help).*
  b) *If the IAC valve assembly has no collar, compress the pintle retaining spring toward the body of the IAC and try to turn the pintle clockwise. If the pintle will turn, continue turning it until the 1-1/8 inch dimension is reached. Return the spring to its original position with the straight part of the spring end lined up with the flat surface under the pintle head. If the pintle will not turn, use firm hand pressure to retract it.*
9   Installation is the reverse of removal. Be sure to use a new gasket and tighten the IAC securely. **Note:** *No adjustment is made to the IAC assembly after reinstallation. IAC resetting is controlled by the ECM when the vehicle is operated.*

Throttle Body

Refer to illustrations 15.14 and 15.15

10   Detach the cable from the negative terminal of the battery. **Caution:** *If the vehicle is equipped with a Delco Loc II audio system, make sure you have the correct activation code before disconnecting the battery. See the information at the front of this manual for the radio re-activation procedure.*
11   Remove the duct between the air cleaner housing and the throttle body.
12   Unplug the IAC, the TPS and the knock sensor electrical connectors.
13   Detach the throttle cable and, if equipped, the cruise control cables. Detach the cables from the bracket (see Section 9).
14   Remove the throttle body mounting nuts **(see illustration)** and separate the throttle body from the plenum/intake manifold assembly.
15   Turn the throttle body until its underside is exposed, loosen both hose clamps and detach the coolant hoses **(see illustration)**.

4

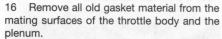

15.21 If you plan to install the same TPS, be sure to make an alignment mark between the plastic TPS body and the aluminum throttle body casting

15.22 You'll need a Torx bit to remove the TPS retaining screws

15.23 The TPS lever (A) must mate with the TPS drive lever (B) when you attach the TPS to the throttle body

16   Remove all old gasket material from the mating surfaces of the throttle body and the plenum.

17   Installation is the reverse of removal. Be sure to use a new gasket and tighten the throttle body mounting nuts to the torque listed in this Chapter's Specifications.

Throttle Position Sensor (TPS)

Refer to illustrations 15.21, 15.22 and 15.23

18   Detach the cable from the negative terminal of the battery. **Caution:** *If the vehicle is equipped with a Delco Loc II audio system, make sure you have the correct activation code before disconnecting the battery. See the information at the front of this manual for the radio re-activation procedure.*

19   Unplug the connector from the TPS.

20   If the TPS on your vehicle is located on the side of the throttle body, proceed to the next Step. If the TPS is attached to the underside of the throttle body (like the one shown in this book), remove the throttle body (see Steps 10 through 14), then proceed to the next Step.

21   If you intend to install the same TPS, scribe or paint an alignment mark between the TPS and the throttle body **(see illustra-**tion). If you are reinstalling a new TPS, you will have to set it with a voltmeter.

22   Using a Torx screwdriver or bit **(see illustration)**, remove the TPS.

23   Installation is the reverse of removal. Be sure to install the TPS onto the throttle body with the throttle valve in the closed position. Make sure that the TPS lever lines up with the TPS drive lever on the throttle shaft **(see illustration)**.

24   Install the TPS screw retainers with the TPS retaining screws. Finger tighten the screws.

25   If you had to remove the throttle body to get at the TPS, install the throttle body at this time (see Steps 16 and 17).

26   Install three jumper wires between the TPS and the wire harness electrical connector.

27   With the ignition turned to On and a digital voltmeter connected to the top and middle, or left and center, terminals (marked A and B on some connectors), adjust the TPS to obtain a reading of 0.55 ± 0.05 volts (V6) or under 1.25 volts (2.0L Turbo four) (some throttle position sensors are not adjustable. If the mounting screw holes aren't elongated, the TPS isn't adjustable).

28   Tighten the TPS mounting screws and recheck your reading to ensure that the adjustment has not changed.

29   Turn the ignition off, remove the jumper wires and connect the wiring harness electrical connector to the TPS.

30   If you removed the throttle body to get at the TPS, install the air intake duct between the air cleaner housing and the throttle body and plug in the MAF and air temperature sensors.

Fuel pressure regulator

Refer to illustrations 15.33 and 15.34

Note: *If you are working on a 2.3L four-cylinder engine, refer to Steps 64 through 66.*

31   Relieve the fuel pressure (see Section 2).

32   Detach the cable from the negative terminal of the battery. **Caution:** *If the vehicle is equipped with a Delco Loc II audio system, make sure you have the correct activation code before disconnecting the battery. See the information at the front of this manual for the radio re-activation procedure.*

33   Detach the vacuum line from the top of the pressure regulator **(see illustration)**.

Note: *On some V6 engines it is necessary to remove the intake plenum for access to the pressure regulator (see Step 67).*

34   Unscrew the fuel line from the fuel pressure regulator. Be sure to use a back-up wrench **(see illustration)**. **Note:** *If your vehicle is equipped with a 2.0L turbo four-cylinder engine, the fuel pressure regulator is located underneath the intake runners instead of atop the fuel rail.*

35   Remove the pressure regulator bracket mounting bolts and remove the regulator.

36   Installation is the reverse of removal.

Fuel rail assembly

Refer to illustrations 15.38a, 15.38b, 15.40, 15.43 and 15.44

Note 1: *If you're working on a 2.3L four-cylinder engine, refer to Steps 53 through 63.*

Note 2: *If you are removing the fuel rail assembly to service or replace an injector, it is not necessary to remove the throttle body.*

15.33 To remove the fuel pressure regulator from the fuel rail, detach the vacuum hose (A), unscrew the fuel return line threaded fitting (B) and remove the bracket mounting bolts (C)

15.34 Use a back-up wrench when disconnecting the fuel line threaded fittings at the pressure regulator

15.38a To detach the fuel injector wiring harness from the engine compartment wiring harness, slide the locking tab sideways with a small screwdriver . . .

15.38b . . . then release the locking tab on top of the plug and pull the two halves of the connector apart

Follow Steps 10 through 13, then continue with the Steps below. If, however, you intend to replace the fuel rail assembly itself, follow Steps 10 through 16, then proceed to the Steps below. Note also that the procedure for removing the fuel rail assembly on the 2.0L Turbo four is slightly different than the procedure outlined below.

37   Relieve the fuel system pressure (see Section 2), then disconnect the cable from the negative terminal of the battery. **Caution:** *If the vehicle is equipped with a Delco Loc II audio system, make sure you have the correct activation code before disconnecting the battery. See the information at the front of this manual for the radio re-activation procedure.* Detach the vacuum hose from the pressure regulator. **Note:** *On 3.1L V6 engines it is necessary to remove the intake plenum (see Step 67).*

38   Unplug the electrical connector from the fuel rail wiring harness **(see illustrations)**.

39   Unscrew the fuel return line from the fuel pressure regulator. Be sure to use a back-up wrench.

40   Unscrew the fuel line from the fuel rail.

Be sure to use a back-up wrench **(see illustration)**.

41   Remove the alternator support bracket nut, if necessary.

42   Unscrew the alternator through-bolt and remove the bracket (see Chapter 5 for further illustrations if necessary).

43   Remove the fuel rail assembly mounting bolts **(see illustration)**.

44   Using a gentle rocking motion, remove the fuel rail and fuel injector assembly **(see illustration)**.

Fuel injectors

Refer to illustrations 15.47, 15.48, 15.49, 15.50 and 15.51

Note: *If you're working on a 2.3L four-cylinder engine, follow Steps 53 through 63.*

45   Relieve the fuel pressure (see Section 2).

46   Detach the cable from the negative terminal of the battery. **Caution:** *If the vehicle is equipped with a Delco Loc II audio system, make sure you have the correct activation code before disconnecting the battery. See*

15.40 Use a back-up wrench when detaching the fuel feed line from the fuel rail assembly

the information at the front of this manual for the radio re-activation procedure.

47   If you intend to service/replace more than one injector on a cylinder bank, it is a good

4

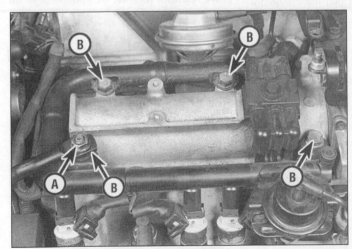

15.43 To detach the fuel rail assembly from the plenum, remove the nut (A) that attaches the alternator bracket to the right front fuel rail mounting bolt, then remove the four fuel rail bolts (B)

15.44 Use a gentle side-to-side rocking motion while pulling straight up to release the injectors from their bores in the intake manifold

15.47 If you plan to remove more than one injector it's a good idea to clearly label them to prevent mixups during reassembly

15.48 To unplug the electrical connectors from the injectors, push the wire retaining clip in and pull the connector straight up

idea to label the injector electrical leads to prevent mix-ups at reassembly **(see illustration)**.

48   To unplug the electrical connectors from the injectors you are going to service/replace, push in the connector wire retaining clip with your index finger **(see illustration)** and pull on the plug.

49   Pop off the fuel injector spring clip(s) with a small screwdriver **(see illustration)**.

50   Using a gentle side-to-side wiggling motion, pull the injector from the fuel rail **(see illustration)**. Use care when removing injectors to prevent damage to the electrical connector pins on the injector and the nozzle. Repeat the above Steps for each injector you wish to service or replace.

51   Even if you intend to reinstall the old injectors, be sure to remove the O-rings from both ends of each injector with a small screwdriver **(see illustration)** and install new ones. Coat the O-rings with a little engine oil and install them on the new injectors. If you are installing new injectors, they must also be fitted with new O-rings lubricated with a little engine oil.

52   Installation is the reverse of removal.

Fuel rail and injectors (2.3L engine) - removal and installation

Refer to illustration 15.59

53   Relieve the fuel system pressure (see Section 2).

54   Disconnect the cable from the negative terminal of the battery. **Caution:** *If the vehicle is equipped with a Delco Loc II audio system, make sure you have the correct activation code before disconnecting the battery. See the information at the front of this manual for the radio re-activation procedure.*

55   Remove the crankcase ventilation oil/air separator.

56   Detach the vacuum hose from the fuel pressure regulator.

57   Remove the fuel rail-to-cylinder head bolts. Remove any fuel line clamp bolts, if necessary.

58   Carefully lift the fuel rail and injectors from the cylinder head, then disconnect the electrical connectors from the injectors. To disconnect the electrical connectors, push in on the wire clips, then pull the connector

from the injector.

59   Remove the fuel return line clamp bolt and clamp from the fuel pressure regulator **(see illustration)**, slide the clamp off, then separate the line from the regulator.

60   Disconnect the fuel inlet line from the end of the fuel rail, using a backup wrench on the fuel rail fitting.

61   Lift the fuel rail from the engine.

62   To remove fuel injector(s) refer to steps 49 through 51.

63   Installation of the fuel rail is the reverse of the removal procedure, but be sure to tighten the return line clamp bolt and the fuel rail mounting bolts to the torque figures listed in this Chapter's Specification.

Fuel pressure regulator (2.3L engine) - removal and installation

Refer to illustration 15.65

64   Remove the fuel rail (see Steps 53 through 61).

65   Remove the screws from the fuel pressure regulator retainer, slide the retainer off

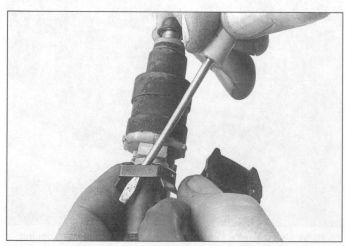

15.49 To detach an injector from the fuel rail assembly, pop off the spring clip with a small screwdriver . . .

15.50 . . . then pull on the injector while rocking it until the upper O-ring breaks loose from the fuel rail

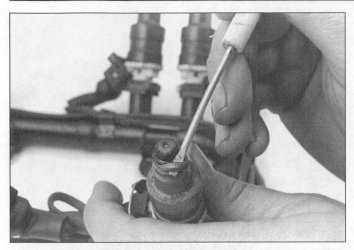

15.51 If you plan to reuse the same injector, always remove the old O-rings with a small screwdriver

15.59 Remove the fuel return line clamp retaining bolt from the pressure regulator (arrow)

the fuel rail, then separate the regulator from the rail (see illustration).

66   Installation of the fuel pressure regulator is the reverse of removal, but be sure to use a new O-ring between the regulator and the fuel rail.

Air intake plenum (3.1L V6 engines only)

Note: This component is sometimes referred to as the upper intake manifold.

Removal

67   Disconnect the cable from the negative terminal of the battery. Caution: If the vehicle is equipped with a Delco Loc II audio system, make sure you have the correct activation code before disconnecting the battery. See the information at the front of this manual for the radio re-activation procedure.

68   Detach the air intake duct from the throttle body.

69   Disconnect the accelerator cable, transmission control cable and cruise control cable (if equipped) from the throttle lever. Unbolt the accelerator cable bracket and position the bracket and cables aside (see Section 9).

70   Detach any hoses and electrical connectors from the throttle body and plenum. If necessary, mark them with pieces of numbered tape to avoid confusion during reassembly.

71   Remove the EGR valve (see Chapter 6).

72   Remove the ignition coil assembly.

73   Remove the plenum bolts and lift the plenum from the intake manifold. If the plenum sticks, use a block of wood and a hammer to dislodge it. Don't pry between the sealing flanges, as this will damage the machined surfaces and could cause vacuum leaks to develop.

74   Remove all traces of old gasket material from the plenum and intake manifold mating surfaces. It's a good idea to stuff rags into the intake manifold openings to prevent debris from falling in.

Installation

75   Install the new gasket and set the plenum into position.

76   Install the plenum bolts and tighten them in a criss-cross pattern to the torque listed in this Chapter's Specifications.

77   The remainder of installation is the reverse or removal.

16   Turbocharger - removal and installation

Warning: Wait until the engine is completely cool before beginning this procedure.

1   Detach the cable from the negative terminal of the battery. Caution: If the vehicle is equipped with a Delco Loc II audio system, make sure you have the correct activation code before disconnecting the battery. See the information at the front of this manual for the radio re-activation procedure.

2   Raise the vehicle and support it securely on jackstands.

3   Remove the lower fan retaining screw.

4   Detach the exhaust pipe from the tur-

bocharger outlet elbow.

5   Remove the rear air conditioning compressor support bracket bolt and loosen the remaining bolts.

6   Remove the turbocharger support bracket-to-engine bolt.

7   Remove the oil drain hose from the turbocharger.

8   Remove the water return pipe.

9   Lower the vehicle.

10   Remove the coolant recovery pipe and move it to one side.

11   Remove the turbocharger induction tube.

12   Remove the engine cooling fan (see Chapter 3).

13   Remove the oxygen sensor.

14   Disconnect the oil feed hose.

15   Remove the water feed pipe.

16   Remove the air intake duct and vacuum hose at the actuator.

17   Remove the turbocharger-to-exhaust manifold fasteners and remove the turbocharger.

18   Installation is the reverse of removal. Tighten all fasteners to the torque values listed in this Chapter's Specifications.

4

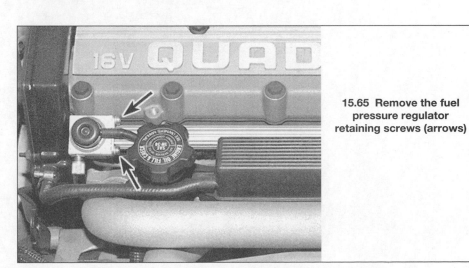

15.65 Remove the fuel pressure regulator retaining screws (arrows)

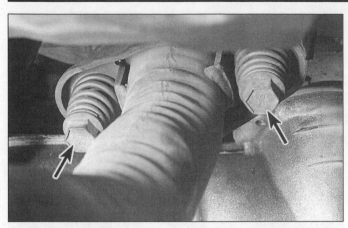

17.3 The exhaust pipe to exhaust manifold flange bolts - make sure you don't lose the springs when removing these bolts

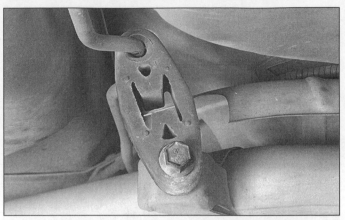

17.4 To detach this rubber block type hanger from the exhaust pipe, remove the bolt

17 Exhaust system components - general information, removal and installation

Refer to illustrations 17.3 and 17.4

Warning: *The vehicle's exhaust system generates very high temperatures and should be allowed to cool down completely before any of the components are touched. Be especially careful around the catalytic converter, where the highest temperatures are generated.*

1   Disconnect the cable from the negative terminal of the battery. **Caution:** *If the vehicle is equipped with a Delco Loc II audio system, make sure you have the correct activation code before disconnecting the battery. See the information at the front of this manual for the radio re-activation procedure.*

2   Raise the vehicle and support it securely on jackstands.

3   Disconnect the exhaust pipe from the exhaust manifold flange by removing the two flange bolts **(see illustration)**.

4   Remove the bolt from the exhaust pipe rubber hanger just in front of the fuel tank **(see illustration)**.

5   Remove the bolt and detach the hanger from the forward end of the muffler.

6   Remove the bolt and detach the hanger from the rear end of the muffler.

7   Remove the exhaust pipe, catalytic converter and muffler as an assembly. **Note:** *These components cannot be separated without cutting. If you need to replace any of these parts, take the entire assembly to a dealer or a muffler shop for further service.*

Chapter 5
Engine electrical systems

Contents

Component location

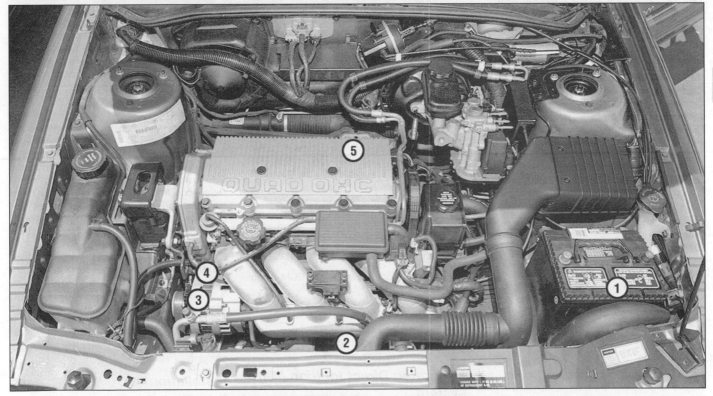

Typical 2.3L (Quad-4) engine electrical system

1 Battery
2 Starter (under manifold)
3 Serpentine drive belt
4 Alternator
5 Integrated Direct Ignition system (IDI)

1 Ignition system - general information

Warning: *Because of the very high voltage generated by the ignition system, extreme care should be taken whenever an operation involving ignition components is performed. This not only includes the distributor, coil(s), module and spark plug wires, but related items that are connected to the systems as well, such as the plug connections, tachometer and testing equipment.*

Early models are equipped with High Energy Ignition (HEI) systems, consisting of an ignition switch, battery, coil, primary (low tension) and secondary (high tension) wiring circuits, a distributor and spark plugs. Later models are equipped with a distributorless ignition system (either DIS, C3I or IDI - see below for further information).

High Energy Ignition (HEI) distributor

HEI equipped models use a special HEI distributor with Electronic Spark Timing (EST). Some HEI distributors combine all the ignition components into one unit with the ignition coil in the distributor cap. On other HEI distributors, the coil is mounted separately.

All spark timing changes in the HEI/EST distributor are carried out by the Electronic Control Module (ECM), which monitors data from various engine sensors, computes the desired spark timing and signals the distributor to change the timing accordingly. No vacuum or mechanical advance is used.

Electronic Spark Control (ESC)

Some engines are equipped with an Electronic Spark Control (ESC), which uses a knock sensor in connection with the ECM to control spark timing to allow the engine to have maximum spark advance without spark knock. This improves driveability and fuel economy.

Direct Ignition System (DIS)

All distributorless 2.5L four-cylinder and 3.0L V6 models use an ignition system called the Direct Ignition System (DIS). It uses a "waste spark" method of spark distribution. Each cylinder is paired with its opposing cylinder in the firing order (1-4, 2-3 on a four, 1-4, 2-5, 3-6 on a V6) so that one cylinder on compression fires simultaneously with its opposing cylinder on exhaust. Since the cylinder on exhaust requires very little of the available voltage to fire its plug, most of the voltage is used to fire the cylinder on compression.

The DIS system includes a coil pack, an ignition module, a crankshaft reluctor ring, a magnetic crankshaft sensor and the ECM. The ignition module is located under the coil pack and is connected to the ECM.

The magnetic crankshaft sensor protrudes through the engine block, within about 0.050-inch of the crankshaft reluctor ring. The reluctor ring is a special disc cast into the crankshaft, which acts as a signal generator for the ignition timing.

The system uses Electronic Spark Timing (EST) and control wires from the ECM, just like conventional distributor systems. The ECM controls timing using crankshaft position, engine rpm, engine temperature and manifold absolute pressure (MAP) sensing.

Computer Controlled Coil Ignition (C3I) system

The Computer Controlled Coil Ignition (C3I) distributorless ignition system is used on later V6 models. It is very similar to the DIS system, consisting of the ECM, ignition module, ignition coils, a "Hall effect" camshaft position sensor, the crankshaft position sensor and the connecting wires. On some models, the crank and cam sensor functions are combined into one dual sensor, called a combination sensor, which is mounted at the harmonic balancer.

Two types of module/coil assemblies are commonly used. They can be distinguished by the configuration of their coil towers: Type I module/coil assemblies have evenly spaced towers, with three on either side; Type IIs have all six towers (two per coil) placed on one side. The wiring harness and sensors, however, are interchangeable between either type.

The C3I system uses a waste spark method spark distribution. Each cylinder is paired with its opposite cylinder, i.e. 1-4, 5-2, 3-6. The spark occurs simultaneously in the cylinder coming up on compression and the cylinder coming up on exhaust.

The cylinder, on exhaust, requires very little of the available voltage to fire the spark plug. The remaining high voltage can then be used, as required, by the cylinder on compression.

The spark distribution is accomplished by a signal from the crank sensor, which is used by the ignition module to determine the proper time to trigger the next ignition coil. This signal is also processed by the C3I module into the reference signal used by the ECM.

The C3I system uses the Electronic Spark Timing (EST) signal from the crankshaft, just like an HEI distributor ignition system equipped with EST, to control spark timing.

Timing is controlled by the ECM using the following inputs:

Crankshaft position
Engine speed (rpm)
Engine temperature
Amount of air entering the intake (mass air flow sensor)

Integrated Direct Ignition (IDI) system

The 2.3 liter engine (both single and double overhead camshaft versions) uses an Integrated Direct Ignition (IDI) system, which

2.1 Detach the battery cables (arrows) from the battery, starting with the negative cable first

operates in a similar manner to the Direct Ignition System. The IDI system uses two ignition coils, an ignition module, a crankshaft sensor, and a secondary conductor housing, which takes the place of the spark plug wires. The crankshaft sensor is mounted on the bottom of the engine block, just above the oil pan rail. This sensor picks up signals from a reluctor ring cast into the crankshaft, which acts as a signal generator for the ignition timing.

2 Battery - removal and installation

Refer to illustrations 2.1 and 2.2
Warning: *Hydrogen gas is produced by the battery, so keep open flames and lighted cigarettes away from it at all times. Always wear eye protection when working around a battery. Rinse off spilled electrolyte immediately with large amounts of water.*

Removal

1   Detach the cables from the negative and positive terminals of the battery. **Caution 1:** *To prevent arcing, disconnect the negative (-) cable first, then remove the positive (+) cable.* **Caution 2:** *If the vehicle is equipped with a Delco Loc II audio system, make sure you have the correct activation code before disconnecting the battery. See the information at the front of this manual for the radio re-activation procedure* **(see illustration)**.
2   Remove the hold-down clamp bolt **(see illustration)** and the clamp from the battery carrier.
3   Carefully lift the battery from the carrier. **Warning:** *Always keep the battery in an upright position to reduce the likelihood of electrolyte spillage. If you spill electrolyte on your skin, rinse it off immediately with large amounts of water.*

Installation

Note: *The battery carrier and hold-down clamp should be clean and free from corrosion before installing the battery. Make certain that there are no parts in the carrier*

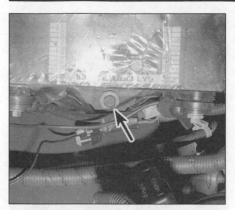

2.2 Remove the battery hold down clamp bolt (arrow)

before installing the battery.
4   Set the battery in position in its carrier. Don't tilt it.
5   Install the hold-down clamp and bolt. The bolt should be snug, but over-tightening it may damage the battery case.
6   Install both battery cables, positive first, then the negative. **Note:** *The battery terminals and cable ends should be cleaned prior to connection (see Chapter 1).*

3   Battery - emergency jump starting

Refer to the *Booster battery (jump) starting* procedure at the front of this manual.

4   Battery cables - check and replacement

Refer to illustration 4.1
1   Periodically inspect the entire length of each battery cable for damage, cracked or burned insulation and corrosion **(see illustration)**. Poor battery cable connections can cause starting problems and decreased engine performance.
2   Check the cable-to-terminal connections at the ends of the cables for cracks, loose wire strands and corrosion. The presence of white, fluffy deposits under the insulation at the cable terminal connection is a sign the cable is corroded and should be replaced. Check the terminals for distortion, missing mounting bolts or nuts and corrosion.
3   If only the positive cable is to be replaced, be sure to disconnect the negative cable from the battery first. **Caution:** *If the vehicle is equipped with a Delco Loc II audio system, make sure you have the correct activation code before disconnecting the battery. See the information at the front of this manual for the radio re-activation procedure.*
4   Disconnect and remove the cable. Make sure the replacement cable is the same length and diameter.
5   Clean the threads of the starter or ground connection with a wire brush to

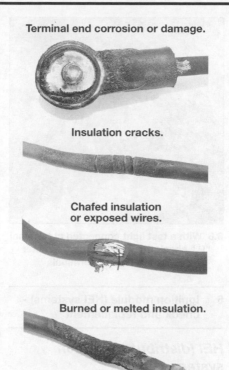

Terminal end corrosion or damage.

Insulation cracks.

Chafed insulation or exposed wires.

Burned or melted insulation.

4.1 Typical battery cable problems

remove rust and corrosion. Apply a light coat of petroleum jelly to the threads to ease installation and prevent future corrosion.
6   Attach the cable to the starter or ground connection and tighten the mounting nut securely.
7   Before connecting the new cable to the battery, make sure it reaches the terminals without having to be stretched.
8   Connect the positive cable first, followed by the negative cable.

5   HEI ignition system - check

Refer to illustrations 5.1 and 5.4
Warning: *Because of the very high voltage generated by the ignition system, extreme care should be taken whenever an operation*

5.1 A typical spark tester

is performed involving ignition components. This not only includes the distributor, coil(s), control module and spark plug wires, but related items that are connected to the system as well, such as the plug connections, tachometer and any test equipment.
1   Disconnect any one spark plug wire and attach a spark tester **(see illustration)**. Crank the engine and observe the spark tester. If there is spark, check the fuel system, spark plugs, ignition timing and compression. If no spark, repeat the test on another wire. If there still is no spark, see Step 2.
2   Disconnect the distributor four-wire connector and check for spark at the spark tester while cranking. If there is spark, replace the pick-up coil. If there is no spark, see Step 3.
3   Check for spark at the coil wire while cranking. If there is spark, check the distributor cap and rotor for moisture or cracks. If OK, replace the rotor. If there is no spark, check the coil wire resistance. It should be less than 15,000 ohms. If OK, see Step 4.
4   Disconnect the distributor module two-terminal "C/+" connector. Turn the ignition switch on, engine stopped. Check the voltage at the distributor electrical connector "C/+" with a voltmeter to ground **(see illustration)**. If terminal "C" only is less than 10 volts, check for an open or ground in the wire from terminal "C" to the ignition coil. If the wire is OK, check the connections to the coil. If OK, replace the coil. If both terminals are under 10 volts, inspect and repair the wire

5

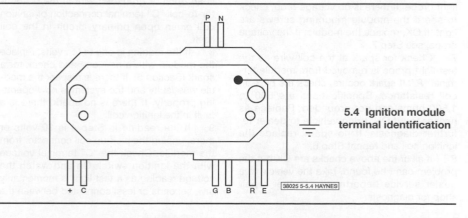

5.4 Ignition module terminal identification

6.4 To check the module for voltage, insert the voltmeter probe into the module positive terminal (arrow)

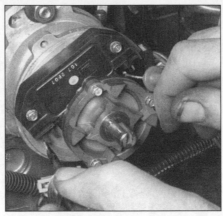

6.6 With a test light connected at terminal "P," check the voltage with the meter probe at the "C" terminal

6.11 As the test light probe (1) is removed, check for a spark at the coil wire (2)

from the module "+" terminal to the black connector at the ignition coil. If OK, check the primary circuit to the ignition switch. If both terminals are 10 volts or more, see Step 5.

5   Reattach the distributor "C/+" connector and with the ignition "on", check the voltage from the distributor tach terminal to ground. The tachometer wire is usually a white wire with a small black connector taped in the wiring harness within 12-inches of the ignition coil. If you measure 1 to 10 volts, replace the distributor module and check for spark as in Step 1. If there is spark, the system is OK. If no spark, replace the coil. If you measure under 1 volt, check and repair an open in the tach lead and repeat Step 5. If you measure over 10 volts, connect a 12-volt test light from the tach lead to ground. Crank the engine and observe the light. If the light is on steady, see Step 6. If the light blinks, check the ignition coil. If the light doesn't blink, check the module (see Section 6).

6   Disconnect the distributor four-terminal connector. Remove the distributor cap and carefully disconnect the pick-up coil connector from the module. Connect a voltmeter from the tach terminal to ground. Turn the ignition on. Using electrical tape, wrap the 12-volt test light probe, leaving 1/4-inch of the tip exposed. Connect the test light lead to the vehicle battery "positive" terminal. Observe the voltmeter as you momentarily touch terminal "P" of the module with the test light probe. If there is no voltage drop, check to see if the module mounting screws are tight. If OK, replace the module. If the voltage drops, see Step 7.

7   Check for spark at the coil wire as the test light probe is removed from module terminal "P". If spark occurs, check the pick-up coil resistance. Specifications are 500 to 1,500 ohms and not grounded. Replace as necessary. If OK, bring vehicle to dealer for further diagnosis. If no spark, replace the ignition coil and repeat Step 6.

8   If all of the above checks are OK but the problem can't be found, take the vehicle to a dealer service department or other repair shop for diagnosis.

6   Ignition module (HEI systems) - check and replacement

HEI (distributor) ignition system

Note: *It is not necessary to remove the distributor to check or replace the module.*

Check

Refer to illustrations 6.4, 6.6 and 6.11

1   Disconnect the tachometer wire (if so equipped) at the distributor.

2   Using a spark tester, check for a spark at the coil and spark plug wires (see illustration 5.1).

3   If there is no spark, remove the distributor cap. Remove the ignition module from the distributor but leave the connector plugged in.

4   With the ignition switch turned On, check for voltage at the module positive terminal (see illustration).

5   If the reading is less than ten volts, there is a fault in the wire between the module positive (+) terminal and the ignition coil positive connector or the ignition coil and primary circuit-to-ignition switch.

6   If the reading is ten volts or more, check the "C" terminal on the module (see illustration).

7   If the reading is less than one volt, there is an open or grounded wire in the distributor-to-coil "C" terminal connection or ignition coil or an open primary circuit in the coil itself.

8   If the reading is one to ten volts, replace the module with a new one and check for a spark (Section 5). If there is a spark the module was faulty and the system is now operating properly. If there is no spark, there is a fault in the ignition coil.

9   If the reading in Step 4 is 10 volts or more, unplug the pick-up coil connector from the module. Check the "C" terminal voltage with the ignition switch On and watch the voltage reading as a test light is momentarily (five seconds or less) connected between the

battery positive (+) terminal and the module "P" terminal.

10   If there is no drop in voltage, check the module ground and, if it is good, replace the module with a new one.

11   If the voltage drops, check for spark at the coil wire as the test light is removed from the module terminal (see illustration). **Warning:** *Don't hold the wire any further than 1/4-inch from a good ground.* If there is no spark, the module is faulty and should be replaced with a new one. If there is a spark, the pick-up coil or connections are faulty or not grounded.

Replacement

Refer to illustration 6.16

12   Detach the cable from the negative terminal of the battery. **Caution:** *If the vehicle is equipped with a Delco Loc II audio system, make sure you have the correct activation code before disconnecting the battery. See the information at the front of this manual for the radio re-activation procedure.*

13   Remove the distributor cap and rotor (see Chapter 1).

14   Remove both module attaching screws and lift the module up and away from the distributor.

15   Disconnect the electrical connectors from the module. Note that they cannot be interchanged.

16   Do not wipe the grease from the module or the distributor base if the same module is to be reinstalled. If a new module is to be installed, a package of silicone grease will be included with it. Wipe the distributor base and the new module clean, then apply the silicone grease on the face of the module and on the distributor base where the module seats (see illustration). This grease is necessary for heat dissipation. If it is not applied, the module will rapidly fail.

17   Install the module and attach the electrical connectors.

18   Install the distributor rotor and cap (see Chapter 1).

19   Attach the cable to the negative terminal of the battery.

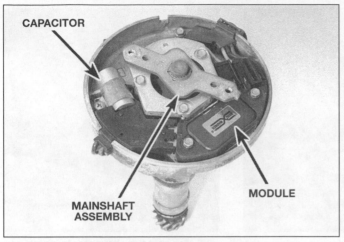

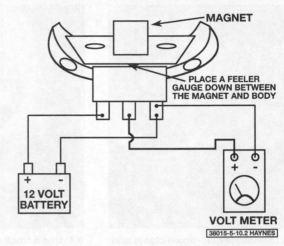

6.16 Silicone lubricant applied to the distributor base in the area under the ignition module dissipates heat and prevents module failure - (coil-in-cap models)

7.2 Hall effect switch test connections

7 Hall effect switch (HEI systems) - check and replacement

Refer to illustration 7.2

1   Some HEI distributors are equipped with a Hall effect switch which is located above the pick-up coil assembly. The Hall effect switch is used in place of the R terminal of the HEI distributor to send engine RPM information to the ECM.

2   Test the switch by connecting a 12-volt power supply and voltmeter as shown **(see illustration)**. Check the polarity markings carefully before making any connections.

3   When a feeler gauge is not inserted against the magnet, the voltmeter should read less than 0.5 volts. If the reading is more, the Hall effect switch is faulty and must be replaced by a new one.

4   With the feeler gauge inserted, the voltmeter should read within 0.5 volts of battery voltage. Replace the switch with a new one if the reading is more.

5   Remove the Hall effect switch by un-plugging the electrical connector and removing the retaining screws.

6   Installation is the reverse of removal.

8 Distributor (HEI systems) - removal and installation

Removal

Refer to illustrations 8.4a, 8.4b, 8.4c and 8.5

1   Disconnect the cable from the negative battery terminal. **Caution:** *If the vehicle is equipped with a Delco Loc II audio system, make sure you have the correct activation code before disconnecting the battery. See the information at the front of this manual for the radio re-activation procedure.*

2   Remove the coil wire or small-wire electrical connections from the distributor cap.

3   Remove the distributor cap (see Chapter 1).

4   Note the position of the rotor and the distributor-to-block alignment. Make an alignment mark on the distributor to indicate

the position of the rotor **(see illustration)**. Also make a mark to indicate distributor-to-block relationship. On the 2.0L OHC engine, the rotor must be pointing straight up. **(see illustrations)**.

8.4a The distributor rotor must be pointed straight up (in the direction of the arrow) prior to removal (2.0L OHC turbo four) (arrow)

5

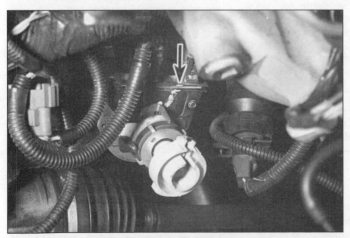

8.4b Mark the position of the rotor to the distributor housing before removing the rotor (HEI distributor on 2.5L engine shown) (arrow)

8.4c A line scribed across the distributor and block (arrow) will make installation easier (2.0L OHC turbo engine shown)

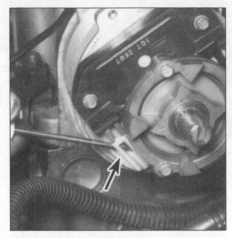

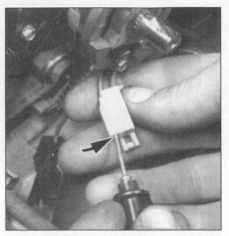

8.5 The distributor hold-down clamp and bolt must be removed before the distributor can be removed from the engine (HEI distributor on 2.5L engine shown)

9.4 Use a small screwdriver to release the clip (arrow) on the pickup coil electrical connector

9.5 Connect the ohmmeter to a pick-up coil terminal and the distributor body. If continuity is indicated, there is a short from the pick-up coil wiring to the distributor body

5   Remove the distributor hold-down clamp bolt and clamp **(see illustration)**. Remove the distributor from the engine. **Caution:** *Do not turn the crankshaft while the distributor is removed from the engine. If the crankshaft is turned, the position of the rotor will be altered and the engine will have to be re-timed.*

Installation (crankshaft not turned after distributor removal)

6   Insert the distributor into the engine in exactly the same relation to the block in which it was removed. To mesh the gears, it may be necessary to turn the rotor slightly. At this point the distributor may not seat down against the block completely. This is due to the lower end of the distributor shaft not mating properly with the oil pump shaft. If this is the case, check again to make sure the distributor is aligned with the block in the same position it was in before removal and that the rotor is correctly aligned with the distributor body. The gear on the distributor shaft is engaged with the gear on the camshaft, and this relationship cannot change as long as the distributor is not lifted from the engine. Use a socket and breaker bar on the crankshaft bolt to turn the engine over in the normal direction of rotation. The rotor will turn, but the oil pump shaft will not because the two shafts are not engaged. When the proper alignment is reached the distributor will drop down over the oil pump shaft, and the distributor body will seat properly against the block.
7   Install the hold-down clamp and tighten the bolt securely.
8   Install the distributor cap and coil wire.
9   Connect the cable to the negative terminal of the battery.

Installation (crankshaft turned after distributor removal)

10   Remove the number one spark plug.
11   Place your finger over the spark plug hole while turning the crankshaft in the normal direction of rotation with a wrench on the pulley bolt at the front of the engine.
12   When you feel compression, continue turning the crankshaft slowly until the timing mark on the crankshaft pulley is aligned with the "0" on the engine timing indicator.
13   Position the rotor to point between the number one and number three distributor terminals.
14   Insert the distributor into the engine in exactly the same relation to the block in which it was removed. To mesh the gears, it may be necessary to turn the rotor slightly. If the distributor does not seat fully against the block it is because the oil pump shaft has not seated in the distributor shaft. Make sure the distributor drive gear is fully engaged with the camshaft gear, then use a socket on the crankshaft bolt to turn the engine over in the normal direction of rotation until the two shafts engage and the distributor seats against the block.
15   Install the hold-down clamp and tighten the bolt securely.
16   Install the distributor cap and coil wire.
17   Connect the cable to the negative terminal of the battery.

9   Ignition pick-up coil (HEI systems) - check and replacement

Refer to illustrations 9.4, 9.5, 9.6, 9.9a, 9.9b, 9.13a and 9.13b

Check

1   Detach the cable from the negative terminal of the battery. **Caution:** *If the vehicle is equipped with a Delco Loc II audio system, make sure you have the correct activation*

9.6 Connect the ohmmeter to the pick-up coil terminals as shown and measure the resistance. It should be between 500 and 1,500 ohms

code before disconnecting the battery. See the information at the front of this manual for the radio re-activation procedure.
2   Remove the distributor cap and rotor (see Chapter 1).
3   Remove the distributor from the engine (see Section 6). **Note:** *This Step is necessary on most models, since it is difficult to gain access to the pick-up coil wires in the distributor. If access on your vehicle is relatively unrestricted, this Step may not be necessary.*
4   Detach the pick-up coil wires from the module **(see illustration)**.
5   Connect one lead of an ohmmeter to the terminal of the pick-up coil lead and the other to ground as shown **(see illustration)**. The ohmmeter should indicate infinite resistance at all times. If it doesn't, the pick-up coil is defective and must be replaced.
6   Connect the ohmmeter leads to both terminals of the pick-up coil wires **(see Illustration)**. Flex the wires by hand to check for intermittent opens. The ohmmeter should

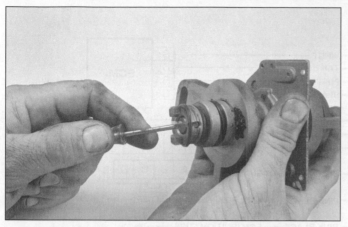

9.9a Remove the spring from the drive coupling

9.9b Use a punch and drive the retaining pin from the shaft

read one steady value between 500 and 1500 ohms as the leads are flexed by hand. If it doesn't, the pick-up coil is defective and must be replaced.

Replacement

7   Remove the distributor, if not already done, then remove the spring from the distributor shaft.
8   Mark the distributor drive gear (or tang) and shaft so that they can be reassembled in the same position.
9   Carefully mount the distributor in a soft-jawed vise and, using a hammer and punch, remove the roll pin from the distributor shaft and gear (see illustrations). Pull the shaft out of the distributor body. Caution: If the shaft binds when being pulled out, you may need to lightly sand the lower shaft area so it will pull through without binding.
10   To remove the pick-up coil, remove the thin "C" washer. Note: On some models, you may have to unbolt a shield to gain access to the "C" washer.
11   Lift the pick-up coil assembly straight up and remove it from the distributor.
12   Reassembly is the reverse of disassembly.
13   Installation is the reverse of removal. Make sure the tensioner assembly, if equipped, is properly assembled (see illustrations)

---

10   Distributorless ignition systems - check and component replacement

Warning: Because of the very high voltage generated by the ignition system, extreme care must be taken whenever an operation involving ignition system components is performed.
Note: These tests require a special fuel injector harness test light, which is available at most auto parts stores. Also, a digital multimeter will be needed (analog meters may damage some of the sensitive components).

Check

Direct Ignition System (DIS)

Engine misfire

1   With the engine idling at normal operating temperature, disconnect the Idle Air Control Motor. Using insulated pliers, momentarily disconnect each spark plug wire. All cylinders should have an equal RPM drop.
2   After you have isolated the cylinder(s) that have less RPM drop than the others, turn the ignition off and install a spark tester (see illustration 5.1) the affected plug wire(s). Crank the engine - spark should be observed at the tester while cranking. If there is spark, check for faulty, worn or damaged spark plugs, engine compression and fuel system. If there is no spark, see Step 3.
3   With the ignition off, ground the opposite plug wire of the affected coil at the spark plug end of the wire, crank the engine. Sparks should be observed at the tester while cranking the engine. If there is spark, replace the spark plug for the wire that was grounded. If the miss is still present, repeat Step 1. If there is no spark while cranking, see Step 4.
4   Using an ohmmeter, check the affected

spark plug wires resistance. It should be less than 30,000 ohms. Inspect the wire for cuts or abrasions in the silicone insulation that may cause a ground. If a problem is found, replace the suspect wire(s). If the wires check OK, see Step 5.
5   Remove the ignition coils. They should be free of carbon tracking and physical damage. If carbon tracking or damage is found, replace the affected coil. If the coils appear to be OK, switch the suspected bad coil with one of the good coils. Sparks should be present at the plug wire(s) while cranking. Remember even though the coils have been switched, you are still checking the cylinders that had the original miss.
6   If you now have spark, the original coil was bad and will have to be replaced. If you do not have spark in the original cylinders that had the miss, replace the ignition module.

Computer Controlled Coil Ignition (C3I)

Refer to illustrations 10.7 and 10.9
Note: Determining whether the module/coil assembly in your vehicle is Type I or II is very important because Type I diagnostics will not

5

9.13a Be sure that the tensioner assembly is properly assembled

9.13b This is how the tensioner assembly looks when it is properly installed in the distributor body

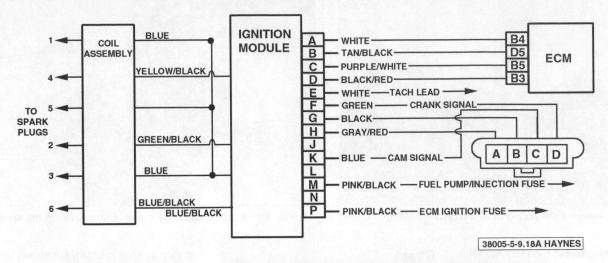

10.7 Computer Controlled Coil Ignition (C31) system schematic

38005-5-9.18A HAYNES

work on a Type II system, or vice-versa. On the Type I module/coil assembly, there are three spark plug wire terminals on each side of the assembly. On the Type II module/coil assembly, all of the spark plug wire terminals are on the same side.

Type 1 module/coil assembly

7 Check for spark with a spark tester **(see illustration 5.1)** or equivalent on each spark plug lead while cranking. Leave wires not being tested connected to the spark plugs and coils. If all have spark, the system is working OK **(see illustration)**. If there is no spark on all cylinders, see Step 31. If no spark on 1 or 2 cylinders, see Step 27.

8 Check the resistance of the spark plug lead and the coil resistance at the plug lead tower of the affected cylinders. Plug lead resistance should not exceed 30,000 ohms. Coil secondary resistance should not exceed 15,000 ohms. Replace any coil/wire exceeding specifications. If OK, see Step 9.

9 Remove the six-coil assembly retaining screws. Lift and tilt the coil to gain access to the coil primary wiring. Disconnect the affected coil's control wire from the module **(see illustration)**.

10 Connect a test light between the common feed wire, usually blue, and the control wire of the coil being tested. Crank the engine and observe the light. If the light blinks, check the primary feed and control wires at the coil. If they are clean and secure, replace the ignition coil assembly. If the light is off or on steadily, see Step 11.

11 Check the primary resistance of the affected coil - it should be over .50 ohms. If OK, replace the ignition module. If not .50 ohms, replace the coil and module.

12 Disconnect any injector and install an injector test light (see Chapter 4, if necessary) in the injector harness. Observe the light as the engine is cranked. If the light blinks, replace the ignition module. If the light remains off while cranking, see Step 13.

13 Disconnect the dual crank sensor electrical connector. With the ignition on, momentarily jump sensor harness terminals "C" to "B". Injector test light should flash each time the terminals are jumped. If the light flashes, see Step 14. If it does not flash, see Step 15.

14 Check voltage at sensor harness terminal "A". Voltage should be over 10 volts. If OK, check the sensor connection and replace the sensor. If the voltage is less than 10 volts, check for battery voltage at module terminal "H". Check the ECM and ignition fuses. Check for battery voltage at module terminal "P" with key on. If all are OK, replace the ignition module.

15 Connect the voltmeter between sensor harness terminals "B" and "C" which should be 6 to 9 volts. Connect a voltmeter between terminals "B" and "D" which should be 6 to 9 volts. If OK, check for an open circuit from fuel pump/inj. fuse to terminal "M" at the module. If OK, check connections and replace the module. If not 6 to 9 volts, see Step 16.

16 Connect a voltmeter between sensor harness terminals "C" to ground and note the voltage. Connect the voltmeter between ter-

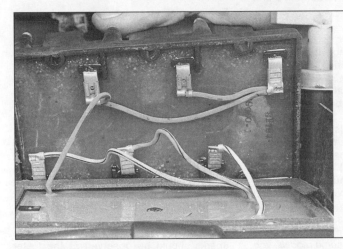

10.9 After removing the Torx screws that hold the coil and module assemblies together, label, then detach, the wires from the module

minal "D" to ground; the voltage in either test should be 6 to 9 volts. If it is 6 to 9 volts, check for an open in the ground wire to terminal "G" at the module. If OK, replace the module. If not 6 to 9 volts, see Step 17.

17 Check for an open in the ground wire to module terminal "G" from the sensor or the signal wire from the sensor to the module terminal "K". If OK, replace the ignition module.

Type II module/coil assembly

18 Check for spark with a spark tester **(see illustration 5.1)** or equivalent at each spark plug lead while cranking the engine. Leave the remaining wires attached to the plugs and coils. If there is spark on all cylinders, the ignition system is working OK. If you have no spark on one or two cylinders, see Step 19. If there is no spark on all cylinders, see Step 22.

19 Check the resistance of the spark plug wire and the coil at the plug lead towers of the affected coil. Plug wire resistance should not exceed 30,000 ohms. Coil secondary resistance should not exceed 7,000 ohms. Replace any coil or wire not within specifications. If OK, see Step 20.

20 Remove the two mounting nuts and

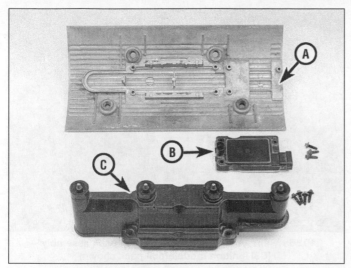

10.32 Exploded view of the Ignition module/coil assemblies on the 2.3L (Quad-4) engine

A Cover
B Ignition module

C Coil housing

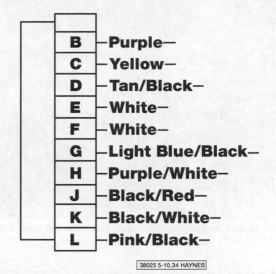

B	—Purple—
C	—Yellow—
D	—Tan/Black—
E	—White—
F	—White—
G	—Light Blue/Black—
H	—Purple/White—
J	—Black/Red—
K	—Black/White—
L	—Pink/Black—

38025 5-10.34 HAYNES

10.34 IDI unit electrical connector details

detach the affected coil. With a 12-volt test light connected between the coil primary terminals on the module, crank the engine and observe the light. If the light is off or on steadily, replace the module. If the light blinks, see Step 21.

21   Inspect the module terminals for dirt and corrosion. If corrosion is found, clean the terminals and re-test the coil as in Step 18. If you have spark, the system is OK. If there is no corrosion or the re-test results in no spark, replace the coil.

22   Disconnect any injector lead and install an injector test light (see Chapter 4, if necessary). Crank the engine and observe the light. If the light is "on" all the time, the ECM is probably faulty. If the light is "off", see Step 27. If the light blinks, see Step 23.

23   Disconnect the cam/crank sensor and install a jumper wire from harness terminals "B" to "D". Install a spark tester (see illustration 5.1) on number 6 plug wire and ground number 3 plug wire coil tower terminal. Disconnect all other plug wires at the spark plugs. With the ignition On momentarily jump harness terminals "C" to "B" while observing the spark tester. If there is no spark, see Step 25. If there is spark, see Step 24.

24   Check the voltage at the crank sensor harness terminal "A". It should be battery voltage. If it is battery voltage, replace the sensor. If it is not battery voltage, check for an open in the wire from terminal "H" at the ignition module to terminal "A" at the sensor. If it is OK, replace the module.

25   Check voltage between sensor harness terminals "B" and "D". Voltage should be between 7 and 9 volts. If voltage is within specifications, replace the module. If it is not within specifications, check the voltage from sensor harness "D" to ground. Voltage should be between 7 and 9 volts.

26   If the voltage is within 7 to 9 volts, check

for an open circuit between module terminal "G" and the sensor harness terminal "B". If the voltage is not within 7 to 9 volts, check the wire from module terminal "F" to sensor harness terminal "D" for an open or grounded circuit. If all is OK, replace the module.

27   Check the fuel pump/ign fuse. If it is blown, replace the fuse and determine the cause. If it is OK, disconnect the crank sensor connector. With the ignition "on" momentarily jump sensor harness terminals "C" to "B" while observing the injector test light. If the light is Off, see Step 28. If the light flashes, check the voltage at sensor harness terminal "A". It should be battery voltage. If it is battery voltage, replace the sensor. If it is not battery voltage, check for an open from module terminal "H" to sensor harness terminal "A". If OK, replace the module.

28   Check voltage between sensor harness terminals "C" and "B". It should be 7 to 9 volts. If voltage is within specification, check for a short to ground at module terminal "F". If OK, replace the module. If voltage is not within specifications, check voltage between sensor harness terminal "C" to ground. It should be 7 to 9 volts. If not 7 to 9 volts, see Step 30. If 7 to 9 volts, see Step 29.

29   If voltage is 7 to 9 volts, check for an open wire from module terminal "G" to sensor terminal "B". If it is OK, replace the module.

30   If voltage was not 7 to 9 volts, check the wire from module terminal "K" to sensor terminal "C" for an open or short to ground. If a short or open is found, repair the wire. If the wire is OK, see Step 31.

31   Disconnect the 14-pin connector at the module. With the ignition On, check the voltage at the module harness connector terminal "M". It should be battery voltage. If it is not battery voltage, check the fuel pump/ign fuse. If the fuse is OK, check the wire at ter-

minal "M" for an open circuit. Repair as necessary. If battery voltage is at terminal "M", replace the module.

Integrated Direct Ignition (IDI) system

Refer to illustration 10.32

32   The Quad-4 engine uses an Integrated Direct Ignition (IDI) system, which operates in a similar manner to the Direct Ignition System **(see illustration)**. The IDI system uses two ignition coils, an ignition module, a crankshaft sensor and a secondary conductor housing, which takes the place of the spark plug wires. The crankshaft sensor is mounted on the engine block, just above the oil pan rail. This sensor picks up signals from a reluctor ring cast into the crankshaft, which acts as a signal generator for the ignition timing. The IDI unit is mounted between the camshaft housings.

Engine cranks over but won't start

Refer to illustration 10.34

33   Check all the fuses.

34   Disconnect the 11-wire electrical connector from the IDI unit. Turn the ignition to the On position and connect a test light between terminals K and L **(see illustration)**. The test light should come on.

35   If the light doesn't come on, check the wiring harness for an open circuit condition.

36   If it does come on, connect the test light to the battery positive terminal. Unplug an electrical connector from one of the fuel injectors and install an injector harness test light. Touch the 12-volt test light to terminal H of the IDI unit electrical connector. The light in the fuel injector connector should blink. If it doesn't, check for an open or shorted circuit in the IDI wiring harness or the fuel injector harness. There is also the possibility that the ECM is malfunctioning.

5

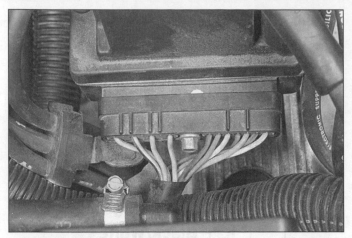

10.54 Unbolt and unplug the connector from the end of the C3I ignition coil/module assembly

10.56a Remove the bolts from the coil pack assembly - (C3I ignition module/coil pack shown)

37   If the light in the injector connector does blink, connect a digital multi-meter, set on the 2-volt AC scale, between terminals B and C of the IDI unit electrical connector. Crank the engine and read the voltage (an assistant would be helpful here). The voltage should be more than 20-mV. If it is, a defective IDI module is indicated.

38   If the voltage is less than 20-mV, remove the crankshaft sensor from the cylinder block. Connect the digital multi-meter, set on the 2K-ohm scale, across the terminals of the sensor. The reading should be between 500 and 900 ohms. If not, replace the sensor.

39   If the resistance reading is OK, check the sensor to make sure it is still magnetic. If it isn't, replace it. If it is, check the wiring to the sensor for an open or shorted circuit condition.

40   If these checks still don't pinpoint the problem, take the vehicle to a dealer service department or other repair shop for further diagnosis.

Engine runs but misfires

Note: *These checks assume that the engine is in good mechanical condition.*

41   Remove the crankcase ventilation oil/air separator for access to the injector electrical connectors.

42   Disconnect the Idle Air Control (IAC) valve electrical connector from the IAC valve (mounted on the throttle body).

43   Start the engine and momentarily disconnect each injector electrical connector, one at a time. As an injector is disconnected, the engine rpm should drop noticeably. If it doesn't, the particular injector that was disconnected wasn't working to begin with, or the cylinder isn't receiving a spark.

44   Connect a fuel injector harness test light to the electrical connector of the injector that didn't result in an rpm drop when it was disconnected. Start the engine and watch the light - it should blink, indicating the signal to the injector is present.

45   If it doesn't blink, there is a problem with the harness to the injector or a faulty ECM.

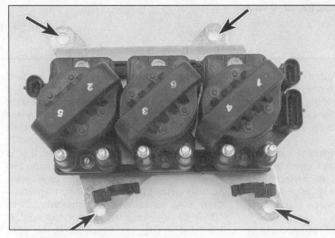

10.56b Remove the ignition module/coil pack bracket bolts (arrows) (DIS ignition module/coil pack shown) - module/coil pack removed for clarity

46   If the light does blink, as it's supposed to, the signal to the fuel injector is OK. Check the resistance value of that injector - the resistance reading should be between 1.8 and 2.2 ohms. If any injector measures less than 1.8 ohms, replace it. If the problem persists, take the vehicle to a dealer service department or other repair shop for further diagnosis.

47   If the injector resistance is OK, remove the IDI unit from between the camshaft housings and connect spark plug jumper wires between the IDI unit and the spark plugs. Disconnect the spark plug wire from the spark plug of the affected cylinder and attach a spark tester (available at most auto parts stores).

48   Crank the engine over and see if there is spark present at the tester. If there is spark, there may be a problem with the fuel injector. Check the rest of the cylinders with the spark tester in the same way, but if they all spark normally it is recommended the vehicle be taken to a dealer service department or other repair shop for further diagnosis.

49   If there isn't any spark present, detach the spark plug boot assemblies from the affected coil. Using a digital multi-meter set on the 20K-ohms scale, measure the resistance between the coil terminals (pair for cylinders

one and four, or cylinders two and three). The resistance should be less than 10K-ohms - if it's higher, replace the coil.

50   Now check the resistance between the coil terminals to the cover plate - the reading should be infinite. If it isn't, replace the coil.

51   If the resistance values are OK, disconnect the coil electrical connector at the module. Connect a test light (at the module) between the battery positive terminal to the coil (terminal A) and terminal B or C. Crank the engine over and watch the light. If the light blinks, check for an open or shorted circuit in the coil wiring harness, or a faulty coil or boot. If the light doesn't blink, check for a bad connection between the coil and the module. If the connection is OK, the IDI module is defective.

Component replacement

Ignition module replacement (DIS or C3I systems)

Refer to illustrations 10.54, 10.56a, 10.56b, 10.58 and 10.59

52   Detach the cable from the negative terminal of the battery. **Caution:** *If the vehicle is equipped with a Delco Loc II audio system, make sure you have the correct activation code before disconnecting the battery. See the information at the front of this manual for*

10.58 To detach the C3I module from the support bracket, remove the three nuts

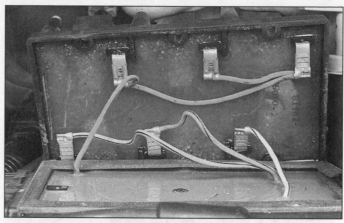

10.59 After removing the Torx screws that hold the coil and module assemblies together, label, then detach, the wires from the module

the radio re-activation procedure.

53   Clearly label, then disconnect, all spark plug wires from the DIS or C3I assembly.
54   Unbolt or unplug the electrical connector at the module **(see illustration)**.
55   If equipped, detach the vacuum lines and the electrical connector from the EGR valve solenoid on the left end of the coil/module assembly.
56   Unbolt and remove the DIS or C3I and support bracket assembly **(see illustrations)**. **Caution:** *On 2.5L four-cylinder models, lift off the assembly very carefully, since the crankshaft position sensor, which protrudes into the engine block, is attached to the bottom of the assembly.*
57   Using a Torx screwdriver or bit (most models), remove the coil-to-module attaching screws.
58   Separate the coil and module assemblies. Separate the module from the bracket on some models **(see illustration)**.
59   Open the coil and module halves as shown **(see illustration)**. Label, then detach, the wires between the module and the coil assemblies from the spade terminals on the underside of the coils.
60   Unbolt the module from the support bracket.
61   Installation is the reverse of removal. Be sure to attach the wires of the new module to the coil assembly spade terminals in exactly the same order in which they were removed.

Crankshaft or combination sensor replacement (DIS or C3I systems)

3.0L and 3.3L V6 models
Refer to illustration 10.63

62   Remove the crankshaft balancer (vibration dampener) (see Chapter 2, Part E).
63   Disconnect the electrical connector for the sensor **(see illustration)**.
64   Unbolt and remove the sensor.
65   Check the interrupter rings on the back of the crankshaft balancer for damage and bends. Replace the balancer as an assembly if any problems exist. Use the appropriate tool to check the rings for bending by inserting the

long post into the balancer and rotating the tool. If the tabs on the tool touch the rings, the rings are bent.
66   Installation is the reverse of removal. Before tightening the mounting bolts, adjust the sensor. If the special tool isn't available, slide the balancer onto the crankshaft and adjust the sensor so the rings on the balancer are positioned midway between each pick-up on the sensor, then tighten the mounting bolts or adjusting screw. **Note:** *Not all crank sensors are adjustable.*

2.5L four-cylinder models
67   The crankshaft sensor is attached to the bottom of the DIS assembly. After carefully lifting the assembly off the engine block, unbolt the sensor from the bottom of the base plate. Installation is the reverse of removal.

3.1L V6 models
Refer to illustration 10.68
68   Unplug the electrical connector, remove the bolt and carefully lift the sensor out of the engine block **(see illustration)**. Installation is the reverse of the removal procedure, but be sure to check the O-ring for hardness, cracking and general deterioration, which may cause a leak. Replace the O-ring if necessary. Lubricate the O-ring with engine oil before installing the sensor.

IDI unit (IDI systems only)
69   Disconnect the cable from the negative terminal of the battery.
70   Unplug the electrical connector from the IDI unit.
71   Remove the four bolts that retain the IDI unit to the camshaft housings.
72   Pull the IDI unit straight up, disconnecting it from the spark plugs.
73   Installation is the reverse of removal.

Ignition coil(s) (IDI systems only)
74   Remove the IDI unit from the engine.
75   Remove the coil housing-to-cover screws and remove the cover **(see illustration 10.32)**.

76   Unplug the electrical connectors from the coil. Lift the coils from the housing.
77   Installation is the reverse of the removal procedure.

Ignition module (IDI systems only)
78   Remove the IDI unit from the engine.
79   Disconnect the module-to-coil electrical connector.
80   Remove the module-to-cover screws

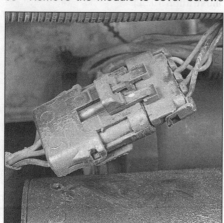

10.63 The electrical connector for the crankshaft sensor is located near the starter motor

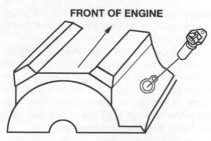

10.68 The 3.1L V6 engine crankshaft sensor is bolted to the firewall side of the engine block

5

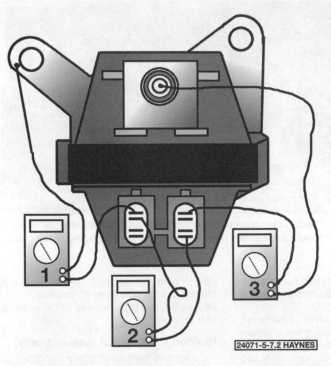

11.12 To check the ignition coil, use an ohmmeter to perform the following three checks

1   On the high scale, the ohmmeter should read infinity
2   On the low scale, the ohmmeter should read very low or zero
3   On the high scale, the ohmmeter should read high but not infinite (if the coil fails any of these tests, replace it)

24071-5-7.2 HAYNES

and separate the module from the cover **(see illustration 10.32)**.
81   Installation is the reverse of the removal procedure.

Crankshaft sensor (IDI systems only)

82   Unplug the electrical connector at the sensor.
83   Remove the bolt that retains the sensor to the engine **(see illustration 10.68)**.
84   Pull the sensor from the cylinder block.
85   Installation is the reverse of the removal procedure, but be sure to check the O-ring for hardness, cracking and general deterioration, which may cause a leak. Replace the O-ring if necessary. Lubricate the O-ring with engine oil before installing the sensor.

11   Ignition coil - removal, check and installation

Note: *Refer to section 10 for the coil checking procedure on Integrated Direct Ignition (IDI) systems.*
1   Disconnect the cable from the negative terminal of the battery. **Caution:** *If the vehicle is equipped with a Delco Loc II audio system, make sure you have the correct activation code before disconnecting the battery. See the information at the front of this manual for the radio re-activation procedure.*

HEI (distributor) ignition systems

Removal

2   On models with a separately mounted coil, unplug the coil high tension wire and the primary (low voltage) electrical connectors from the coil.
3   Remove both mounting nuts and remove the coil from the engine.
4   On models with the coil in the distributor cap, remove the coil cover screws and lift off the cover. **Note:** *If you are just checking the coil, it is not necessary to remove the coil from the cap. Refer to the checking procedure below.*
5   Push the coil electrical leads through the top of the hood with a small screwdriver.
6   Remove the coil mounting screws and lift the coil, with the leads, from the cap.

Check

Coil-in cap models

7   It is not necessary to remove the coil from the distributor cap on coil-in-cap models to test the coil.
8   Disconnect the negative cable from the battery. **Caution:** *If the vehicle is equipped with a Delco Loc II audio system, make sure you have the correct activation code before disconnecting the battery. See the information at the front of this manual for the radio re-activation procedure.*
9   Remove the distributor cap and turn it over so the coil electrical connectors are visible.
10   Connect an ohmmeter to the two outer coil terminals. It should indicate zero resistance. If it doesn't, replace the coil.
11   Connect the ohmmeter between one of the outer terminals and the central coil-to-rotor contact with the ohmmeter on the high scale. Repeat the test using the other terminal. If both terminals show infinite resistance, replace the coil.

Models with a separately mounted coil

Refer to illustration 11.12
12   On models with a separately mounted coil, check the coil for opens and grounds by performing the following three tests with an ohmmeter **(see illustration)**.
13   Using the ohmmeter's high scale, hook up the ohmmeter leads as illustrated (see test #1 in illustration 11.12). The ohmmeter should indicate a very high, or infinite, resistance value. If it doesn't, replace the coil.
14   Using the low scale, hook up the leads as illustrated (see test #2 in illustration 11.12). The ohmmeter should indicate a very low, or zero, resistance value. If it doesn't, replace the coil.
15   Using the high scale, hook up the leads as illustrated (see test #3 in illustration 11.12). The ohmmeter should not indicate an infinite resistance. If it does, replace the coil.

Installation

16   Installation of the coil is the reverse of the removal procedure.

Direct Ignition System (DIS) - 2.5L four-cylinder engine

Removal

17   Detach the cable from the negative terminal of the battery.
18   Unplug the electrical connectors from the module.
19   Detach the plug wires at the coil assembly.
20   Remove the module/coil assembly attaching bolts **(see illustration 10.56a)**.
21   Remove the module/coil assembly. **Caution:** *The crankshaft sensor is attached to the underside of the module. To avoid damage to the sensor, remove the module slowly and carefully.*
22   Remove the bolts that attach the coils to the module and separate the two assemblies.

Check

23   Refer to section 10 for the coil checking procedure.

Installation

24   Installation is the reverse of removal. Be careful when inserting the module/coil assembly to avoid damage to the sensor.

Computer Controlled Coil Ignition (C3I) - V6 engines

Refer to illustrations 11.34a and 11.34b

Removal

25   Detach the cable from the negative terminal of the battery.
26   Clearly label, then disconnect, all six spark plug wires from the coil.
27   Unbolt and unplug the electrical connector at the module.
28   Detach the vacuum lines and the electrical connector from the EGR valve solenoid on the left end of the coil/module assembly (see Chapter 6 if necessary).

11.34a Using the low scale on the ohmmeter, check the resistance between the positive terminal and the negative terminal

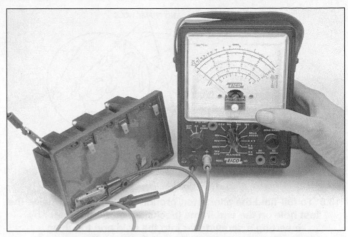

11.34b Using the high scale on the ohmmeter, check the resistance between the negative terminal of the coil and the high tension tower - it should be infinite

29   Remove the front bracket leg mounting nut from the stud on the intake manifold (next to the EGR valve) and the two rear bracket nuts from the studs protruding from the exhaust manifold side of the rear cylinder head.

30   Remove the coil/module and support bracket assembly.

31   Using a Torx screwdriver or bit, remove the coil-to-module attaching screws and separate the coil and module assemblies.

32   Open the coil and module halves **(see illustration 10.59)**. Clearly label, then detach, the wires between the module and the coil assemblies from the spade terminals on the underside of the coil(s).

33   Check the gasket for wear. If it's worn, replace it.

Check

34   The three-part checking procedure for the C3I coil is the same as the procedure outlined above for the HEI type coil. However, the primary terminals are not marked; refer to the accompanying photos **(see illustrations)**.

Installation

35   Installation is the reverse of removal. Be sure to attach the wires of the new module to the coil assembly spade terminals in exactly the same order in which they were removed.

---

12   Charging system - general information and precautions

Caution: *If the vehicle is equipped with a Delco Loc II audio system, make sure you have the correct activation code before disconnecting the battery. See the information at the front of this manual for the radio re-activation procedure.*

The charging system consists of a belt-driven alternator with an integral voltage regulator and the battery. These components work together to supply electrical power for the ignition system, the lights and all accessories.

There are two types of alternators used. Earlier vehicles use the SI type and later models are equipped with the CS type. There are two types of CS alternators in use, the CS-130 and the CS-144. All types use a conventional pulley and fan.

To determine which type of alternator is fitted to your vehicle, look at the fasteners employed to attach the two halves of the alternator housing. All CS models use rivets instead of screws. CS alternators are rebuildable once the rivets are drilled out. However, we don't recommend this practice. For all intents and purposes, CS types should be considered non-serviceable and, if found to be faulty, should be exchanged as cores for new or rebuilt units.

The purpose of the voltage regulator is to limit the alternator's voltage to a preset value. This prevents power surges, circuit overloads, etc., during peak voltage output. On all models with which this manual is concerned, the voltage regulator is contained within the alternator housing.

The charging system does not ordinarily require periodic maintenance. The drivebelts, electrical wiring and connections should, however, be inspected at the intervals suggested in Chapter 1.

Take extreme care when making circuit connections to a vehicle equipped with an alternator and note the following. When making connections to the alternator from a battery, always match correct polarity. Before using arc welding equipment to repair any part of the vehicle, disconnect the wires from the alternator and the battery terminals. Never start the engine with a battery charger connected. Always disconnect both battery leads before using a battery charger.

The charging indicator light on the dash lights when the ignition switch is turned on and goes out when the engine starts. If the light stays on or comes on once the engine is running, a charging system problem has occurred. See Section 13 for the proper diagnosis procedure for each type of alternator.

---

13   Charging system - check

Refer to illustration 13.5

1   Determine the type of generator your vehicle has; SI or CS. SI alternators are bolted together - CS alternators are held together by rivets. If a malfunction occurs in the charging circuit, do not immediately assume that the alternator is causing the problem. First check the following items:

a) *The battery cables where they connect to the battery. Make sure the connections are clean and tight.*

b) *The battery electrolyte specific gravity. If it is low, charge the battery.*

c) *Check the external alternator wiring and connections. They must be in good condition.*

d) *Check the drivebelt condition and tension (see Chapter 1).*

e) *Make sure the alternator mounting bolts are tight.*

f) *Run the engine and check the alternator for abnormal noise (may be caused by a loose drive pulley, loose mounting bolts, worn or dirty bearings, defective diode or defective stator).*

SI type alternator

2   Using a voltmeter, check the battery voltage with the engine off. It should be approximately 12 volts.

3   Start the engine and check the battery voltage again. It should now be approximately 14 to 15 volts.

4   Locate the test hole in the back of the alternator. **Note:** *If there is no test hole, your vehicle is equipped with a CS type alternator. Further testing of this type of alternator must be done by a dealer service department or automotive electrical shop.*

5   Ground the tab that is located inside the hole by inserting a screwdriver blade into the hole and touching the tab and the case at the same time **(see illustration)**. **Caution:** *Do not run the engine with the tab grounded any*

5

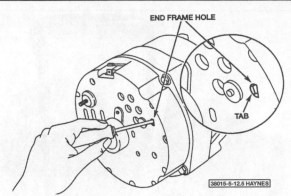

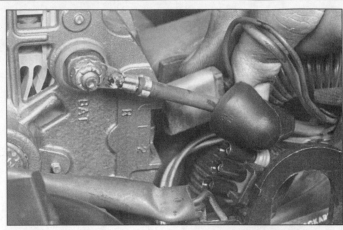

13.5 To full-field the alternator, ground the tab located inside the test hole on the end frame (backside) of the alternator by inserting a screwdriver into the hole and touching the tab and the case at the same time

14.2 Detach the alternator electrical connectors

longer than necessary to obtain a voltmeter reading. If the alternator is charging, it is running unregulated during the test. This condition may overload the electrical system and cause damage to the components.

6   The reading on the voltmeter should be 15 volts or higher with the tab grounded in the test hole.

7   If the voltmeter indicates low battery voltage, the alternator is faulty and should be replaced with a new one (see Section 14).

8   If the voltage reading is 15 volts or higher and a no charge condition is present, the regulator or field circuit is the problem. Remove the alternator (see Section 14) and have it checked further by an auto electric shop.

CS type alternator

Testing of this type of alternator must be done by a dealer service department or automotive electrical shop.

14   Alternator - removal and installation

Refer to illustration 14.2

1   Detach the cable from the negative ter-

minal of the battery. **Caution**: *If the vehicle is equipped with a Delco Loc II audio system, make sure you have the correct activation code before disconnecting the battery. See the information at the front of this manual for the radio re-activation procedure.*

2   Clearly label, if necessary, then unplug and unbolt the electrical connectors from the alternator **(see illustration)**.

3   Remove the drivebelt (see Chapter 1).

4   Remove the alternator mounting bolts and remove the alternator.

5   Installation is the reverse of removal.

15   Alternator brushes - replacement

Refer to illustrations 15.2, 15.3, 15.4, 15.5, 15.6 and 15.10

Note: *The following procedure applies only to SI type alternators. CS types have riveted housings and cannot be disassembled.*

1   Remove the alternator from the vehicle (see Section 14).

2   Scribe or paint marks on the front and rear end frame housings of the alternator to facilitate reassembly **(see illustration)**.

3   Remove the four through-bolts holding the front and rear end frames together, then separate the drive end frame from the rectifier end frame **(see illustration)**.

4   Remove the bolts holding the stator to the rear end frame and separate the stator from the end frame **(see illustration)**.

5   Remove the nuts attaching the diode trio to the rectifier bridge and remove the trio **(see illustration)**.

6   Remove the brush holder screws and remove the brush holder **(see illustration)**.

7   Slide the brushes out of the holder.

8   Remove the springs from the brush holder.

9   Installation is the reverse of the removal procedure, noting the following:

10   When installing the brushes in the brush holder, install the brush closest to the end frame first. Slip a straightened-out paper clip through the rear of the end frame to hold the brush, then insert the second brush and push the paper clip in to hold both brushes while reassembly is completed **(see illustration)**. The paper clip should not be removed until the front and rear end frames have been bolted together.

15.2 Mark the drive end frame and rectifier end frame assemblies with a scribe or paint before separating the two halves

15.3 With the through-bolts removed, carefully separate the drive end frame and the rectifier end frame

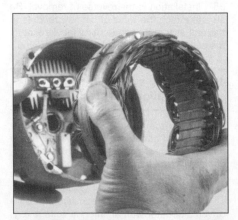

15.4 After removing the bolts holding the stator assembly to the end frame, remove the stator

15.5 Remove the nuts attaching the diode trio to the rectifier bridge and remove the trio

15.6 Remove the screws and detach the brush holder

15.10 To hold the brushes in place during reassembly, insert a paper clip through the hole in the end frame nearest to the rotor shaft

16 Starting system - general information

Caution: *If the vehicle is equipped with a Delco Loc II audio system, make sure you have the correct activation code before disconnecting the battery. See the information at the front of this manual for the radio re-activation procedure.*

The function of the starting system is to crank the engine over quickly enough for it to start. It is composed of a starter motor, solenoid and battery. The battery supplies the electrical energy to the solenoid, which then completes the circuit to the starting motor, which does the actual work of cranking the engine.

The solenoid and starter motor are mounted together at the lower front side of the engine. No periodic lubrication or maintenance is required.

The electrical circuitry of the vehicle is arranged so that the starter motor can only be operated when the clutch pedal is depressed (manual transaxle) or the transaxle selector lever is in Park or Neutral (automatic transaxle).

Never operate the starter motor for more than 15 seconds at a time without pausing to allow it to cool for at least two minutes. Excessive cranking can cause overheating, which can seriously damage the starter.

17 Starter motor - testing in vehicle

Refer to illustration 17.6
1   If the starter motor does not turn at all when the switch is operated, make sure that the shift lever is in Neutral or Park (automatic transaxle) or that the clutch pedal is depressed (manual transaxle).
2   Make sure that the battery is charged and that all cables, both at the battery and starter solenoid terminals, are secure.
3   If the starter motor spins but the engine is not cranking, the overrunning clutch in the

starter motor is slipping and the motor must be removed from the engine for replacement.
4   If, when the switch is actuated, the starter motor does not operate at all but the solenoid clicks, then the problem lies with either the battery, the main solenoid contacts or the starter motor itself. **Note:** *Before diagnosing starter problems, make sure that the battery is fully charged.*
5   If the solenoid plunger cannot be heard when the switch is actuated, the solenoid itself is defective or the solenoid circuit is open.
6   To check the solenoid, connect a jumper lead between the battery (+) and the "S" terminal on the solenoid **(see illustration)**. If the starter motor now operates, the solenoid is OK and the problem is in the ignition switch, neutral start switch or in the wiring.
7   If the starter motor still does not operate, remove the starter/solenoid assembly for

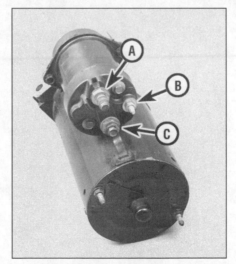

17.6 There are three terminals on the end of the typical starter solenoid

A   Battery terminal
B   Switch terminal (S)
C   Motor terminal (M)

disassembly, testing and repair.
8   If the starter motor cranks the engine at an abnormally slow speed, first make sure that the battery is charged and that all terminal connections are tight. If the engine is partially seized, or has the wrong viscosity oil in it, it will crank slowly.
9   Run the engine until normal operating temperature is reached, then disconnect the coil wire from the distributor cap and ground it on the engine.
10   Connect a voltmeter positive lead to the starter motor terminal of the solenoid and then connect the negative lead to ground.
11   Crank the engine and take the voltmeter readings as soon as a steady figure is indicated. Do not allow the starter motor to turn for more than 15 seconds at a time. A reading of 9 volts or more, with the starter motor turning at normal cranking speed, is normal. If the reading is 9 volts or more but the cranking speed is slow, the motor is faulty. If the reading is less than 9 volts and the cranking speed is slow, the solenoid contacts are probably burned.

5

18 Starter motor - removal and installation

Refer to illustration 18.4

All except 2.3L (Quad 4) models

1   Disconnect the negative battery cable. **Caution:** *If the vehicle is equipped with a Delco Loc II audio system, make sure you have the correct activation code before disconnecting the battery. See the information at the front of this manual for the radio re-activation procedure.*
2   Raise the front of the vehicle and support it securely on jackstands.
3   From under the vehicle, disconnect the solenoid wire and battery cable from the terminals on the rear of the solenoid.

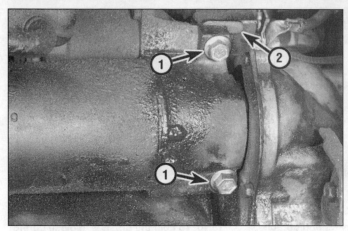

18.4 Typical starter motor mounting for 2.5L four-cylinder and 3.0L V6 applications

1   *Starter bolts*   2   *Shim*

19.5 To remove the solenoid housing from the starter motor, remove the screws and turn it clockwise

4   Remove the starter motor bolts **(see illustration)**.
5   Remove the starter motor. Note the location of the spacer shim(s).
6   Installation is the reverse of removal. Be sure to install the spacer shim(s) in exactly the same location.

2.3L (Quad-4) models

7   Disconnect the cable from the negative battery terminal. **Caution:** *If the vehicle is equipped with a Delco Loc II audio system, make sure you have the correct activation code before disconnecting the battery. See the information at the front of this manual for the radio re-activation procedure.*
8   Remove the intake air duct.
9   Remove the engine cooling fan (see Chapter 3).
10   Remove the oil filter (see Chapter 1).

11   Remove the starter mounting bolts and pull the starter out enough to disconnect the battery cable and wiring harness from the solenoid.
12   Carefully lift the starter out between the intake manifold and radiator.
13   Installation is the reverse of removal.

19   Starter solenoid - removal and installation

Refer to illustration 19.5

1   Disconnect the cable from the negative terminal of the battery. **Caution:** *If the vehicle is equipped with a Delco Loc II audio system, make sure you have the correct activation code before disconnecting the battery. See the information at the front of this manual for the radio re-activation procedure.*

2   Remove the starter motor (see Section 18).

Removal

3   Disconnect the strap from the solenoid to the starter motor terminal.
4   Remove the two screws which secure the solenoid to the starter motor.
5   Twist the solenoid in a clockwise direction to disengage the flange from the starter body **(see illustration)**.

Installation

6   To install, first make sure the return spring is in position on the plunger, then insert the solenoid body into the starter housing and turn the solenoid counterclockwise to engage the flange.
7   Install the two solenoid screws and connect the motor strap.

Chapter 6
Emissions and engine control systems

Contents

Component location

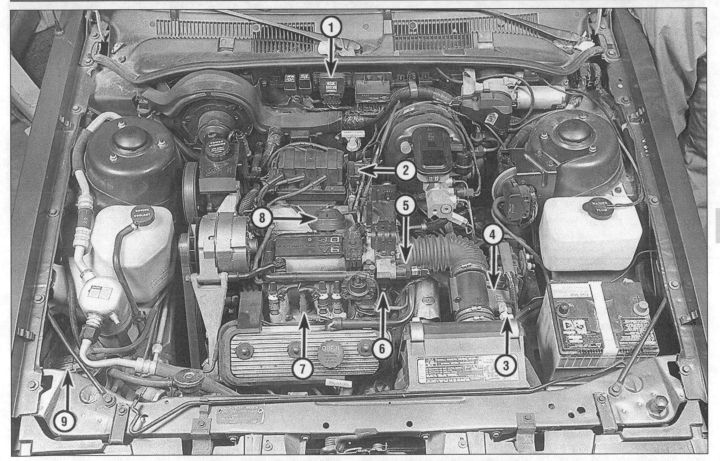

Emissions and engine control system components - 3.0L V6 engine

1 Electronic Spark Control (ESC) module
2 Exhaust Gas Recirculation (EGR) solenoid
3 Intake Air Temperature (IAT) sensor
4 Mass Air Flow (MAF) sensor
5 Idle Air Control (IAC) motor
6 Throttle Position Sensor (TPS)
7 Positive Crankcase Ventilation (PCV) valve
8 Exhaust Gas Recirculation (EGR) valve
9 Charcoal canister

6

Component location

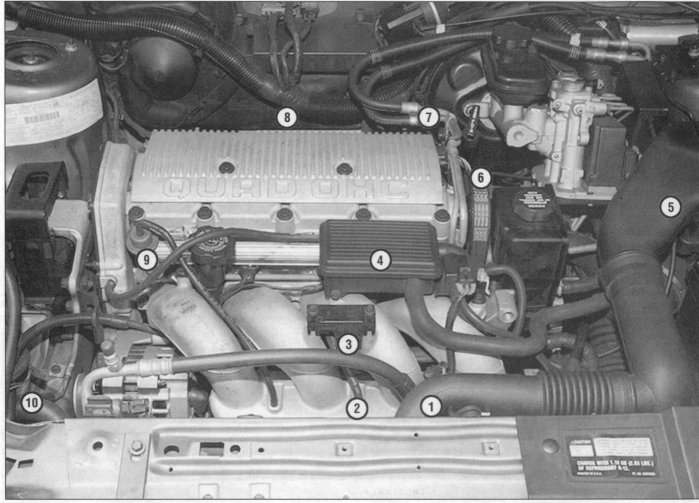

Emissions control system and related component locations - 2.3L MPFI four-cylinder (Quad-4) engine

1   Throttle Position Sensor (TPS) (on throttle body)
2   Intake Air Temperature (IAT) sensor
3   Manifold Absolute Pressure (MAP) sensor
4   Crankcase vent oil/air separator
5   Air cleaner housing
6   Coolant temperature sensor
7   ESC knock sensor (below manifold)
8   Exhaust oxygen sensor
9   Fuel pressure regulator
10 Fuel vapor canister

1   General information

Refer to illustration 1.6

To prevent pollution of the atmosphere from burned and evaporating gases, a number of emissions control systems are incorporated on the vehicles covered by this manual. The combination of systems used depends on the year in which the vehicle was manufactured, the locality to which it was originally delivered and the engine type. The major systems incorporated on the vehicles with which this manual is concerned include the:

Fuel Control System
Electronic Spark Control (ESC) system
Electronic Spark Timing (EST) system
Exhaust Gas Recirculation (EGR) system
Evaporative Emissions Control (EECS) system
Transmission Converter Clutch (TCC)
Positive Crankcase Ventilation (PCV) system
Catalytic converter

All of these systems are linked, directly or indirectly, to the Computer Command Control System (CCCS).

The Sections in this Chapter include general descriptions, checking procedures (where possible) and component replacement procedures (where applicable) for each of the systems listed above.

Before assuming that an emissions control system is malfunctioning, check the fuel and ignition systems carefully. In some cases special tools and equipment, as well as specialized training, are required to accurately diagnose the causes of a rough running or difficult to start engine. If checking and servicing become too difficult, or if a procedure is beyond the scope of the home mechanic, consult your dealer service department. This does not necessarily mean, however, that the emissions control systems are particularly difficult to maintain and repair. You can quickly and easily perform many checks and do most (if not all) of the regular maintenance at home with common tune-up and hand tools. **Note:** *The most frequent cause of emissions system problems is simply a loose or broken vacuum hose or wiring connection. Therefore, always check the hose and wiring connections first.*

Component location

Emissions control system and related component locations - 3.1L V6 engine

1 ESC knock sensor (below manifold)	7 Exhaust Gas Recirculation (EGR) valve
2 Positive Crankcase Ventilation (PCV) valve	8 Manifold Absolute Pressure (MAP) sensor
3 Throttle Position Sensor (TPS)	9 Exhaust oxygen sensor (in exhaust manifold)
4 Intake Air Temperature (IAT) sensor	10 Camshaft position sensor
5 Air cleaner housing	11 Fuel vapor canister
6 Fuel pressure regulator	

Pay close attention to any special precautions outlined in this Chapter. It should be noted that the illustrations of the various systems may not exactly match the system installed on your particular vehicle due to changes made by the manufacturer during production or from year to year.

A *Vehicle Emissions Control Information* (VECI) label is located in the engine compartment of all vehicles with which this manual is concerned **(see illustration)**. This label contains important emissions specifications and setting procedures, as well as a vacuum hose schematic with emissions components identified. When servicing the engine or emissions systems, the VECI label in your particular vehicle should always be checked for up-

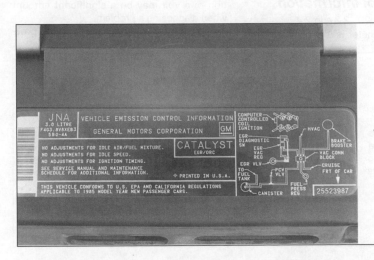

1.6 Look for your vehicle's VECI label under the hood

to-date information. **Note:** *Because of a federally mandated extended warranty which covers the emission control system components (and any components which have a primary purpose other than emission control but have significant effects on emissions), check with your dealer about warranty coverage before working on any emission related systems.*

The number of emissions control system components on later model fuel-injected vehicles has actually decreased due to the high efficiency of the new fuel injection and ignition systems. No longer needed are the AIR pump (most models), early fuel evaporation (EFE) system (except for TBI models), dual bed catalytic converter (although a single bed or monolithic converter is still used) and many of the confusing thermal vacuum switches, valves and hoses as installed on the carbureted engines.

2   Self-diagnosis system and trouble codes

Note: *1995 and earlier models are equipped with the OBD I self diagnosis system, while 1996 models are equipped with the OBD II self diagnosis system. 1994 and later models require the use of a Scan tool to access trouble codes. However, many of the information sensor checks and replacement procedures do apply to both systems. Because 1994 and later systems require a special SCAN tool to access the trouble codes, have the vehicle diagnosed by a dealer service department or other qualified automotive repair facility if the proper SCAN tool is not available. 1994 V6 models and all 1996 models utilize five-digit trouble codes. These "generic" trouble codes listed in the following table do not include the manufacturer's specific trouble codes. Consult a dealer service department or other qualified repair shop for additional information. Refer to the troubleshooting tips in the beginning of this manual and the information described in Section 4 to gain some insight to the most likely causes of a problem.*

Diagnostic tool information

Refer to illustrations 2.1, 2.2 and 2.4

1   A digital multimeter is a necessary tool

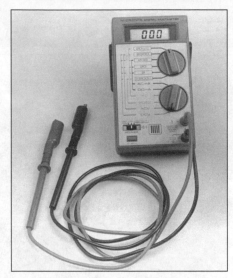

2.1 Digital multimeters can be used for testing all types of circuits; because of their high impedance, they are much more accurate than analog meters for measuring millivolts in low-voltage computer circuits

for checking fuel injection and emission related components **(see illustration)**. A digital volt-ohmmeter is preferred over the older style analog multimeter for several reasons. The analog multimeter cannot display the volts-ohms or amps measurement in hundredths and thousandths increments. When working with electronic circuits which are often very low voltage, this accurate reading is most important. Another good reason for the digital multimeter is the high impedance circuit. The digital multimeter is equipped with high resistance internal circuitry (10 million ohms). Because a voltmeter is hooked up in parallel with the circuit when testing, it is vital that none of the voltage being measured should be allowed to travel the parallel path set up by the meter itself. This dilemma does not show itself when measuring larger amounts of voltage (9 to 12 volt circuits) but if you are measuring a low voltage circuit such as the oxygen sensor signal voltage, a fraction of a volt may be a significant amount when diagnosing a problem.

2   Hand-held scanners are the most pow-

2.2 Scanners like the Actron Scantool and the AutoXray XP240 are powerful diagnostic aids - programmed with comprehensive diagnostic information, they can tell you just about anything you want to know about your engine management system, but they are expensive

erful and versatile tools for analyzing engine management systems used on later model vehicles **(see illustration)**. Unfortunately, they are the most expensive. Early model scanners handle codes and some diagnostics for many OBD I systems. Each brand scan tool must be examined carefully to match the year, make and model of the vehicle you are working on. Often interchangeable cartridges are available to access the particular manufacturer; Ford, GM, Chrysler, etc.). Some manufacturers will specify by continent; Asia, Europe, USA, etc.

3   With the arrival of the federally mandated emission control system (OBD II), a specially designed scanner must also be developed. At this time, several manufacturers plan to release OBD II scan tools for the home mechanic. Ask the parts salesperson at a local auto parts store for additional information concerning dates and costs. **Note:** *Although 1994 and 1995 OBDI and 1996 OBD II codes cannot be accessed without a Scan tool, follow the simple component checks in Section 4.*

4   Another type of code reader is available at parts stores **(see illustration)**. These tools simplify the procedure for extracting codes from the engine management computer by simply "plugging in" to the diagnostic connector on the vehicle wiring harness and are much less expensive (however, they will not work on models that require the use of a scan tool to extract codes).

General description

5   The electronically controlled fuel and emissions system is linked with many other related engine management systems. It consists mainly of sensors, output actuators and an Electronic Control Module (ECM) or Pow-

2.4 Trouble code tools simplify the task of extracting the trouble codes

2.11a The 12-pin Assembly Line Data Link (ALDL) terminal identification

A   Ground   B   Diagnostic TEST terminal

2.11b The 16 pin Data Link Connector (DLC) found on models equipped with OBD II

...ertrain Control Module (PCM) (see Section 1). Completing the system are various other components which respond to commands from the ECM/PCM.

6   In many ways, this system can be compared to the central nervous system in the human body. The sensors (nerve endings) constantly gather information and send this data to the ECM/PCM (brain), which processes the data and, if necessary, sends out a command for some type of vehicle change (limbs).

7   Here's a specific example of how one portion of this system operates: An oxygen sensor, mounted in the exhaust manifold and protruding into the exhaust gas stream, constantly monitors the oxygen content of the exhaust gas as it travels through the exhaust pipe. If the percentage of oxygen in the exhaust gas is incorrect, an electrical signal is sent to the ECM/PCM. The ECM/PCM takes this information, processes it and then sends a command to the fuel injectors, telling it to change the fuel/air mixture. To be effective, all this happens in a fraction of a second, and it goes on continuously while the engine is running. The end result is a fuel/air mixture which is constantly kept at a predetermined ratio, regardless of driving conditions.

Obtaining trouble codes

Refer to illustrations 2.11a and 2.11b

8   One might think that a system which uses exotic electrical sensors and is controlled by an on-board computer would be difficult to diagnose. This is not necessarily the case.

9   The On Board Diagnostic (OBD) system has a built-in self-diagnostic system, which indicates a problem by turning on a "SERVICE ENGINE SOON" light on the instrument panel when a fault has been detected. **Note:** *Since some of the trouble codes do not set the CHECK ENGINE or SERVICE ENGINE SOON light, it is a good idea to access the OBD system and look for any trouble codes that may have been recorded and need tending.*

10   Perhaps more importantly, the ECM/PCM will recognize this fault, in a particular system monitored by one of the various information sensors, and store it in its memory in the form of a trouble code.

Although the trouble code cannot reveal the exact cause of the malfunction, it greatly facilitates diagnosis as you or a dealer mechanic can "tap into" the ECM/PCM's memory and be directed to the problem area.

11   To retrieve this information from the ECM on 1993 and earlier models, you must use a short jumper wire to ground a diagnostic terminal. The terminal is part of an electrical connector called the Assembly Line Data Link (ALDL) **(see illustrations)**. The ALDL is located just behind the dashboard, next to the steering column. On some models a small rectangular plate is used to cover the connector and must be pried off to provide access to the terminals. With the electrical connector exposed, push one end of the jumper wire into the diagnostic TEST terminal and the other end into the GROUND terminal. **Note:** *1994 and 1995 models with a 12-pin diagnostic connector do not have a terminal B present in the connector. On these models a scan tool is required to access trouble codes.*

12   On 1994 and later models, a scan tool must be connected to the Assembly Line Data Link (ALDL). The scan tool is a hand held digital computer scanner that interfaces with the on-board computer. The scan tool is a very powerful tool; it not only reads the trouble codes but also displays the actual operating conditions of the sensors and actuators. Scan tools are expensive, but they are necessary to accurately diagnose a modern computerized fuel-injected engine. Scan tools are available from auto parts stores and specialty tool companies.

13   It should be noted that the self-diagnosis feature built into this system does not detect all possible faults. If you suspect a problem with the On Board Diagnostic (OBD) system, but the CHECK ENGINE or SERVICE ENGINE SOON light has not come on and no trouble codes have been stored, and performing the checks described in Section 4 doesn't pinpoint a problem, take the vehicle to a dealer service department or other qualified repair shop for diagnosis.

14   Furthermore, when diagnosing an engine performance, fuel economy or exhaust emissions problem (which is not accompanied by a CHECK ENGINE or SERVICE ENGINE SOON light) do not automatically assume the fault lies in this system. Perform

all standard troubleshooting procedures, as indicated elsewhere in this manual, before turning to the On Board Diagnostic (OBD) system.

15   Finally, since this is an electronic system, you should have a basic knowledge of automotive electronics before attempting any diagnosis. Damage to the ECM/PCM, Programmable Read Only Memory (PROM) calibration unit or related components can easily occur if care is not exercised.

Clearing trouble codes

16   To clear the trouble codes from the ECM's memory on a 1993 or earlier model, unplug the ECM electrical pigtail at the positive battery cable and wait at least 30 seconds before plugging it back in. If the vehicle you are working on does not have this connector, disconnect the cable from the negative terminal of the battery for at least 30 seconds. **Caution 1:** *To prevent damage to the ECM, the ignition switch must be turned OFF when disconnecting or connecting power to the ECM.* **Caution 2:** *If the vehicle is equipped with a Delco Loc II audio system, make sure you have the correct activation code before disconnecting the battery. See the information at the front of this manual for the radio reactivation procedure.*

17   To clear the codes from the ECM/PCM memory on 1994 and later models, install the SCAN tool, scroll the menu for the function that describes "CLEARING CODES" and follow the prescribed method for that particular SCAN tool or momentarily remove the PCM/IGN fuse from the fuse box for 30 seconds. Clearing codes may also be accomplished by removing the fusible link (main power fuse) located near the battery positive terminal (see Chapter 12) or by disconnecting the cable from the positive terminal (+) of the battery. **Caution:** *If the vehicle is equipped with a Delco Loc II audio system, make sure you have the correct activation code before disconnecting the battery. See the information at the front of this manual for the radio reactivation procedure.*

18   Disconnecting the power to the ECM/PCM to clear the memory can be an important diagnostic tool, especially on intermittent problems.

19   **Note:** *Not all codes apply to all models.*

6

2-digit trouble codes

Code	Code definition
12	Diagnostic mode
13	Oxygen sensor or circuit
14	Coolant sensor or circuit/high temperature indicated
15	Coolant sensor or circuit/low temperature indicated
16	System voltage out of range
19	Crankshaft position sensor or circuit
21	Throttle Position Sensor (TPS) or circuit - voltage high
22	Throttle Position Sensor (TPS) or circuit - voltage low
23	Mixture Control (M/C) solenoid or circuit (carbureted models)
23	Manifold Air Temperature (MAT) sensor or circuit (1990 and earlier models)
23	Intake Air Temperature (IAT) sensor circuit (fuel-injected models)
24	Vehicle Speed Sensor (VSS) or circuit
25	Manifold Air Temperature (MAT) sensor or circuit - high temperature indicated (1990 and earlier models)
25	Intake Air Temperature (IAT) sensor or circuit - high temperature indicated (1991 and later models)
26	Quad Driver module circuit
27	Quad Driver module circuit
28	Quad Driver module circuit
29	Quad Driver module circuit
31	Park/Neutral Position (PNP) switch circuit
32	BARO sensor or circuit (carbureted models)
32	EGR circuit (fuel-injected models)
33	Manifold Absolute Pressure (MAP) sensor signal voltage high
33	Mass Air Flow (MAF) sensor or circuit - excessive airflow indicated
34	Manifold Absolute Pressure (MAP) sensor signal voltage low
34	Mass Air Flow (MAF) sensor signal - low airflow indicated
35	Idle Speed Control (ISC) switch or circuit (shorted) (carbureted models)
35	Idle Air Control (IAC) valve or circuit
38	Brake switch circuit
39	Torque Converter Clutch (TCC) circuit
41	No distributor signals to ECM, or faulty ignition module (carbureted models)
41	Cylinder select error - MEM-CAL or ECM problem (fuel-injected models)
41	Cam sensor circuit (3.8L engine)
42	Bypass or Electronic Spark Timing (EST) circuit
43	Low voltage at ECM terminal L (carbureted models)
43	Knock sensor circuit
44	Oxygen sensor or circuit - lean exhaust detected
45	Oxygen sensor or circuit - rich exhaust detected
46	Power steering pressure switch circuit
48	Misfire diagnosis
51	PROM, MEM-CAL or ECM problem
52	CALPAK or ECM problem
53	EGR fault (carbureted models only)
53	System over-voltage (ECM over 17.7 volts)
54	Mixture Control (M/C) solenoid or circuit (carbureted models)
54	Fuel pump circuit (1986 and later models)
55	Oxygen sensor circuit or ECM
55	Fuel lean monitor (2.2L engine)
61	Oxygen sensor signal faulty (possible contaminated sensor)
62	Transaxle gear switch signal circuits
63	Manifold Absolute Pressure (MAP) sensor voltage high (low vacuum detected)
64	Manifold Absolute Pressure (MAP) sensor voltage low (high vacuum detected)
66	Air conditioning pressure sensor or circuit

5-digit trouble codes

Code	Code definition
P0101	Mass Air Flow (MAF) sensor error
P0102	Mass Air Flow (MAF) sensor circuit - low frequency detected
P0103	Mass Air Flow (MAF) sensor - high frequency detected
P0106	Manifold Absolute Pressure (MAP) sensor performance fault
P0107	Manifold Absolute Pressure (MAP) sensor circuit low input
P0108	Manifold Absolute Pressure (MAP) sensor circuit high input
P0112	Intake Air Temperature (IAT) sensor circuit low input
P0113	Intake Air Temperature (IAT) sensor circuit high input
P0117	Engine Coolant Temperature (ECT) sensor circuit - low input
P0118	Engine Coolant Temperature (ECT) sensor circuit - high input
P0121	Throttle Position Sensor (TPS) range/performance fault
P0122	Throttle Position Sensor (TPS) circuit low input
P0123	Throttle Position Sensor (TPS) circuit high input
P0125	Engine Coolant Temperature (ECT) takes too long to enter closed loop
P0131	Upstream heated O2 sensor circuit - low voltage (Bank 1, Sensor 1)
P0132	Upstream heated O2 sensor circuit - high voltage (Bank 1, Sensor 1)
P0133	Upstream heated O2 sensor slow response (lazy sensor) (Bank 1, Sensor 1)
P0134	Upstream heated O2 sensor insufficient activity (Bank 1, Sensor 1)
P0135	Upstream heated O2 sensor - heater circuit fault (Bank 1, Sensor 1)
P0137	Downstream heated O2 sensor circuit - low voltage (Bank 1, Sensor 2)
P0138	Downstream heated O2 sensor circuit high voltage (Bank 1, Sensor 2)
P0140	Downstream heated O2 sensor insufficient activity (Bank 1, Sensor 2)
P0141	O2 sensor heater circuit fault (Bank 1, Sensor 2)
P0171	System Adaptive fuel too lean
P0172	System Adaptive fuel too rich
P0191	Injector Pressure sensor system performance
P0192	Injector Pressure sensor circuit low input
P0193	Injector Pressure sensor circuit high input
P0300	Cylinder misfire detected (random)
P0301	Cylinder number 1 misfire detected
P0302	Cylinder number 2 misfire detected
P0303	Cylinder number 3 misfire detected
P0304	Cylinder number 4 misfire detected
P0305	Cylinder number 5 misfire detected
P0306	Cylinder number 6 misfire detected
P0321	Crankshaft Position sensor circuit fault
P0325	Knock sensor circuit fault
P0326	Knock sensor circuit performance
P0327	Knock sensor noise channel - low voltage
P0335	Crankshaft Position sensor circuit
P0336	Crankshaft reference signal circuit
P0341	Camshaft Position sensor circuit
P0342	Camshaft Position sensor circuit
P0401	Exhaust Gas Recirculation (EGR) system flow insufficient
P0420	Three Way Catalyst (TWC) system - low efficiency
P0441	EVAP system - no flow during purge cycle
P0351	COP ignition coil 1 primary circuit fault
P0352	COP ignition coil 2 primary circuit fault
P0353	COP ignition coil 3 primary circuit fault
P0354	COP ignition coil 4 primary circuit fault
P0400	EGR flow fault
P0401	EGR insufficient flow detected

6

5-digit trouble codes

Code	Code definition
P0402	EGR excessive flow detected
P0420	Catalyst system efficiency below threshold (Bank 1)
P0421	Catalyst system efficiency below threshold (Bank 1)
P0430	Catalyst system efficiency below threshold (Bank 2)
P0431	Catalyst system efficiency below threshold (Bank 2)
P0441	EVAP incorrect purge flow
P0443	EVAP VMV circuit fault
P0452	EVAP fuel tank pressure sensor low input
P0453	EVAP fuel tank pressure sensor high input
P0502	VSS circuit low input
P0503	VSS circuit range performance
P0506	IAC system rpm lower than expected
P0507	IAC system rpm higher than expected
P0530	A/C refrigerant pressure sensor circuit
P0560	System voltage out of range
P0600	PCM serial data communication link fault
P0601	PCM memory problem
P0602	PCM control module programming error
P0650	Quad driver module circuit
P0703	TCC brake switch input circuit fault
P0705	Transaxle Range sensor circuit malfunction
P0706	Transaxle Range sensor performance
P0712	Transaxle fluid temperature sensor circuit low input
P0713	Transaxle fluid temperature sensor circuit high input
P0740	TCC circuit fault
P0755	Shift solenoid circuit fault

3   Electronic Control Module (ECM)

ECM replacement

Refer to illustration 3.4

Caution: *Prior to servicing the ECM, PROM, CALPAK or MEM-CAL, it is essential the ignition be "off" and the negative battery cable be disconnected. Failure to do so will result in either the ECM, PROM or both to be damaged either on removal or on installation.*

Warning: *Sensitive electronic components, such as PROMS, MEMCALS and CALPAKS can be damaged internally by Electro Static Discharge (ESD). This is the normal build up of static electricity in your body. As little as 100 volts can damage components. It takes approximately 4,000 volts before you would notice the snap and feel the shock from static electricity. It is not unusual for voltages in your body to build up in excess of 25,000 volts. Before handling any electronic component, discharge yourself by touching a good ground such as a door jamb switch or unpainted metal surface. It may be necessary to discharge yourself several times during a repair.*

Note: *The ECM for the 1994 and later 3.1L engine does not have a replaceable PROM. What appears to be a PROM, is actually the ESC module. The ECM must be programmed*

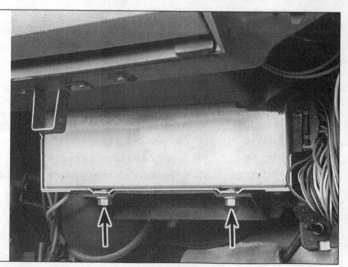

3.4 To remove the Electronic Control Module (ECM) from the vehicle, remove the mounting bolts (arrows) and slide it out far enough to unplug the electrical connectors

prior to its installation. This can only be done at the dealership.

1   The Electronic Control Module (ECM) is located under the instrument panel on the right (passenger) side on the passenger compartment.

2   Disconnect the cable from the negative battery terminal. **Caution:** *If the vehicle is equipped with a Delco Loc II audio system, make sure you have the correct activation code before disconnecting the battery. See*

the information at the front of this manual for the radio re-activation procedure.

3   Remove the right sound insulator panel retaining screws and detach the panel (under the right side of the dashboard).

4   Remove the retaining bolts **(see illustration)** and carefully slide the ECM out far enough to unplug the electrical connector.

5   Unplug the electrical connectors from the ECM.

6   Installation is the reverse of removal.

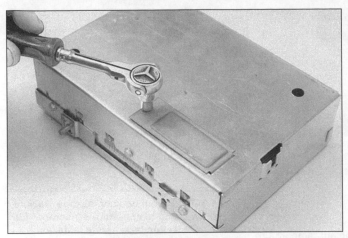

3.8 A typical electrical control module (ECM) - the PROM, CALPAK or MEM-CAL unit is located under the access cover

3.9 Using two fingers, push the retaining clips (arrows) back away from the MEM-CAL and simultaneously grasp it at both ends and lift it up out of the socket

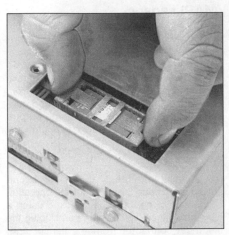

3.10 To install the MEM-CAL, press only on the ends (arrows) until the retaining clips snap into the ends of the MEM-CAL - make sure that the notches in the MEM-CAL are aligned with the small notches in the socket

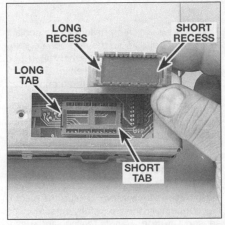

3.12 Note how the notch in the PROM is matched up with the smaller notch in the carrier

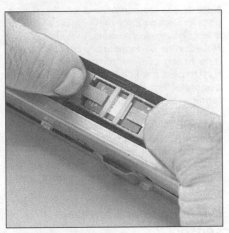

3.13 Press only on the ends of the PROM carrier - pressure on the area in between could result in bent or broken pins or damage to the PROM

PROM, CALPAK or MEM-CAL replacement

Refer to illustration 3.8

7   To allow one model of ECM to be used for many different vehicles, a device called a PROM (Programmable Read Only Memory), CALPAK (calibration pack) or MEM-CAL (memory and calibration) is used. Some models use a combination of two of these. This device is located inside the ECM and contains information on the vehicle's weight, engine, transaxle, axle ratio, etc. One ECM part number can be used by many GM vehicles but the PROM, CALPAK or MEM-CAL is very specific and must be used only in the vehicle for which it was designed. For this reason, it's essential to check the latest parts book and Service Bulletin information for the correct part number when replacing one of these components. A replacement ECM doesn't come with a PROM, CALPAK or MEM-CAL. It (or they) must be carefully removed from the old ECM and installed in

the new ECM.
8   Remove the access cover **(see illustration)**.

MEM-CAL

Refer to illustrations 3.9 and 3.10

9   To remove a MEM-CAL, push both retaining clips back away from the MEM-CAL **(see illustration)**. At the same time, grasp the unit at both ends and lift it up out of the socket. Don't remove the MEM-CAL cover itself. **Caution:** *Use of unapproved removal or installation methods may damage the MEM-CAL or socket.*
10   To install the MEM-CAL, press only on the ends. The small notches in the MEM-CAL must be aligned with the small notches in the MEM-CAL socket. Press on the ends of the MEM-CAL until the retaining clips snap into the ends of the MEM-CAL. Don't press on the middle of the MEM-CAL - press only on the ends **(see illustration)**.

PROM/CALPAK

Refer to illustrations 3.12 and 3.13

11   To remove a PROM or CALPAK, a special removal tool should be used. These usu-

ally are supplied when a replacement ECM is purchased. **Caution:** *Removal without this tool or with any other type of tool may cause damage.* Grasp the PROM carrier at the narrow ends. Gently rock the carrier from end-to-end while carefully pulling up.
12   Note the reference end of the PROM/CALPAK carrier **(see illustration)** before setting it aside.
13   Position the PROM or CALPAK and carrier assembly squarely over the socket with the small notched end of the carrier aligned with the small notch in the socket. Press on the carrier until it seats firmly in the socket **(see illustration)**. **Caution:** *Don't press on the PROM or CALPAK - press only on the carrier. Also, if the unit is installed backwards, it will be destroyed when the ignition switch is turned on.*

Final installation

14   The remainder of the installation is the reverse of removal.
15   Once the new MEM-CAL is installed in the old ECM (or the old unit is installed in the new ECM), check the installation to verify it

6

has been installed properly by doing the following test:

a) *Turn the ignition switch on.*
b) *Enter the diagnostics mode at the DLC (see Section 2).*
c) *Allow code 12 to flash four times to verify that no other codes are present. This indicates the PROM, CALPAK or MEM-CAL is properly installed and the ECM is functioning properly.*

16   If trouble codes 41, 42, 43, 51 or 52 occur, or if the Check Engine or Service Engine Soon light is on constantly but isn't flashing any codes, the unit is either not completely seated or it's defective. If it's not seated, press firmly on the ends once again.

---

4   Information sensors

Note 1: *See the component location illustrations in Section 2 for the location of the following information sensors.*
Note 2: *After performing any checking procedure to any of the information sensors, be sure to clear the ECM of all trouble codes by disconnecting the cable from the negative terminal of the battery for at least ten seconds.*
Caution: *If the vehicle is equipped with a Delco Loc II audio system, make sure you have the correct activation code before disconnecting the battery. See the information at the front of this manual for the radio re-activation procedure.*

Engine coolant temperature sensor

Refer to illustrations 4.2 and 4.3

General description and check

1   The coolant sensor is a thermistor (a resistor which varies the value of its voltage output in accordance with temperature changes). A failure in the coolant sensor circuit should set either a Code 14 or a Code 15.

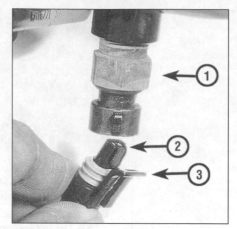

4.2 Typical engine coolant temperature sensor (1) electrical connector (2) - locking tab (3) must be released to unplug the connector

These codes indicate a failure in the coolant temperature circuit, so the appropriate solution to the problem will be either repair of a wire or replacement of the sensor. The sensor can also be checked with an ohmmeter, by measuring its resistance when cold, then warming up the engine and taking another measurement. If the difference in resistance readings is not approximately 500 ohms, or more, the sensor is probably bad.

Replacement

2   To remove the sensor, release the locking tab **(see illustration)**, unplug the electrical connector, then carefully unscrew the sensor. **Caution:** *Handle the coolant sensor with care. Damage to this sensor will affect the operation of the entire fuel injection system.*

3   Before installing the new sensor, wrap the threads with Teflon sealing tape to prevent leakage and thread corrosion **(see illustration)**.

4   Installation is the reverse of removal.

4.3 To prevent coolant leakage, be sure to wrap the temperature sensor threads with Teflon tape before installation

Manifold Absolute Pressure (MAP) sensor

Refer to illustrations 4.5 and 4.7

General description

5   The Manifold Absolute Pressure (MAP) sensor **(see illustration)** monitors the intake manifold pressure changes resulting from changes in engine load and speed and converts the information into a voltage output. The ECM uses the MAP sensor to control fuel delivery and ignition timing.

Check

6   A failure in the MAP sensor circuit should set a code 33 or 34 but the operation of the sensor can also be checked using a high-impedance digital voltmeter. Unplug the electrical connector from the sensor and, using jumper wires, connect terminals A and C (the two outside terminals) to their corresponding terminals in the electrical connector. Connect the positive lead of the voltmeter to terminal B (the center terminal) of the sensor and the negative lead to ground. With the ignition On (engine not running) the voltage reading should be about 4.5 to 5

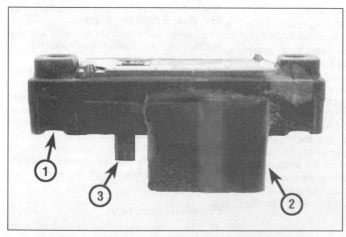

4.5 Typical Manifold Absolute Pressure (MAP) sensor

1   *Sensor assembly*   3   *Manifold vacuum port*
2   *Electrical connector*

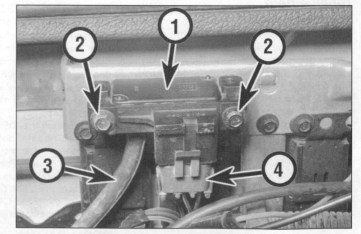

4.7 Typical MAP sensor installation details

1   *MAP sensor*   3   *Vacuum line*
2   *Mounting screws*   4   *Electrical connector*

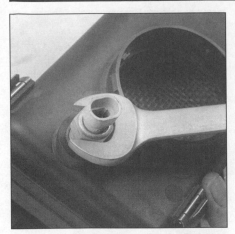

4.10 Remove the MAT sensor from the air cleaner housing

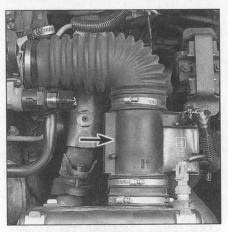

4.12 Typical Mass Air Flow (MAF) sensor installation (arrow)

4.16 The oxygen sensor (arrow) threads into the exhaust manifold

volts. Start the engine and let it warm up. The reading should now be different from the original reading, and should fluctuate with changes in engine rpm. If it doesn't, check the vacuum hose for breaks or blockage. If the hose is OK, the sensor is probably bad.

Replacement

7   To replace the sensor, detach the vacuum hose, unplug the electrical connector and remove the mounting screws **(see illustration)**. Installation is the reverse of removal.

Manifold Air Temperature (MAT) sensor or Intake Air Temperature (IAT) sensor

Refer to illustration 4.10

General description

8   This sensor, located in the intake manifold air cleaner housing or air duct, is a thermistor (a resistor which changes the value of its voltage output as the temperature changes). The ECM uses the this signal to delay EGR until the manifold air temperature reaches 40-degrees F.

Check

9   A failure in the MAT/IAT sensor circuit should set either a Code 23 or a Code 25. The sensor can also be checked with an ohmmeter, by measuring its resistance when cold, then warming it up (a hair dryer can be used for this) and taking another measurement. If the difference in resistance readings is not approximately 500 ohms, or more, the sensor is probably bad.

Replacement

10   To remove a MAT/IAT sensor, unplug the electrical connector and remove the sensor with a wrench **(see illustration)**.
11   Installation is the reverse of removal.

Mass Air Flow (MAF) sensor

Refer to illustration 4.12

General description

12   The Mass Air Flow (MAF) sensor, which

is located in a housing between the air cleaner housing and the intake duct **(see illustration)**, measures the amount of air entering the engine. The ECM uses this information to control fuel delivery. A large quantity of air indicates acceleration, while a small quantity indicates deceleration or idle.

Check

13   If the sensor fails at a high frequency, a Code 33 should set and if it fails at a low frequency or power is lost to the sensor, a Code 34 should set. A Code 44 or 45 may also result if the MAF sensor is faulty. A quick check of the sensor can also be made by tapping the flat portion of the sensor body with a screwdriver handle as the engine is running. If the engine stumbles or dies, the sensor is faulty.

Replacement

14   To replace the MAF sensor, unplug the electrical connector, loosen the clamps and detach the sensor from the air ducts.
15   Installation is the reverse of removal.

Oxygen sensor

Refer to illustration 4.16

General description

16   The oxygen sensor is mounted in the exhaust system where it monitor's the oxygen content of the exhaust gas stream **(see illustration)**. The ECM constantly monitors the variable voltage output of the oxygen sensor to determine the ratio of oxygen to fuel in the mixture. The ECM alters the air/fuel mixture ratio by controlling the pulse width (open time) of the fuel injectors.
17   The oxygen sensor produces no voltage when it's below its normal operating temperature of about 600-degrees F. During this initial period before warm-up, the ECM operates in open loop mode.
18   If the engine reaches normal operating temperature and/or has been running for two or more minutes, and if the oxygen sensor is producing a steady signal voltage between 0.35 and 0.55-volt, even though the TPS indicates the engine isn't at idle, the ECM will set

a Code 13.
19   A delay of two minutes or more between engine start-up and normal operation or the sensor, followed by a low voltage signal or a short in the sensor circuit, will cause the ECM to set a Code 44. If a high voltage signal occurs, The ECM will set a Code 45.
20   When any of the above codes occur, the ECM operates in the open loop mode - that is it controls fuel delivery in accordance with a programmed default value instead of feedback information from the oxygen sensor.

Check

21   An open in the oxygen sensor circuit should set a Code 13. A low voltage in the circuit should set a Code 44. A high voltage in the circuit should set a Code 45. Codes 44 and 45 may also be set as a result of fuel system problems.
22   The sensor can also be checked with a high-impedance digital voltmeter. Warm up the engine to normal operating temperature, then turn the engine off. Unplug the oxygen sensor electrical connector and connect the positive probe of the voltmeter to the sensor side of the connector. **Caution:** *Don't let the sensor wire or the voltmeter lead touch the exhaust pipe or manifold.* Ground the negative probe of the meter, turn the meter to the millivolt setting and start the engine.
23   The reading on the voltmeter should fluctuate between 100 and 1,000 millivolts (0.1 and 1.0 volts). If the meter reading doesn't fluctuate, the sensor is probably bad (although a fuel system problem could be the cause).

Replacement

24   Disconnect the negative battery cable.
25   Disconnect the oxygen sensor electrical connector.
26   Remove the oxygen sensor from the exhaust manifold or exhaust pipe.
27   Installation is the reverse of removal.
Note: *If you are going to reuse the same oxygen sensor, a small amount of anti-seize compound should be applied to the threads before reinstallation. New sensors come with anti-seize applied to the threads.*

6

Throttle Position Sensor (TPS)

28   The Throttle Position Sensor (TPS) is located on the TBI unit or throttle body.

29   By monitoring the output voltage from the TPS, the ECM can determine fuel delivery based on throttle valve angle (driver demand). A broken or loose TPS can cause intermittent bursts of fuel from the injector and an unstable idle because the ECM thinks the throttle is moving.

30   A problem in any of the TPS circuits will set either a Code 21 or 22. Once a trouble code is set, the ECM will use an artificial default value for TPS and some vehicle performance will return.

31   Checking and replacement procedures for the TPS are contained in Chapter 4.

Park/Neutral (P/N) switch

32   The Park/Neutral (P/N) switch, located on the rear upper part of the automatic transaxle, indicates to the ECM when the transaxle is in Park or Neutral. This information is used for Transaxle Converter Clutch (TCC), Exhaust Gas Recirculation (EGR) and Idle Air Control (IAC) valve operation. **Caution:** *The vehicle should not be driven with the Park/Neutral switch disconnected because idle quality will be adversely affected and a false Code 24 (failure in the Vehicle Speed Sensor circuit) may be set.*

33   For more information regarding the P/N switch, which is part of the Neutral-Start and Back-up light switch assembly, see Chapter 7B.

Air conditioning (A/C) On Signal

34   This signal tells the ECM the A/C selector switch is in the On position and the high side low pressure switch is closed. The ECM uses this information to turn on the A/C and adjust the idle speed when the air conditioning system is working. If this signal isn't available to the ECM, idle may be rough, especially when the A/C compressor cycles.

35   Diagnosis of the circuit between the A/C On signal and the ECM should be left to a dealer service department or other repair shop.

Vehicle Speed Sensor (VSS)

36   The Vehicle Speed Sensor (VSS) sends a pulsing voltage signal to the ECM, which the ECM converts to miles per hour. This sensor controls the operation of the Torque Converter Clutch (TCC) system.

Crankshaft Position sensor

37   The crankshaft sensor sends a signal to the ECM to tell it both engine rpm and crankshaft position. See Chapter 5, for further information.

5   Electronic Spark Timing (EST) system

1   Electronic Spark Timing is used on all engines with which this manual is concerned. The EST distributor contains no vacuum or centrifugal advance, depending on commands from the ECM instead. The ECM receives a reference pulse from the distributor, indicating both engine rpm and crankshaft position, determines the proper spark advance for the engine operating conditions and sends an EST pulse to the distributor. **Note:** *On later models, the ECM controls spark advance by receiving information from the crankshaft sensor and sending an EST pulse to the DIS module.*

2   Under normal operating conditions, the ECM will always control the spark advance. However, under certain conditions, such as cranking or setting base timing, the distributor can operate independent of ECM control. This condition is called Bypass mode and is determined by the bypass lead from the ECM to the distributor. When the bypass lead voltage is over two volts, the ECM will control the spark. Disconnecting the four terminal EST connector, or grounding the bypass lead, will cause the engine to operate in the bypass mode.

3   For further information (and checking and component replacement procedures) regarding the EST distributor, refer to Chapter 5.

6   Electronic Spark Control (ESC) system

Refer to illustrations 6.3 and 6.14

General description

1   Irregular octane levels in modern gasoline can cause detonation in an engine. Detonation is sometimes referred to as "spark knock."

2   The Electronic Spark Control (ESC) system is designed to retard spark timing up to 20-degrees to reduce spark knock in the engine. This allows the engine to use maximum spark advance to improve driveability and fuel economy.

3   The ESC knock sensor, which is located on the engine block **(see illustration)**, sends a voltage signal of 8 to 10-volts to the ECM when no spark knock is occurring and the ECM provides normal advance. When the knock sensor detects abnormal vibration (spark knock), the ESC module turns off the circuit to the ECM and the voltage at the ECM drops to zero volts. The ECM then retards the timing until spark knock is eliminated.

4   Failure of the ESC knock sensor signal or loss of ground at the ESC module will cause the signal to the ECM to remain high. This condition will result in the ECM controlling the EST as if no spark knock is occurring. Therefore, no retard will occur and spark knock may become severe under heavy engine load conditions. At this point, the ECM will set a Code 43.

5   Loss of the ESC signal to the ECM will cause the ECM to constantly retard EST. This

6.3 Typical Electronic Spark Control (ESC) knock sensor (arrow) located on the engine block

will result in sluggish performance and cause the ECM to set a Code 43.

Check

6   Connect a timing light in accordance with the tool manufacturer's instructions. Start the engine and allow it to reach normal operating temperature.

7   With an assistant pointing the timing light at the timing marks, tap on the engine block with a hammer in the area of the ESC (knock) sensor. The ignition timing should retard noticeably each time the hammer strikes the block. If the timing retards, the system is operating properly.

8   If the timing does not retard, stop the engine and unplug the electrical connector from the sensor.

9   Using a digital voltmeter set on the 2-volt AC scale, probe the knock sensor single wire terminal with the positive probe and ground the negative probe to the engine block. Tap on the engine block with a hammer near the knock sensor and check for a small AC signal generated by the sensor as it detects the knock. If no signal is detected, the knock sensor is not functioning; replace the ESC knock sensor. If a signal is detected, the knock signal is functioning properly, the ESC module or the ECM may be defective; have further diagnosis performed by a dealership service department or other qualified repair facility.

ESC sensor replacement

10   Disconnect the electrical connector from the ESC sensor.

11   Remove the ESC sensor from the block.

12   Installation is the reverse of removal.

ESC module replacement

13   Detach the cable from the negative terminal of the battery.

14   Detach the wiring harness electrical connector from the module **(see illustration)**.

15   Remove the module mounting bolts and remove the module.

16   Installation is the reverse of removal.

6.14 The ESC module is located on the firewall, between the A/C compressor relay and the engine coolant fan relay - to remove it, unplug the connector (A) and remove the two mounting bolts (B)

7 Exhaust Gas Recirculation (EGR) system

General description (non-digital EGR system)

1   An EGR system is used on all engines except the 2.3L and the 3.3L V6 engines. Due to camshaft profile, an EGR valve is not required on the 2.3L engine.

2   The Exhaust Gas Recirculation (EGR) system is used to lower NOx (oxides of nitrogen) emission levels caused by high combustion temperatures. It does this by decreasing combustion temperature. The main element of the system is the EGR valve, which feeds small amounts of exhaust gas back into the combustion chamber.

3   The EGR valve is usually open during warm engine operation and anytime the engine is running above idle speed. The amount of gas recirculated is controlled by variations in vacuum and exhaust backpressure.

4   There are three types of EGR valves. Their names refer to the means by which they are controlled:

   Positive backpressure
   Negative backpressure (2.5L four-cylinder engine only)
   Ported vacuum

Positive backpressure EGR valve

5   The positive backpressure valve has an air bleed, located inside the EGR valve assembly, which acts as a vacuum regulator. This bleed valve controls the amount of vacuum in the vacuum chamber by bleeding vacuum to the atmosphere during the open phase of the cycle. When the bleed valve receives sufficient exhaust backpressure through the hollow shaft, it closes the bleed. At this point, maximum available vacuum is applied to the diaphragm and the EGR valve opens.

6   If there is little or no vacuum in the vac-

7.14 To check an EGR valve for freedom of movement and clear passages, warm up the engine, remove the air cleaner assembly (if necessary) and, using a rag to protect your fingers, push up on the diaphragm - the engine should stumble and stall

uum chamber, such as at idle or wide open throttle, or if there is little or no pressure in the exhaust manifold, the EGR valve will not open. This type of valve will not open if vacuum is applied to it with the engine stopped or idling.

Negative backpressure EGR valve

7   The negative backpressure EGR valve is similar to the positive backpressure EGR valve except that the bleed valve spring is moved from above the valve to below and the valve is normally closed.

Ported vacuum EGR valve

8   The ported vacuum EGR valve uses ported vacuum connected directly to the EGR valve. The amount of exhaust gas recirculated is controlled by the throttle opening and the amount of manifold vacuum.

Ported EGR valve (computer controlled)

9   This valve is controlled by a flexible diaphragm which is spring loaded to hold the valve closed. Ported vacuum applied to the top side of the diaphragm overcomes the spring pressure and opens the valve in the exhaust gas port.

10   The EGR vacuum control has a vacuum solenoid that uses *pulse width modulation*. This means that the ECM turns the solenoid on and off many times a second and varies the amount of on time (the pulse width) to vary the amount of exhaust gas recirculated.

11   A diagnostic switch is part of the control and monitors vacuum to the EGR valve. This switch will trigger a *Check Engine or Service Engine Soon* light and set a Code 32 in the event of a vacuum circuit failure.

EGR valve identification

12   A series of numbers is stamped into the top of every EGR valve. This identification

number indicates the assembly plant code, part number, date built and type of EGR valve.

   a) *Positive backpressure EGR valves will have a P stamped on the top side of the valve after the part number.*
   b) *Negative backpressure EGR valves will have an N stamped on the top side of the valve after the part number.*
   c) *Ported vacuum EGR valves have no identification stamped after the part number.*

Check

Refer to illustration 7.14

Non-computer controlled EGR valves

13   Hold the top of the EGR valve and try to rotate it back and forth. If looseness is felt, replace the valve.

14   If no looseness is felt, place the transaxle in Neutral (manual) or Park (automatic), set the parking brake and block the drive wheels. Start the engine and run the engine at idle until it warms up to at least 195 F. Push up on the underside of the EGR valve diaphragm, lifting the valve off its seat **(see illustration);** the rpm should drop. If there is no change in rpm, clean the EGR passages. If there is still no change in rpm when the valve is opened, replace the valve. If the rpm drops when the valve is opened, check for movement of the EGR valve diaphragm as the rpm is changed from idle to approximately 2000 rpm. If the diaphragm moves, there is no problem.

15   If the diaphragm does not move when the engine is accelerated, check the vacuum signal at the EGR valve as the engine rpm is changed from idle to approximately 2000 rpm.

16   If the vacuum is over six inches, replace the EGR valve. If it is under six inches, check the vacuum hoses for restrictions, leaks or poor connections.

Computer controlled ported type EGR valves

17   Disconnect the EGR solenoid vacuum harness. Rotate the harness and reinstall only the EGR valve side. Install a vacuum pump with gauge on the manifold side of the EGR solenoid. Turn the ignition to On (engine not running). Apply vacuum. Observe the EGR valve. The valve should not move.

18   If the valve moves, disconnect the EGR solenoid electrical connector and repeat the test. If the valve still moves, replace the solenoid.

19   If the valve does not move, ground the diagnostic terminal (12-pin DLC only, see Section 2) and repeat the test. If the valve still does not move, replace the EGR valve.

20   If the valve does move, start the engine. Lift up on the EGR valve and note the idle speed.

21   If there is no change in the idle, remove the EGR valve and check the passages for blockage. If the passages are not plugged, replace the EGR valve.

22   If the idle roughens, reconnect the EGR

6

7.30 Deposits can be removed from the EGR pintle seating area by taping the end of the pintle lightly with a soft-face hammer

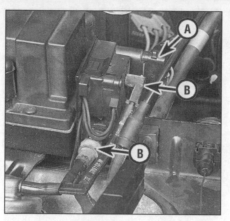

7.40 Typical EGR valve control solenoid - to remove it, unplug the electrical connector (A) and label and detach the vacuum hoses (B)

7.45 Typical digital EGR valve (arrow)

solenoid. Connect a vacuum gauge to the vacuum harness at the EGR valve. Warm up the engine to normal operating temperature. If your transaxle is an automatic, set the park brake, block the drive wheels and place the gear selector in Drive. Hold the brakes firmly and accelerate momentarily up to about 1800 rpm. Observe the gauge. It should indicate over two but less than ten inches of vacuum.

23   If it is zero or less than two inches of vacuum, check for restrictions in the vacuum lines. If there are no restrictions in the vacuum lines, the park/neutral switch is probably faulty (see Chapter 7B).

24   If there is over ten inches of vacuum, replace the EGR filter.

25   If the vacuum is within two to ten inches, the EGR system is functioning properly.

Component replacement

Refer to illustrations 7.30 and 7.40

EGR valve

26   Disconnect the vacuum hose from the EGR valve.

27   Remove the nuts or bolts which secure the valve to the intake manifold or adapter and remove the valve.

EGR valve cleaning

28   Inspect the valve pintle for deposits.

29   Depress the valve diaphragm and check for deposits around the valve seating area.

30   Hold the valve securely and tap lightly on the round pintle with a plastic hammer, using a light snapping action, to remove any deposits from the valve seat (see illustration). Make sure to empty any loose particles from the valve. Depress the valve diaphragm again and inspect the valve seating area, repeating the cleaning operation as necessary.

31   Use a wire brush to carefully clean deposits from the pintle.

32   Remove any deposits from the valve outlet using a screwdriver.

33   If EGR passages in the intake manifold show an excessive build-up of deposits, the passages should be cleaned. Care should be

taken to ensure that all loose particles are completely removed to prevent them from clogging the EGR valve or from being ingested into the engine. **Note:** *It is a good idea to place a rag in the passage opening to keep debris from entering while cleaning the manifold.*

34   With a wire wheel, buff the exhaust deposits from the mounting surface.

35   Look for exhaust deposits in the valve outlet. Remove deposit build-up with a screwdriver.

36   Clean the mounting surfaces of the EGR valve. Remove all traces of old gasket material.

37   Install the new EGR valve, with a new lithium-based grease coated gasket, on the intake manifold or adapter.

38   Connect the vacuum signal hose to the EGR valve.

EGR control solenoid

39   Disconnect the negative battery cable.

40   Unplug the solenoid electrical connector (see illustration).

41   Clearly label, then detach, the vacuum hoses.

42   Remove the mounting screws/nuts and the solenoid.

43   Installation is the reverse of removal.

General description (digital EGR valve)

Refer to illustration 7.45

44   The digital EGR valve feeds small amounts of exhaust gas back into the intake manifold and then into the combustion chamber.

45   The digital EGR valve is designed to accurately supply EGR to an engine, independent of intake manifold vacuum. The valve controls EGR flow from the exhaust to the intake manifold through three orifices, which increment in size, to produce seven combinations. When a solenoid is energized, the armature, with attached shaft and swivel pintle, is lifted, opening the orifice. The flow accuracy is dependent on metering orifice

size only, which results in improved control (see illustration).

46   The digital EGR valve is opened by the ECM, grounding each solenoid circuit. This activates the solenoid, raises the pintle, and allows exhaust gas flow into the intake manifold. The exhaust gas then moves with the air/fuel mixture into the combustion chamber.

Check

47   A special "scan" tool is needed to check this valve and should be left to a dealer service department or other repair shop.

Replacement

48   Disconnect the electrical connector from the EGR valve.

49   Remove the two mounting bolts and remove the EGR valve from the intake manifold.

50   Remove the EGR valve gasket.

51   Clean the mounting surface of the EGR valve. Remove all traces of gasket material from the intake manifold and from the valve if it is to be reinstalled. Clean both mating surface with a cloth dipped in lacquer thinner or acetone.

52   Install a new gasket and the EGR valve and tighten the bolts securely.

53   Connect the electrical connector onto the EGR valve.

8   Evaporative Emissions Control System (EECS)

Refer to illustration 8.2

General description

1   This system is designed to trap and store fuel vapors that evaporate from the fuel tank, throttle body and intake manifold.

2   The Evaporative Emission Control System (EECS) consists of a charcoal-filled canister and the lines connecting the canister to the fuel tank, ported vacuum and on some models, intake manifold vacuum (see illustration).

3   Fuel vapors are transferred from the fuel

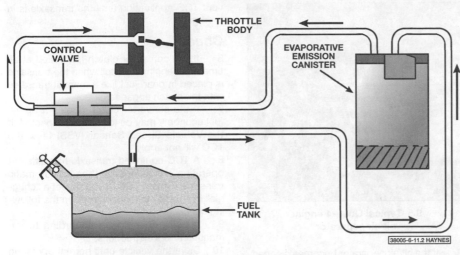

8.2 Details of a typical EECS system

8.16 Unplug the canister solenoid electrical connectors (arrows) to remove either the solenoid or the canister

tank, throttle body and intake manifold to a canister where they are stored when the engine is not operating. When the engine is running, the fuel vapors are purged from the canister by intake air flow and consumed in the normal combustion process.

4 On some models with MPFI, the ECM operates a solenoid valve (located on top of the canister) which controls vacuum to the purge valve in the charcoal canister. Under cold engine or idle conditions, the solenoid is turned on by the ECM, which closes the valve and blocks vacuum to the canister purge valve. The ECM turns off the solenoid valve and allows purge when the engine is warm.

Check

5 Poor idle, stalling and poor driveability can be caused by an inoperative purge valve, a damaged canister, split or cracked hoses or hoses connected to the wrong tubes.
6 Evidence of fuel loss or fuel odor can be caused by liquid fuel leaking from fuel lines or the TBI, a cracked or damaged canister, an inoperative purge valve, disconnected, mis-routed, kinked, deteriorated or damaged vapor or control hoses or an improperly seated air cleaner or air cleaner gasket.
7 Inspect each hose attached to the canister for kinks, leaks and breaks along its entire length. Repair or replace as necessary.
8 Inspect the canister. If it is cracked or damaged, replace it.
9 Look for fuel leaking from the bottom of the canister. If fuel is leaking, replace the canister and check the hoses and hose routing.
10 Check the filer at the bottom of the canister. If it is dirty, plugged or damaged, replace the filter.
11 Apply a short length of hose to the lower tube of the purge valve assembly and attempt to blow through it. Little or no air should pass into the canister (a small amount of air will pass because the canister has a constant purge hole).
12 With a hand vacuum pump, apply vac-

uum through the control vacuum signal tube to the purge valve diaphragm.
13 If the diaphragm does not hold vacuum for at least 20 seconds, the diaphragm is leaking and the canister must be replaced.
14 If the diaphragm holds vacuum, again try to blow through the hose while vacuum is still being applied. An increased flow of air should be noted. If it isn't, replace the canister.

Component replacement

Refer to illustrations 8.16, 8.18, 8.22, 8.23 and 8.24

Fuel vapor canister solenoid (if equipped)

15 Detach the cable from the negative terminal of the battery.
16 Unplug the solenoid electrical connectors (see illustration).
17 Clearly label, then detach, the vacuum hoses from the solenoid.
18 Remove the solenoid from the canister (see illustration).
19 Installation is the reverse of removal.

Fuel vapor canister/filter (some models)

20 Detach the electrical connector and vacuum lines from the solenoid, if equipped.
21 Clearly label, then detach, any remaining vacuum lines from the canister.
22 Remove the A/C accumulator bracket bolt and the canister bracket bolt (see illustration).
23 Move the accumulator out of the way and remove the canister by pulling it straight up (see illustration).

8.18 To remove the solenoid from the canister, pry the two locking tangs apart with a small screwdriver and lift up on the solenoid

6

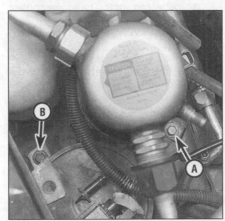

8.22 To remove the canister, remove the accumulator bracket bolt (A) and the canister bracket bolt (B) . . .

8.23 . . . then push the accumulator aside and lift the canister out

8.24　To replace the evaporative canister filter, simply remove it and install another one

24　Check the filter and replace it if it is dirty **(see illustration)** (not applicable to the 2.0L Turbo canister, which has no externally accessible filter on the bottom).
25　Installation is the reverse of removal.

9　Positive Crankcase Ventilation (PCV) system

1　The Positive Crankcase Ventilation (PCV) system reduces hydrocarbon emissions by scavenging crankcase vapors. It does this by circulating fresh air from the air cleaner through the crankcase, where it mixes with blow-by gasses and is then rerouted through a PCV valve to the intake manifold.
2　The main components of the PCV system are the PCV valve, a fresh air filtered inlet and the vacuum hoses connecting these two components with the engine and the EECS system.
3　To maintain idle quality, the PCV valve restricts the flow when the intake manifold vacuum is high. If abnormal operating conditions arise, the system is designed to allow excessive amounts of blow-by gasses to flow back through the crankcase vent tube into the air cleaner to be consumed by normal combustion.
4　Checking and replacement of the PCV valve and filter is covered in Chapter 1.

2.3L Quad-4 engine
General information
Refer to illustration 9.5
5　Instead of a ventilating the crankcase the conventional way, using a PCV valve, the Quad-4 engine uses an oil/air separator crankcase breather arrangement. Blow-by gases are continuously drawn through a crankcase ventilation oil/air separator and into the intake manifold. The oil/air separator causes oil droplets, which may be suspended in the blow-by gases, to be separated from the gases and allows them to drain back into the crankcase through a hose **(see illustration)**.

9.5　Typical Quad-4 engine oil/air separator

6　If the oil/air separator becomes clogged, it must be replaced as a unit.

Oil/air separator - removal and installation
7　Label and remove all hoses from the oil/air separator.
8　Remove the mounting bolts and detach it from the engine.
9　Installation is the reverse of removal.

10　Transaxle Converter Clutch (TCC)

General description
1　The Transaxle Converter Clutch (TCC) uses a solenoid-operated valve in the automatic transaxle to mechanically couple the engine flywheel to the output shaft of the transaxle through the torque converter. This reduces the slippage losses in the converter, reducing emissions because engine rpm at any given speed is reduced. It also increases fuel economy.
2　For the converter clutch to operate properly, two conditions must be met:
　a)　*The engine must be warmed up before the clutch can apply. The engine coolant temperature sensor (see Section 4) tells the ECM when the engine is at operating temperature.*
　b)　*The vehicle must be traveling at the necessary minimum speed to raise the pressure to the level necessary to apply the valve. If the hydraulic pressure is correct, the ECM signals the solenoid to apply the converter clutch.*
3　After the converter clutch applies, the ECM uses the information from the TPS to release the clutch when the car is accelerating or decelerating at a certain rate.
4　Another switch used in the TCC circuits is a brake switch, which opens the power supply to the TCC solenoid when the brake is applied.
5　A third gear switch is placed in series on the battery side of the TCC solenoid to pre-

vent TCC application until the transaxle is in third gear.

Check
6　If the converter clutch is applied at all times, the engine will stall when the transaxle is placed in gear, just like a manual transaxle with the clutch engaged.
7　If the converter clutch does not apply, fuel economy may be lower than expected. If the Vehicle Speed Sensor (VSS) fails, the TCC will not apply.
8　A TCC-equipped transaxle has different operating characteristics than an automatic transaxle without TCC. If you detect a "chuggle" or "surge" condition, perform the following check.
9　Install a tachometer according to the manufacturers instructions.
10　Drive the vehicle until normal operating temperature is reached, then maintain a 50 to 55 mph speed.
11　Lightly touch the brake pedal and check it for a slight bumpy sensation, indicating that the TCC is releasing. A slight increase in rpm should be also noted.
12　Release the brake and check for reapplication of the converter clutch and a slight decrease in engine rpm.
13　If the TCC fails to perform satisfactorily during this test, take your vehicle to a dealer to have the TCC serviced.

11　Catalytic converter

General description
1　The catalytic converter is an emission control device added to the exhaust system to reduce pollutants from the exhaust gas stream. There are two types of converters used. One converter contains pellets coated with the three way catalysts while the monolithic converter contains a honeycomb mesh which is also coated with three catalysts. The coating on the three way catalyst contains platinum and rhodium, which lowers the levels of oxides of nitrogen (NOx) as well as hydrocarbons (HC) and carbon monoxide (CO) emissions.

Check
2　The test equipment for a catalytic converter is expensive and highly sophisticated. If you suspect the converter is malfunctioning, take it to a dealer service department or authorized emissions inspection facility for diagnosis and repair.
3　Whenever the vehicle is raised for service of underbody components, check the converter for leaks, corrosion and other damage. If damage is discovered, the converter should be replaced.
4　Because the converter is welded to the exhaust system, converter replacement requires removal of the exhaust pipe assembly (see Chapter 4). Take the vehicle, or the exhaust system, to a dealer service department or a muffler shop.

Chapter 7 Part A
Manual transaxle

Contents

Specifications

Torque specifications
	Ft-lbs
Shift lever nut (Muncie transaxle)	61
Transaxle-to-engine bolts..	55

1   General information

The vehicles covered by this manual are equipped with either a 5-speed manual or a 3-speed automatic transaxle. Information on the manual transaxle is included in this Part of Chapter 7. Information on the automatic transaxle can be found in Part B of this Chapter.

The 5-speed manual transaxle used in these vehicles is essentially a transmission and a differential integrated into a single assembly. Transaxles are supplied by two different manufacturers - Isuzu and Muncie - but they're very similar in design.

Because of their complexity, the special tools needed to service them, and the difficulty in obtaining replacement parts, internal repair is not recommended for the home mechanic. The information contained within this manual will be limited to general diagno-sis, external adjustments, and removal and installation.

Depending on the expense involved in having a faulty transaxle overhauled, it may be more cost effective to replace it with either a new or rebuilt unit. Your local dealer or transmission shop should be able to supply you with information concerning cost, avail-ability and exchange policy. Regardless of how you decide to remedy a faulty transaxle problem, however, you can still save consid-erable expense by removing and installing the unit yourself.

2   Shift cables (Muncie transaxle) - removal and installation

Warning: *Some models covered by this man-ual are equipped with airbags. Always turn the steering wheel to the straight ahead posi-tion, place the ignition switch in the Lock position disable the airbag system before working in the vicinity of the impact sensors, steering column or instrument panel to avoid the possibility of accidental deployment of the airbag(s), which could cause personal injury (see Chapter 12 for the airbag disarm-ing procedure). Do not use electrical test equipment on any of the airbag system wiring or tamper with them in any way.*

Removal
Refer to illustration 2.2
Caution: *If the vehicle is equipped with a Delco Loc II audio system, make sure you have the correct activation code before dis-connecting the battery. See the information at the front of this manual for the radio re-activa-tion procedure.*
1   Disconnect the negative cable at the battery. Place the cable out of the way so it cannot accidentally come in contact with the negative terminal of the battery, as this would

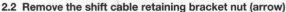

2.2 Remove the shift cable retaining bracket nut (arrow)   **3.3 Remove the shift lever nut (arrow)**

once again allow power into the electrical system of the vehicle.

2   Remove the nuts retaining the selector and shift cables to the transaxle levers **(see illustration)**.

3   Remove the console (see Chapter 11).

4   Use a small screwdriver to pry the cable free of the shift control ball sockets.

5   Remove the screws from the carpeting sill plate in the left front corner of the passenger compartment, remove the plate and then pull the carpet back for access to the cables.

6   Remove the cable retainer and grommet screws at the floor pan and pry up the two retaining tabs.

7   Pull the cables through into the passenger compartment and remove them from the vehicle.

Installation

8   Push the cable assembly through the opening from the passenger compartment into the engine compartment.

9   Install the grommet and cable retainer screws and bend down the two retaining tabs.

10   Install the carpet and sill plate.

11   Connect the cable ends to the shifter.

12   Install the console.

13   Connect the cable assembly to the transaxle bracket and shift levers.

---

3   Shift shaft seal (Muncie transaxle) - removal and installation

Refer to illustration 3.3

Caution: *If the vehicle is equipped with a Delco Loc II audio system, make sure you have the correct activation code before disconnecting the battery. See the information at the front of this manual for the radio re-activation procedure.*

Note: *The term "shift lever" as used in this Section, refers to the shift lever on the transaxle, not the one inside the vehicle.*

1   Disconnect the negative cable at the battery. Place the cable out of the way so it

cannot accidentally come in contact with the negative terminal of the battery, as this would once again allow power into the electrical system of the vehicle.

2   Disconnect the shift cables from the shift lever.

3   Remove the shift lever nut, making sure the shift lever itself does not move while the nut is loosened **(see illustration)**.

4   Remove the shift lever assembly, keeping all of the components in order.

5   Pry out the old seal with a screwdriver or suitably hooked tool.

6   Install the new seal evenly into the bore and tap it fully into place, using a suitable size socket and hammer.

7   Installation of the remaining components is the reverse of removal. Be sure to tighten the shift lever nut to the torque listed in this Chapter's Specifications.

---

4   Shift cables (Isuzu transaxle) - removal, installation and adjustment

Warning: *Some models covered by this manual are equipped with airbags. Always turn the steering wheel to the straight ahead position, place the ignition switch in the Lock position disable the airbag system before working in the vicinity of the impact sensors, steering column or instrument panel to avoid the possibility of accidental deployment of the airbag(s), which could cause personal injury (see Chapter 12 for the airbag disarming procedure). Do not use electrical test equipment on any of the airbag system wiring or tamper with them in any way.*

Removal

Caution: *If the vehicle is equipped with a Delco Loc II audio system, make sure you have the correct activation code before disconnecting the battery. See the information at the front of this manual for the radio re-activation procedure.*

1   Disconnect the negative cable at the battery. Place the cable out of the way so it

cannot accidentally come in contact with the negative terminal of the battery, as this would once again allow power into the electrical system of the vehicle.

2   In the engine compartment, remove the clamps and nuts retaining the cables to the shift lever at the transaxle.

3   In the passenger compartment, remove the shift knob, console and boot (see Chapter 11).

4   Disconnect the shift cables from the shifter by prying the cable ends loose from the shifter ballstuds with a screwdriver.

5   Remove the spring clips retaining the cables to the shifter.

6   Remove the right front floor carpet sill and carpet for access to the shift cables.

7   Remove the cable grommet screws, lift off the cover, pull the cable assembly through and remove it from the vehicle.

Installation

8   Insert the cable assembly through the floor and install the cable grommet cover.

9   Connect the shift cables to the shifter by placing them in position and popping them onto the ballstuds.

10   Install the cable retainer spring clips.

11   Install the carpet and sill cover.

12   Install the console, shift knob and boot, unless the cables are to be adjusted.

13   In the engine compartment, connect the cables to the shift lever.

Adjustment

14   If adjustment is necessary, shift the transaxle into 3rd gear and lock it in 3rd by removing the locking pin (H) and installing it upside down.

15   Loosen the shift cable nuts at the shift levers.

16   Install a 5/32-inch (No. 22) drill bit into the upper shifter alignment hole).

17   Line up the hole in the selector lever with the slot in the shifter plate and insert a 3/16-inch drill bit.

18   Tighten the shift lever nuts at the shift levers.

19   Remove the drill bits and install the lock-

6.5 Transaxle removal and installation will be much easier if the special engine support fixture is used

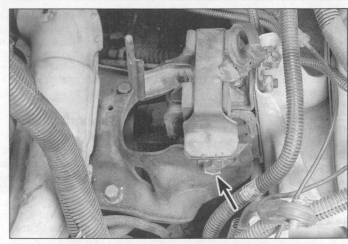

6.9 Remove the transaxle-to-frame mounting bolt

ing pin in the proper direction.
20   Install the console, shift knob and boot.
21   Connect the negative battery cable and test drive the vehicle. Make sure there is sufficient neutral gate feel. It may be necessary to repeat the adjustment procedure to obtain the proper neutral gate and shifting action.

5   Shift lever (all models) - removal and installation

Warning: *Some models covered by this manual are equipped with airbags. Always turn the steering wheel to the straight ahead position, place the ignition switch in the Lock position disable the airbag system before working in the vicinity of the impact sensors, steering column or instrument panel to avoid the possibility of accidental deployment of the airbag(s), which could cause personal injury (see Chapter 12 for the airbag disarming procedure). Do not use electrical test equipment on any of the airbag system wiring or tamper with them in any way.*

Removal

Caution: *If the vehicle is equipped with a Delco Loc II audio system, make sure you have the correct activation code before disconnecting the battery. See the information at the front of this manual for the radio re-activation procedure.*
1   Disconnect the negative cable at the battery. Place the cable out of the way so it cannot accidentally come in contact with the negative terminal of the battery, as this would once again allow power into the electrical system of the vehicle.
2   Remove the console, shift boot and knob (see Chapter 11).
3   Disconnect the shift cables from the shifter.
4   Remove the shift cable retaining clips.
5   Remove the retaining nuts and lift the shift lever assembly from the vehicle.

Installation

6   Place the shift control assembly in position and install the retaining nuts.
7   Connect the shift cables to the shift control assembly.
8   Install the console.
9   Connect the negative battery cable.

6   Manual transaxle - removal and installation

Removal

Refer to illustrations 6.5, 6.9 and 6.10
Caution: *If the vehicle is equipped with a Delco Loc II audio system, make sure you have the correct activation code before disconnecting the battery. See the information at the front of this manual for the radio re-activation procedure.*
1   Disconnect the negative cable at the battery. Place the cable out of the way so that it cannot accidentally come into contact with the terminal, which would again allow current flow.
2   Inside the passenger compartment, remove the left hush panel.

3   Disconnect the clutch release system (see Chapter 8).
4   Disconnect the ground cable, shift cables and clamp from the transaxle.
5   The engine must be supported during transaxle removal and this can be accomplished using an engine support tool **(see illustration)**. Install a 1/4-inch by 2-inch bolt in the hole in the right front engine mount to maintain driveline alignment if the support tool is used. If this tool is not available, support the engine with a lifting device that will allow the transaxle to be lowered from the engine compartment with the vehicle raised.
6   Install the engine support or connect a lifting device and raise the engine sufficiently to take the weight off the engine mounts. Raise the vehicle as necessary to allow the transaxle to be removed. Support it securely on jackstands and remove the front wheels.
7   Remove the left front brake caliper, hang it out of the way on a piece of wire and remove the disc (see Chapter 9).
8   Drain the transaxle fluid (see Chapter 1).
9   Remove the transaxle mount-to-frame bolts **(see illustration)**.
10   Remove the front transaxle engine strut and bracket **(see illustration)**.
11   Remove the clutch housing cover bolts.

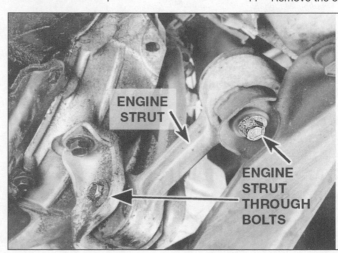

ENGINE STRUT

ENGINE STRUT THROUGH BOLTS

6.10 Typical transaxle/engine strut layout

12   Disconnect the speedometer cable or sensor at the transaxle.

13   Disconnect the stabilizer bar at the control arm and suspension support.

14   Disconnect the balljoint and remove the left suspension support with the lower suspension arm (see Chapter 10).

15   Remove the left front fender liner (see Chapter 11).

16   Disconnect the right driveaxle from the transaxle and remove the left driveaxle (see Chapter 10).

17   Support the transaxle with a jack, preferably a transmission jack made for this purpose.

18   Remove the bellhousing-to-engine bolts.

19   Make a final check that all wiring, cables, etc. are disconnected from the transaxle.

20   Separate the transaxle from the engine by prying the bellhousing away from the engine.

21   Lower the transaxle and remove it from the left side of the engine compartment.

22   The clutch components can now be inspected (see Chapter 8). In most cases, new clutch components should be installed as a matter of course if the transaxle is removed.

Installation

23   With the clutch components installed and properly aligned (see Chapter 8), carefully raise the transaxle into place. Guide the right side driveaxle into the transaxle and slide the input shaft into place in the clutch splines.

24   Install the transaxle-to-engine bolts. Tighten the bolts to the torque listed in this Chapter's Specifications.

25   Install the left driveaxle.

26   Install the suspension support (see Chapter 10).

27   Connect the speedometer cable or sensor.

28   Install the clutch housing cover. Tighten the bolts securely.

29   Install the front strut bracket and the strut. Tighten the bolts securely.

30   Install the transaxle mount bolts. Tighten the bolts securely.

31   Install the front fender liner (see Chapter 11).

32   Install the brake caliper (see Chapter 9).

33   Install the wheels and lower the vehicle.

34   Connect the ground cable.

35   Connect the clutch linkage. On hydraulic clutch equipped models, install the clutch release system (see Chapter 8).

36   Connect the shift linkage.

37   Remove the engine support.

38   Fill the transaxle with the specified lubricant (see Chapter 1).

39   Connect the battery negative cable.

Chapter 7 Part B
Automatic transaxle

Contents

Specifications

Torque specifications

Ft-lbs (unless otherwise indicated)

Shift lever nuts	17
Transaxle-to-engine bolts	55
Torque converter-to-driveplate bolts	35
TV cable-to-transaxle case bolt	84 in-lbs

1   General information

Refer to illustration 1.1

Because of the complexity of the clutches and the hydraulic control system, and because of the special tools and expertise needed, automatic transaxle overhaul should be left to a professional transmission mechanic. The procedures in this Chapter are limited to general diagnosis, routine maintenance, adjustment, and transaxle removal and installation **(see illustration)**.

If the transaxle requires major repair work, it should be left to a dealer service department or an automotive or transmission repair shop. You can, however, remove and install the transaxle yourself and save the expense, even if the repair work is done by a transmission specialist.

Replacement and adjustment procedures that the home mechanic can perform include those involving the throttle valve (TV) cable and the shift linkage. **Caution:** *Never tow a disabled vehicle with an automatic transaxle at speeds greater than 35 mph or distances over 50 miles.*

Component location

1.1 Underside view of a typical automatic transaxle

1	Transaxle fluid pan	3	Driveplate	5	Left driveaxle
2	Right driveaxle	4	Transaxle/engine strut		

2   Diagnosis - general

Note: *Automatic transaxle malfunctions may be caused by five general conditions: poor engine performance, improper adjustments, hydraulic malfunctions, mechanical malfunctions or malfunctions in the computer or its signal network. Diagnosis of these problems should always begin with a check of the easily repaired items: fluid level and condition (see Chapter 1), shift linkage adjustment and throttle linkage adjustment. Next, perform a road test to determine if the problem has been corrected or if more diagnosis is necessary. If the problem persists after the preliminary tests and corrections are completed, additional diagnosis should be done by a dealer service department or transmission repair shop. Refer to the Troubleshooting section at the front of this manual for information on symptoms of transaxle problems.*

Preliminary checks

1   Drive the vehicle to warm the transaxle to normal operating temperature.
2   Check the fluid level as described in Chapter 1:

a) *If the fluid level is unusually low, add enough fluid to bring the level within the designated area of the dipstick, then check for external leaks (see below).*
b) *If the fluid level is abnormally high, drain off the excess, then check the drained fluid for contamination by coolant. The presence of engine coolant in the automatic transmission fluid indicates that a failure has occurred in the internal radiator walls that separate the coolant from the transmission fluid (see Chapter 3).*
c) *If the fluid is foaming, drain it and refill the transaxle, then check for coolant in the fluid, or a high fluid level.*

3   Check the engine idle speed. **Note:** *If*

the engine is malfunctioning, do not proceed with the preliminary checks until it has been repaired and runs normally.

4   Check the throttle valve cable for freedom of movement. Adjust it if necessary (see Section 3). **Note:** *The throttle valve cable may function properly when the engine is shut off and cold, but it may malfunction once the engine is hot. Check it cold and at normal engine operating temperature.*

5   Inspect the shift control linkage (see Section 3). Make sure that it's properly adjusted and that the linkage operates smoothly.

Fluid leak diagnosis

6   Most fluid leaks are easy to locate visually. Repair usually consists of replacing a seal or gasket. If a leak is difficult to find, the following procedure may help.

7   Identify the fluid. Make sure it's transmission fluid and not engine oil or brake fluid

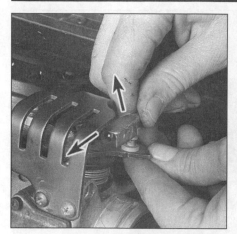

3.2 Move the TV cable connector forward and then lift up to detach it from the throttle lever pin (arrows)

3.3 Use a screwdriver to compress the TV cable tangs (arrows) and then push the housing back through the bracket (arrow)

3.5 Remove the TV cable bolt (arrow) and pull up on the cable until it's out of the transaxle

3.6 Hold the transaxle TV link with needle nose pliers and slide the cable link off the pin

(automatic transmission fluid is a deep red color).

8   Try to pinpoint the source of the leak. Drive the vehicle several miles, then park it over a large sheet of cardboard. After a minute or two, you should be able to locate the leak by determining the source of the fluid dripping onto the cardboard.

9   Make a careful visual inspection of the suspected component and the area immediately around it. Pay particular attention to gasket mating surfaces. A mirror is often helpful for finding leaks in areas that are hard to see.

10   If the leak still cannot be found, clean the suspected area thoroughly with a degreaser or solvent, then dry it.

11   Drive the vehicle for several miles at normal operating temperature and varying speeds. After driving the vehicle, visually inspect the suspected component again.

12   Once the leak has been located, the cause must be determined before it can be properly repaired. If a gasket is replaced but the sealing flange is bent, the new gasket will not stop the leak. The bent flange must be straightened.

13   Before attempting to repair a leak, check to make sure that the following conditions are corrected or they may cause another leak. **Note:** *Some of the following conditions cannot be fixed without highly specialized tools and expertise. Such problems must be referred to a transmission shop or a dealer service department.*

Gasket leaks

14   Check the pan periodically. Make sure the bolts are tight, no bolts are missing, the gasket is in good condition and the pan is flat (dents in the pan may indicate damage to the valve body inside).

15   If the pan gasket is leaking, the fluid level or the fluid pressure may be too high, the vent may be plugged, the pan bolts may be too tight, the pan sealing flange may be warped, the sealing surface of the transaxle

housing may be damaged, the gasket may be damaged or the transaxle casting may be cracked or porous. If sealant instead of gasket material has been used to form a seal between the pan and the transaxle housing, it may be the wrong sealant.

Seal leaks

16   If a transaxle seal is leaking, the fluid level or pressure may be too high, the vent may be plugged, the seal bore may be damaged, the seal itself may be damaged or improperly installed, the surface of the shaft protruding through the seal may be damaged or a loose bearing may be causing excessive shaft movement.

17   Make sure the dipstick tube seal is in good condition and the tube is properly seated. Periodically check the area around the speedometer gear or sensor for leakage. If transmission fluid is evident, check the O-ring for damage.

Case leaks

18   If the case itself appears to be leaking, the casting is porous and will have to be repaired or replaced.

19   Make sure the oil cooler hose fittings are tight and in good condition.

Fluid comes out vent pipe or fill tube

20   If this condition occurs, the transaxle is overfilled, there is coolant in the fluid, the case is porous, the dipstick is incorrect, the vent is plugged or the drain-back holes are plugged.

3   Throttle valve (TV) cable - replacement and adjustment

Refer to illustrations 3.2, 3.3, 3.5, 3.6, 3.9a and 3.9b

Replacement

1   Remove the air cleaner assembly.

2   Disconnect the TV cable from the throttle lever by grasping the connector, pulling it forward to disconnect it and then lifting up and off the lever pin **(see illustration)**.

3   Disconnect the TV cable housing from the bracket by compressing the tangs and pushing the housing back through the bracket **(see illustration)**.

4   Disconnect any clips or straps retaining the cable to the transaxle.

5   Remove the bolt retaining the cable to the transaxle **(see illustration)**.

6   Pull up on the cover until the end of the cable can be seen and then disconnect it from the transaxle TV link **(see illustration)**. Remove the cable from the vehicle.

7   To install, connect the cable to the transaxle TV link and install the bolt. Tighten the bolt to the torque listed in this Chapter's Specifications and push the cover securely over the cable. Route the cable to the top of the engine, push the housing through the bracket until it clicks into place, place the connector over the throttle lever pin and pull back to lock it. Secure the cable with any retaining clips or straps.

7B

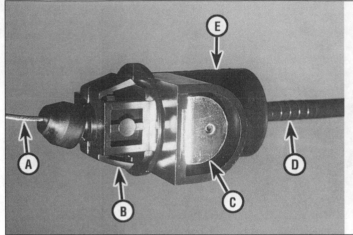

3.9b TV cable adjuster details

A   TV cable
B   Locking lugs
C   Release tab
D   Cable casing
E   Slider

3.9a Press down on the TV cable re-adjust tab and then move the adjuster back against the fitting (arrows)

Adjustment

8 The engine should not be running during this adjustment.
9 Depress the adjuster tab and move the slider until it stops against the fitting **(see illustrations)**.
10 Release the adjuster tab.
11 Manually turn the throttle lever to the "wide open throttle" position, which will automatically adjust the cable. Release the throttle lever. **Note:** *Do not use excessive force at the throttle lever to adjust the TV cable. If great effort is required to adjust the cable, disconnect the cable at the transaxle end and check for free operation. If it is still difficult, replace the cable. If it is now free, suspect a bent TV link in the transaxle or a problem with the throttle lever.*

4   Neutral safety switch - check, adjustment and replacement

Check

1 Verify that the engine starts in the Park and Neutral positions.

2 Verify that the back-up lights come on when the shift lever is in the Reverse position.
3 If the neutral safety switch isn't operating correctly, adjust it (see below). If the switch still fails to operate correctly after adjustment, replace it.

Replacement

Refer to illustrations 4.7 and 4.8
Caution: *If the vehicle is equipped with a Delco Loc II audio system, make sure you have the correct activation code before disconnecting the battery. See the information at the front of this manual for the radio re-activation procedure.*
4 Disconnect the negative cable at the battery. Place the cable out of the way so it cannot accidentally come in contact with the negative terminal of the battery, as this would once again allow power into the electrical system of the vehicle.
5 Shift the transaxle into Neutral.
6 Disconnect the shift linkage.
7 Lift the T-latch out of the connector and then unplug the connector **(see illustration)**. It may be necessary to remove the heat shield covering the switch for access.
8 Remove the attaching bolts and lift the

switch off the shift shaft **(see illustration)**.
9 To install, line up the flats on the shift shaft with the flats in the switch and lower the switch onto the shaft.
10 Install the bolts. If the switch is new and the shaft has not been moved, tighten the bolts. If the switch requires adjustment, leave the bolts loose and follow the adjustment procedure below. The remainder of replacement is the reverse of removal.

Adjustment

11 Insert a 3/32 inch drill bit into the switch gauge hole.
12 Rotate the switch until the drill bit can be felt dropping into the switch, indicating that it is now in the Neutral position. Tighten the switch bolts.
13 Connect the battery negative cable and verify that the engine will start only in Neutral or Park.

5   Shift cable - replacement and adjustment

Refer to illustrations 5.2a, 5.2b and 5.6
Warning: *Some models covered by this man-*

4.7 Typical neutral safety switch details

1   Switch retaining bolts   3   Transaxle shift lever shaft
2   T-latch

4.8 Remove the neutral start switch bolts (arrows)

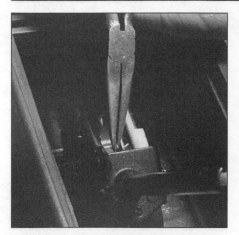

5.2a To disconnect the cable at the shift control, pull off the clip with needle nose pliers . . .

5.2b . . . and pry the cable off the lever pin with a screwdriver

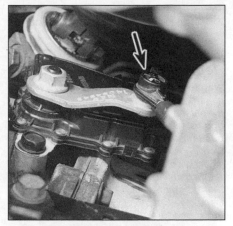

5.6 Pry the cable end (arrow) until it releases from the stud on the transaxle lever

ual are equipped with airbags. Always turn the steering wheel to the straight ahead position, place the ignition switch in the Lock position disable the airbag system before working in the vicinity of the impact sensors, steering column or instrument panel to avoid the possibility of accidental deployment of the airbag(s), which could cause personal injury (see Chapter 12 for the airbag disarming procedure). Do not use electrical test equipment on any of the airbag system wiring or tamper with them in any way.

Caution: *If the vehicle is equipped with a Delco Loc II audio system, make sure you have the correct activation code before disconnecting the battery. See the information at the front of this manual for the radio re-activation procedure.*

1   Disconnect the negative cable at the battery. Place the cable out of the way so that it cannot accidentally come into contact with the terminal, which would once again allow current flow.

Removal

Console shift

2   Remove the console (see Chapter 11) and disconnect the shift cable at the transaxle lever and the shift control lever **(see illustrations)**.
3   Remove the right and left side sound insulators from the under dash portion of the console and then pull back the carpet for access to the cable.
4   Disengage the grommet in the firewall and withdraw the cable assembly.
5   Installation is the reverse of removal. After installation, adjust the cable as described below.

Column shift

6   In the engine compartment, disconnect the cable from the transaxle lever and bracket **(see illustration)**.
7   In the passenger compartment, remove the left sound insulator located under the dash.
8   Disconnect the cable bracket on the

steering column and separate the cable from the shift lever.
9   Dislodge the grommet in the firewall and withdraw the cable from the vehicle.
10   Installation is the reverse of removal. After installation, adjust the cable as described below.

Adjustment

11   Place the shift control lever and the transaxle shift lever in Neutral, then push the locking tab on the shift cable to automatically adjust the cable.
12   Connect the negative battery cable.

---

6   Shift lever - removal and installation

Refer to illustration 6.4
Warning: *Some models covered by this manual are equipped with airbags. Always turn the steering wheel to the straight ahead position, place the ignition switch in the Lock position disable the airbag system before working in the vicinity of the impact sensors, steering column or instrument panel to avoid the possibility of accidental deployment of*

the airbag(s), which could cause personal injury (see Chapter 12 for the airbag disarming procedure). Do not use electrical test equipment on any of the airbag system wiring or tamper with them in any way.

Caution: *If the vehicle is equipped with a Delco Loc II audio system, make sure you have the correct activation code before disconnecting the battery. See the information at the front of this manual for the radio re-activation procedure.*

1   Disconnect the negative cable at the battery. Place the cable out of the way so it cannot accidentally come in contact with the negative terminal of the battery, as this would once again allow power into the electrical system of the vehicle.
2   Remove the console (see Chapter 11).
3   Disconnect the shift cable from the shift lever (see Section 5).
4   Remove the retaining nuts and lift the shift lever from the vehicle **(see illustration)**.
5   Place the shift lever in position on the mounting studs and install the nuts. Tighten the nuts to the torque listed in this Chapter's Specifications.
6   Connect the shift cables.
7   Install the console.
8   Connect the battery negative cable.

6.4 Shift lever assembly mounting nuts (arrows)

7B

7   Park/lock cable - removal and installation

Removal

Warning: *Some models covered by this manual are equipped with airbags. Always turn the steering wheel to the straight ahead position, place the ignition switch in the Lock position disable the airbag system before working in the vicinity of the impact sensors, steering column or instrument panel to avoid the possibility of accidental deployment of the airbag(s), which could cause personal injury (see Chapter 12 for the airbag disarming procedure). Do not use electrical test equipment on any of the airbag system wiring or tamper with them in any way.*

Caution: *If the vehicle is equipped with a Delco Loc II audio system, make sure you have the correct activation code before disconnecting the battery. See the information at the front of this manual for the radio re-activation procedure.*

1   Disconnect the negative cable at the battery. Place the cable out of the way so it cannot accidentally come in contact with the negative terminal of the battery, as this would once again allow power into the electrical system of the vehicle.

2   Remove the console (see Chapter 11).

3   Place the transaxle shift lever in Park and the ignition key switch in the Run position.

4   Insert a screwdriver blade into the slot in the ignition switch inhibitor, depress the cable latch and detach the cable.

5   Push the cable connector lock button located at the shift control base to the up position and detach the cable from the park lock lever pin. Depress the two cable connector latches and remove the cable from the shift control base.

6   Remove the cable clips.

Installation

7   Make sure the cable lock button is in the up position and the shift lever is in Park. Snap the cable connector into the shift control base.

8   With the ignition key in the Run position (this is very important), snap the cable into the inhibitor housing.

9   Turn the ignition key to the Lock position.

10   Snap the end of the cable onto the shifter park/lock pin.

11   Push the nose of the cable connector forward to remove the slack.

12   With no load on the connector nose, snap the cable connector lock button onto the nose.

13   Check the operation of the park/lock cable as follows:

a) *With the shift lever in Park and the key in Lock, make sure the shift lever cannot be moved to another position and the key can be removed.*

8.3 The rubber-type differential seal (arrow) can be pried out of the housing with a screwdriver. Be careful not to damage the splines of the axleshaft (transaxle removed for clarity)

b) *With the key in Run and the shift lever in Neutral, make sure the key cannot be turned to Lock.*

14   If it operates as described above, the park/lock cable system is properly adjusted.

15   If the park/lock system does not operate as described, return the cable connector lock to the up position and repeat the adjustment procedure. Push the cable connector down and recheck the operation.

16   If the key cannot be removed in the Park position, snap the lock button to the up position and move the nose of the cable connector rearward until the key can be removed from the ignition switch.

17   Install the cable into the retaining clips.

8   Seal replacement

Refer to illustrations 8.3 and 8.4

Caution: *If the vehicle is equipped with a Delco Loc II audio system, make sure you have the correct activation code before disconnecting the battery. See the information at the front of this manual for the radio re-activation procedure.*

Differential side-gear seals

1   Raise the vehicle and support it securely on jackstands.

2   Remove the driveaxle(s) (see Chapter 8).

3   On the rubber-type seal, use a seal remover or a long screwdriver to pry it from the transaxle, taking care not to damage the splines on the output shaft **(see illustration)**.

4   On the metal-type seal, use a hammer and chisel to work around the outer circumference of the seal to dislodge it so it can be pried from the housing **(see illustration)**.

5   Compare the new seal with the old to make sure they are the same.

6   Coat the lips of the new seal with transmission fluid.

7   Place the new seal into position and tap

8.4 Dislodge the metal type differential seal by working around the outer circumference with a chisel and hammer (transaxle removed for clarity)

it into the bore using a large socket or a piece of pipe that is the same diameter as the seal.

8   Reinstall the various components in the reverse order of removal, referring to the necessary Chapters as needed.

Speedometer driven gear/speed sensor seal

9   The speedometer driven gear/speed sensor assembly is located on top of the transaxle.

10   If the vehicle has a mechanically driven speedometer, disconnect the speedometer cable from the driven-gear assembly; if it has an electric speedometer, unplug the electrical connector from the speed sensor housing.

11   Remove the driven-gear assembly (mechanical) or the speed sensor housing (electric).

12   Remove the O-ring from the driven-gear assembly or the speed sensor housing.

13   Coat the new O-ring with clean engine oil and install it.

14   The remainder of reassembly is otherwise the reverse of disassembly.

9   Automatic transaxle - removal and installation

Removal

Refer to illustrations 9.3, 9.5, 9.8a, 9.8b, 9.8c, 9.9, 9.13, 9.14, 9.15, 9.19, 9.23, 9.26a, 9.26b, 9.28, 9.30, 9.31a, 9.31b and 9.32

Warning: *Some models covered by this manual are equipped with airbags. Always turn the steering wheel to the straight ahead position, place the ignition switch in the Lock position disable the airbag system before working in the vicinity of the impact sensors, steering column or instrument panel to avoid the possibility of accidental deployment of the airbag(s), which could cause personal injury (see Chapter 12 for the airbag disarming procedure). Do not use electrical test*

9.3 On V6 models the heat shield must be removed for access to the transaxle lever (transaxle removed for clarity)

9.5 Pry the shift lever clip (arrow) off the pin with a screwdriver

assembly in place during transaxle removal.

8   The engine must be supported during transaxle removal and this can be accomplished using an engine support tool **(see illustrations)**. Insert a 2-inch long bolt of the appropriate diameter in the hole in the right front motor mount to maintain driveline alignment if the support tool is used. If the tool is not available, support the engine with a lifting device that can hold it high enough to allow the transaxle to be lowered from the engine compartment with the vehicle raised **(see illustration)**.

9   Install the engine support or connect a lifting device and raise the engine sufficiently to take the weight off the engine mounts. Raise the vehicle as necessary to remove the transaxle, support it securely on jackstands and remove the front wheels **(see illustration)**.

10   Drain the transaxle fluid (see Chapter 1).

11   Unplug the speed sensor and Torque Converter Clutch (TCC) connectors and disconnect the ground cable.

12   Unplug the starter safety switch by lifting the lock pin and pulling on the harness connector body. Do not remove the switch mounting bolts as this will require readjust-

equipment on any of the airbag system wiring or tamper with them in any way.

Caution: *If the vehicle is equipped with a Delco Loc II audio system, make sure you have the correct activation code before disconnecting the battery. See the information at the front of this manual for the radio re-activation procedure.*

1   Disconnect the negative cable at the battery. Place the cable out of the way so that it cannot accidentally come into contact with the terminal, which would again allow current flow.

2   Remove the hood (see Chapter 11).

3   On V6 engine equipped models, remove the air cleaner and mass air flow sensor assembly (see Chapter 4). Remove the exhaust crossover pipe followed by the heat shield covering the transaxle shift lever (four bolts, two of which are accessible from underneath) **(see illustration)**.

4   Remove the nut holding the wiring harness to the transaxle and move the harness out of the way.

5   Pry the shift cable from the shift lever, unbolt the cable bracket from the transaxle

complete with cables and move the assembly out of the way **(see illustration)**.

6   Disconnect the throttle valve (TV) cable at the throttle lever (see Section 3).

7   Remove the transaxle fluid dipstick tube-to-manifold bolt. Disengage the tube from the tab in the transaxle and leave the

9.8a The engine must be supported from above - the best way is with a special fixture like this one

9.8b If an engine support tool is not available, connect a chain to the lifting eyes and raise the weight off the engine mounts with a suitable lifting device

9.9 Measure the height of the transaxle, then raise the vehicle sufficiently to allow clearance for the transaxle to be removed from under the vehicle

7B

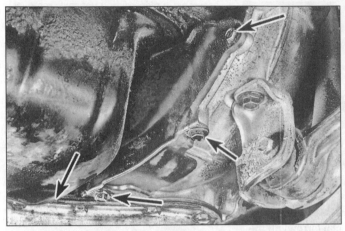

9.13 Torque converter shield mounting bolts (arrows)

9.14 Lock the driveplate starter ring gear teeth with a screwdriver
and remove the torque converter bolts

9.15 One of the upper transaxle bolts can only be reached
through the right side wheel well, using a long extension

9.19 Transaxle/engine strut through-bolts (arrows)

ment of the switch.

13   Remove the torque converter shield **(see illustration)**.

14   Mark the relationship of the torque converter and driveplate with paint or a scribe. Lock the driveplate using a screwdriver inserted in the starter gear teeth and remove the driveplate-to-torque converter bolts **(see illustration)**. Turn the engine over with a wrench on the crankshaft pulley bolt for

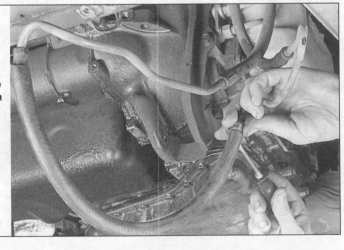

9.23 A simple way to plug the transaxle fluid tubes is to push a piece of rubber tubing on the open ends and secure it with hose clamps

access to each torque converter bolt in turn until they are all removed. Push the torque converter back toward the transaxle on the input shaft to make sure it will be removed along with the transaxle.

15   Remove the two upper transaxle-to-engine bolts. It will be necessary to work through the right wheel well to reach one of the bolts because it is only accessible from this side. A 30-inch long extension with a uni-

versal or wobble-type socket will be necessary to reach this bolt **(see illustration)**.

16   Disconnect the transaxle vent hose.

17   Remove the remaining upper transaxle-to-engine bolts.

18   Remove the left driveaxle and disconnect the right driveaxle from the transaxle (see Chapter 8).

19   Remove the transaxle/engine strut **(see illustration)**.

20   Remove the brake caliper, hang it out of the way on a piece of wire and remove the disc (see Chapter 9).

21   Remove the front suspension support together with lower suspension arm (see Chapter 10).

22   Remove the left front fender liner (see Chapter 11).

23   Disconnect the cooler lines at the radiator, push a piece of hose over the connections and secure at both ends with hose clamps so the fluid won't drain out **(see illustration)**.

24   Support the transaxle with a jack, preferably a transmission jack made for this purpose.

25   Remove the remaining transaxle-to-engine bolts.

26   Remove the transaxle mount through-

9.26a Use a wrench to hold the nut while removing the through-bolt with a ratchet and socket

9.26b Remove the transaxle mount bracket-to-bellhousing bolts. After unbolting it, the bracket can be left in place and removed with the transaxle

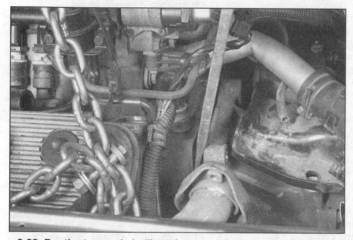

9.28 Pry the transaxle bellhousing away from the engine with a large screwdriver

9.30 Pull the hub/strut assembly back for clearance when removing the transaxle from under the vehicle

bolt, followed by the mount-to-transaxle bolts **(see illustrations)**. The mount bracket can now be pushed back allowing clearance for the transaxle to moved away from the engine sufficiently to allow removal.

27 Make a final check that all wiring, cables, etc. which could interfere with transaxle removal are disconnected or moved out of the way.

28 Separate the transaxle from the engine by prying the bellhousing away from the engine **(see illustration)**. As this is done make sure the torque converter is held back against the transaxle.

29 Disconnect the right driveaxle from the transaxle.

30 Lower the transaxle and remove it from the left side of the engine compartment **(see illustration)**.

31 Remove the driveplate and inspect it for missing weights, cracks, corrosion and dam-

9.31a Check the driveplate for loose weights (arrows) and cracks around the bolt holes (arrows)

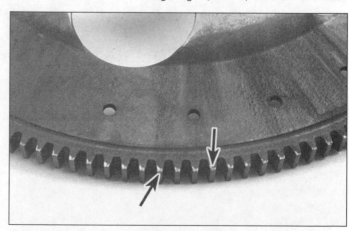

9.31b Inspect the driveplate for broken or worn starter gear teeth (arrows)

7B

9.32 With the driveplate removed, inspect the sealing joints around the crankshaft for leaks (arrows)

9.35 Lubricate the torque converter hub with grease

aged or broken starter gear teeth **(see illustrations)**.

32 Inspect the crankshaft seal area for damage and signs of oil leakage, indicating that the rear seal or oil pan gasket require replacement **(see illustration)**.

33 Inspect the hoses and cables that attach to the transaxle for damage, replacing as necessary.

Installation

Refer to illustration 9.35

34 Remove the rubber gasket from the dipstick tube and install it on the transaxle for ease of installation of the tube as the transaxle is raised into place.

35 Lubricate the torque converter hub with a light coat of chassis grease **(see illustration)**.

36 Move the transaxle under the vehicle and raise it into position.

37 With the help of two assistants, one to guide it into place and the other to move any cables or brackets that would interfere with installation out of the way, raise the transaxle into the engine compartment.

38 Raise the transaxle into position while an assistant guides the right driveaxle into place. Push the dipstick tube into place and install the retaining bolt. Install the mounting bracket, making sure the wiring harness passes under it.

39 Install the transaxle-to-engine bolts.

40 Install the transaxle mount and through-bolt.

41 Connect the transaxle cooler lines.

42 Move the torque converter to the marked position against the driveplate. Make sure the weld nuts on the converter are flush with the driveplate and the converter rotates freely. Install the bolts and tighten to the torque listed in this Chapter's Specifications.

Install the torque converter shield.

43 Install the transaxle mounting strut.

44 Install the left driveaxle, suspension support and the brake caliper.

45 Install the fender liner.

46 Connect the transaxle vent hose.

47 Plug in the starter safety switch, TCC switch and speed sensor connectors.

48 Remove the jack and engine support.

49 Install the shift cable bracket and connect the shift cable.

50 Install the wiring harness retaining nut.

51 Connect the TV cable.

52 Install the components that were removed. Refer to the appropriate Chapters where necessary for additional information.

53 Fill the transaxle with the specified fluid (see Chapter 1).

54 After all components are installed, adjust the shift control cable (see Section 5) and TV cable (see Section 3).

Chapter 8
Clutch and driveaxles

Contents

Specifications

Clutch

Fluid type	See Chapter 1
Disc runout	0.020 inch maximum
Slave cylinder pushrod travel	7/16-inch minimum

Driveaxles

CV joint boot dimension	
Tri-pot design	5-1/16 inches
Double-offset design	5-7/32 inches

Torque specifications

	Ft-lbs (unless otherwise indicated)
Clutch	
Release lever bolt	30 to 45
Pressure plate-to-flywheel bolts	
1985 through 1987	14 to 18
1988 through 1990	22
1991 on	
2.5L	22
2.3L	
Initial	15
Final	Tighten and additional 30-degrees
Master cylinder mounting nuts	15 to 25
Slave cylinder mounting nuts	14 to 20

Driveaxle/hub nut

1983 through 1992	
Initial	70
Final	185
1993 on	
Initial	103
Final	Tighten an additional 20-degrees

8

1   General information

The information in this Chapter deals with components from the flywheel to the drive wheels, except for the transaxle. Chapters 7A and 7B cover transaxle service. For the purposes of this Chapter, these components are grouped into two categories: clutch and driveaxles. Separate sections within this Chapter offer general descriptions and checking procedures for each of these groups.

Many of the procedures covered in this Chapter involve working under the vehicle. Make sure the vehicle is firmly supported on jackstands or a hoist where it can be easily raised and lowered.

2   Clutch - description and check

Refer to illustration 2.1

1   All vehicles with a manual transaxle use a single dry-plate, diaphragm-spring clutch **(see illustration)**. The clutch disc has a splined hub that allows it to slide along the splines of the transaxle input shaft. The clutch and pressure plate are held in contact by spring pressure exerted by the diaphragm in the pressure plate.

2   The clutch release system is operated by hydraulic pressure on some models, while on others a mechanical system is used.

3   The hydraulic release system consists of the clutch pedal, the master cylinder, the hydraulic line and the slave cylinder that actuates the clutch release (or throwout) bearing. The clutch slave on 1993 and later 2.3 liter DOHC (Quad-4) models is mounted inside the transaxle bellhousing, around the input shaft. The release bearing is pressed onto the actuating piston of the clutch slave cylinder.

4   The mechanical release system includes the pedal with adjuster mechanism, a clutch cable that actuates the clutch release lever and the release bearing.

5   When pressure is applied to the clutch pedal to release the clutch, hydraulic or mechanical pressure is exerted against the release bearing.

The bearing pushes against the fingers of the diaphragm spring of the pressure plate assembly, which in turn releases the clutch plate.

6   Other than to replace components with obvious damage, some preliminary checks should be performed to diagnose a clutch system failure.

a) *The first check should be of the fluid level in the clutch master cylinder. If the fluid is low, add fluid as necessary and inspect the hydraulic clutch system for leaks. If the master cylinder reservoir has run dry, bleed the system as described in Section 4 and re-test the clutch operation.*

b) *To check "clutch spin down time," run*

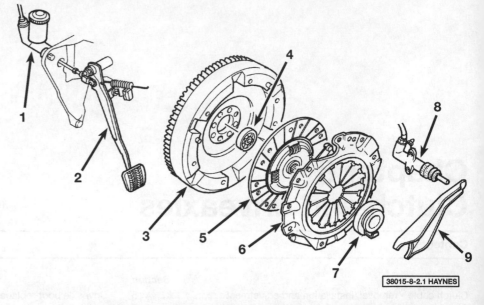

2.1 Exploded view of the clutch components - external slave type

1	Clutch master cylinder	4	Pilot bearing	7	Clutch release bearing
2	Clutch pedal	5	Clutch disc	8	Clutch slave cylinder
3	Flywheel	6	Clutch cover	9	Clutch release lever

c) *To check for complete clutch release, run the engine with the parking brake on to prevent movement) and hold the clutch pedal approximately 1/2-inch from the floor. Shift the transaxle between 1st gear and Reverse several times. If the shift is not smooth a component failure is indicated. On vehicles with a hydraulic release system and an external slave cylinder, measure the slave cylinder pushrod travel. With the clutch pedal compressed completely the slave cylinder pushrod should extend a minimum of 7/16-inch. If the pushrod doesn't meet this requirement, check the fluid in the clutch master cylinder.*

d) *Visually inspect the clutch pedal bushing at the top of the clutch pedal to make sure there is no sticking or excessive wear.*

e) *On vehicles with mechanical release systems, a clutch pedal that is difficult to operate is most likely caused by a faulty clutch cable. Check the cable where it enters the casing for fraying, rust or corrosion. If it looks good, lubricate the cable with penetrating oil. If pedal operation improves, the cable is worn out and should be replaced.*

3   Clutch hydraulic release system - removal and installation

Note: *The clutch slave cylinder on 1993 and later 2.3 liter DOHC (Quad-4) models is mounted inside the transaxle bellhousing,*

around the input shaft. The release bearing is pressed onto the actuating piston of the clutch slave cylinder and is serviced with the clutch slave cylinder as an assembly. The transaxle must be removed to service the slave cylinder. On all other models the clutch release system is serviced as a complete assembly and individual components are not available. Replacing the entire system or bleeding the system of air are the only service procedures possible. There are no provisions for adjustment of clutch pedal height or freeplay on either system.

Removal

Refer to illustration 3.4

Caution: *If the vehicle is equipped with a Delco Loc II audio system, make sure you have the correct activation code before disconnecting the battery. See the information at the front of this manual for the radio re-activation procedure.*

Warning: *Some models covered by this manual are equipped with airbags. Always turn the steering wheel to the straight ahead position, place the ignition switch in the Lock position disable the airbag system before working in the vicinity of the impact sensors, steering column or instrument panel to avoid the possibility of accidental deployment of the airbag(s), which could cause personal injury (see Chapter 12 for the airbag disarming procedure). Do not use electrical test equipment on any of the airbag system wiring or tamper with them in any way.*

1   Disconnect the cable from the negative battery terminal.

2   Remove the left under-dash panel.

3.4 Remove the clutch master cylinder retaining nuts (arrows)

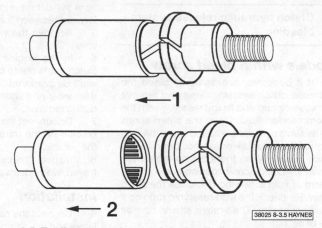

3.5 To disconnect the clutch hydraulic line, push the flange toward the connector (1), hold it there and pull the connector away (2) (1993 and later 2.3L DOHC models)

3.22 To connect the clutch hydraulic lines, push the flange (1) back against its stop, hold it there and insert that line into the connector (2) on the end of the other line (1993 and later 2.3L DOHC models)

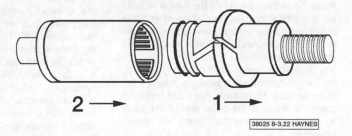

3 Remove the retaining clip from the clutch master cylinder pushrod and slide the pushrod off the pedal pin.

4 If the system is equipped with a remote fluid reservoir, disconnect the hose at the clutch master cylinder and plug it. Remove the two master cylinder mounting nuts (see illustration).

1993 and later 2.3L DOHC models

Refer to illustration 3.5

5 Locate the quick disconnect on the clutch hydraulic line, at the transaxle. Push the quick-disconnect flange *toward* the connector (the smooth, cylindrically shaped part), hold it there and pull the two lines apart (see illustration). Be prepared for some leakage of hydraulic fluid when the line separates from the connector.

6 Remove the clutch master cylinder and hydraulic line as a unit.

7 Remove the transaxle assembly (see Chapter 7 Part A).

8 Remove the clutch slave and clutch release bearing as an assembly.

All other four-cylinder models

9 Remove the clutch slave cylinder mounting nuts, then remove the slave cylinder, hydraulic line and master cylinder as a single assembly.

V6 models

10 Remove the intake duct from the air cleaner.

11 Disconnect the positive battery cable

from the battery.

12 Remove the left fender brace above the battery.

13 Remove the battery from the vehicle.

14 Using pieces of numbered tape, mark and remove the electrical connectors at the air cleaner and the Mass Air Flow sensor.

15 Remove the PCV pipe clamp from the intake duct and the intake duct clamp at the throttle body.

16 Remove the Mass Air Flow sensor mounting bolt and the air cleaner bracket mounting bolts. Remove the air cleaner, Mass Air Flow sensor and the intake duct as an assembly (see Chapter 4).

17 Remove the two bolts retaining the windshield washer bottle to the left inner fender well then remove the bottle.

18 If your vehicle is equipped with cruise control, unbolt the servo bracket nuts from the left strut tower and move the servo assembly.

19 Remove the clutch slave cylinder mounting nuts and detach the slave cylinder, the hydraulic line and the master cylinder from the vehicle as a unit.

Installation

1993 and later 2.3L DOHC engine models

Refer to illustration 3.22

20 Install the slave and release bearing assembly.

21 Install the transaxle (see Chapter 7 Part A).

22 Install the clutch master cylinder and hydraulic line. To reconnect the hydraulic line, push back the release flange as far as it will go, hold it there and push the lines together (see illustration). You should hear a click when the connector is properly engaged.

23 The remainder of the installation is the reverse of the removal procedure.

24 Bleed the clutch hydraulic system (see Section 4).

All other models

25 Install the new slave cylinder into the support bracket and insert the pushrod into the cup on the clutch release lever. Tighten the nuts evenly, a little at a time, to the torque listed in this Chapter's Specifications. **Note:** *Do not remove the plastic strap that holds the pushrod in position. It is designed to break off the first time the clutch pedal is depressed. If the original slave cylinder is being installed or if air is in the system, bleed the hydraulic system before installing the slave cylinder to the transaxle (see Section 4, models without bleed screw).*

26 Mount the clutch master cylinder to the firewall and install the nuts. Tighten the nuts evenly, a little at a time, to the torque listed in this Chapter's Specifications. If the vehicle is equipped with a remote fluid reservoir, reconnect the hose to the clutch master cylinder.

27 Remove the plastic pedal restrictor from the master cylinder pushrod. Coat the inside of the pushrod bushing with multi-purpose grease, connect the pushrod to the brake pedal pin and install the retaining clip. If the vehicle is equipped with cruise control, check to see that the disengage switch on the clutch pedal bracket is in contact with the clutch pedal when the pedal is at rest. If it isn't, adjust it accordingly.

28 Pump the clutch pedal several times to break the slave cylinder retaining strap. Leave the remaining plastic button under the pushrod in place.

29 The remainder of the installation is the reverse of the removal procedure.

4   Clutch hydraulic release system - bleeding

Models with a bleed screw

1   If it becomes necessary to bleed the hydraulic clutch system, clean and remove the reservoir cap and fill the reservoir with the recommended fluid. Open the bleed screw on the slave cylinder body and allow the fluid to drip into a container (do not depress the clutch pedal). When there are no more bubbles at the bleed screw opening and a steady stream of fluid is flowing out, close the bleed screw. Re-check the fluid reservoir, topping it up as necessary. The system should now be free of air.
2   You can verify that the system is free of air by measuring the slave cylinder pushrod travel as described in Section 2.

Models without a bleed screw

3   Loosen the clutch master cylinder mounting nuts until they are on the end of the studs. Allow the master cylinder to move away from the firewall to take any pressure off the pushrod. Don't remove the master cylinder from the mounting studs.
4   Remove the clutch slave assembly from the transaxle. It is important to keep the slave cylinder lower than the master cylinder while performing the following procedure.
5   Clean and remove the fluid reservoir cap and diaphragm.
6   Fill the reservoir with the recommended fluid.
7   Hold the slave cylinder vertically with the pushrod facing down and press the pushrod into the slave cylinder 3/4-inch.
8   While holding the pushrod in the slave cylinder, install the fluid reservoir diaphragm and cap. Tighten the fluid reservoir cap.
9   Release the slave cylinder pushrod. This will pull fluid into the slave cylinder.
10   With the slave cylinder still in a vertical position, press and release the pushrod with 3/8-inch strokes. Watch for air in the reservoir. Continue this until no air bubbles are present in the fluid reservoir.
11   Install the slave cylinder and tighten the master cylinder nuts. Recheck the fluid reservoir, topping it up as necessary.

5   Clutch cable - removal, installation and adjustment

Removal

1   Pull the clutch pedal rearward and support it against the bumper stop so that the adjuster pawl is released.
2   Disconnect the clutch cable from the release lever at the transaxle, taking care not to let it snap rearward, which could damage the adjusting mechanism.
3   Remove the left side under-dash panel.
4   Disconnect the clutch cable from the tangs of the detent, lift the locking pawl away

from the detent and carefully slide the cable forward between the detent and pawl.
5   Remove the windshield washer reservoir.
6   In the engine compartment, pull the clutch cable out to disengage it from the firewall. Be prepared to retrieve the insulators, dampener and washers, which may separate during removal.
7   Disconnect the cable from the mounting bracket on the transaxle and remove it from the vehicle.
8   Inspect the cable and replace it if it is frayed, worn, damaged or kinked.

Installation

9   Connect the cable into both of the insulators and the damper and washers. Lubricating the rear insulator with a small amount of light oil will ease the installation into the pedal mounting bracket.
10   Inside the passenger compartment, route the cable casing into the rubber isolator on the pedal bracket and then attach the cable end to the detent. Make sure the cable is routed underneath the pawl and into the detent cable groove.
11   Install the under-dash panel.
12   Hold the clutch pedal up against the bumper stop to release the pawl from the detent and install the other end of the cable to the release lever and transaxle mount brackets.
13   Install the windshield washer reservoir.
14   Lift the clutch pedal up several times to allow the mechanism to adjust the cable length, then depress it several times to mesh the pawl with the detent teeth.

6   Clutch release bearing - removal and installation

Note: *The clutch slave cylinder on the 1993 and later 2.3 liter DOHC (Quad-4) model is mounted inside the transaxle bellhousing, around the input shaft. The release bearing is pressed onto the actuating piston of the clutch slave cylinder and is serviced with the clutch slave cylinder as an assembly. The transaxle must be removed to service the slave cylinder. Refer to Section 3 for clutch slave cylinder replacement procedures.*

Removal

Refer to illustration 6.4
Caution: *If the vehicle is equipped with a Delco Loc II audio system, make sure you have the correct activation code before disconnecting the battery. See the information at the front of this manual for the radio re-activation procedure.*
Warning: *Some models covered by this manual are equipped with airbags. Always turn the steering wheel to the straight ahead position, place the ignition switch in the Lock position disable the airbag system before working in the vicinity of the impact sensors, steering column or instrument panel to avoid*

6.4   Before removing the release bearing from the transaxle, index the bearing pad to the clutch release fork, then disengage the retaining spring (arrow)

the possibility of accidental deployment of the airbag(s), which could cause personal injury (see Chapter 12 for the airbag disarming procedure). Do not use electrical test equipment on any of the airbag system wiring or tamper with them in any way.
1   Disconnect the negative cable from the battery.
2   On vehicles with hydraulic release systems, and an external clutch slave cylinder, remove the under-dash panel and disconnect the clutch master cylinder pushrod from the clutch pedal pin.
3   Remove the transaxle (see Chapter 7).
4   Remove the clutch release bearing from the clutch fork. Place a mark on the release bearing pad and the release fork so the bearing can be returned to its original position if it is to be re-used **(see illustration)**. Remove the bearing retaining spring from the release fork holes and remove the bearing.
5   Hold the center of the bearing and spin the outer portion. If the bearing doesn't turn smoothly or if it is noisy, replace it with a new one. Wipe the bearing with a clean rag and inspect it for damage, wear or cracks. Do not immerse the bearing in solvent - it is sealed for life and to do so would ruin it.

Installation

Refer to illustrations 6.6a and 6.6b
6   Lubricate the clutch fork ends where they contact the bearing lightly with white lithium base grease. Pack the inner diameter of the bearing with this grease **(see illustrations)**.
7   Install the release bearing on the transaxle retainer so that both of the fork tangs fit into the outer diameter of the bearing groove. Be sure the bearing pads are resting on the fork ends with the previously inscribed marks aligned, then install the retaining spring. The spring must be fully seated in the retaining groove and both ends secured in the clutch fork holes.
8   Install the transaxle, making sure that the clutch lever does not move toward the flywheel until the transaxle is bolted to the engine.

6.6a A small brush makes it easier to lubricate the fork ends

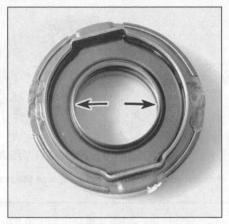

6.6b Fill the groove in the inner diameter of the release bearing with lithium-base grease (arrows)

9   On models with hydraulic release systems, reconnect the clutch master cylinder pushrod and install the under-dash cover.

10   Check the clutch operation. Adjust the clutch cable and depress the pedal slowly several times to mesh the pawl with the detent teeth (mechanically actuated systems).

7   Clutch components - removal, inspection and installation

Warning 1: *Dust produced by clutch wear and deposited on clutch components may contain ASBESTOS, which is hazardous to your health. DO NOT blow it out with compressed air and DO NOT inhale it. DO NOT use gasoline or petroleum-based solvents to remove the dust. Brake system cleaner should be used to flush the dust into a drain pan. After the clutch components are wiped clean with a rag, dispose of the contaminated rags and cleaner in a covered container.*

Warning 2: *Some models covered by this manual are equipped with airbags. Always*

turn the steering wheel to the straight ahead position, place the ignition switch in the Lock position disable the airbag system before working in the vicinity of the impact sensors, steering column or instrument panel to avoid the possibility of accidental deployment of the airbag(s), which could cause personal injury (see Chapter 12 for the airbag disarming procedure). Do not use electrical test equipment on any of the airbag system wiring or tamper with them in any way.

Caution: *If the vehicle is equipped with a Delco Loc II audio system, make sure you have the correct activation code before disconnecting the battery. See the information at the front of this manual for the radio re-activation procedure.*

Removal

Refer to illustration 7.5

1   Access to the clutch components is normally accomplished by removing the transaxle, leaving the engine in the vehicle. If, of course, the engine is being removed for major overhaul, then the opportunity should

always be taken to check the clutch for wear and replace worn components as necessary. The following procedures assume that the engine will stay in place.

2   Remove the left side under-dash panel and disconnect the clutch master cylinder pushrod from the clutch pedal (hydraulic release systems).

3   Referring to Chapter 7 Part A, remove the transaxle from the vehicle. Remove the release bearing as described in Section 6).

4   To support the clutch disc during removal, install a clutch alignment tool through the middle of the clutch.

5   Mark the relationship of the pressure plate-to-flywheel so it can be installed in the same relative position **(see illustration)**.

6   Turning each bolt a little at a time, loosen the pressure plate-to-flywheel bolts. Work in a criss-cross pattern, again, loosening only a little at a time until all spring pressure is relieved. Support the pressure plate and completely remove the bolts, followed by the pressure plate and clutch disc.

Inspection

Refer to illustrations 7.9 and 7.11

7   Ordinarily, when a fault is found in the clutch system, it can be attributed to wear of the clutch driveplate assembly (clutch disc). However, all components should be inspected at this time.

8   Inspect the flywheel for cracks, heat checking, grooves or other signs of obvious defects. If the imperfections are slight, a machine shop can machine the surface flat and smooth, which is highly recommended regardless of the surface appearance. Refer to Chapter 2 for the flywheel removal and installation procedure.

9   Inspect the facing on the clutch disc. There should be at least 1/16-inch of lining above the rivet heads. Check for loose rivets, distortion, cracks, broken springs or any obvious damage **(see illustration)**. As mentioned above, the disc is usually replaced as

8

7.5 After removal of the transmission, this will be the view of the clutch components

1   *Pressure plate assembly (clutch disc inside)*
2   *Flywheel*

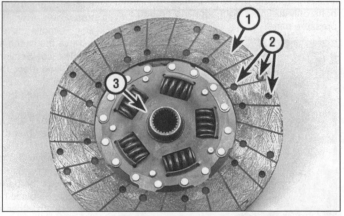

7.9 The clutch disc

1   **Facing** - *this will wear down in use*
2   **Rivets** - *these secure the facing and will damage the flywheel or pressure plate if allowed to contact the surfaces*
3   **Markings** - *"Flywheel side" or similar*

NORMAL FINGER WEAR

EXCESSIVE WEAR →

EXCESSIVE FINGER WEAR

BROKEN OR BENT FINGERS

7.11 If any of these conditions are noted, replace the pressure plate

a matter of course, so if in any doubt about the quality, replace it with a new one.

10   Ordinarily, the release bearing is also replaced along with the clutch disc (see Section 6).

11   Check the machined surfaces of the pressure plate **(see illustration)**. If the surface is grooved or otherwise damaged, take it to a machine shop for possible machining or replacement. Also check for obvious damage, distortion, cracking, etc. Light glazing can be removed with medium grit emery cloth. If a new pressure plate is indicated, new or factory-rebuilt units are available.

Installation

Refer to illustrations 7.13

12   Before installation, carefully wipe clean the flywheel and pressure plate machined surfaces. It is important that no oil or grease is on these surfaces or the facing of the clutch disc. Handle these parts only with clean hands.

13   Position the clutch disc and pressure plate with the clutch disc held in place with an alignment tool **(see illustration)**. Make sure the disc is installed properly. Most replacement discs are marked "flywheel side". If the disc is not marked, install the it with the damper springs toward the transaxle.

14   Tighten the pressure plate-to-flywheel bolts only to finger tight, working around the pressure plate.

7.13 Center the clutch disc in the pressure plate with an alignment tool

15   Center the clutch disc by inserting the alignment tool through the splined hub and into the bore on the crankshaft. Tighten the pressure plate-to-flywheel bolts a little at a time, working in a criss-cross pattern to prevent distorting the cover. After all the bolts are snug, tighten them to the torque listed in this Chapter's Specifications. Remove the alignment tool.

16   Using high temperature grease, lubricate the inner groove of the release bearing (see Section 6). Also place grease on the fork fingers.

17   Install the clutch release bearing as described in Section 6.

18   Install the transaxle, slave cylinder and all components that were removed previously.

19   Adjust the shift linkage as outlined in Chapter 7 Part A.

8   Clutch pedal - removal and installation

Mechanically actuated clutch

Removal

1   Pull back on the clutch pedal and support it in the raised position. Disconnect the clutch cable from the release lever at the transaxle.

2   Remove the left under-dash panel, then remove the clutch switch from the pedal and bracket (see Section 9).

3   Disconnect the clutch cable from the tangs of the detent, lift the pawl away and slide the cable between the detent and the pawl.

4   Remove the pivot bolt. Remove the spring, pawl and spacer from the pedal assembly.

5   Remove the detent spacer, bushings, spring and pawl.

6   Clean the parts and inspect for wear or damage. Replace both the pawl and detent if the teeth on either are damaged or worn.

Installation

7   Position the detent spring in the side of the detent and install the detent into the clutch pedal opening, hooking the spring onto the pedal.

8   Install the bushings onto the pedal assembly.

9   Install the pawl, spring, spacer and pivot mounting bolt. Tighten the bolt securely.

10   Attach the clutch pedal to the mounting bracket and install the pivot bolt and nut. Both the pivot and pawl bolts must be installed from the driver's side through to the passenger side.

11   Check the pawl and detent for proper operation to make sure the pawl disengages when pulled to the upper position and the detent rotates freely in both directions.

12   Attach the cable end to the pawl, making sure to route the cable underneath the pawl and into the detent cable groove.

13   Install the clutch switch.

14   Hold the clutch pedal up against the bumper stop and release the pawl from the detent.

15   Check the clutch pedal mechanism for proper operation and adjust the cable length by lifting the pedal. Depress the pedal slowly several times so the pawl meshes properly with the detent teeth.

16   Install the under-dash panel.

Hydraulically actuated clutch

Removal

17   Remove the left under-dash panel.

18   Remove the clutch switch from the pedal and bracket (see Section 9).

19   Remove the clutch pushrod retaining clip and slide the pushrod off the pedal pin.

20   Remove the clutch pedal pivot bolt and pull the pedal from the mounting bracket. Extract the bushings and spacer and inspect for wear, replacing them as necessary.

Installation

21   Lubricate the spacer and bushings with multi-purpose grease and install them on the clutch pedal. Position the pedal in the bracket and install the pivot bolt.

22   Lubricate the master cylinder pushrod bushing with multi-purpose grease, slide it onto the pedal pin and install the retaining clip.

23   Install and adjust the neutral start switch (see Section 9).

24   If the vehicle is equipped with cruise control, check the adjustment of the clutch switch (see Chapter 12).

25   Install the under-dash panel.

9 Starter safety switch - check and replacement

1 The clutch switch allows the vehicle to be started only with the clutch pedal fully depressed.

Check

2 Place the shift lever in Neutral and try to start the engine without depressing the clutch; it shouldn't start. Then depress the clutch pedal to the floor and try to start the engine again; it should now start. If the engine starts when the pedal is not depressed, or doesn't start when the pedal is depressed, replace the switch.

Replacement

3 Disconnect the negative cable at the battery. Place the cable out of the way so it cannot accidentally come in contact with the negative terminal of the battery, as this would once again allow power into the electrical system of the vehicle.

4 Remove the left side under-dash panel to gain access to the top of the clutch pedal.

Cable-actuated clutch

5 Near the top of the clutch pedal, a small rod connects the switch to the pedal. Remove the clip from the end of this rod.

6 Remove the screw that secures the clutch switch to the clutch pedal support bracket.

7 Disconnect the electrical lead to the switch, disengage the switch rod from the clutch pedal and remove the switch.

Hydraulic clutch

8 Remove the switch mounting nuts, pull off the instrument panel wiring harness bracket and remove the switch.

9 Unplug the electrical connector.

All models

10 Install the new switch in the reverse order of removal. Test to be sure that the vehicle can be started only when the clutch pedal is fully depressed. Be sure to perform this test with the transaxle placed in neutral.

10 Driveaxles - general information and inspection

1 Power is transmitted from the transaxle to the wheels through a pair of driveaxles. The inner end of each driveaxle is splined into the differential side gears, or onto a splined intermediate axleshaft. The outer ends of the driveaxles are splined to the axle hubs and locked in place by a large nut.

2 The inner ends of the driveaxles are equipped with sliding constant velocity joints, which are capable of both angular and axial motion. Some inner joint assemblies consist of a tripot bearing and a joint housing (outer race) in which the joint is free to slide in and out as the driveaxle moves up and down with the wheel. Other inner joints are "ball-and-cage" type, which consists of six ball bearings riding between an inner race and outer race and held in position by a cage. The inner joints can be disassembled, cleaned, inspected and repacked, but they cannot be overhauled. If any parts are damaged, an inner joint must be replaced as a unit.

3 The outer CV joints are the cross-groove," or "ball-and-cage," type. The outer joints are capable of angular but not axial movement. The outer joints can be disassembled, cleaned, inspected and repacked, but they cannot be overhauled. If any parts are damaged, an outer joint must be replaced as a unit.

4 The boots should be inspected periodically for damage and leaking lubricant. Torn CV joint boots must be replaced immediately or the joints can be damaged. Boot replacement involves removal of the driveaxle (see Section 11). **Note:** *Some auto parts stores carry "split" type replacement boots, which can be installed without removing the driveaxle from the vehicle. This is a convenient alternative; however, the driveaxle should be removed and the CV joint disassembled and cleaned to ensure the joint is free from contaminants such as moisture and dirt which will accelerate CV joint wear. The most common symptom of worn or damaged CV joints, besides lubricant leaks, is a click-*ing noise in turns, a clunk when accelerating after coasting and vibration at highway speeds. To check for wear in the CV joints and driveaxle shafts, grasp each axle (one at a time) and rotate it in both directions while holding the CV joint housings, feeling for play indicating worn splines or sloppy CV joints. Also check the driveaxle shafts for cracks, dents and distortion.

11 Driveaxle - removal and installation

Removal

Refer to illustrations 11.5, 11.6, 11.9 and 11.10

1 Disconnect the cable from the negative terminal of the battery. **Caution:** *If the stereo in your vehicle is equipped with an anti-theft system, make sure you have the correct activation code before disconnecting the battery.*

2 Set the parking brake.

3 Loosen the front wheel lug nuts, raise the vehicle and support it securely on jackstands.

4 Remove the wheel.

5 Remove the driveaxle/hub nut and washer. To prevent the disc/hub from turning, wedge a long punch into the brake disc cooling vanes and allow it to rest against the caliper anchor **(see illustration)**.

6 To loosen the driveaxle from the hub splines, tap the end of the driveaxle with a soft-faced hammer or a hammer and a brass punch **(see illustration)**. **Note:** *Don't attempt to push the end of the driveaxle through the hub yet. Applying force to the end of the driveaxle, beyond just breaking it loose from the hub, can damage the driveaxle or transaxle. If the driveaxle is stuck in the hub splines and won't move, it may be necessary to remove the brake disc (see Chapter 9) and push it from the hub with a two-jaw puller after Step 8 is performed.*

7 Place a drain pan underneath the transaxle to catch the lubricant that will spill out when the driveaxles are removed.

8 Separate the strut from the steering

11.5 To hold the hub/disc while breaking loose the driveaxle hub nut, jam a punch into the cooling vanes of the disc

11.6 Using a brass punch, strike the end of the driveaxle sharply with a hammer; when it breaks free, it will move noticeably

8

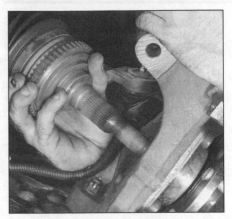

11.9 Pull the steering knuckle out and slide the end of the driveaxle out of the hub

11.10 To separate the inner end of the driveaxle from the transaxle, pry on the CV joint housing like this with a large screwdriver or prybar - you may need to give the prybar a sharp rap with a brass hammer

12.3a Cut off the boot seal retaining clamps, using wire cutters or a chisel and hammer

knuckle (see Chapter 10).

9   Pull out on the steering knuckle and detach the driveaxle from the hub **(see illustration)**. Don't let the driveaxle hang by the inner CV joint after the outer end has been detached from the steering knuckle, as the inner joint could become damaged. Support the outer end of the driveaxle with a piece of wire, if necessary.

10   Carefully pry the inner CV joint out of the transaxle **(see illustration)** or off the splined end of the intermediate shaft (right driveaxle only, on vehicles so equipped).

11   Refer to Chapter 7 for the driveaxle oil seal replacement procedure.

Installation

12   Installation is the reverse of the removal procedure, but with the following additional points:

   a) *Seat the inner CV joint in the differential side gear by positioning the end of a large screwdriver in the groove in the CV joint housing and tapping it into position with a hammer. Once this has been done pull out on the joint housing to make sure the retaining ring has seated.*

   b) *Tighten the strut-to-knuckle bolts/nuts to the torque listed in the Chapter 10*

Specifications.

   c) *Install a new driveaxle/hub nut and tighten it to the torque listed in this Chapter's Specifications.*

   d) *Install the wheel and lug nuts, lower the vehicle and tighten the lug nuts to the torque listed in the Chapter 1 Specifications.*

   e) *Check the transaxle lubricant and add, if necessary, to bring it to the proper level (see Chapter 1).*

12   Driveaxle boot - replacement

Note: *If the CV joint boots must be replaced, explore all options before beginning the job. Complete rebuilt driveaxles are available on an exchange basis, which eliminates much time and work. Whichever route you choose to take, check on the cost and availability of parts before disassembling the vehicle.*

1   Remove the driveaxle (see Section 11).

2   Place the driveaxle in a vise lined with rags to avoid damage to the axleshaft. Check

the CV joint for excessive play in the radial direction, which indicates worn parts. Check for smooth operation throughout the full range of motion for each CV joint. If a boot is torn, disassemble the joint, clean the components and inspect for damage due to loss of lubrication and possible contamination by foreign matter.

Inner CV joint

Refer to illustrations 12.3a through 12.3w

Note: *Some models use a "ball-and-cage" type inner CV joint instead of the usual tripot design. Aside from a wire retainer ring which must be removed before the ball-and-cage assembly can be removed from the CV joint housing, this unit is similar in construction to the outer CV joint, which is covered in the sequence beginning with illustration 11.4a.*

3   To replace the inner boot, refer to the accompanying illustrations **(see illustrations 11.3a through 11.3w)**.

Outer CV joint

Refer to illustrations 12.4a through 12.4t

4   Refer to the accompanying illustrations and perform the outer CV joint boot replacement procedure **(see illustrations 12.4a through 12.4t)**.

12.3b Slide the housing off the spider assembly

12.3c On models with a ball-and-cage inner joint, pry out the wire ring bearing retainer with a screwdriver

12.3d Slide the boot towards the center of the driveaxle

12.3e Spread the ends of the stop ring apart and slide it towards the center of the shaft

12.3f Slide the spider assembly back to expose the retaining ring and pry off the ring

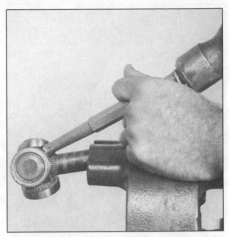

12.3g Carefully tap the spider off the axleshaft with a brass punch (but don't hit it so hard that it flies off, or you'll be picking up needle bearings!)

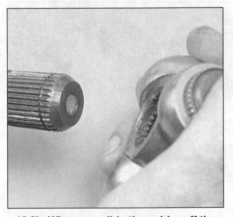

12.3h When you slide the spider off the driveaxle, hold the bearings in place with your hand; even better, use tape or a cloth wrapped around the spider bearing assembly to retain them

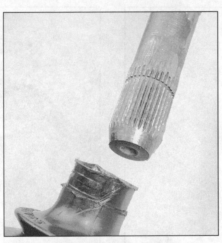

12.3i Slide the boot off the axleshaft (and the stop ring, if equipped)

12.3j Clean all of the old grease out of the housing and spider assembly, then remove each bearing, one at time

12.3k Carefully disassemble each section of the spider assembly, clean the needle bearings with solvent and inspect the rollers, spider cross, bearings and housing for scoring, pitting and other signs of abnormal wear

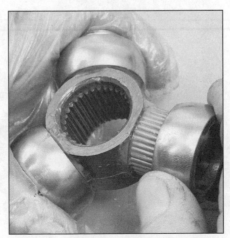

12.3l Apply a coat of CV joint grease to the inner bearing surfaces to hold the needle bearings in place and slide the bearing over them

12.3m Wrap the axleshaft splines with tape to avoid damaging the boot, then slide the small clamp and boot onto the axleshaft

8

12.3n Remove the tape and slide the stop ring onto the axleshaft, past the groove in which it seats

12.3o Install the spider assembly with the recess in the counterbore facing the end of the driveaxle

12.3p On ball-and-cage type inner joints, the small-diameter side of the cage must face the center of the axleshaft

12.3q Use a screwdriver to install the spider retaining ring, then slide the spider assembly against it and install the stop ring

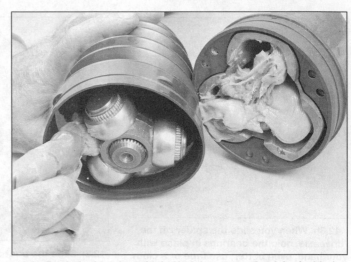

12.3r Pack the housing with half of the grease furnished with the new boot and place the remainder in the boot

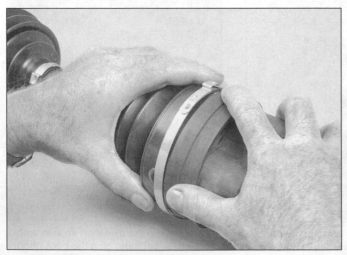

12.3s With the retaining clamps in place (but not tightened), install the tripot housing

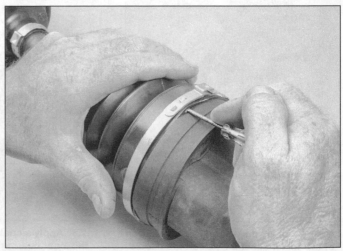

12.3t Seat the boot in the housing and axle seal grooves - a small screwdriver can make the job easier (make sure the boot isn't dimpled, stretched or out of shape)

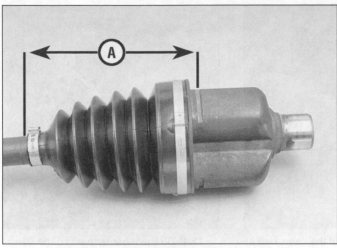

12.3u Adjust the length of the joint (A) to the dimension listed in this Chapter's Specifications

12.3v Equalize the pressure inside the boot by inserting a *dull* screwdriver between the boot and the outer race . .

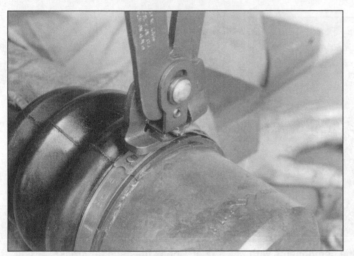

12.3w . . then secure the boot clamps with special pliers (available at auto parts stores)

12.4a Cut off the band retaining the boot to the shaft, then slide the boot toward the center of the shaft

12.4b On models with a retaining ring, tap around the circumference of the retaining ring to remove it from the housing

12.4c Expand the snap-ring, slide the joint off the shaft and remove the old boot

8

12.4d Press down on the inner race far enough to allow a ball bearing to be removed - if it's difficult to tilt, gently tap the cage and inner race with a brass punch and hammer

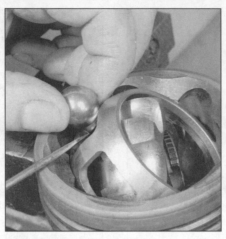

12.4e Pry the balls out of the cage, one at a time

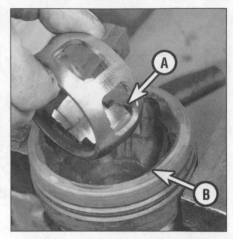

12.4f Tilt the inner race and cage 90-degrees, then align the windows in the cage (A) with the lands of the housing (B) and rotate the inner race up and out of the outer race

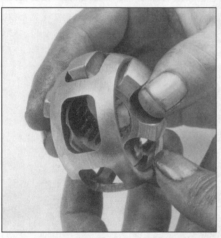

12.4g Align the inner race lands with the cage window and rotate the inner race out of the cage

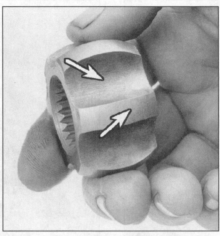

12.4h After cleaning the components with solvent, check the inner race lands and grooves for pitting and score marks

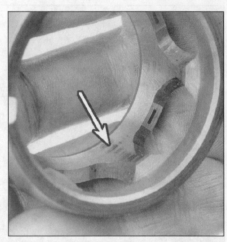

12.4i Check the cage for cracks, pitting and score marks - shiny spots are normal and don't affect operation

12.4j With the race and cage tilted at 90-degrees, lower the assembly into the housing

12.4k Rotate the assembly by gently tapping with a hammer and brass punch, then . . .

12.4l . . . press the balls into the cage windows, repeating until all of the balls are installed

12.4m Use needle-nose pliers to lower a new snap-ring into the groove . . .

12.4n . . . then seat it into the groove with snap-ring pliers

12.4o Apply grease through the splined hole, then insert a wooden dowel (with a diameter slightly less than that of the axle) through the splined hole and push down - the dowel will force the grease into the joint - repeat until the bearing is completely packed

12.4p Install the small clamp and the boot on the driveaxle and apply grease to the inside of the axle boot until . . .

12.4q . . . the level is up to the end of axle

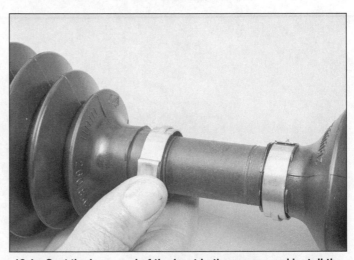

12.4r Position the CV joint assembly on the driveaxle, aligning the splines, then use a soft-face hammer to drive the joint onto the driveaxle until the snap-ring is seated in the groove

12.4s Seat the inner end of the boot in the groove and install the retaining clamp, then do the same on the other end of the boot - tighten boot clamps with the special tool (see illustration 12.3w)

8

12.4t   On models with a retaining ring, carefully tap around the circumference of the retaining ring to install it on the housing

13   Intermediate axleshaft (2.0L turbo models) - removal and installation

Removal

1   Loosen the right front wheel lug nuts, raise the vehicle and support it securely on jackstands. Remove the wheel.

2   Disconnect the stabilizer bar from the right control arm (see Chapter 10).

3   Remove the balljoint stud nut and separate the control arm from the steering knuckle (see Chapter 10).

4   Pull the inboard of the right driveaxle from the intermediate shaft and support it with a piece of wire. Do not let it hang, or damage to the outer CV joint may occur.

5   Disconnect the detonation (knock) sensor electrical connector and remove the sensor (see Chapter 6).

6   Remove the power steering pump brace (see Chapter 10).

7   Remove the intermediate shaft bracket bolts and pull the shaft from the transaxle.

Installation

8   Lubricate the lips of the differential seal with multi-purpose grease and slide the intermediate shaft into the transaxle. Install the bolts and tighten them to the torque listed in this Chapter's Specifications.

9   Install the power steering pump brace.

10   Install the detonation sensor and reconnect the electrical connector.

11   Apply multi-purpose grease to the intermediate shaft splines and install the driveaxle to the shaft.

12   Insert the balljoint stud into the steering knuckle and tighten the nut. Be sure to use a new cotter pin.

13   Install the stabilizer bar-to-control arm bolt (see Chapter 10).

14   Install the wheel and tighten the lug nuts to the torque.

Chapter 9 Brakes

Contents

Specifications

Disc brakes

Minimum (discard) thickness...	Cast into disc
Disc runout (maximum)..	0.003 inch
Disc thickness variation (parallelism)...	0.0005 inch
Caliper-to-bracket stop clearance...	0.005 to 0.012 inch

Drum brakes

Drum maximum (discard) diameter..	Cast into drum
Out-of-round (maximum)..	0.006 inch

Torque Specifications

	Ft-lbs (unless otherwise indicated)
Caliper mounting bolts..	38
Bleeder valve...	80 in-lbs
Brake hose-to-caliper banjo bolt...	33
Booster-to-firewall nuts..	18
Master cylinder-to-booster nuts..	22
Proportioner valve caps..	20
Switch piston plugs..	24 to 48 in-lbs

9

Component location

Typical front disc brake assembly

1 Disc	2 Caliper	3 Outer brake pad	4 Brake hose

1   General information

Conventional (non-ABS) system

All vehicles covered by this manual are equipped with hydraulically operated front and rear brake systems. The front brakes are disc type, and the rear brakes are drum type. All brakes are self-adjusting. The front disc brakes automatically compensate for pad wear, while the rear drum brakes incorporate an adjustment mechanism that is activated as the brakes are applied when the vehicle is driven in reverse.

The hydraulic system consists of two separate circuits. Models without an Anti-lock Brake System (ABS) are split diagonally. Models with ABS have separate front and rear circuits. The master cylinder has separate reservoirs for the two circuits, and in the event of a leak or failure in one hydraulic circuit, the other circuit will remain operative. A visual warning of circuit failure, air in the system, or other pressure differential conditions in the brake system is given by a warning light activated by a failure warning switch in the master cylinder.

The parking brake mechanically operates the rear brakes only. It is activated by a pull-handle in the center console between the front seats or a pedal mounted next to the left kick panel.

The power brake booster, located in the engine compartment on the firewall, uses engine manifold vacuum and atmospheric pressure to provide assistance to the hydraulically operated brakes.

After completing any operation involving the disassembly of any part of the brake system, always test drive the vehicle to check for proper braking performance before resuming normal driving. Test the brakes while driving on a clean, dry, flat surface. Conditions other than these can lead to inaccurate test results. Test the brakes at various speeds with both light and heavy pedal pressure. The vehicle should stop evenly without pulling to one side or the other. Avoid locking the brakes because this slides the tires and diminishes braking efficiency and control.

Tires, vehicle load and front end alignment are factors that also affect braking performance.

Anti-lock Brake System (ABS)

Refer to illustration 1.7
Warning: *Do not disassemble or disconnect*

Component location

Leading/trailing drum brake components (1994 and later models) - left side shown

1	Actuating spring	3	Retractor spring	5	Adjusting screw	7	Wheel cylinder
2	Trailing shoe	4	Leading shoe	6	Actuator lever	8	Backing plate

ABS system components or controls. Refer vehicle to a dealer service center or qualified repair shop for component repair or replacement.

This system is standard equipment on 1993 and later models and was available as an option on some earlier models. It consists of all the components and design of the conventional (non-ABS) brake system, and in addition it uses individual speed sensors at each wheel, a four-valve electro-hydraulic fluid modulator mounted on the master cylinder and an electronic module to process wheel speed input and control the modulator **(see illustration)**.

It is designed to control pressure in the hydraulic brake system during normal and hard braking. Wheel speeds are electronically sensed. Should any individual wheel slow disproportionately or should any wheel begin to lock up, the modulator valve opens, reducing hydraulic pressure to the affected wheel. As soon as the rotating speed of the affected wheel matches that of the other wheels, the modulator valve closes. This opening-and-closing cycle can occur several times a second.

Under light braking, the brake system operates in the conventional mode. During ABS system failure, fluid moves through a bypass port in the modulator valve to the front brakes which will then operate in the conventional mode. Diagnosis of the ABS system is beyond the scope of the home mechanic and should be referred to a repair facility equipped with an ABS diagnostic computer capable of accessing the control module for system failure codes.

1.7 Typical electro-hydraulic modulator and electronic module

9

2.5 A large C-clamp can be used to compress the piston into the caliper for removal

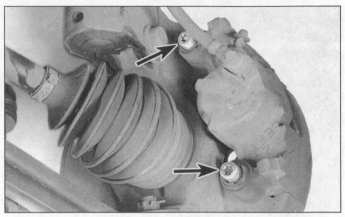

2.6a Remove the caliper mounting bolts (arrows). Early models have Allen-head bolts. On later models, a No. 50 Torx bit must be used - don't attempt to loosen Torx-head bolts with an Allen wrench, because the bolt heads could be damaged

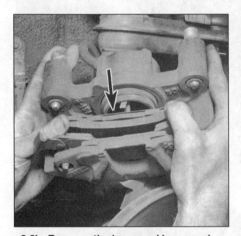

2.6b Remove the inner pad by snapping it out of the piston in the direction shown (arrow)

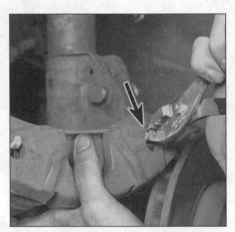

2.6c On 1990 and earlier models, remove the outer pad by bending the tabs (arrow) straight out with pliers . . .

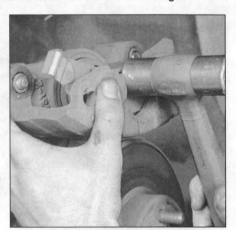

2.6d . . . then dislodge the pad from the caliper with a hammer

2 Disc brake pads - replacement

Refer to illustrations 2.5 and 2.6a through 2.6l

Warning: *Disc brake pads must be replaced on both front wheels at the same time - never replace the pads on only one wheel. Also, the dust created by the brake system may contain asbestos, which is harmful to your health. Never blow it out with compressed air and do not inhale any of it. An approved filtering mask should be worn whenever servicing the brake system. Do not, under any circumstances, use petroleum-based solvents to clean brake parts. Use brake system cleaner only.*

1   Remove the cover from the brake fluid reservoir, siphon off about two-thirds of the fluid into a container and discard it. **Warning:** *Don't start the siphoning action by mouth! Use a siphon pump or a suction gun.*

2   Loosen the wheel lug nuts, raise the vehicle and support it securely on jackstands.

3   Remove the front wheel, then reinstall two wheel nuts (flat side toward the disc) to hold the disc in place. Work on one brake assembly at a time, using the assembled

2.6e On 1991 and later models, pry the ends of the retaining clip out of the holes in the caliper

brake for reference if necessary.

4   Inspect the disc carefully as outlined in Section 4. If machining is necessary, follow the information in that Section to remove the disc, at which time the pads can be removed from the calipers as well.

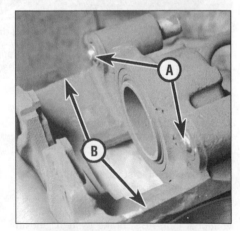

2.6f Inspect the caliper bolts and bushings (A) for damage and the contact surfaces (B) for corrosion

5   Push the piston back into its bore. If necessary, a C-clamp can be used **(see illustration)**, but a prybar will usually do the job. As the piston is depressed to the bottom of the caliper bore, the fluid in the master cylinder will rise. Make sure that it does not over-

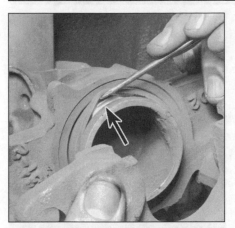

2.6g Carefully peel back the edge of the piston boot and check for corrosion and leaking fluid

2.6h Snap the inner pad retainer spring into the new pad in the direction shown (arrow)

2.6i Lightly lubricate the lower steering knuckle contact surface with high-temperature grease

2.6j Also apply a light coat of high-temperature grease to the upper steering knuckle contact surface

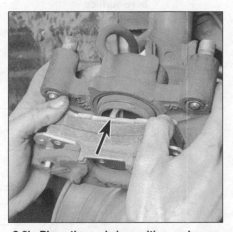

2.6k Place the pads in position and snap the inner pad into place in the piston (arrow)

2.6l After installing the caliper, tighten the bolts to the torque listed in this Chapter's Specifications. On models with tabs that protrude through the caliper frame, insert a large screwdriver between the outer pad flange and the disc hat to seat the pad and bend the tabs over with a hammer - on models with a retaining clip make sure the ends of the clip on the outer pad fit into the holes in the caliper frame

flow. If necessary, siphon off more of the fluid as directed in Step 1.

6   Refer to the accompanying photographs and perform the procedure illustrated. Start with **illustration 2.6a**.

7   When reinstalling the caliper, be sure to tighten the mounting bolts to the torque listed in this Chapter's Specifications. After the job has been completed, firmly depress the brake pedal a few times to bring the pads into contact with the disc.

3   Disc brake caliper - removal, overhaul and installation

Warning: *Dust created by the brake system may contain asbestos, which is harmful to your health. Never blow it out with compressed air and do not inhale any of it. An approved filtering mask should be worn whenever servicing the brake system. Do not, under any circumstances, use petroleum-based solvents to clean brake parts. Use brake system cleaner only.*

Note: *If an overhaul is indicated (usually because of fluid leakage) explore all options before beginning the job. New and factory*

rebuilt calipers are available on an exchange basis, which makes this job quite easy. If it is decided to rebuild the calipers, make sure that a rebuild kit is available before proceeding.

Removal

Refer to illustration 3.5

1   Remove the cover from the brake fluid reservoir, siphon off two thirds of the fluid into a container and discard it. **Warning:** *Don't start the siphoning action by mouth! Use a siphon pump or a suction gun.*

2   Loosen the wheel lug nuts, raise the front of the vehicle and support it securely on jackstands. Remove the front wheels.

3   Reinstall two lug nuts on each disc, flat side against the disc, to hold the disc in place.

4   Bottom the piston in the caliper bore. This is accomplished by pushing on the caliper, although it may be necessary to carefully use a flat prybar or a C-clamp **(see illustration 2.5)**.

5   Remove the brake hose-to-caliper banjo bolt and detach the hose from the caliper. Have a rag handy to catch the spilling fluid, but be sure to plug the brake hose to prevent excessive fluid loss **(see illustration)**.

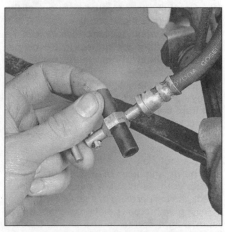

3.5 Use a piece of rubber hose to plug the brake hose-to-caliper fitting

9

3.9 With the caliper padded to catch the piston, use compressed air to force the piston out of its bore - make sure your hands or fingers are not between the piston and caliper!

3.10 Carefully pry the dust boot out of the housing, taking care not to scratch the bore surface

3.11 To remove the seal from the caliper bore, use a plastic or wooden tool, such as a pencil

6   Remove the two mounting bolts and lift the caliper from the vehicle **(see illustration 2.6a)**.

Overhaul

Refer to illustrations 3.9, 3.10, 3.11, 3.12, 3.15, 3.16, 3.17 and 3.18

7   Remove the brake pads from the caliper (see Section 2).

8   Clean the exterior of the caliper with brake system cleaner. Never use gasoline, kerosene or any petroleum-based cleaning solvents. Place the caliper on a clean workbench.

9   Position a wooden block or numerous shop rags in the caliper as a cushion, then use compressed air to remove the piston from the caliper **(see illustration)**. Use only enough air pressure to ease the piston out of the bore. If the piston is blown out, even with the cushion in place, it may be damaged. **Warning:** *Never place your fingers in front of the piston in an attempt to catch or protect it when applying compressed air, as serious injury could occur.*

10   Carefully pry the dust boot out of the caliper bore **(see illustration)**.

11   Using a wood or plastic tool, remove the piston seal from the groove in the caliper bore **(see illustration)**. Metal tools may cause bore damage.

12   Remove the caliper bleeder valve, then remove and discard the sleeves and bushings from the caliper ears. Discard all rubber parts **(see illustration)**.

13   Clean the remaining parts with brake system cleaner.

14   Carefully examine the piston for nicks and burrs and loss of plating. If surface defects are present, parts must be replaced. Check the caliper bore in a similar way. Light polishing with crocus cloth is permissible to remove light corrosion and stains. Discard the mounting bolts if they are corroded or damaged.

15   When assembling, lubricate the piston

bores and seal with clean brake fluid. Position the seal in the caliper bore groove **(see illustration)**.

16   Lubricate the piston with clean brake fluid, then install a new boot in the piston groove with the fold toward the open end of

the piston **(see illustration)**.

17   Insert the piston squarely into the caliper bore, then apply force to bottom the piston in the bore **(see illustration)**.

18   Position the dust boot in the caliper bore, then use a drift punch to drive it into

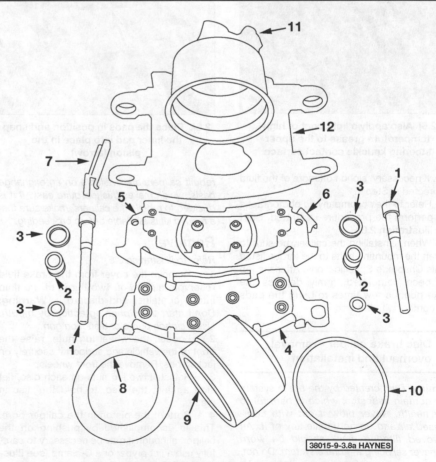

3.12 Exploded view of the disc brake caliper components

1	Mounting bolt	5	Inner pad	9	Piston
2	Sleeve	6	Wear sensor	10	Piston seal
3	Bushing	7	Pad retainer	11	Bleeder valve
4	Outer pad	8	Dust boot	12	Caliper housing

3.15 Position the seal in the caliper bore groove, making sure it is not twisted

3.16 Install the new dust boot in the piston groove with the folds toward the open end of the piston

3.17 Install the piston squarely into the caliper bore

position **(see illustration)**. Make sure that the boot is evenly installed below the caliper face.
19   Install the bleeder valve.
20   Install new bushings in the mounting bolt holes and fill the area between the bushings with silicone grease, supplied in the rebuild kit. Push the sleeves into the mounting bolt holes.

Installation

Refer to illustration 3.23
21   Inspect the mounting bolts for excessive corrosion.
22   Install the brake pads (see Section 2). Place the caliper in position over the disc and mounting bracket, install the bolts and tighten them to the torque listed in this Chapter's Specifications.
23   Check to make sure the clearance between the caliper and the bracket stops is between 0.005 and 0.012 inch **(see illustration)**.
24   Install the brake hose-to-caliper banjo bolt, using new sealing washers, then tighten the bolt to the torque listed in this Chapter's Specifications. It will be necessary to bleed the brakes (see Section 9).
25   Install the wheels and lower the vehicle.
26   After the job has been completed, lightly pump the brake pedal a few times to bring the pads into contact with the disc before test driving.

4   Brake disc - inspection, removal and installation

Inspection

Refer to illustrations 4.2, 4.3, 4.4a, 4.4b, 4.5a and 4.5b
1   Loosen the wheel lug nuts, raise the vehicle and support it securely on jackstands. Remove the wheel and install two lug nuts to hold the disc in place.
2   Remove the brake caliper as outlined in Section 3. It is not necessary to disconnect the brake hose. After removing the caliper bolts, suspend the caliper out of the way with

3.18 Use a seal driver to seat the boot - if a seal driver isn't available, carefully tap around the circumference of the boot with a drift punch until it is seated

a piece of wire **(see illustration)**.
3   Visually inspect the disc surface for scoring or damage. Light scratches and shallow grooves are normal after use and may

3.23 Measure the clearance between the caliper and bracket stops at the top and bottom

not always be detrimental to brake operation, but deep scoring - over 0.015 inch (0.38 mm) - requires disc removal and refinishing by an automotive machine shop. Be sure to check both sides of the disc **(see illustration)**. If

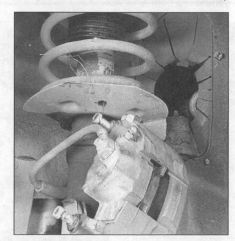

4.2 Suspend the caliper with a piece of wire whenever it is necessary to reposition it. Do not let it hang by the brake hose!

4.3 The brake pads on this vehicle were obviously neglected, as they wore down to the rivets and cut deep grooves into the disc - wear this severe means the disc must be replaced

9

4.4a Check for runout with a dial indicator, mounted with the indicator needle about 1/2-inch from the outside edge

4.4b If you elect not to have the discs machined, at the very least be sure to break the glaze on the disc surface with sandpaper or emery cloth

4.5a The minimum wear (or discard) thickness (arrow) is cast into the inside of the disc

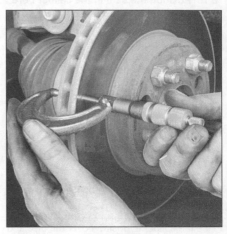

4.5b Measure the thickness of the disc with a micrometer

pulsating has been noticed during application of the brakes, suspect disc runout.

4   To check disc runout, place a dial indicator at a point about 1/2-inch from the outer edge of the disc **(see illustration)**. Set the indicator to zero and turn the disc. The indicator reading should not exceed the specified allowable runout limit. If it does, the disc should be refinished by an automotive machine shop. **Note:** *It is recommended that the discs be resurfaced regardless of the dial indicator reading, as this will impart a smooth finish and ensure a perfectly flat surface, eliminating any brake pedal pulsation or other undesirable symptoms related to questionable discs. At the very least, if you elect not to have the discs resurfaced, remove the glazing from the surface with sandpaper or emery cloth using a swirling motion* **(see illustration)**.

5   It is absolutely critical that the disc not be machined to a thickness under the specified minimum allowable disc refinish thickness. The minimum wear (or discard) thickness is cast into the inside of the disc **(see**

illustration). The disc thickness can be checked with a micrometer **(see illustration)**.

Removal

6   Remove the two lug nuts that were put on to hold the disc in place and remove the disc from the hub.

Installation

7   Place the disc in position over the threaded studs.
8   Install the caliper and brake pad assembly over the disc and position it on the steering knuckle (see Section 3 for the caliper installation procedure, if necessary). Tighten the caliper bolts to the torque listed in this Chapter's Specifications.
9   Install the wheel, then lower the vehicle to the ground. Depress the brake pedal a few times to bring the brake pads into contact with the disc. Bleeding of the system will not be necessary unless the fluid hose was disconnected from the caliper. Check the operation of the brakes carefully before placing the vehicle into normal service.

5   Rear brake shoes - inspection and replacement

Refer to illustrations 5.4a through 5.4ae, 5.5a and 5.5b
Warning: *Drum brake shoes must be replaced on both wheels at the same time - never replace the shoes on only one wheel.*

5.4a If the brake drum will not come off easily, it may be necessary to remove the lanced cutout with a hammer and chisel, then turn the adjuster screw to move the brake shoes away from the drum

5.4b Before removing anything, clean the brake assembly with brake system cleaner - DO NOT use compressed air to blow the dust from the brake assembly!

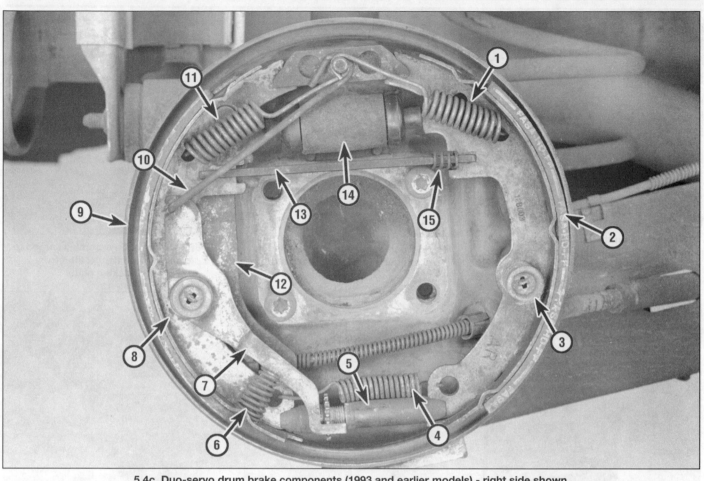

5.4c Duo-servo drum brake components (1993 and earlier models) - right side shown

1	Return spring	6	Lever return spring	11	Return spring
2	Primary shoe	7	Actuator lever	12	Parking brake lever
3	Hold-down spring	8	Hold-down spring	13	Parking brake strut
4	Adjuster screw spring	9	Secondary shoe	14	Wheel cylinder
5	Adjuster screw assembly	10	Actuator link	15	Strut spring

Also, the dust created by the brake system may contain asbestos, which is harmful to your health. Never blow it out with compressed air and do not inhale any of it. An approved filtering mask should be worn whenever servicing the brake system. Do not, under any circumstances, use petroleum-based solvents to clean brake parts. Use brake system cleaner only.

Caution: *Whenever the brake shoes are replaced, the retractor and hold down springs should also be replaced. Due to the continuous heating/cooling cycle that the springs are subjected to, they lose their tension over a period of time and may allow the shoes to drag on the drum and wear at a much faster rate than normal.*

1   Loosen the wheel lug nuts, raise the vehicle and support it securely on jackstands.
2   Release the parking brake.
3   Remove the wheel. **Note:** *All four rear shoes must be replaced at the same time, but to avoid mixing up parts, work on only one brake assembly at a time.*
4   Refer to the accompanying photographs and perform the brake shoe inspection and, if

necessary, the replacement procedure. If you're working on a duo-servo type brake, start with **illustration 5.4a**. If you're working on a leading/trailing type brake, start with

illustration 5.4z. If you don't know which kind of brake you have, compare your brake with illustrations 5.4c and 5.4z. **Note:** *If the brake drum cannot be easily removed, make*

5.4d Remove the return springs using a brake spring tool

5.4e Remove the hold down springs and pins. To do this, push down on the retainer, turn it 1/4-turn to align the slot in the retainer with the blade on the pin, then release

9

5.4f Lift up on the actuator lever and remove the actuating link from the anchor pin pivot along with the actuator lever and return spring (arrows)

5.4g Spread the shoes apart at the top and remove the parking brake strut

5.4h With the shoe assembly spread to clear the hub flange, lift it from the backing plate

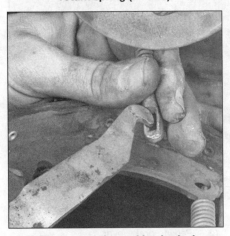

5.4i Disconnect the parking brake lever from the cable and remove the shoe assembly

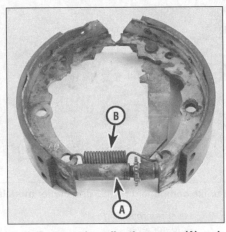

5.4j Remove the adjusting screw (A) and spring (B) from the shoe assembly, making sure to note the direction in which they are installed

5.4k Remove the parking brake lever by prying off the C-clip

sure that the parking brake is completely released, then squirt some penetrating oil around the center hub area. Allow the oil to soak in then try to pull the drum off. If the drum still cannot be pulled off, the brake shoes will have to be retracted. This is

accomplished on duo-servo designs by first removing the lanced cutout in the brake drum with a hammer and chisel (see illustration 5.4a), or on leading/trailing designs by

removing the rubber plug in the backing plate. With the cutout or plug removed, pull the lever off the adjusting screw wheel with one small screwdriver while turning the adjusting wheel with another small screwdriver, moving the shoes away from the drum. The drum may now be pulled off.

5.4l Install the parking brake lever on the new brake shoe and press the C-clip into place with needle-nose pliers

5.4m Lubricate the contact surfaces of the backing plate with a light film of high-temperature grease

5.4n Lubricate the adjuster screw with high-temperature grease prior to installation

5.4o Join the brake shoes with the adjusting screw spring, install the adjuster screw (with the long end pointing towards the front of the vehicle), then connect the parking brake lever to the cable

5.4p Spread the brake assembly apart sufficiently to clear the hub flange and raise it into position

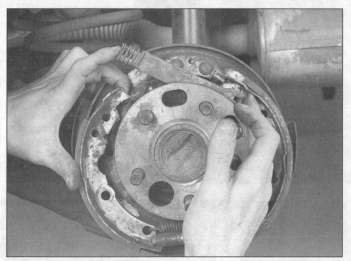

5.4q Install the parking brake and spring

5.4r Make sure the parking brake strut is positioned in the shoes properly (arrows)

5.4s Install the hold-down pin and spring on the primary brake shoe

5.4t Install the actuator link and lever to the secondary brake shoe

5.4u Install the actuator lever return spring

9

5.4v Install the hold-down pin and spring on the secondary brake shoe

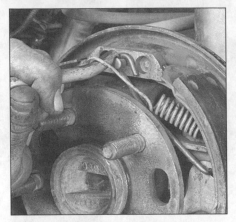

5.4w Install the return springs

5.4x Center the brake shoe assembly so the drum will slide over it

5.4y Adjust the star wheel so the drum fits snugly over the shoes, then after the drum has been installed, turn the star wheel so the drum doesn't drag

5.4z Drum brake components - 1994 and later models

1 Actuator spring
2 Trailing shoe
3 Retractor spring
4 Leading shoe
5 Adjusting screw
6 Actuator lever
7 Wheel cylinder
8 Backing plate

5.4aa Use a pair of needle-nose pliers to remove the actuator spring

5.4ab Wedge a flat-bladed screwdriver under the spring and pry it out of the leading brake shoe, then remove the shoe, adjusting screw and actuator lever

5.4ac Lift the retractor spring from the trailing brake shoe and swing the shoe out from the hub area to gain access to the parking brake cable

5   Before reinstalling the drum it should be checked for cracks, score marks, deep scratches and hard spots, which will appear as small discolored areas. If the hard spots cannot be removed with sandpaper or emery cloth or if any of the other conditions listed above exist, the drum must be taken to an automotive machine shop to have it resurfaced. **Note:** *It is recommended that the drums be resurfaced regardless of the sur-*

face appearance, as this will impart a smooth finish and ensure a perfectly round drum, eliminating any brake pedal pulsation or other undesirable symptoms related to questionable drums. At the very least, if you elect not to have the drums resurfaced, remove the glazing from the surface with sandpaper or emery cloth using a swirling motion **(see**

illustration). *If the drum will not "clean up" before the maximum service limit is reached in the machining operation, it will have to be replaced with a new one. The maximum wear diameter is cast into the each brake drum* **(see illustration)**. *This should not be confused with the service limit (the dimension at which the drum should be thrown away).*

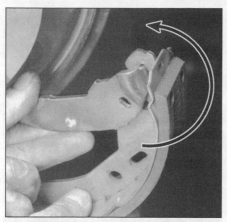

5.4ad Rotate the brake shoe to release the parking brake lever from the shoe

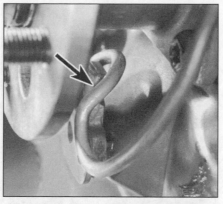

5.4ae Use a screwdriver to pry the retractor spring over the alignment peg (arrow) - to install the new shoes on these models, perform Steps 5.4m and 5.4n, then reverse the removal steps and proceed to Steps 5.4x and 5.4y

5.5a Remove the glaze from the drum braking surface with sandpaper or emery cloth, working in a circular motion

5.5b The drum has a maximum permissible diameter cast into it (arrow) which is a wear dimension, not a refinish dimension

6   Install the brake drum on the axle flange.
7   Mount the wheel, install the lug nuts, then lower the vehicle.
8   Make a number of forward and reverse stops to adjust the brakes until a satisfactory pedal action is obtained.

6   Rear wheel cylinder - removal, overhaul and installation

Note: *If an overhaul is indicated (usually because of fluid leakage or sticky operation) explore all options before beginning the job. New wheel cylinders are available, which makes this job quite easy. If it is decided to rebuild the wheel cylinder, make sure that a rebuild kit is available before proceeding.*

Removal

Refer to illustrations 6.4 and 6.5
1   Raise the rear of the vehicle and support it securely on jackstands.
2   Remove the brake shoe assembly (see Section 5).
3   Carefully clean all dirt and foreign material from around the wheel cylinder.

6.4 A flare-nut wrench should be used to disconnect the brake line (arrow)

4   Using a flare-nut wrench, if available, disconnect the brake fluid inlet line **(see illustration)**. Do not pull the brake line away from the wheel cylinder.
5   Two types of wheel cylinder fasteners are used to retain the wheel cylinder to the backing plate; either two screws or a ring-type retainer. If equipped with the ring-type retainer, pry off the retainer using two small

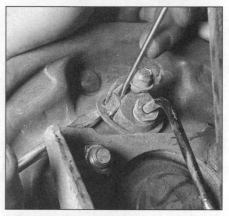

6.5 If equipped with the ring-type retainer, pry the retainer off using two small screwdrivers

screwdrivers **(see illustration)**.
6   Remove the wheel cylinder from the brake backing plate and place it on a clean workbench. Immediately plug the brake line to prevent fluid loss and contamination.

Overhaul

Refer to illustration 6.7
7   Remove the bleeder valve, seals, pis-

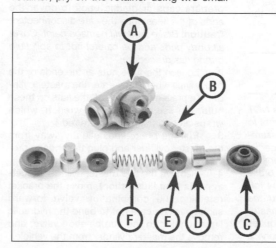

6.7 Wheel cylinder components - exploded view

A	Wheel cylinder body
B	Bleeder valve
C	Boot
D	Piston
E	Seal
F	Spring assembly

9

6.13 A wood block (arrow) should be used to hold the wheel cylinder in position

7.4 Remove the master cylinder mounting nuts (arrows)

7.8 Pry the plastic reservoir from the cylinder body

7.9 Remove the proportioner valves (1987 and earlier models shown)

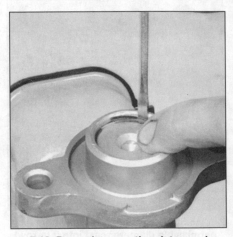

7.10 Press down on the piston and remove the lock ring

tons, boots and spring assembly from the cylinder body **(see illustration)**.

8   Clean the wheel cylinder with brake system cleaner. **Warning:** *Do not, under any circumstances, use petroleum based solvents to clean brake parts.*

9   Use filtered, unlubricated compressed air to remove excess fluid from the wheel cylinder and to blow out the passages.

10   Check the cylinder bore for corrosion and scoring. Crocus cloth may be used to remove light corrosion and stains, but the cylinder must be replaced with a new one if the defects cannot be removed easily, or if the bore is scored.

11   Lubricate the new seals with brake fluid.

12   Assemble the brake cylinder, making sure the boots are properly seated.

Installation

Refer to illustration 6.13

13   Place the wheel cylinder in position and use a wooden block wedged between the axle flange and the cylinder body to hold it in place **(see illustration)**

14   Install the two screws and tighten them securely, or if equipped with the ring-type retainer, use a 1-1/8 deep socket to drive the retainer on. Make sure the tabs are securely locked into place.

15   Connect the brake line and install the brake shoe assembly.

7   Master cylinder - removal, overhaul and installation

Warning: *The following procedure does NOT apply to vehicles with ABS. Do NOT attempt to remove the master cylinder/modulator assembly on an ABS-equipped model. Special equipment is needed to relieve gear tension inside the modulator before the metal brake hydraulic lines can be disconnected. The following procedure is therefore beyond the scope of the home mechanic. If the master cylinder on an ABS-equipped model requires service, it must be handled by a dealer service*

department or other qualified repair shop.
Note: *Before deciding to overhaul the master cylinder, investigate the availability and cost of a new or factory-rebuilt unit and also the availability of a rebuild kit.*

Removal

Refer to illustration 7.4

1   Place rags under the fluid fittings and prepare caps or plastic bags to cover the ends of the lines once they are disconnected. **Caution:** *Brake fluid will damage paint. Cover all body parts and be careful not to spill fluid during this procedure.*

2   Loosen the tube nuts at the ends of the brake lines where they enter the master cylinder. To prevent rounding off the flats on these nuts, the use of a flare-nut wrench, which wraps around the nut, is preferred.

3   Pull the brake lines slightly away from the master cylinder and plug the ends to prevent contamination.

4   Remove the two master cylinder mounting nuts **(see illustration)**, move the bracket retaining the combination valve forward slightly, taking care not to bend the hydraulic lines running to the combination valve, and remove the master cylinder from the vehicle.

Overhaul

Refer to illustrations 7.8, 7.9, 7.10, 7.11, 7.14a, 7.14b, 7.20, 7.22, 7.24, 7.25a through 7.25f, 7.26 and 7.27a through 7.27e

5   Remove the reservoir cover and reservoir diaphragm, then discard any remaining fluid in the reservoir.

6   Mount the master cylinder in a vise. Be sure to line the vise jaws with blocks of wood to prevent damage to the cylinder body.

7   On 1988 and later models, drive out the spring pins with a narrow punch. Be careful not to damage the reservoir or the master cylinder body when driving out the pins.

8   On 1987 and earlier models, pry the reservoir from the master cylinder body with a prybar **(see illustration)** On 1988 and later models, remove the reservoir by pulling it straight up. Remove the reservoir grommets or O rings.

9   Remove the proportioner valves (1987 and earlier models) or the proportioner valve caps (1988 and later models) **(see illustration)**. You may have to use needle-nose pliers to remove the proportioner valve pistons. Be careful not to scratch or damage the piston stems.

7.11 Remove the primary piston assembly

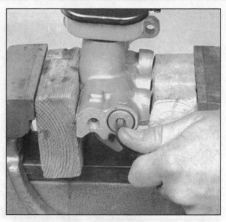

7.14a Remove the switch piston plug (1987 and earlier models)

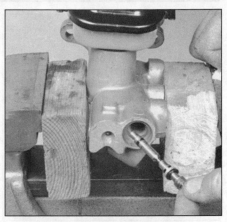

7.14b Remove the switch piston assembly (1987 and earlier models)

10   Remove the primary piston lock ring by depressing the piston and prying the ring out with a screwdriver (see illustration).

11   Remove the primary piston assembly from the cylinder bore (see illustration).

12   Remove the secondary piston assembly from the cylinder bore. It may be necessary to remove the master cylinder from the vise and invert it, carefully tapping it against a block of wood to expel the piston.

13   Do not attempt to remove the quick take-up valve from the cylinder body, as this valve is not serviceable.

14   On 1987 and earlier models, remove the pressure differential warning switch plug and the switch piston assembly (see illustrations). It may be necessary to lightly tap the master cylinder to remove the piston.

15   Clean all parts with brake system cleaner.

16   Inspect the cylinder bore for corrosion and damage. If any corrosion or damage is found, replace the master cylinder body with a new one, as abrasives cannot be used on the bore.

17   On 1987 and earlier models, install the proportioner valve assemblies into the master cylinder body (see illustration 7.9a).

18   On 1988 and later models, lubricate the new O-rings, proportioner valve seals and proportioner valve pistons with silicone grease. Install the new seals on the proportioner valve pistons with the seal lips facing up, towards the valve cap (see illustration 7.9b). Install the proportioner valve pistons

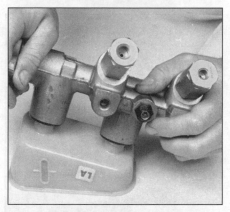

7.20 Use a rocking motion when pressing the reservoir onto the master cylinder

and seals into the master cylinder body. Install the valve springs. Install new O-rings onto the valve caps and install the caps into the master cylinder. Tighten the caps to the torque listed in this Chapters' Specifications.

19   Lubricate the new reservoir grommets with silicone lubricant and press the grommets into the master cylinder body, making sure they are properly seated.

20   Lay the reservoir on a hard surface and press the master cylinder body onto the reservoir, using a rocking motion (see illustration).

21   Drive in the spring pins to retain the reservoir, using care not to damage the reservoir or master cylinder body (1988 and later models).

22   Remove the old seals from the sec-

7.22 The secondary piston seals must be installed with the lips facing out as shown

ondary piston assembly and install the new seals so that the cups face away from each other (see illustration).

23   Attach the spring retainer to the secondary piston assembly.

24   Lubricate the cylinder bore with clean brake fluid and install the spring and secondary piston assembly in the cylinder (see illustration).

25   Disassemble the primary piston assembly, noting the position of the parts, then lubricate the new seals with clean brake fluid

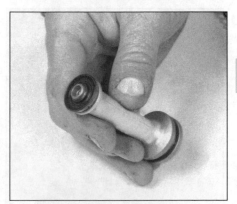

7.25a The primary piston seal must be installed with the lip facing away from the piston

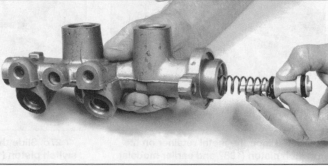

7.24 Install the secondary piston assembly

9

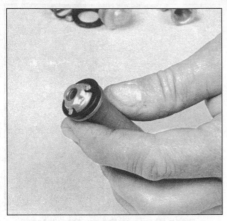

7.25b   Install the seal guard over the seal

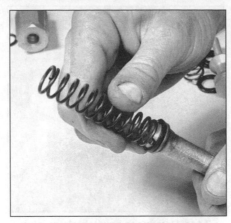

7.25c   Place the primary piston spring in position

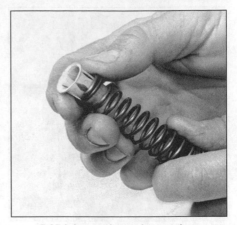

7.25d   Insert the spring retainer into the spring

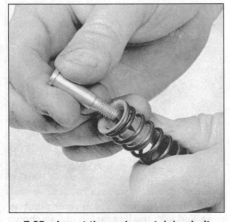

7.25e   Insert the spring retaining bolt through the retainer and spring and thread it into the piston

7.25f   Install the O-ring on the piston

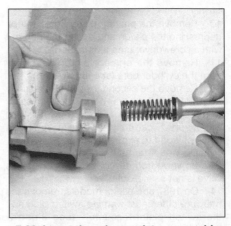

7.26   Insert the primary piston assembly into the body

and install them on the piston **(see illustrations)**.

26   Install the primary piston assembly in the cylinder bore **(see illustration)**, depress it and install the lock ring.

27   On 1987 and earlier models, install the new O-rings on the switch piston, lubricate the piston with silicone grease and carefully

insert it back into the master cylinder **(see illustrations)**. Install a new O-ring on the piston plug, install the plug and tighten it to the torque listed in this Chapter's Specifications.

28   Inspect the reservoir cover and diaphragm for cracks and deformation. Replace any damaged parts with new ones.

29   **Note:** *Whenever the master cylinder is removed, the complete hydraulic system must be bled. The time required to bleed the*

system can be reduced if the master cylinder is filled with fluid and bench bled (see Steps 29 through 32) before the master cylinder is installed on the vehicle. Insert threaded plugs of the correct size into the cylinder outlet holes and fill the reservoirs with brake fluid. The master cylinder should be supported in such a manner that brake fluid will not spill during the bench bleeding procedure.

30   Loosen one plug at a time and push the

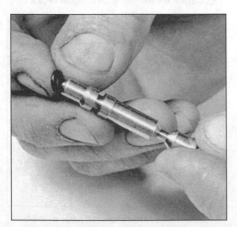

7.27a   Install the small O-ring on the switch piston (1987 and earlier models)

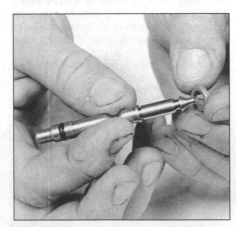

7.27b   Place the metal retainer on the switch piston (1987 and earlier models)

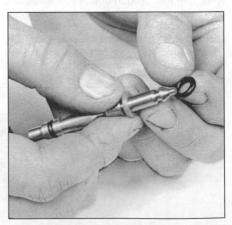

7.27c   Slide the large O-ring onto the switch piston (1987 and earlier models)

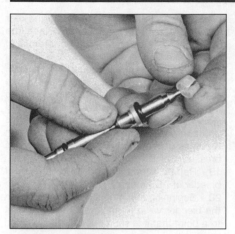

7.27d Install the plastic retainer on the switch piston (1987 and earlier models)

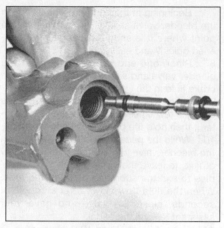

7.27e Insert the switch piston assembly into the cylinder body (1987 and earlier models)

piston assembly into the bore to force air from the master cylinder. To prevent air from being drawn back into the cylinder, the appropriate plug must be replaced before allowing the piston to return to its original position.

31   Stroke the piston three or four times for each outlet to assure that all air has been expelled.

32   Since high pressure is not involved in the bench bleeding procedure, an alternative to the removal and replacement of the plugs with each stroke of the piston assembly is available. Before pushing in on the piston assembly, remove one of the plugs completely. Before releasing the piston, however, instead of replacing the plug, simply put your finger tightly over the hole to keep air from being drawn back into the master cylinder. Wait several seconds for the brake fluid to be drawn from the reservoir to the piston bore, then repeat the procedure. When you push down on the piston it will force your finger off the hole, allowing the air inside to be expelled. When only brake fluid is being ejected from the hole, replace the plug and

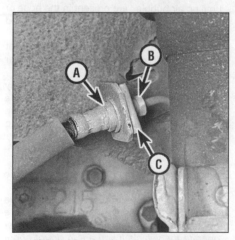

8.2 Using a back-up wrench on the flexible hose side of the fitting (A), loosen the tube nut (B) with a flare-nut wrench and remove the U-clip (C) from the hose fitting

go on to the other port.

33   Refill the master cylinder reservoirs and install the diaphragm and cover assembly. **Note:** *The reservoirs should only be filled to the top of the reservoir divider to prevent overflowing when the cover is installed.*

Installation

34   Install the master cylinder by reversing the removal steps, then bleed the brakes as necessary (see Section 9). Be sure to tighten the master cylinder-to-booster mounting nuts to the torque listed in this Chapter's Specifications.

8   Brake hoses and lines - inspection and replacement

1   About every six months, with the vehicle raised and placed securely on jackstands, the flexible hoses that connect the steel brake lines with the front and rear brake assemblies should be inspected for cracks, chafing of the outer cover, leaks, blisters and other damage. These are important and vulnerable parts of the brake system and inspection should be complete. A light and mirror will prove helpful for a thorough check. If a hose exhibits any of the above conditions, replace it with a new one.

Front brake hose

Refer to illustration 8.2

2   Using a back-up wrench, disconnect the brake line from the hose fitting, being careful not to bend the frame bracket or brake line **(see illustration)**.

3   Use pliers to remove the U-clip from the female fitting at the bracket, then remove the hose from the bracket.

4   At the caliper end of the hose, remove the bolt from the fitting block, then remove the hose and the sealing washers on either side of the fitting block.

5   When installing the hose, always use new sealing washers on either side of the fit-

ting block and lubricate all bolt threads with clean brake fluid before installation.

6   With the fitting flange engaged with the caliper locating ledge, attach the hose to the caliper.

7   Without twisting the hose, install the female fitting in the hose bracket. It will fit the bracket in only one position.

8   Install the U-clip retaining the female fitting to the frame bracket.

9   Using a back-up wrench, attach the brake line to the hose fitting.

10   When the brake hose installation is complete, there should be no kinks in the hose. Make sure the hose does not contact any part of the suspension. Check this by turning the wheels to the extreme left and right positions. If the hose makes contact, remove the hose and correct the installation as necessary.

Rear brake hose

11   Using a back-up wrench, disconnect the hose at both ends, being careful not to bend the bracket or steel lines **(see illustration 8.2)**.

12   Remove the two U-clips with pliers and separate the female fittings from the brackets.

13   Unbolt the hose retaining clip and remove the hose.

14   Without twisting the hose, install the female ends of the hose in the frame brackets. It will fit the bracket in only one position.

15   Install the U-clips retaining the female end to the bracket.

16   Using a back-up wrench, attach the steel line fittings to the female fittings. Again, be careful not to bend the bracket or steel line.

17   Check that the hose installation did not loosen the frame bracket. Tighten the bracket if necessary.

18   Fill the fluid reservoir and bleed the system (see Section 9).

Metal brake lines

19   When replacing brake lines it is important that the proper replacements be purchased. Do not use copper pipe for any brake system connections. Purchase proper brake line from an auto parts store, dealer or brake specialist.

20   Prefabricated brake lines with the tube ends already flared and connectors installed, are available at auto parts stores or dealers.

21   If necessary, carefully bend the line to the proper shape. A tube bender is recommended for this. **Caution:** *Do not crimp or damage the line.*

22   When installing the new line make sure it is well supported in the brackets and has plenty of clearance between moving or hot components.

23   After installation, check the fluid level and add fluid as necessary. Bleed the brake system as outlined in Section 9 and test the brakes before placing the vehicle into normal service.

9

9   Brake system bleeding

Warning: *Wear eye protection whenever bleeding the brake system. If the fluid comes in contact with your eyes, immediately rinse them with water and seek a physician's advice.*

Note: *Bleeding the hydraulic system is necessary to remove any air in the system or when the system has been opened for repairs.*

1   It will probably be necessary to bleed the system at all four brakes if air has entered the system due to low fluid level.

2   If a brake line was disconnected only at a wheel, then only that caliper or wheel cylinder must be bled unless the system is allowed to drain through the open line.

3   If a brake line is disconnected at a fitting located between the master cylinder and any of the brakes, the part of the system served by the disconnected line must be bled.

4   Remove the master cylinder reservoir cover and fill the reservoir with brake fluid. Reinstall the cover. **Note:** *Check the fluid level often during the bleeding operation and add fluid as necessary to prevent the fluid level from falling low enough to allow air bubbles into the master cylinder.*

5   Have an assistant on hand, as well as a supply of new brake fluid, an empty clear plastic container, a length of 3/16-inch plastic, rubber or vinyl tubing to fit over the bleeder valve and a wrench to open and close the bleeder valve.

Conventional (non-ABS) system

Refer to illustration 9.8

6   Remove any residual vacuum from the brake power booster by applying the brake several times with the engine off.

9.8 When bleeding the brakes, a hose is connected to the bleeder valve at the caliper (or wheel cylinder) and then submerged in brake fluid. Air will be seen as bubbles in the container or in the tube. All air must be expelled before continuing to the next wheel

7   Beginning at the right rear wheel, loosen the bleeder valve slightly, then tighten it to a point where it is snug but can still be loosened quickly and easily.

8   Place one end of the tubing over the bleeder valve and submerge the other end in brake fluid in the container **(see illustration)**.

9   Have the assistant pump the brakes slowly a few times to get pressure in the system, then hold the pedal firmly depressed.

10   While the pedal is held depressed, open the bleeder valve just enough to allow a flow of fluid to leave the valve. Watch for air bubbles to exit the submerged end of the tube. When the fluid flow slows after a couple of seconds, close the valve and have your assistant release the pedal.

11   Repeat Steps 9 and 10 until no more air is seen leaving the tube, then tighten the bleeder valve and proceed to the left rear wheel, the right front wheel and the left front wheel, in that order, and perform the same procedure. Be sure to check the fluid in the master cylinder reservoir frequently.

12   Never use old brake fluid. It contains moisture that will deteriorate the brake system components.

13   Refill the master cylinder with fluid at the end of the operation.

14   Check the operation of the brakes. The pedal should feel solid when depressed, with no sponginess. If necessary, repeat the entire process. **Warning:** *Do not operate the vehicle if you are in doubt about the effectiveness of the brake system.*

Anti-lock Brake System (ABS)

Warning: *To properly bleed the ABS system on these vehicles, this entire bleeding procedure must be followed. This method can only be used if the ABS warning lamp is not illuminated and the ABS control system is functioning properly. Do not press on the brake pedal during this procedure unless you are directed to do so.*

15   With your foot off the brake pedal, start the engine and run it for at least 10 seconds while observing the ABS warning lamp. The warning lamp should light for approximately three seconds and then go off.

16   Repeat Step 15. If the warning lamp fails to come on at all or if it stays on after 10 seconds, this procedure must be stopped and the ABS system must be diagnosed and repaired before bleeding. If the warning lamp comes on for approximately three seconds and then goes off, proceed to Step 17.

Note: *The ABS modulator valve is mounted on the side of the master cylinder. There are two bleeder valves on the front of the ABS modulator valve assembly. The innermost bleeder, closest to the fluid reservoir, is referred to as the rear bleeder. The outermost bleeder is referred to as the front bleeder. Check the fluid reservoir throughout this procedure and make sure it is kept filled to the proper level.*

17   Repeat Step 15 five times to correctly position the pistons in the modulator valve.

Place one end of a clear hose onto the rear bleeder of the ABS modulator. Place the other end into a partially filled container of clean brake fluid.

18   Open the rear bleeder 3/4 of a turn. Have an assistant press down the brake pedal and hold it until brake fluid begins to flow into the tube. Close the bleeder and slowly release the brake pedal. Repeat this procedure until no air bubbles are visible in the hose or the container when the pedal is pressed down.

19   Repeat Steps 17 and 18 on the front bleeder of ABS modulator.

20   Beginning at the right rear wheel, loosen the bleeder valve slightly, and then tighten it to a point that it is snug but can be loosened easily.

21   Place one end of a clear hose onto the bleeder and the other end into a partially filled container of clean brake fluid **(see illustration 9.8)**.

22   Open the bleeder valve and have the assistant slowly press down on the brake pedal. Close the bleeder and slowly release the pedal.

23   Wait at least five seconds and repeat Step 22.

24   Repeat Steps 22 and 23 until no air bubbles are present in the hose or the container when the pedal is pressed down. Tighten the bleeder valve.

25   Repeat Steps 20 through 24 on the left rear wheel, the right front wheel and the left front wheel, in that order. Be sure to check the fluid level in the master cylinder reservoir frequently.

26   Place one end of a clear bleeder hose onto the rear bleeder of the ABS modulator. Place the other end into a partially filled container of clean brake fluid.

27   Have the assistant press down on the brake pedal with moderate force and slowly open the rear bleeder 3/4 of a turn to release pressure. Close the bleeder and have the assistant slowly release the brake pedal.

28   Wait five seconds and repeat Step 27 until no air bubbles are present in the hose or the container when the pedal is pressed down. Tighten the bleeder valve.

29   Repeat Steps 27 and 28 on the front bleeder of ABS modulator. Top up the master cylinder fluid reservoir.

30   Turn the ignition switch on and apply moderate pressure to the brake pedal. The pedal travel should not be excessive and the pedal should feel firm. If not, proceed to Step 32.

31   Start the engine and apply moderate pressure to the brake pedal. If the pedal travel is not excessive and the pedal feels firm, proceed to Step 33.

32   If the pedal feels soft or has excessive travel, repeat the entire bleeding procedure beginning with Step 17. **Warning:** *Never operate the vehicle if you are in doubt about the effectiveness of the brake system.*

33   Road test the vehicle making several normal stops from a moderate speed. Test the brakes while driving on a clean, dry, flat

10.4 With a pair of locking pliers clamped to the end of the threaded rod to prevent it from turning, turn the adjusting nut until the right rear wheel can just be turned in a rearward direction but not in the forward direction

surface. Then test the brakes at various speeds with both light and heavy pedal pressure. The vehicle should stop evenly without pulling to one side or the other.

10 Parking brake - adjustment

Refer to illustration 10.4

1 Apply the parking brake lever exactly three ratchet clicks.
2 Raise the vehicle and support it securely on jackstands.
3 Before adjusting, make sure the equalizer nut groove is lubricated with multi-purpose grease.
4 Tighten the adjusting nut **(see illustration)** until the right rear wheel can just be turned rearward with two hands, but locks when forward motion is attempted.
5 Release the parking brake lever and check to make sure the rear wheels turn freely in both directions with no drag.
6 Lower the vehicle.

11 Parking brake cables - removal and installation

Front cable

Hand brake models

1 Remove the console trim to gain access to the parking brake handle mechanism (see Chapter 11).
2 Remove the cable nut from the cable at the hand brake lever and push the cable and housing through the floorpan.
3 Raise the rear of the vehicle and support it securely on jackstands.
4 Pull the cable casing from the L-shaped guide just above the rear of the exhaust pipe heat shield.
5 Maneuver the cable out of the wire

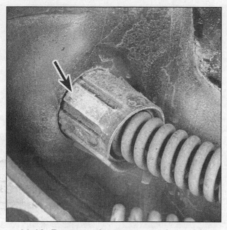

11.19 Depress the tangs on the cable casing retainer and push it through the backing plate

bracket at the left rear suspension pivot.
6 Slide the cable casing out of the equalizer and disconnect the cable from the cable joiner.
7 Installation is the reverse of the removal procedure. Adjust the cable (see Section 10).

Foot lever models

8 Raise the rear of the vehicle and support it securely on jackstands.
9 Maneuver the cable out of the wire bracket at the left rear suspension pivot.
10 Open the tangs connecting the front cable to the right rear cable at the cable joiner on the rear axle. Disconnect the cable from the cable joiner and slide the cable housing out of the equalizer.
11 Remove the left door sill plate and the left front kick panel.
12 Disconnect the cable from the lever assembly. Press down the tangs on the cable housing retainer and remove the housing from the lever assembly.
13 Remove the clips holding the cable housing in the rocker panel. Remove the cable housing grommet from the floor pan, below the rear seat cushion, and pull the front cable out from beneath the vehicle.
14 Installation is the reverse of the removal procedure. Adjust the cable (see Section 10).

Left cable

Refer to illustration 11.19

15 Raise the vehicle and support it securely on jackstands.
16 Loosen the equalizer adjusting screw and disconnect the left cable from the equalizer.
17 Disconnect the cable casing at the frame mounting bracket by depressing the tangs on the retainer with a pair of pliers.
18 Remove the brake shoes as described in Section 5. Disconnect the parking brake cable from the parking brake lever.
19 Using a pair of pliers, depress the tangs on the cable casing retainer and push cable and casing out through the backing plate **(see illustration)**.

20 Installation is the reverse of the removal procedure. Be sure to adjust the cable as described in Section 10.

Right cable

21 Raise the rear of the vehicle and support it securely on jackstands.
22 Remove enough tension at the equalizer to enable the cable to be removed from the cable joiner.
23 Disconnect the cable casing at the frame mounting bracket by depressing the tangs on the retainer with a pair of pliers.
24 Remove the brake drum and brake shoes as described in Section 5. Disconnect the parking brake cable from the parking brake lever.
25 Using a pair of pliers, depress the tangs on the cable casing retainer and push the cable and casing out through the backing plate **(see illustration 11.19)**.
26 Installation is the reverse of the removal procedure. Be sure to adjust the cable as described in Section 10.

12 Power brake booster - check, removal and installation

1 The power brake unit requires no special maintenance apart from periodic inspection of the hoses and inspection of the air filter beneath the boot at the pedal pushrod end. Early models have an in-line filter that should be inspected periodically and replaced if clogged or damaged.
2 Dismantling of the power brake unit requires special tools. If a problem develops, it is recommended that a new or factory-exchange unit be installed rather than trying to overhaul the original booster.

Operating check

3 Depress the brake pedal several times with the engine off and make sure there's no change in the pedal reserve distance.
4 Depress the pedal and start the engine. If the pedal goes down slightly, operation is normal.

Airtightness check

5 Start the engine and turn it off after one or two minutes. Depress the brake pedal slowly several times. If pedal resistance increases each time (gets harder to push down), the booster is airtight.
6 Depress the brake pedal while the engine is running, then stop the engine with the pedal depressed. If there's no change in the pedal reserve travel after holding the pedal for 30 seconds, the booster is airtight.

Removal and installation

Refer to illustrations 12.9a and 12.9b

7 Remove the mounting nuts which hold the master cylinder to the power brake unit. Position the master cylinder out of the way, being careful not to strain the lines leading to

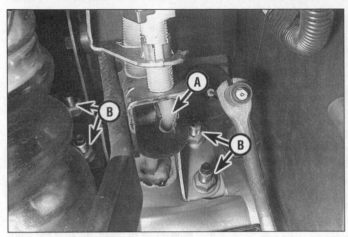

12.9a Remove the retaining clip and slide the power brake pushrod (A) off of the brake pedal pin, then remove the booster-to-firewall nuts (B)

12.9b Remove the brake booster mounting nuts (arrows)

the master cylinder. If there is any doubt as to the flexibility of the lines, disconnect them at the cylinder and plug the ends.

8   Disconnect the vacuum hose leading to the front of the power brake booster. Cover the end of the hose.

9   Inside the vehicle, disconnect the power brake pushrod from the brake pedal. Do not force the pushrod to the side when disconnecting it **(see illustrations)**.

10   Remove the four booster mounting nuts and carefully lift the unit out of the engine compartment.

11   When installing, loosely install the four mounting nuts and connect the pushrod to the brake pedal. Tighten the nuts to the torque listed in this Chapter's Specifications and reconnect the vacuum hose and master cylinder. If the hydraulic brake lines were disconnected, the entire brake system must be bled to eliminate any air which has entered the system (see Section 9).

---

13   Brake light switch - removal, installation and adjustment

Removal

Refer to illustration 13.3

1   The brake light switch, or stop light switch as it is sometimes called, is located on a bracket at the top of the brake pedal. The switch activates the brake lights at the rear of the vehicle whenever the pedal is depressed.

2   Remove the under dash cover and disconnect the wiring to the courtesy lamp in this panel.

3   Locate the switch at the top of the brake pedal **(see illustration)**. If equipped with cruise control, there will be another switch very similar in appearance. The brake light switch is the one towards the end of the bracket.

4   Disconnect the negative battery cable from the battery. **Caution:** *If the vehicle is equipped with a Delco Loc II audio system, make sure you have the correct activation code before disconnecting the battery. See the information at the front of this manual for the radio re-activation procedure.*

5   Disconnect the wiring connectors at the brake light switch.

6   Depress the brake pedal and pull the switch out of its clip. The switch appears to be threaded, but it is designed to be pushed into and out of the clip and not turned.

Installation and adjustment

7   With the brake pedal depressed, push the new switch into the clip.

8   Pull the brake pedal fully rearward

13.3 The brake light switch (arrow) is located to the right of the steering column at the end of the mounting bracket

against the pedal stop until the clicking sounds can no longer be heard. This action will automatically move the switch the proper amount and no further adjustment will be required. **Caution:** *Do not apply excessive force during this adjustment procedure, as power booster damage may result.*

9   Connect the wiring at the switch and the battery. With an assistant, check that the rear brake lights are functioning properly.

Chapter 10
Steering and suspension systems

Contents

Specifications

Torque specifications | Ft-lbs

Front suspension

Control arm pivot bolts	
Through 1994	60
1995	89
Control arm rear (vertical) bolt (1994 and 1995 only)	111
Suspension support (in the following order)	
Center bolts	
Through 1994	66
1995	89
Front bolts	
Through 1994	65
1995	89
Rear bolts	
Through 1994	65
1995	89
Balljoint-to-steering knuckle nut	55
Stabilizer bar-to-control arm nut	15
Stabilizer bar bushing clamp nuts	15
Front hub and wheel bearing assembly bolts	70
Strut-to-steering knuckle nuts	133
Strut-to-body nuts	18
Strut damper shaft nut	60

Rear suspension

Rear hub and wheel bearing assembly bolts	44
Rear axle assembly pivot bolts	63

Steering system

Steering gear-to-firewall clamp nuts	28
Coupling-to-steering column pinch bolt	34
Coupling-to-stub shaft pinch bolt	37
Inner tie rod-to-rack bolts	65
Tie rod end-to-steering knuckle nut	35
Steering wheel hub nut	30
Steering column support bolts/nuts	20

10

Component location

1.1 Front suspension components

A　Control arm
B　Stabilizer bar

C　Suspension support
D　Balljoint

1　General information

Refer to illustrations 1.1 and 1.2
Warning: *Whenever any of the suspension or steering fasteners are loosened or removed they must be inspected and if necessary, be replaced with new ones of the same part number or of original equipment quality and design. Torque specifications must be followed for proper reassembly and component retention. Never attempt to heat or straighten any suspension or steering components. Instead, replace any bent or damaged part with a new one.*

The front suspension is a MacPherson strut design. The steering knuckles are located by lower control arms which are mounted to longitudinally positioned, removable frame members. The control arms are connected by a sway bar, which reduces body lean during cornering **(see illustration).**

The rear suspension is semi-independent with a cross-beam axle with integrated trailing arms, two coil springs and insulator assemblies, two shock absorbers and a stabilizer bar. The axle assembly attaches to the vehicle at two points, one on each side of the vehicle at the underbody side rails **(see illustration).** Models through 1991 use a tubular-type axle assembly, while some 1992 and later models use a "spring-on-center" axle assembly that aligns the center of the spring mount with the axle centerline.

The rack-and-pinion steering gear is located behind the engine/transaxle assembly on the firewall and actuates the steering arms which protrude from the strut housings. Most vehicles are equipped with power steering. The steering column is connected to the steering gear through an insulated coupler. The steering column is designed to collapse in the event of an accident. **Note:** *These vehicles use a combination of standard and metric fasteners on the various suspension and steering components, so it would be a good idea to have both types of tools available when beginning work.*

2　Front stabilizer bar and bushings - removal and installation

Removal

Refer to illustrations 2.2, 2.4a, 2.4b, 2.5, 2.6 and 2.7
Caution: *If the vehicle is equipped with a Delco Loc II audio system, make sure you have the correct activation code before disconnecting the battery. See the information at the front of this manual for the radio re-activation procedure.*

1　Loosen the lug nuts on both front wheels, raise the vehicle and support it securely on jackstands. Remove the front wheels.

2　Remove the stabilizer bar-to-control arm bolts, taking note how the link bushings, spacers and washers are arranged **(see illustration).**

3　Remove the four stabilizer bar bushing clamp nuts through the access holes in the

Component location

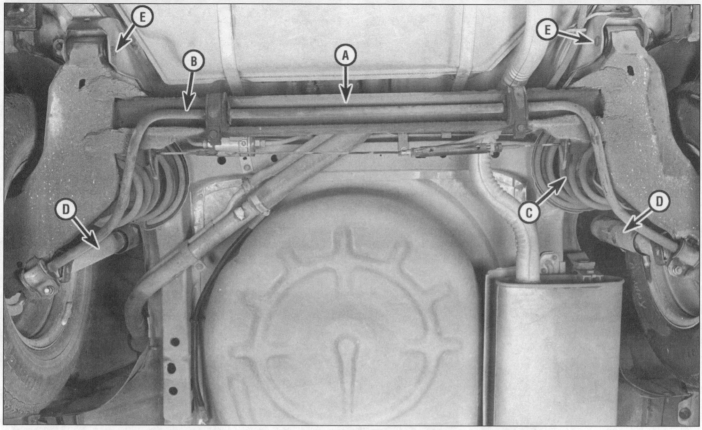

1.2 Typical rear suspension components (tubular-type axle shown)

A   Rear axle assembly
B   Stabilizer bar
C   Coil spring
D   Shock absorber
E   Rear axle-to-underbody bracket mounting point

suspension supports **(see illustration 2.4a)**.
4   Working on one side at a time, place a jack under the suspension support then remove the two rear and the two center

mounting bolts from the suspension support. Slowly lower the jack and allow the support to drop down. It may also be necessary to slightly loosen the two front support mount-

ing bolts on each side to provide adequate clearance for stabilizer bar removal **(see illustrations)**.
5   Push up on the stabilizer bar while

2.2 The stabilizer bar link uses washers, rubber bushings and spacers to connect the stabilizer bar to the control arm

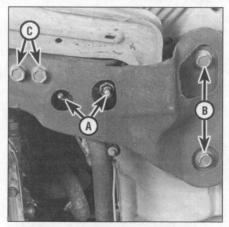

2.4a After removing the stabilizer bar bushing clamp nuts (A), place a jack under the suspension support and remove the rear (B) and center (C) mounting bolts

2.4b If the suspension support doesn't hang down far enough to allow stabilizer bar removal, loosen the two front mounting bolts (arrows) on each suspension support

10

2.5 Separate the stabilizer bar from the suspension support

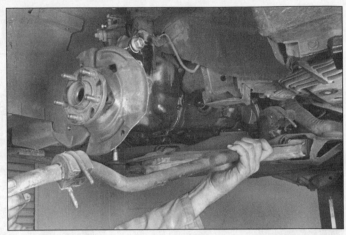

2.6 Guide the stabilizer bar out through the wheel well

2.7 Pry the stabilizer bar bushing clamp off of the bushing

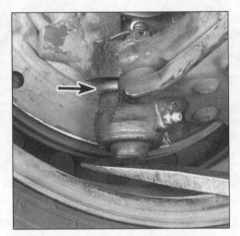

3.3a Check for movement between the balljoint and steering knuckle (arrow) when prying up

3.3b With the pry bar positioned between the steering knuckle boss and the balljoint, pry down and check for play in the balljoint. If there is any play, replace it.

pulling down on the suspension support to separate the bushing clamp from the support **(see illustration)**.

6   Remove the stabilizer bar through the wheel well **(see illustration)**.

7   Inspect the bushings for wear or damage and replace them if necessary. To remove them, pry the bushing clamp off with a screwdriver **(see illustration)** and pull the bushings off of the bar. To ease installation, spray the inside and outside of the bushings with a silicone-based lubricant. Do not use petroleum-based lubricants on any rubber suspension part!

Installation

8   Assemble the shaft bushings and clamps on the bar, guide the bar through the wheel well, over the suspension supports and into position.

9   Insert the clamp studs through the suspension support and install the nuts finger tight.

10   Raise the suspension supports (one at a time) and install the bolts loosely.

11   Center the bar in the vehicle and install the stabilizer bar-to-control arm bolts, spac-

ers, bushings and washers. Tighten all of the fasteners to the torque listed in this Chapter's Specifications at this time.

12   Install the wheels and lower the vehicle. Tighten the lug nuts to the torque listed in the Chapter 1 Specifications.

3   Balljoint - check and replacement

Check

Refer to illustrations 3.3a and 3.3b

1   Raise the vehicle and support it securely on jackstands.

2   Visually inspect the rubber seal for cuts, tears or leaking grease. If any of these conditions are noticed, the balljoint should be replaced.

3   Place a large pry bar under the balljoint and attempt to push the balljoint ups. Next, position the pry bar between the steering knuckle and the control arm and apply down pressure **(see illustrations)**. If any movement is seen or felt during either of these checks, a worn out balljoint is indicated.

4   Have an assistant grasp the tire at the top and bottom and shake the top of the tire in an in-and-out motion. Touch the balljoint stud castellated nut. If any looseness is felt, suspect a worn out balljoint stud or a widened hole in the steering knuckle boss. If the latter problem exists, the steering knuckle should be replaced as well as the balljoint.

5   Separate the lower control arm from the steering knuckle (Section 4). Using your fingers (don't use pliers), try to twist the stud in its socket. If the stud turns, replace the balljoint.

Replacement

Refer to illustration 3.11

6   Loosen the wheel lug nuts, raise the vehicle and support it securely on jackstands. Remove the wheel.

7   Separate the control arm from the steering knuckle (Section 4). Temporarily insert the balljoint stud back into the steering knuckle (loosely). This will ease balljoint removal after Step 9 has been performed, as well as hold the assembly stationary while drilling out the rivets.

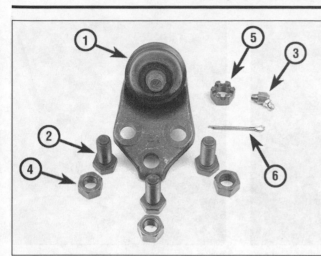

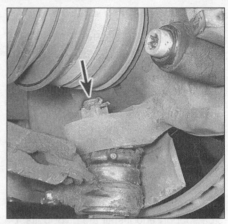

3.11 Replacement balljoint details (typical) - be sure to tighten the bolts to the torque specified on the instruction sheet

1   Replacement balljoint
2   Bolt
3   Grease fitting
4   Nut
5   Castellated nut
6   Cotter pin

4.3 Remove the cotter pin and castellated nut (arrow) from the balljoint stud

4.4 Pry the balljoint out of the steering knuckle. If it is stubborn and won't come out, strike the steering knuckle boss on both sides (arrow) with a hammer, then try again

4.5a The control arm mounting bolts are accessible through the reliefs in the suspension support at the rear . . .

4.5b . . . and at the front

8   Using a 1/8-inch drill bit, drill a pilot hole into the center of each balljoint-to-control arm rivet. Be careful not to damage the CV joint boot in the process.

9   Using a 1/2-inch drill bit, drill the head off each rivet. Work slowly and cautiously so as not to deform the holes in the control arm.

10   Loosen (but do not remove) the stabilizer bar-to-control arm nut. Pull the control arm and balljoint down to remove the balljoint stud from the steering knuckle, then dislodge the balljoint from the control arm.

11   Position the new balljoint on the control arm and install the bolts (supplied in the balljoint kit) from the top of the control arm **(see illustration)**. Tighten the bolts to the torque specified in the new balljoint instruction sheet.

12   Insert the balljoint into the steering knuckle, install the castellated nut, tighten it to the torque listed in this Chapter's Specifications and install a new cotter pin. It may be necessary to turn the nut a bit more to align the cotter pin hole with an opening in the nut, which is acceptable. Never loosen the castellated nut to allow cotter pin insertion.

13   Tighten the stabilizer bar-to-control arm nut to the torque listed in this Chapter's Specifications.

14   Install the wheel, lower the vehicle and tighten the lug nuts to the torque listed in the Chapter 1 Specifications. It is a good idea to take the vehicle to a dealer service department or garage to have the front end alignment checked and if necessary, adjusted.

4   Control arm and suspension support - removal and installation

Removal

Refer to illustrations 4.3, 4.4, 4.5a and 4.5b
Warning: *Some models covered by this manual are equipped with airbags. Always disable the airbag system before working in the vicinity of the impact sensors, steering column or instrument panel to avoid the possibility of accidental deployment of the airbag(s), which could cause personal injury (see Chapter 12 for the airbag disarming procedure). The yellow wires and connectors routed through the instrument panel are for this system. Do not*

use electrical test equipment on these yellow wires or tamper with them in any way while working under the instrument panel.
Caution: *If the vehicle is equipped with a Delco Loc II audio system, make sure you have the correct activation code before disconnecting the battery. See the information at the front of this manual for the radio re-activation procedure.*

1   Loosen the wheel lug nuts, raise the vehicle and support it securely on jackstands. Remove the wheel.

2   If only one control arm is being removed, disconnect only that end of the stabilizer bar. If both control arms are to be removed, disconnect both ends (see Section 2 if necessary).

3   Remove the balljoint stud-to-steering knuckle castellated nut and cotter pin **(see illustration)**.

4   With a large pry bar positioned between the control arm and steering knuckle, "pop" the balljoint out of the knuckle **(see illustration)**. **Caution:** *When removing the balljoint from the knuckle be careful not to overextend the inner CV joint or damage to the joint may occur.*

5   Remove the two control arm pivot bolts and remove the control arm **(see illustrations)**. **Note:** *On 1994 and later models, the*

10

rear of the control arm is secured by one vertical bolt and no nut.

6   The control arm bushings are replaceable, but special tools and expertise are necessary to perform the job. Carefully inspect the bushings for hardening, excessive wear or cracking, and if they appear to be in need of replacement, take the control arm to a dealer service department or repair shop.

7   The suspension support may also be removed if desired. Refer to **illustrations 2.4a and 2.4b** and remove the mounting bolts and support assembly.

Installation

8   Position the control arm in the suspension support and install the pivot bolts. Do not tighten them fully at this time.

9   Insert the balljoint stud in the steering knuckle boss, install the castellated nut and tighten it to the torque listed in this Chapter's Specifications. If necessary, tighten the nut a little more if the cotter pin hole doesn't line up with an opening on the nut. Install a new cotter pin.

10   Install the stabilizer bar-to-control arm bolt, spacer, bushings and washers and tighten the nut to the torque listed in this Chapter's Specifications.

11   Install the wheel and lower the vehicle. Tighten the lug nuts to the torque listed in the Chapter 1 Specifications.

12   With the weight of the vehicle now on the suspension, tighten the control arm pivot bolts to the torque listed in this Chapter's Specifications. **Caution:** *If the bolts aren't tightened with the weight of the vehicle on the suspension, control arm bushing damage may occur.*

13   Drive the vehicle to a dealer service department or an alignment shop to have the front wheel alignment checked and if necessary, adjusted.

---

5   Front strut and spring assembly - removal, inspection and installation

Removal

Refer to illustrations 5.2, 5.4, 5.5 and 5.6

1   Loosen the wheel lug nuts, raise the vehicle and support it securely on jackstands. Remove the wheel.

2   Using white paint or a scribe, place a mark from the strut to the steering knuckle and also around the strut-to-steering knuckle nuts **(see illustration)**.

3   Separate the tie-rod end from the steering arm as described in Section 15.

4   Remove the strut-to-knuckle nuts **(see illustration)** and knock the bolts out with a brass or plastic faced hammer.

5   Separate the strut from the steering knuckle **(see illustration)**. Be careful not to overextend the inner CV joint or stretch the brake hose.

6   Support the strut and spring assembly

5.2 Mark the relationship of the strut to the steering knuckle and around the nuts using paint or a scribe

5.5 Push in on the strut while pulling out on the top of the brake rotor to separate the knuckle from the strut

with one hand and remove the three strut-to-shock tower nuts **(see illustration)**. Remove the assembly out from the fender well.

Inspection

7   Check the strut body for leaking fluid, dents, cracks and other obvious damage which would warrant repair or replacement.

8   Check the coil spring for chips or cracks in the spring coating (this will cause premature spring failure due to corrosion). Inspect the spring seat for cuts, hardness and general deterioration.

9   If any undesirable conditions exist, proceed to Section 6 for the strut disassembly procedure.

Installation

10   Verify that the flat in the upper spring seat is in line with the steering knuckle flange. Guide the strut assembly up into the fender well and insert the three upper mounting studs through the holes in the shock tower.

5.4 Remove the strut-to-knuckle nuts and bolts. The bolts are splined and must be driven out with a brass or plastic faced hammer

5.6 Remove the three strut-to-shock tower nuts (arrows) while supporting the strut assembly

Once the three studs protrude from the shock tower, install the nuts so the strut won't fall back through. This is most easily accomplished with the help of an assistant, as the strut is quite heavy and awkward.

11   Slide the steering knuckle into the strut flange and insert the two bolts. These should be positioned with the flats situated horizontally. Install the nuts, align the previously applied marks and tighten them to the torque listed in this Chapter's Specifications.

12   Install the tie-rod end into the steering arm and tighten the castellated nut to the torque listed in this Chapter's Specifications. Install a new cotter pin. If the cotter pin will not pass through, tighten the nut a little more, but just enough to align the hole in the stud with a castellation on the nut (do not loosen the nut).

13   Install the wheel, lower the vehicle and tighten the lug nuts to the torque listed in the Chapter 1 Specifications.

14   Tighten the three upper mounting nuts to the torque listed in this Chapter's Specifications.

6.4 After the spring has been compressed, remove the damper shaft nut

6.5a Remove the bearing cap . . .

6.5b . . . and the upper spring seat and insulator from the damper shaft

6.8a Install the upper spring seat with the flat (arrow) facing the steering knuckle flange

6.8b The bearing cap must also be positioned with the flat (arrow) facing the knuckle flange

6   Strut assembly - replacement

Refer to illustrations 6.4, 6.5a, 6.5b, 6.8a and 6.8b

1   If the struts exhibit the telltale signs of wear (leaking fluid, loss of dampening capability) explore all options before beginning any work. The strut cartridges can be replaced. However, rebuilt strut assemblies (some complete with springs) are available on an exchange basis which eliminates much time and work. Whichever route you choose to take, check on the cost and availability of parts before disassembling your vehicle. **Warning:** *Disassembling a strut is potentially dangerous. Use only a high quality spring compressor and carefully follow the manufacturer's instructions furnished with the tool. After removing the coil spring from the strut assembly, set it aside in a safe, isolated area.*

2   Remove the strut and spring assembly following the procedure described in the Section 5. Mount the strut assembly in a vise with the jaws of the vise cushioned with rags or blocks of wood.

3   Following the tool manufacturers instructions, install the spring compressor (which can be obtained at most auto parts stores or equipment yards on a daily rental basis) on the spring and compress it sufficiently to relieve all pressure from the spring seat. This can be verified by wiggling the spring seat.

4   Loosen the damper shaft nut while using a socket wrench on the shaft hex to prevent it from turning **(see illustration)**.

5   Lift the bearing cap, upper spring seat and upper insulator off of the damper shaft **(see illustrations)**. Inspect the bearing in the spring seat for smooth operation and replace it if necessary.

6   Carefully remove the compressed spring assembly and set it in a safe place. **Warning:** *Never place your head near the end of the spring!*

7   Fully extend the damper shaft of the new strut assembly and hold it in place with a clothes pin placed at the bottom of the rod.

8   Assemble the strut beginning with the lower spring insulator and spring, then the upper spring insulator, spring seat and bearing cap. Position the spring seat and bearing cap with the flats facing the steering knuckle

flange **(see illustrations)**.

9   Install the damper shaft nut and tighten it to the torque listed in this Chapter's Specifications. Remove the clothes pin from the damper shaft.

10   Install the strut and spring assembly on the vehicle as outlined in Section 5.

7   Front hub and wheel bearing assembly - removal and installation

Refer to illustrations 7.6, 7.7, 7.8 and 7.9
Note: *The front hub and wheel bearing assembly is sealed-for-life and must be replaced as a unit.*

1   Loosen the wheel lug nuts, raise the front of the vehicle and support it securely on jackstands. Remove the wheel.

2   Disconnect the stabilizer bar from the control arm (see Section 2).

3   Remove the balljoint-to-steering knuckle nut and separate the control arm from the knuckle (see Section 4).

4   Remove the caliper from the steering

10

7.6 A No. 55 Torx bit is necessary to remove the hub bolts. Don't use an Allen wrench, as the bolts may be damaged

7.7 Pull the hub and bearing assembly and the rotor shield from the steering knuckle

knuckle and hang it out of the way with a piece of wire (see Chapter 9).

5   Pull the rotor from the hub and remove the driveaxle (see Chapter 8 if necessary).

6   Using a No. 55 Torx bit, remove the three hub retaining bolts through the opening in the hub flange **(see illustration)**.

7   Wiggle the hub and bearing assembly back-and-forth and pull it from the steering knuckle, along with the disc shield **(see illustration)**.

8   If the hub and bearing assembly is being replaced with a new one, it is a good idea to replace the dust seal in the back of the steering knuckle. Pry it out of the knuckle using a screwdriver **(see illustration)**.

9   Drive the new dust seal into the knuckle using a large socket or a seal driver **(see illustration)**. Try not to cock the seal in the bore.

10   Install a new O-ring around the rear of the bearing and push it up against the bearing flange.

11   Clean the mating surfaces on the steering knuckle and bearing flange, and the knuckle bore. Lubricate the outside diameter of the bearing and the seal lips with high temperature grease and insert the hub and bearing into the steering knuckle. Position the rotor shield and install the three bolts, tightening them securely.

12   Install the driveaxle (see Chapter 8).

13   Attach the control arm to the steering knuckle (see Section 4).

14   Reconnect the stabilizer bar to the control arm (see Section 2).

15   Install the brake rotor and caliper (see Chapter 9).

16   Install the hub nut and tighten it to the initial torque listed in the Chapter 8 Specifications to seat the driveaxle into the hub. Prevent the axle from turning by inserting a screwdriver through the caliper and into a disc cooling vane (see Chapter 8 if necessary).

17   Install the wheel, lower the vehicle and tighten the lug nuts to the torque listed in the Chapter 1 Specifications.

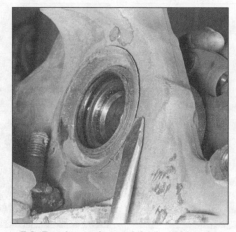

7.8 Pry the seal out of the knuckle with a screwdriver

7.9 Using a large socket, drive the new seal into place

18   Tighten the hub nut to the final torque listed in the Chapter 8 Specifications.

---

8   Steering knuckle and hub - removal and installation

Removal

1   Loosen the wheel lug nuts, raise the vehicle and support it securely on jackstands. Remove the wheel.

2   Remove the hub nut. Insert a screwdriver through the caliper and into a rotor cooling vane to prevent the driveaxle from turning.

3   Remove the caliper and suspend it out of the way with a piece of wire. Lift the rotor off of the hub.

4   Mark the position of the two strut-to-knuckle nuts and remove them **(see illustration 5.2)**. Do not drive out the bolts at this time.

5   Separate the control arm balljoint from the steering knuckle (see Section 4 if necessary).

6   Attach a puller to the hub flange and push the driveaxle from the hub (see Chap-

ter 8). Hang the driveaxle with a piece of wire to prevent damage to the inner CV joint.

7   Support the knuckle and drive out the two strut-to-knuckle bolts with a brass or plastic faced hammer. Remove the steering knuckle assembly from the strut.

Installation

8   Position the knuckle in the strut and insert the two splined bolts, with the flats on the bolt heads in the horizontal position. Tap the bolts into place and install the nuts, but do not tighten them at this time.

9   Install the driveaxle into the hub.

10   Connect the control arm to the steering knuckle and tighten the castellated balljoint nut to the torque listed in this Chapter's Specifications. Install a new cotter pin.

11   Align the strut-to-knuckle nuts with the previously applied marks and tighten them to the torque listed in this Chapter's Specifications.

12   Install the brake rotor and caliper.

13   Tighten the hub nut to the initial torque listed in the Chapter 8 Specifications to seat the driveaxle in the hub.

14   Install the wheel, lower the vehicle and

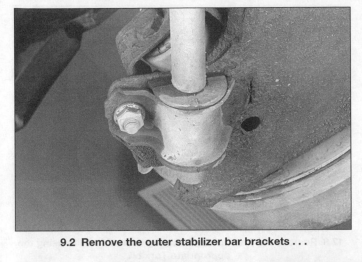

9.2 Remove the outer stabilizer bar brackets . . .

9.3 . . . then disconnect the inner bushing clamps and remove the stabilizer bar

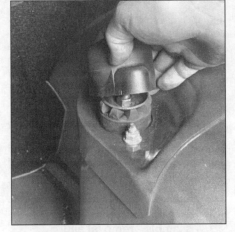

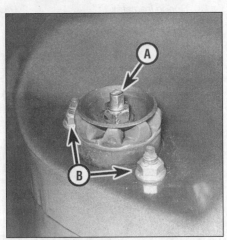

10.2 Remove the lower shock mounting bolt (arrow). Be sure to support the trailing arm with a jack

10.3 Locate the upper shock mount behind the trunk compartment side panel trim and remove the upper mount cover

10.4 Using an open-end wrench on the damper shaft flats, remove the shaft-to-upper mount nut (A). The upper mount is held in place by two nuts (B)

tighten the lug nuts to the torque listed in this Chapter's Specifications.

15   Tighten the hub nut to the final torque listed in the Chapter 8 Specifications.

9   Rear stabilizer bar - removal and installation

Refer to illustrations 9.2 and 9.3

1   Raise the rear of the vehicle and support it securely on jackstands.

2   Remove the outer stabilizer bar bushing bracket nuts and bolts and remove the brackets from the trailing arms **(see illustration)**.

3   Remove the two inner stabilizer bushing clamp bolts and nuts **(see illustration)** and remove the stabilizer bar.

4   Inspect the bushings for cracking, hardness and other signs of wear, replacing them if necessary.

5   Installation is the reverse of the removal procedure. Before tightening the bolts, make sure the stabilizer bar is centered from side-to-side in the rear axle assembly.

10   Rear shock absorber - removal and installation

Refer to illustrations 10.2, 10.3 and 10.4
Caution: *Do not remove both shock absorbers at one time. They limit the downward travel of the rear suspension and damage to the brake hoses and lines may occur if the suspension is allowed to hang.*

1   Loosen the wheel lug nuts, raise the rear of the vehicle and remove the wheel.

2   Support the trailing arm with a jack and remove the lower shock absorber mounting bolt **(see illustration)**.

3   Open the trunk lid and peel back the side trim panel to expose the upper shock mount. Pull the plastic cap off of the mount **(see illustration)**.

4   Remove the damper shaft-to-upper mount nut and remove the shock absorber from the vehicle. Inspect the upper mount for cracks, hardness, separation or other damage. If any of these conditions are noted, unscrew the two mounting nuts and remove the mount from the fender well **(see illustration)**.

5   Installation is the reverse of the removal procedure.

11   Rear springs and insulators - removal and installation

Removal

1   Loosen the wheel lug nuts, raise the rear of the vehicle and support it securely on jackstands. Remove both rear wheels.

2   Locate the right and left brake line brackets and unbolt them from the frame, allowing the lines to hang freely.

3   Place a floor jack under the center of the axle beam to support it. Remove both lower shock mounting bolts and slowly lower the jack until the coil spring is fully extended. Keep an eye on the brake hoses to make sure that they don't become hung-up on anything.

4   Remove the coil spring, compression bumper and the upper spring insulator. Inspect the rubber components for cracks, hardening and general deterioration and replace them if necessary.

10

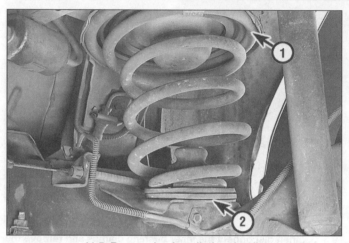

11.5 Rear spring installation details

1   Spring insulator   2   Compression bumper

12.3 Remove the four hub and bearing assembly bolts using the appropriate Torx bit

12.4a Angle the hub and bearing assembly out through the brake assembly

Installation

Refer to illustration 11.5

5   Position the compression bumpers on the lower spring pockets and place the coil springs on the axle assembly. Install the upper spring insulators on top of the springs **(see illustration)** and raise the axle, guiding the springs into place. The help of an assistant may be necessary to accomplish this.

6   If difficulty is encountered in keeping the upper spring insulators in place, glue them to the contact area on the body with spray adhesive.

7   Install the lower shock absorber mounting bolts.

8   Attach the brake line brackets to the frame.

9   Install the wheels, lower the vehicle and tighten the wheel lug nuts to the torque listed in the Chapter 1 Specifications.

12   Rear hub and wheel bearing assembly - removal and installation

Note: *The rear hub and wheel bearing assembly is sealed-for-life and must be replaced as a unit.*

Removal

Refer to illustrations 12.3, 12.4a and 12.4b

1   Loosen the wheel lug nuts, raise the vehicle and support it securely on jackstands.

Remove the wheel.

2   Pull the brake drum from the hub. If difficulty is encountered, refer to Chapter 9 for the removal procedure.

3   Using a Torx bit, remove the four hub-to-trailing arm bolts, accessible by turning the hub flange so that the circular cutout exposes each bolt **(see illustration)**. Save the upper rear bolt for last, because there isn't much clearance between the bolt and the parking brake strut.

4   Remove the hub and bearing assembly from its seat, maneuvering it out through the brake assembly. Reinstall two bolts through the brake backing plate into the trailing arm to avoid hanging the brake assembly by the hydraulic line **(see illustrations)**.

Installation

Refer to illustration 12.5

5   Position the hub and bearing assembly to the trailing arm and align the holes in the backing plate. Install the bolts, beginning with the upper rear bolt. A magnet is useful in guiding the bolts through the hub flange and into position **(see illustration)**. After all four bolts have been installed, tighten them to the torque listed in this Chapter's Specifications.

12.4b Temporarily reinstall two bolts (arrows) to retain the brake assembly to the trailing arm, rather than let it hang by the hydraulic line

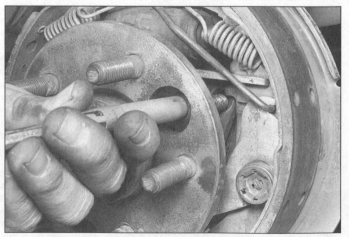

12.5 A magnet is useful for installing the bolts

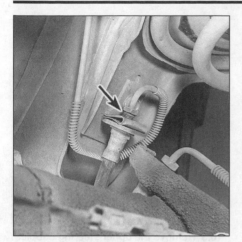

13.6 Loosen the brake line tube nuts and remove the hose retaining clips

13.7 Remove the rear axle assembly pivot bolt (arrow) and carefully lower the axle to the ground

15.2 Before disconnecting the tie-rod end from the steering arm, loosen the pinch bolt (arrow)

6   Install the brake drum and wheel. Lower the vehicle and tighten the wheel lug nuts to the torque listed in the Chapter 1 Specifications.

13 Rear axle assembly - removal and installation

Removal

Refer to illustrations 13.6 and 13.7

1   Loosen the wheel lug nuts, raise the vehicle and support it securely on jackstands. Remove the wheels.
2   If the axle assembly is to be replaced, remove the stabilizer bar as outlined in Section 9.
3   Remove the brake drums from the hubs. See Chapter 9 if any difficulty is encountered.
4   Remove the coil springs (see Section 11).
5   Disconnect the parking brake cable at the equalizer (see Chapter 9).
6   Loosen the brake line tube nuts and remove the brake hose retaining clips, disconnecting the brake lines from the rear axle assembly **(see illustration)**.
7   With a floor jack supporting the axle assembly, unbolt the axle from the vehicle at the pivot points on the underbody side rails **(see illustration)**. Lower the axle assembly to the ground.

Installation

8   If a new axle assembly is being installed, transfer the hub and bearing assemblies, the brake assemblies, the parking brake cables and the hydraulic lines to the new axle.
9   Place the new axle on the jack and raise it into position. Install the pivot bolts, but don't tighten them fully yet.
10   Install the coil springs and insulators and connect the shock absorbers (see Section 11).
11   Reconnect the brake lines.
12   Reconnect the parking brake cable to the equalizer and position it in the cable guide.

13   Install the stabilizer bar.
14   Install the brake drums.
15   Bleed the brake system of all air, following the procedure described in Chapter 9.
16   Install the wheels, lower the vehicle and tighten the lug nuts to the torque listed in the Chapter 1 Specifications.
17   With the vehicle standing at normal ride height, tighten the axle pivot bolts to the torque listed in this Chapter's Specifications.

14 Steering system - general information

Warning: *Whenever any of the steering fasteners are removed they must be inspected and if necessary, be replaced with new ones of the same part number or of original equipment quality and design. Torque specifications must be followed for proper reassembly and component retention. Never attempt to heat or straighten any suspension or steering components. Instead, replace any bent or damaged part with a new one.*

All vehicles covered by this manual use power rack-and-pinion steering systems. The components making up the system are the steering wheel, the steering column, the rack-and-pinion assembly, the tie-rods and the tie-rod ends. The power steering system uses a belt-driven pump to provide hydraulic pressure.

In the power steering system, the motion of turning the steering wheel is transferred through the column to the pinion shaft in the rack-and-pinion assembly. Teeth on the pinion shaft are meshed with teeth on the rack, so when the shaft is turned, the rack is moved left or right in the housing. A rotary control valve in the rack-and-pinion unit directs hydraulic fluid under pressure from the power steering pump to either side of the integral rack piston, which is connected to the rack thereby reducing manual steering force. Depending on which side of the piston this hydraulic pressure is applied to, the rack

will be forced either left or right, which moves the tie-rods, etc. If the power steering system loses its hydraulic pressure it will still function manually, though with increased effort.

The steering column is of the collapsible, energy-absorbing type, designed to compress in the event of a front end collision to minimize injury to the driver. The column also houses the ignition switch lock, key warning buzzer, turn signal controls, headlight dimmer control and windshield wiper controls. The ignition and steering wheel can both be locked while the car is parked to inhibit theft.

Due to the column's collapsible design, it is important that only the specified screws, bolts and nuts be used as designated and that they be tightened to the torque listed in this Chapter's Specifications. Other precautions particular to this design are noted in appropriate Sections.

In addition to the standard steering column, optional tilt and key-release versions are also offered. The tilt model can be set in five different positions, while with the key release model the ignition key is locked in the column until a lever is depressed to extract it.

Because disassembly of the steering column is more often performed to repair a switch or other electrical part than to correct a problem in the steering, the upper steering column disassembly and reassembly procedure is included in Chapter 12.

15 Tie-rod ends - removal and installation

Removal

Refer to illustrations 15.2, 15.3 and 15.4

1   Loosen the wheel lug nuts, raise the vehicle and support it securely on jackstands. Remove the wheel.
2   Loosen the tie-rod end pinch bolt **(see illustration)**.
3   Disconnect the tie-rod from the steering

10

15.3 A two jaw puller works well for separating the tie-rod end from the steering arm. Do not pound on the stud!

15.4 Using white paint, mark the relationship of the tie-rod end to the threaded adjuster

16.3 Remove the upper steering coupler pinch bolt (arrow)

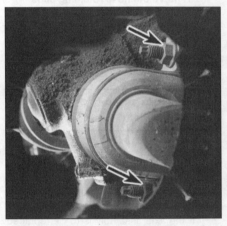

16.4 Remove the steering gear mounting clamp nuts (arrows) - left side shown

knuckle arm with a puller **(see illustration)**.
4   Mark the relationship of the tie-rod end to the threaded adjuster **(see illustration)**. This will ensure that the toe-in setting is restored when reassembled.
5   Unscrew the tie-rod end from the tie-rod.

Installation

6   Thread the tie-rod end onto the tie-rod to the marked position and connect the tie-rod end to the steering arm. Install the castellated nut and tighten it to the torque listed in this Chapter's Specifications. Install a new cotter pin.
7   Tighten the pinch bolt securely and install the wheel. Lower the vehicle and tighten the lug nuts to the torque listed in the Chapter 1 Specifications.
8   Have the front end steering geometry checked by a dealer service department or an alignment shop.

16   Steering gear - removal and installation

Refer to illustrations 16.3 and 16.4
Warning: *Make sure the steering shaft is not turned while the steering gear is removed or you could damage the airbag system. To prevent the shaft from turning, place the ignition key in the LOCK position or thread the seat belt through the steering wheel and clip it into place.*
Caution: *If the vehicle is equipped with a Delco Loc II audio system, make sure you have the correct activation code before disconnecting the battery. See the information at the front of this manual for the radio re-activation procedure.*
1   Disconnect the cable from the negative battery terminal.
2   Remove the left side under-dash panel.
3   Roll back the boot at the bottom of the steering column to expose the flange and steering coupler assembly. Mark the coupler to the steering column shaft and remove the

upper pinch bolt **(see illustration)**.
4   Remove the two left side steering gear-to-firewall clamp nuts and the right upper clamp nut **(see illustration)**.
5   Remove the pressure hose retainer from the support bracket at the center of the rack.
6   Place a drain pan or tray under the vehicle, positioned beneath the left side of the steering gear. Using a flare nut wrench, disconnect the pressure and return lines from the steering gear (the two lines closest to the firewall, angled toward the left side of the vehicle). Plug the lines to prevent excessive fluid loss.
7   Loosen the front wheel lug nuts, raise the vehicle and support it securely on jackstands. Remove both front wheels.
8   Remove the lower right side clamp nut.
9   Separate the tie-rod ends from the steering arms (see Section 15).
10   Move the steering gear forward and remove the lower pinch bolt from the coupler. Slide the coupler off of the pinion shaft.
11   Support the steering gear and carefully maneuver the entire assembly out through the left side wheel opening.
12   If any of the mounting studs came out with the clamps, apply a thread locking compound to the firewall side of the threads and install them snugly into the firewall.
13   Pass the steering gear assembly through the left wheel opening into approximate position.
14   Install the coupler and tighten the lower pinch bolt securely.
15   Center the steering gear, ensuring that the dash seal is installed properly. Have an assistant guide the coupler onto the steering column shaft, with the previously applied marks aligned. Position the right side clamp and install the lower clamp nut, tightening it to the torque listed in this Chapter's Specifications.
16   Install the tie-rod ends in the steering arms and tighten the nuts to the torque listed in this Chapter's Specifications. Install new cotter pins.
17   Install the front wheels, lower the vehicle and tighten the lug nuts to the torque listed in

the Chapter 1 Specifications.
18   Install the pressure and return lines to the steering gear. Connect the line retainer to the support bracket.
19   Install the left side clamp and nuts and the upper right side clamp nut, tightening them to the torque listed in this Chapter's Specifications.
20   Install the upper pinch bolt in the coupler and tighten it to the torque listed in this Chapter's Specifications.
21   Install the under-dash panel.
22   Reconnect the negative battery cable.
23   Fill the power steering pump with the recommended fluid, bleed the system of air (see Section 19) and recheck the fluid level. Check for leaks.
24   Have the front end steering geometry checked by a dealer service department or an alignment shop.

17   Steering gear boots - replacement

Refer to illustrations 17.2 and 17.3
Warning: *Some models covered by this manual are equipped with airbags. Always disable the airbag system before working in the vicin-*

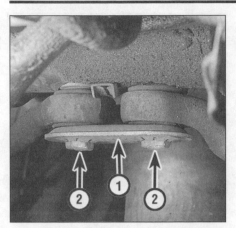

17.2 Remove the lock plate (1), and then remove the inner tie-rod bolts (2)

17.3 Use a flare nut wrench to loosen the steering gear lines

18.3 Loosen the return line hose clamp and separate the line from the pump (V6 engine shown)

18.4 Disconnect the pressure hose from the pump. Use a flare nut wrench and a backup wrench to avoid damage to the pipe and fitting (V6 engine shown)

18.5 Using a socket and short extension inserted through one of the holes in the pulley (arrow), remove the three pump mounting bolts - rotate the pulley to access each bolt

ity of the impact sensors, steering column or instrument panel to avoid the possibility of accidental deployment of the airbag(s), which could cause personal injury (see Chapter 12 for the airbag disarming procedure). The yellow wires and connectors routed through the instrument panel are for this system. Do not use electrical test equipment on these yellow wires or tamper with them in any way while working under the instrument panel.

Caution: *If the vehicle is equipped with a Delco Loc II audio system, make sure you have the correct activation code before disconnecting the battery. See the information at the front of this manual for the radio re-activation procedure.*

1   Remove the steering gear from the vehicle (see Section 16).
2   Remove the tie-rods from the steering gear **(see illustration)**.
3   Using a flare nut wrench, remove the hydraulic cylinder lines from the steering gear assembly **(see illustration)**.
4   Remove the right mounting grommet from the rack housing.
5   Cut off both boot clamps and discard them.
6   Slide the cylinder end (right end) of the boot toward the center of the steering gear, enough to expose the boot groove. Place a rubber band in the groove to occupy the space then slide the boot off of the steering gear.
7   Install a new clamp on the left end of the boot and insert the boot retaining bushing into the end of the boot. Apply multi-purpose grease to the inside diameter of the bushing and slide the boot onto the steering gear housing.
8   Press the center housing cover washers into the center housing cover.
9   Align the center housing bolt holes with the rack guide assembly and install the two tie-rod bolts. This will ensure proper alignment of the center housing, rack and rack guide.
10   Tighten the left side boot clamp.
11   Slide the right end of the boot onto the housing, remove the rubber band and seat the boot into the boot groove. Install the

clamp and tighten it.
12   Install the hydraulic cylinder lines.
13   Install the tie-rods and tighten the bolts to the torque listed in this Chapter's Specifications.
14   Install the mounting grommet.
15   Install the steering gear assembly.

---

18   Power steering pump - removal and installation

Removal

Refer to illustrations 18.3, 18.4 and 18.5

1   Disconnect the cable from the negative battery terminal.
2   Remove the serpentine drivebelt (V6) or the power steering pump drivebelt (four cylinder engines).
3   Position a drain pan under the vehicle. Remove as much fluid as possible with a suction gun, then remove the return line from the pump **(see illustration)**.
4   Using a flare nut wrench and a backup wrench, disconnect the pressure hose at the pump **(see illustration)**. Disconnect the elec-

trical connector from the EVO actuator, if equipped.
5   Remove the pump mounting bolts and lift the pump from the vehicle, being careful not spill the remaining fluid **(see illustration)**.

Installation

6   Position the pump on the mounting bracket and install the bolts. On 2.5L four cylinder models, install the front adjustment bracket-to engine bolt and spacer first, then the front adjustment bracket-to-rear adjustment bracket bolt.
7   Connect the pressure and return lines to the pump.
8   Fill the reservoir with the recommended fluid and bleed the system, following the procedure described in the next Section.

---

19   Power steering system - bleeding

---

1   Following any operation in which the power steering fluid lines have been disconnected, the power steering system must be bled of air to obtain proper steering performance.

10

20.3 Use a Torx bit to remove the airbag module screws from behind the steering wheel

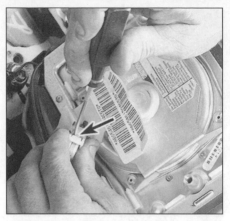

20.4a Use a small screwdriver to release the plastic locking clip (arrow) from the airbag module connector, then . . .

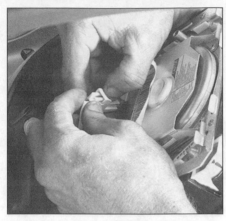

20.4b . . . squeeze the tab and separate the airbag connector

2   With the front wheels turned all the way to the left, check the power steering fluid level and, if low, add fluid until it reaches the Cold mark on the dipstick.

3   Start the engine and allow it to run at fast idle. Recheck the fluid level and add more if necessary to reach the Cold mark on the dipstick.

4   Bleed the system by turning the wheels from side to side, without hitting the stops. This will work the air out of the system. Be careful that the reservoir does not run empty of fluid.

5   When the air is worked out of the system, return the wheels to the straight ahead position and leave the car running for several minutes before shutting it off. Recheck the fluid level.

6   Road test the car to be sure the steering system is functioning normally and is free from noise.

7   Recheck the fluid level to be sure it is up to the Hot mark on the dipstick while the engine is at normal operating temperature. Add fluid if necessary.

20 Steering wheel - removal and installation

Refer to illustrations 20.3, 20.4a, 20.4b, 20.5a, 20.5b, 20.6, 20.7, 20.8 and 20.9

Warning: *Some models covered by this manual are equipped with airbags. Always turn the steering wheel to the straight ahead position, place the ignition switch in the Lock position disable the airbag system before working in the vicinity of the impact sensors, steering column or instrument panel to avoid the possibility of accidental deployment of the airbag(s), which could cause personal injury (see Chapter 12 for the airbag disarming procedure). Do not use electrical test equipment on any of the airbag system wiring or tamper with them in any way.*

Caution: *If the vehicle is equipped with a Delco Loc II or Theftlock audio system, make sure you have the correct activation code before disconnecting the battery.*

20.5a Remove the steering wheel nut retainer

1   Park the vehicle with the wheels pointing straight ahead. Disconnect the cable from the negative terminal of the battery. On airbag equipped models, also disconnect the positive terminal, then wait two minutes before proceeding.

2   On models without an airbag, the horn pad is attached to the steering wheel with various combinations of clips and/or screws.

3   On airbag models use a number 30 Torx bit, remove the two screws that secure the airbag module to the steering wheel **(see illustration)**.

4   Lift the airbag module carefully away from the steering wheel and disconnect the yellow airbag electrical connector. This is a two-part disconnection, as there is a plastic clip that must be removed before the connector can be disconnected **(see illustrations)**. Remove the module. **Warning:** *When carrying the airbag module, keep the driver's side of it away from your body, and when you place it on the bench, have the driver's side facing up.*

5   Remove the steering wheel nut retainer (if equipped) and the steering wheel nut **(see illustrations)**.

6   Mark the relationship of the steering wheel to the shaft **(see illustration)**.

20.5b Remove the steering wheel nut with a deep socket

7   Install a steering wheel puller (available at most auto parts stores) and turn the center bolt until the wheel is free **(see illustration)**.

8   Remove the puller and disconnect the horn and ground connector **(see illustration)**. Remove the steering wheel. **Warning:** *Don't allow the steering shaft to turn with the steering wheel removed. If the shaft turns, the airbag SIR coil assembly (the mechanism*

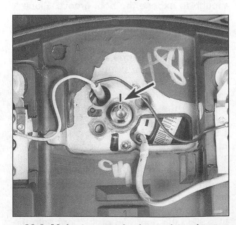

20.6 Make two marks (arrow) to show alignment of the wheel to the shaft

20.7 A steering wheel puller threads into two holes in the steering wheel - tightening the center bolt removes the wheel

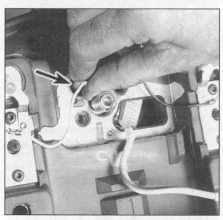

20.8 Disconnect the horn and ground wire connector

20.9 When properly aligned, the airbag coil will be centered with the marks aligned (in circle here) and the tab fitted between the projections on the top of the steering column (arrow)

21.2 Pressing a wheel stud out of the hub flange

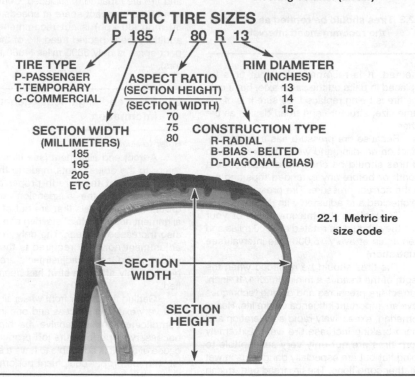

METRIC TIRE SIZES

P 185 / 80 R 13

TIRE TYPE
P-PASSENGER
T-TEMPORARY
C-COMMERCIAL

ASPECT RATIO
(SECTION HEIGHT)
―――――――――
(SECTION WIDTH)
70
75
80

RIM DIAMETER
(INCHES)
13
14
15

SECTION WIDTH
(MILLIMETERS)
185
195
205
ETC

CONSTRUCTION TYPE
R-RADIAL
B-BIAS - BELTED
D-DIAGONAL (BIAS)

22.1 Metric tire size code

SECTION WIDTH

SECTION HEIGHT

21.3 Install washers or a spacer and a lug nut on the stud, then tighten the nut to draw the stud into place

which protects the airbag wiring when the steering wheel is turned) will become uncentered, which may cause the airbag harness to break when the vehicle is returned to service.
9   Installation is reverse of removal. On airbag models, before the steering wheel is installed, make sure the SIR coil is centered **(see illustration)**. If it isn't, see Chapter 12, Section 23 for the centering procedure. Con-

nect the airbag connector to the back of the airbag module just as it was before steering wheel removal, i.e. with the plastic locking device in place. Be sure to tighten the steering wheel nut and airbag screws to the torque listed in this Chapter's Specifications.
10   Refer to chapter 12 for the procedure to enable the airbag system.

21   Wheel studs - replacement

Refer to illustrations 21.2 and 21.3
Note: *This procedure applies to either the front or rear wheel studs.*
1   Install a lug nut part way onto the stud to be replaced.
2   Push the stud from the hub flange using a press tool, available at most auto parts

stores **(see illustration)**.
3   Insert the new stud into the hub flange from the backside and install four flat washers and a lug nut on the stud **(see illustration)**.
4   Tighten the lug nut until the stud is fully seated in the flange.

22   Wheels and tires - general information

Refer to illustrations 22.1 and 22.3
All vehicles covered by this manual are equipped with metric-sized fiberglass or steel belted radial tires **(see illustration)**. Use of other size or type of tires may affect the ride and handling of the car. Do not mix different types of tires, such as radials and bias belted, on the same car as handling may be seriously

10

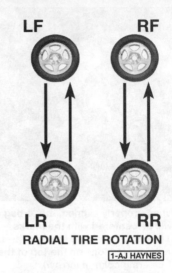

RADIAL TIRE ROTATION

1-AJ HAYNES

22.3 Tires should be rotated as shown at the recommended intervals

affected. It is recommended that tires be replaced in pairs on the same axle, but if only one tire is being replaced, be sure it is of the same size, structure and tread design as the other.

Because tire pressure has a substantial effect on handling and wear, the pressure on all tires should be checked at least once a month or before any extended trips and set to the correct pressure. Tire pressure should be checked and adjusted with the tires cold.

To achieve the maximum life of your tires they should be rotated at 7500 miles and then again at every 15,000-mile interval **(see illustration)**.

The tires should be replaced when the depth of the tread is a minimum of 1/16-inch. Correct tire pressures and driving techniques have an important influence on tire life. Heavy cornering, excessively rapid acceleration and sharp braking increase tire wear. Extremely worn tires are not only very susceptible to going flat but are especially dangerous in wet weather conditions. The tire tread pattern can give a good indication of problems in the maintenance or adjustment of tires, suspension and front end components (see Chapter 1).

Wheels must be replaced if they are bent, dented, leak air, have elongated bolt holes, are heavily rusted, out of vertical symmetry or if the lug nuts won't stay tight. Wheel repairs that use welding or peening are not recommended, as this can weaken the metal.

Tire and wheel balance is important in the overall handling, braking and performance of the car. Unbalanced wheels can

adversely affect handling and ride characteristics as well as tire life. Whenever a tire is installed on a wheel, the tire and wheel should be balanced by a shop with the proper equipment.

All vehicles covered by this manual are equipped with a compact spare tire, which is designed to save space in the trunk as well as being easier to handle due to its lighter weight. The spare tire pressure should be checked at least once a month, and maintained at 70 psi (412 kPa). The compact spare tire and wheel are designed for use with each other only, and neither the tire nor the wheel should be coupled with other types or size of wheels and tires. Because the compact spare is designed as a temporary replacement for an out-of-service standard wheel and tire, the compact spare should be used on the car only until the standard wheel and tire are repaired or replaced. Continuous use of the compact spare at speeds of over 50 mph (80 kph) is not recommended. In addition, the expected tread life of the compact spare is only 3000 miles (4800 kilometers).

23 Front end alignment - general information

Refer to illustration 23.1

A front end alignment **(see illustration)** refers to the adjustments made to the front wheels so that they are in proper angular relationship to the suspension and the ground. Front wheels that are out of proper alignment not only affect steering control, but also increase tire wear. The only front end adjustment normally required is the toe-in adjustment. Camber adjustments are possible, but only after the strut has been modified.

Getting the proper front wheel alignment is a very exacting process and one in which complicated and expensive machines are necessary to perform the job properly. Because of this, it is advisable to have a specialist with the proper equipment perform these tasks. We will, however, use this space to give you a basic idea of what is involved with front end alignment so you can better understand the process and deal intelligently with shops which do this work.

Toe-in is the turning in of the front wheels. The purpose of a toe specification is to ensure parallel rolling of the front wheels. In a car with zero toe-in, the distance between the front edges of the wheels will be the same as the distance between the rear edges of the wheels. The actual amount of toe-in is normally only a fraction of an inch. Toe-in adjustment is controlled by the tie-rod

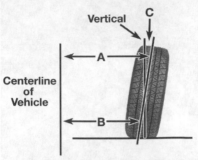

CAMBER ANGLE (FRONT VIEW)

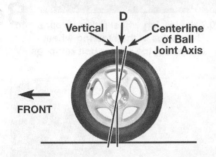

CASTER ANGLE (SIDE VIEW)

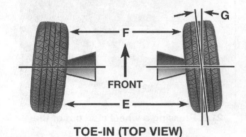

TOE-IN (TOP VIEW)

23.1 A front end alignment on these vehicles normally consists of a toe-in adjustment only. However, camber adjustment is possible after strut modification

end position on the inner tie-rod. Incorrect toe-in will cause the tires to wear improperly by making them scrub against the road surface.

Camber is the tilting of the front wheels from the vertical when viewed from the front of the vehicle. When the wheels tilt out at the top, the camber is said to be positive (+). When the wheels tilt in at the top the camber is negative (-). The amount of tilt is measured in degrees from the vertical and this measurement is called the camber angle. This angle affects the amount of tire tread which contacts the road and compensates for changes in the suspension geometry when the car is cornering or traveling over undulating surface.

Chapter 11 Body

Contents

Specifications

Torque specifications

	Ft-lbs (unless otherwise indicated)
Door hinge-to-body pillar nuts and bolts	
1991 and earlier..	36 to 40
1992 and later	16 to 18
Door latch striker bolt	
1991 and earlier..	36 to 40
1992 and later	16 to 18
Front seat-to-floor pan nut	15 to 21
Rear seat cushion bolt	14 to 20
Trunk lid latch striker nut	108 to 144 in-lbs

1 General information

The vehicles covered in this manual are available in 2-door coupe and 4-door sedan body styles. The body and chassis are of unitized construction and are designed to provide vehicle rigidity so that a separate frame is not necessary. Front and rear frame side rails, integral with the body, support the front end sheet metal, front and rear suspension systems and other mechanical components. Due to this type of construction, it is very important that, in the event of collision damage, the underbody be thoroughly checked by a facility with the proper equipment to do so.

Body maintenance is an important part of the retention of the vehicle's market value. It is far less costly to handle small problems before they grow into larger ones.

Major body components which are particularly vulnerable in accidents are removable. These include the hood, front fenders, grille, doors, trunk lid and tail light assembly. It is often cheaper and less time consuming to replace an entire panel than it is to attempt a restoration of the old one. However, this must be decided on a case-by-case basis.

Only general body maintenance and body panel repair procedures within the scope of the do-it-yourselfer are included in this Chapter.

2 Maintenance - body

1 The condition of your vehicle's body is very important, because it is on this that the second hand value will mainly depend. It is much more difficult to repair a neglected or damaged body than it is to repair mechanical components. The hidden areas of the body, such as the fender wells, the frame, and the engine compartment, are equally important, although they obviously do not require as frequent attention as the rest of the body.

2 Once a year, or every 12,000 miles, it's a good idea to have the underside of the body and the frame steam cleaned. All traces of dirt and oil will be removed and the underside

11

These photos illustrate a method of repairing simple dents. They are intended to supplement *Body repair - minor damage* in this Chapter and should not be used as the sole instructions for body repair on these vehicles.

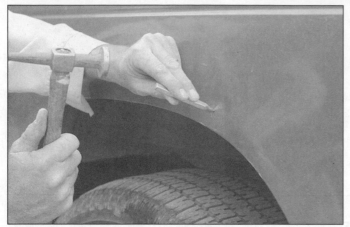

1   If you can't access the backside of the body panel to hammer out the dent, pull it out with a slide-hammer-type dent puller. In the deepest portion of the dent or along the crease line, drill or punch hole(s) at least one inch apart . . .

2   . . . then screw the slide-hammer into the hole and operate it. Tap with a hammer near the edge of the dent to help 'pop' the metal back to its original shape. When you're finished, the dent area should be close to its original contour and about 1/8-inch below the surface of the surrounding metal

3   Using coarse-grit sandpaper, remove the paint down to the bare metal. Hand sanding works fine, but the disc sander shown here makes the job faster. Use finer (about 320-grit) sandpaper to feather-edge the paint at least one inch around the dent area

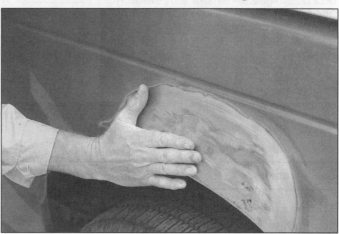

4   When the paint is removed, touch will probably be more helpful than sight for telling if the metal is straight. Hammer down the high spots or raise the low spots as necessary. Clean the repair area with wax/silicone remover

5   Following label instructions, mix up a batch of plastic filler and hardener. The ratio of filler to hardener is critical, and, if you mix it incorrectly, it will either not cure properly or cure too quickly (you won't have time to file and sand it into shape)

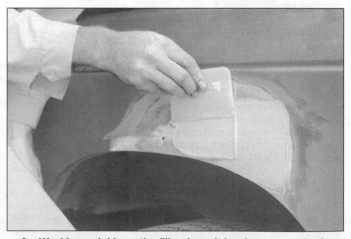

6   Working quickly so the filler doesn't harden, use a plastic applicator to press the body filler firmly into the metal, assuring it bonds completely. Work the filler until it matches the original contour and is slightly above the surrounding metal

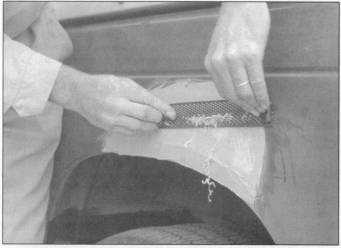

7   Let the filler harden until you can just dent it with your fingernail. Use a body file or Surform tool (shown here) to rough-shape the filler

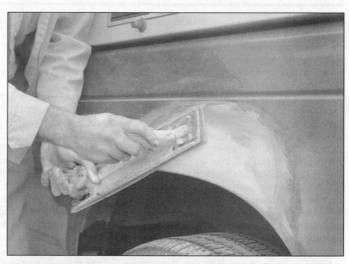

8   Use coarse-grit sandpaper and a sanding board or block to work the filler down until it's smooth and even. Work down to finer grits of sandpaper - always using a board or block - ending up with 360 or 400 grit

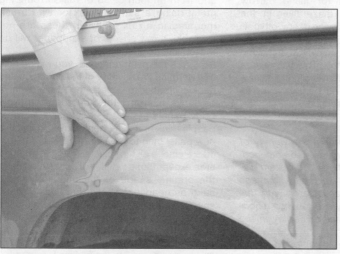

9   You shouldn't be able to feel any ridge at the transition from the filler to the bare metal or from the bare metal to the old paint. As soon as the repair is flat and uniform, remove the dust and mask off the adjacent panels or trim pieces

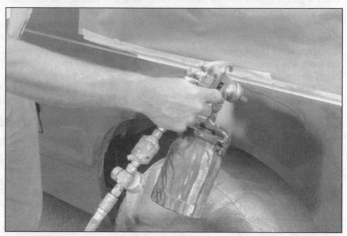

10   Apply several layers of primer to the area. Don't spray the primer on too heavy, so it sags or runs, and make sure each coat is dry before you spray on the next one. A professional-type spray gun is being used here, but aerosol spray primer is available inexpensively from auto parts stores

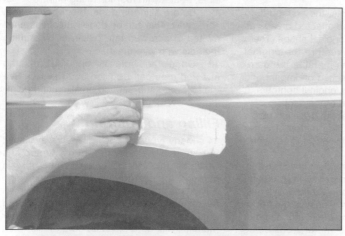

11   The primer will help reveal imperfections or scratches. Fill these with glazing compound. Follow the label instructions and sand it with 360 or 400-grit sandpaper until it's smooth. Repeat the glazing, sanding and respraying until the primer reveals a perfectly smooth surface

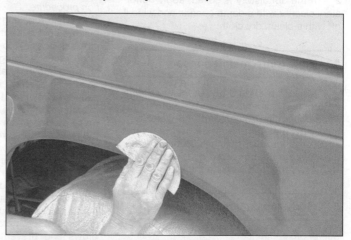

12   Finish sand the primer with very fine sandpaper (400 or 600-grit) to remove the primer overspray. Clean the area with water and allow it to dry. Use a tack rag to remove any dust, then apply the finish coat. Don't attempt to rub out or wax the repair area until the paint has dried completely (at least two weeks)

can then be inspected carefully for rust, damaged brake lines, frayed electrical wiring, damaged cables and other problems. The front suspension components should be greased after completion of this job.

3   At the same time, clean the engine and the engine compartment using either a steam cleaner or a water soluble degreaser. Caution: Do not steam clean or spray water onto electronic components, wiring harnesses, wiring connectors, ignition system components or electronic fuel injection components. Water can migrate down wiring looms to sensitive electrical components and corrode connectors or disable unit.

4   The fender wells should be given particular attention, as undercoating can peel away and stones and dirt thrown up by the tires can cause the paint to chip and flake, allowing rust to set in. If rust is found, clean down to the bare metal and apply an anti-rust paint.

5   The body should be washed as needed. Wet the vehicle thoroughly to soften the dirt, then wash it down with a soft sponge and plenty of clean soapy water. If the surplus dirt is not washed off very carefully, it will in time wear down the paint.

6   Spots of tar or asphalt coating thrown up from the road should be removed with a cloth soaked in solvent.

7   Once every six months, give the body and chrome trim a thorough waxing. If a chrome cleaner is used to remove rust from any of the vehicle's plated parts, remember that the cleaner also removes part of the chrome, so use it sparingly.

3   Maintenance - upholstery and carpets

1   Every three months remove the carpets or mats and clean the interior of the vehicle (more frequently if necessary). Vacuum the upholstery and carpets to remove loose dirt and dust.

2   If the upholstery is soiled, apply upholstery cleaner with a damp sponge and wipe it off with a clean, dry cloth.

4   Vinyl trim - maintenance

Vinyl trim should not be cleaned with detergents, caustic soaps or petroleum-based cleaners. Plain soap and water or a mild vinyl cleaner is best for stains. Test a small area for color fastness. Bubbles under the vinyl can be corrected by piercing them with a pin and then working the air out.

5   Body repair - minor damage

See photo sequence

Repair of minor scratches

1   If the scratch is superficial and does not penetrate to the metal of the body, repair is

very simple. Lightly rub the scratched area with a fine rubbing compound to remove loose paint and built up wax. Rinse the area with clean water.

2   Apply touch-up paint to the scratch, using a small brush. Continue to apply thin layers of paint until the surface of the paint in the scratch is level with the surrounding paint. Allow the new paint at least two weeks to harden, then blend it into the surrounding paint by rubbing with a very fine rubbing compound. Finally, apply a coat of wax to the scratch area.

3   If the scratch has penetrated the paint and exposed the metal of the body, causing the metal to rust, a different repair technique is required. Remove all loose rust from the bottom of the scratch with a pocket knife, then apply rust inhibiting paint to prevent the formation of rust in the future. Using a rubber or nylon applicator, coat the scratched area with glaze-type filler. If required, the filler can be mixed with thinner to provide a very thin paste, which is ideal for filling narrow scratches. Before the glaze filler in the scratch hardens, wrap a piece of smooth cotton cloth around the tip of a finger. Dip the cloth in thinner and then quickly wipe it along the surface of the scratch. This will ensure that the surface of the filler is slightly hollow. The scratch can now be painted over as described earlier in this section.

Repair of dents

Warning: *Before working in the vicinity of airbag components (on models so equipped) refer to Chapter 12 for the airbag system disarming procedure. Use care not to damage any wiring or sensors associated with this system or the airbag may deploy when reconnecting the battery or fail to deploy in the event of an accident.*
Caution: *If the vehicle is equipped with a Delco Loc II audio system, make sure you have the correct activation code before disconnecting the battery. See the information at the front of this manual for the radio re-activation procedure.*

4   When repairing dents, the first job is to pull the dent out until the affected area is as close as possible to its original shape. There is no point in trying to restore the original shape completely as the metal in the damaged area will have stretched on impact and cannot be restored to its original contours. It is better to bring the level of the dent up to a point which is about 1/8-inch below the level of the surrounding metal. In cases where the dent is very shallow, it is not worth trying to pull it out at all.

5   If the back side of the dent is accessible, it can be hammered out gently from behind using a soft-face hammer. While doing this, hold a block of wood firmly against the opposite side of the metal to absorb the hammer blows and prevent the metal from being stretched.

6   If the dent is in a section of the body which has double layers, or some other factor makes it inaccessible from behind, a different

technique is required. Drill several small holes through the metal inside the damaged area, particularly in the deeper sections. Screw long, self tapping screws into the holes just enough for them to get a good grip in the metal. Now the dent can be pulled out by pulling on the protruding heads of the screws with locking pliers.

7   The next stage of repair is the removal of paint from the damaged area and from an inch or so of the surrounding metal. This is easily done with a wire brush or sanding disk in a drill motor, although it can be done just as effectively by hand with sandpaper. To complete the preparation for filling, score the surface of the bare metal with a screwdriver or the tang of a file or drill small holes in the affected area. This will provide a good grip for the filler material. To complete the repair, see the Section on filling and painting.

Repair of rust holes or gashes

8   Remove all paint from the affected area and from an inch or so of the surrounding metal using a sanding disk or wire brush mounted in a drill motor. If these are not available, a few sheets of sandpaper will do the job just as effectively.

9   With the paint removed, you will be able to determine the severity of the corrosion and decide whether to replace the whole panel, if possible, or repair the affected area. New body panels are not as expensive as most people think and it is often quicker to install a new panel than to repair large areas of rust.

10   Remove all trim pieces from the affected area except those which will act as a guide to the original shape of the damaged body, such as headlight shells, etc. Using metal snips or a hacksaw blade, remove all loose metal and any other metal that is badly affected by rust. Hammer the edges of the hole in to create a slight depression for the filler material.

11   Wire brush the affected area to remove the powdery rust from the surface of the metal. If the back of the rusted area is accessible, treat it with rust-inhibiting paint.

12   Before filling is done, block the hole in some way. This can be done with sheet metal riveted or screwed into place, or by stuffing the hole with wire mesh.

13   Once the hole is blocked off, the affected area can be filled and painted. See the following sub-section on filling and painting.

Filling and painting

14   Many types of body fillers are available, but generally speaking, body repair kits which contain filler paste and a tube of resin hardener are best for this type of repair work. A wide, flexible plastic or nylon applicator will be necessary for imparting a smooth and contoured finish to the surface of the filler material. Mix up a small amount of filler on a clean piece of wood or cardboard (use the hardener sparingly). Follow the manufacturer's instructions on the package, otherwise the filler will set incorrectly.

15   Using the applicator, apply the filler paste to the prepared area. Draw the applicator across the surface of the filler to achieve the desired contour and to level the filler surface. As soon as a contour that approximates the original one is achieved, stop working the paste. If you continue, the paste will begin to stick to the applicator. Continue to add thin layers of paste at 20-minute intervals until the level of the filler is just above the surrounding metal.

16   Once the filler has hardened, the excess can be removed with a body file. From then on, progressively finer grades of sandpaper should be used, starting with a 180-grit paper and finishing with 600-grit wet or-dry paper. Always wrap the sandpaper around a flat rubber or wooden block, otherwise the surface of the filler will not be completely flat. During the sanding of the filler surface, the wet-or-dry paper should be periodically rinsed in water. This will ensure that a very smooth finish is produced in the final stage.

17   At this point, the repair area should be surrounded by a ring of bare metal, which in turn should be encircled by the finely feathered edge of good paint. Rinse the repair area with clean water until all of the dust produced by the sanding operation is gone.

18   Spray the entire area with a light coat of primer. This will reveal any imperfections in the surface of the filler. Repair the imperfections with fresh filler paste or glaze filler and once more smooth the surface with sandpaper. Repeat this spray-and-repair procedure until you are satisfied that the surface of the filler and the feathered edge of the paint are perfect. Rinse the area with clean water and allow it to dry completely.

19   The repair area is now ready for painting. Spray painting must be carried out in a warm, dry, windless and dust free atmosphere. These conditions can be created if you have access to a large indoor work area, but if you are forced to work in the open, you will have to pick the day very carefully. If you are working indoors, dousing the floor in the work area with water will help settle the dust which would otherwise be in the air. If the repair area is confined to one body panel,

mask off the surrounding panels. This will help minimize the effects of a slight mismatch in paint color. Trim pieces such as chrome strips, door handles, etc., will also need to be masked off or removed. Use masking tape and several thickness of newspaper for the masking operations.

20   Before spraying, shake the paint can thoroughly, then spray a test area until the spray painting technique is mastered. Cover the repair area with a thick coat of primer. The thickness should be built up using several thin layers of primer rather than one thick one. Using 600-grit wet-or-dry sandpaper, rub down the surface of the primer until it is very smooth. While doing this, the work area should be thoroughly rinsed with water and the wet-or-dry sandpaper periodically rinsed as well. Allow the primer to dry before spraying additional coats.

21   Spray on the top coat, again building up the thickness by using several thin layers of paint. Begin spraying in the center of the repair area and then, using a circular motion, work out until the whole repair area and about two inches of the surrounding original paint is covered. Remove all masking material 10 to 15 minutes after spraying on the final coat of paint. Allow the new paint at least two weeks to harden, then use a very fine rubbing compound to blend the edges of the new paint into the existing paint. Finally, apply a coat of wax.

6   Body repair - major damage

1   Major damage must be repaired by an auto body/frame repair shop with the necessary welding and hydraulic straightening equipment.

2   If the damage has been serious, it is vital that the structure be checked for proper alignment or the vehicle's handling characteristics may be adversely affected. Other problems, such as excessive tire wear and wear in the driveline and steering may occur.

3   Due to the fact that all of the major body components (hood, fenders, etc.) are separate and replaceable units, any seriously

damaged components should be replaced rather than repaired. Sometimes these components can be found in a wrecking yard that specializes in used vehicle components, often at considerable savings over the cost of new parts.

7   Maintenance - hinges and locks

Every 3000 miles or three months, the door, hood and trunk lid hinges should be lubricated with a few drops of oil. The door striker plates should also be given a thin coat of white lithium-base grease to reduce wear and ensure free movement.

8   Windshield and fixed glass - replacement

1   Replacement of the windshield and fixed glass requires the use of special fast-setting adhesive/caulk materials. These operations should be left to a dealer or a shop specializing in glass work.

2   The windshield-mounted rear view mirror support is prone to falling off after years of exposure to sunlight. Most auto parts stores carry adhesive kits designed specifically for reattaching the support anchor plate to the windshield, as the bond to the glass also requires special tools and adhesives.

9   Hood - removal and installation

Refer to illustrations 9.1, 9.2 and 9.3

1   Use rags or pads to protect the windshield from the rear of the hood **(see illustration)**.

2   Scribe or paint alignment marks around the hinge bolts **(see illustration)**.

3   On models so equipped, detach the support strut **(see illustration)**.

4   Remove the bolts and, with the help of an assistant, detach the hood from the vehicle.

5   Installation is the reverse of removal.

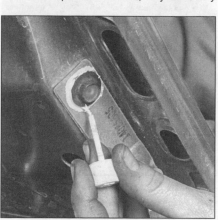

9.2 Mark the hood bolt positions in relation to the hinges

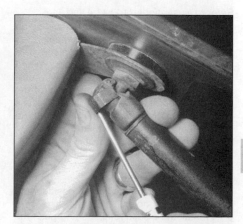

9.3 Use a screwdriver to pry the retaining clip from the support

9.1 Pad the back corners of the hood with rags so the windshield won't be damaged if the hood accidentally swings rearward

11

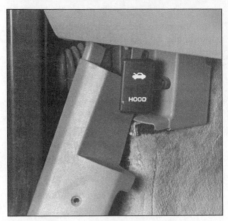

10.1 Pull the trim panel down for access to the two screws behind the hood latch handle

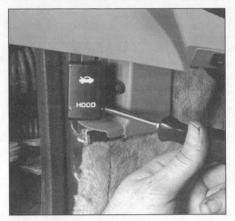

10.2 Remove the two screws with a Phillips head screwdriver

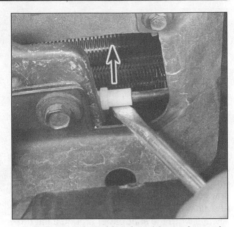

10.3 Pry the hood latch cable up (arrow) to detach it from the clip

10 Hood latch cable - replacement

Refer to illustrations 10.1, 10.2, 10.3 and 10.4

1 In the passenger compartment, remove the trim panel **(see illustration)**.
2 Remove the latch handle retaining screws and detach the handle **(see illustration)**.
3 In the engine compartment, pry the cable grommet out of the clip **(see illustration)**.
4 Spread the clip with a screwdriver and detach the end of the cable from the latch **(see illustration)**.
5 Connect a piece of string or thin wire of suitable length to the end of the wire to the cable and pull the cable through into the passenger compartment.
6 Connect the string or wire to the new cable and pull it back into the engine compartment.
7 Connect the cable and install the latch screws and trim panel.

11 Front fender liner - removal and installation

Refer to illustrations 11.2, 11.4 and 11.6

1 Raise the vehicle, support it securely on jackstands and remove the front wheel.
2 The fender liner is held in place with bolts or special plastic retainers. When removing the plastic retainers, use wire cutters or a similar tool to pry the heads of the retainers out of the retainer bodies to release them **(see illustration)**. Pry the heads out, do not cut them off to remove them.
3 Once all of the bolts or retainers are released, remove them from the fender liner.
4 Detach the liner and remove it from the vehicle **(see illustration)**.
5 To install, place the liner in position and align the retainer holes.
6 Install the plastic retainers and push the heads in to securely lock them in place **(see illustration)**.

10.4 Pry the clip back and lift the cable up to detach it

11.4 Grasp the fender liner and pull the ends in to detach it from the fender well

12 Front fender - removal and installation

Warning: *Before working in the vicinity of airbag components (on models so equipped) refer to Chapter 12 for the airbag system disarming procedure. Use care not to damage any wiring or sensors associated with this*

11.2 Pry the head out of the retainer body - do not cut the head off

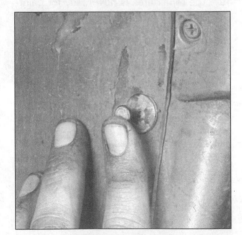

11.6 Push the head of the retainer into the body until it locks in place

system or the airbag may deploy when reconnecting the battery or fail to deploy in the event of an accident.

1 Raise the front of the vehicle, support it securely on jackstands and remove the front wheel.
2 Remove the front fender liner (see Section 11).
3 Remove the retaining nuts and detach

13.2 The radiator grille is held in place by either Phillips or Torx head screws

13.3 Tilt the grille forward to detach it from the clips

14.1 Use a screwdriver to remove the door panel screws

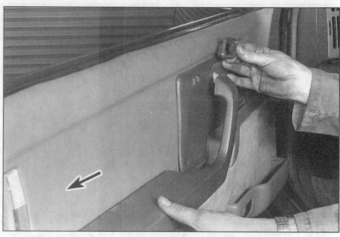

14.2 Move the armrest rearward to disengage it

the fender from the vehicle.
4   To install, place the fender in position and install the retaining nuts. Tighten the nuts securely.
5   The remainder of installation is the reverse of removal.

13   Radiator grille - removal and installation

Refer to illustrations 13.2 and 13.3
Warning: *Before working in the vicinity of airbag components (on models so equipped) refer to Chapter 12 for the airbag system disarming procedure. Use care not to damage any wiring or sensors associated with this system or the airbag may deploy when reconnecting the battery or fail to deploy in the event of an accident.*
1   Open the hood.
2   Remove the retaining screws **(see illustration)**.
3   Rotate the top of the grille out and lift it from the vehicle **(see illustration)**.
4   Installation is the reverse of removal.

14   Door trim panel - removal and installation

Refer to illustrations 14.1, 14.2, 14.3a, 14.3b, 14.4, 14.5 and 14.6
1   Remove door glass regulator handle (if equipped) (see Section 17), and the visible

door panel screws from the door trim panel **(see illustration)**.
2   Once the screws are removed from the arm rest (if equipped) slide it to the rear to disengage the clips and then lift it off **(see illustration)**.
3   Pry out any escutcheon screw covers and remove the screws **(see illustrations)**.

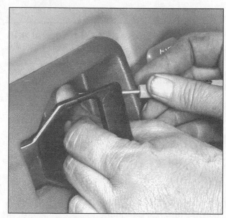

14.3a Use a small screwdriver to pry out the screw covers

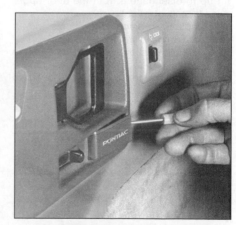

14.3b Some screws are hidden under decorative panels

11

14.4 Slide the escutcheon forward to remove it (some models)

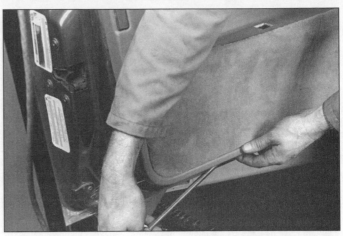

14.5 Pry around the outer circumference of the door panel to disengage the clips

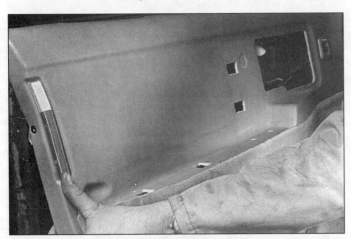

14.6 Lift the door panel up and out of the top edge of the door to disengage it

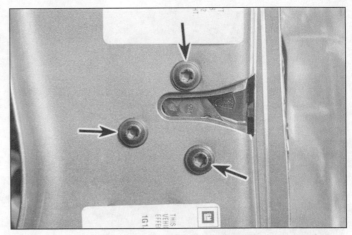

15.3 To detach the lock assembly from the door, remove these three bolts (arrows)

4   Disengage the escutcheon and remove it by sliding it forward off the clips **(see illustration)**.

5   Pry around the outer circumference of the door panel with a pry bar or large screwdriver to disengage the clips **(see illustration)**.

6   Grasp the door trim panel securely and lift up to disengage it from the door upper edge **(see illustration)**.

7   Unplug any electrical switches and lift the door trim panel from the vehicle.

8   Carefully peel the water shield from the door for access to the inner door components. Take care not to tear the water shield as it must be reinstalled.

9   Installation is the reverse of removal.

15   Door lock assembly - removal and installation

Refer to illustration 15.3

1   With the window glass in the full up position, remove the door trim panel and water shield (see Section 14).

2   Disconnect spring clips from the remote

control connecting rods at the lock assembly.

3   Remove the lock assembly-to-door bolts and lift the assembly from the door **(see illustration)**.

4   To install, place the assembly in position and install the retaining screws.

5   Connect the lock rods.

6   Install the water shield and door trim panel.

16   Door window glass - removal and installation

Refer to illustration 16.4

1   With the window glass in the full up position, remove the door trim panel and water shield (see Section 14).

Front door
Removal

2   Remove the outside mirror (see Section 28).

3   Remove the rubber stop bumper, screws and run channel.

4   On early models, lower the glass to the bottom of the door, slide the window regula-

16.4 Lower the window partially and remove the glass channel mounting bolts (arrows)

tor guide block off the sash channel and tilt the glass inboard of the door frame to remove it. On later models, lower the glass half way for access, then remove the retaining nuts. Lower the glass all the way and slide it rearward, then rotate it up and out of the door **(see illustration)**.

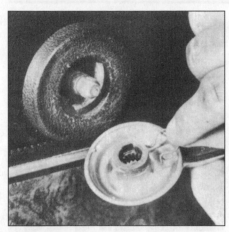

17.2a Disengage the manual door glass regulator handle spring clip and withdraw the assembly from the door

Installation

5   Insert the glass into the door and engage the regulator guide block to the sash channel. Engage the rear guide clip on the glass to the rear run channel weather-strip.
6   Raise the glass to the half way up position. Install the run channel bolts finger tight. On later models install the glass retaining nuts and tighten them securely.
7   Engage the front clip on the glass to the run channel and tighten the bolts securely.
8   Install the rubber stop bumper.
9   The remainder of installation is the reverse of removal.

Rear door

Removal

10   On early models, remove the bolts retaining the regulator block to the window glass.
11   Disengage the glass and lower it to the bottom of the door.
12   Remove the run channel from the door frame at the front and rear of the glass division channel.
13   Lift the glass from the door.
14   On later models, pry out the inner door sealing strip from the glass opening.
15   Lower the glass halfway for access and remove the retaining nuts, then lift the glass up and out of the opening, toward the inboard side.

Installation

16   On early models, insert the glass into the door and connect the division channel, making sure to engage the glass guide securely to the channel.
17   Connect the regulator guide block to the glass sash channel and install the bolts. Tighten the bolts securely.
18   On later models, lower the glass into the door from the inboard side, place it in position over the stud, then install the nuts and tighten them securely.
19   The remainder of installation is the reverse of removal.

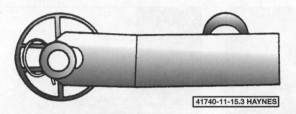

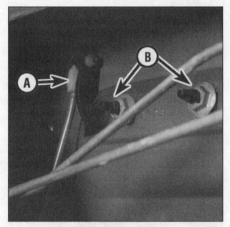

18.2 Push the outside handle rod clip (A) off and remove the two handle retaining nuts (B)

17   Door glass regulator - removal and installation

Refer to illustrations 17.2a and 17.2b

Removal

Caution: *If the vehicle is equipped with a Delco Loc II audio system, make sure you have the correct activation code before disconnecting the battery. See the information at the front of this manual for the radio re-activation procedure.*
1   On power window equipped models, disconnect the negative battery cable.
2   On manual window glass regulator equipped models, remove the handle by pressing the bearing plate and door trim panel in and, with a piece of hooked wire, pulling off the spring clip **(see illustration)**. A special tool is available for this purpose **(see illustration)** but its use is not essential. With the clip removed, take off the handle and the bearing plate.
3   With the window glass in the full up position, remove the door trim panel and water shield (see Section 14).
4   Secure the window glass in the up position with strong adhesive tape fastened to the glass and wrapped over the door frame.
5   Punch out the center pins of the rivets that secure the window regulator and drill the rivets out with a 1/4-inch drill bit.
6   On power window equipped models, unplug the electrical connector.
7   Remove the retaining bolts and move the regulator until it is disengaged from the sash channel. Lift the regulator from the door.

17.2b A special tool like this one (available at most auto parts stores) makes it easier to remove the spring clip retainer

18.4 Rotate the plastic retainer off and detach the rod, then drill out the rivets (arrows) and remove the handle - on installation, install new rivets with a pop-riveting tool

Installation

8   Place the regulator in position in the door and engage it to the sash channel.
9   Secure the regulator to the door using 3/16-inch rivets and a rivet tool.
10   Install the bolts and tighten them securely.
11   Plug in the electrical connector (if equipped).
12   Install the water shield, door trim panel and window regulator handle. Connect the negative battery cable.

18   Door handles - removal and installation

Refer to illustrations 18.2 and 18.4
1   With the window glass in the full up position, remove the door trim panel and water shield (see Section 14).

Outside handle

2   Pry the remote rod out of the handle with a small screwdriver, remove the nuts and lift the handle off **(see illustration)**.
3   Installation is the reverse of removal.

Inside handle

4   Disconnect the rod from the handle **(see illustration)**.
5   Punch out the center pins of the rivets that secure the inside handle and drill the rivets out.
6   Lift the handle from the door.

11

19.3 To detach the lock cylinder from the door, insert a large screwdriver through the small hole above the lock cylinder and pry off this retainer

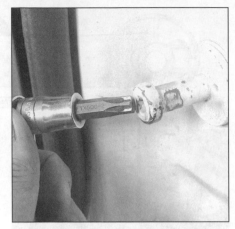

20.2 Use a Torx bit to remove the striker bolt

22.2 Mark the position of the trunk lid bolts before removing them

23.2 Use a 5/32-inch drill bit to remove the rivet (arrow) holding the lock cylinder retaining clip

24.1 Insert a small screwdriver into the solenoid connector, depress the retaining tab and then pull the cable out

7   To install, place the handle in position and secure it to the door, using pop rivets and a rivet tool.

8   The remainder of installation is the reverse of removal.

19 Door lock cylinder - removal and installation

Refer to illustration 19.3

1   With the window glass in the full up position, remove the door trim panel and water shield (see Section 14).

2   Disconnect the rod from the lock cylinder.

3   Use a screwdriver to pry the retainer off and withdraw the lock cylinder from the door **(see illustration 15.2)**.

4   Installation is the reverse of removal.

20 Door lock striker - removal and installation

Refer to illustration 20.2

1   Mark the position of the striker bolt on the door pillar with a pencil.

2   It will be necessary to use a Torx-bit to fit the star-shaped recess in the striker bolt head. Unscrew the bolt and remove it **(see illustration)**.

3   To install, screw the lock striker bolt into the tapped cage plate in the door pillar and tighten it finger tight at the marked position. Tighten the bolt to the torque listed in this Chapter's Specifications.

21 Door - removal and installation

1   Remove the door trim panel and water shield.

2   Unplug any wiring connectors.

3   Open the door all the way and support it

on jacks or blocks covered with cloth or pads to prevent damage to the paint.

4   Scribe around the hinges to ensure correct realignment during installation.

5   Remove the bolts/nuts retaining the hinges to the door and with the help of an assistant lift the door away.

6   Install the door by reversing the removal procedure. Tighten the nuts and bolts to the torque listed in this Chapter's Specifications.

22 Trunk lid - removal and installation

Refer to illustration 22.2

1   Open the trunk lid and unplug any electrical connectors and disconnect the solenoid (if equipped).

2   Scribe or mark around the heads of the retaining bolts to mark their locations for ease of reinstallation **(see illustration)**.

3   With an assistant supporting the trunk lid, remove the bolts. Lift the trunk lid from the vehicle.

4   Installation is the reverse of removal.

23 Trunk lock cylinder - removal and installation

Refer to illustration 23.2

1   Open the trunk lid.

2   Punch out the center pin in the retaining clip mounting rivets and drill out the rivets with a 5/32-inch drill bit **(see illustration)**.

3   Pry the retaining clip off and withdraw the lock cylinder from the vehicle.

4   To install, place the lock cylinder in place and secure it with the retaining clip. Use 5/32 by 7/16-inch long steel rivets and a rivet tool to attach the clip to the trunk lid.

24 Trunk latch and striker - removal and installation

Refer to illustration 24.1, 24.2 and 24.3

1   On models so equipped, disconnect the trunk lock cylinder cable by inserting small screwdriver into the connector to hold the release tab down and them pull the cable out of the solenoid **(see illustration)**.

2   Remove the electric solenoid (if

24.2 Lock release solenoid

1   Solenoid   3   Screw
2   Connector

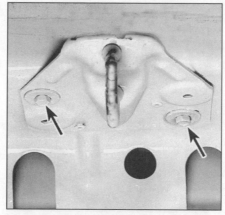

24.3 Remove the striker retaining bolt(s) (arrow) and remove the striker

25.2a Unscrew the plastic retaining wing nuts and . . .

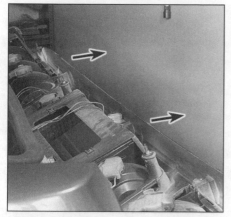

25.2b . . . rotate the lens assembly away from the rear of the vehicle (arrows) for access to the bulb holders

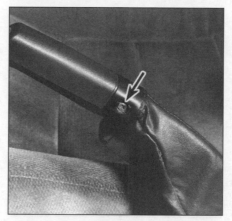

26.3 Use a screwdriver to remove the parking brake handle screw (arrow)

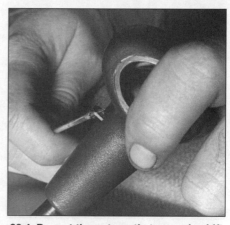

26.4 Pry out the automatic transaxle shift handle retaining clip

equipped) and unbolt and remove the latch and (if equipped) the ajar switch **(see illustration)**.
3   Remove the retaining nut and lift off the striker **(see illustration)**.
4   Installation is the reverse of removal.

25 Rear lens assembly - removal and installation

Refer to illustrations 25.2a and 25.2b
1   Open the trunk lid and remove the rear trim panel.
2   Unscrew the plastic wing nuts, pull the lens assembly out and lean it back **(see illustrations)**. Disconnect the bulb holders (Chapter 12) and lift the assembly from the vehicle.
3   Installation is the reverse of removal.

26 Console - removal and installation

Refer to illustrations 26.3, 26.4, 26.5a, 26.5b, 26.6a, 26.6b, 26.7 and 26.8
Caution: *If the vehicle is equipped with a*

Delco Loc II audio system, make sure you have the correct activation code before disconnecting the battery. See the information at the front of this manual for the radio re-activation procedure.
1   Disconnect the negative battery cable.
2   Remove the ash receptacle and cigarette lighter.
3   Remove the retaining screw at the base of the parking brake handle **(see illustration)**.

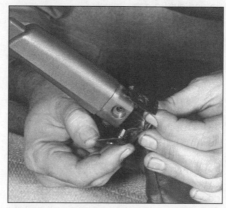

26.5a Pull the parking brake cover snap retainer apart and . . .

4   Use a small screwdriver to pry the retaining clip out of the automatic transaxle shift handle **(see illustration)**. On manual transaxle equipped models, remove the shift knob retaining screw (if equipped). Pull the handle or knob off the shift lever or unthread the knob.
5   Unsnap the cover and pull the parking brake handle off **(see illustrations)**.
6   Pry around the outer edge of the con-

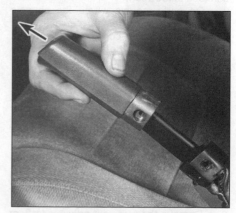

26.5b . . . pull the handle off (arrow)

11

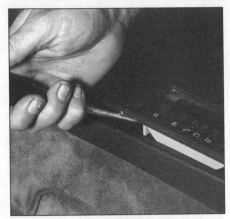

26.6a Use a screwdriver to pry the console trim plate and . . .

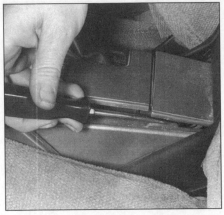

26.6b . . . the rear cover free of the clips

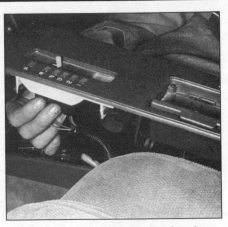

26.7 Raise the console trim plate for access to the electrical connectors

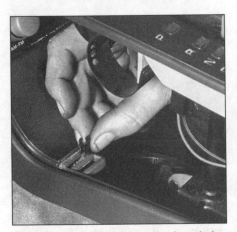

26.8 Insert the retaining clips into their holders before pressing the console trim plate into place

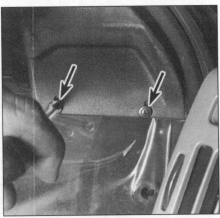

28.2 The mirror escutcheon is held in place by two screws (arrows)

28.3 This Allen head screw must be removed to release the control cable from the escutcheon

sole trim plate until the assembly is free and then pry the rear piece loose and then pull the console trim plate up **(see illustrations)**.

7   Lift the console trim plate up for access and unplug the electrical connectors **(see illustration)**.

8   Some or all of the retaining clips will probably come out during removal, so be sure to reinstall them prior to console installation **(see illustration)**.

9   On early models where the console extends up the center of the instrument panel, remove the air conditioning panel and the radio. Remove the bolts securing the console to the body and remove the console.

10   Installation is the reverse of removal.

27   Seats - removal and installation

Front seat

1   Move the seat all the way forward.

2   Remove the seat track covers and pull the carpet away from the adjuster and retaining nuts.

3   Remove the rear seat adjuster-to-floor panel retaining nuts.

4   Move the seat all the way to the rear.

5   Remove the front seat retaining nuts. On power seats, unplug the electrical connector. Lift the seat from the vehicle.

6   Installation is the reverse of removal. Tighten the adjuster-to-floor panel nuts to the torque listed in this Chapter's Specifications.

Rear seat

7   Remove the seat cushion retaining bolts, detach the seat cushion and remove it up and out from the vehicle.

8   Remove the rear seat back retaining bolts at the bottom of the seat back. Pull up then out to disengage the upper frame from the hangers and remove seat back from the vehicle.

9   Installation is the reverse of removal.

28   Outside mirror - removal and installation

Refer to illustrations 28.2, 28.3 and 28.6

1   On 1991 and earlier models, remove the door trim panel (see Section 14).

2   Remove retaining screws and pull the escutcheon back **(see illustration)**.

3   On manual mirrors, loosen the Allen

screw holding the control on the escutcheon **(see illustration)**.

4   On power mirrors, unplug the electrical connector.

5   Remove the escutcheon.

6   Remove the three nuts and lift off the mirror assembly **(see illustration)**.

7   Installation is the reverse of removal.

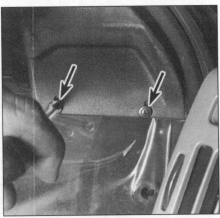

28.6 Remove the mirror retaining nuts (arrows)

Chapter 12
Chassis electrical system

Contents

1 General information

The electrical system is a 12-volt, negative ground type. Power for the lights and all electrical accessories is supplied by a lead/acid-type battery that is charged by the alternator.

This Chapter covers repair and service procedures for the various electrical components not associated with the engine. Information on the battery, alternator, distributor and starter motor can be found in Chapter 5.

It should be noted that whenever portions of the electrical system are serviced, the negative battery cable should be disconnected at the battery to prevent electrical shorts and/or fires.

Caution: *If the vehicle is equipped with a Delco Loc II audio system, make sure you have the correct activation code before disconnecting the battery. See the information at the front of this manual for the radio re-activation procedure.*

Note: *Information concerning digital instrumentation and dash related accessories is not included in this manual. Problems involving these components should be referred to a dealer service department.*

2 Electrical troubleshooting - general information

A typical electrical circuit consists of an electrical component, any switches, relays, motors, etc. related to that component and the wiring and connectors that connect the component to both the battery and the chassis. To aid in locating a problem in any electrical circuit, wiring diagrams are included at the end of this book.

Before tackling any troublesome electrical circuit, first study the appropriate diagrams to get a complete understanding of what makes up that individual circuit. Trouble spots, for instance, can often be narrowed down by noting if other components related to that circuit are operating properly or not. If several components or circuits fail at one time, chances are the problem lies in the fuse or ground connection, as several circuits are often routed through the same fuse and ground connection.

Electrical problems often stem from simple causes, such as loose or corroded connections, a blown fuse or a melted fusible link. Always visually inspect the condition of the fuse, wires and connections in a problem circuit before troubleshooting it.

If testing instruments are going to be utilized, use the diagrams to plan ahead of time where you will make the necessary connections in order to accurately pinpoint the trouble spot.

The basic tools needed for electrical troubleshooting include a circuit tester or voltmeter (a 12-volt bulb with a set of test leads can also be used), a continuity tester, and a jumper wire, preferably with a circuit breaker incorporated, which can be used to bypass electrical components.

Voltage checks should be performed if a circuit is not functioning properly. Connect one lead of a circuit tester to either the negative battery terminal or a known good ground. Connect the other lead to a connector in the circuit being tested, preferably nearest to the battery or fuse. If the bulb of the tester lights, voltage is present, which means that the part of the circuit between the connector and the battery is problem free. Continue checking the rest of the circuit in the same fashion. When you reach a point at which no voltage is present, the problem lies between that point and the last test point with voltage. Most of the time the problem can be traced to a loose connection. **Note:** *Keep in mind that some*

12

3.1 The fuse box is located above a small swing-down door on the left underside of the dashboard

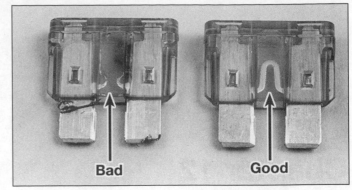

3.3 When a fuse blows, the element between the terminal melts - the fuse on the left is blown, the fuse on the right is good

circuits receive voltage only when the ignition key is in the Accessory or Run position.

One method of finding shorts in a circuit is to remove the fuse and connect a test light or voltmeter in its place to the fuse terminals. There should be no voltage present in the circuit. Move the wiring harness from side-to-side while watching the test light. If the bulb goes on, there is a short to ground somewhere in that area, probably where the insulation has rubbed through. The same test can be performed on each component in the circuit, even a switch.

Perform a ground test to check whether a component is properly grounded. Disconnect the battery and connect one lead of a self powered test light, known as a continuity tester, to a known good ground. Connect the other lead to the wire or ground connection being tested. If the bulb goes on, the ground is good. If the bulb does not go on, the ground is not good.

A continuity check is done to determine if there are any breaks in a circuit - if it is passing electricity properly. With the circuit off (no power in the circuit), a self-powered continuity tester can be used to check the circuit. Connect the test leads to both ends of the circuit (or to the "power" end and a good ground), and if the test light comes on the circuit is passing current properly. If the light doesn't come on, there is a break somewhere in the circuit. The same procedure can be used to test a switch, by connecting the continuity tester to the power in and power out sides of the switch. With the switch turned On, the test light should come on.

When diagnosing for possible open circuits, it is often difficult to locate them by sight because oxidation or terminal misalignment are hidden by the connectors. Merely wiggling a connector on a sensor or in the wiring harness may correct the open circuit condition. Remember this when an open circuit is indicated when troubleshooting a circuit. Intermittent problems may also be caused by oxidized or loose connections.

Electrical troubleshooting is simple if you keep in mind that all electrical circuits are basically electricity running from the battery, through the wires, switches, relays, fuses and fusible links to each electrical component

(light bulb, motor, etc.) and to ground, from which it is passed back to the battery. Any electrical problem is an interruption in the flow of electricity to and from the battery.

3 Fuses - general information

Refer to illustrations 3.1 and 3.3

The electrical circuits of the vehicle are protected by a combination of fuses, circuit breakers and fusible links. The fuse block is located under the instrument panel on the left side of the dashboard **(see illustration)**.

Each of the fuses is designed to protect a specific circuit, and the various circuits are identified on the fuse panel itself.

Miniaturized fuses are employed in the fuse block. These compact fuses, with blade terminal design, allow fingertip removal and replacement. If an electrical component fails, always check the fuse first. The easiest way to check fuses is with a test light. Check for power at the exposed terminal tips of each fuse. If power is present on one side of the fuse but not the other, the fuse is blown. A blown fuse can also be confirmed by visually inspecting it **(see illustration)**.

Be sure to replace blown fuses with the correct replacement. Fuses of different ratings are physically interchangeable, but only fuses of the proper rating should be used. Replacing a fuse with one of a higher or lower value than specified is not recommended. Each electrical circuit needs a specific amount of protection. The amperage value of each fuse is molded into the fuse body. **Caution:** *At no time should a fuse be bypassed with pieces of metal or foil. Serious damage to the electrical system could result.*

If the replacement fuse immediately fails, do not replace it again until the cause of the problem is isolated and corrected. In most cases, this will be a short circuit in the wiring caused by a broken or deteriorated wire.

4 Fusible links - general information

Some circuits are protected by fusible

links. These links are used in circuits that are not ordinarily fused, such as the ignition circuit.

Although the fusible links appear to be a heavier gauge than the wire they are protecting, the appearance is due to the thick insulation. All fusible links are four wire gauges smaller than the wire they are designed to protect. The location of the fusible links on your particular vehicle may be determined by referring to the wiring diagrams at the end of this book.

Fusible links cannot be repaired, but a new link of the same size wire can be put in its place. The procedure is as follows:

a) *Disconnect the negative cable at the battery.*

b) *Disconnect the fusible link from the wiring harness.*

c) *Cut the damaged fusible link out of the wiring just behind the connector.*

d) *Strip the insulation approximately 1/2-inch.*

e) *Position the connector on the new fusible link and crimp it into place.*

f) *Use rosin core solder at each end of the new link to obtain a good solder joint.*

g) *Use plenty of electrical tape around the soldered joint. No wires should be exposed.*

h) *Connect the battery ground cable. Test the circuit for proper operation.*

5 Circuit breakers - general information

Circuit breakers, which are located in the main fuse block, protect accessories such as power windows, power door locks and the rear window defogger.

The headlight wiring is also protected by a circuit breaker. An electrical overload in the system will cause the lights to go off and come on or, in some cases, to remain off. If this happens, check the headlight circuit immediately. The circuit breaker will function normally once the overload condition is corrected. Refer to the wiring diagrams at the end of this book for the location of the circuit breakers in your vehicle.

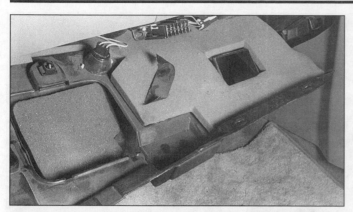

6.2a To gain access to the turn signal flasher and convenience center (or the connectors for most instrument panel related electrical devices), remove the screws from the under-dash panel and allow it to hang down

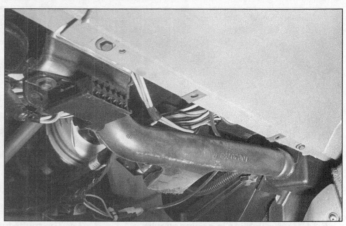

6.2b Remove the screws from the smaller panel under the steering column and remove it

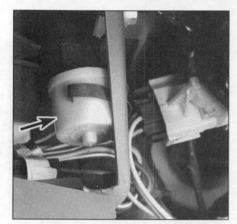

6.4 To remove the turn signal flasher (arrow), pop it loose from its retaining clip and unplug it

6.6 To gain access to the hazard flasher, remove the retaining screws and remove the left side console extension panel

6.7 To remove the hazard flasher (arrow), pop it loose from its retaining clip and unplug it

6 Turn signal flasher, hazard flasher, chime and convenience center - replacement

Refer to illustrations 6.2a, 6.2b, 6.4, 6.6, 6.7, 6.10 and 6.14

1 Disconnect the cable from the negative terminal of the battery.
Caution: *If the vehicle is equipped with a Delco Loc II audio system, make sure you have the correct activation code before disconnecting the battery. See the information at the front of this manual for the radio re-activation procedure.*

Turn signal flasher

2 The two-piece panel under the instrument panel must be removed to gain access to the flasher unit. Remove the screws retaining the under-dash panel and allow it to hang down **(see illustration)**. Remove the retaining screws **(see illustration)** from the steering column filler plate panel (under the steering column) and remove it.
3 Some vehicles are equipped with a steering column collar and steering column filler plate that must be removed to gain access to the under dash sound insulator

panel. If your vehicle is equipped with a collar and filler plate, pinch together the four slide clips along the bottom seam between the collar filler plate and detach them, slide the collar up the steering column and unscrew and remove the filler plate **(see the illustration in Section 15)**. Remove the sound insulator panel as described above.
4 Locate the turn signal flasher **(see illustration)**, remove it from its retaining clip and unplug it.
5 Installation is the reverse of removal.

Hazard flasher

6 Remove the left side console extension panel **(see illustration)**.
7 Locate the hazard flasher **(see illustration)**, remove it from its retaining clip and unplug it.
8 Installation is the reverse of removal.

Chime

9 On some vehicles, the chime is located immediately above the glove box.
10 Remove the glove box mounting screws

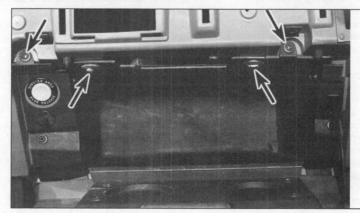

6.10 The chime is located above the glove box on some models - to remove the glove box, remove the mounting screws (arrows)

12

6.14 If your vehicle is equipped with a "convenience center" for the turn signal flasher, hazard flasher, chime, etc., it is probably located under the dash, in the vicinity of the steering column

7.4 The multi-function lever electrical connector is located under the dash to the right side of the steering column

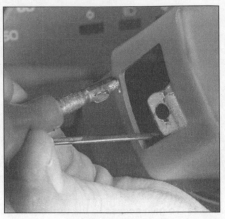

7.6 To detach the multi-function lever from the steering column, pull straight out

(see illustration) and remove the glove box.
11   Remove the chime mounting bracket screws and unplug the chime electrical connector.
12   Remove the chime.
13   Installation is the reverse of removal.

Convenience center

14   The turn signal flasher, hazard flasher and chime units are not always located as described above. Some vehicles are equipped with a "convenience center," which is a small junction block, usually located in the vicinity of the steering column, to which the turn signal and hazard flashers, chime and other devices are attached **(see illustration)**.
15   After removing the under dash panel(s), look for a junction block similar to the one in the accompanying illustration.
16   To remove either flasher unit, unplug it and install a new one.

---

7   Multi-function lever - replacement

Refer to illustrations 7.4 and 7.6
Warning: *Before working in the vicinity of airbag components (on models so equipped) refer to Section 23 for the airbag system disarming procedure. Use care not to damage any wiring or sensors associated with this system or the airbag may deploy when reconnecting the battery or fail to deploy in the event of an accident.*
1   Disconnect the cable from the negative terminal of the battery. **Caution:** *If the vehicle is equipped with a Delco Loc II audio system, make sure you have the correct activation code before disconnecting the battery. See the information at the front of this manual for the radio re-activation procedure.*
2   The panels under the instrument panel must be removed to gain access to the multi-function stalk pigtail electrical connector. Remove the screws retaining the under-dash

panel and allow it to hang down **(see illustration 6.2a)**.
3   Remove the retaining screws from the smaller panel under the steering column and remove it (as you remove the panel, note how the tabs along the upper edge fit into the dash).
4   Locate the multi-function stalk electrical connector **(see illustration)** and unplug it.
5   Attach a suitable length of wire to the pigtail to pull the pigtail back through on installation.
6   Pull the stalk straight out from the steering column **(see illustration)**.
7   Pull the multi-function stalk pigtail lead up through the steering column. Detach the wire from the pigtail lead and attach it to the lead of the new multi-function stalk.
8   Carefully thread the new connector and lead back through the steering column.
9   Installation is the reverse of removal.

---

8   Steering column switches and ignition lock cylinder - replacement

1   Disconnect the cable from the negative

8.3 Remove the shaft lock plate cover

8.4 Depress the shaft lock plate and remove the retaining clip with a scribe or small screwdriver

terminal of the battery.
Caution: *If the vehicle is equipped with a Delco Loc II audio system, make sure you have the correct activation code before disconnecting the battery. See the information at the front of this manual for the radio re-activation procedure.*

1991 and earlier models

Turn signal switch
Refer to illustrations 8.3, 8.4, 8.5, 8.6 and 8.8
2   Remove the steering wheel (see Chapter 10).
3   Remove the shaft lock plate cover **(see illustration)**.
4   Depress the shaft lock plate and remove the retaining clip **(see illustration)**. Remove the shaft lock plate. **Note:** *Special lock plate depressor tools are available at most auto parts stores.*
5   Remove the turn signal canceling cam and the spring **(see illustration)**.
6   Remove the hazard flasher button **(see illustration)**.
7   Remove the signal switch lever by pulling the lever straight out of the turn signal

8.5 Remove the turn signal canceling cam and spring

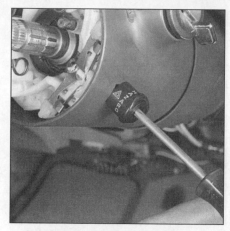

8.6 Unscrew and remove the hazard flasher button

8.8 Remove the three turn signal switch retaining screws (arrows)

8.11 To remove the key warning buzzer switch, stick a paper clip into the space (A) between the switch and the steering column assembly and pry it out - don't lose the small retainer (B) underneath the switch

8.12 Remove the key lock cylinder lock screw (arrow)

8.13 Turn the lock cylinder to the Run position and pull it out

8.16 Remove the bolts (arrows) and the two retaining nuts on the steering column support (arrows)

switch (make sure the lever is in the center or off position).

8   Remove the three turn signal switch screws **(see illustration)**.

9   Disconnect the turn signal switch electrical connector located near the base of the steering column and remove the harness cover.

10   Pull the turn signal switch up and off while guiding the wire harness up through the steering column. Installation is the reverse of removal using a stiff wire taped to the electrical connector to guide the harness through the column.

Ignition lock cylinder

Refer to illustrations 8.11, 8.12 and 8.13

11   Perform steps 1 through 10 above. Remove the key warning buzzer switch **(see illustration)**. The easiest way to get the buzzer switch out is to use a paper clip to pry it out. **Note:** *Don't lose the small retainer clip that holds the buzzer switch in place. This clip must be installed in exactly the same position*

during reassembly.

12   Remove the lock retaining screw **(see illustration)**. This will require a Torx bit on most models

13   Turn the lock cylinder to the Run position and pull it out **(see illustration)**.

14   Installation is the reverse of removal.

Ignition switch

Refer to illustrations 8.16 and 8.19

Note: *The ignition switch is located on the*

top, lower section of the steering column and can be replaced without removing the key lock cylinder.

15   Remove the screws securing the center panel under the steering column and remove the panel.

16   Remove the bolts securing the steering column support bracket to the dash panel. Lower and support the steering column **(see illustration)**.

17   Place the ignition switch in the lock

12

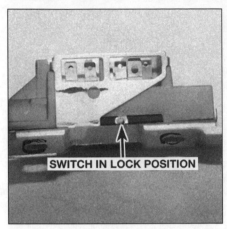

8.19 The ignition switch must be in the lock position before installing

8.30 Remove the Torx-head bolts (arrows) and remove the housing from the steering column

8.31 Use a small punch to drive the pivot pin (arrow) from the switch and pivot assembly

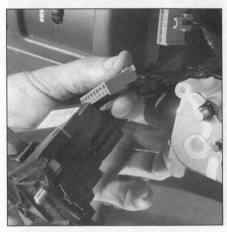

8.34 Detach the combination switch from the steering column housing assembly and unplug the electrical connector

position. If the lock cylinder has been removed, pull the actuating rod up until a definite stop can be felt and then move down one detent.

18   Disconnect the electrical connector to the ignition switch, remove the retaining screws and lift the switch off the steering column.

19   Prior to installation, make sure the ignition switch is in the lock position **(see illustration)**.

20   Connect the actuating rod to the switch. Press the switch into position, install the screws and the electrical connector.

21   Move the steering column back into position and install the nuts and bolts, tightening them to the torque listed in Chapter 10 specifications. Reconnect the battery cable and turn the ignition key to the Start position, making sure the engine cranks over. If it doesn't, loosen the switch mounting screws, slide the switch up the column slightly, then tighten the screws and repeat the test.

22   Install the lower trim panel.

Headlight dimmer switch

Note: *The dimmer switch is located on the lower section of the steering column and actuated by a rod connected to the turn signal lever.*

23   Perform steps 15 and 16 above.

24   Disconnect the dimmer switch electrical connector.

25   Remove the screws retaining the switch to the column and remove the switch.

26   Depressing the switch slightly, install a 3/32-inch drill bit into the alignment hole in the new switch. Install the switch on the column, applying slight pressure toward the top of the column removing all lash between the switch and the actuator rod.

27   Tighten the retaining screws securely and remove the drill bit.

28   Perform steps 21 and 22 above.

Windshield wiper/washer switch

Refer to illustrations 8.30 and 8.31

29   Perform steps 1 through 13 above. Disconnect the electrical connector at the base

of the column and remove the tilt lever, if equipped.

30   Remove the Torx head bolts securing the housing to the column and remove the housing **(see illustration)**.

31   Using the appropriate size punch, drive the pivot pin from the housing and remove the switch assembly **(see illustration)**.

32   Installation is the reverse of removal.

1992 and later models

Refer to illustration 8.34

Warning: *Before working in the vicinity of airbag components (on models so equipped) refer to Section 23 for the airbag system disarming procedure. Use care not to damage any wiring or sensors associated with this system or the airbag may deploy when reconnecting the battery or fail to deploy in the event of an accident.*

Combination switch

Note: *The combination switch includes the headlight, dimmer, turn signal, cruise control and hazard switches.*

33   Remove the steering wheel (see Chapter 10) and upper steering column covers.

34   Remove the combination switch from the steering column and disconnect the electrical connector **(see illustration)**.

35   Installation is the reverse of removal.

Windshield wiper/washer switch

36   Remove the steering wheel (see Chapter 10) and upper steering column covers.

37   Remove the wiper/washer switch and disconnect the electrical connector.

38   Installation is the reverse of removal.

Ignition switch

39   Turn the key to the Off/Lock position and remove the key from the lock.

40   Remove the steering wheel (see Chapter 10) and upper steering column covers.

41   Disconnect the electrical connector to the ignition switch, remove the screws securing the switch to the lock cylinder housing and remove the switch.

42   Installation is the reverse of removal.

Ignition lock cylinder

43   Remove the steering wheel (see Chapter 10) and upper steering column covers.

44   Insert the key into the lock and turn to the On position.

45   Using a 1/4-inch drill bit, drill off the heads of the shear bolts securing the lock cylinder housing to the steering column.

46   Remove the lock cylinder. Remove the ignition switch and the park lock cable.

47   Remove the threaded portion of the shear bolts from the steering column and clean all metal shavings from the column after drilling.

48   Installation is the reverse of removal. Install the lock cylinder with two shear bolts (supplied with the new lock cylinder housing) and tighten the bolts until the heads separate from the body.

---

9   Headlight switch - replacement

Refer to illustrations 9.3a and 9.3b

Note: *For headlight switch replacement on 1992 and later models, see Section 8.*

9.3a If the headlight switch pod on your vehicle looks like this, remove this screw and pull the pod off

1   Disconnect the cable from the negative terminal of the battery.
Caution: *If the vehicle is equipped with a Delco Loc II audio system, make sure you have the correct activation code before disconnecting the battery. See the information at the front of this manual for the radio re-activation procedure.*
2   On some vehicles, the steering column collar must be detached to remove the headlight switch pod assembly.
3   Remove the headlight switch pod retaining screw(s) **(see illustrations)** and pull the pod out from the dash.
4   Unplug the electrical connectors and remove the headlight switch.
5   Installation is the reverse of removal.

10   Headlight - removal and installation

Refer to illustrations 10.2 and 10.3
1   Most earlier vehicles are equipped with conventional dual rectangular sealed beam headlights. Some later vehicles are equipped

9.3b If the headlight switch looks like this, remove the headlight switch mounting screws (arrows) and unplug the electrical connections

with a single-piece "composite" type headlight assembly.

Sealed beam type

2   Remove the headlight trim ring screws **(see illustration)** and the trim ring.
3   Remove the headlight bezel screws **(see illustration)** and the headlight.
4   Unplug the headlight electrical connector and remove the headlight.
5   Installation is the reverse of removal.
6   Adjust the headlights (Section 11).

Composite type bulb

Caution: *Halogen gas filled bulbs are under pressure and may shatter if the surface is scratched or the bulb is dropped. Wear eye protection and handle the bulbs carefully, grasping only the base whenever possible. Do not touch the surface of the bulb with your fingers because the oil from your skin will cause hotspots and the bulb will prematurely fail. If you do happen to touch the bulb surface, clean it with rubbing alcohol.*

7   If your vehicle is equipped with composite type headlights, it is not necessary to replace the entire assembly just to change a bulb.
8   Locate the bulb lock ring on the back of the headlight assembly and turn it counterclockwise until it is loose.
9   With a vertical rocking motion, pull the bulb rearward.
10   With one hand, grip the wire harness end of the bulb. Do not grip the wires. With the other hand, grip the base of the bulb. Do not touch the bulb glass. Pull the bulb and base apart.
11   Installation is the reverse of removal.

Composite headlight assembly

12   There are two basic composite headlight types. To remove the first type, loosen the two top thumbscrews. Tilt the lamp assembly forward and lift. Unplug the electrical connector, loosen the rotating lock and remove the bulb. **Note:** *The bulbs for high and low beam are the same and have two separate filaments. Instead of using a new bulb for a burned out light, low and high beam bulbs can be interchanged.*
13   On other composite headlight assemblies, it is necessary to remove the headlight bezel, front bumper fascia screws, lens housing bolts and headlight lens assembly screws.
14   Installation is the reverse of removal.
15   Adjust the headlights (Section 11).

11   Headlights - adjustment

Refer to illustrations 11.2 and 11.4
1   It is important that the headlights be aimed correctly. If adjusted incorrectly they could blind an oncoming car and cause a serious accident or seriously reduce the your ability to see the road. The headlights should be checked for proper aim every 12 months and any time a new sealed beam headlight is installed or front end body work is performed.
2   Each headlight has two adjusting screws,

10.2 Remove the headlight trim ring screws (arrows)

10.3 Remove the headlight bezel screws (arrows)

12

11.2 Each headlight has a vertical (A) and a horizontal (B) adjusting screw

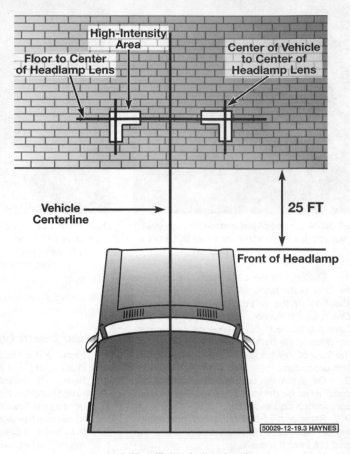

11.4 Headlight aiming details

12.2 To replace the turn signal/side marker bulb, remove both lens assembly retaining screws

one on the top controlling up and down movement and one on the side controlling left and right movement **(see illustration)**. There are several methods of adjusting the headlights. The simplest method uses an empty wall 25 feet in front of the vehicle and a level floor.

3   Park the vehicle on a level floor 25 feet from the wall.

4   Position masking tape vertically on the wall in reference to the vehicle centerline and the centerlines of both headlights **(see illustration)**.

5   Position a horizontal tape line in reference to the centerline of all the headlights. **Note:** *It may be easier to position the tape on the wall with the vehicle parked only a few inches away.*

6   Adjustment should be made with the vehicle sitting level, the gas tank half-full and no unusually heavy load in the vehicle.

7   Starting with the low beam adjustment, position the high intensity zone so it is two inches below the horizontal line and two inches to the right of the headlight vertical line. Adjustment is made by turning the top adjusting screw clockwise to raise the beam and counterclockwise to lower the beam. The adjusting screw on the side should be used in the same manner to move the beam left or right.

8   With the high beams on, the high intensity zone should be vertically centered with the exact center just below the horizontal line. **Note:** *It may not be possible to position the headlight aim exactly for both high and low beams. If a compromise must be used, keep in mind that the low beams are the most used and have the greatest effect on driver safety.*

12 Bulb replacement

Refer to illustrations 12.2, 12.3, 12.20, 12.22, 12.24, 12.28 and 12.34

1   Disconnect the cable from the negative terminal of the battery before attempting to replace any of the following bulbs. **Caution:** *If the vehicle is equipped with a Delco Loc II audio system, make sure you have the correct activation code before disconnecting the battery. See the information at the front of this manual for the radio re-activation procedure.*

Front turn signal/side marker lights

2   Remove the outer headlight (see Section 10) and remove both turn signal lens retaining screws **(see illustration)**.

3   Pull the turn signal lens assembly forward until the retaining clip **(see illustration)** slides free of the front fender.

4   Turn the bulb holder counterclockwise and remove it from the turn signal lens assembly.

5   Turn the bulb counterclockwise and remove it from the bulb holder.

6   Installation is the reverse of removal.

12.3 Pull the lens assembly forward until the retaining clip pops loose from the fender

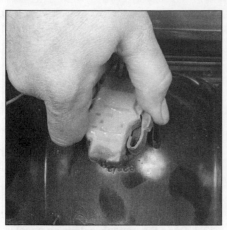

12.20 To release a bulb holder from the tail light lens assembly, depress the locking lever with your thumb and turn the holder counterclockwise

12.22 When installing the slide-out type lens assembly, make sure that the tabs on the bottom of the lens assembly slide into the grooves along the edge of the rear trim section

12.24 To remove the backup lens assembly, remove the license plate and this retaining screw

Front parking lights

7   Reach under the bumper and locate the bulb holder. Turn it counterclockwise and pull it out of the lamp assembly.
8   To remove the bulb from the holder, depress it and turn it counterclockwise.
9   Installation is the reverse of removal.

Fog lights (if equipped)

10   Some vehicles are equipped with optional fog lights. Bulb replacement requires disassembly of the unit.
11   Unplug the electrical connector from the fog light pigtail lead and remove the fog light assembly from the mounting bracket.
12   Disassemble the unit, remove the old bulb, install a new one and reassemble the fog light.
13   Install the fog light on the mounting bracket.

Rear turn signal and brake lights

14   If the turn signal lens on your vehicle is retained by screws at the top of the lens, refer to Steps 15 and 16.
15   Raise the trunk lid and remove both turn signal lens retaining screws from the rear tail-light trim section.
16   Slide the lens assembly toward the side of the vehicle until it is free.
17   If the turn signal lens on your vehicle is retained by plastic nuts inside the trunk, refer to Steps 18 and 19.
18   Open the trunk lid and remove the plastic wing nuts inside the back wall of the trunk.
19   Pull the lens assembly out of the rear trim section.
20   To remove the bulb holder (all types), depress the locking lever with your thumb **(see illustration)** and turn the holder counterclockwise.
21   Turn the bulb counterclockwise and remove it.
22   Installation is the reverse of removal for

both types of turn signal assemblies. If you are installing the slide-out type lens assembly, note that the tabs on the bottom of the lens assembly slide into slots in the rear trim section **(see illustration)**.

Backup lights

23   On 1991 and earlier models, remove the license plate.
24   On all models, remove the backup lens assembly retaining screw **(see illustration)** and remove the lens assembly.
25   To remove the bulb holder, turn it counterclockwise.
26   Remove the bulb from the holder.
27   Installation is the reverse of removal.

Dome light

28   Pry off the plastic dome light lens with a small screwdriver **(see illustration)**.
29   Pull the bulb straight out.
30   Installation is the reverse of removal.

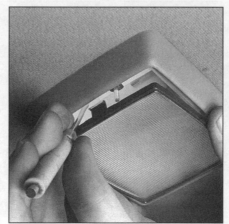

12.28 To replace a dome light, pop the lens cover loose with a small screwdriver and pull the old bulb straight out of the holder

12.34 A typical courtesy light located in the swing-down under-dash panel - turn the holder counterclockwise to detach it from the panel

Courtesy lights

31   Courtesy lights are located in various spots. Most vehicles have a light under the left side of the dash and one in the glove box.
32   To replace a bulb in the glovebox, open the glovebox door, pry loose the lens located in the ceiling of the glove box and pull the bulb straight out. Installation is the reverse of removal.
33   To replace a bulb in the panel under the dash, remove the two screws retaining the under-dash panel and allow it to hang down.
34   Turn the bulb holder **(see illustration)** counterclockwise and remove it from the under-dash panel.
35   To remove the bulb from the holder, turn it counterclockwise and pull out.
36   Installation is the reverse of removal.

Instrument panel lights

37   Remove the instrument panel (Section 15).
38   Turn the instrument panel upside down

12

13.2 Prior to removing the radio console trim plate, pop loose the forward end of the console trim plate or you will damage the lower end of the radio trim plate during removal

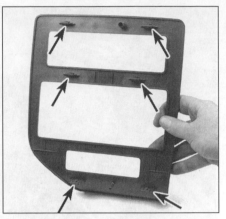

13.3 The radio trim plate has six tabs (arrows) on the back - when prying it loose from the dashboard, concentrate your prying efforts to these areas to prevent damage to the plate

13.5 Once the console extension panel is removed, remove the console heater duct

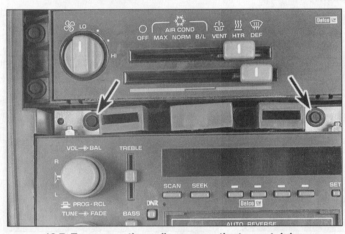

13.7 To remove the radio, remove the two retaining screws (arrows)

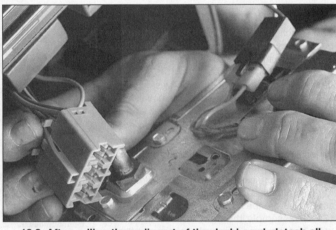

13.8 After pulling the radio out of the dashboard, detach all electrical connectors

and lay it down on a clean work surface or shop rag.

39 Turn the bulb holder counterclockwise and pull it out of the back of the instrument panel case.

40 Pull the bulb straight out from the bulb holder.

41 Installation is the reverse of removal.

Center high mount brake lights

42 Pull down on plastic brake light cover until it unsnaps from the base plate.

43 Push in on the small retainer tab holding the lamp bulbs into the base plate and withdraw the bulb and holder. Carefully unplug the bulb from the bulb socket. **Note:** *If the bulb is being replaced, be sure to use the correct type and wattage.*

---

13 Radio and speakers - removal and installation

Warning: *Before working in the vicinity of airbag components (on models so equipped)*

refer to Section 23 for the airbag system disarming procedure. Use care not to damage any wiring or sensors associated with this system or the airbag may deploy when reconnecting the battery or fail to deploy in the event of an accident.

1 Disconnect the cable from the negative terminal of the battery prior to performing any of the following procedures.

Caution: *If the vehicle is equipped with a Delco Loc II audio system, make sure you have the correct activation code before disconnecting the battery. See the information at the front of this manual for the radio re-activation procedure.*

Radio

Refer to illustrations 13.2, 13.3, 13.5, 13.7 and 13.8

2 Remove the instrument cluster trim plate. On 1991 and earlier models with a console, carefully pry up the forward end of the console trim plate **(see illustration)**. **Caution:** *If you attempt to remove the radio trim plate without loosening the forward end of the console trim plate you will damage the lower end of the radio trim plate.*

3 Carefully pry the console radio trim plate loose. The back of the trim plate has six tabs **(see illustration)** that must be pried loose from their respective metal clips in the dashboard.

4 Remove the right side console extension panel screws and remove the panel.

5 Remove the console heater duct **(see illustration)**.

6 Reach behind the radio and disconnect the antenna lead.

7 Remove the radio retaining screws/nuts **(see illustration)**.

8 Pull the radio out of the console and detach the electrical connectors **(see illustration)**.

9 Remove the radio.

10 Installation is the reverse of removal.

Speakers

Refer to illustrations 13.16a, 13.16b, 13.21, 13.22, 13.23 and 13.24

Dashboard speakers

11 Remove the pod retaining screws from the pods on either side of the instrument panel and remove both pods.

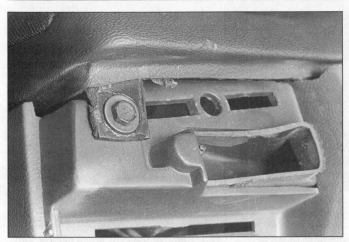

13.16a To remove the dashboard cover, remove the screw from each control pod cavity (not shown) and the bolts from both ends of the dashboard (left end shown) . . .

13.16b . . . and the two bolts (arrows) immediately above the instrument panel (not visible or accessible unless you have removed the retaining plate along the top of the instrument panel)

12   Remove both retaining screws from the instrument panel retaining plate along the upper edge of the instrument panel.

13   Pop loose the dashboard pad above the glove box.

14   Remove the screws from the lower edge of the center heating and air conditioning vent and remove the vent. Remove the retaining screws from the vents at both ends of the dashboard and remove both vents.

15   Pop loose and remove the defroster vent covers from the top of the dashboard cover.

16   Remove all dashboard cover retaining bolts (see illustrations). Note: Don't forget the screws hidden in the top of each control pod cavity (not shown in the above illustrations).

17   Raise the dashboard cover and detach the electrical connectors from both speakers, then remove the cover from the vehicle.

18   Turn the dashboard cover upside down and remove the speaker screws.

19   Installation is the reverse of removal.

Rear speakers

1991 and earlier

20   Open the trunk lid and locate the speakers (they're affixed to the underside of the package tray).

21   Remove the plastic wing nuts (see illustration) from the inner end of the speaker enclosure.

22   The outer end of the speaker enclosure has a hooked lip (see illustration) that hangs from a body reinforcement member. To disengage it from the reinforcement member, lift it up. Remove the enclosure.

23   Detach the speaker retaining clip (see illustration) from the underside of the package tray.

24   Allow the speaker assembly to swing down, then detach the outer end (see illustration) from the reinforcement member.

25   Unplug the electrical connector from the speaker and remove the speaker assembly.

26   Installation is the reverse of removal.

13.21 To remove either of the rear speaker enclosures, first remove the plastic wing nuts from the inner end of the enclosure

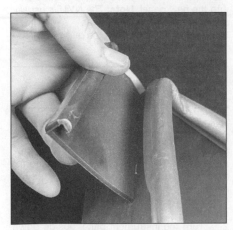

13.22 Lift the outer, hooked end (removed from the vehicle for clarity in this photo) off its corresponding tab on the package tray reinforcement member and remove the enclosure

13.23 To remove the speaker assembly from the vehicle, first disconnect this wire retaining clip from its corresponding hook on the underside of the package tray . . .

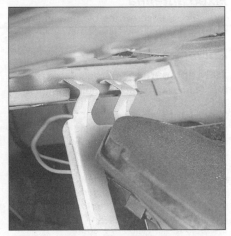

13.24 . . . then unhook the other end of the speaker from the slots in the package tray reinforcement member and lower the speaker far enough to unplug the electrical connector and remove the speaker assembly

12

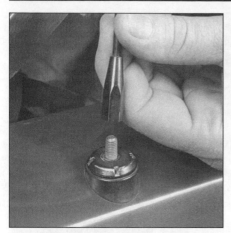

14.1 If the antenna on your vehicle is fixed, simply loosen it with a wrench and remove

14.2 Use a pair of needle-nose pliers to remove the antenna locking nut

15.1 Remove the instrument cluster trim screws (arrows) and remove the trim panel

1992 and later

27   Remove the rear seat cushion and rear seat back.
28   Remove the right and left rear quarter trim panels.
29   Remove the rear shelf panel.
30   Remove the fasteners, lift the speaker out and disconnect the electrical connector.
31   Installation is the reverse of removal.

Door speakers

32   Remove the door trim panel.
33   Remove the fasteners, lift the speaker out and disconnect the electrical connector.
34   Installation is the reverse of removal.

14   Radio antenna - removal and installation

Refer to illustrations 14.1 and 14.2

Fixed antenna

1   Simply unscrew the old antenna mast **(see illustration)** and install a new unit.

Power antenna

1991 and earlier

2   Remove the locking nut **(see illustration)**.
3   Turn the ignition to ACC and turn the radio on to extend the antenna and toothed cable out of the motor assembly.
4   Disconnect the cable from the negative terminal of the battery. **Caution:** *If the vehicle is equipped with a Delco Loc II audio system, make sure you have the correct activation code before disconnecting the battery. See the information at the front of this manual for the radio re-activation procedure.*
5   Remove the contact spring from the antenna and clean it.
6   Insert the new antenna into the antenna drive assembly. **Note:** *The toothed side of the plastic cable must face the antenna motor to prevent damage to the motor assembly* **(see**

illustration 14.2).
7   Insert the plastic cable into the tube assembly until resistance is felt (about 12 inches).
8   Install the battery cable, turn the radio off and hold the toothed cable and antenna in position until they retract into the antenna assembly.
9   Insert the antenna into the antenna assembly and install the contact spring with the flanged end facing up.
10   Install the nut.
11   Cycle the antenna several times to check its operation. At first, the antenna may only extend or retract halfway. Cycle it until it fully extends and retracts.

1992 and later

12   Disconnect the cable from the negative battery terminal.
13   Working inside the trunk, remove the rear compartment trim to access the antenna assembly.
14   Disconnect the electrical connector at the relay, the ground cable screw and the cable lead from the base.
15   Remove the brace screw, the insulator nut at the quarter panel and remove the antenna assembly.
16   Installation is the reverse of removal.

15   Instrument cluster - removal and installation

Refer to illustration 15.1
Warning: *Before working in the vicinity of airbag components (on models so equipped) refer to Section 23 for the airbag system disarming procedure. Use care not to damage any wiring or sensors associated with this system or the airbag may deploy when reconnecting the battery or fail to deploy in the event of an accident.*
1   Disconnect the negative terminal from the battery. **Caution:** *If the vehicle is equipped with a Delco Loc II audio system, make sure you have the correct activation*

code before disconnecting the battery. See the information at the front of this manual for the radio re-activation procedure. Remove the instrument panel trim plate or top cover **(see illustration)**.
2   Some 1991 and earlier vehicles that are equipped with a steering column collar and steering column filler plate which must be removed before the instrument panel can be removed. If your vehicle is equipped with a collar and filler plate, pinch together the four slide clips along the bottom seam between the collar filler plate and detach them and slide the collar up the steering column.
3   On 1992 and later vehicles, remove the screws retaining the left and right steering column filler plates and remove the plates.
4   Remove the instrument panel retaining screws. Pull the instrument panel from its cavity in the dashboard and unplug all electrical connectors, then remove the instrument panel.
5   If you are replacing the old instrument panel with a new one, be sure to remove the non-volatile memory (NVM) chip and install it into the new panel. **Note:** *The NVM is usually somewhere near the odometer.*
6   Installation is the reverse of removal.

16   Instruments - removal and installation

Refer to illustrations 16.3, 16.4 and 16.5
Note: *The gages on 1992 and later vehicles are not serviced separately from the instrument panel. The panel can be exchanged for a remanufactured or new unit if it needs repair.*
1   Remove the instrument panel (see Section 15).
2   Turn the instrument panel upside down and lay it down on a clean work surface.
3   Remove the printed circuit/case assembly screws and separate the case from the cluster assembly **(see illustration)**.
4   Remove the screws retaining the faulty

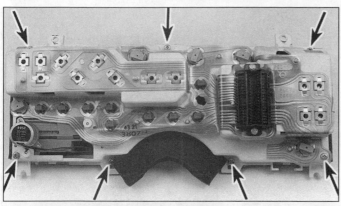

16.3 The printed circuit/case side of a typical instrument cluster assembly - to remove it, take out the six screws (arrows)

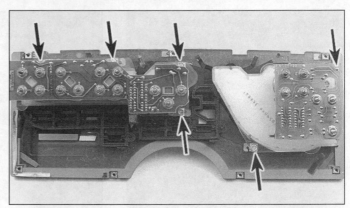

16.4 A typical instrument panel as seen from the back - to remove an instrument from the panel, remove the retaining screws (arrows)

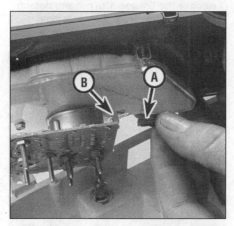

16.5 When removing the speedometer from an instrument cluster, be sure to detach the electrical connector (A) from the spade terminal (B) on the back of the speedometer printed circuit

17.4 When measuring the voltage at the rear window defogger grid, wrap a piece of aluminum foil around the negative probe of the voltmeter and press the foil against the wire with your finger

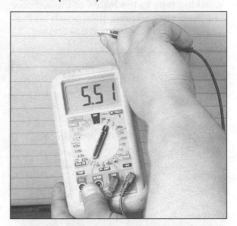

17.5 To determine if a heating element has broken, check the voltage at the center of each element - if the voltage is 6-volts, the element is unbroken - if the voltage is 12-volts, the element is broken between the center and the positive end - if there is no voltage, the element is broken between the center and ground

instrument(s) (see illustration). Note: Some instruments can be replaced individually but others can only be replaced as an assembly. Consult your dealer for information regarding the various replacement gauges for the instrument cluster in your vehicle.

5   Remove the instrument. Note: If you are replacing the speedometer, there may be a pigtail lead plugged into a spade type terminal on the printed circuit board behind the speedometer. Be sure to unplug it (see illustration).

6   Installation is the reverse of removal.

17 Rear window defogger - check and repair

1   The rear window defogger consists of a number of horizontal elements baked onto the glass surface.

2   Small breaks in the element can be repaired without removing the rear window.

Check

Refer to illustrations 17.4, 17.5 and 17.7

3   Turn the ignition switch and defogger

system switches to the ON position.

4   When measuring voltage during the next two tests, wrap a piece of aluminum foil around the tip of the voltmeter negative probe and press the foil against the heating element with your finger (see illustration).

5   Check the voltage at the center of each heating element (see illustration). If the voltage is 6-volts, the element is okay (there is no break). If the voltage is 12-volts, the element is broken between the center of the element and the positive end. If the voltage is 0-volts the element is broken between the center of the element and ground.

6   Connect the negative lead to a good body ground. The reading should stay the same.

7   To find the break, place the voltmeter positive lead against the defogger positive terminal. Place the voltmeter negative lead with the foil strip against the heating element at the positive terminal end and slide it toward the negative terminal end. The point at which the voltmeter deflects from zero to several volts is the point at which the heating element is broken (see illustration).

17.7 To find the break, place the voltmeter positive lead against the defogger positive terminal, place the voltmeter negative lead with the foil strip against the heating element at the positive terminal end and slide it toward the negative terminal end - the point at which the voltmeter reading changes abruptly is the point at which the element is broken

12

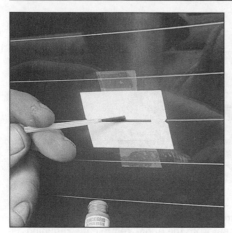

17.13 To use a defogger repair kit, apply masking tape to the inside of the window at the damaged area, then brush on the special conductive coating

18.4 Remove the vent grille screws, raise the vent, then remove the washer hose nozzle retaining screw and detach the washer hose and nozzle from the vent grille

18.5 Once the vent grille is out of the way, remove the linkage arm nut and detach the linkage from the windshield wiper motor

18.6 Remove the windshield wiper mounting bolts (arrows) - the third bolt, which is at the bottom of the motor, is not visible in this photo

18.9a To remove the windshield washer pump from the wiper motor, pry out the clip (arrow) with a small screwdriver

18.9b To detach the washer pump from the windshield wiper motor, pull straight down - the pump is sealed by a rubber O-ring and the top end of the pump is plugged into a socket at the top of the pump cavity so you will encounter some resistance until the pump pulls loose

Repair

Refer to illustration 17.13

8   Repair the break in the element using a repair kit specifically recommended for this purpose. Included in this kit is plastic conductive epoxy.

9   Prior to repairing a break, turn off the system and allow it to cool off for a few minutes.

10   Lightly buff the element area with fine steel wool, then clean it thoroughly with rubbing alcohol.

11   Use masking tape to mask off the area being repaired.

12   Thoroughly mix the epoxy, following the instructions provided with the repair kit.

13   Apply the epoxy material to the slit in the masking tape, overlapping the undamaged area about 3/4-inch on either end **(see illustration).**

14   Allow the repair to cure for 24 hours before removing the tape and using the system.

18 Windshield wiper motor, washer pump and switch - removal and installation

Refer to illustrations 18.4, 18.5, 18.6, 18.9a and 18.9b

Note: *For wiper switch replacement on steering column mounted switch, see Section 8.*

1   Disconnect the cable from the negative terminal of the battery before performing either of the following procedures.

Caution: *If the vehicle is equipped with a Delco Loc II audio system, make sure you have the correct activation code before disconnecting the battery. See the information at the front of this manual for the radio re-activation procedure.*

Windshield wiper motor

2   Unplug the electrical connectors from the motor and the pump.

3   Detach the hoses from the washer pump.

4   Remove the vent grille from the left side

of the vehicle. Be sure to detach the washer hose and nozzle **(see illustration).** **Note:** *The grilles in some vehicles are retained with plastic pop fasteners instead of screws. Be careful when removing these fasteners or you will break them.*

5   Disconnect the transmission linkage arm **(see illustration).**

6   Remove the motor mounting bolts and remove the motor **(see illustration).**

7   Installation is the reverse of removal. If you are replacing the motor, be sure to switch the washer pump to the new motor (if equipped).

Washer pump

8   If the washer pump is located at the washer fluid reservoir, drain the fluid from the reservoir or be prepared to catch the fluid as the pump is removed (on some models it may be easier to remove the reservoir from the vehicle to replace the pump). Disconnect the

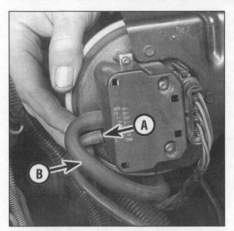

20.2 Periodically inspect the vacuum hoses between the vacuum diaphragm/servo and the intake manifold (A) and the cruise/vacuum release valve assembly (B)

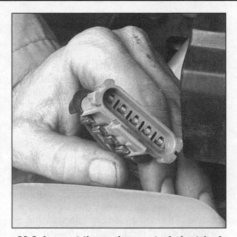

20.3 Inspect the cruise control electrical connector for the presence of dirt, moisture or corrosion

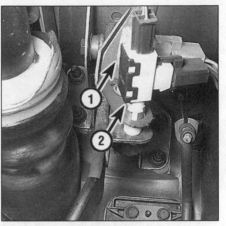

20.5 Typical self-adjusting cruise release/vacuum release valve assembly (1) and brake switch (2)

electrical connector and washer hose from the pump. Remove the pump from the reservoir.

9   If the washer pump is located at the motor, disconnect the washer hose, remove the small locking clip **(see illustration)** and pull the pump from the bottom of the motor **(see illustration)**. Installation is the reverse of removal.

Switch

10   Remove the mounting screw(s) from the windshield wiper motor switch.
11   Remove the switch from the dash and unplug the electrical connectors.
12   Installation is the reverse of removal.

19 Horn - removal and installation

1   Disconnect the cable from the negative terminal of the battery. **Caution:** *If the vehicle is equipped with a Delco Loc II audio system, make sure you have the correct activation code before disconnecting the battery. See the information at the front of this manual for the radio re-activation procedure.*
2   Locate the horn behind the front bumper.
3   Unplug the electrical connector to the horn.
4   Remove the horn mounting bracket bolt.
5   Remove the horn.
6   Installation is the reverse of removal.

20 Cruise control system - general check and repair

Refer to illustrations 20.2, 20.3 and 20.5
1   Servicing the cruise control system requires special test equipment and techniques. However, there are a few simple visual inspections you should make to ensure that the cruise control on your vehicle

remains in good working order.
2   Inspect the vacuum hoses **(see illustration)**. Make sure that they are in good condition and firmly attached to their respective fittings. If any hose is cracked or damaged, replace it.
3   Check the electrical connector **(see illustration)** for a tight fit and inspect it for any evidence of dirt, corrosion or moisture. If any of these symptoms are evident, clean the plug thoroughly.
4   Inspect the servo diaphragm for tears or other damage. If such damage is evident, have it replaced.

Cruise release/vacuum release valves

5   If your vehicle's cruise control system fails to release when the brake pedal is applied on a vehicle equipped with an automatic transaxle, or when the brake or clutch pedal are applied on a vehicle equipped with a manual transaxle, check the cruise release valve or vacuum release valve at the pedal **(see illustration)**.
6   If your vehicle is equipped with an automatic transaxle, make sure that the electrical connectors are firmly attached to the vacuum release valve assembly and the switch assembly and the vacuum line is firmly attached to the vacuum release valve assembly.
7   If your vehicle is equipped with a manual transaxle, make sure that the electrical connector is firmly attached to the switch assembly and the vacuum line is firmly attached to the cruise release valve assembly.
8   If everything looks properly attached, the cruise release valve (manual transaxle) or the vacuum release valve (automatic transaxle) is faulty.
9   To remove the cruise release/vacuum release valve, unplug the electrical connector (automatic only) and detach the vacuum hose, turn the retainer counterclockwise and pull out the retainer and cruise/vacuum release valve assembly.

10   Separate the retainer and cruise/vacuum release valve.
11   Install the retainer.
12   With the brake pedal depressed, insert the valve into the tubular retainer until the valve seats on the retainer. Note that "clicks" can be heard as the threaded portion of the valve is pushed through the retainer toward the brake pedal.
13   Pull the brake pedal fully rearward against the pedal stop until the "click" sounds cease. The valve is now adjusted.
14   Release the brake pedal and repeat Step 13 to verify that no "click" sounds can be heard.

21 Power door lock system - general information

The power door lock system operates the door lock actuators mounted in each door. The system consists of the switches, actuators and associated electrical wiring. Diagnosis can usually be limited to simple checks of the wiring connectors and actuators for minor faults which can be easily repaired. These include:

a) *Check the system fuse and circuit breaker.*
b) *Check the switch wiring for damage or loose connections.*
c) *Check the switch for continuity in the closed position. Also check the switches for sticking. If a switch sticks closed the actuator internal circuit breaker will trip and stay tripped until voltage is removed.*
d) *Remove the door panel(s) and check the actuator electrical connections for looseness or damage. Inspect the actuator rods and door lock linkage to make sure they are not bent, damaged or binding.*
e) *Remove the electrical connector at the actuator and with a test light or voltmeter, check for available voltage to the*

12

actuator as you cycle the switch. If voltage is present, but the actuator doesn't operate when connected, the actuator is probably defective. If no voltage is present at the connector, the switch, relay (if equipped) or wiring is probably defective.

22 Power window system - general information

The power window system operates the electric motors mounted in the doors which raise and lower the windows. The system consists of the control switches, motors, door glass regulators and associated wiring. As a convenience feature, later models may be equipped with an "express down" feature that allows the drivers door window to be fully opened by holding the left front switch in the down position for more than 0.3 seconds. This system uses a power window control module located in the drivers door.

Diagnosis can usually be limited to simple checks of the electrical connections and motors for minor faults which can be easily repaired. These include:

a) *Check the system fuse and circuit breaker.*

b) *Check the switch wiring for damage or loose connections.*

c) *Check the switches for continuity in the closed position. Also check the switches for sticking. If a switch sticks closed the power window motor internal circuit breaker will trip and stay tripped until voltage is removed.*

d) *Remove the door panel(s) and check the window motor electrical connections for looseness or damage. Inspect the door glass regulator for damage which could cause binding.*

e) *Remove the electrical connector at the window motor and with a test light or voltmeter, check for available voltage to the motor as you cycle the switch. If voltage is present, but the motor doesn't operate when connected, the motor is probably defective. If no voltage is present at the connector, the switch, control module (if equipped) or wiring is probably defective.*

23 Airbag - general information

General information

1   Some later models are equipped with a Supplement Inflatable Restraint (SIR) system, more commonly known as an airbag. This system is designed to protect the driver from serious injury in the event of a head-on or frontal collision. It consists of an airbag module in the center of the steering wheel, two discriminating (crash) sensors mounted at the front and interior of the vehicle, an arming sensor located behind the glove box, an SIR

coil assembly mounted under the steering wheel and a diagnostic module located inside the passenger compartment under the dash.

Airbag module and SIR

2   The airbag inflator module contains a housing incorporating the cushion (airbag) and inflator unit, mounted in the center of the steering wheel. The inflator assembly is mounted on the back of the housing over a hole through which gas is expelled, inflating the bag almost instantaneously when an electrical signal is sent from the system. The airbag steering column coil assembly is mounted on the steering column under the steering wheel and carries this signal to the module. The coil assembly can transmit an electrical signal regardless of steering wheel position.

Sensor

3   The system has three sensors: a forward discriminating sensor mounted on the radiator support and a passenger compartment discriminating sensor mounted under the front of the center console. These sensors are basically pressure sensitive switches that complete an electrical circuit during an impact of sufficient G force. The electrical signal from these sensors is sent to the arming sensor which then completes the circuit and inflates the airbag.

Diagnostic Energy Reserve Module (DERM)

4   The DERM supplies the current to the airbag system in the event of the collision, even if battery power is cut off. It checks this system every time the vehicle is started, causing the "AIR BAG" light to go on then off, if the system is operating properly. If there is a fault in the system, the light will go on and stay on and the DERM will store fault codes indicating the nature of the fault. If the "AIR BAG" light goes on and stays on, the vehicle should be taken to your dealer immediately for service.

Operation

5   For the airbag(s) to deploy, an impact of sufficient force must occur within 30-degrees of the vehicle centerline. When this condition occurs, the circuit to the airbag inflator is closed and the airbag inflates. If the battery is destroyed by the impact, or is too low to power the inflator, a back-up power supply inside the diagnostic/energy reserve module supplies current to the airbag.

Self-diagnosis system

6   A self-diagnosis circuit in the module displays a light when the ignition switch is turned to the On position. If the system is operating normally, the light should go out after seven flashes. If the light doesn't come on, or doesn't go out after seven flashes, or if it comes on while you're driving the vehicle, there's a malfunction in the SIR system. Have it inspected and repaired as soon as possible. Do not attempt to troubleshoot or service

the SIR system yourself. Even a small mistake could cause the SIR system to malfunction when you need it.

Servicing components near the SIR system

7   Nevertheless, there are times when you need to remove the steering wheel, radio or service other components on or near the instrument panel or at the front of the vehicle. At these times, you'll be working around components and wiring harnesses for the SIR system. SIR system wiring is easy to identify; they're all covered by a bright yellow conduit. Do not unplug the connectors for the SIR system wiring, except to disable the system. And do not use electrical test equipment on the SIR system wiring. **Always disable the SIR system before working near the SIR system components or related wiring.**

Disabling the SIR system

Refer to illustration 23.10

8   Turn the steering wheel to the straight ahead position, place the ignition switch key in the Lock position and remove the key. Remove the airbag fuse from the fuse block. It's also a good idea to disconnect the cable from the negative terminal of the battery, although this is not actually specified by the manufacturer. **Caution:** *If the vehicle is equipped with a Delco Loc ll audio system, make sure you have the correct activation code before disconnecting the battery. See the information at the front of this manual for the radio re-activation procedure.*

9   Remove the steering column covers and the left sound insulator panel below the instrument panel (see Chapter 11).

10   Unplug the yellow Connector Position Assurance (CPA) steering column harness connector **(see illustration)**.

Enabling the SIR system

11   After you've disabled the airbag and performed the necessary service, plug in the steering column CPA connectors. Reinstall

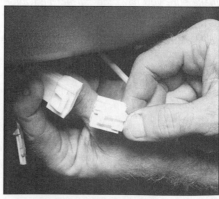

23.10 The driver's side airbag Connector Position Assurance (CPA) connector is located at the base of the steering column; always unplug it before removing the steering wheel or working in the area of the steering wheel

23.15a To release the SIR coil from the steering shaft, remove this snap ring . . .

23.15b . . . then remove the coil

the steering column lower trim panel, and the sound insulator panel.

12   Install the airbag fuse. Connect the negative battery terminal, if it was disconnected.

Removing, centering and installing the SIR coil

Refer to illustrations 23.15a, 23.15b, 23.16 and 23.18

13   Anytime some part of the steering system is disassembled for service or replacement, the steering column should be immobilized to ensure that the SIR coil doesn't become uncentered (moved). This can occur, for example, if the steering column is separated from the steering gear, or if the centering spring is pushed down, allowing the hub to rotate while the coil is removed from the steering column. If the coil becomes accidentally uncentered, re-center it as follows

before reassembling the steering system:

14   Make sure that the wheels are pointed straight ahead.

15   Remove the coil assembly snap-ring **(see illustration)** and remove the coil assembly **(see illustration)**.

16   Holding the coil assembly with its bottom side facing up, depress the spring lock **(see illustration)** and rotate the hub in the direction of the arrow until it stops (the arrow is on the back of the coil assembly). The coil ribbon should be wound up snug against the center hub.

17   Rotate the coil hub in the opposite direction two and three-quarters turns, then release the spring lock. The coil is now centered.

18   Install the SIR coil and secure it with the snap-ring. The tab will be at the top and the marks aligned when the coil is properly installed **(see illustration)**.

24   Wiring diagrams - general information

Since it isn't possible to include all wiring diagrams for every year covered by this manual, the following diagrams are those that are typical and most commonly used.

Prior to troubleshooting any circuits, check the fuse and circuit breaker, if equipped, to make sure they're in good condition. Make sure the battery is properly charged and check the cable connections (see Chapter 1).

When checking a circuit, make sure that all connections are clean and tight with no broken or loose terminals. When unplugging a connector, do not pull on the wires. Pull only on the connector housings themselves.

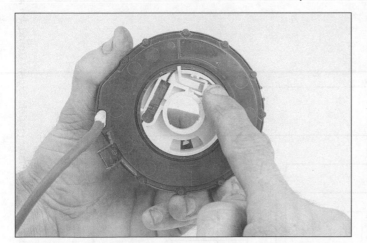

23.16 To center the SIR coil, hold it with its underside facing up, depress the spring lock and rotate the hub in the direction of the arrow on the coil assembly until it stops, then turn it in the opposite direction 2-3/4 turns and release the spring lock

23.18 When properly installed, the airbag coil will be centered with the marks aligned (circle) and the tab fitted between the projections on the top of the steering column shroud (arrow)

12

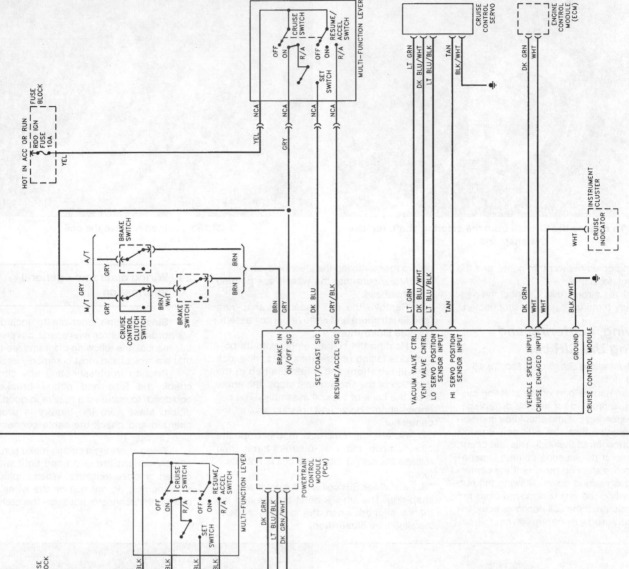

Cruise control system (1988 thru 1992 models except Grand Am and Skylark)

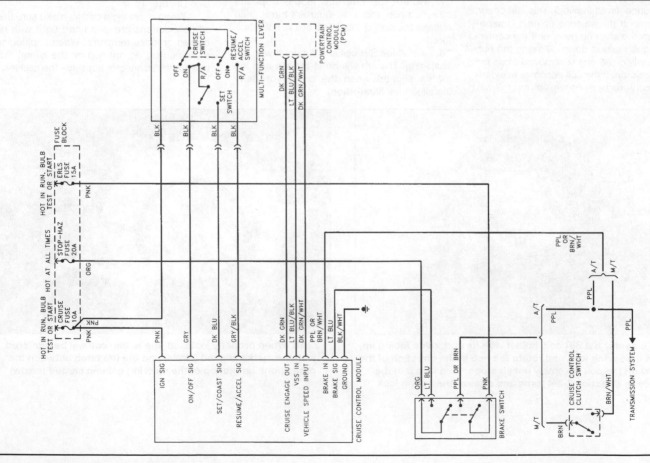

Cruise control system (1993 and later models except Grand Am and Skylark)

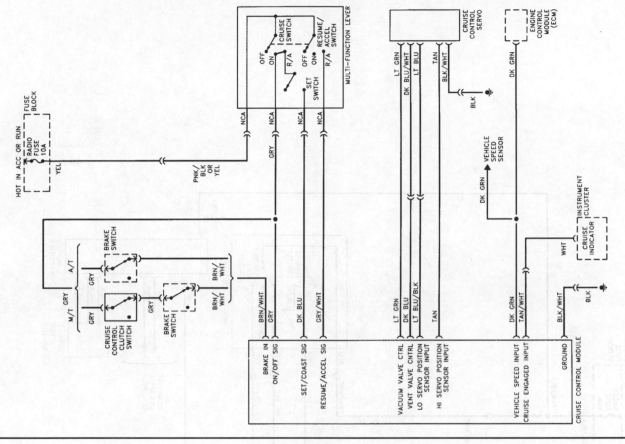

Cruise control system (Grand Am and Skylark models without a 2.5L engine)

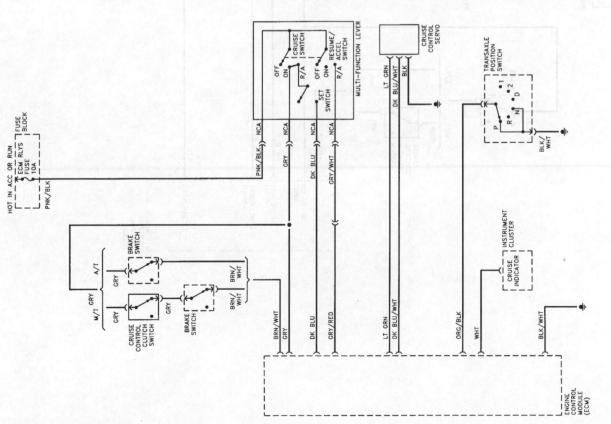

Cruise control system (Grand Am and Skylark models with a 2.5L engine)

12

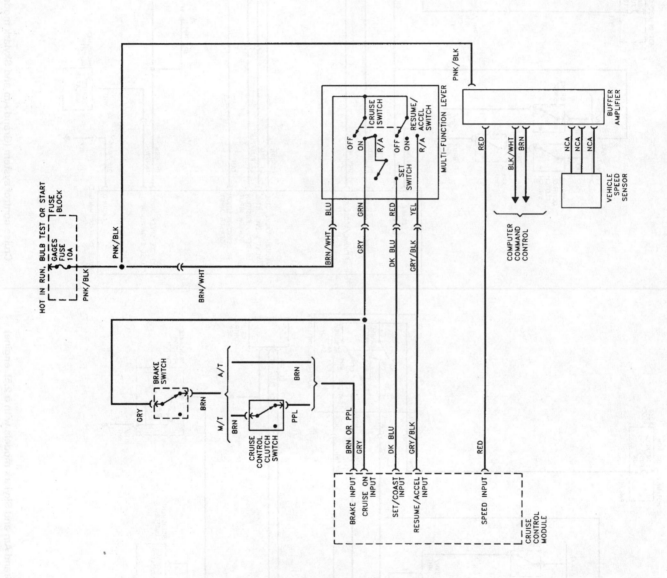

Cruise control system (1987 and earlier except Grand Am and Skylark models)

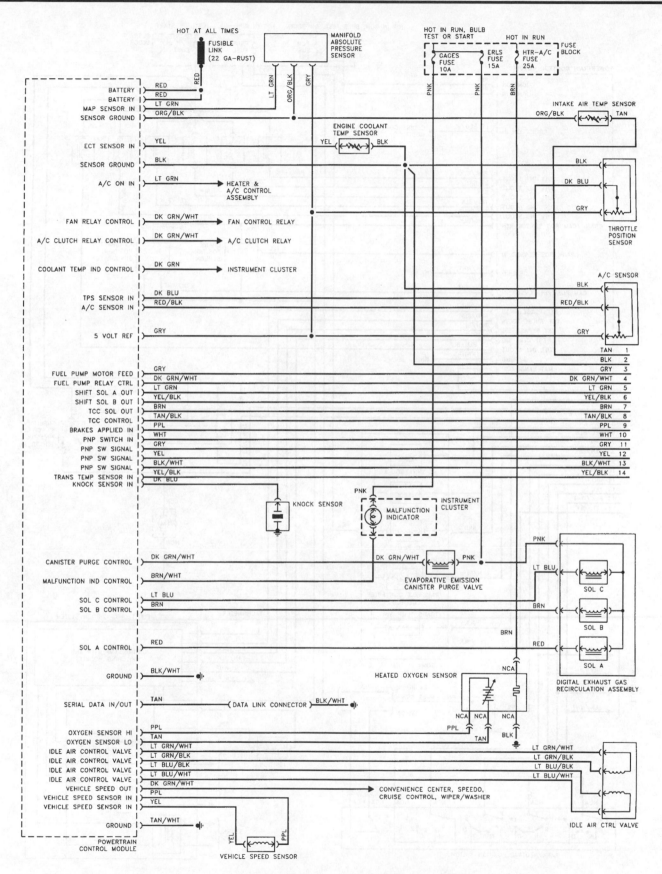

Typical 3.1L engine controls (1 of 2)

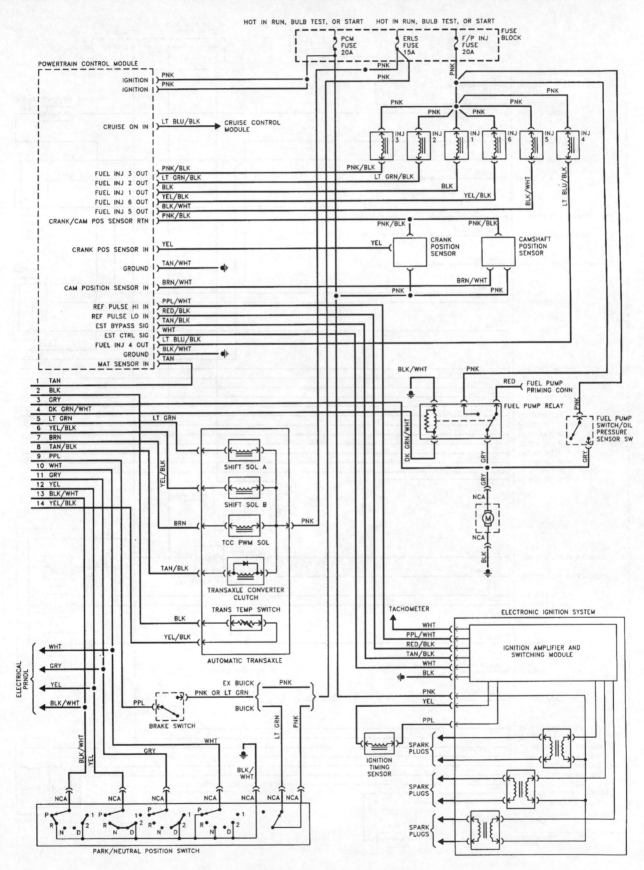

Typical 3.1L engine controls (2 of 2)

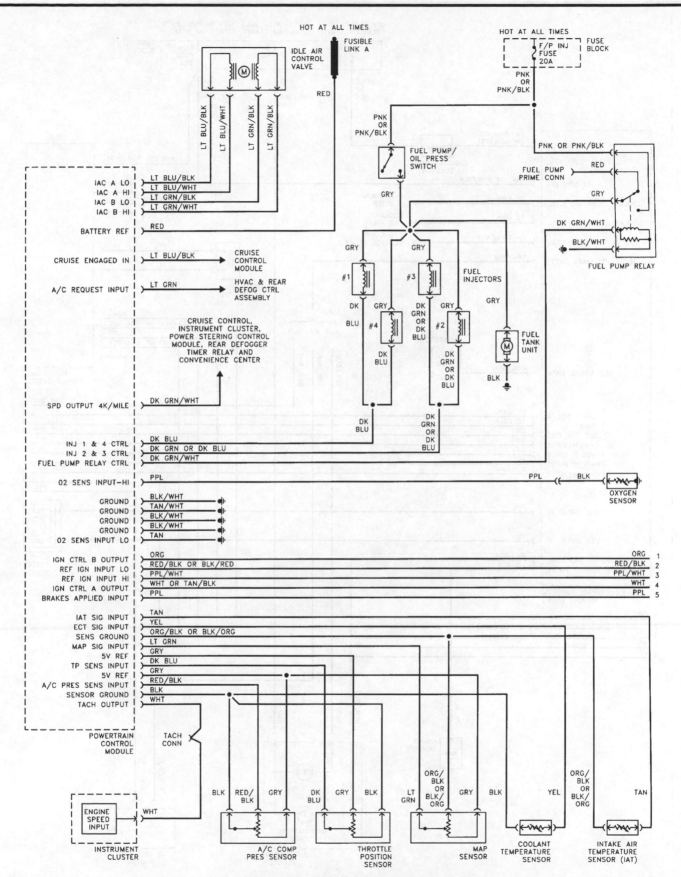

2.3L engine controls (1991 and later models) (1 of 3)

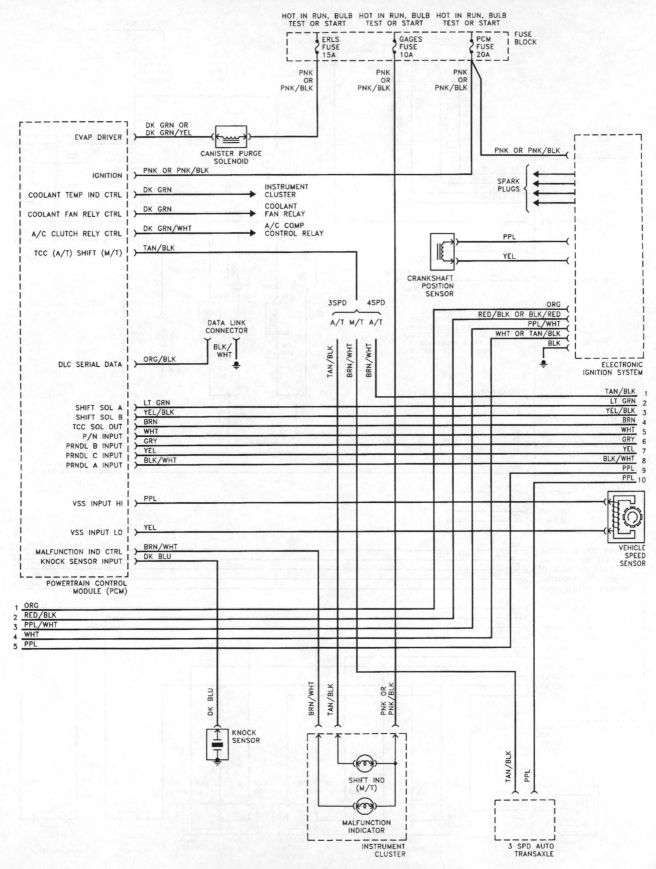

2.3L engine controls (1991 and later models) (2 of 3)

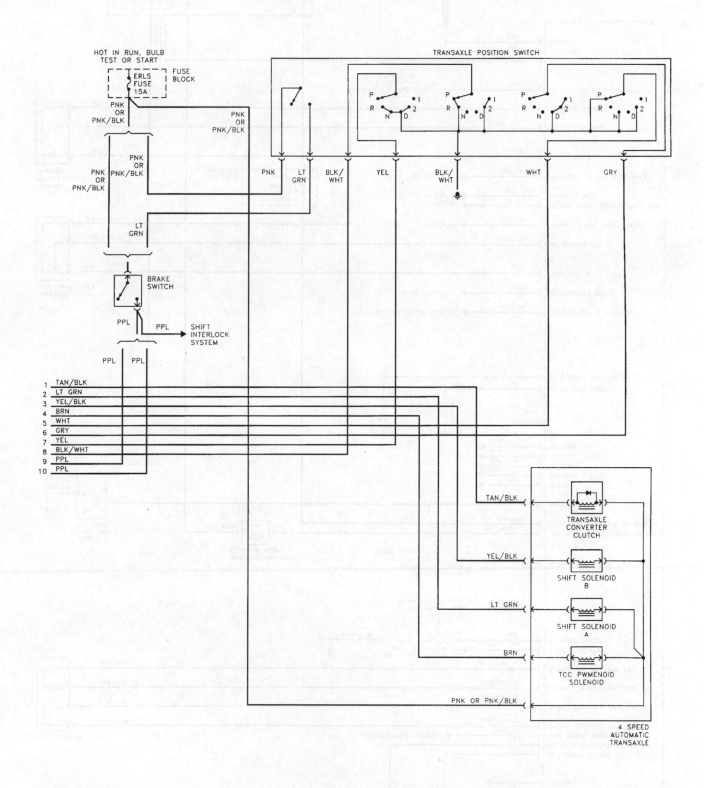

2.3L engine controls (1991 and later models) (3 of 3)

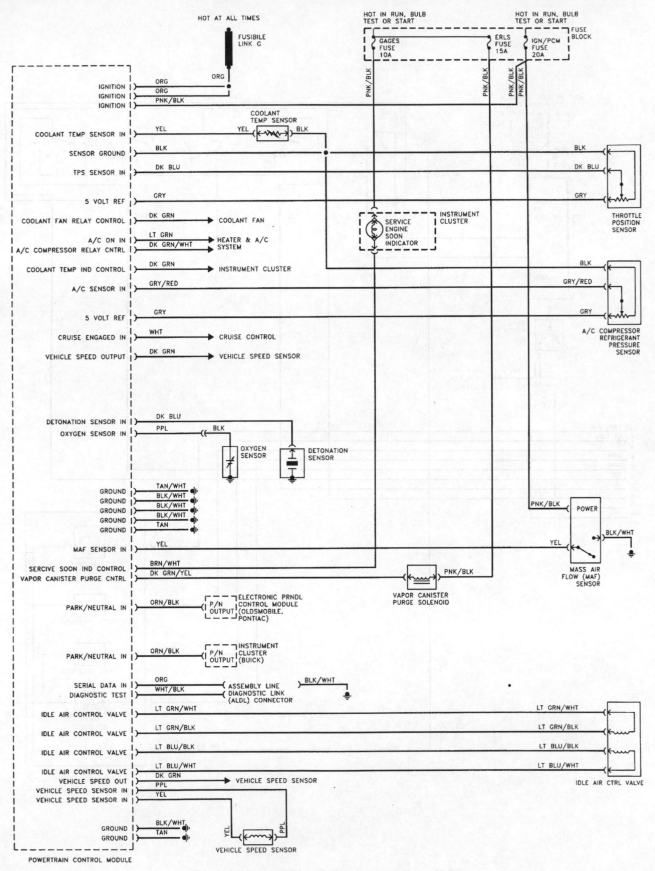

Typical 3.3L engine controls (1 of 2)

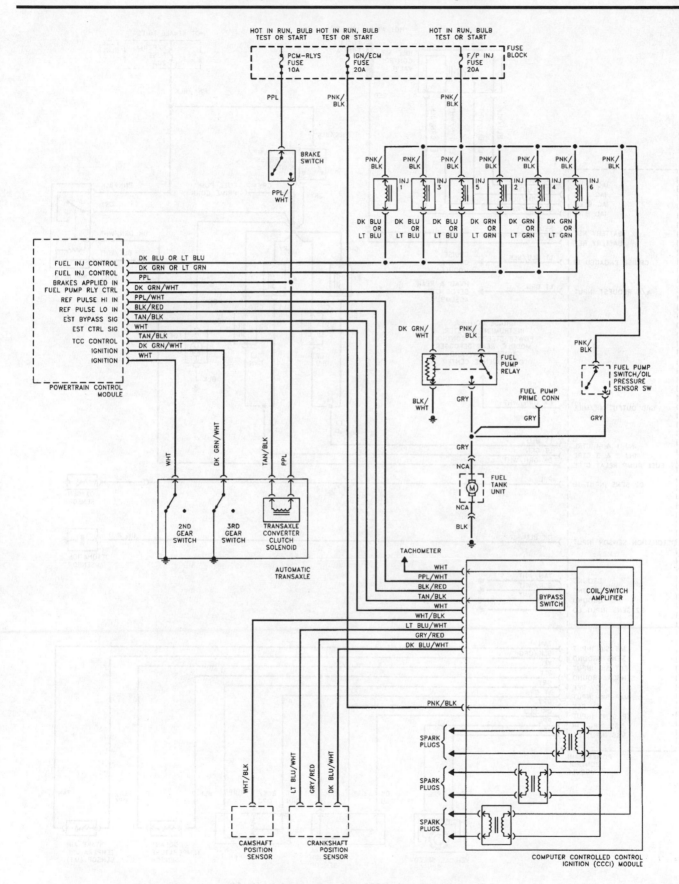

Typical 3.3L engine controls (2 of 2)

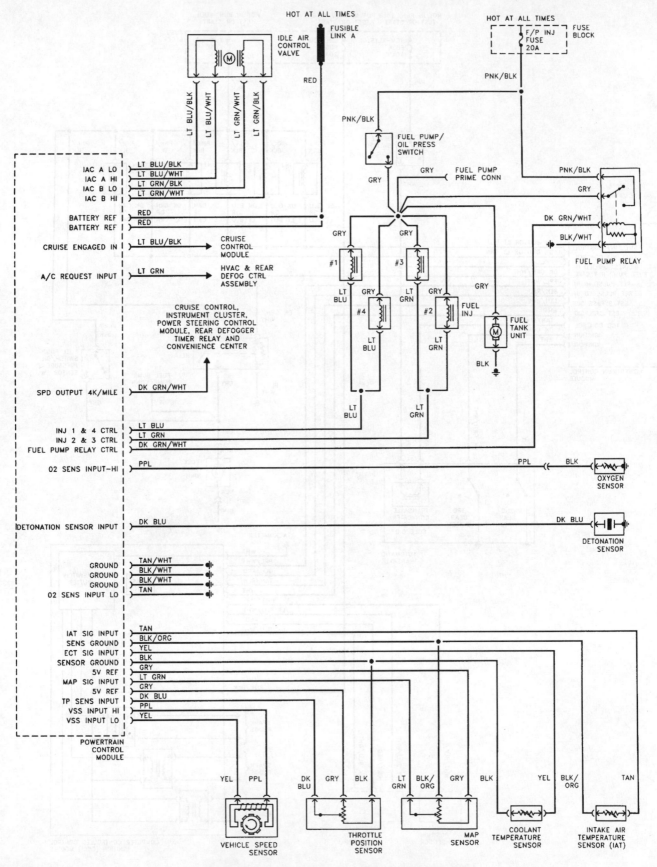

2.3L engine controls (1990 and earlier models) (1 of 2)

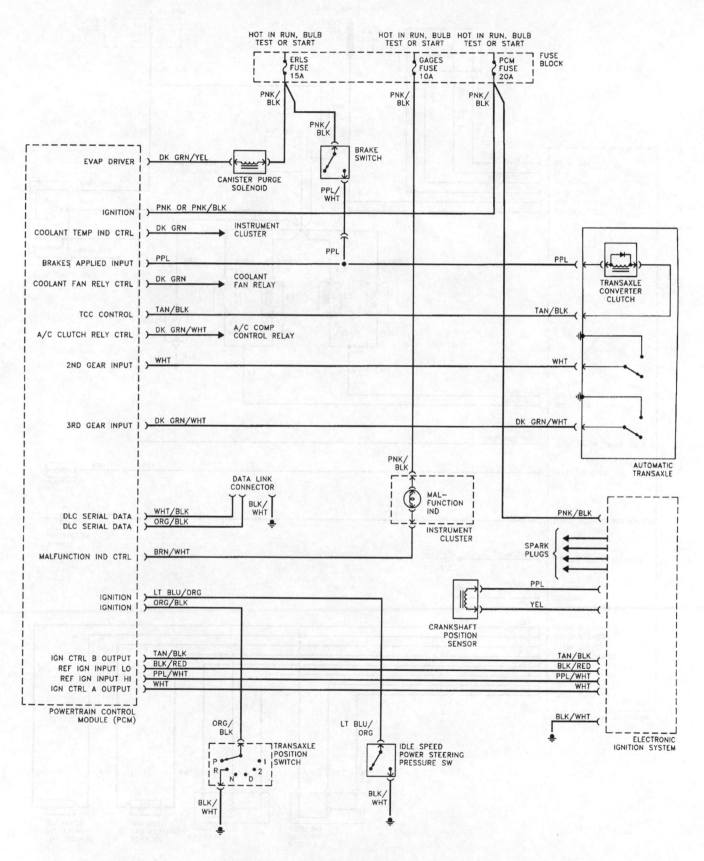

2.3L engine controls (1990 and earlier models) (2 of 2)

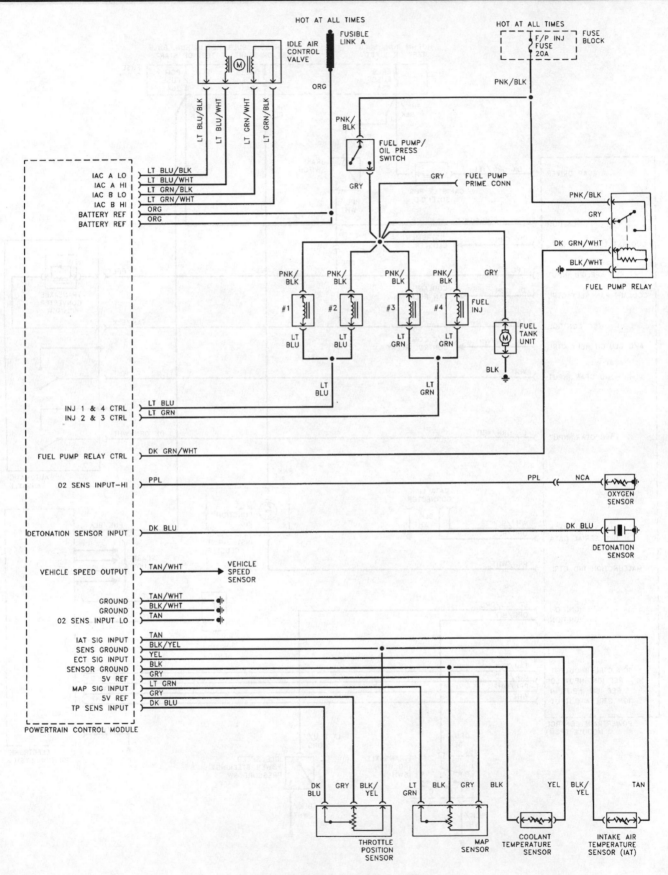

Typical 2.0L engine controls (1 of 2)

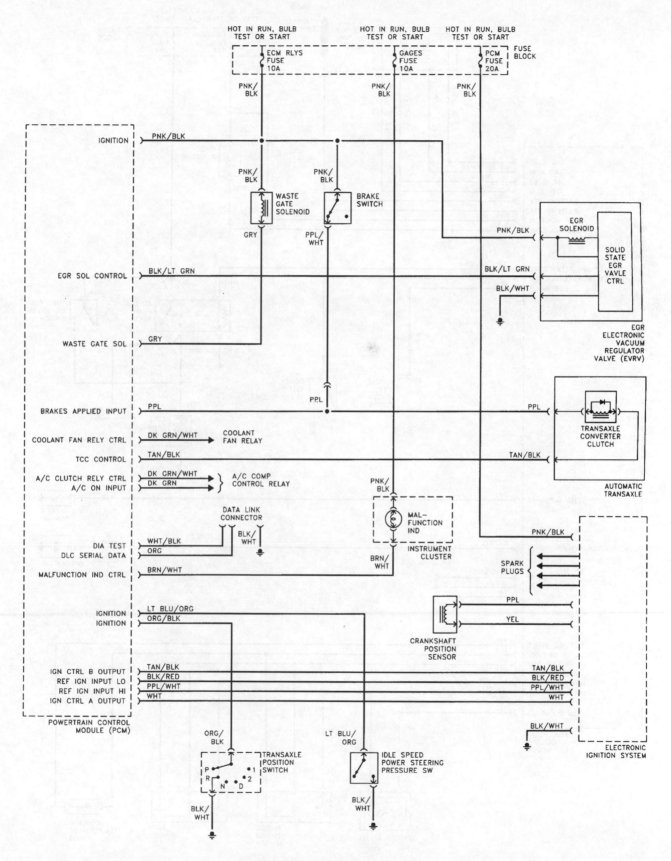

Typical 2.0L engine controls (2 of 2)

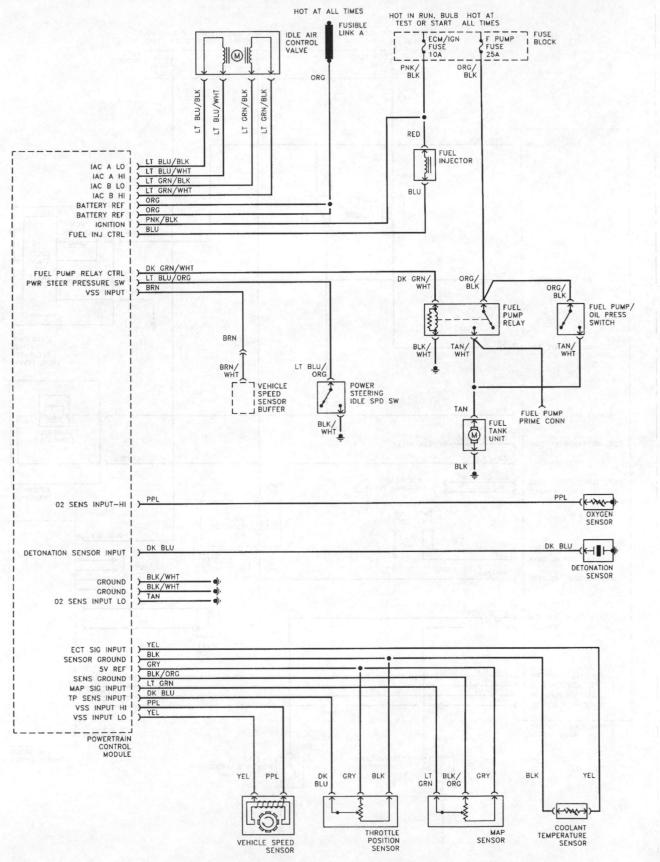

2.5L engine controls (1987 and earlier models) (1 of 2)

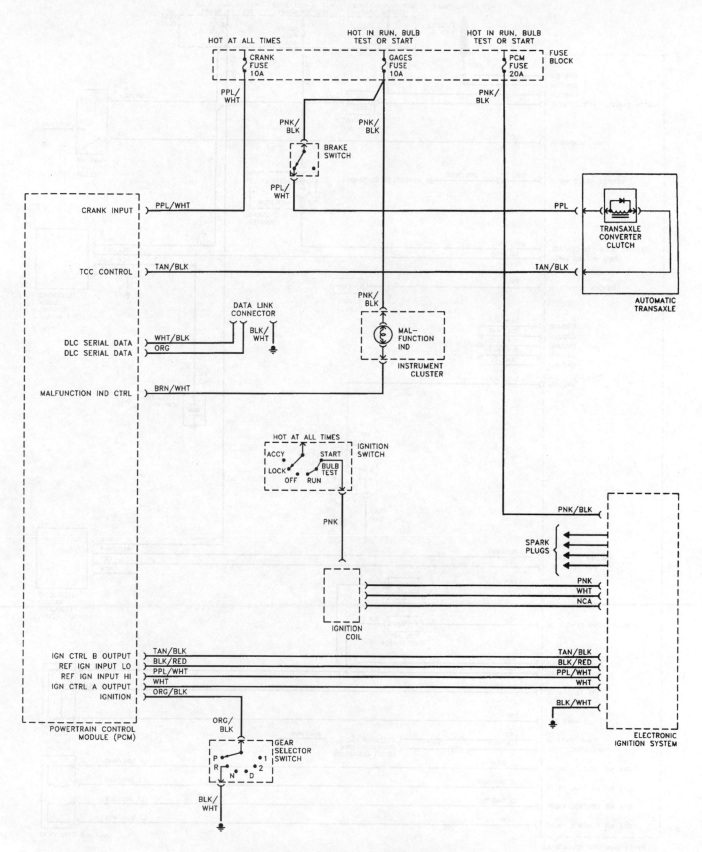

2.5L engine controls (1987 and earlier models) (2 of 2)

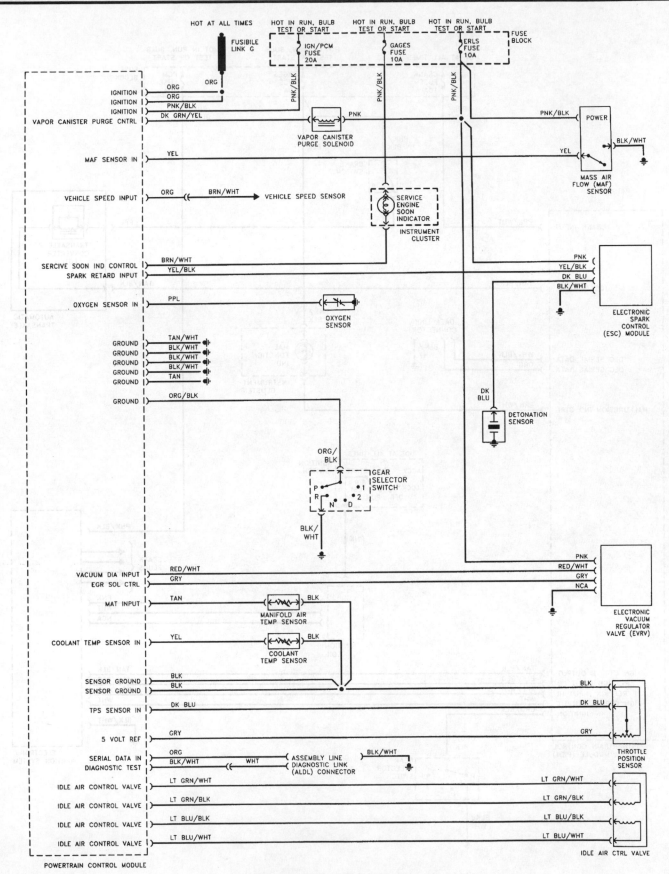

Typical 3.0L engine controls (1 of 2)

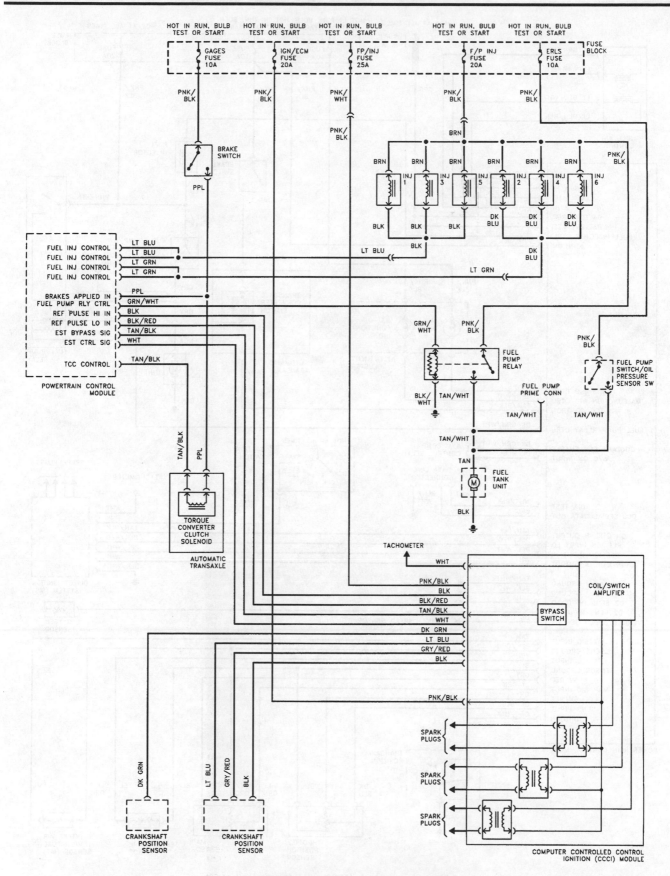

Typical 3.0L engine controls (2 of 2)

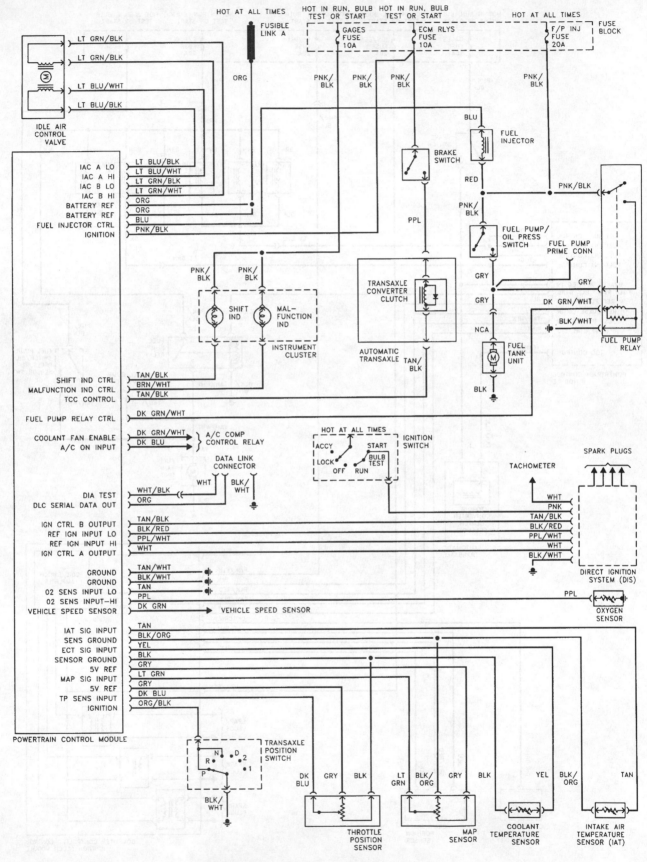

2.5L engine controls (1988 and later models)

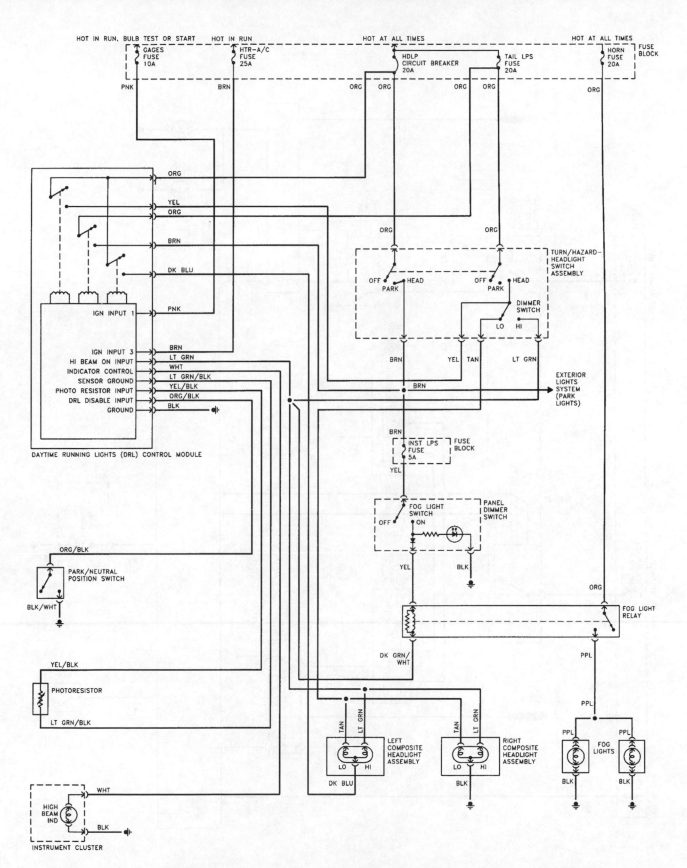

Headlight system with daytime running lights (1994 and later models)

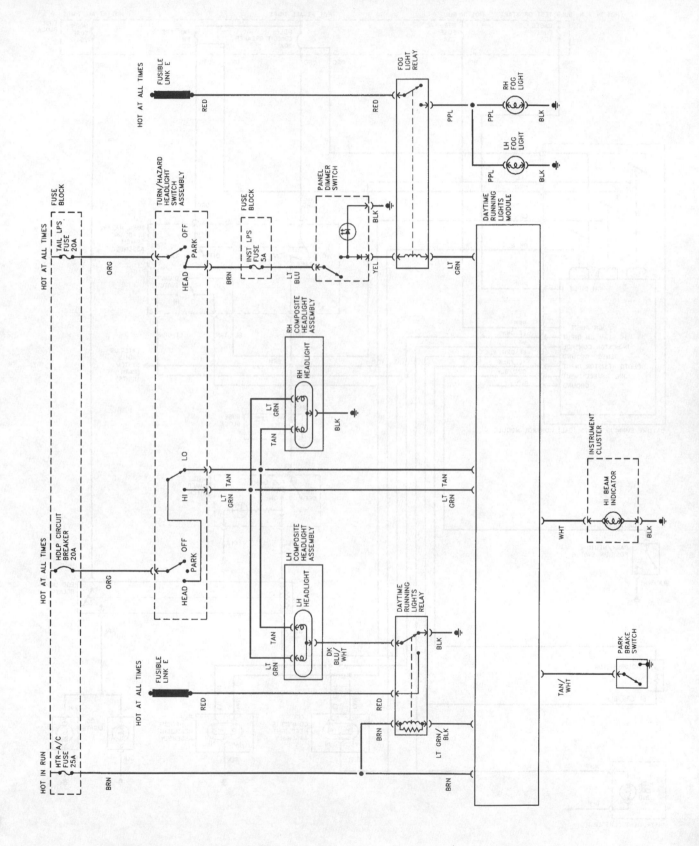

Headlight system with daytime running lights (1993 and earlier models)

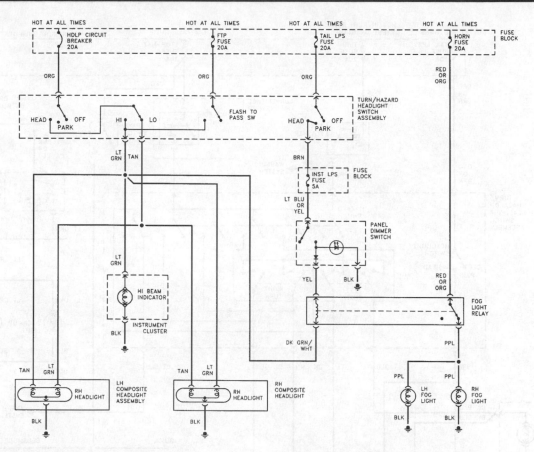

Typical headlight system without daytime running lights (except Grand Am and Skylark models)

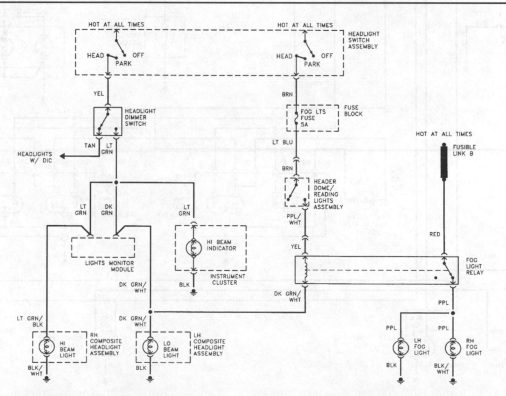

Typical headlight system without daytime running lights (Grand Am and Skylark models)

12

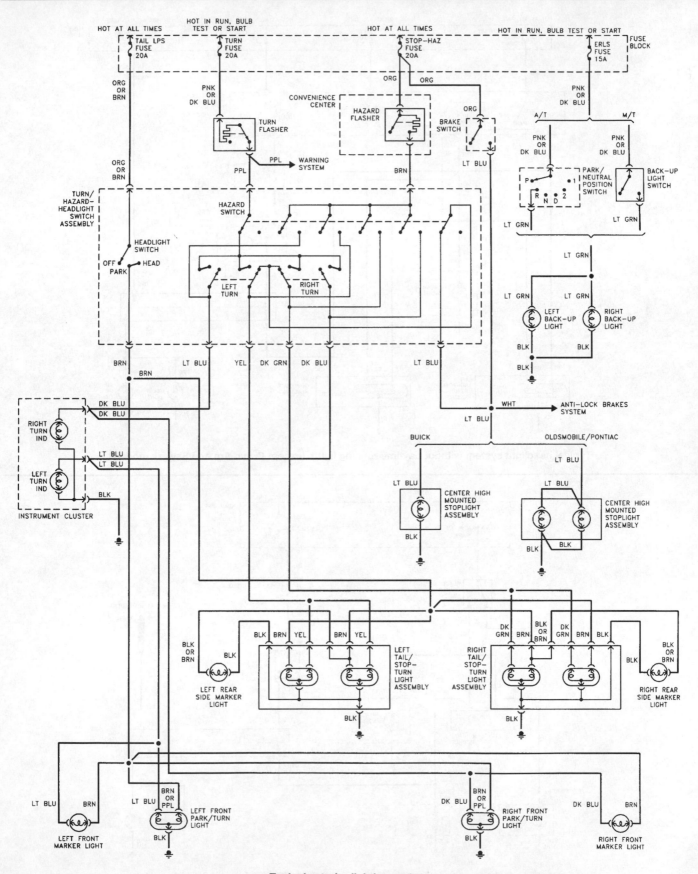

Typical exterior lighting system

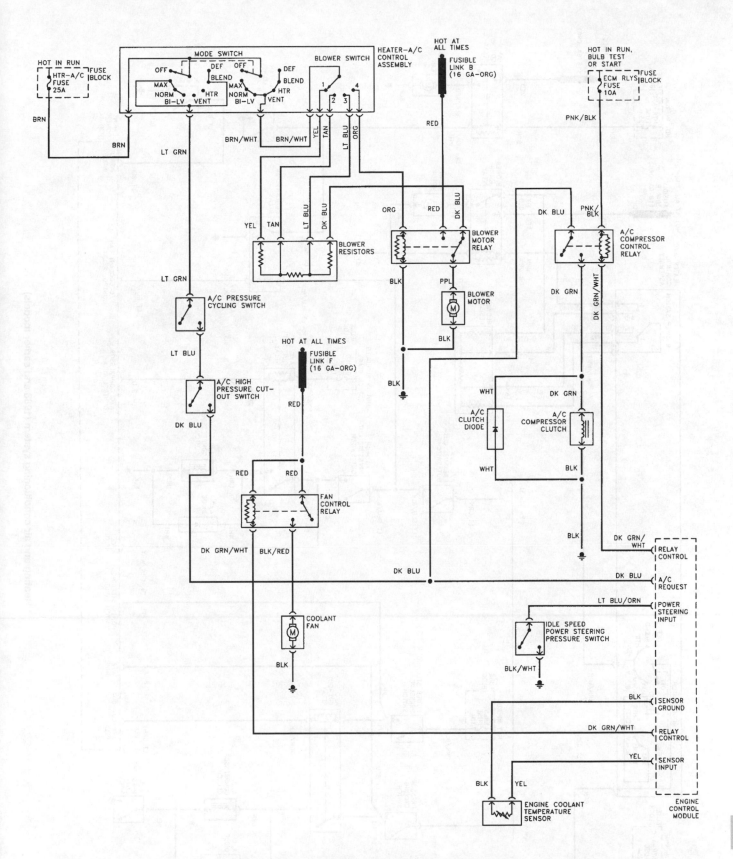

Heating and air conditioning system (1989 and later models)

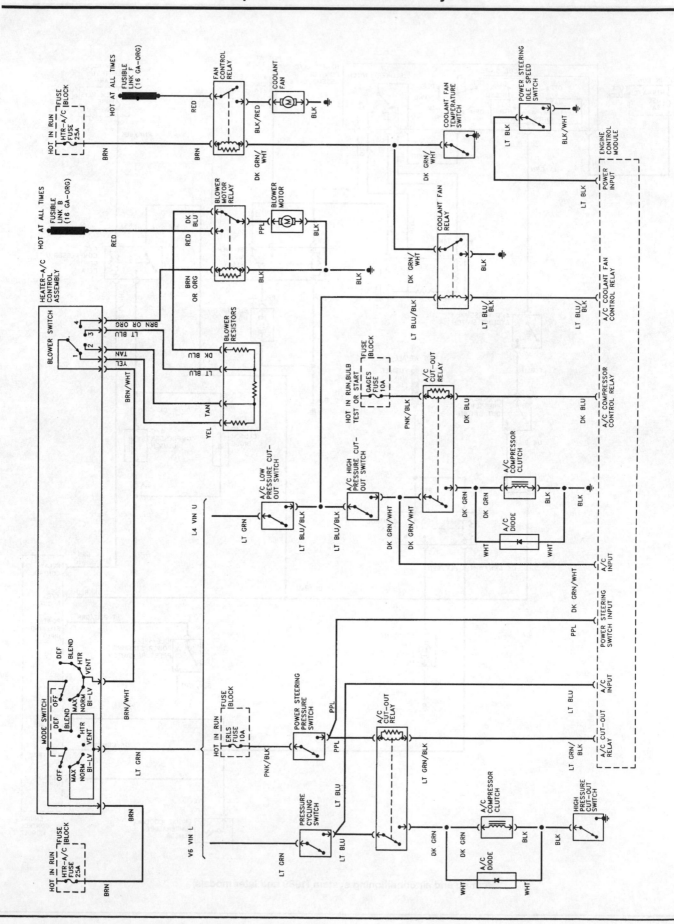

Heating and air conditioning system (1988 and earlier models)

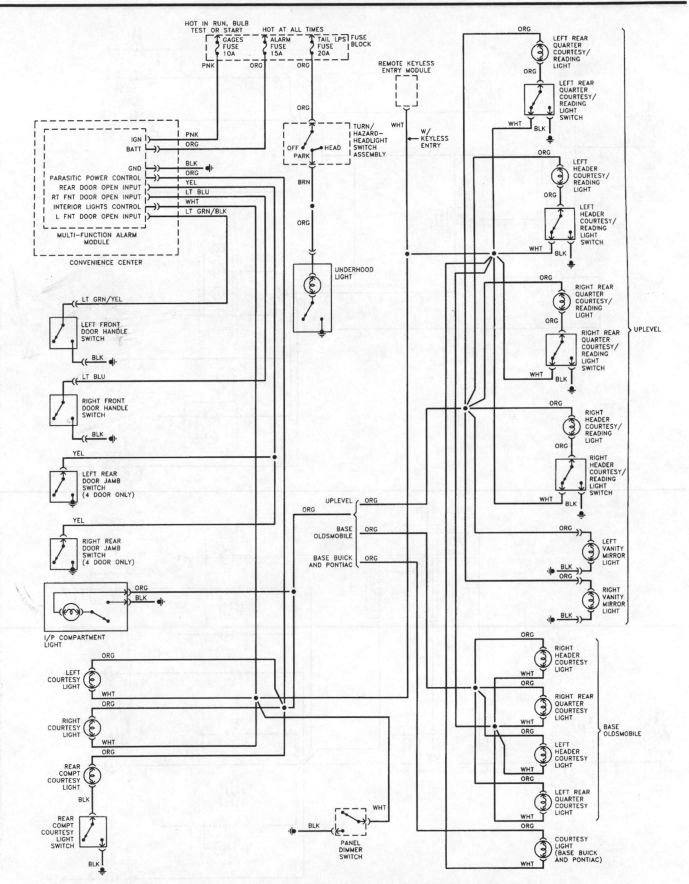

Typical courtesy lamp system (except Grand Am and Skylark models)

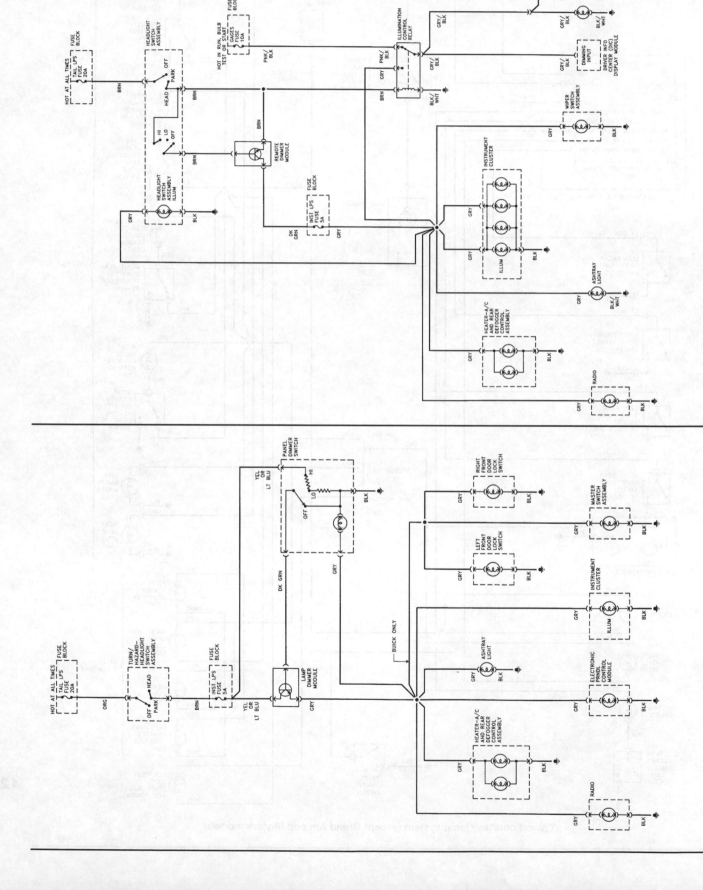

Typical illumination system (except Grand Am and Skylark models)

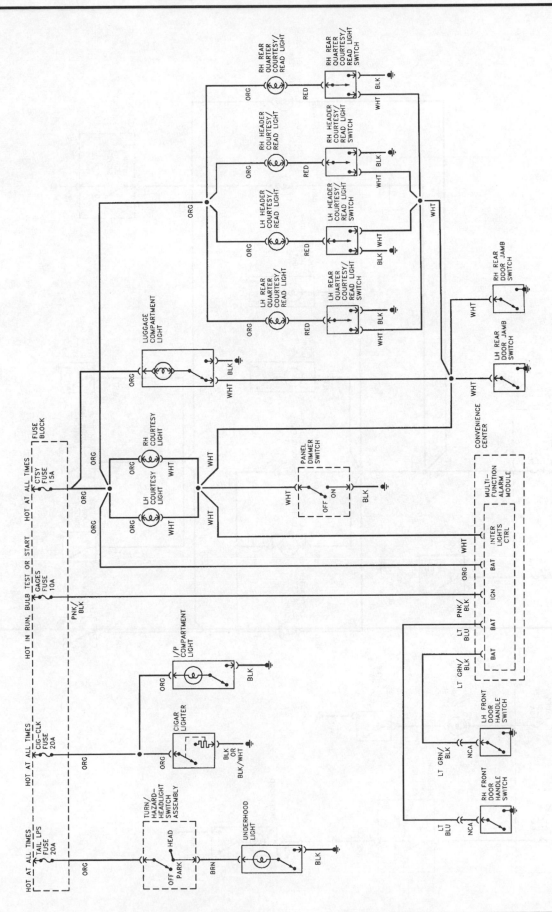

Courtesy lamp system (1990 and later Grand Am and Skylark models)

12

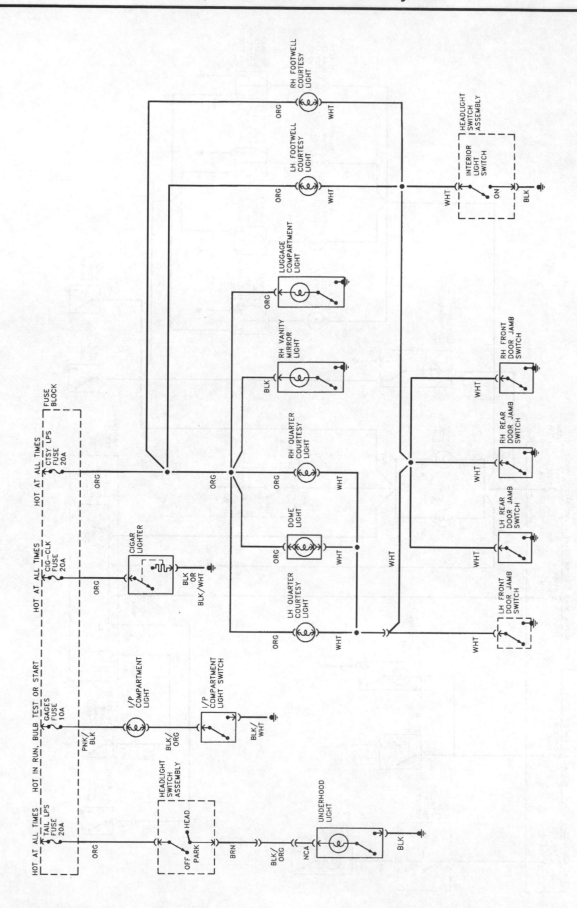

Courtesy lamp system (1989 and earlier Grand Am and Skylark models)

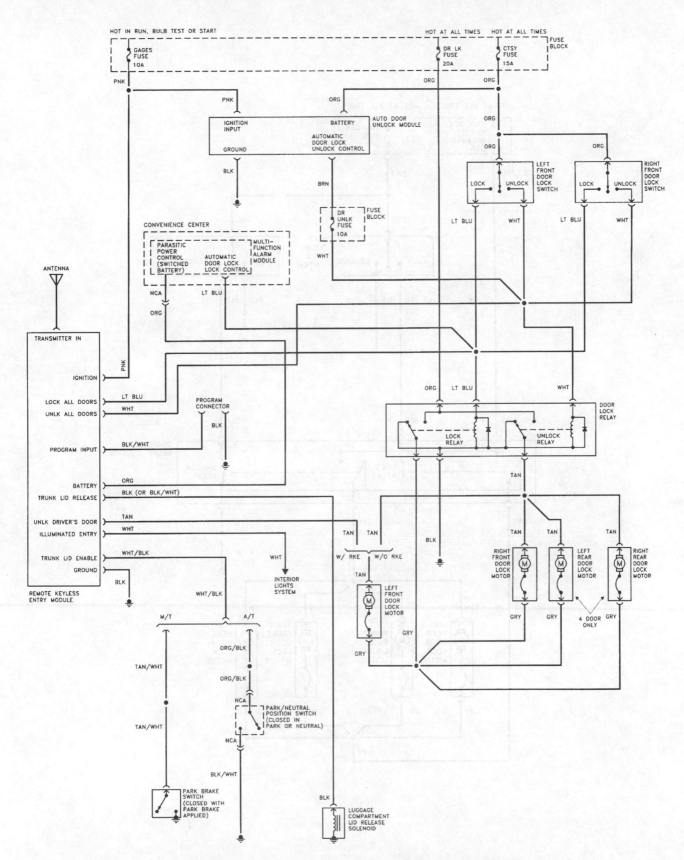

Typical power window system (except Grand Am and Skylark models)

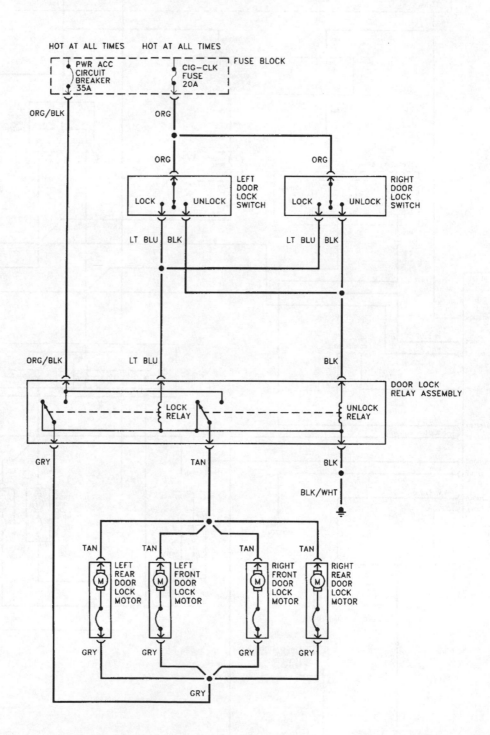

Typical power window system (Grand Am and Skylark models)

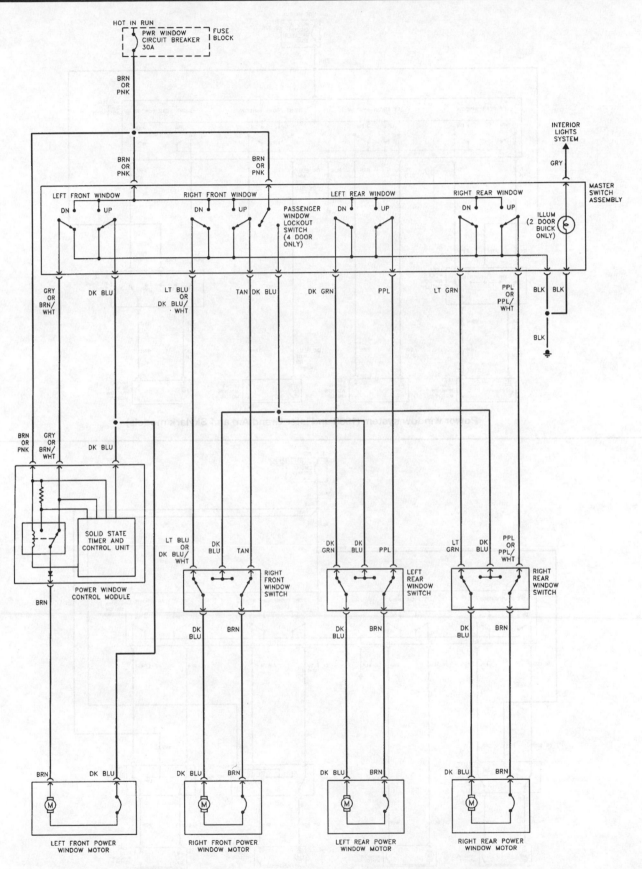

Typical power window system (except Grand Am and Skylark models)

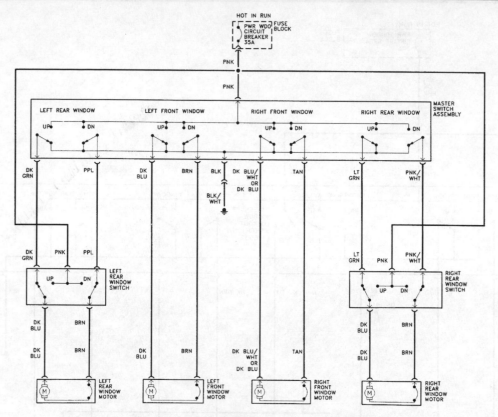

Power window system (1988 and later Grand Am and Skylark models)

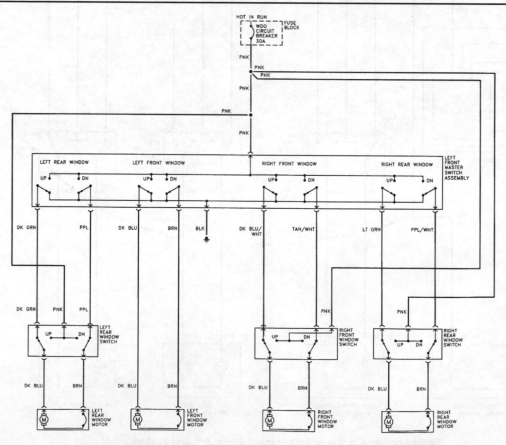

Power window system (1987 and earlier Grand Am and Skylark models)

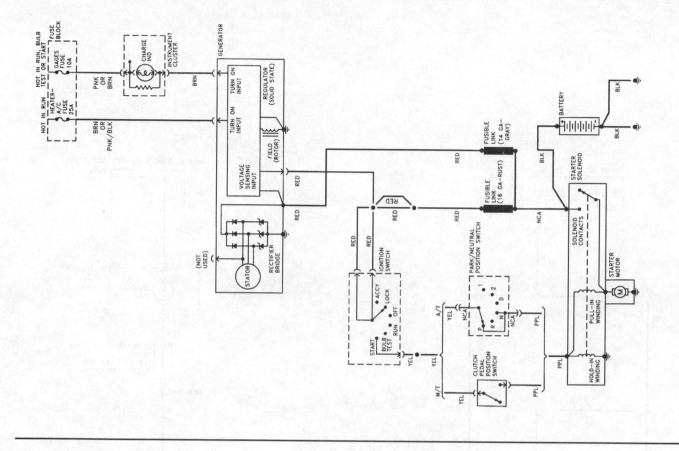

Typical starting and charging system (except Grand Am and Skylark models)

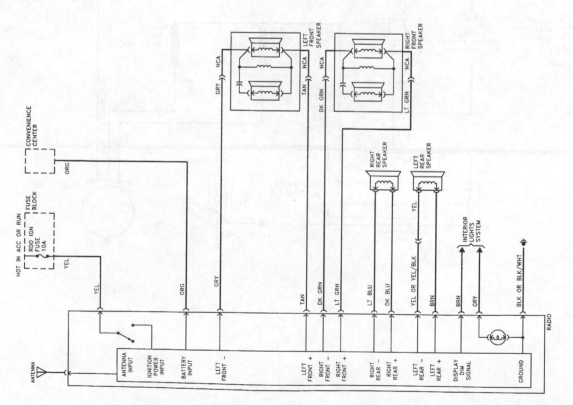

Typical radio system

12

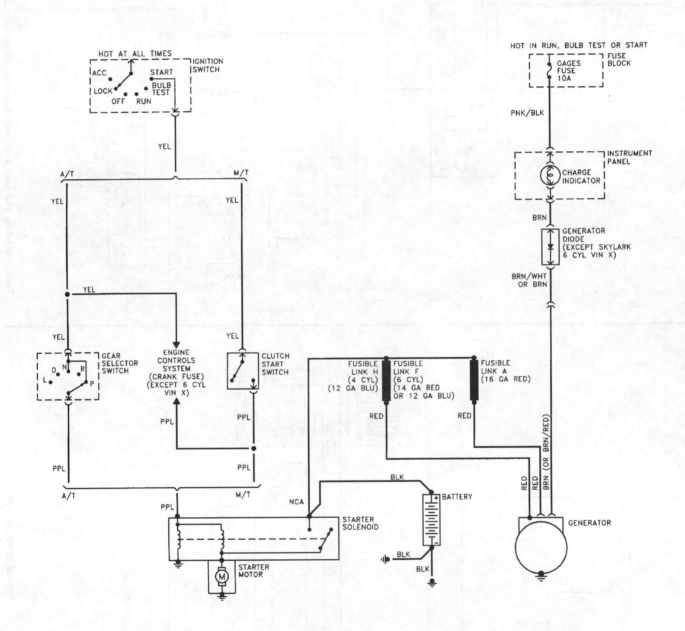

Typical starting and charging system (Grand Am and Skylark models)

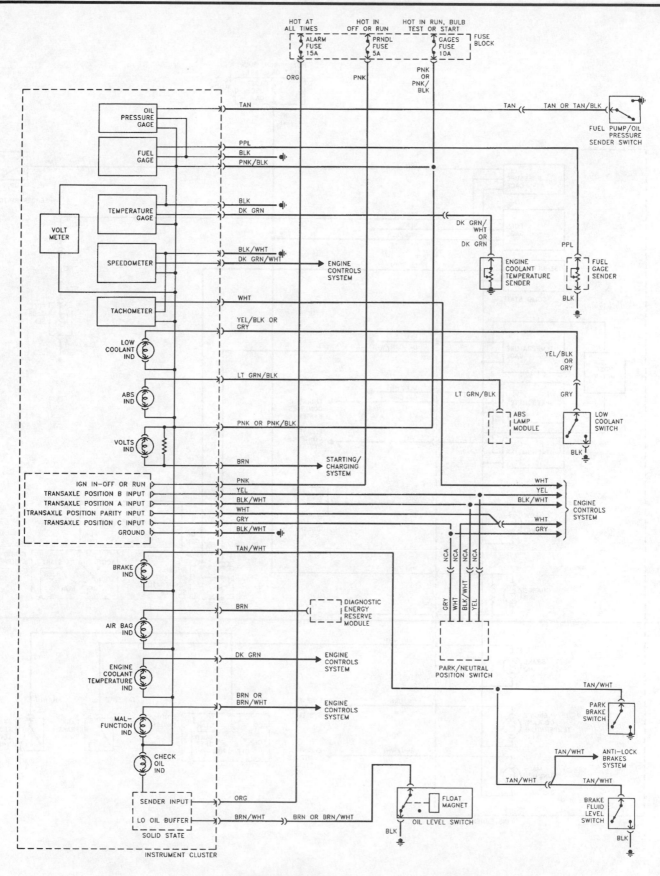

Typical warning system (except Grand Am and Skylark models)

12

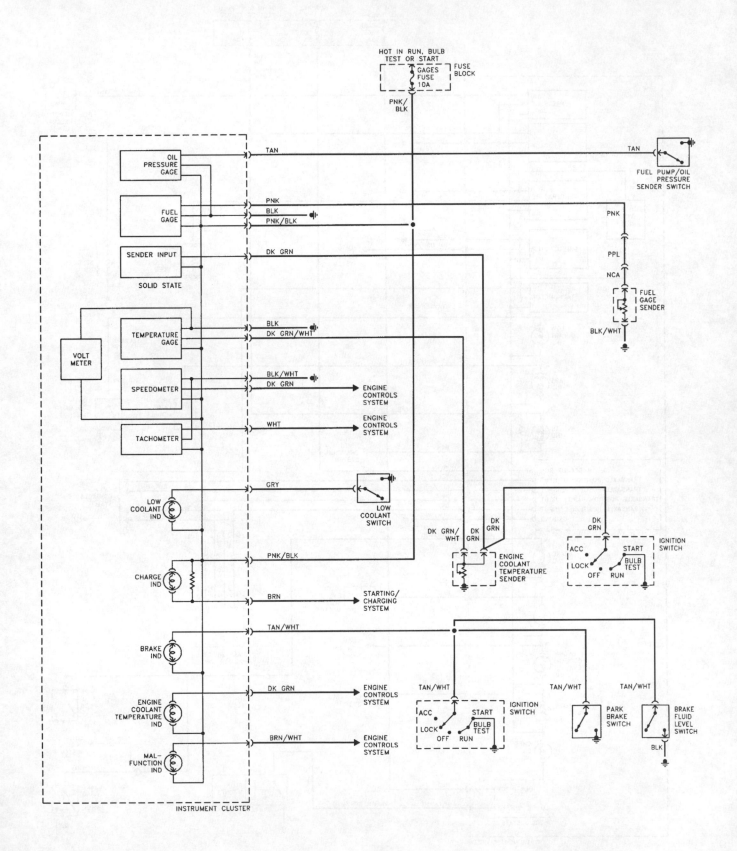

Typical warning system (Grand Am and Skylark models)

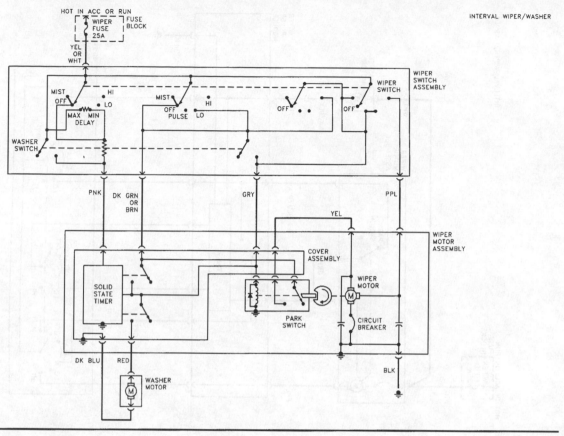

INTERVAL WIPER/WASHER

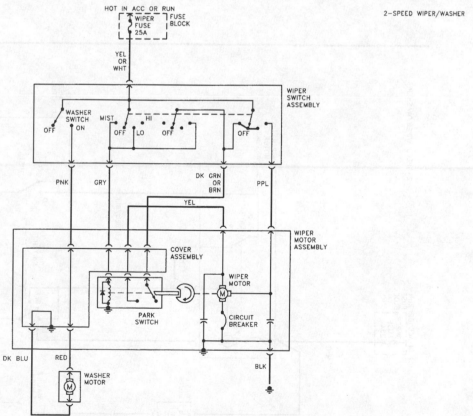

2-SPEED WIPER/WASHER

Typical wiper/washer system (except Grand Am and Skylark models)

12

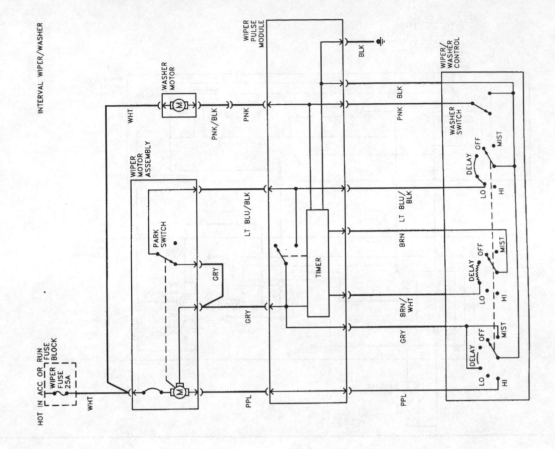

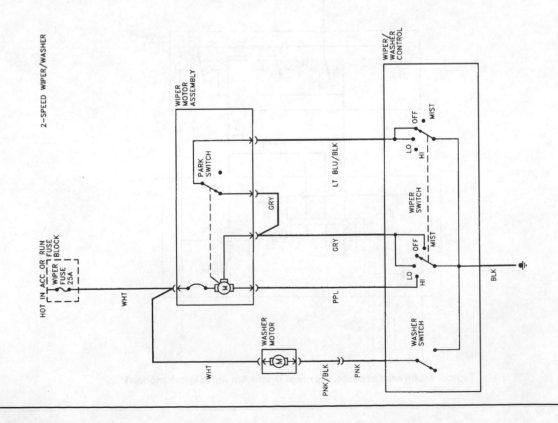

Typical wiper/washer system (Grand Am and Skylark models)

Index

Haynes Automotive Manuals

NOTE: New manuals are added to this list on a periodic basis. If you do not see a listing for your vehicle, consult your local Haynes dealer for the latest product information.

ACURA
*12020 **Integra** '86 thru '89 **& Legend** '86 thru '90

AMC
Jeep CJ - see *JEEP (50020)*
14020 **Mid-size models,** Concord, Hornet, Gremlin & Spirit '70 thru '83
14025 **(Renault) Alliance & Encore** '83 thru '87

AUDI
15020 **4000** all models '80 thru '87
15025 **5000** all models '77 thru '83
15026 **5000** all models '84 thru '88

AUSTIN-HEALEY
Sprite - see *MG Midget (66015)*

BMW
*18020 **3/5 Series** not including diesel or all-wheel drive models '82 thru '92
*18021 **3 Series** except 325iX models '92 thru '97
18025 **320i** all 4 cyl models '75 thru '83
18035 **528i & 530i** all models '75 thru '80
18050 **1500 thru 2002** except Turbo '59 thru '77

BUICK
Century (front wheel drive) - see *GM (829)*
*19020 **Buick, Oldsmobile & Pontiac Full-size (Front wheel drive)** all models '85 thru '98
Buick Electra, LeSabre and Park Avenue; Oldsmobile Delta 88 Royale, Ninety Eight and Regency; Pontiac Bonneville
19025 **Buick Oldsmobile & Pontiac Full-size (Rear wheel drive)**
Buick Estate '70 thru '90, Electra'70 thru '84, LeSabre '70 thru '85, Limited '74 thru '79
Oldsmobile Custom Cruiser '70 thru '90, Delta 88 '70 thru '85,Ninety-eight '70 thru '84
Pontiac Bonneville '70 thru '81, Catalina '70 thru '81, Grandville '70 thru '75, Parisienne '83 thru '86
19030 **Mid-size Regal & Century** all rear-drive models with V6, V8 and Turbo '74 thru '87
Regal - see *GENERAL MOTORS (38010)*
Riviera - see *GENERAL MOTORS (38030)*
Roadmaster - see *CHEVROLET (24046)*
Skyhawk - see *GENERAL MOTORS (38015)*
Skylark '80 thru '85 - see *GM (38020)*
Skylark '86 on - see *GM (38025)*
Somerset - see *GENERAL MOTORS (38025)*

CADILLAC
*21030 **Cadillac Rear Wheel Drive** all gasoline models '70 thru '93
Cimarron - see *GENERAL MOTORS (38015)*
Eldorado - see *GENERAL MOTORS (38030)*
Seville '80 thru '85 - see *GM (38030)*

CHEVROLET
*24010 **Astro & GMC Safari Mini-vans** '85 thru '93
24015 **Camaro V8** all models '70 thru '81
24016 **Camaro** all models '82 thru '92
Cavalier - see *GENERAL MOTORS (38015)*
Celebrity - see *GENERAL MOTORS (38005)*
24017 **Camaro & Firebird** '93 thru '97
24020 **Chevelle, Malibu & El Camino** '69 thru '87
24024 **Chevette & Pontiac T1000** '76 thru '87
Citation - see *GENERAL MOTORS (38020)*
*24032 **Corsica/Beretta** all models '87 thru '96
24040 **Corvette** all V8 models '68 thru '82
*24041 **Corvette** all models '84 thru '96
10305 **Chevrolet Engine Overhaul Manual**
24045 **Full-size Sedans** Caprice, Impala, Biscayne, Bel Air & Wagons '69 thru '90
24046 **Impala SS & Caprice and Buick Roadmaster** '91 thru '96
Lumina - see *GENERAL MOTORS (38010)*

24048 **Lumina & Monte Carlo** '95 thru '98
Lumina APV - see *GM (38035)*
24050 **Luv Pick-up** all 2WD & 4WD '72 thru '82
*24055 **Monte Carlo** all models '70 thru '88
Monte Carlo '95 thru '98 - see *LUMINA (24048)*
24059 **Nova** all V8 models '69 thru '79
*24060 **Nova and Geo Prizm** '85 thru '92
24064 **Pick-ups '67 thru '87** - Chevrolet & GMC, all V8 & in-line 6 cyl, 2WD & 4WD '67 thru '87; Suburbans, Blazers & Jimmys '67 thru '91
*24065 **Pick-ups '88 thru '98** - Chevrolet & GMC, all full-size pick-ups, '88 thru '98; Blazer & Jimmy '92 thru '94; Suburban '92 thru '98; Tahoe & Yukon '98
24070 **S-10 & S-15 Pick-ups** '82 thru '93, **Blazer & Jimmy** '83 thru '94,
*24071 **S-10 & S-15 Pick-ups** '94 thru '96 **Blazer & Jimmy** '95 thru '96
*24075 **Sprint & Geo Metro** '85 thru '94
*24080 **Vans - Chevrolet & GMC,** V8 & in-line 6 cylinder models '68 thru '96

CHRYSLER
25015 **Chrysler Cirrus, Dodge Stratus, Plymouth Breeze** '95 thru '98
25025 **Chrysler Concorde, New Yorker & LHS, Dodge Intrepid, Eagle** Vision, '93 thru '97
10310 **Chrysler Engine Overhaul Manual**
*25020 **Full-size Front-Wheel Drive** '88 thru '93
K-Cars - see *DODGE Aries (30008)*
Laser - see *DODGE Daytona (30030)*
*25030 **Chrysler & Plymouth Mid-size** front wheel drive '82 thru '95
Rear-wheel Drive - see *Dodge (30050)*

DATSUN
28005 **200SX** all models '80 thru '83
28007 **B-210** all models '73 thru '78
28009 **210** all models '79 thru '82
28012 **240Z, 260Z & 280Z** Coupe '70 thru '78
28014 **280ZX** Coupe & 2+2 '79 thru '83
300ZX - see *NISSAN (72010)*
28016 **310** all models '78 thru '82
28018 **510 & PL521 Pick-up** '68 thru '73
28020 **510** all models '78 thru '81
28022 **620 Series Pick-up** all models '73 thru '79
720 Series Pick-up - see *NISSAN (72030)*
28025 **810/Maxima** all gasoline models, '77 thru '84

DODGE
400 & 600 - see *CHRYSLER (25030)*
*30008 **Aries & Plymouth Reliant** '81 thru '89
30010 **Caravan & Plymouth Voyager Mini-Vans** all models '84 thru '95
*30011 **Caravan & Plymouth Voyager Mini-Vans** all models '96 thru '98
30012 **Challenger/Plymouth Saporro** '78 thru '83
30016 **Colt & Plymouth Champ (front wheel drive)** all models '78 thru '87
*30020 **Dakota Pick-ups** all models '87 thru '96
30025 **Dart, Demon, Plymouth Barracuda, Duster & Valiant** 6 cyl models '67 thru '76
*30030 **Daytona & Chrysler Laser** '84 thru '89
Intrepid - see *CHRYSLER (25025)*
*30034 **Neon** all models '95 thru '97
*30035 **Omni & Plymouth Horizon** '78 thru '90
*30040 **Pick-ups** all full-size models '74 thru '93
*30041 **Pick-ups** all full-size models '94 thru '96
*30045 **Ram 50/D50 Pick-ups & Raider and Plymouth Arrow Pick-ups** '79 thru '93
30050 **Dodge/Plymouth/Chrysler** rear wheel drive '71 thru '89
*30055 **Shadow & Plymouth Sundance** '87 thru '94
*30060 **Spirit & Plymouth Acclaim** '89 thru '95
*30065 **Vans - Dodge & Plymouth** '71 thru '96

EAGLE
Talon - see *Mitsubishi Eclipse (68030)*
Vision - see *CHRYSLER (25025)*

FIAT
34010 **124 Sport Coupe & Spider** '68 thru '78
34025 **X1/9** all models '74 thru '80

FORD
10355 **Ford Automatic Transmission Overhaul**
*36004 **Aerostar Mini-vans** all models '86 thru '96
*36006 **Contour & Mercury Mystique** '95 thru '98
36008 **Courier Pick-up** all models '72 thru '82
36012 **Crown Victoria & Mercury Grand Marquis** '88 thru '96
10320 **Ford Engine Overhaul Manual**
36016 **Escort/Mercury Lynx** all models '81 thru '90
*36020 **Escort/Mercury Tracer** '91 thru '96
*36024 **Explorer & Mazda Navajo** '91 thru '95
36028 **Fairmont & Mercury Zephyr** '78 thru '83
36030 **Festiva & Aspire** '88 thru '97
36032 **Fiesta** all models '77 thru '80
36036 **Ford & Mercury Full-size,**
Ford LTD & Mercury Marquis ('75 thru '82); Ford Custom 500,Country Squire, Crown Victoria & Mercury Colony Park ('75 thru '87); Ford LTD Crown Victoria & Mercury Gran Marquis ('83 thru '87)
36040 **Granada & Mercury Monarch** '75 thru '80
36044 **Ford & Mercury Mid-size,**
Ford Thunderbird & Mercury Cougar ('75 thru '82); Ford LTD & Mercury Marquis ('83 thru '86); Ford Torino,Gran Torino, Elite, Ranchero pick-up, LTD II, Mercury Montego, Comet, XR-7 & Lincoln Versailles ('75 thru '86)
36048 **Mustang V8** all models '64-1/2 thru '73
36049 **Mustang II** 4 cyl, V6 & V8 models '74 thru '78
36050 **Mustang & Mercury Capri** all models Mustang, '79 thru '93; Capri, '79 thru '86
*36051 **Mustang** all models '94 thru '97
36054 **Pick-ups & Bronco** '73 thru '79
36058 **Pick-ups & Bronco** '80 thru '96
36059 **Pick-ups, Expedition & Mercury Navigator** '97 thru '98
36062 **Pinto & Mercury Bobcat** '75 thru '80
36066 **Probe** all models '89 thru '92
36070 **Ranger/Bronco II** gasoline models '83 thru '92
*36071 **Ranger** '93 thru '97 & **Mazda Pick-ups** '94 thru '97
36074 **Taurus & Mercury Sable** '86 thru '95
*36075 **Taurus & Mercury Sable** '96 thru '98
*36078 **Tempo & Mercury Topaz** '84 thru '94
36082 **Thunderbird/Mercury Cougar** '83 thru '88
*36086 **Thunderbird/Mercury Cougar** '89 and '97
36090 **Vans** all V8 Econoline models '69 thru '91
*36094 **Vans** full size '92-'95
*36097 **Windstar Mini-van** '95-'98

GENERAL MOTORS
*10360 **GM Automatic Transmission Overhaul**
*38005 **Buick Century, Chevrolet Celebrity, Oldsmobile Cutlass Ciera & Pontiac 6000** all models '82 thru '96
*38010 **Buick Regal, Chevrolet Lumina, Oldsmobile Cutlass Supreme & Pontiac Grand Prix** front-wheel drive models '88 thru '95
*38015 **Buick Skyhawk, Cadillac Cimarron, Chevrolet Cavalier, Oldsmobile Firenza & Pontiac J-2000 & Sunbird** '82 thru '94
*38016 **Chevrolet Cavalier & Pontiac Sunfire** '95 thru '98
38020 **Buick Skylark, Chevrolet Citation, Olds Omega, Pontiac Phoenix** '80 thru '85
38025 **Buick Skylark & Somerset, Oldsmobile Achieva & Calais and Pontiac Grand Am** all models '85 thru '95
38030 **Cadillac Eldorado** '71 thru '85, **Seville** '80 thru '85, **Oldsmobile Toronado** '71 thru '85 **& Buick Riviera** '79 thru '85
*38035 **Chevrolet Lumina APV, Olds Silhouette & Pontiac Trans Sport** all models '90 thru '95
General Motors Full-size Rear-wheel Drive - see *BUICK (19025)*

(Continued on other side)

* Listings shown with an asterisk (*) indicate model coverage as of this printing. These titles will be periodically updated to include later model years - consult your Haynes dealer for more information.

Haynes North America, Inc., 861 Lawrence Drive, Newbury Park, CA 91320-1514 • (805) 498-6703

Haynes Automotive Manuals (continued)

NOTE: New manuals are added to this list on a periodic basis. If you do not see a listing for your vehicle, consult your local Haynes dealer for the latest product information.

GEO
Metro - *see CHEVROLET Sprint (24075)*
Prizm - *'85 thru '92 see CHEVY (24060), '93 thru '96 see TOYOTA Corolla (92036)*
*40030 Storm all models '90 thru '93
Tracker - *see SUZUKI Samurai (90010)*

GMC
Safari - *see CHEVROLET ASTRO (24010)*
Vans & Pick-ups - *see CHEVROLET*

HONDA
42010 Accord CVCC all models '76 thru '83
42011 Accord all models '84 thru '89
42012 Accord all models '90 thru '93
42013 Accord all models '94 thru '95
42020 Civic 1200 all models '73 thru '79
42021 Civic 1300 & 1500 CVCC '80 thru '83
42022 Civic 1500 CVCC all models '75 thru '79
42023 Civic all models '84 thru '91
*42024 Civic & del Sol '92 thru '95
*42040 Prelude CVCC all models '79 thru '89

HYUNDAI
*43015 Excel all models '86 thru '94

ISUZU
Hombre - *see CHEVROLET S-10 (24071)*
*47017 Rodeo '91 thru '97; Amigo '89 thru '94; Honda Passport '95 thru '97
*47020 Trooper & Pick-up, all gasoline models Pick-up, '81 thru '93; Trooper, '84 thru '91

JAGUAR
*49010 XJ6 all 6 cyl models '68 thru '86
*49011 XJ6 all models '88 thru '94
*49015 XJ12 & XJS all 12 cyl models '72 thru '85

JEEP
*50010 Cherokee, Comanche & Wagoneer Limited all models '84 thru '96
50020 CJ all models '49 thru '86
*50025 Grand Cherokee all models '93 thru '98
50029 Grand Wagoneer & Pick-up '72 thru '91 Grand Wagoneer '84 thru '91, Cherokee & Wagoneer '72 thru '83, Pick-up '72 thru '88
*50030 Wrangler all models '87 thru '95

LINCOLN
Navigator - *see FORD Pick-up (36059)*
59010 Rear Wheel Drive all models '70 thru '96

MAZDA
61010 GLC Hatchback (rear wheel drive) '77 thru '83
61011 GLC (front wheel drive) '81 thru '85
*61015 323 & Protogé '90 thru '97
*61016 MX-5 Miata '90 thru '97
*61020 MPV all models '89 thru '94
Navajo - *see Ford Explorer (36024)*
61030 Pick-ups '72 thru '93
Pick-ups '94 thru '96 - *see Ford Ranger (36071)*
61035 RX-7 all models '79 thru '85
*61036 RX-7 all models '86 thru '91
61040 626 (rear wheel drive) all models '79 thru '82
*61041 626/MX-6 (front wheel drive) '83 thru '91

MERCEDES-BENZ
63012 123 Series Diesel '76 thru '85
*63015 190 Series four-cyl gas models, '84 thru '88
63020 230/250/280 6 cyl sohc models '68 thru '72
63025 280 123 Series gasoline models '77 thru '81
63030 350 & 450 all models '71 thru '80

MERCURY
See *FORD Listing.*

MG
66010 MGB Roadster & GT Coupe '62 thru '80
66015 MG Midget, Austin Healey Sprite '58 thru '80

MITSUBISHI
*68020 Cordia, Tredia, Galant, Precis & Mirage '83 thru '93
*68030 Eclipse, Eagle Talon & Ply. Laser '90 thru '94
*68040 Pick-up '83 thru '96 & Montero '83 thru '93

NISSAN
72010 300ZX all models including Turbo '84 thru '89
*72015 Altima all models '93 thru '97
*72020 Maxima all models '85 thru '91
*72030 Pick-ups '80 thru '96 Pathfinder '87 thru '95
72040 Pulsar all models '83 thru '86
*72050 Sentra all models '82 thru '94
*72051 Sentra & 200SX all models '95 thru '98
*72060 Stanza all models '82 thru '90

OLDSMOBILE
*73015 Cutlass V6 & V8 gas models '74 thru '88
For other OLDSMOBILE titles, see BUICK, CHEVROLET or GENERAL MOTORS listing.

PLYMOUTH
For PLYMOUTH titles, see DODGE listing.

PONTIAC
79008 Fiero all models '84 thru '88
79018 Firebird V8 models except Turbo '70 thru '81
79019 Firebird all models '82 thru '92
For other PONTIAC titles, see BUICK, CHEVROLET or GENERAL MOTORS listing.

PORSCHE
*80020 911 except Turbo & Carrera 4 '65 thru '89
80025 914 all 4 cyl models '69 thru '76
80030 924 all models including Turbo '76 thru '82
*80035 944 all models including Turbo '83 thru '89

RENAULT
Alliance & Encore - *see AMC (14020)*

SAAB
*84010 900 all models including Turbo '79 thru '88

SATURN
87010 Saturn all models '91 thru '96

SUBARU
89002 1100, 1300, 1400 & 1600 '71 thru '79
*89003 1600 & 1800 2WD & 4WD '80 thru '94

SUZUKI
*90010 Samurai/Sidekick & Geo Tracker '86 thru '96

TOYOTA
92005 Camry all models '83 thru '91
92006 Camry all models '92 thru '96
92015 Celica Rear Wheel Drive '71 thru '85
*92020 Celica Front Wheel Drive '86 thru '93
92025 Celica Supra all models '79 thru '92
92030 Corolla all models '75 thru '79
92032 Corolla all rear wheel drive models '80 thru '87
92035 Corolla all front wheel drive models '84 thru '92
*92036 Corolla & Geo Prizm '93 thru '97
92040 Corolla Tercel all models '80 thru '82
92045 Corona all models '74 thru '82
92050 Cressida all models '78 thru '82
92055 Land Cruiser FJ40, 43, 45, 55 '68 thru '82
92056 Land Cruiser FJ60, 62, 80, FZJ80 '80 thru '96
*92065 MR2 all models '85 thru '87
92070 Pick-up all models '69 thru '78
*92075 Pick-up all models '79 thru '95
*92076 Tacoma '95 thru '98, 4Runner '96 thru '98, & T100 '93 thru '98
*92080 Previa all models '91 thru '95
92085 Tercel all models '87 thru '94

TRIUMPH
94007 Spitfire all models '62 thru '81
94010 TR7 all models '75 thru '81

VW
96008 Beetle & Karmann Ghia '54 thru '79
96012 Dasher all gasoline models '74 thru '81
*96016 Rabbit, Jetta, Scirocco, & Pick-up gas models '74 thru '91 & Convertible '80 thru '92
96017 Golf & Jetta all models '93 thru '97
96020 Rabbit, Jetta & Pick-up diesel '77 thru '84
96030 Transporter 1600 all models '68 thru '79
96035 Transporter 1700, 1800 & 2000 '72 thru '79
96040 Type 3 1500 & 1600 all models '63 thru '73
96045 Vanagon all air-cooled models '80 thru '83

VOLVO
97010 120, 130 Series & 1800 Sports '61 thru '73
97015 140 Series all models '66 thru '74
*97020 240 Series all models '76 thru '93
97025 260 Series all models '75 thru '82
*97040 740 & 760 Series all models '82 thru '88

TECHBOOK MANUALS
10205 Automotive Computer Codes
10210 Automotive Emissions Control Manual
10215 Fuel Injection Manual, 1978 thru 1985
10220 Fuel Injection Manual, 1986 thru 1996
10225 Holley Carburetor Manual
10230 Rochester Carburetor Manual
10240 Weber/Zenith/Stromberg/SU Carburetors
10305 Chevrolet Engine Overhaul Manual
10310 Chrysler Engine Overhaul Manual
10320 Ford Engine Overhaul Manual
10330 GM and Ford Diesel Engine Repair Manual
10340 Small Engine Repair Manual
10345 Suspension, Steering & Driveline Manual
10355 Ford Automatic Transmission Overhaul
10360 GM Automatic Transmission Overhaul
10405 Automotive Body Repair & Painting
10410 Automotive Brake Manual
10415 Automotive Detailing Manual
10420 Automotive Eelectrical Manual
10425 Automotive Heating & Air Conditioning
10430 Automotive Reference Manual & Dictionary
10435 Automotive Tools Manual
10440 Used Car Buying Guide
10445 Welding Manual
10450 ATV Basics

SPANISH MANUALS
98903 Reparación de Carrocería & Pintura
98905 Códigos Automotrices de la Computadora
98910 Frenos Automotriz
98915 Inyección de Combustible 1986 al 1994
99040 Chevrolet & GMC Camionetas '67 al '87 Incluye Suburban, Blazer & Jimmy '67 al '91
99041 Chevrolet & GMC Camionetas '88 al '95 Incluye Suburban '92 al '95, Blazer & Jimmy '92 al '94, Tahoe y Yukon '95
99042 Chevrolet & GMC Camionetas Cerradas '68 al '95
99055 Dodge Caravan & Plymouth Voyager '84 al '95
99075 Ford Camionetas y Bronco '80 al '94
99077 Ford Camionetas Cerradas '69 al '91
99083 Ford Modelos de Tamaño Grande '75 al '87
99088 Ford Modelos de Tamaño Mediano '75 al '86
99091 Ford Taurus & Mercury Sable '86 al '95
99095 GM Modelos de Tamaño Grande '70 al '90
99100 GM Modelos de Tamaño Mediano '70 al '88
99110 Nissan Camionetas '80 al '96, Pathfinder '87 al '95
99118 Nissan Sentra '82 al '94
99125 Toyota Camionetas y 4Runner '79 al '95

Over 100 Haynes motorcycle manuals also available

5-98

* Listings shown with an asterisk (*) indicate model coverage as of this printing. These titles will be periodically updated to include later model years - consult your Haynes dealer for more information.

Haynes North America, Inc., 861 Lawrence Drive, Newbury Park, CA 91320-1514 • (805) 498-6703